A
DICTIONARY
OF THE PUKKHTO OR PUKSHTO LANGUAGE

A DICTIONARY OF THE PUKKHTO OR PUKSHTO LANGUAGE

IN WHICH THE WORDS ARE TRACED TO THEIR SOURCES
IN THE

INDIAN AND PERSIAN LANGUAGES.

BY

H. W. BELLEW

ASSISTANT SURGEON, BENGAL ARMY

GYAN

Published by

Gyan Publishing House
5, Ansari Road
Daryaganj, New Delhi-110002
Phone: 011-47034999, 9811692060
E-mail: books@gyanbooks.com

Distribution Network
gyanbooks.com
India, USA, Canada, UK, Australia, France

ISBN : 978-81-212-4297-4 (PB)
First Published, 1901

2nd Impression 2020

Printed at: Gyan Press, Delhi.

A
Dictionary of the Pukkhto or Pukshto Language
Author: H. W. Bellew

A DICTIONARY

OF THE

PUKKHTO OR PUKSHTO LANGUAGE,

IN WHICH THE WORDS ARE TRACED TO THEIR SOURCES

IN THE

INDIAN AND PERSIAN LANGUAGES.

BY

HENRY WALTER BELLEW,

ASSISTANT SURGEON, BENGAL ARMY.

LAHORE:

RAI SAHIB M. GULAB SINGH & SONS,

GOVERNMENT PUBLISHERS, PRINTERS, AND BOOKSELLERS;

PROPRIETORS, MUFID-I-'AM PRESS.

MDCCCCI.

A

DICTIONARY

OF THE

PUKKHTO OR PUKSHTO LANGUAGE.

DEDICATED

TO

COLONEL SIR HERBERT BENJAMIN EDWARDES,

K.C.B., K.C.S.I., ETC.,

BY

HIS OBEDIENT HUMBLE SERVANT,

H. W. BELLEW.

PREFACE.

In compiling this Dictionary of the Pukkhto or Pukshto Language (Pukkhto-English and English-Pukkhto), I have experienced considerable difficulty in deciding upon the words of foreign origin—principally Arabic and Persian, but still of common use in the Pukkhto—that should find a place in these pages.

As a rule, words of the Arabic and Persian that are used in an unaltered form in the Pukkhto have been omitted, excepting only those of very common or general use; for to have given place to all the words of those languages used in an unchanged form by Pukkhtūn authors, would have added unnecessarily to the bulk of the work without, in return, being of any practical utility in the study of the language, since their use is almost solely confined to literary works or to discussions on theological subjects.

Of the words purely Pukkhto, the most, it will be observed, are derived from the Persian, from which country, indeed, the Afghans appear to have derived most of their literature. In most instances I have endeavoured to point out their sources in those languages, by quoting in brackets with each word the original form from which it may be derived, with a preceding capital letter for the initial of the language to which each belongs.

In some instances the changes are very slight, in others more complex, and in a few complete, but still in general accordance with the regular laws of philology, which in Pukkhto are very variously illustrated according to the diverse vocal and phonetic peculiarities of the different tribes (for the most part illiterate) composing the Afghan nation.

I have not had leisure to follow out this enquiry as fully as the subject demands, owing to the scant opportunities at my disposal in the intervals between my professional and military duties. I have considered it necessary, however, to allude to the subject, and to note in brief some instances that have attracted my attention, in the hope that they will, whilst serving as illustrations of the changes which words from the Persian and Indian languages undergo on becoming Pukkhto, at the same time suffice to guide the student desirous of a further investigation of the subject. For illustration of the grammatical structure of the language, see the Preface to my Pukkhto Grammar.

As stated in the text of my Grammar (Art. 5) the letters *ch* and *j* of foreign words adopted into the Pukkhto, generally become changed to *ts* and *dz* respectively: as in *tsādar* (a sheet) for *chādar*, *trats* (awry) from *tirchhā*, *tskhedal* (to hop), or *tskhe kawul* (to romp), from *chakhīdan*, etc.; and in *dzigar* (liver) for *jigar*, *zandzīr* (a chain) for *zanjīr*, etc.

The letters of cognate sound with *j*, viz. *ĵ* and *z*, in Pukkhto are often replaced by *g* and *dz* respectively, as in *kog* (crooked) from *kaj*, *gala-ī* (hail from *jālah*, and *nmūndz* (prayer) from *namāz*. By some tribes, as the Yusufzais and Eastern Afghans generally, the letters *ĵ* and *g* are habitually pronounced, and generally also written, as *j* and *g* respectively.

The letter *d* in words introduced from a foreign source, in the Pukkhto generally becomes replaced by *l*, as in *las* (ten) from the Hindī *das*, and *lewar* (husband's brother) from the Hindī *dewar*, and in *lās* (hand) from *dast*, *lūm* (a net) from *dām*, *plār* (father) from *padar*, *plandar* (stepfather) from *padandar*, *lūr* (daughter) from *dukhtar*, *lewanai* (mad) from *diwānah*, *lwashal* (to milk) from *doshīdan*, etc., all from the Persian.

The letters *rd*, when coming together without an intervening vowel, are rendered in Pukkhto by *ṛ* as in *wṛal* (to carry) from *burdan*, *rāwṛal* (to fetch) from *āwurdan*, *khwaṛal* (to eat) from *khurdan*, *mṛal* (to die) from *murdan*, *kṛal*

which I have added a reversed part in English and Pukkhto, my acknowledgments are due for the aid derived from Raverty's Dictionary, though, in many instances, we differ as to the meaning of certain words, such as *tsakkhkūrai, māndah, kishor*, etc., etc., as well as in more important particulars respecting the family and structure of the language.

With the view to economising space, the present, active, and passive participles have been generally omitted from the first part of the work, as also have derivative adjectives and verbs, the rules with examples for forming these several parts of speech having been fully detailed in the Grammar.

For the rest I must crave the forbearance of the student for some imperfections in the volume, which, under the pressure of unavoidable circumstances, I have been forced to complete in a much more hurried manner than was anticipated at the time when I entered upon the task.

Such as it is, however, I trust it will be found useful, especially as regards the second or English and Pukkhto part; and with the Grammar and the Exercises and Dialogues added to it, be serviceable in facilitating the study of the language of the Afghans, and paving the way to the easy acquisition of a practical knowledge of the Pukkhto colloquial.

H. W. B.

LONDON,
19TH MARCH, 1867.

PUBLISHERS' NOTICE TO THE SECOND EDITION.

THIS new edition is brought out by Rai Sahib Munshi Gulab Singh & Sons to meet the demand, and at the special request of Mrs. Bellew.

A

DICTIONARY;

PUKKHTO OR PUKSHTO AND ENGLISH.

ABBREVIATIONS.

a. adjective; ad. adverb; c. conjunction: in. interjection; pl. plural; s.m. substantive masculine; s.f. substantive feminine; v.a. verb active; v.n. verb neuter; p. preposition; pr. pronoun; part. particle: Irr. irregular; Def. defective.

A. Arabic; P. Persian; S. Sanskrit; H. Hindī; T. Turkī.

N.B. The letters ځ *dz* and ج *j*, څ *ts* and چ *ch*, ج *j* and ز *z*, or ژ *ĵ*, ق *q* and ک *k* are sometimes used the one for the other. The long vowels ا *ā*, و *o* or *ū*, and ي *e* or *ī* are often replaced by their corresponding short vowels َ *a*, ُ *u*, and ِ *i*. The letter م *m* preceding ب *b* in a word is often changed to ن *n*.

The letter ژ *ĵ* has the sound of *z* in *azure* amongst the Western Afghans, and of *j* in *just* amongst the Eastern Afghans. ږ *g̣* has the same sound as ژ *ĵ* amongst the Western tribes, and the sound of ګ *g*, for which it is often changed, amongst the Eastern tribes. ښ has the sound of *kkh* amongst the Eastern Afghans, and of *ksh* amongst the Western Afghans, by whom it is often changed to ش *sh*.

ا ***alif***, The first letter of the Pukkhto alphabet; is often interchanged with the short vowel *zabar*, especially in the vocative case; is sometimes added as the initial letter to words commencing with و or ي, as in اورور *oror* for ورور *wror*, ايواځي *īwādzai* for يواځي *yawādzai*.

آب ***āb***, s.m. Water; lustre; reputation, honour. P.

ابا ***abā***, in. Father! A. *ibā*, s.f. Denial, refusal. A.

آباد ***ābād***, a. Cultivated, peopled, prosperous. P.

آبادي ***ābādī***, s.f. Cultivation, prosperity. P.

اباسين ***abāsīn***, s.m. The father of rivers. The Indus. Also written *abāsīnd*.

ابتدا ***ibtidā***, s.f. Beginning, commencement. A.

ابد ***abad***, s.m. Eternity. A. *abadan*, a. Eternal.

ابدال ***abdāl***, s.m. A saint. A.

ابدالي ***abdālī***, s.m. Name of an Afghan clan in the country between Kandahar and Herat. *abdālai*, s.m. A man of the tribe.

آبرو ***ābrū***, s.m. Honour, reputation, name, renown. P. *abrū*, s.m. The eyebrow. P.

ابره ***abra***, s.f. The outer cloth of a garment; a sash for the waist. P.

ابريښم ***abrekkham*** or ***abreksham***, s.m. New silk, floss silk. P. (*abresham*).

ابل ***abl***, a. Barefooted, unshod; powerless, weak. S. (*abal*). *kkhpa-abla*, a. Barefooted, unshod.

ابله ***ablah***, a. Foolish, silly, stupid. A.

ابئي ***aba-ī***, s.f. A mother.

آبرين ***āparīn***, in. Bravo! well done! P. (*āfarīn*).

اپريدي ***aprīdī***, s.m. Name of a tribe of Pathans in the Kohat hills. Also written *afrīdī*.

اپس‌ډنډئي ***apas-ḍanḍa-ī***, s.f. Name of a game; tip-cat; bat and ball.

اپلت ***aplat***, a. Obscene, dirty, filthy.

اپوټه ***apūṭah***, a. Inverted, reversed, inside-out. H.

اترنگ ***atrang***, s.m. Name of a plant, used in dyeing and medicine (*asclepias echinata*). H.

آتش ***ātash***, s.m. Fire (in comp. only). P.

اتفاق ***ittifāq***, s.m. Agreement, concord. A.

اتفاقي ***ittifāqī***, a. Accidental. A.

اتم ***atam***, a. The eighth.

اتڼ or اتن ***ataṉr***, s.m. A kind of dance, a jig, a reel, round dance.

اتوار ***itwār***, s.m. Sunday. S.

اتوب ***atob***, s.m. Gruel, pap.

اته ***atah***, s.m. Eight. *atah-las*, s.m. Eighteen.

اتيا ***atiyā***, a. Eighty. *atiyāyam*, a. Eightieth.

اټال ***aṭāl***, a. Idle, unemployed, out of work.

اټکل ***aṭkal***, s.m. Conjecture, guess. H.

اټه ***aṭa***, s.f. A ball, reel, or skein of thread. H. (*aṭṭī*).

اټيران ***aṭerān***, s.m. A reel for thread. H.

اټيرل ***aṭeral***, v.n. To be dyspeptic.

اټيرنه ***aṭerana***, s.f. Indigestion, dyspepsia.

اټيه ***aṭiya***, | اټيهه ***aṭeha***, } s.f. See اټه.

اثبات ***is̱bāt***, s.m. Confirmation, proof. A.

اثر ***as̱r***, s.m. Effect, mark, sign. A.

اجاره ***ijāra***, s.f. Farm, hire, rent. A.

اجازت ***ijāzat***, s.m. Leave, permission, order. A.

اجر ***ajar***, | اجرت ***ujrat***, } s.m. Hire, wages, reward. A.

اجل ***ajal***, s.m. Fate, death. A.

اڅنرل ***atsaṉral***, v.a. To arrange, harmonize, level, smooth.

اچت ***uchat***, a. Elevated, high, lofty. s. (*unchā*).

اچرلي ***ucharlai***, s.m. The forehead, brow.

آچو ***āchū***, s.f. A raspberry; the bush and fruit.

آچول ***āchawul***, v.a. To cast, throw, fling.

آخ ***ākh***, in. Ah! Good! Well! How good! A.

اخاړه ***akhāṛah***, s.m. Plaster; daubing, plastering.

اخبار ***akhbār***, s.m. Intelligence, news; a newspaper (pl. of خبر A.).

اختر ***akhtar***, s.m. A star; good omen, good fortune; a festival. *loe-akhtar*, the great festival; name of a month corresponding with *z̤ī-hijja*. *wṛūkai-akhtar*, the little festival, or the month corresponding with *shawāl*. P.

آخته ***ākhtah***, a. Castrated; involved, caught, entangled, trammeled. P.

اختيار ***ikhtiyār***, s.m. Authority, power; option, choice. A.

آخر ***ākhir***, s.m. Conclusion, end. ad. At last, finally. A.

آخرت ***ākhirat***, s.m. Futurity. A.

آخستل ***ākhistal***, v.a. To accept, take; appropriate, seize, capture. A. (*akhaz̤*)?

آخښ ***ākhkkh*** or ***ākhksh***, in. Alas! Heigho! See آخ.

اخگر ***akhgar***, s.m. Live coal, hot ember. P.

اخلاص ***ikhlāṣ***, s.m. Sincerity, kindness, affection. A.

آخون ***ākhūn***, s.m. A tutor, teacher, master. Also written *ākhūnd*. P.

اخيړل ***akheṛal***, v.a. To daub, plaster, smear.

ادا ***adā***, s.f. Payment, performance. A.

ادب ***adab***, s.m. Courtesy, politeness, respect. A.

ادنا ***adnā***, a. Inferior, mean, small. A.

ادوبدو ***adūbadū***, a. Distended, tumefied, blown, swelled.

ادينه ***adīna***, s.f. Friday; Sabbath. P.

ادئ *aḍa-ī*, s.f. Fields, plots of land round a village. Mother.

آذان *āẕān*, s.m. Call to prayer. A.

اذن *iẕn*, s.m. Leave, permission, order. A.

آذوقه *āẕūqa*, s.f. Food, provisions, victuals. A.

اراخ *arā<u>kh</u>*, s.m. A brook, rivulet, watercourse.

اراده *irāda*, s.f. Design, desire, wish. A.

آراسته *ārāstah*, a. Adorned, arranged, composed. P.

آرام *ārām*, s.m. Comfort, ease, rest. P.

ارباب *arbāb*, s.m. A noble, chief, lord (pl. of رب A.).

اربوز *urbūz*, s.m. The snout, muzzle.

ارت *art*, a. Loose, open, wide. *aratawul*, v.a. To loosen.

ارتاو *arṭāw*, s.m. See پرتاب.

ارتول *artawul*, v.a. To break wind; widen.

آرته *ārta* or ښپه آرته *<u>kkh</u>pa·ārta*, s.f. Name of a wedding ceremony; the first visit of a lover at the house of his affianced, on the third day after betrothal; he takes some present for his affianced bride and is in return regaled with sherbet and cakes. After this ceremony, but not before, he can visit at the bride's house whenever convenient. S. (*ārtā*). *<u>kkh</u>pa·ārtūn*, s.m. Courtship.

ارتينه *artīna*, s.f. A woman, wife; female. A. (*'aurat*).

ارجل برجل *arjal·barjal*, a. Entangled, noosed, trapped.

آرخښ *ār<u>kh</u>a<u>kkh</u>*, s.m. A gasp, gurgle.

اردو *urdū*, s.m. A camp, cantonment. T.

ارز *arz*, s.m. Price, value. P.

ارزان *arzān*, a. Cheap, inexpensive. P.

آرزو *ārzū*, s.m. Desire, want, wish. P.

ارزيدل *arzedal*, v.n. To be worth, fetch.

ارږمي *argamai*, s.m. A belch, eructation.

ارږي *argai*, s.m. See preceding. P. (*āro<u>gh</u>*).

آرسئ *ārsa-ī*, s.f. A small mirror worn on the thumb by women. H.

ارغند *ar<u>gh</u>und*, s.m. A. knuckle bone.

ارګ *arg*, s.m. A citadel, palace. P.

ارګجه *argajah*, a. Mixed, miscellaneous. H.

ارمان *armān*, s.m. Regret, sorrow; desire, wish. in. Woe! Alas!

اروته *arwata*, s.f. A woman, wife, female. A. (*'aurat*).

آرويدل *ārwedal*, v.a. To hear, listen.

آره *āra*, s.f. A base, foundation. *ara*, s.f. A saw. P.

ارهټ *arhaṭ*, s.m. An irrigation well worked by wheels. H.

ارهر *arhar*, s.m. Name of a pulse, "pigeon pea" (*Cytisus cajan*). H.

ارهنډه *arhanḍa*, s.m. The castor-oil tree (*Ricinus communis*). S.

آري *āre*, ad. Yea, yes, verily, aye. P.

اریړئ *areṛai*, s.f. A stop, catch, bolt; the small cross-bars to which the waterpots of an irrigation wheel are fastened.

آړ *āṛ*, s.m. Difficulty, obstruction; a screen; shelter; a fetter, bond. H.

اړمکي *aṛamkai*, s.m. A shepherd's crook.

اړخ *aṛ<u>kh</u>*, s.m. Armpit; flank, side.

اړم *aṛam*, s.m. A buttress, prop, support.

اړمي *aṛamai*, s.m. A small prop, a bar; the bar of a door.

اړنګ بړنګ *aṛang·baṛang*, a. Confused, entangled.

اړول *aṛawul*, v.a. To overturn, upset, invert, turn over.

اړيکي *aṛekai*, s.m. The bar or bolt of a door or window; a small prop or support; hindrance, obstacle.

آزاد *āzād*, a. Free, liberated, loose. P.

آزار *āzār*, s.m. Affliction, distress. P. *izār*, s.m. Trowsers, drawers. P.

آزرده *āzurdah*, a. Sad, sorrowful, grieved. P.

ازغن *az<u>gh</u>an*, a. Thorny, prickly.

ازغي *az<u>gh</u>ai*, s.m. A thorn, prickle.

آزمايښت *āzmāyi<u>kkh</u>t* or آزمېښت *āzme<u>kkh</u>t*, s.m. Proof, trial, test. P. (*āzmā-ī<u>sh</u>*).

آزمايل **āzmāyal** or آزمويل **āzmoyal,** v.a. To examine, prove, test, try. P. (*āzmūdan*).

اڼريل **agayal,** v.a. To wattle, net; stitch, sew; to provoke, urge, incite, instigate.

آس **ās,** s.m. A horse. P. (*asp*).

اسامي **asāmī,** s.m. A tenant, client; defendant. A.

آسان **āsān,** a. Easy, facile. P.

اسباب **asbāb,** s.m. Chattels, goods (pl. of سبب A.).

اسپغول **ispaghol,** s.m. Name of a herb (*Plantago ispaghula*). The seeds are used in medicine. P.

اسپند **ispand,** s.m. Name of a plant; the Syrian rue (*Peganum harmala*). The seeds are used in medicine, and the dried herb as incense to drive away evil spirits. P.

آسپه **āspa,** s.f. A mare. *aspa,* s.f. Quinsy; scurvy.

استاځي **astādzai,** s.m. A messenger, delegate, apostle.

استاذ **ustāz,** s.m. A master, teacher. P. (*ustād*).

آستان **āstān,** s.m. A threshold; shrine of a saint; family, house. P.

استر **astar,** s.m. The lining of a dress. P.

استره **astura,** s.f. A razor. P.

استوژه **astoja,** / استوګه **astoga,** } s.f. Abode, dwelling, residence. Also *astogana*.

استوګونکي **astogūnkai,** s.m. Resident, dweller.

استيفا **istīfā,** s.f. Renouncing; resignation. A.

آستين **āstīn,** s.m. A sleeve. P.

آستول **āstawul,** v.a. To send, transmit, despatch, depute. P. (*firistādan*).

آستيدل **āstedal,** v.n. To abide, dwell, reside. P. (*istādan*). See *osedal.*

اسراف **isrāf,** s.m. Extravagance, prodigality, waste. A. (*isrāf*).

آسره **āsra,** s.f. Hope, refuge, trust, reliance. S. (*āsrā*).

اسلام **islām,** s.m. The Muhammadan religion. A.

آسمان **āsmān,** s.m. The sky, heaven. P.

اسو **asū,** s.m. Name of the sixth Hindu month. September-October. S. (*āsin*).

آسوده **āsūdah,** a. Contented, tranquil, quiet. P.

اسويلي **aswelai,** s.m. A gape, sigh, yawn.

اسي **asī,** a. Unfortunate, unlucky. *asa-ī,* s.f. Hoarfrost.

آسيا **āsiyā,** s.f. A water-mill. P.

اسير **asīr,** s.m. A captive, prisoner. P.

اشارت **ishārat,** s.m. A hint, nod, sign, wink. A.

اشاري **ashārai,** s.m. A dried apricot.

اشر **asharr,** a. Abusive, wicked, vicious, obscene. A.

اشتوکه **ashtoka,** s.f. Concord, peace. P. (*āshtī*).

اشتها **ishtihā,** s.f. Appetite, desire. A.

آشناي **āshnāe,** s.m. A friend, lover. P. (*āshnā*). *āshnā-ī,* s.f. Friendship, intimacy.

آښل **ākkhal,** v.a. To knead or mix dough. Def. in pres. ten. See آغړل.

آښلي **ākkhalai,** s.m. Dough. a. Kneaded.

اصل **asl,** s.m. Lineage, origin, source; capital. A.

اصلي **aslī,** a. Genuine, original. A.

اصيل **asīl,** a. Noble, well bred. A.

اطلاع **ittilā',** s.f. Notice, information. A.

اعتبار **i'tibār,** s.m. Credit, trust, reliance. A.

اعجوبه **a'jūbah,** s.m. A miracle, prodigy, wonder. A.

اغ‌دغ **agh·dugh,** s.m. Fraud, deceit, imposture.

اغر **aghar,** s.m. Fixing the arrow on the bow-string preparatory to shooting.

آغزکي **āghzakai,** s.m. Name of a thorny plant.

آغزن **āghzan,** a. Thorny, prickly.

آغزي **āghzai,** s.m. A thorn, prickle.

آغړل **āghagal,** v.a. To knead or mix dough. Def. in past ten. See آښل. P. (*āghishtan*).

اغلب **aghlab,** ad. Most likely, most probably. A.

آغله **āghalah,** a. Mixed, kneaded; good, pleasing.

آغوستل *āghūstal*, v.a. To dress, put on clothes, attire. P. (*āghastan, āghandan*).

آغوستن *āghostan*, s.m. Apparel, dress, raiment, clothing.

آغوستول *āghostawul*, v.a. To attire, clothe, dress.

آغيرل *āgheṛal*, v.n. s. (*ajīran*). See اتيرل.

آفت *āfat*, s.m. Calamity, misfortune. A.

افسوس *afsos*, s.m. Grief, sorrow, regret. in. Alas! pity! ah! P.

افغان *afghān*, s.m. An Afghān.

افيم *afīm*, s.m. Opium. A. (*afiyūn*).

اقبال *iqbāl*, s.m. Good fortune, prestige, good auspices. A.

اقرار *iqrār*, s.m. Agreement, assurance, confession. A.

اقليم *iqlīm*, s.m. Country, climate, region. A.

اكا *akā*, s.m. A paternal uncle.

اكثر *akṣar*, a. Most. ad. Mostly, generally. A.

اكر *akar*, s.m. Giddiness, vertigo.

اكوبكو *akū·bakū*, s.m. Name of a bird; name of a game; it is played with cakes of moist clay of a globular shape, hollowed out, and made to explode by being dashed on a hard surface with the opening downwards.

اكور *akoṛ*, s.m. A walnut; the tree.

اكوري *akoṛai*, s.m. A kind of leather tanned red.

آگاه *āgāh*, a. Apprized, aware, informed. P.

اگر *agar*, s.m. A captive, slave, bondsman. P. c. If. P.

اگرچه *agarchi*, c. Although, though. P.

اگرمي *agramai*, s.m. See اريمي.

اگن *agan*, s.m. Name of a bird; the skylark. H.

اگي *aga-ī*, s.f. An egg.

آل *āl*, s.m. Children, progeny. A.

الاج *alāj*, s.m. A carder or comber of cotton. A. (*ḥallāj*).

الاجي *alājī*, s.f. A comb for clearing cotton of its seeds.

الاستي *alāstī*, a. Absent, invisible.

البتة *albatta*, ad. Certainly, undoubtedly, of course. A.

الجه *ulja*, s.f. Booty, plunder.

السي *alsī*, s.f. Linseed. H.

الفت *ulfat*, s.m. Familiarity, friendship, intimacy, kindness. A.

آلفته *āluftah*, a. Vexed, troubled, distressed. P.

القصه *alqiṣṣa*, ad. In fine, in short. A.

الله *allah*, s.m. God. in. Good God! My God! Oh God! A. *allah·bāsh*, s.m. Greeting, shaking hands.

آلو *ālū*, s.m. A kind of plum; a plum. P.

الوان *alwān*, s.m. A kind of cotton cloth dyed red; coloured cloth. A.

آلوتل *ālwatal*, v.n. To fly, float in the air.

الوچه *alūcha*, s.f. A kind of plum. P.

آلوده *ālūdah*, a. Soiled, stained, spattered. P.

آلوزول *ālwuzawul*, v.a. To make fly; to sift or winnow corn, etc., by throwing it up in the air against the wind.

الوس *ulūs*, s.m. A clan, people, tribe. T.

الول *aluwal*, a. All of a heap, by the run, all in a lump.

الوويل *alwoyal*, v.a. To parch, roast, scorch, burn.

الوي *alawai*, a. Parched, roasted, scorched, burnt.

الهنگ *alhang*, s.m. Crying, sobbing, blubbering.

امام *imām*, s.m. The chief priest of a mosque; the large bead of a rosary. A.

امان *amān*, s.m. Protection, quarter, safety. A.

امانت *amānat*, s.m. Deposit, trust. A.

اماني *amānī*, a. All, entire, whole. ad. Entirely, wholly. s.f. Deposit, security, trust. A.

امبار *ambār*, s.m. A heap, a store of grain, etc. P.

امبور *ambūr*, s.m. Forceps, pincers, pliers. P.

آمدني *āmadanī*, s.f. Income, revenue; import. P.

آمدرفت *āmad-raft*, s.m. Coming and going, intercourse, thoroughfare. P.

امر *amr*, s.m. Command, order; affair, business. A.

امرسه *amrasa*, s.f. A kind of sweetmeat.

امسا *amsā*, s.f. A staff, stick. A. (*'aṣā*).

امكان *imkān* s.m. Possibility. A.

امل *amal*, s.m. Intoxication; habitude.

املي *amalī*, s.m. A man addicted to intoxicating drugs.

املوك *amlūk*, s.m. Name of a tree that bears an edible fruit (*Diospyros sp.*).

امن *aman*, s.m. Safety, security, asylum. A.

آموخته *āmo<u>kh</u>tah*, a. Learned, taught; experienced, habituated, accustomed. P.

اميد *umed*, s.m. Expectation, hope; pregnancy. P.

امير *amīr*, s.m. A noble, grandee, ruler. A.

اميل *amel*, s.m. An ornament for the neck; a necklace of charms, etc. A. (*ḥimā-il*).

آمين *āmīn*, ad. Amen, so be it. A. *amīn*, s.m. A guardian, umpire, trustee. a. Constant, faithful, trusty. A.

انا *anā*, s.f. A grandmother, paternal or maternal. *warla-anā*, s.f. A great grandmother.

انار *anār*, s.m. A pomegranate. P.

انبالي *anbāla-ī*, s.f. A howdah; a sedan or litter for women, carried on a pole by men. A. (*'amārī*).

انجام *anjām*, s.m. Accomplishment, end. P.

انجير *anjīr*, s.m. Scrofula; diseased glands in the neck.

انځي *an<u>ts</u>a-ī*, s.f. Cord, string, twine. H. (*āns*).

اند *and*, s.m. An age, cycle of five hundred years; idea, thought, fancy; testicle, egg. S.

اندازه *andāza*, s.f. Measure, quantity; guess. P.

اندرپايه *andarpāya*, s.f. A ladder, steps, stairs.

اندركه *andraka*, s.f. A coat, doublet. S. (*angarkhā*).

اندرور *andror*, s.f. A husband's sister. See ندرور.

انده *inda*, s.f. A sip, gulp, mouthful.

انديښ *ande<u>kkh</u>* or *ande<u>ksh</u>*, s.m. Meditating, cogitating, thinking. P. (*ande<u>sh</u>*).

انديښنه *ande<u>kkh</u>na*, s.f. Anxiety, care, thought, dread. Also *ande<u>kkh</u>nā*.

اندوخړ *anḍo<u>kh</u>aṛ*, s.m. Name of a game; baste the bear. Called also *swara-ḍabala-ī*, The basters riding on the backs of other boys round the bear.

اندي *anḍai*, s.m. A bundle, package.

انديري *anḍerai*, s.m. A mat made of palm leaves.

انذور *an<u>z</u>or* or انځور *an<u>dz</u>or*, s.m. Ornament, decoration, embellishment.

انسان *insān*, s.m. Man, mankind. A.

انسټ *ansiṭ*, s.m. Name of a plant.

انصاف *inṣāf*, s.m. Equity, justice. A.

انعام *in'ām*, s.m. A favour, gift, present. A.

انكار *inkār*, s.m. Denial, negation. A.

انگازه *angāza*, s.f. Echo, resonance, reverberation.

انگبين *angabīn*, s.m. Honey; the comb. P.

انگړ *angaṛ*, s.m. A house, mansion.

انگڼ *anga<u>nr</u>*, s.m. An area, court, yard. S. (*āngan*).

انگولا *angolā*, s.f. The howl of a wild animal.

انگه *inga*, s.f. A bride's maid or attendant for the first few days after marriage. *anga*, s.f. A frock, coat. S. (*angā*).

انگي *anga-ī*, s.f. Name of a game; prisoners' bars.

انگيټي *angeṭa-ī*, s.f. A chafing dish. H. (*angeṭhī*).

انگيرل *angeral*, v.a. To fancy, imagine, suppose, think. P. (*ingārdan*).

اننگ *anang*, s.m. A pomegranate; the space between the thumb and fore-finger; a short span.

اننگوري *anangūṛai*, s.m. A small pomegranate.

اننگي *anangai*, s.m. The cheek.

آنه *āna*, s.f. The pommel of a saddle.

انني *ana-ī*, s.f. A woman's name; Annie.

انړل *anṛal*, v.a. To grind, powder, triturate.

انړول *anṛawul*, v.a. To choose, gather, pick, select, separate, sort.

انوټ *anwaṭ*, s.m. A ring for the thumb or great toe. H.

او *aw*, c. And, also. *ao*, ad. Aye, yes. *o*, in. Oh! Halloa! Hie!

اوار *awār*, s.m. Booty, plunder, spoil; injustice, delay, tyranny. P.

آواره *āwārah*, a. Dissolute, vagabond; spiritless, mean.

آواز *āwāz*, s.m. Voice, sound, report. P.

آوازه *āwāza*, s.f. Rumour, report, fame, celebrity.

اوبال *obāl*, s.m. A crime, fault, sin. A.

اوبړي *obṛa-ī*, s.f. The green vegetation in ponds, etc. Confervæ; duckweed.

اوبنړه *obanṛa*, s.f. The caul; the membrane enveloping the fœtus.

اوبه *oba*, s.f. Water, liquid, fluid. P. (*āb*). A splint in the leg of a horse, etc. *oblan*, a. Watery, sodden.

اوپره *ūprah*, a. Foreign, strange.

اوتر *awtar*, a. Ruined, spoiled; dissolute, wanton, deranged. A. (*abtar*).

اوجاړ *ūjāṛ*, a. Desert, waste, desolated, ruined. S.

اوجري *ūjrai*, s.m. An entrail, gut; tripe. H. (*ūjh*).

اوڅار *awtsār*, a. Clear, evident, manifest. s.m. symptom, sign, evidence, mark. H. (*ūjāl*).

اوچت *ūchat*, a. High, lofty, raised, elevated. S. (*ūnchā*).

اودرول *odrawul*, v.a. To fix, set up, pitch (as a tent); to halt, stop, stay (as a boat, cattle, etc.); to make stand.

اودريدل *ūdaredal*, v.n. To abide, halt, stop, stay, stand up, stand still.

اودس *awdas*, s.m. Washing the hands; a form of ablution before prayers; purification. P. (*āb-dast*).

اودل *ūdal*, v.a. To weave, braid, net. P. (*āwīdan*).

اوده *ūdah*, a. Asleep, sleeping. *ūda*, s.f. A charm, blowing, breathing upon by way of charm; mesmerism. (The power is supposed to be acquired by direct commission from above, or by inheritance.) Also written *hūda*. A. (*'uhda*).

اوډني *oḍana-ī*, s.f. A woman's veil or mantle. H. (*oṛhnā*).

اور *or*, s.m. Fire. H. (*āg*).

اوراوره‌کي *or-orahkai*, s.m. Name of a plant; the wild onion or leek; it is used as a condiment.

اوربوشه *orbūsha*, s.f. A barley corn. *orbūshe*, pl. Barley.

اوربوشينه *orbūshīna*, s.f. Barley-meal, barley-bread.

اوربل *orbal*, s.m. A curl, ringlet, or lock of hair on the forehead.

اورپښت *orpukkht*, s.m. A moth.

اورلړوني *or-laṛūnai*, s.m. A fire-poker.

اورمير *ormeg*, s.m. The neck, throat.

اورنړي *oranṛai*, s.m. A swaddling-cloth, a baby's winding sheet. H. (*oṛhnī*).

آورول *āwrawul*, v.a. To cause to hear.

اوره *orah*, s.m. A cloud, the clouds. P. (*abr*).

اوره‌کي *orahkai*, s.m. A firefly, glow-worm.

آوري *āwrai*, s.m. Mustard seed; name of a herb; wild mustard.

اوري *ora-ī*, s.f. The gums; quick of the nails.

اوريځ *oryadz*, / اوريځه *oryadza*, } s.f. A cloud.

آوريدل *āwredal*, v.a. To hear, listen, P. (*āwrīdan*).

اوريدل *oredal*, v.n. To rain, drizzle. P. (*bārīdan*).

اوړ *oṛ*, s.m. A weaver's tool; the web through which the woof passes.

اورنبي *oṛunbe*, ad. Firstly, first, formerly, previously. Also written *wṛūnbe*. *oṛunbanai* or *wṛunbanai*, a. Former, previous.

اورنئ *oṛana-ī*, s.f. See اودنئ.

اوروَل *oṛawul*, v.a. To powder, grind, pulverize.

اوړه *oṛah*, s.m. Flour, meal, powder.

اوري *oṛai*, s.m. Summer.

اوژغونه *oǰghūna*, s.f. A goat's hair. *oǰghune*, pl. Goat's hair.

اوږد *ūgd*, a. Long, extended.

اوږمکئ *ugmaka-ī*, s.f. The moon; moonlight.

اوږه *ūga*, s.f. Garlic. *oga*, s.f. The shoulder.

اوږي *ogai*, s.m. A measure of grain, etc. equal to 14lbs. *oga-ī*, s.f. An ornament for the neck; a necklet or collar of silver or gold.

اوس *os*, ad. Now, at this time.

اوسپانخړي *ospankhaṛai*, s.m. Iron slag or dross.

اوسپنه *ospana*, s.f. Iron.

اوسط *awsaṭ*, a. Medium, mean, middling. A.

اوسن *osan*, a. Existing, present.

اوسني *osanai*, a. Modern, late, recent.

اوسي *osai*, s.m. A deer, gazelle.

اوسيدل *osedal*, v.n. To abide, exist, remain, dwell, reside, stay. See *āstedal*.

اوښ *ūkkh*, s.m. A camel. P. (*ūshtur*).

اوښبه *ūkkhbah* or *ūkshbah*, s.m. A camelman, an owner of camels.

آوښتل *āwukkhtal*, v.a. To change, turn, alter. P. (*bāz-gashtan*).

اوښه *okkha*, s.f. A tear. P. (*ashk*).

اوښي *awkkhai*, s.m., A brother-in-law: wife's brother; sister's husband. A. (*akh*, brother). *okkhī*, s.m. The mane of a horse.

اوغان *awghān*, s.m. An Afghan.

اوغز *ūghz*, s.m. A walnut.

اوگره *ogra*, s.f. Porridge, pap, gruel. P. (*oghrā*).

اوگړائي *ūgṛā-ī*, s.f. A portion, part, instalment; a debt paid at different times. H.

اول *awwal*, a. First, foremost. A.

اولاد *awlād*, s.m. Progeny, issue, children. A. Also written *alwād*.

اولو *awlū*, s.m. Treacle, molasses.

اوله *olah*, s.m. A flock of lambs kept separate from their mothers.

اوم *om* or *ūm*, a. Crude, raw, uncooked, unripe, immature. P. (*khām*). *awam*, a. The seventh.

اومه *omah*, s.m. Name of a plant. It is used in tanning, and is added to snuff to increase its pungency.

اونگئ *ūnga-ī*, s.f. The moon.

اوني *ūnai*, s.m. A babbler, chatterer.

اووم *owom*, a. The seventh.

اووه *owah*, a. Seven.

اووي *owī*, s.m. A cock's comb; a horse's mane.

اوه *owoh*, a. Seven. *awa*, s.f. A pimple, pustule, vesicle.

اوي *oe*, s.m. Consent, promise, pledge.

اويا *awiyā*, a. Seventy.

اويزاند *awezānd*, a. Hanging, pendant, suspended. P. (*ānez*).

اوينه *oenah*, s.m. The white ant.

اهاړ *ahāṛ*, s.m. Name of the third Hindu month. June-July.

اي *ai*, in. Oh! Halloa! sign of the vocative case. P.

آيا *āyā*, in. No! Is it! Really! How odd! P. ad. No, not at all, never.

ايړى *erṛai*, s.m. The long-tailed sheep. S. (*bheṛī*).

ايره *īra*, s.f. Ash. *īre*, pl. Ashes.

ايړي *eṛai*, s.m. See ايړوي.

ايسار *īsār*, a. Hindered, stopped, surrounded. s.m. A castle, fort; embarrassment; perplexity. A. (*ḥiṣār*).

ايستل *estal*, v.a. To draw out, extract, expel. Also *yastal*. Def. in pres. ten. See باسل.

ايشنه *eshana*, s.f. Agitation, ferment, ebullition, effervescence. P. (*josh*).

ايشول *eshawul*, v.a. To boil, heat, make boil. P. (*joshandan*).

ايشيدل *eshedal*, v.n. To boil, bubble, effervesce. P. (*joshīdan*).

اېښل *ekkhal* or *īkkhal*, v.a. To lay, put, place, set. Also *yakkhal*. Def. in pres. ten. See ږدل. P. (*nishāndan*).

اېښودل *ekkhodal* or *īkkhodal*, } v.a. See اېښل.
اېښول *ekkhawul* or *īkkhawul*, }

ايل *el* or *īl*, T. Domestic, tame, not wild.

ايله *elah*, T. Free, liberated. P. (*yalah*).

ايمان *īmān*, s.m. Faith, religious belief. A.

ايمن *eman*, a. Calm, gentle, patient.

ايمنه *emna*, s.f. A woman's name.

اينځر *indzar*, s.m. A fig; the tree. P. (*anjīr*).

آئين *ā-īn*, s.m. Law, rule, regulation. P.

آئينه *ā-īna*, s.f. A mirror, looking-glass; the liver, the gall bladder.

اينه *īna*, s.f. The gall bladder, the liver, lungs and heart, the vitals.

ايوه *īwa*, s.f. A plough, ploughing.

ب

ب *be*. The second letter of the Pukkhto alphabet. It is often changed for و in words adopted from Persian and Sanscrit.

بَ *ba* or به *ba*, part. The sign of the future and continuative past tenses of verbs.

با *bā*, p. With, by. Only used in comp. with words from Persian. P.

باب *bāb*, s.m. Account, business, matter; chapter or section of a book; door, gate. A.

بابا *bābā*, in. Father! Sire! A term of affection and respect used towards old men, and by children to a grandfather. T.

بابت *bābat*, s.m. Affair, business; item, article; account, on account of. A.

بابړ *bābaṛ*, s.m. Name of an Afghan clan.

بابكو *bābako*, in. Dear child! A term of affectionate address to a child.

بابو *bābū*, in. Father! Sire! A term of affection or esteem used towards a father or old man.

بابي *bābī*, s.f. A brother's wife, sister-in-law. in. Mother! Granny dear! s.m. Name of an Afghan clan.

باتور *bātūr*, s.m. An eagle; brave, valiant (corrupt: of P. *bahādur*). *bātor*, s.m. The pupil of the eye.

باتۍ *bāta-ī*, s.f. A wick, match, candle, spile; bougie, a tent for a wound. S. (*battī*).

باټ *bāṭ*, s.m. A hone, grindstone.

باټينګنړ *bāṭingaṇṛ*, s.m. The egg-plant (*solanum longum*). H. (*baingan*).

باج *bāj*, s.m. Tax, toll, impost, duty. P.

باجره *bājra*, s.f. Indian corn, spiked millet (*Holcus spicatus*). P. (*bājrā*).

باجه *bājah*, s.m. Wife's sister's husband, brother-in-law.

باد *bād*, s.m. Air, wind; rheumatism. P.

بادام *bādām*, s.m. An almond. P.

بادخور *bād-khor*, s.m. A disease of horses; œdema. Name of a kind of hawk. P.

بادخورک *bād-khorak*, s.m. The sparrow-hawk. P.

بادرنګ *bādrang*, s.m. A cucumber. P.

بادرو *bādro*, s.m. Name of the fifth Hindu month. August-September. S. (*bhādon*). *bādraw*, s.m. An air-hole, ventilator. Also *bād-khāna*. P.

بادشاه *bādshāh*, s.m. Monarch, sovereign, king. P.

بادکښ *bād-kakkh*, s.m. A ventilator, chimney. P. (*bād-kash*).

بادګوله *bād-gola*, s.f. Colic, flatulent colic. P.

بادوان *bād-wān*, s.m. A sail, wing; a shade or screen for a lamp. P.

بادهوا *bād-hawā*, s.f. A paper kite. P.

بادي *bādī*, a. Flatulent, windy; haughty, proud.

بادګول *bāḍgol*, s.m. A leading string, rein, head rope of a horse. H. (*bāgḍor*).

بار *bār*, s.m. A burden, load; time, occasion, turn, place. P.

باران *bārān*, s.m. Rain; a shower, downpour. P.

بارخو *bār<u>kh</u>o*, s.f. The cheek, side of the face.

بارک *bārak*, s.m. A man's name, Barak. *bārakzī*, s.m. The clan Barak. *bārakzai*, s.m. A man of the clan Barak. *bārakza-ī*, s.f. A woman of the clan Barak. The late Amir Dost Muhammad Khan was the head of this now famous clan.

بارکښ *bār-ka<u>kkh</u>*, s.m. A rope, cord, etc., for tying up baggage; a beast of burden. a. burthen-bearing; meek, humble. P. (*bār-ka<u>sh</u>*).

باره *bāra*, s.f. A rampart, fortification, enclosure, ditch, entrenchment, fence. P.

باریک *bārīk*, a. Fine, narrow, slender, subtile. P.

باري *bāre*, ad. Once; at length; then.

باړ *bāṛ*, s.m. A volley of musketry. An iron dish for roasting grain. S.

باړه *bāṛa*, s.f. An enclosure, sheepfold. S. (*bāṛā*).

باړینچغ *bāṛen<u>ch</u>agh*, s.m. A whirligig; a cross bar balanced on the top of an upright post, on which as a pivot it is made to revolve by the riders, who sit in chairs attached to the ends of the cross bar.

باز *bāz*, s.f. A female falcon. P. See جرړه.

بازار *bāzār*, s.m. A market, mart. P.

بازو *bāzū*, s.m. The arm; side of a bedstead; fold of a door; the flank, side of anything. P.

بازوبند *bāzū-band*, s.m. An ornament for the arm. P.

بازي *bāzī*, s.f. Cheat, trick, deception, stratagem; play, sport, game. P.

بازیګر *bāzī-gar*, s.m. A tumbler, rope-dancer, juggler; cheat, impostor.

باس *bās*, s.m. A privy, necessary; odour, smell. S.

باسل *bāsal*, v.a. To extract, draw out, pull out. Def. in past tense. See ایستل.

باښه *bā<u>kkh</u>a*, s.f. A sparrow-hawk. P. (*bā<u>sh</u>a*).

باښین *bā<u>kkh</u>īn*, s.m. A sparrow-hawk. P. (*bā<u>sh</u>īn*).

باطل *bāṭil*, a. Futile, useless, vain. A.

باطن *bāṭin*, a. Concealed, internal. A.

باعث *bā'is̤*, s.m. Account, cause, reason. A.

باغ *bā<u>gh</u>*, s.m. A garden, grove, orchard. P.

باغوان *bā<u>gh</u>wān*, s.m. A gardener.

باقي *bāqī*, s.m. Arrears, balance, remnant; existing, remaining. A.

باک *bāk*, s.m. Anxiety, dread, fear. P.

باکي *bāka-ī*, s.f. Nausea, sickness. H. (*ūbkā-ī*).

باګو *bāgū*, or باګولي *bāgola-ī*, s.f. } A bogy, goblin, ghost.

بالښت *bāli<u>kkh</u>t*, s.m. A bolster, pillow. P. (*bāli<u>sh</u>*). *bāli<u>kkh</u>t-goṭai*, s.m. A cushion.

بالښتک *bāli<u>kkh</u>tak*, s.m. A cushion, pad.

بالغ *bāli<u>gh</u>*, a. Adult, mature, full-grown. A.

بالڼ *bāla<u>nr</u>*, s.m. Fuel, fire-wood.

بالین *bālīn*, s.m. A bolster, pillow, cushion, pad. P.

بام *bām*, s.m. The roof of a house. P.

بامبڼ *bāmba<u>nr</u>*, s.m. A Brahmin. S. (*bāmhan*).

بامبڼه *bāmba<u>nr</u>a*, s.f. A blaze, conflagration. A Brahmin woman.

بامبیلکي *bāmbī-lakai*, s.m. A kind of butterfly.

باندِ *bāndi*, باندي *bānde*, } p. Above, atop, on, upon.

بانډه *bānḍa*, s.f. A cattle or sheep pen; a hamlet. S. (*bāṛā*).

باڼ *bā<u>nr</u>*, s.m. Cordage made of palm-leaves.

باڼه *bā<u>nr</u>a*, s.f. The eyelash.

بانکیا *bānkiyā*, s.m. A fop, beau. H. (*bānkā*).

بانګ *bāng*, s.m. A call, cry, shout. P.

بانگيدل *bāngedal*, v.n. To low, bleat, bellow.

بانه *bāna*, s.f. An excuse, pretence, sham, pretext. P. (*bahāna*).

باور *bāwar*, s.m. Belief, faith, credit, trust. P.

باوسير *bāwsīr*, s.m. Hemorrhoids, piles. A. (*bawāsīr*).

باولي *bāolī*, s.f. The drag on which hawks, dogs, etc. are trained and taught to hunt. A well, with steps to the water. H. *bāolī-warkawul*, v.a. To initiate, train, teach.

باهر *bāhar*, ad. Outside, without, beyond, foreign. S.

باهو *bāhū*, s.m. An ornament for the arm.

بائيده *bā-īdah*, a. Fit, proper, necessary, suitable. ad. Necessarily, of necessity, it behoves.

بائيكر *bā-īkar*, s.m. Name of a shrub (*Adhatoda vasica*). H. (*bākar*).

بايلل *bā-elal*, v.a. To fail, forfeit, lose. P. (*bākhtan*).

ببر *babar*, a. Hairy, shaggy. P.

ببوزي *babozai*, s.m. A fan made of palm leaves, a fan. Name of a bird, the kingfisher.

ببئ *baba-ī*, s.f. Name of a bird. An affectionate term for "mother."

بت *but*, s.m. An image, idol, figure, form, model. One of the walls that supports the cross-beam of a Persian wheel.

بتان *batān*, s.m. See پتان.

بتر *batar*, a. Worse, very bad. P. (*badtar*).

بتك *batak*, s.m. A water cruse, in the shape of a double convex disc, made of leather or pottery.

بتكي *batakai*, s.m. Dimin. of preceding.

بته *bata*, s.f. A heron, crane.

بتي *batī*, s.f. Glue, paste, starch, size.

بټ *baṭ*, s.m. A furnace, kiln; an iron pot or dish for roasting grain; bark, rind, husk; prosperity, good luck.

بټه *baṭa*, s.f. Husked or pounded barley.

بجز *bajuz*, p. Except, besides, save, without. P.

بجل *bujal*, s.m. Ankle-joint, knuckle-bone. P.

بڅخه *butskha*, s.f. A clothes-bag, bundle of clothes. T. (*buqcha*).

بڅخكي *butskhaka-ī*, s.f. A reticule, small bag for collyrium, needles, etc.

بڅري *batsarai*, } s.m. A spark, scintillation.
بڅركي *batsarkai*, }

بچاو *bachāo*, s.m. Escape, protection, shelter. H. *bachawul*, v.a. To save, shelter, etc.

بچري *bachrai*, s.m. An ass's colt, young donkey.

بچكري *bachakarai*, s.m. The lash of a whip; end of a sling.

بچو *bachū*, in. Dear babe! Baby dear! Baby! A term of affectionate address to a child.

بچونګري *bachūngaṛai*, s.m. A babe, infant, a very young animal.

بچوي *bachawai*, s.m. The lash of a whip; end of a sling; a band or ribbon for fastening women's hair; a tassel of braided cords attached to the back hair of women.

بچي *bachai*, s.m. A babe, infant, child, young one. P. (*bacha*).

بحث *bahs*, s.m. Argument, discussion, controversy. A.

بحر *bahr*, s.m. The ocean, sea. A.

بخت *bakht*, s.m. Fate, fortune, luck. P.

بخره *bakhra*, s.f. Lot, portion, share. P.

بخښ *bakhkhsh*, s.m. Lot, share, portion; bestowing, giving; forgiveness. P. (*bakhsh*).

بخښښ *bakhkhshiksh*, s.m. Donation, gift, grant. P. (*bakhshish*).

بخښل *bakhkkhal* or *bakhkshal*, v.a. See ببهل.
P. (*bakhshīdan*).

بخښنه *bakhkkhana*, s.f. Pardon, forgiveness, forgiving; giving, bestowing.

بخملي *bak͟hmala-ī*, s.f. Name of an insect of a scarlet colour, the scarlet lady; called also *bībī-pāto*. (From A. *mak͟hmal*.)

بخيل *bak͟hīl*, s.m. A miser, niggard. a. Vicious, ill-tempered, spiteful, stingy. A.

بخيلي *bak͟hīlī*, s.f. Avarice, stinginess; obstinacy, vice, ill-temper, spite.

بد *bad*, a. Bad, evil, vicious. P.

بدر *badar*, s.m. The silky cotton tree (*Bombax heptaphyllum*). *badar-kand* or *badar-kāṉṟai*, s.m. The gum resin of the tree: used in medicine. The silky cotton is used as a stuffing for pillows.

بدرگه *badraga*, s.f. A convoy, escort, guide. A. (*badraqa*).

بدري *badra-ī*, s.f. A woman's name. *budrī*, s.f. A stumble, trip; loss, injury, damage.

بدعا *bad'uā*, s.f. A curse, malediction. P. (*bad d'uā*).

بدل *badal*, s.m. Exchange; revenge, retaliation. A. *badalawul*, v.a. To exchange, etc.

بدلمن *bad-laman*, a. Wanton, dissolute, unchaste.

بدله *badala*, s.f. Melody, music, tune.

بدن *badan*, s.m. The body. A.

بدي *badī*, s.f. Enmity, evil, mischief.

بداݨي *baḍā-ī*, s.f. Dignity, rank; magnitude, greatness. S. (*baṛā-ī*).

بدګال *baḍagāl*, s.m. The silky down on the flower spike of the bullrush. H. (*baṛā gālā*). See لوخه.

بدړه *baḍa*, s.f. A bribe, douceur; the upper hem of a pair of trousers through which passes the fastening band.

بر *bar*, a. High, upper, top; victorious, successful. s.m. A stroke of the moon, moonblast. *bar wahalai*, a. Moon-struck.

برابر *barābar*, a. Abreast, equal, even, level, alike, smooth, straight.

برايه *barāya*, ad. Last night, yesternight.

برباد *barbād*, a. Ruined, wasted, thrown away. P.

بربره *burbura*, s.f. A bubble. P. (*bulbulā*).

بربست *barbast*, s.m. Chattels, effects, goods. P.

بربند *barbanḍ*, a. Bare, naked, uncovered. P. (*barahna*).

برپا *barpā*, a. Raised, set on foot, commenced. P.

برج *bruj*, s.m. A turret, tower, bastion. P. (*burj*).

برجو *barjo*, s.f. A hone, whetstone. Also *barjo kāṉṟai*.

برڅير *barts̱er*, a. Clear, manifest, evident, visible.

برڅيرن *barts̱eran*, ad. Apparently, manifestly, visibly, clearly.

برخه *brak͟ha*, s.f. See بخره.

برړه *baraṛa*, s.f. Name of a shrub (*Periploca aphylla*).

برطرف *barṯaraf*, a. Apart, aside, dismissed, turned off, discharged. A.

برغ *bragh*, s.m. A fold, layer, plait; duplication, multiplication, fold.

برغټ *barghuṭ*, s.m. A wild cat.

برغنډ *barghanḍ*, s.m. A notch, dent, nick.

برغو *bargho*, s.m. The cleaning rod of a gun.

برغوټي *bar ghoṭa-ī*, s.f. A disease of the parotid gland, mumps.

برغوږ *barghwag*, s.m. An ear-drop, pendant, or ring.

برغولي *bargholai*, s.m. A dish-cover, lid.

برغوني *braghūnai*, s.m. A twin, one of twins.

برکت *barakat*, s.m. Blessing, prosperity, fortune. A.

برکتي *barakatī*, a. Blessed, fortunate, prosperous.

برګ *brag*, a. Spotted, speckled, streaked. s.m. A leper.

برګړندي *bargaṛandai*, s.m. Embracing, hugging, cuddling.

برگستوان *bargastawān*, s.m. Mail armour for a horse; sword proof trappings. P. (*barga-stān*).

برگویت *bargweṭ*, s.m. A man's name. One of the great ancestors of Khaṭak clan.

برگه *barga*, s.f. A beam, rafter. H. (*bargā*).

برگي *bragai*, s.m. Leprosy, a leper.

برم *bram*, s.m. Force, power, strength; guard, protection. P. (*barm*).

برمته *baramta*, s.f. Reprisal, seizing the property or persons of an offending tribe or family in retaliation for injuries done, and as pledges or hostages for restitution or settlement.

برمند *barmanḍ*, a. See برند.

برمه *barma*, s.f. An auger, gimlet, centre-bit or borer, worked with a bow and string. H. (*barmā*).

برند *brand*, a. Frowning, scowling, staring. P. (*barham*).

برندول *brandawul*, v.a. To frown, scowl.

برندي *barandai*, s.m. A spindle for twisting thread. A teetotum, spun by two strings pulled in opposite directions.

برني *baranai*, a. Stale, old, yesterday's.

برروړه *baroṛa*, s.f. A wood-louse; crab-louse; name of a venomous insect. Nettlerash, hives. *broṛah*, s.m. Mixed meal of pulses and cereals. See رارړه.

برونړي *barwanṛa-ī*, s.f. The socket in which the pivot of an irrigation wheel works.

بروي *barwai*, a. Viscid, glutinous, sticky, starchy.

بره *barrah*, s.m. A kid, lamb, sheep. P.

برهگړه *bara-gaṛa*, s.f. Embrace, hug.

برهم *barham*, a Confused, disconcerted, vexed. P.

بري *barai*, s.m. Victory, success, triumph.

بريت *bret*, s.m. the mustache. P. (*burūt*). *brīt*, s.m. Boundary, limit, separation. P. (*burīd*).

بريږن *bregan*, s.m. The bleat of a goat or sheep.

بريښ *brekkh*, s.m. Piercing, lancing, pricking or stabbing pain; a throb, spasm, cramp, stitch; a cutting pain. P. (*burrish*).

بريښنا *brekkhnā*, s.f. Brilliancy, lustre, splendour; lightning.

بريښيدل *brekkhedal*, v.n. To glitter, shine; lighten. A. (*baraq*).

بړاس *bṛās*, s.m. Heat, steam, vapour.

بړانډه *baṛānḍa*, s.f. A conflagration, blaze.

بړبړ *baṛbaṛ*, ad. Often, repeatedly, frequently. P. (*bārbār*).

بړبړي *baṛbaṛai*, s.m. A prattler, gabbler, chatterbox.

بړبوکي *baṛbūka-ī*, s.f. A dust devil, whirlwind.

بړستن *bṛastan*, s.f. Coverlet, quilt, counterpane.

بړني *baṛanai*, s.m. Name of a tree.

بړوا *baṛwā*, s.m. A pimp. H. (*bhaṛwā*).

بړوټ *bṛūṭ*, s.m. Name of a grass (*Cyperus verticillatus*).

بړوس *bṛūs*, a. Angry, furious, savage, enraged. *bṛus-wālai*, s.m. Anger, rage, wrath.

بز *buz*, s.m. A he-goat. P.

بزاز *bazāz*, s.m. Cloth-merchant, draper, mercer. P.

بزغاله *buzghālah*, s.m. A kid. P.

بزغلي *buzghalai*, s.m, A bud, sprout, young shoot.

بزه *baza*, s.f. Sin, crime. P. Name of a shrub. See بائيکر. *bza*, s.f. A she-goat; a curlew. P.

بژه *bjah*, a. Chopped, minced, cut up.

بس *bas*, a. Enough, plenty, sufficient.

بساط *bisāṭ*, s.m. A display, show, or spread of things, as furniture, merchandize, etc., bedding, sheeting, flooring. A.

بسمه *basma*, s.f. Indigo. S.

بسمل *bismil*, a. Sacrificed. *bismil kawul*, v.a. To sacrifice.

بسم الله *bismillah*, In the name of God. *bismillah kawul*, v.a. To commence, begin.

بسيا *basiyā*, a. Cultivated, peopled, inhabited. s.

بشپړ *bashpaṛ*, a. Complete, entire, perfect.

بشر *bashar*, s.m. Man, mankind. A.

بشره *bashra*, s.f. Face, visage, countenance.

بشري *basharī*, a. Human, of man.

بشکه *bushka*, s.f. Name of a plant, used as a pot-herb; goosefoot (*Chenopodium album*).

بشنج *bashanj*, s.m. Character, reputation, name.

بښل *bakkhal*, v.a. To give, pardon, forgive, excuse. See بخښل.

بښنه *bakkhana*, s.f. A gift, pardon, forgiveness.

بط *baṭ*, s.m. A duck. A.

بعد *b'ad*, ad. After, subsequently. A.

بعيد *b'aīd*, a. Far, remote. A.

بغارګ *bghārg*, a. Double, duplex, two-fold.

بغاره *baghāra*, s.f. A scream, shriek.

بغبغو *baghbagho*, s.m. The rice bird (*Ardea torra*).

بغدر *baghdar*, s.m. Hammer, mallet. s. (*mugdar*).

بغرګ *bagharg*, s.m. Rebound, recoil, return. Double, duplex.

بغرګه *bgharga*, s.f. A breach, gap; a deep wound. P. (*bughāra*).

بغرئي *baghra-i*, s.m. A pimp; term of abuse. *baghara-ī*, s.f. A mortar; *vulva*; a term of abuse. P. (*ghubāra*).

بغض *bughz*, s.m. Hatred, malice, rancour, spite. A.

بغل *baghal*, s.m. The armpit, side; embrace. P.

بغير *baghair*, ad. Besides, except, without. A.

بقا *baqā*, s.f. Eternity, perpetuity. A.

بقال *baqāl*, s.m. A corn chandler, grocer. A.

بک *bak*, s.m. Jabber, gabble, prattle, talk. s.

بک بکي *bak·bakai*, s.m. A gabbler, prattler, chatterbox.

بکاره *bakārah*, s.m. Courier, messenger. H. (*bakārā*).

بکاول *bakāwul*, s.m. A cook, victualler. P.

بکرئي *bakra-ī*, s.f. A flint, quartz.

بکيانړه *bakyāṇra*, s.m. Name of a tree (*Melia sempervirens*). H. (*bukāyan*).

بګلولئي *bagalola-ī*, s.f. A bogy, goblin, scarecrow, hag.

بګلي *baglai*, s.m. A crane, heron, the rice bird. H. (*baglā*).

بګنيدل *bugnedal*, v.n. To shy, start, fear. *bugnawul*, v.a. To frighten, scare, start.

بګوړه *bagoṛa*, s.f. A kind of cheese; dry curds; the Persian *qurūt*.

بګوه *bagwa*, s.f. Red ochre, red clay.

بل *bul*, a. Another, other, different. *bal*, a. Burnt, fired, ignited, kindled, lighted.

بلا *balā*, s.f. Affliction, calamity, misfortune.

بلابتر *balā·batar*, s.m. Lumber, trash, rubbish.

بلاربه *blārba*, a. Pregnant, with young.

بلاربيدل *blārbedal*, v.n. To conceive, become pregnant. *blārbawul*, v.a. To make pregnant.

بلاغنډ *balāghunḍ*, s.m. Name of a tree and its fruit (*Ægle marmelos*), and a snuff box.

بلانړه *bilāṇrah*, s.m. A moan, groan, wail.

بلاوه *bulāwa*, s f. Mistake, error. H. (*bhūl*).

بلبل *bulbul*, s.m. A nightingale; a shrike. A kind of dance, a reel. P.

بلد *balad*, s.m. A guide, resident. a. Acquainted, familiar. P.

بلغاک *bulghāk*, s.m. The twitter of birds.

بلغم *balgham*, s.m. Phlegm, mucus. P.

بلکه *balki*, ad. But, nay, rather. A

بلګه *bilga*, s.f. A clue, trace, track, etc., of stolen goods.

بلل *balal*, v.a. To call, summon, convoke. H. (*bulānā*).

بلماز *bilmāz*, a. Prayerless, profane, unholy, impure, corrupt. P. (*be·namāz*).

بلمګي *bilmagai*, } a. Saltless, tasteless, without flavour. (Corrupt: of *be·mālge*).
بلمنګي *bilmangai*, }

بلند *buland*, a. High, lofty, tall. P.

بلندي *bulandai*, s.m. An eminence, height, elevation.

بلو *balaw*, s.m. A hone, razor-strop, whetstone.

بلوا *balwā*, s.f. Mutiny, riot, tumult. A.

بلوڅ *balots*, s.m. A Baloch; the tribe.

بلودل *blodal*, v.a. To chafe, fret, abrade, graze, rub, touch; to vex, annoy, worry. P. (*burīdan*).

بلور *bilaur*, s.m. Crystal, glass. P.

بلوس *blos*, s.m. A rub, graze, touch; annoyance, vexation.

بلوسيدل *blosedal*, v.a. See بلودل.

بلوغت *bulūghat*, s.m. Puberty, adolescence, youth. A.

بلول *balawul*, v.a. To burn, kindle, set alight, fire, ignite.

بلونګړي *bilūngaṛai*, s.m. A squirrel.

بله *bala*, s.f. A javelin, dart, pike. H. (*ballā*).

بلئ *bala-ī*, s.f. The edge of a roof, eaves; door-bolt, boat-hook, barge-pole. H. (*ballī*).

بليدل *baledal*, v.n. To burn, blaze, take fire, ignite. H. (*balnā*).

بليږدل *blegdal*, v.a. To swaddle, swathe.

بم *bam*, s.m. A bass, deep, or hollow sound. A.

بمبره *bambara*, s.f. A wasp, hornet.

بڼ *ba-an*, s.f. A cotemporary or rival wife; each of a man's several wives is *ba-an* to the other. The children by one wife are *ba-anzī* to those by the others. See بڼزی.

بنا *binā*, s.f. Preparation; foundation, building, edifice. A.

بنات *banāt*, s.m. Broad-cloth, woollen cloth. H.

بنبل *banbal*, s.m. The beard of grasses, etc.

بنبوله *banbola*, s.f. A wicker box coated with clay for the storing of grain.

بنج *banj*, s.m. The horse chestnut tree, the fruit. *banaj*, s.m. Trade, merchandise. S.

بنجاري *banjārī*, s.m. A trader, peddler, grain merchant. S. (*banjārā*).

بنجخ *banjakh*, s.m. Name of a plant, the seed of which contains cowitch.

بنجئ *banja-ī*, s.f. The Cassia tree.

بند *band*, s.m. A band, fastening, knot, tie; a joint, knuckle; arrest, captivity, imprisonment; artifice, dodge, trick. P.

بندر *bandar*, s.m. An emporium, seaport. P.

بندلئ *bindla-ī*, s.f. A flute, fife, whistle.

بندڼ *bandaṉr*, s.m. Promise, covenant. S. (*bandhan*).

بندوخ *bandūkh*, s.m. A gun, matchlock. T. (*bandūq*).

بندوبست *bandobast*, s.m. Arrangement, management, settlement. P.

بنده *bandah*, s.m. A servant, slave, bondsman; a creature. P.

بندي *bandī*, s.m. A captive, prisoner. S.

banda-ī, s.f. An ornament for the neck; an ornamental shoulder sling worn by women. S.

بڼزي *ba-anzai*, s.m. Step-son; son of the husband by another wife. (See پرکټي.)

ba-anza-ī, s.f. Step-daughter; a former or other wife's daughter.

بنګ *bang*, s.m. The hemp plant (*Cannabis Indicus*). H. (*bhang*).

بنګي *bangī*, s.m. One addicted to the use of bang, or any other intoxicating drug; a drunkard.

بنګښ *bangakkh*, s.m. Name of a Pathan tribe located about Kohat.

بنګول *bangawul*, v.a. To taint, corrupt, pollute.

بنئ *bana-ī*, s.f. A wallet or bag made of an entire kid's skin; bellows made of a pair of such skins attached to one nozzle.

بنياد *bunyād*, s.m. Base, origin, foundation. A.

بنڼ *baṉr*, s.m. A wood, forest. S. (*ban*).

بنڼمانو *baṉr-mānū*, s.m. A kind of monkey, man of the woods. S. (*ban-manukh*).

بنړه *banṛa*, s.f. A quill, large feather; a feather.

بنړکه *banṛaka*, s.f. A feather, small feather.

بنړئ *banṛa-ī*, s.f. Name of a tree; mistletoe. *banṛai*, a. Red-haired, rufus; shock-headed.

بنړيه *banṛiyah*, s.m. A Hindu shopkeeper. s. (*baniyā*).

بنفشه *binafsha*, s.f. A violet, the plant. P.

بو *bū* or *bo*, s.m. Odour, scent, smell. P. *baw*, s.m. A goblin, scare-crow.

بوتکي *būtkī*, s.f. Name of a gold coin; Belgian ducat.

بوتلل *botlal*, v.a. To carry away, conduct, lead, convey. Only applied to animate objects. See بيول.

بوته *bota*, s.f. Carrying away, leading off, etc. See برمته.

بوتي *botai*, s.m. A young camel. P.

بوټ *būṭ*, a. Surly, cross, sullen, ill-tempered. Also *sūṭ-būṭ*.

بوټسوړي *būṭsūṛī*, s.m. Chaff, bran, husks, shell, etc.

بوټي *būṭai*, s.m. A plant, herb, bush, shrub. *būṭī*, pl. Drugs, vegetable medicines; flowers embroidered, painted, or carved. H. (*būṭā*).

بوجه *būja*, s.f. A bung, cork, stopper, plug.

بوڅکئ *butska-ī*, s.f. The lobe of the ear.

بود *būd*, s.m. Existence, being; profit, gain.

بوده *būda*, s.f. (In weaving) the woof of the web. P.

بوډاګي *būḍāgai*, s.m. A decrepid old man. H. (*būṛhā*).

بور *baur*, s.m. A panther, leopard. *bor*, s.m. A dent, chip, flaw, fracture. a. Grey, brown; a grey horse. H. (*bhūrā*). *būr*, s.m. Husk, skin, chaff; the linear leaves of the pine, tamarisk, and similar trees. A father who has lost a child by death.

بورا *baurā*, s.m. A large black bee. s. (*bhaunra*).

بورجل *borjal*, s.f. An abode, home, house, resort; a place of resort, assignment, or meeting. A. (*marja'*).

بورګي *baurgai*, s.m. A panther, small leopard.

بورنه *bornah*, s.m. Dredging, flour, meal, etc., used to sprinkle upon meat, dough, etc. Also بورنړه.

بوره *būra*, s.f. A woman who has lost her child by death.

بورئ *baura-ī*, s.f. A bunion, corn.

بوړه *bauṛa*, s.f. An elevated plateau, table-land, or flat bit of land on a hill side.

بوړي *būṛai*, s.m. The cog of a Persian wheel. a. Chipped, cracked (as a cup); clipped, slit, split (as the nose or ears). *būṛa-ī*, s.f. Name of a disease (*prolapsus ani*).

بوزه *boza*, s.f. Fermented liquor. P.

بوزينه *bozīna*, s.f. Leather of a red colour, prepared from goat skins. P.

بوږ *bog*, a. Hoarse, rough, husky voice. s.m. A sore throat, aphonia, loss of voice.

بوس *būs*, s.m. Chaff, chopped straw. H. (*bhūs*).

بوساړه *būsāṛa*, s.f. A stack of būs.

بوستان *bostān*, s.m. A flower-garden. P.

بوښت *bokkht*, a. Sticky, adhesive. s.m. A quicksand, bog, quagmire.

بوښتنه *bokkhtana*, s.f. A bog, quicksand.

بوغ *būgh*, s.m. A wooden bowl or cup.

بوق *būq*, A bugle, clarion. A.

بوکه *boka*, s.f. A water-bucket. H.

بوکي *bokī*, s.m. Name of an Afghan clan.

بوګري *bogarai*, s.m. Church land, glebe; land given to priests and holy men free of rent; ploughing and sowing, free of cost, for priests, etc., or for one another.

بول *baul*, s.f. Urine. A. *waṛa-baul kawul*, v.a. To make water, urinate. *loya-baul kawul*, v.a. To go to stool, ease oneself.

بولاق *bolāq*, s.m. An ornament for the nose. H.

بولقه *bolqa*, s.f. A sheet or mantle with eyelets to see through: it is a woman's outdoor dress, and covers the whole body from head to foot: it is only used by women living in cities or large towns. A. (*burqa'*).

بوم *būm*, s.m. A country; an owl; a native or home-bred person; a guide. a. Acquainted, familiar, habituated. P.

بوميا *būmiyā*, s.m. A conductor, guide, resident.

بونست *bonsaṭ*, s.m. Foundation, origin, root; name of a plant.

بونگه *būnga*, s.f. Black-mail, ransom.

بونړ *būnṟ*, s.m. A disease of the nose, ozœna; one afflicted with the disease. Cordage made of palm leaves, and used for netting of beds, etc. H. (*bān*). *bonṟ*, s.m. A buzz, hum (as of a bee or fly).

بونړيدل *bonṟedal*, v.n. To buzz, hum; putrefy, rot, become fly-blown, tainted, etc. *bonṟawul*, v.a. To taint, fly-blow, pollute, etc.

بوهار *būhār*, s.m. Spring. P. (*bahār*).

بوهاري *būhārai*, s.m. A weanling, an animal newly weaned from its mother.

بويه *boyah*, a. Necessary, proper, indispensable. ad. Necessarily, properly, fitly.

به *ba*, A particle used as a sign of the future and continuative past tenses. Also written ب.

بها *bahā*, s.f. Cost, price, value. A.

بهادر *bahādur*, s.m. A champion, hero. a. Courageous, brave. P.

بهادري *bahādurī*, s.f. Bravery, courage. *bahādurai*, s.m. A little hero, a coward.

بهانړ *bihānṟ*, s.m. A colt, young horse.

بهانيه *bahāniyah*, a. Costly, expensive, valuable, precious.

بهبود *bihbūd*, a. Advantageous, profitable. P.

بهبودي *bihbūdī*, s.f. Advantage, profit, gain, good. A large knife, dagger.

بهتان *buhtān*, s.m. Calumny, defamation; lying. A.

بهتر *bihtar*, a. Better, preferable, well. P.

بهتري *bihtarī*, s.f. Advantage, welfare.

بهره *bahra*, s.f. Lot, share; gain, profit. P.

بهښت *bihikkht*, s.m. Heaven, paradise. P. (*bihisht*).

بهگنړ *bhaganṟ*, s.m. A fly, gadfly.

بهم *baham*, ad. Together, one with another. P.

بهنه *bahna*, s.f. A top, whip-top. P.

بهي *baha-ī*, s.f A masonry tank or reservoir, with steps leading down to the water. *bihī*, s.f. A quince, the tree. P.

بهيدل *bahedal*, v.n. To float, flow, stream, pass, rush, gush. S. (*bahnā*).

بي *be*, part. Without, void of. Used in composition as a privative particle, and equivalent to the English prefixes *in-*, *im-*, *ir-*, *un-*, etc., and the affix *-less*. Ex. *be-hokkh*, insensible; *be-ṣabr*, impatient; *be-adab*, irreverent; *be-wafā*, unfaithful; *be-shakk*, doubtless, etc. P.

بيا *biyā*, ad. Again, afresh, once more. P. (*bāz*).

بيابان *bayābān*, s.m. A desert, waste, wilderness. P.

بياتي *biyātī*, s.m. Scissors, shears, clippers.

بياسته *biyāsta*, s.f. Cable, cord, rope; the rope of a Persian wheel, to which the water-pots are fastened.

بيامونډل *biyāmūndal*, v.a. To acquire, gain, get, find, recover, regain. obtain.

بيان *bayān*, s.m. Explanation, recital, relation. P.

بيانول *bayānawul*, v.a. To explain, recite, relate, tell, say, describe.

بيايل *biyāyal*, v.a. Def. in past ten. See بيول.

بيبي *bībī*, s.f. A lady, married woman. H. *bebe*, in. Sister dear! (to an elder sister).

بيپرتي *be-partai*, or *be-pratai*, a. Gormandizing, surfeiting; gluttonous, greedy.

بيت **bait**, s.m. A couplet, verse; house, temple. A. *bet*, s.m. A cane, rattan. S.

بيټ **baiṭ**, s.m. The name of one of the three sons of Kais. He is also called بټن *baṭan*, and the tribe descended from him بټني *baṭanī*. See قيس.

بيخ **bekh**, s.m. A root; origin, foundation. P.

بيخرتي **be·khratai**, a. Excessive, much, very much; unseasonable, inopportune, out of time; unbounded, without limit.

بيد **bed**, s.m. A willow tree. P.

بيدار **baidār**, a. Awake, vigilant, alert, watchful; conscious, sensible. P. (*bedār*).

بيداري **baidārī**, s.f. Wakefulness, sleeplessness; vigilance, alertness, watching. P.

بيدو **bedū**, ad. Identical, the same, exactly.

بيده **beda**, s.f. The coil or twist into which lucerne, vetches, etc. are rolled, preparatory to storing for winter use. *bīdah*, a. Asleep, sleeping.

بيديا **bediyā**, s.f. A desert, wilderness. A. (*bādiyā*).

بيرته **biyarta**, ad. Back, back again, return; aside, apart, away.

بيرغ **bairagh**, s.m. Banner, standard. A. (*bairaq*).

بيرنړ **beranṛ**, s.m. A kind of grass.

بيره **bera**, s.f. Name of a thorny bush (*zizyphus jujuba*); the berry. S. (*ber*). A fetter, manacle. H.

بيړه **beṛa**, s.f. A float, raft. S. (*beṛā*).

بيړئ **beṛa-ī**, s.f. A boat, barge.

بيزل **bezal**, v.a. To darn, hem, baste.

بيزار **bezār**, a. Annoyed, vexed; disgusted, sick of. P.

بيزو **bīzo**, s.m. A monkey.

بيساک **baisāk**, s.m. Name of the first Hindu month. April-May. S. (*baisākh*).

بيستئ **biyasta-ī**, s.f. Coarse cloth, canvass, baize.

بيسر **bīsar**, s.m. A small nose-ring, worn as an ornament by women. H.

بيش **besh**, a. More; superior (in comp. only). P.

بيشه **besha**, s.f. A forest, wood. P.

بيعه **bai'a**, s.f. Barter, exchange, trade. A. (*bai'*).

بيعانه **bai'āna**, s.f. Deposit, security, earnest-money.

بيک **biyak**, s.m. Harpoon, five-pronged fork.

بيگا **begā**, s.f. See بيگاه.

بيگار **begār** or **bīgār**, s.m. A pressed labourer (with or without pay). H.

بيگاري **bīgārī**, s.f. Forced labour. s.m. A pressed labourer. H.

بيگانه **begānah**, a. Foreign, strange, unknown. P.

بيگانگي **begānagī**, s.f. Strangeness, being foreign, not of the same house, not domestic. P.

بيگاني **begānai**, a. Last preceding, last past, preceding, stale, last night's, yesterday's.

بيگاه **begāh**, s.m. The evening. Also بيگا *begā*.

بيل **biyal** or **bel**, a. Apart, distinct, separate. H. (*byorā*). *bel*, s.m. Name of a tree and its fruit (*Ægle marmelos*); a creeper, climbing plant.

بيلاو **belāw**, s.m. A hone, razor strop.

بيلتون **biyaltūn**, s.m. Absence, separation difference, distinction.

بيلچه **belcha**, s.f. A mattock, hoe. P.

بيلک **belak**, s.m. A wedding-gift from bridegroom to the bride; an enemy, rival, guardian; an arrow tip. P.

بيلگه **belga**, s.f. See بلگه.

بيله **bela**, s.f. An island, delta, sandbank.

بيم **bīm**, s.m. Awe, fear, dread. P.

بيمار **bīmār**, a. Sick, ill. s.m. A sick man. P.

بيماري **bīmārī**, s.f. Disease, sickness. P.

بينا **bīnā**, a. Seeing, having sight. P.

بيند **bend**, s.m. See بيده *beda*.

بينش *bensh*, s.m. A beam, rafter.

بيوره *benrah*, a. Clear, manifest, simple, plain.

بيول *bīnul*, v.a. To conduct, lead, take along, convey. Applied only to animate objects. See بوتلل. P. (*bi·bur*)?

بيوه *bewa*, s.f. A widow. P.

بيه *baia*, s.f. Price, value. A. (*bai'*).

بيهودگي *behūdagī*, s.f. Absurdity, nonsense, folly.

بيهوده *behūdah*, a. Absurd, idle, foolish, frivolous. P.

پ

پ *pe*, The third letter of the Pukkhto alphabet. It is frequently used for ف. Ex. آپرين *āparīn* for آفرين *āfarīn*, etc.

پَ *pa*, p. By, with, for; in, into, within; above, on, upon. Also written به. P. (*bā*).

پا *pā*, s.m. The foot, leg. Used in comp. only. Ex. *pā·band*, s.m. A hobble, fetter. a. Bound, clogged, fettered, tethered. P.

پاپره *pāpra*, s.f. The herb fumitory (*Fumaria officinalis*). H. (*phāphrī*).

پاتو *pāto*, s.f. Name of a scarlet insect. See بخملي.

پاتي *pātai*, a. Left, remaining; abiding, staying.

پاتيدل *pātedal*, v.n. To remain, survive, be left. Also *pātai·kedal*.

پاټئ *pāṭa-ī*, s.f. The cup or pan of a sling or pellet bow.

پاڅول *pātsawul*, v.a. To arouse, awaken, stir up; raise, set up, elevate.

پاڅيدل *pātsedal*, v.n. To arise, rise, get up, sit up.

پاداش *pādāsh*, s.m. Revenge, requital, retaliation. P.

پادشاه *pādshāh*, s.m. Sovereign, king, emperor. P.

پادشاهي *pādshāhī*, s.f. Royal, regal; empire, kingdom. P.

پارا *pārā*, s.f. Mercury, quicksilver. S.

پارچنگ *pārchang*, s.m. A ladder, steps, stairs.

پارچه *pārcha*, s.f. A bit, fragment, scrap, shred; the water trough of an irrigation well. P.

پارو *pārū*, s.m. A kind of rake.

پارول *pārawul*, v.a. To annoy, vex, disturb, irritate, excite, stir up.

پاره *pāra*, s.f. A bit, scrap, slip, shred. P.

پاړبنج *pāṛbanj*, s.m. Name of a tree, horse chestnut.

پاړو *pāṛū*, s.m. A snake charmer. *pāṛū·k.*, v.a. To charm.

پاړه *pāṛa*, s.f. A patch of unploughed land in a field; unfinished work, incomplete action; a kind of rake.

پاړي *pāṛai*, s.m. The hog deer (*cervus porcinus*). H. (*pāṛhā*).

پازه *pāzah*, s.m. Action, effect, operation, result.

پازيگه *pāzīgah*, a. See پاکيزه.

پاس *pās*, p. Above, aloft, on, upon. s.m. Attention, observation, watch. P. An ointment made of oil and lime, and used as a remedy for mangy camels.

پاسخ *pāsukh*, s.m. Answer, reply. P.

پاسلول *pāslawul*, v.a. To entrust, commit, recommend.

پاسنگ *pāsang*, s.m. Balance, weight. P.

پاسني *pāsanai*, a. Upper, higher, high, superior.

پاسو *pāsū*, a. Ill-bred, vulgar, low, mean.

پاسوان *pāswān*, s.m. A shepherd, watchman, guard, sentinel. P. (*pāsbān*).

پاسواني *pāswānī*, s.f. Guarding, watching, keeping; protection; occupation of a shepherd.

پاشنه *pā<u>sh</u>na*, s.f. The heel of a door; the socket in which it revolves; the heel. P. (*pā<u>sh</u>nā*).

پاښ *pā<u>kkh</u>*, s.f. Name of a mountain near the Kāsī<u>gh</u>ar hill in the Ta<u>kh</u>ti-Sulaimān range. It is described as the spot first colonized by the Pu<u>kkh</u>tūn nation on their arrival from the West.

پاغنده *pā<u>gh</u>unda*, s.f. A ball or roll of carded cotton ready for spinning. P.

پاك *pāk*, a. Clean, pure; holy, innocent. P.

پاك لمن *pāk-laman*, a. Chaste, modest; holy, pure. P. (*pāk-dāman*).

پاكول *pākawul*, v.a. To cleanse, purify, wash.

پاكي *pākī*, s.f. Cleanliness, purity; cleaning, purifying; chastity, innocence; a razor. P.

پاكيزه *pākīzah*, a. Chaste, clean, pure, holy. P.

پال *pāl*, s.m. Abstinence, diet, regimen; augury, omen, presage. A. (*fāl*).

پالان *pālān*, s.m. A pack saddle. P.

پالك *pālak*, s.m. Garden spinach. H.

پالل *pālal*, v.a. To cherish, rear, educate, protect. S. (*pālnā*).

پالنگ *pālang*, s.m. A bedstead, bed. S. (*palang*).

پالوده *pālūda*, s.f. A kind of vermicelli. P. (*fālūda*). A kind of wild plum.

پاله *pāla*, s.f. A ploughshare. S. (*phāl*).

پالهنگ *pālhang*, s.m. A tether; a log tied to the neck of an ox, etc. to prevent its straying. P.

پاليز *pālez*, s.m. A melon field. P. (*fālez*).

پانشنبه *pān<u>sh</u>amba*, s.f. Thursday. P. (*panj-<u>sh</u>amba*).

پانه *pāna*, s.f. A wedge for splitting wood; thumbscrew, mode of torture. H. (*phanī*).

پانړ *pā<u>n</u>r*, s.m. A cliff, precipice, steep bank.

پانړه *pā<u>n</u>ra*, s.f. A leaf, leaf of a tree or book. S. (*pannā*).

پاو *pāo*, s.m. A fourth, quarter. S.

پائي *pā-ī*, s.f. A halter, leading string; pins used by weavers in weaving. H. *pāe*, s.m. The foot. P.

پاياب *pāyāb*, } a. Fordable, within depth. P.
پاياو *pāyāo*,

پايابه *pāyāba*, s.f. A float, a buoy.

پائيدل *pā-edal*, v.n. To endure, last, remain, tarry, survive. P. (*pā-īdan*).

پائيكو *pā-eko*, s.f. A crusher, pounder, thresher, flail, roller.

پائيله *pā-ela*, s.f. An anklet with bells; an ornament for the feet.

پائيمال *pā-emāl*, a. Trampled, ruined, crushed.

پاينده *pāyandah*, a. Constant, durable, lasting.

پائيڅه *pā-en<u>ts</u>a*, s.f. The leg of a pair of drawers. P. (*pā-en<u>ch</u>ā*).

پائينك *pā-enak*, s.m. The mounting at the end of a sword scabbard.

پايه *pāya*, s.f. A step; dignity, rank; foundation. P.

پپئي *pupa-ī*, s.f. A kiss on the cheek.

پت *pat*, s.m. Character, reputation, honour. S.

پتاو *pitāo*, s.m. Sunshine, sun's rays. P. (*partau*).

پتري *patrai*, s.m. A clamp, metal binding; the boss of a shield. H. (*pattar*).

پتنگ *patang*, s.m. A moth; paper kite. S.

پتنه *patna*, s.f. Anarchy, civil war, strife; sedition, rebellion. P. (*fitna*).

پتنړ *pata<u>n</u>r*, s.m. The stand of a spinning wheel; a ferry, passage across a river. H. (*pātan*).

پتون *patūn*, s.m. The thigh, shank.

پته *pata*, s.f. A card, ticket.

پتيره *patīra*, s.f. Unleavened bread.

پټ *paṭ*, s.m. Delirium, madness; bark of a tree. *puṭ*, a. Concealed, secret, hidden, covered.

پټ پټانړي *puṭ-puṭā<u>n</u>rai*, s.m. Name of a game; hide and seek.

پتخ *paṭakh*, a. Hard, tough; decayed, worn. s.m. A razor strop.

پتکه *paṭka*, s.f. A girdle, sash, waist-cloth. s. (*paṭkā*).

پتکي *paṭkai*, s.m. A small turban. *paṭakī*, ad. Immediately, instantly, on the spot; the same, very same, identical.

پتګني *puṭgana-ī*, s.f. Ambuscade, ambush, lair, cover.

پتو *patū*, s.m. A kind of woollen cloth. s.

پتوار *paṭwār*, s.m. Bailiff, land steward, village accountant. H.

پتوسکي *paṭūskai*, a. A little, very little, some, few.

پتول *puṭawul*, v.a. To conceal, cover, hide, veil.

پته *paṭa*, s.f. A shoulder belt, sword belt.

پتي *paṭai*, s.m. A field, patch of cultivated land. *paṭa-ī*, s.f. The alphabet; writing tablet; bandage, plaster.

پتيدل *puṭedal*, v.n. To abscond, hide.

پتيره *paṭera*, s.f. A beam, rafter, large timber.

پتيلنړ *paṭelanṛ*, s.m. See پليتنړ H. (*paṭelā*).

پجه *paja*, s.f. A furnace, kiln. H. (*pajāwā*).

پڅ *pa-ats* or *p-uts*, a. Blunt, dull, obtuse.

پڅاني *pitsāṇrai*, a. Small, little, few, some.

پڅکه *pitska*, s.f. Corner, end, nib, point.

پڅيدل *pa-atsedal* or *p-utsedal*, v.n. To become blunt, obtuse, dull.

پچنه *pachana*, s.f. A scratch, prick, prod, cut; a scarifier, cupping instrument.

پچني *pachanai*, a. Scarified, cupped, pricked.

پچواړي *pachwāṛa-ī*, s.f. Heel ropes for a horse. H.

پچه *pucha*, s.f. Orbicular dung (as of camels, deer, etc.); a lot or share of land; a ripple or catspaw on the surface of water.

پخ *pa-akh*, or *p-ukh*, s.m. Scurf, dandriff, scab, scale. *pakh*, s.m. A hiss, spit (as of a cat, etc.). *pakh-wahal*, v.a. To hiss, spit (as a cat).

پخپله *pakhpula*, ad. Spontaneously, voluntarily, of own accord.

پخته *pukhtah*, a. Baked, cooked, dressed, ripe; shrewd, expert, knowing; firm, solid, strong. P.

پخساک *pakhsāk*, s.m. Distress, grief, sorrow, solicitude. P. (*pakhshā*).

پخسول *pakhsawul*, v.a. To distress, annoy, trouble, worry.

پخسه *pakhsa*, s.f. Stiff clay or mud, used to build walls; mire, mud, slush.

پخسيدل *pakhsedal*, v.n. To desire, fret, pine, yearn, long.

پخلا *pakhulā*, a. Appeased, conciliated, pacified, reconciled, on speaking terms.

پخلي *pakhalai*, a. Cooked, prepared, dressed; cooking, dressing, preparing (food); firm, solid, sound; experience, maturity, ripeness. *pukhalai*, s.m. The hooping cough.

پخوا *pakhwā*, a. Former, previous, prior. ad. Before, ere now, previously.

پخواني *pakhwānai*, a. Ancient, former, preceding.

پخول *pakhawul*, v.a. To cook, dress, prepare.

پخوندي *pakhwandai*, s.m. A button hole, loop; an ornament for the feet, anklet.

پخه *pa-akha* or *p-ukha*, s.f. Chaff, husk, skin; leafy covering of the ear of Indian corn.

پخي *pa-akhai* or *p-ukhai*, a. Scabby, scurfy.

پخيدل *pakhedal*, v.n. To ripen, mature; boil; suppurate.

پخيل *pakhiyal*, s.m. Perspiring, sweating.

پدود *padod*, ad. As if, just as, like, similarly. P.

پديد *padīd*, a. Clear, evident, manifest. P.

پده *paḍa*, s.f. A species of willow.

پر *par*, s.m. A feather, quill; wing; the flat board of a water or other wheel. s. *pur*, a. Complete, full, loaded (in comp. only). P. *parr*, s.m. The whirr of a snipe, quail, etc. taking wing. H. (*phurr*). *pri*, p. On, upon, atop (in comp.). See پري.

پراټه *parāṭa*, s.f. A kind of bread made in thin layers of pastry. H. (*parāṭhā*).

پراچه *parāchah*, s.m. A pedlar, hawker, travelling merchant; mule driver; descendant of a Hindu converted to Islam.

پراچگي *parāchaga-ī*, s.f. A female of the preceding.

پراګنده *parāgandah*, a. Dispersed, scattered. P.

پرانتل *prānetal*, v.a. To loose, open, undo, untie. P. (*farākhtan, farāzīdan*).

پرت *prat*, a. Absurd, fruitless, idle, vain; distant, far, remote.

پرتاب *partāb*, s.m. Bowshot, gunshot, range of an arrow, etc. P.

پرتل *partal*, s.m. Baggage for a journey, baggage of an army. H. Name of a game, marbles.

پرتوړ *partūg*, s.m. See پرتوګ.

پرتوغاښ *partūghākkh*, s.m. The band or string for tying the *partūg*.

پرتوګ *partūg*, s.m. Loose trousers, drawers.

پرَڅِکي *parchata-ī*, s.f. Thatch or coping of a mud wall, eaves. H. (*parchhatī*).

پرخم *parkham*, s.m. A tassel, tuft; the tuft at the end of a cow's tail. P. (*parcham*).

پرخه *pa-arkha*, s.f. Dew, hoarfrost. *parkha*, s.f. A boulder, rock.

پرداخت *pardākht*, s.m. Attention, service, care. P.

پرداز *pardāz*, s.m. Finishing, performing (in comp.). P.

پرده *parda*, s.f. A veil, curtain, screen; secrecy, privacy. P.

پردي *pradai*, a. Foreign, strange. H. (*pardes*).

پرزو *pirzo*, a. Becoming, fit, proper, suitable; inclined, partial, longing. P. (*pazīr*).

پرزول *parzawul*, v.a. To overthrow, floor; struggle, wrestle.

پرزوه *pirzawa*, s.f. Desire, wish, bent, fancy.

پرزيدل *parzedal*, v.n. To be floored, thrown, upset, prostrated, etc. in wrestling.

پرسان *pursān*, s.m. Asking, enquiry. P.

پرست *parast*, s.m. Adorer, worshipper (in comp.). P.

پرستي *parastī*, s.f. Worship, devotion, adoration. P.

پرسش *pursish*, s.m. Inquiry, interrogation. P.

پرش *prash*, s.m. A snort, sniff; sneeze.

پرشکال *parshakāl*, s.m. The hot weather rains; rainy season; name of the fourth Hindu month. July-August. S. (*barshakāl*).

پرغز *par ghaz*, s.m. Convulsion, fainting fit, hysterics.

پرغزي *parghazī*, a. Stunned, faint, senseless, convulsed.

پرکار *purkār*, a. Coarse, thick, fat; well made P.

پرکټي *parkaṭai*, s.m. A step-son: wife's son by a former husband.

پرکي *parkai*, s.m. A butterfly.

پرکار *parkār*, s.m. A pair of compasses. P.

پرګنه *pargana*, s.f. A district, province, shire. P.

پرنا *parnā*, s.f. A doze, nap; nodding, sleeping. *parnā-wṛal*, v.a. To doze, nap, nod, sleep.

پرناله *parnāla*, s.f. A gutter, drain, scupper. H.

پرنج *pranj*, } s.m. A sneeze.
پرنجي *pranjai*, }

پرنجيدل *pranjedal*, v.n. To sneeze.

پرنړ *pranr*, s.m. Curdled, sour, or turned milk. a. Clotted, curdled (as blood, etc.).

پرو *paro*, s.m. A hot wind. S. (*purwā*).

پروا *parwā*, s.f. Anxiety, care, concern; dread, fear; wish, desire. P.

پروانه *parwāna*, s.f. An order, license, pass, warrant. P.

پروت *prot*, a. Prostrate, fallen, lying down.

پرور *parwar*, a. Cherisher, protector (in comp. only). P.

پروردګار *parwardagār*, s.m. The nourisher, God. P.

پرورده *parwardah*, a. Cherished, nourished, bred. s.m. Dependent, protegé. P.

پرورش *parwarish*, s.m. Maintenance, support, patronage; cherishing, nourishing. P.

پروړل *parwaral*, v.a. To cherish, foster, feed, support. P. (*parwardan*).

پروړ *proṛ*, s.m. Chaff; husk of Indian corn.

پروړه *proṛa*, s.f. Chaff; husk of rice, millet, etc.

پروسکال *paroskāl*, ad. Last year.

پروسګني *parosganai*, a. Last year's, of last season.

پرولل *prolal*, }
پروړل *prowul*, } v.a. To barter, exchange, sell, trade. P. (*farokhtan*).

پرون *parūn*, ad. Yesterday.

پروني *parūnai*, a. Yesterday's, last, last past, yester.

پرويزي *parwezai*, s.m. A sieve. P. (*parwezan*).

پره *para*, s.f. The plate or board of a water or spinning wheel; a row, rank, line, file; faction, party, set. H. (*parā*).

پرهار *parhār*, }
پرهر *parhar*, } s.m. A cut, laceration, wound. H. (*prahār*).

پرهرژلي *parhar-jalai*, a. Wounded, cut.

پرهيز *parhez*, s.m. Abstinence, continence; sobriety, regimen. P.

پرهيزګار *parhezgār*, a. Abstemious, continent, sober, frugal. P.

پرهيزګاري *parhezgārī*, s.f. Abstinence, sobriety.

پري *pre*, p. On, upon, above, atop. *parī*, s.f. A fairy. P.

پريباسل *prebāsal*, v.a. To cast upon, fling, throw, discharge upon. Def. See پريبستل.

پريدل *predal*, }
پرېږدل *pregdal*, } v.a. To abandon, desert, give up; cease, desist, leave off; relinquish, let go, set free. Def. See پريښول. P. (*farohīdan*).

پريشان *pareshān*, a. Confused, perplexed. P.

پريشاني *pareshānī*, s.f. Perplexity, confusion.

پريښودل *prekkhodal*, }
پريښول *prekkhawul*, } v.a. To abandon, desert; let go, etc. See پرېږدل. P. (*faroshāndan*).

پريکول *prekawul*, v.a. To cut, sever, divide, lop off.

پريو *paryo*, s.m. A follower, pursuer. P. (*pairau*).

پريوان *prewān*, s.m. The after-birth, placenta. H. (*puren*). a. Copious, abundant, much. P. (*farāwān*).

پريواني *prewānī*, s.f. Abundance, plenty.

پريوتل *prewatal*, v.n. To drop, fall down, tumble; to alight, fall upon, come upon. P. (*faro uftādan*).

پريوتي *prewatai*, a. Fallen. s.m. Name of a plant.

پريوستل *prewastal*, }
پريېستل *preyastal*, } v.a. To cast, throw, fling, etc. upon. Def. See پريباسل.

پريېښل *preyakkhal*, v.a. See پريښودل.

پړ *paṛ*, s.m. A gaming house, where dice are played. H. (*phaṛ*). *pa-aṛ*, or *p-ūṛ*, a. Beaten, conquered, overcome; losing, unsuccessful. *p-uṛ* or *pa-aṛ-kawul*, v.a. To conquer, subdue, overcome. *pa-aṛ* or *p-uṛ-kedal*, v.n. To lose, be beaten, overcome, subdued.

پړانګ *pṛāng*, s.m. A leopard, panther. P. (*palang*).

پړانګ پيش *pṛāng-pīsh*, s.m. A wild cat, lynx.

پړانه وړانه *pa-aṛāna wa-aṛāna*, s.f. Loss and gain; betting, gambling, wagering.

پړپوس *paṛpūs*, s.m. The lungs. H. (*phephṛā*).

پړسوب *paṛsob*, s.m. Tumour, swelling, inflammation.

پړسول *paṛsawul*, v.a. To dilate, distend, expand. H. (*pasārnā*).

پړسيدل *paṛsedal*, v.n. To swell, tumefy, dilate.

پړق *paṛaq*, s.m. A razor strop.

پرک *parak*, s.m. Agitation, flutter. H. (*pharak*). *park*, s.m. A crowd, mob, bevy, herd.

پرکول *parakawul*, v.a. To agitate, shake, stir.

پرکه *parka*, s.f. A kind of bird trap, gin.

پرکي *parkai*, s.m. The leg below the knee, the calf.

پرکيدل *parakedal*, v.n. To flutter, quiver, hover.

پرمخ *pa-armakh*, a. Prone, face downwards, upset.

پرنگ *prang*, s.m. A cry, whimper, whine.

پروکي *parūkai*, s.m. A riband, shred, strip, tatter.

پروني *parūnai*, s.m. A woman's mantle, or veil.

پژه *pa-ara*, s.f. Defeat, failure, loss at play.

پري *purai*, s.m. A cable, rope, cord.

پرين *prīn*, s.m. Diaphragm, hypogastrium.

پس *pas*, ad. After, behind; then, next, therefore, at length. P. *pa-as*, s.m. Flatus, wind from the bowels. *pus-pus*, s.m. Whispering. H. (*phus*).

پسات *pasāt*, s.m. Mutiny, rebellion, sedition; depravity, iniquity, mischief. A. (*fasād*).

پساتي *pasātī*, a. Mischievous, quarrelsome, seditious.

پسان *psān*, s.m. A grindstone, whetstone. S. (*sān*).

پست *past*, a. Low, below; abject, mean. P.

پستنه *pastana*, ad. After, behind, back, in rear; since, subsequently.

پستو *pastū*, s.m. An inner room, cell.

پستوني *pastawunai*, s.m. Name of a tree (*Grewia Asiatica*).

پسخاک *paskhāk*, s.m. See پخساک P.

پسخه *paskha*, s.f. Stiff mud or clay, used to build walls.

پسرلي *psarlai*, s.m. The Spring.

پسکي *puska-ī*, s.f. Flatus, wind from the bowels. *puska-ī-āchawul*, v.a. To break wind.

پسند *pasand*, s.m. Approbation, choice. a. Chosen, approved. P.

پسندول *pasandawul*, v.a. To choose, approve.

پسنديدل *pasandedal*, v.n. To be chosen, approved. P. (*pasandidan*).

پسور *psor*, a. Broad, wide.

پسول *psol*, s.m. A necklace of coins; ornament.

پسولول *psolawul*, v.a. To adorn, decorate, ornament.

پسوني *pasūnai*, s.m. Ambush, cover, lair.

پسه *psah*, s.m. Goats, sheep; goat species.

پسينه *pasīnah*, a. Late, last, late sown crops. P.

پش *pa-ash*, s.m. A wheeze, sound of air forced from a bag; a blacksmith. *pash-pash*, in. Call to a cat, puss! puss!

پشت *pusht*, s.m. Ancestry; a generation of progenitors; the back; a ridge; a prop, support, help; an assistant; reservoir of a canal. P.

پشته *pushta*, s.f. A buttress, prop, support. in. A word used to drive away a cat—away puss!

پشتي *pushtī*, s.f. A prop, buttress, support; aid, succour, help. P. *pishtai*, s.m. A terrier dog.

پشرلي *psharlai*, s.m. A yearling kid.

پشقاب *pashqāb*, s.m. A salver, tray, platter.

پشک *pishak*, s.m. A disease of the skin; ringworm; the bald-headed vulture.

پشکالي *pashkālai*, s.m. Hay, dry fodder.

پشم *pashm*, s.m. Wool, down, fur, hair. P.

پشمي *pashmī*, a. Woolly, downy.

پشمينه *pashmīnah*, a. Woollen. *pashmīna*, s.f. A kind of woollen cloth. P.

پشو *pisho*, s.m. and f. A cat.

پشوخت *pishokhut*, s.m. Tonquin bean; the seed of a climbing plant, the seed pod of which is covered with cowhage; the bean is used as a charm against evil eye, etc.

پشه *pasha*, s.f. A musquito, gnat. in. A word used to drive away a cat. P.

پښ *pakkh*, s.m. See پاښ.

پښت *pukkht*, s.m. Ancestry, lineage; back, ridge; a mountain range. P. (*pusht*).

پښتنه *pukkhtana*, s.f. Enquiry, investigation, interrogation, questioning. An Afghan or Pathan woman, a female Pukkhtūn.

پښتو *pukkhto*, s.f. The Afghan language.

پښتورگه *pukkhtawarga*, s.f. A kidney.

پښتون *pukkhtūn*, s.m. An Afghan, a Pathan; one whose language is Pukkhto. *bar-pukkhtūn*, s.m. An upper or highland Afghan. *lar-pukkhtūn*, s.m. A lower or lowland Afghan.

پښتونخوا *pukkhtūn-khwā*, s.f. Afghanistan, the country of the Afghans, or Pathans.

پښتونوالي *pukkhtūnwālai*, } s.m. The Afghan
پښتونولي *pukkhtūnwalī*, } constitution, Pukkhtūn code, the manners and customs of the Pathans.

پښته *pukkhta*, s.f. A small hill. P. (*pushta*).

پښتۍ *pukkhta-ī*, s.f. A rib, the ribs. *pukkhtī*, s.f. Enquiry, investigation, questioning.

پښتيدل *pukkhtedal*, v.a. To ask, question, interrogate, enquire. S. (*pūchhnā*).

پښويه *pakkhwaya*, or *pakkhoya*, s.f. Orthography, spelling, naming or forming words.

پښه *pksha*, or *pkkha*, s.f. The foot.

پښيمان *pakkhemān*, a. Penitent, repentant, sorry. P. (*pashemān*).

پښيماني *pakkhemānī*, s.f. Penitence, regret, sorrow.

پقير *paqīr*, s.m. A beggar, mendicant; hermit, recluse. A. (*faqīr*).

پک *puk*, s.m. Chance, opportunity, turn, time.

پکار *pakār*, a. Effective, useful, serviceable. Also په کار.

پکل *pakal*, v.a. To chuck, or jerk anything into the mouth from the palm of the hand. H. (*phānknā*). s.m. A railing, fence, screen, lattice of reeds, etc.

پکو *pako*, a. Bothered, confused, amazed.

پکه *paka*, s.f. A palm full, enough to fill the palm for a chuck into the mouth. H. (*phankā*). *paka-wahal*, v.a. To chuck into the mouth (as grain, etc.).

پگړۍ *pagṛa-ī*, s.f. A turband. H. (*pagṛī*).

پگڼ *pagaṇr*, s.m. Name of the eleventh Hindu month. February-March. S. (*phāgan*).

پل *pal*, s.m. A millstone; potter's wheel; footprint, trace; wheel, truck-wheel; one side of a pair of scales. P. (*pallā*). *pul*, s.m. A bridge, ridge, bank, embankment. P. *pul*, a. Let off, excused, acquitted, absolved.

پلا *plā*, s.f. Period, turn, time, round.

پلار *plār*, s.m. A father. P. (*padar*).

پلارگني *plārganai*, s.m. Paternal relation; father's family, connexions, household, etc.

پلاله *palāla*, s.f. Rice straw, straw of millet, corn, etc. (unbroken). S. (*parāl*). P. (*pulāl*).

پلاڼره *palāṇra*, s.f. A pack-saddle. P. (*pālān*). Mule load of water; water skins.

پلاو *pulāo*, s.m. A kind of dish made of rice, meat, fruits, spices, etc. cooked together. P.

پلټن *palṭan*, s.f. A battalion, regiment, peloton. H.

پلټل *palaṭal*, v.a. To return, turn back, retreat; to overturn; turn, wind. H. (*palaṭnā*).

پلغت *palaghat*, ad. Quickly. P.

پلک *palak*, s.m. The eyelid; an instant, moment; a wink. P. *pa-alk*, s.m. A sledge hammer; a ploughshare.

پلکه *palka*, s.f. The blade of a sword.

پلمه *palma*, s.f. Calumny, slander; deception, falsehood, prevarication. P.

پلن *plan*, a. Broad, wide, spacious. P. (*pahan*).

پلندر *plandar*, s.m. Step-father: father to wife's children by a former husband. P. (*padandar*).

پلنده *palanda*, s.f. A bog, quagmire.

پلنول *planawul*, v.a. To widen, make broad.

پلو *palau*, s.m. Border, hem, skirt of a dress; side, direction, quarter; margin, edge, verge. P. (*pahlū*). H. (*pallā*).

پلواښه *pulwākkha*, s.f. Button-hole, loop, noose, slip-knot, lasso.

پلور *plor*, s.m. Buying and selling, trade.

پلورل *ploral*, v.a. To sell, vend. See پرول.

پلوسه *palosa*, s.f. Name of a tree (*Acacia modesta*).

پلوشه *palwasha*, s.f. A ray of light, glitter of a star, radiance of the moon; light, glitter.

پلول *pulawul*, v.a. To acquit, absolve, excuse.

پلوند *palwanḍ*, a. Foolish, stupid.

پله *pala*, s.f. Nerve, sinew, tendon; direction, quarter, side.

پلي *palai*, s.m. A pod, legume. S. (*phallī*). *pala-ī*, s.f. The spoke of a wheel. Name of a tree (*Butea frondosa*). S. (*palās*). *palai*, a. Afoot, on foot.

پليت *palīt*, a. Defiled, polluted, unclean. P. (*palīd*).

پليته *palīta*, s.f. A wick, match, torch. P. (*falīta*).

پليتي *palītī*, s.f. Impurity, pollution.

پليټنر *paleṭanr*, s.m. A weaver's beam. See پټيلنر.

پلينه *plenah*, } پليون *plewan*, } s.m. Name of a tree (*Salvadora Persica*), the root of which is used as a tooth-brush. S. (*pīlū*).

پم *pam*, s.m. Mange, itch.

پماني *pamānai*, s.m. Name of a tree (*Vitex negundo*).

پمبه *pumba*, s.f. The cotton plant. P.

پمبيچو *pumbechu*, s.f. A cotton pod; the withered stalks of the plant.

پمن *paman*, a. Mangy, scabby.

پنا } پناه } *panā*, s.f. Refuge, shelter, protection, aid. P.

پنبه *punba*, s.f. See پمبه.

پنځوس *pandzos*, a. Fifty.

پنځه *pindzah*, a. Five. P. (*panj*). *pindzah-binā*, s.f. The five foundations (of religion), viz. The belief, prayer, fasting, pilgrimage, and alms.

پنجره *pinjra*, s.f. A cage; lattice. S. (*pinjrā*).

پنجكي *panjakai*, s.m. The cross bar between the strings of a pellet-bow; a latch, catch, stop.

پنجه *panja*, s.f. A claw, hand, paw. P.

پند *pand*, s.m. Advice, counsel. P. Distance, journey. S. (*penḍ*).

پندانه *pundāna*, s.f. Cotton seed.

پندوک *pandūk*, s.m. A bud, blossom.

پنده *punda*, s.f. The heel.

پندۍ *punda-ī*, s.f. The iron top of a spear; a disease of the fetlock, the grease.

پنډ *panḍ*, s.m. A package, bundle, load for the head. *punḍ*, s.m. A steel for striking fire from a flint. *punḍ-bakra-ī*, flint and steel. *punḍ*, s.m. A band, herd, flock; tumour, bump, swelling; *vulva*. a. Corpulent, fat, stout. P.

پنډاوچرګ *panḍāw-chirg*, s.m. A game cock; fowl of a large breed with big bones and few feathers.

پنډغالي *panḍ-ghālai*, s.m. A common or open space outside a village on which the cattle are collected on going to and returning from pasture.

پنډوس *panḍos*, s.m. } پنډوسکي *panḍoskai*, } A ball, a play ball, a cricket ball.

پنډوکي *panḍūkai*, s.m. A bundle, parcel, package.

پندولي *panḍolī*, s.f. A portion or share of a cotton crop allotted to the women who pick it, by way of perquisite or hire for their labour. *panḍol·gara*, s.f. A woman who picks the cotton crop.

پنده *panḍa*, s.f. A small load, bundle.

پندئي *panḍa-ī*, s.f. The calf of the leg. H. (*pindlī*). *punḍa-ī*, s.f. The heel; iron tip of a spear.

پنديدل *punḍedal*, v.n. To swell, expand, distend, tumefy. P. (*pundīdan*).

پنگه *panga*, s.f. Capital, reserve, stock. S. (*punjī*).

پنهم *pinham*, a. Concealed, hidden, secret. P. (*pinhān*).

پني *panai*, s.m. Name of a scented grass (*Andropogon muricatum*). *pannī*, s.m. Name of a Pathan tribe.

پنير *panīr*, s.m. Cheese. P.

پنيرک *panīrak*, s.m. Name of a potherb (*Malva parviflora*). The seeds and root are used in medicine.

پنړه *panṛa*, s.f. A shoe, slipper. S. (*panhī*).

پو *pū*, a. Light, smooth, slight. s.m. Enquiry, search; a puff, blast, blow, breath. P.

پوپکه *pūpaka*, s.f. A bump, swelling, tumour.

پوتي *pūtai*, s.m. A heap, mound, lump, mass.

پوټ *poṭ*, s.m. Bark, rind, shell, crust, skin. P. (*post*).

پوټسوري *poṭ·sūrī*, s.m. Bran, chaff, husk.

پوټکي *poṭakai*, s.m. Scurf, dandriff, scab.

پوټوسکي *poṭūskai*, a. Diminutive, wee, tiny, small. s.m. An atom, jot, tittle, bit.

پوټي *pūṭai*, a. Small, puny, wee, tiny. s.m. A bit, pinch, crumb, little bit; a dwarf, pigmy.

پوجي *pūjī*, s.f. Weeding, thinning, pruning.

پوڅکۍ *potsaka-ī*, s.f. A mushroom, fungus. *pūtsaka-ī*, s.f. The lobe of the ear.

پوڅه *potsa*, s.f. Curds, cream-cheese, dry curds.

پوڅۍ *pūtsa-ī*, s.f. The lobe of the ear.

پوچ *pūch*, a. Obscene, absurd, useless, foolish. P.

پوچګوئي *pūch·goī*, s.f. Obscenity, nonsense, rigmarole. *pūch·goe*, s.m. A talker of nonsense, smut, bosh, etc.

پوخ *pokh*, a. Ripe, mature; cooked, dressed; firm, strong; expert, shrewd, knowing.

پوخلي *pukhalai*, s.m. Hooping-cough; croup.

پوده *pūda*, s.f. Cloth in the loom; the warp or web. P. (*pud*). *pūdah*, a. Crumbling, decayed, rotten, mildewed. P.

پور *por*, s.m. A loan, advance; debt. *pori*, ad. To, up to; till, whilst; over, across, beyond; at, upon; as far as, near, close to. H. (*par*). See پوري.

پورتني *portanai*, a. Upper, superior, upmost.

پورته *porta*, ad. Above, atop, on, upon, over, up. a. More, greater, superior. *porta·kawul*, v.a. To raise, erect, lift, exalt. *porta·kedal*, v.n. To ascend, arise, rise.

پوروړي *porawuṛai*, s.m. A debtor; creditor; avenger.

پوره *pūrah*, a. Complete, entire, full, perfect. S. (*pūrā*).

پوري *pore*, ad. To, up to; as far as, near, close to; upon, at; till, whilst; over, across, beyond. H. (*par*). *pore·ore*, or *pore·rā·pore*, Through and through, in and out, right through, from end to end, etc. *pore·kawul*, v.a. To apply, attach, fix, shut, set, place, etc.

پوري ژني *pore·ǰanai*, a. Ejected, expelled, cast out. Also پوري جني *pore·janai*.

پوړ *poṛ*, a. Half cooked (as food), half ripe, (as fruit), half-grown, or near puberty (as an animal). *pauṛ*, s.m. Cord, cable, rope, hobble, tether.

پوړه *poṛa*, s.f. A rake, shovel for removing stable litter. s. (*phāorī*).

پوړۍ *pauṛa-ī*, s.f. A ladder. H. (*pauṛī*).

پوزه *poza*, s.f. The nose, snout. P.

پوزي *pūzai*, s.m. A small mat made of palm leaves.

پوږ *pūg*, s.m. A blow, puff, squirt; a bellows. *pūg-wahal*, v.a. To puff, blow (as on fire); to squirt, sprinkle from the mouth (as water on cloth, etc.).

پوس *pos*, } پوست *post*, } a. Soft, supple, pliant, ductile, elastic, tender, tractable.

پوست *post*, s.m. Bark, crust, hide, shell, skin, etc.; poppy-head or capsule. P. *post-bāsal* or *kāgal*, v.a. To flay, skin, peel, bark, shell, etc.

پوستکي *postakai*, s.m. Crust, scab, bark, rind; an untanned hide.

پوستي *postī*, s.m. A drunkard, sot; one addicted to the use of the intoxicating liquor prepared from the fresh poppy-head. P.

پوستين *postīn*, s.m. A fur coat; sheep-skin coat. P.

پوسلل *poslal*, v.a. To attire, clothe, dress.

پوش *posh*, in. Look out! Clear the way! Stand by! Have a care! H. (*pocsh*) or for *poh sha* (imperative). *posh* (in comp.), Covering, wearing. P.

پوښ *pokkh*, s.m. Apparel, clothing, dress. P. (*posh*).

پوښاک *pokkhāk*, s.m. Clothes, garments. P. (*poshāk*).

پوښښ *pokkhikkh*, s.m. Covering, dress, vestment. P. (*poshish*).

پوښل *pokkhal*, v.a. To clothe, cover, dress, hide, screen; to cheer, console, sympathize, etc. P. (*poshīdan*).

پوغله *poghla*, s.f. Dung of young animals, of kids and lambs before it becomes orbicular.

پوک *pūk*, s.m. A puff, blow, squirt, etc. from the mouth. P. (*phūnk*).

پوکل *pūkal*, v.a. } پوکول *pūkawul*, } To blow, puff, breathe on, inflate; to squirt from the mouth.

پوکنړۍ *pukanṛa-ī*, s.f. A bladder, the urinary bladder. H. (*phuknā*).

پوکي *pūkai*, s.m. A puff, blow, whiff.

پول *pūl*, s.m. An aqueduct; gutter, trough. P. *pūl*, s.m. A film over the eye, albugo. s. (*phūlī*).

پولاد *polād*, s.m. Fine steel. P. (*fūlād*).

پولک *pūlak*, s.m. A clamp, bit, or wedge to fix the share to the plough.

پوله *pūla*, s.f. A ridge, bank, hedge; limit, boundary, or division line or mark. *pūlah*, s.m. Parched grain. s.

پولۍ *pūla-ī*, s.f. A vesicle, blister, bleb. H. (*pholā*).

پون *pūn*, s.m. The mange.

پونه *pūna*, s.f. Drizzle, mist, small rain. H. (*phūnhī*).

پونړۍ *pūnṛa-ī*, s.f. A ball or roll of cotton prepared for spinning. H. (*pūnī*).

پوول *powul*, v.a. To graze; lead cattle to pasture. Def. in pres. ten. See پيايل.

پوه *poh*, a. Clever, intelligent, knowing, wise.

پوهاند *pohānd*, a. Clever, intelligent, learned, wise.

پوهړ *pūhaṛ*, a. Careless, untidy, slovenly, dirty; foolish, stupid, sottish. H. (*phūhaṛ*). *pohuṛ*, s.m. A large mat made of palm leaves. H.

پوهول *pohawul*, v.a. To acquaint, inform, explain, etc.

پوهه *poha*, s.f. Judgment, intellect, understanding. P. (*fahm*).

پوهيدل *pohedal*, v.n. To understand, appreciate, perceive, know. P. (*fahmīdan*).

پويه *poya*, s.f. A canter, gallop. P.

په *pa*, p. See پَ.

په *pah*, } in. Pooh! pooh! bosh! fudge!
پها *phā*, }

پهار *pahār*, s.m. A measure of time; about three hours. S. (*pahar*).

پهره *pahra*, s.f. A watch, vigil; tour of watch; guard, sentinel. S. (*pahrā*).

پهلواړي *phulwāṛai*, s.m. A white rose; strips of clean straw, used by women to plait with the back hair (as an ornament).

پهلوان *pahlawān*, s.m. An athlete, champion, wrestler, hero, gladiator. P.

پهلواني *pahlwānī*, s.f. Heroism, athletics, wrestling.

پهم *pahm*, s.m. Intellect, mind, reason, sense. P. (*fahm*).

پهمول *pahmawul*, v.a. To acquaint, inform, etc. P. (*fahmāndan*).

پهميدل *pahmedal*, v.n. To understand, perceive, know. P. (*fahmīdan*).

پهورته *pahorta*, ad. See پورته.

پهه *paha*, s.f. A poultice, ointment, plaster.

پئ *pa-ī*, s.f. Milk; the sap of trees. S. (*pai*). *pai*, s.m. The foot; a sinew; tendon of the leg; footing, basis; track, trace; a ford. P. *pai-oba*, Fordable, within depth. *pai-kawul*, v.a. To hamstring; cut a tree close to the roots. *pai-wṛal*, v.a. To know, follow, catch at the meaning, etc. *pai*, ad. After, behind, following. *pai-ā-pai*, In succession, one after another. P.

پياڅه *piyātsa*, s.m. Bread made from millet or rye.

پياخله *piyākhla*, s.f. Collar, cuff, wristband. Exhaling, perspiring, sweating.

پيادہ *piyādah*, s.m. A footman; foot soldier. a. On foot, afoot. P.

پيارمه *piyārma*, s.f. A brace for tightening the netting of a bedstead; the crupper of a saddle; the strap of a spinning-wheel, etc.

پياز *piyāz*, s.m. An onion. P.

پيازكي *piyāzakai*, s.m. Wild onion; squill.

پيازه *piyāza*, s.f. Abortion; aborting, miscarrying; clearing, dividing, splitting.

پياله *piyāla*, s.f. A cup, goblet; fire-pan of a gun. P.

پياوي *payāwai*, s.m. A float, buoy, angler's float.

پيايل *piyāyal*, v.a. To graze or pasture cattle, to tend flocks. See پوول.

پيپنئ *pepna-ī*, s.f. A chemise, shift, shirt.

پيتي *paitī*, s.f. Cooked peas or pulse.

پيټ *peṭ*, s.m. } A bundle, load, package,
پيټي *peṭai*, } burden; tumbril, box, parcel. H. (*peṭī*).

پيټي مو *peṭī-mo*, in. Fie on thee! A curse on you! The devil seize thee! H. (*phiṭe-munh*).

پيجمخي *pejmakhai*, a. Handsome; beardless, smooth-faced; light or fair complexioned.

پيڅل *petsal*, v.a. To bear, endure, suffer, undergo. P. (*pechīdan*).

پيچ *pech*, s.m. A coil, twist; screw; complication, deceit, difficulty. P.

پيچش *pechish*, s.m. Contortion, twist, gripes. P.

پيچک *pechak*, s.m. A skein or hank of thread; a reel. P.

پيچومه *pechūma*, s.f. Zigzag; elevation, rise.

پيچيدل *pechedal*, v.n. To wind, twist, writhe, coil, etc. P. (*pechīdan*).

پيخاره *paikhāra*, s.f. See پوغله.

پيخال *paikhāl*, s.m. Dung of birds. P.

پيخل *paikhal*, s.m. See پخيل.

پيدا *paidā*, a. Born, created, produced. P.

پير *pīr*, s.m. A saint; spiritual guide; descendant of a saint; old man; Monday. P. *per*, s.m. Bend, curve, turn, wind, twist. H. (*pher*).

پيرامن *pairāman*, s.m. Circumference. ad. Around, about, roundabout. P.

پيراهن *pairāhan*, s.m. A frock, long shirt. P.

پيړ *peraṛ*, a. Corpulent, fat, bulky, large.

پيرزو *pīrzo*, a. See پرزو.

پيرل *pīral*, v.a. See پيرودل.

پيروان *perwān*, s.m. See پريوان.

پيروي *pairawai*, s.m. Cream; a suckling.

پيرودل *pīrodal*, v.a. To buy, purchase. P. (*farokhtan*).

پيروني *perone*, s.f. The Pleiades.

پيري *pere*, s.m. A demon, evil spirit, one of the genii; a devil. *periyān*, pl. (*met.*) Hysterics.

پيرياني *periyānai*, s.m. A demoniac, one possessed with a devil. *periyāna-ī*, s.f. A hysterical woman.

پيړ *peṛ*, a. Fat, obese, gross; coarse, thick; bulky.

پيرزه *perza*, s.f. A mound, hillock, detached hill.

پيړه *peṛa*, s.f. A lump of dough; a kind of sweetmeat. S. (*peṛā*).

پيړۍ *peṛa-ī*, s.f. A chair, settle, ottoman; a generation of ancestors. S. (*pīṛhī*).

پيزار *paizār*, s.m. A shoe, slipper, sandal. P.

پيزل *pezal*, v.a. To darn, repair, mend, stitch.

پيزنه *pezna*, s.f. A sieve. P.

پيزوان *pezwān*, s.m. A nose-ring. An ornament worn in the nose by women.

پيزواني *pezwānai*, s.m. A bullock with its nose bored for a ring or bridle.

پيزه *peza*, s.f. Apex, tip, summit, top, peak.

پيزي *pezai*, a. Faded, decayed, withered. *peza-ī*, s.f. Spelling, forming syllables, joining letters. The name of a woman.

پيژانده *pejāndah*, a. Recognized, known, familiar. s.m. Recognition, remembrance.

پيژندگلي *pejandgalī*, s.f. Acquaintance, knowledge, recognition, familiarity.

پيژندل *pejandal*, v.a. To distinguish, recognize, know, recollect. H. (*pahchānnā*).

پيس *pes*, s.m. Leprosy; a leper. P.

پيسانړي *pīsāṉrai*, s.m. A little, bit, fraction, atom, pinch, jot, etc.

پيسه *paisa*, s.f. Name of a copper coin. H. (*paisā*).

پيسي *pesai*, a. Leprous. s.m. A leper.

پيش *pesh*, a. Before, in front. The vowel point ـُ *u*. P.

پيشاب *peshāb*, s.m. Urine. P.

پيشتر *peshtar*, ad. Before, formerly. P.

پيشکار *peshkār*, s.m. An agent, deputy, manager. P.

پيشگي *peshagī*, s.m. Advance of money or wages, etc. P.

پيشلمي *peshlamai*, پيشمني *peshmanai*, } s.m. The meal before sunrise during the month of Ramaẓān; an early breakfast.

پيشوا *peshwā*, s.m. A guide, leader. P.

پيشواز *peshwāz*, s.m. A gown; an open frock worn by dancing women. P.

پيشه *pesha*, s.f. Calling, trade, profession; habit, custom. P.

پيشه‌ور *pesha·war*, s.m. A mechanic, artificer.

پيشۍ *pīsha-ī*, s.f. A caterpillar; a small nose-ring worn as an ornament by women; a leather bag or wallet.

پيښ *pekkh*, a. Before, in front, advanced. P. (*pesh*).

پيښاور *pekhāwar*, s.m. Name of a city and province: Peshāwar.

پيښ‌کښ *pekkh·kakkh*, s.m. Offering, present, tribute. P. (*pesh·kash*).

پيښول *pekkhawul*, v.a. To bring forward, introduce, bring together, cause to meet.

پيښه *pekkha*, s.f. Mockery, ridicule, caricature. H. (*pekhnā*). *pekkhe·kawul*, v.a. To make faces, ridicule, ape, mock.

پيښيدل *pekkhedal*, v.n. To happen, occur, befall; to meet, encounter. P. (*peshīdan*).

پيښين *pekkhīn*, a. Ancient, prior, former. s.m. Noon, afternoon. P. (*peshīn*).

پیغام *paighām*, s.m. A message. P.

پیغامبر *paighāmbar*, s.m. A messenger, prophet. P.

پیغله *peghla*, s.f. A damsel, maid, virgin.

پیغور *peghor*, s.m. Reproach, abuse, raillery; calumny, slander. P. (*peghāra*). *peghor-markawul*, v.a. To reproach, rail at, abuse; calumniate, slander.

پیک *paik*, s.m. A messenger, porter, runner. P.

پیکار *paikār*, s.m. Contest, battle, war. P. A pedlar.

پیکان *paikān*, s.m. The head of an arrow. P.

پیکر *paikar*, s.m. Countenance, face, form; likeness, portrait. P.

پیکره *paikara*, s.f. An anklet, ornament for the ankle; fetter, hobble.

پیکل *pekal*, s.m. A clothes-line, rope to hang clothes upon.

پیکوي *pekawai*, s.m. See پیبوي.

پیل *pīl*, s.m. An elephant. P.

پیله *pela*, s.f. Silkworm's cocoon; silkworm. P.

پیمان *paimān*, s.m. Promise, oath, contract. P.

پیمانه *paimāna*, s.f. A goblet; a dry measure. P.

پیمائش *paimā-īsh*, s.m. Measure, limit. P.

پیمخي *paimakhai*, a. See پیاجمخي. Also پي مخي *pa-ī-makhai*.

پینځه *pīndzah*, a. Five.

پینڅه *paintsa*, s.f. The leg of a pair of trousers. P. (*pāencha*).

پینل *pīnal*, v.a. To chuck into the mouth from the hand.

پینه *pīna*, s.f. A trencher, wooden bowl, kneading trough.

پیودل *pewdal*, v.a. To thread, file, string, spit. H. (*pironā*).

پیودلي *pewdalai*, a. Filed, strung, threaded.

پیوره *paiwara*, a. Milky, milk-giving, milch, full of milk. Also پي وره *pa-ī-wara*.

پیوست *pewast* or *paiwast*, s.m. Connection, junction; relationship, friendship. P.

پیوستون *pewastūn*, s.m. Adhesion, connection, attachment; contiguity, proximity, relationship.

پیوسته *pewastah*, a. Connected, joined, attached. P.

پیوند *pewand*, s.m. A joint, patch, fastening; bud, graft. P.

پیبوي *peyawai*, s.m. A band for the hair; the bunch of braids plaited with the hair of young women and allowed to hang down the back.

ت

ت *te*, The fourth letter of the Pukkhto alphabet.

ت *ta*, or ته *tah*, pr. The second personal pronoun, thou. part. The sign of the dative case, to, unto. It always follows its noun.

تا *tā*, ad. As far as, to, till, whilst, so that. P. s.f. A fold, sheet, layer, plait. P. (*tah*). pr. The inflected form of the second personal pronoun in the oblique cases singular, thee, by thee, thou.

تاب *tāb*, s.m. Heat, fury, rage; endurance, suffering; power, strength; coil, twist; light, splendour. P.

تابدان *tābdān*, s.m. A sky-light, lattice. P.

تابږن *tābǰan*, a. Glittering, shining. P. (*tābān*). Also written تابجن *tābjan*.

تابستان *tābistān*, s.m. The hot weather, summer. P.

تابع *tābiʻ*, s.m. A dependant, subject. A.

تابعدار *tābiʻdār*, a. Obedient, submissive, subject. s.m. A subject, follower, dependant.

تابعداري *tābiʻdārī*, s.f. Obedience, allegiance, fidelity.

تابوت *tābūt*, s.m. A coffin, bier. *tābūt-i-sakīna*, s.f. The ark of the covenant given to Adam from heaven. A.

تابين *tābīn*, s.m. A subject, follower, dependant.

تابه *tāba*, s.f. A frying-pan. P.

تاثير *tāṣīr*, s.m. Effect, operation, impression. A.

تاج *tāj*, s.m. A crown, diadem; crest of a bird. P.

تاجر *tājir*, s.m. A merchant, trader. A.

تاجك *tājik*, s.m. A cultivator, peasant; mechanic. The name of a tribe; they are settled about the large cities of Afghanistan, and form the bulk of the population on the western borders of the country; their language is the Persian, and they are supposed to be descendants of the ancient Persians.

تاخت *tā<u>kh</u>t*, s.m. A gallop, run; foray, raid; attack, invasion; plunder, ravage. P.

تاخير *tā<u>kh</u>īr*, s.m. Delay, procrastination. A.

تار *tār*, s.m. Wire; cord, thread. P. *tār-tār* or *tār-patār*, a. Confused, dispersed, scattered.

تاراج *tārāj*, s.m. Plunder, spoil, booty. P.

تارك *tārik*, s.m. Leaving, forsaking; a deserter. A.

تارو *tārū*, s.m. A black partridge; a drone, humble bee; a kind of wasp without a sting. A kind of saddle cloth.

تاروګي *tārūgai*, s.m. A kind of butterfly.

تارول *tāranul*, v.a. to scatter, disperse.

تاريخ *tārī<u>kh</u>*, s.m. Era, date; annals, history. A.

تاريک *tārīk*, a. Dark, obscure. P.

تاريکي *tārīkī*, s.f. Darkness, obscurity. P.

تاړ *tāṛ*, s m. Plunder, spoil; a gang of robbers.

تاړه *tāṛah*, a. Spoiled, ruined, sacked.

تاړي *tāṛī*, s.m. Clapping the hands to express approbation, or in time to music. H. (*tārī*).

تازه *tāzah*, a. Fresh, new; green, verdant; young, robust; happy, pleased. P.

تازي *tāzī*, s.m. A greyhound; an Arab horse; a hunting dog, hound. P.

تازيانه *tāziyāna*, s.f. A whip, scourge, birch. P.

تاس *tās*, s.m. A goblet or cup of brass; a platter or tray of copper. P. Cards; a game at cards. H.

تاسو *tāsū*, pr. Plural form of the second personal pronoun: ye, you. Also written تاسُ *tāsu*.

تاغه *tā<u>gh</u>ah*, s.m. Name of a tree, the wood of which is used to make charms against the evil eye; the white poplar (*Populus albus*). H. (*tā<u>gh</u>*).

تافته *tāfta*, s.f. A kind of silk, taffeta; a colour of horses, cream colour. P.

تاك *tāk*, s.m. A vine. P. A precipice, cliff; mountain side. a. Odd, single, unique. A. (*ṭāq*).

تاكيد *tākīd*, s.m. Emphasis, injunction; confirmation. A. *tākīd-kanul*, v.a. To enjoin, insist, urge, press.

تاكيدي *tākīdī*, a. Emphatic, decided, confirmed.

تال *tāl*, s.m. Clapping the hands to music; chime. S.

تالاب *tālāb*, تالاو *tālāo*, s.m. A pond, tank, reservoir. P.

تالاش *tālā<u>sh</u>*, s.m. Investigation, inquiry, search. P. (*talā<u>sh</u>*). Name of a valley between Bajawar and Swat.

تالنده *tālanda*, s.f. Thunder.

تالو *tālū*, s.m. The palate; a disease of the palate in cattle. S.

تاله *tāla*, s.f. Booty, spoil, pillage, plunder, ruin; a kind of fine spring grass.

تالي *tālai*, s.m. A metal platter or tray. S. (*thālī*).

تامبه *tāmba*, تانبه *tānba*, s.f. Copper. S. (*tāmbā*).

تامّل *tā-ammul*, s.m. Hesitation, meditation. A.

تان *tān*, s.m. A note in music, tone, tune. S.

تاندوله *tāndola*, s.f. Name of a potherb.
تانده *tāndah*, a. Fresh, green, verdant.
تانسته *tānasta*, s.f. The warp or threads stretched lengthwise on the loom. P.
تانگ *tāng*, s.m. A band, brace, saddle-girth. P. (*tang*).
تانړه *tānṛa*, s.f. A guard, picket; police station. S. (*thānā*).
تاو *tāo*, s.m. See تاب.
تاوان *tāwān*, s.m. Amends, recompense; retaliation; debt, fine, mulct. P. Used in opposition to *qiṣāṣ*, which means actual revenge, —blood for blood, injury for injury, etc. *tāwān-ā**kh**istal*, v.a. To fine, mulct; take the responsibility. *tāwān-kedal*, v.n. To suffer loss, injury, etc. *tāwān-warkawul*, v.a. To make amends, compensate, pay a fine. *tāwān-kawul*, v.a. To expend, incur, etc.
تاواني *tāwānī*, a. Injurious, incurring loss, noxious.
تاوس *tāos*, s.m. A peacock. A. (*ṭāūs*).
تاوون *tāwūn*, s.m. The plague. A. (*ṭā'ūn*).
تاووني *tāwūnai*, s.m. A man afflicted with the plague.
تاويتک *tāwītak*, s.m. An ornamental charm worn on the bosom by women.
تب *tab*, s.m. A poultice, epithem.
تباخ *tabā**kh***, s.m. A charger, plate, dish. A. (*ṭabāq*).
تبار *tabār*, s.m. Race, family, tribe, people. P.
تباه *tabāh*, a. Ruined, spoiled; abject, wretched. P.
تباهي *tabāhī*, s.f. Ruin, wreck; depravity, wretchedness.
تبخي *taba**kh**ai*, s.m. An iron platter for baking cakes on. A. (*ṭabāq*). The pelvis.
تبديل *tabdīl*, s.m. Alteration, change. A.
تبر *tabar*, s.m. An axe, hatchet, cleaver. P. *tabar-zīn*, s.m. A horseman's battle-axe.
تبرک *tabarruk*, s.m. Blessing, benediction. A.
تبړه *tabaṛa*, s.f. A slate, slab of stone.
تبسم *tabassum*, s.m. A smile, simper. A.
تبق *tabaq*, تبخ *taba**kh***, s.m. A disease of cattle, the glanders.
تبه *taba*, s.f. Fever; heat, fervour. P. S. (*tap*).
تبي *taba-ī*, s.f. A flat dish of pottery for baking cakes on.
تپ *tap*, s.m. A mole, freckle; scar or pit of small-pox. *tap-tap*, in. A call to encourage dogs to go into a hole.
تپاس *tapās*, s.m. Labour, toil, search, enquiry. S.
تپاک *tapāk*, s.m. Esteem, regard, affection, love. S.
تپړا *tapṛā*, s.f. A potter's tool; a wooden tapper or mallet; tapping. H. (*thāpī*).
تپک *tapak*, s.m. The roll or sound of a drum. A sledge hammer. P.
تپل *tapal*, v.a. To dab, stick against; daub, smear; heap, mass, pile. H. (*thāpnā*).
تپنړي *tapanṛa-ī*, s.f. See تپړا.
تپور *tapor*, s.m. An ornamental breast-band worn by young women; a stomacher.
تپوس *tapos*, s.m. Enquiry, search. A. (*tafaḥḥuṣ*).
تپه *tapa*, s.f. A district, parish; a clan, tribe. H.
تپي *tapai*, a. Freckled, pitted, scarred, spotted. s.m. A mole, freckle, scar, pit of small-pox.
تت *tat*, a. Close, compact, dense, thick. H. (*ṭhaṭh*).
تتړي *tataṛai*, a. Lisping, stammering. s.m. A lisper, stammerer.
تتمه *tatimma*, s.f. Appendix, supplement. A.
تتوه *tatawa*, s.f. A ring-dove.
تجارت *tajārat*, s.m. Commerce, trade. A.
تجربه *tajriba*, s.f. Experiment, proof, trial, test. A.
تجويز *tajwīz*, s.m. Contrivance, plan, scheme; enquiry, consideration; determination, judgment. A.

تچ *ti<u>ch</u>*, s.m. The scabbard of a sword, sheath of a dagger.

تحرير *taḥrīr*, s.m. Writing correctly; written; dated. A.

تحصيل *taḥṣīl*, s.m. Acquisition, acquirement; profit, gain; collection; collectorate. A.

تحفه *tuḥfah*, a. Curious, rare, choice, excellent. A.

تحقيق *taḥqīq*, a. Authentic, verified, ascertained. ad. Indeed, really, truly. s.m. Precision, exactness. A.

تحقيقات *taḥqīqāt*, s.m. Inquiry, investigation. A.

تحمل *taḥammul*, s.m. Endurance, forbearance. A.

تخت *ta<u>kh</u>t*, s.m. A throne. P.

تخته *ta<u>kh</u>ta*, s.f. A board, plank; sheet of paper; bench, form; bier. *ta<u>kh</u>ta-bandī*, s.f. Boarding, planking, wainscot. *ta<u>kh</u>ta-pok<u>kh</u>*, s.m. A stage, platform, flooring. *ta<u>kh</u>ta·nard*, s.m. Backgammon. P.

تخرگ *ta<u>kh</u>arg*, or *t<u>kh</u>arg*, s.m. The armpit.

تخرگي *ta<u>kh</u>argai*, s.m. The fillet or patch in the armpit of a dress.

تخفيف *ta<u>kh</u>fif*, s.m. Abatement, mitigation, relief. A.

تخم *tu<u>kh</u>m*, s.m. Seed, sperm; an egg; a testicle. P.

تخمخ *ta<u>kh</u>ma<u>kh</u>*, in. Fie! shame!

تخمه *tu<u>kh</u>ma*, s.f. Origin, principle. P. Indigestion. A.

تخميناً *ta<u>kh</u>mīnan*, ad. About, nearly, by guess. A.

تخنول *ta<u>kh</u>nawul*, تخول *ta<u>kh</u>awul*, } v.a. To tickle. P. (*tā<u>kh</u>t*, assault, etc.).

تخنيدل *ta<u>kh</u>nedal*, تخيدل *ta<u>kh</u>edal*, } v.n. To tickle, titillate.

تخه *ta<u>kh</u>a*, s.f. تخي *ta<u>kh</u>ai*, s.m. } Tickling, titillation.

تدارک *tadāruk*, s.m. Chastisement, retaliation; remedy, precaution; provision, preparation. A.

تدبير *tadbīr*, s.m. Advice, counsel, deliberation; contrivance, management, policy; arrangement, order. A.

تدريج *tadrīj*, s.m. Gradation, scale. A.

تذکره *tazkira*, s.f. Biography, memoir. A.

تر *tar*, a. Damp, moist. P. ad. As far as, to, until, up to, etc. It is generally followed by the adverb *pore* or *pori*. Ex. *tar·osa·pore*, until now. *tar·kala·pore*, till when? *tar·kūma·pore*, as long as, etc. *tri*, p. See تري.

ترات *trāṭ*, s.m. A whip, goad.

تراته *trāṭa*, s.f. Piping, or edging of a dress.

تراړه *tarāṛa*, s.f. Gravel, shingle.

ترازو *tarāzū*, s.m. A balance, scale. P.

ترازه *tarāza*, s.f. A slice, shaving, bit. P. (*tarā<u>sh</u>a*).

تراش *tarā<u>sh</u>*, s.m. Cutting, clipping; cut, form, shape; (in comp.) -cutter, -carver. P.

تراغ *tarā<u>gh</u>*, s.m. A coil, plait, twist.

تراک *trāk*, s.m. A crack, fissure; slit, rent, tear. A. Also تراق *trāq*.

ترانه *tarāna*, s.f. Melody, music, song; symphony, tune. P. *tarāne·wayal*, v.a. To sing.

تراوي *tarāwe*, s.f. A prayer comprising twenty genuflexions, performed at bedtime every night during the month of Ramaẓān.

ترب *turb*, s.m. A radish. P.

تربت *turbat*, s.m. A tomb, sepulchre. A.

تربور *tarbūr*, s.m. A cousin: father's brother's son.

تربوزه *tarbūza*, s.f. A water melon. P.

تربيت *tarbiyat*, s.m. Education, instruction, tuition. A.

ترپ *trap*, s.m. A leap, bound, jump; hop, skip.

تَرپَل *trapal,* v.a. To jump, vault, bound, etc.
ترپه *trapa,* s.f. See ترپ.
ترپي *trapai,* s.m. A footfall, sound of steps.
ترتاب *tartāb,* s.m. Remorse, sorrow, regret.
ترتړي *tartaṛai,* s.m. See تتړي.
ترتله *tartala,* ad. Always, ever, continually.
ترتيب *tartīb,* s.m. Arrangement, disposition, order, method. A.
ترتيزک *tartezak,* s.m. Watercress. P. (*tezak*).
ترټل *traṭal,* v.a. To scold, reprimand, taunt; drive away, repel. See رټل, *raṭal.*
ترجمه *tarjuma,* s.f. Translation, interpretation. A.
ترجمان *tarjumān,* s.m. An interpreter. A.
ترڅ *traṯs,* a. Slanting, sloping, aside, wry, crooked. H. (*tirchhā*).
ترخ *trakh,* s.m. The armpit.
ترخان *tarkhān,* s.m. Free, exempted from taxation; name of a tribe of Turks; wormwood.
ترخه *tarkha,* s.f. The herb wormwood, absinth (*Artemisia Judaica*).
ترخئي *tarkha-ī,* s.f. Name of a plant, wild camomile (*Anthemis nobilis*).
تردد *taraddud,* s.m. Hesitation, suspense. A.
ترس *tars,* s.m. Fear, dread, terror. P.
ترسا *tarsā,* s.m. A heretic, infidel, idolator, pagan. P.
ترسان *tarsān,* } ترسناک *tarsnāk,* } a. Timid, fearful, cowardly. P.
ترسري *tarsarai,* } تيرسري *tersarai,* } s.m. A headstall, halter for a horse; a freckle, spot in the skin.
ترش *tursh,* a. Acid, sour; austere, crabbed, cross. P.
ترشي *turshī,* s.f. Acidity, sourness; acids; ill-temper, austerity. P.
ترښځ *tarkkhadz,* } ترښځه *tarkkhadza,* } s.f. An adze; a band, fillet, or strip of cloth let into the side of a dress.

ترغيب *targhīb,* s.m. Incitement, instigation. A.
ترقي *taraqqī,* s.f. A rise, elevation, ascent; promotion, advancement; increase; proficiency. A.
ترک *turk,* s.m. A Turk; a soldier; a robber; (in poetry) a handsome youth. P. *tark,* s.m. Desertion, forsaking. A. *trak,* s.m. A crack, cleft, split; sand-crack, a disease of the hoof in cattle; a crack, the sound of splitting, bursting, tearing, etc.
ترکاڼړ *tarkāṉṛ,* s.m. A carpenter.
ترکښ *tarkakkh,* s.m. A quiver. P. (*tarkash*).
ترکلاڼړي *tarkalāṉṛī,* s.m. Name of a Pathan tribe settled in Bajawur.
ترکه *tarka,* s.f. Legacy, bequest; effects or estate of a deceased person. A.
ترکيب *tarkīb,* s.m. Composition, mixture; make, form. A.
ترګمئي *tarugma-ī,* s.f. A dark, moonless night; obscurity, darkness.
ترله *tarla,* s.f. A cousin: father's brother's daughter.
ترم *turum,* s.m. A stallion, kept only for covering. P.
ترمنه *taramna,* s.f. A bog, quagmire, quicksand.
ترمي ترمي *tarmai-tarmai,* a. Dispersed, scattered, dispelled.
ترناو *tarnāo,* s.m. An aqueduct, trough, gutter.
ترنځ *trandz,* a. Slim, compressed, slight, spare. P. (*taranj*).
ترنج *turanj,* s.m. A citron, lime, lemon. *taranj,* s.m. Name of several plants of the orders *Euphorbia* and *Asclepias,* containing milky sap. *tranj,* s.m. A skein or roll of thread.
ترنجوکي *tranjūkai,* } ترنجي *tranjai,* } s.m. Small skein of thread.
ترنکوڅه *trankūṯsa,* s.f. A sling.

ترنگ **trang**, s.m. Twang, jar, vibration, sound.

ترنگبين **tarangabīn**, | ترنجبين **taranjabīn**, } s.m. Manna produced from the camel's thorn (*Hedysarum alhagi*). Oxymel, honey and limejuice. S. P.

ترنگړ **trangaṛ**, s.m. A net for carrying grass, etc.

ترو **tro**, ad. Consequently, therefore, then, for that; at length, afterwards, at that time.

تروټ **troṭ**, s.m. Damage, injury; loss, deficiency.

تروټه **troṭa**, s.f. Detriment, discount.

ترور **tror**, s.f. Aunt: father's or mother's sister.

ترورۍ **trora-ī**, s.f. A fox.

تروکه **tarūka**, s.f. Sorrel (*Rumex vesicarius*). Wood-sorrel (*Oxalis corniculata*).

تروه **tarwa**, a. See تريو .

تروي **tarwai**, s.m. Name of a purgative plant (*Ipomœa turpethum*). H. (*teorī*). **tarwe**, s.f. (pl. of *tarwa*) Sour milk, whey, curds and whey.

تره **trah**, s.m. Uncle: father's or mother's brother. **tara**, s.f. Greens, vegetables, potherbs. P. A kind of cucumber (*Cucumis acutangulus*). H. (*tura-ī*). Alarm, dread, fear.

ترهاو **tirhāo**, s.m. The third part of an oke. See اوړي .

ترهر **tarhar**, a. Timid, fearful, nervous. s.m. Fear, alarm, dismay. Also ترهور **tarhūr**.

ترهول **tarhawul**, v.a. To alarm, frighten, start, etc. (as game).

ترهيدل **tarhedal**, v.n. To start, fear, shy, etc. (as animals). P. (*tarīdan*).

تري **tarī**, s.f. Moisture; water in opposition to land; moist or brown sugar. ad. By water. P. **tarai**, s.m. An aqueduct or canal on the side of a hill. **turai**, s.m. A kind of cucumber (*Cucumis utilissimus*).

tara-ī, ad. Clandestinely, confidentially, secretly. **tura-ī**, s.f. A. bugle. H. (*turhī*).

تري **tre**, p. From, by, than, with.

ترياک **tariyāk**, s.m. Opium. A. (*tiriyāq*).

تريز **tarīz**, s.m. A patch, piece sewed on to a dress or garment. P.

تريج **tarīj**, a. Strong, violent, rough. A.

تريخ **trīkh**, a. Bitter, nauseous; sour, austere, cross, ill-tempered. f. *tarkha*.

تريخي **trīkhai**, s.m. Bitterness; gall, bile; the gall-bladder; anger, malice, ill-feeling.

تريو **trīw**, a. Acid, sharp, sour; austere, crabbed, morose, cross. f. *tarwa*.

تريه **tariyah**, in. A shepherd's call to drive sheep, etc.

تړاق **tṛāq**, s.m. A knock, rap, tap. H. (*taṛākā*).

تړاقي **taṛāqa-ī**, s.f. A loin clout; a cord tied round the waist, and used as a fastening for the clout covering the privates. H. (*taṛāgī*).

تړپ **tṛap**, s.m. Haste, hurry; flutter; leap. H. (*taṛap*).

تړپول **tṛapawul**, v.a. To agitate, disturb, flurry. H. (*taṛpānā*).

تړپيدل **tṛapedal**, v.n. To flutter, palpitate, writhe. H. (*taṛapnā*).

تړق **tṛaq**, s.m. A pat, tap, rap, knock, slap.

تړل **taṛal**, v.a. To tie, fasten, bind, lash. P. (*tār*, thread, cord).

تړم **taṛam**, a. Lukewarm, tepid.

تړون **taṛūn**, s.m. Binding, fastening, lashing; agreement, bargain, compact, treaty.

تړنه **taṛana**, | تړه **taṛa**, } s.f. See preceding.

تړي **taṛai**, s.m. Lisping; a lisper.

تژن **tuzan**, a. Base, cowardly.

تږي **tagai**, a. Thirsty. P. (*tishna*).

تسبه **tasba**, s.f. The bead of a rosary. A. (*tasbīḥ*). **tasbe**, pl. A rosary, chaplet of beads.

تسخير *tas<u>kh</u>īr*, s.m. Capture, subjection. A.

تسکين *taskīn*, s.m. Comfort, consolation. A.

تسلي *tasallī*, s.m. Comfort, solace, consolation. A.

تسليم *taslīm*, s.m. Resignation, obedience; obeisance, salutation; health, safety. A.

تسمه *tasma*, s.f. A thong, leather strap. H.

تُش *ta-a<u>sh</u>*, a. Empty, void, hollow. ad. Only, merely, simply. P. (*tihī*).

تشبيه *ta<u>sh</u>bīh*, s.m. Comparison, simile. A.

تشت *ta<u>sh</u>t*, s.m. A basin used to wash the hands over. P. A platter, salver, tray.

تشخانه *ta<u>sh</u>k<u>kh</u>āna*, s.f. The fire pan of a gun. P. (*āta<u>sh</u>·<u>kh</u>āna*).

تشخيص *ta<u>sh</u><u>kh</u>īṣ*, s.m. Ascertaining, distinguishing; valuation, assessment. A.

تشويش *ta<u>sh</u>wī<u>sh</u>*, s.m. Anxiety, disquietude. A.

تُشي *ta-a<u>sh</u>ai*, s.m. The flank, side, hypochondrium.

تښتن *ta<u>kkh</u>tan*, s.m. See خښتن.

تښتول *ta<u>kkh</u>tawul*, } v.a. To put to flight, run away with, carry off,
تښول *ta<u>kkh</u>awul*, } elope with, etc. P. (*tā<u>kh</u>tāndan*).

تښتيدل *ta<u>kkh</u>edal*, } v.n. To flee, decamp,
تښل *ta<u>kkh</u>al*, } retire, retreat, run away. P. (*tā<u>kh</u>tan*).

تصديق *taṣdīq*, s.m. Attestation, verification. A.

تصرف *taṣarruf*, s.m. Disposal, use; expenditure, extravagance. A.

تصنيف *taṣnīf*, s.m. Composition, authorship. A.

تصوير *taṣwīr*, s.m. Image, picture, portrait. A.

تعجب *t'ajjub*, s.m. Wonder, surprise, astonishment. A.

تعريف *t'arīf*, s.m. Explaining, praising. A.

تعطيل *ta'ṭīl*, s.m. Vacation; neglecting, abandoning. A.

تعظيم *t'aẓīm*, s.m. Honour, reverence, respect. A.

تعلق *t'alluq*, s.m. Relation, connection; dependence; correspondence, commerce. A.

تعليم *t'alīm*, s.m. Teaching, tuition. A.

تعويذ *t'awīẕ*, s.m. An amulet, charm. A.

تغار *ta<u>gh</u>ār*, s.m. A bread-tray; a bucket, pail. P.

تغارک *ta<u>gh</u>ārak*, s.m. Dropsy; a small pail. P.

تغاري *ta<u>gh</u>ārai*, s.m. A bread-basket; an earthenware dish or platter; a small bucket or pail. A. a. A glutton.

تغمه *ta<u>gh</u>ma*, s.f. A mark, weal, welt; a medal. A.

تغير *ta<u>gh</u>īr*, s.m. }
تغيري *ta<u>gh</u>īrī*, s.f. } Change, alteration. A.
تغيير *ta<u>gh</u>aiyur*, s.m. }

تف *taf*, s.m. Vapour, steam. P. *tuf*, s.m. Saliva. P.

تفاوت *tafāwat*, s.m. Difference, distinction; distance. A.

تفرقه *tafriqa*, s.f. }
تفريق *tafrīq*, s.m. } Division, separation. A.

تفسير *tafsīr*, s.m. Commentary, explanation. A.

تفصيل *tafṣīl*, s.m. Detail, explanation, separation. A.

تفنګ *tufang*, s.m. A musket. P.

تقاضا *taqāẓā*, s.f. Exacting, dunning; importunity. A.

تقدير *taqdīr*, s.m. Destiny, fate, lot. A.

تقرير *taqrīr*, s.m. Detail, relation, recital. A.

تقسيم *taqsīm*, s.m. Dividing, division, distribution. A.

تقصير *taqṣīr*, s.m. Crime, error, fault. A.

تقليد *taqlīd*, s.m. Imitation; forging; copying; believing without enquiry. A.

تقوىٰ *taqwā*, s.f. Piety, the fear of God. A.

تک *tak*, ad. Altogether, wholly, utterly; only used with respect to colour. Ex. *tak·tor·saṛai*, a jet-black man. *taka·spīna·<u>kkh</u>adza*, a snow-white woman.

تکبير *takbīr*, s.m. Repeating the creed, or saying "God is great" (*allahu·akbar*). A.

تکرار *takrār*, s.m. Altercation, contention, dispute. A.

تکراري *takrārī*, s.m. A wrangler, caviller. a. Disputing, importuning, wrangling. A.

تکړه *takṛah*, a. Active, vigorous, strong, robust, healthy. *takaṛa*, s.f. A pebble; boulder.

تکل *takal*, s.m. Attempt, effort, endeavour. See کتل.

تکلاستي *taklāstai*, a. Agile, nimble, smart, active, alert.

تکليف *taklīf*, s.m. Ceremony; difficulty, inconvenience, trouble, ailment, distress, annoyance. A.

تکمه *tukma*, s.f. A button loop; the sac or tubercle of piles. P.

تکيه *takiya*, s.f. A bolster, pillow; a faqīr's stand or hut. *takiya-kalām*, s.m. An expletive, cant phrase. P.

تګ *tag*, s.m. Departure; toiling, running about.

تګاپو *tagāpū*, s.m. Bustle, toil, labour, search. P.

تل *tal*, ad. Always, ever, perpetually. *til*, s.m. Sesamum, the seed. S. *tal*, s.m. The base, bottom, foot, sole. S. (*talā*). *tall*, s.m. A hillock, mound, heap. A.

تلاش *talāsh*, s.m. Enquiry, study, search. P.

تلب *talab*, s.m. Salary, wages, hire, pay. A. (*ṭalab*).

تلتک *taltak*, s.m. Coverlet, counterpane; mattress.

تلخ *talkh*, a. Acrid, bitter, rancid. P.

تلخان *talkhān*, s.m. Meal of parched grain, made into a paste for food on a journey. P.

تلف *talaf*, s.m. Destruction, loss, ruin; prodigality, waste. A.

تلکه *talaka*, s.f. A kind of snare for catching birds, a springe.

تلل *tlal*, v.n. To go, depart, set out, leave. H. (*chalnā*). See لاړل *lāṛal*. *talal*, v.a. To balance, weigh. H. (*tolnā*).

تلوار *talwār*, s.m. Haste, speed, quickness.

تلوسه *talwasa*, s.f. Commotion, distraction. P. (*talwāsa*).

تلول *talwal*, s.m. Dispatch, haste, speed, quickness. *talawul*, v.a. To fry, grill, broil.

تلولي *talwalai*, a. Precipitate, rash, hasty, quick. *talawalai*, a. Broiled, fried, grilled.

تله *tlah*, s.m. Exit, exodus, departure, setting out. *tala*, s.f. Balance, scale; the sole of the foot.

تلي *talai*, s.m. The sole of a shoe; under surface of a thing; sole of the foot; palm of the hand. S. (*talī*). *tilai*, s.m. Form, figure, shape. *tila-ī*, s.f. The shaft of an arrow, stalks of corn, reeds, grasses, etc.; a straw, straw. H. (*tīl*).

تم *tam*, s.m. Continuance, permanence, rest. a. Staying, abiding, tarrying.

تماچه *tamācha*, s.f. A pistol; a blow, cuff, slap. A. (*ṭamāncha*).

تماشا *tamāshā*, } s.f. A show, sight, spectacle,
تماشه *tamāsha*, } amusement, entertainment. A.

تماکو *tamākū*, } s.m. Tobacco.
تمباکو *tambākū*, }

تمام *tamām*, a. Complete, entire, perfect. A.

تمامي *tamāmī*, s.f. Completion, end; perfection.

تمبل *tambal*, s.m. A kettledrum, tambourine. A. (*ṭabal*).

تمبو *tambū*, s.m. A tent. H.

تمبوزک *tambūzak*, s.m. A muzzle; a muzzle of spikes fastened on the nose of a calf to prevent its sucking.

تمبوزي *tambūzai*, s.m. The muzzle, snout; bridge of the nose.

تمبه *tamba*, s.f. The leaf of a door; prop of a door; a group, party, herd.

تمبګي *tambaga-ī*, s.f. The leaf of a window or shutter.

تمبيزه *tambeza*, s.f. } The muzzle, snout.
تمبيزي *tambezai*, s.m. }

تمتراق *tamtarāq*, s.m. Grandeur, magnificence, pomp. A. (*ṯamṯarāq*).

تمسک *tamassuk*, s.m. Note of hand, bond, receipt. A.

تمن *tuman*, s.m. A crowd, troop, party; brotherhood, connection; a score, twenty. P.

تموز *tamūz*, s.m. Heat, warmth; name of a month, July. P.

تمه *tama*, s.f. Avarice, avidity; covetousness, greediness. A. (*ṯama'*).

تميز *tamīz*, s.m. Discretion, sense, judgment. A.

تن *tan*, s.m. Body, person; individual. P.

تنا *tanā*, s.f. Thunder.

تناو *tanāo*, s.m. A cord, rope; strap.

تنبيه *tanbīh*, s.m. Admonition, advice, correction. A.

تنتنا *tantanā*, s.f. Fame, sound, rumour; dignity, pomp. A. (*tanṯanā*).

تنخواه *tankhwāh*, s.m. Salary, wages, pay. P.

تند *tund*, a. Active, fast, quick; hot, spirited, rash; acrid, pungent. P.

تندار *tandār*, s.f. Uncle's wife. See تندور.

تندر *tandar*, s.m. Thunder; a thunder-bolt; eclipse. P.

تندور *tandor*, s.f. Paternal aunt, father's brother's wife. *tandūr*, s.m. An oven. P.

تندوره *tandūra*, s.f. A cascade, waterfall.

تندوري *tindoṛai*, s.m. The cartilage of the nose.

تندوي *tandwai*, s.m. Cartilage, gristle.

تنده *tanda*, s.f. Thirst.

تندي *tundī*, a. Acrimony; impetuosity, fierceness. P. *tandai*, s.m. An infant, babe, suckling; sprout, shoot, young plant; the forehead; the crown of the head, vertex.

تنديارہ *tandyāra*, s.f. Father's brother's wife. See تندار.

تندل *tanḍal*, v.a. To make, form, mend, repair.

تنذري *tanẕarai*, } s.m. A grey partridge.
تنزري *tanzarai*, }

تنکي *tankai*, s.m. A babe, suckling; sprout, shoot, young plant. a. Young, tender, unripe.

تنګ *tang*, a. Confined, narrow, tight; scarce, wanting, barren; distressed, in want; dejected, sad. P. *tung*, s.m. An ewer, vase, long-necked jar. P.

تنګسه *tangsa*, } s.f. Distress, poverty; scarcity, want; narrowness, tightness.
تنګسيا *tangsiyā*, }

تنګه *tanga*, s.f. The stock or stem of a tree; body or centre width of a garment; name of a coin equal to one-third of a rupee. T.

تنګي *tangai*, s.m. A defile, gorge, hill, pass. *tangī*, s.f. Distress, poverty, want; avarice, parsimony, stinginess; narrowness, tightness. P.

تنور *tanūr*, s.m. A furnace; oven. P.

تنومند *tanomand*, a. Corpulent, robust. P.

تنها *tanhā*, a. Alone, solitary; single; apart. ad. Merely, only, singly. P.

تنهائي *tanhā-ī*, s.f. Solitude, loneliness, privacy. P.

تنړا *tanrā*, s.f. Thunder; roar of a wild animal.

تنړاکه *tanrāka*, s.f. A bleb, vesicle, blister.

تنړکار *tanrakār*, s.m. Borax. P. (*tinkār*).

تنړئي *tanra-ī*, s.f. Button loop; strings of a dress; cord, pack-thread, etc. used to tie bundles.

تو *tū*, s.m. Spittle, saliva. H. (*thūk*). *tu-tu*, in. Call to a dog. H.

توا *tawā*, s.f. A frying pan. P.

تواريخ *tawārīkh*, s.m. Annals, dates; history. A.

توان *tuwān*, s.m. Force, power, strength. P.

توانا *tuwānā*, a. Able, powerful, strong. P.

توانګر *tuwāngar*, a. Rich, wealthy; powerful, able. P.

توانګري *tuwāngarī*, s.f. Opulence, wealth; ability, power. P.

توانيدل *tuwānedal*, v.n. To be able. P. (*tuwānīdan*).

توب *tob*, A particle affixed to nouns and adjectives to denote state, pursuit, or quality. Ex. *tang*, a. Tight. *tang·tob*, s.m. Tightness. *spāhī*, s.m. Soldier. *spāhī·tob*, s.m. Soldiering, profession of a soldier. *saṛī*, s.m. Men. *saṛī·tob*, s.m. The state of men, humanity. A. (*tab'a*). See تيا.

توبره *tobra*, s.f. A nose-bag (for a horse); saddle-bag; a beggar's wallet. H. (*tobṛā*).

توبري *tobrai*, s.m. The head of an arrow, dart, etc.

توبه *toba*, s.f. Contrition, penitence, remorse. in. Fie! shame! A.

توبه‌ګار *toba·gār*, a. Penitent, contrite. A.

توپ *top*, s.m. A cannon, gun. T.

توپان *tūpān*, s.m. A hurricane, storm; deluge. A. (*ṭufān*).

توپک *topak*, s.m. A matchlock, musket. T.

توپنګچه *tūpangcha*, s.f. A pistol. P. (*tufangcha*).

توت *tūt*, s.m. The mulberry, tree and fruit. A.

توتا *totā*, s.m. } A parrot; the cock or hammer
توتي *totī*, s.f. } of a gun. H.

توتکي *totakai*, s.m. A swift, swallow.

توتکرکي *totakarkai*, s.m. A sand martin, swallow.

توتکري *totakarai*, s.m. A swift, swallow.

توتنکي *totankai*, s.m. A chip, filing, shaving, fragment. H. (*tūtan*).

توتيا *totiyā*, or نيله‌توتيا *nīla·totiyā*, s.f. Blue vitriol, sulphate of copper. S.

توجه *tawajja*, s.f. Attention, regard; favour. A.

توخي *tokhī*, s.m. Name of a section of the Ghilzai tribe.

تود *tod*, a. Hot, warm. P. (*tūnd*). H. (*tāt*).

تودوخه *todūkha*, s.f. Sultriness, heat, warmth.

تور *tor*, a. Black, dark. P. (*tār*). s.m. Fright, panic; slander, calumny; a net, snare. *tor·pore·kawul*, v.a. To calumniate, blacken, slander.

تورغړي *torgharai*, s.m. The arm above the elbow.

تورلمي *torlamai*, s.m. A badger.

توره *tūra*, s.f. A sword. *tora*, s.f. A copper coin, equal to half an anna.

توره‌آنه *tora·āna*, s.f. Name of a black coloured bird with a forked tail; the king-crow or tyrant fly-catcher. Called also *ḍāng·luka-ī*, club tail.

توره‌غاړه *tora·ghāṛa*, s.f. Hooping cough.

توري *torai*, s.m. The spleen; pupil of the eye. a. Simple, plain, pure, unmixed. *tora-ī*, s.f. A kind of cucumber (*cucumis acutangulus*). H. (*torī*).

توريت *tauret*, s.m. The Pentateuch, Old Testament. A. (*torāt*).

توږل *togal*, v.a. To plane, shave; polish, smooth.

توسن *tausan*, s.m. A war horse; high spirited horse. P.

توسند *tosand*, a. Dry, parched, withered. H. (*tūsā*).

توشدان *toshdān*, s.m. A pouch, cartridge-box. P.

توشک *toshak*, s.m. A mattress, quilt. P.

توښه *tokkha*, s.f. Necessaries, provisions, supplies for a journey. P. (*tosha*).

توغ *togh*, s.m. A banner, ensign, standard. T.

توغل *toghal*, } s.m. A saddle cloth of felt.
توغم *togham*, }

توقه *tūqa*, s.f. A blunt arrow; a small hill. P. (*tukka*).

توک *tūk*, s.m. Spittle. H. (*thūk*).

توکل *tūkal*, v.a. To spit. *tawakkul*, s.m. Faith, hope, reliance, trust in God. A.

توګه *toga*, s.f. Manner, method, way, mode.

تول *tol*, s.m. Gravity, weight. s. *tūl*, s.m. A crop or field ready for reaping. *twal*, a. Equal, even, same weight, six of one and half a dozen of the other.

تولاند *tūlānd*, s.m. A stride, long step; gait of a bird.

تولائي *tolā-ī*, s.f. A mattress, quilted bed.

توله *tola*, s.f. Name of a weight equal to 180 grs. (troy). s. (*tolā*).

تومان *tomān*, s.m. A sum equal to twenty rupees; a myriad; 10,000. P. See تمن.

تومت *tomat*, s.m. See تهمت.

تومنه *tomna*, } s.f. Rennet; ferment, yeast;
تومه *toma*, } essence, origin.

تونبيا *tonbiyā*, s.f. Carded cotton; thread made from carded cotton. H. (*tūmiyā*).

تونگ *tawang*, s.m. A band-box; a reed-basket for the clothes of women. *tuwang*, s.m. Magazine, store, treasury. P. *tūng*, s.f. A maiden, damsel, girl.

تونگي *tawangai*, s.m. A band-box; a small basket made of reeds, and used by women to keep jewelry, ornaments, clothes, etc. in.

تونړي *tawṛa-ī*, s.f. A clothes chest, locker, safe.

توهړ *tohaṛ*, s.m. Cactus, prickly pear. H. (*thūhar*).

توي *toe*, a. Spilt, shed, overflowed, upset (as water from a bowl).

تويول *toyawul*, v.a. To pour out, upset, spill, shed.

تويېدل *toyedal*, v.n. To overflow, flow out, be spilt.

ته *tah*, a. Going, walking, proceeding. pr. The second personal pronoun, thou. *ta*, s.f. Fold, layer, plait; the bottom, under surface. P. *ta-khāna*, s.f. A cellar, vault. P. *tih*, a. Void, empty. P.

تهان *thān*, s.m. A piece, length of cloth; manger, stall for cattle. H.

تهمت *tuhmat*, s.m. Calumny, slander, suspicion, false accusation. A.

تهنال *tahnāl*, s.m. The mounting at the end of a scabbard. P.

تهنه *tahana*, s.f. A hollow, dip in the ground.

تي *tai*, s.m. A teat, nipple.

تيا *tiyā*, A particle added to adjectives in forming nouns denoting possession of their quality. Ex. *ārām*, a. Easy. *ārāmtiyā*, s.f. Easiness. *khamsor*, a. Familiar. *khamsortiyā*, s.f. Familiarity. *grān*, a. Dear. *grāntiyā*, s.f. Dearness.

تيار *tayār* or *taiyār*, a. Ready, complete, prepared, finished.

تياره *tyāra*, s.f. Darkness, gloom, obscurity (pl. of *tor*, black).

تياري *tayārī*, s.f. Readiness; preparation. P.

تيبون *taibūn*, s.m. See تيمم.

تيڅل *tetsal*, v.a. To perforate, pierce; to cram, stuff. A. (*tīsnā*).

تير *ter*, a. Lapsed, passed, gone by. *tīr*, s.m. An arrow; beam, ridge-pole. P.

تيرک *tīrak*, s.m. The iron axle on which the stone of a mill revolves; an axle.

تيرول *terawul*, v.a. To give the male to the female; to cause to pass.

تيره *terah*, a. Acute, keen, sharp. *tera*, a. Ready for the male, in heat. *tīrah*, a. Dark, obscure. P.

تيري *terai*, s.m. Excess; passing, lapsing; excellence, superiority.

تيريدل *teredal*, v.n. To pass, lapse, go by.

تيز *tez*, a. Acute, sharp, keen. P. *tīz*, s.m. Wind from the bowels, flatus. *tīz-āchawul*, v.a. To break wind.

تيزل *tezal*, v.a. To hasten, urge, press.

تيزندي *tezanda-ī*, s.f. A slip-knot; hangman's noose, halter, rope.

تيږه *tīga*, s.f. A boulder, rock; pebble, stone, slab.

تيشه *tesha*, s.f. A carpenter's adze. P.

تیښته *tekkhta*, s.f. Defeat, flight, retreat.

تیغ *tegh*, s.m. A scimitar, sword. P. A sprout, shoot, blade of grass.

تیغنه *teghna*, s.f. An iron plate for baking on.

تیک *tyak*, a. Distended, inflated, expanded.

تیکه *teka*, s.f. } A scabbard, sheath.
تیکي *tekai*, s.m. }

تیل *tel*, s.m. Oil. S.

تیلي *telī*, s.m. An oilman. f. (*telanṛa*).

تیمم *tayammum*, s.m. The ceremonial purification before prayers, with dust or sand, when water is not at hand. A.

تینبوزک *tīnbūzak*, s.m. The muzzle, snout.

تینبوزي *tīnbūzai*, s.m. A muzzle.

تیندک *tīndak*, s.m. A trip, stumble; ricochet, bound.

تییل *teyal*, v.a. To broil, fry, grill, roast.

تییني *teyanai*, s.m. A broil, grill, fry.

ټ

ټ *ṭa*, The fifth letter of the Pukkhto alphabet. It corresponds with the Sanskrit ट, represented by ٹ in the Hindūstānī, and exactly resembles it in sound.

ټاپ *ṭāp*, s.m. An impression; stamp, die, seal. H. (*thāp*).

ټاپو *ṭāpū*, s.m. An island. H.

ټاپوړه *ṭāpoṛa*, s.f. A crutch, a stilt; washerman's board or plank.

ټاپه *ṭāpa*, s.f. A stamp, die, seal, print. H. (*thāpa*).

ټاټ *ṭāṭ*, s.m. Canvas, sackcloth. H. Conceit, vanity, swagger. H. (*ṭhāṭh*).

ټاټوب *ṭāṭob*, s.m. Calmness, composure, rest, repose.

ټاټوکه *ṭāṭūka*, s.f. Name of an edible ground nut.

ټاټي *ṭāṭa-ī*, s.f. Lullaby, rocking, swinging. *ṭāṭī*, s.m. A dandy, fop, beau.

ټاس *ṭās*, s.m. An explosion, pop, snap, bang.

ټاق *ṭāq*, s.m. A bang, explosion, discharge.

ټاقر *ṭāqar*, s.m. A decrepid old man. S. (*ṭhākur*).

ټاک *ṭāk*, s.m. The fruit of the bael tree (*Ægle marmelos*). A bang, rap, knock.

ټاکو *ṭākū*, s.m. A robber, highwayman, pirate. H. (*ḍākū*). Name of a disease in buffaloes.

ټال *ṭāl*, s.m. A swing; the branch of a tree. H. (*ṭhāl*).

ټاله *ṭāla*, s,f. Wholesale, by the lump (pl. of *ṭol*).

ټانټه *ṭānṭa*, s.f. Stalk of Indian corn. H. (*ḍānṭhī*).

ټانګ *ṭāng*, s.m. A period, season, time, term.

ټانګو *ṭāngū*, s.m. } Name of a tree and its
ټانګي *ṭānga-ī*, s.f. } fruit; a kind of pear tree.

ټبر *ṭabar*, s.f. A wife. s.m. Family, household. H.

ټبکي *ṭubkai*, } s.m. A pit, hole, cavity.
ټبلي *ṭublai*, }

ټبي *ṭabai*, s.m. A flat stone, slate, slab of pottery, etc. used to bake cakes upon.

ټپ *ṭap*, a. Weak, haggard, worn, exhausted. s.m. A slap, hit, whack, rap; smack, thud, concussion. ad. Altogether, entirely, totally; used with adjectives to denote intensity. Ex. *ṭap·ṛūnd·saṛai*, s.m. A perfectly blind man. *ṭapa·kanṛa·kkhadza*, s.f. A completely deaf woman.

ټپټپانړي *ṭapṭapānṛai*, s.m. Name of a game played by children.

ټپریدل *ṭaparedal*, v.n. To totter, plod, stagger, creep, etc. (as an old man). P. (*tapīdan*).

ټپړ *ṭapaṛ*, } s.m. Canvas, sackcloth. H.
ټپنړ *ṭapanṛ*, }

ټپل *ṭapal*, v.n. See ټپریدل.

تپوځ *ṭapūts*, s.m. A kite (*Milvus sp.*).

تپي *ṭapai*, s.m. A spot, blotch, or patch of colour on the hide of an animal.

تپيدل *ṭapedal*, v.n. See تپل.

تت *ṭat*, s.m. Conceit, vanity.

تتي *ṭatai*, s.m. A fop, beau, coxcomb; braggart.

تتر *ṭaṭar*, s.m. The breast, chest, thorax. Vertex, poll. H. (*ṭaṭrī*).

تتو *ṭaṭū*, s.m. A pony. H. Bridge of a fiddle.

تتوګي *ṭaṭūgai*, s.m. A small pony.

تتئ *ṭaṭa-ī*, s.f. A matted screen; privy. H. (*ṭaṭṭī*).

تچ *ṭach*, s.m. See تاس.

تخ *ṭukh*, s.m. See توخ.

تر *ṭar*, s.m. Flatus, explosion of wind from behind; bosh, fudge, humbug.

ترتر *ṭarṭar*, s.m. Gabble, chatter, jabber.

ترق *ṭraq*, | ترک *ṭrak*, } s.m. See تق.

تري *ṭarai*, s.m. Gabbler, chatterbox, prattler.

تريدل *ṭaredal*, v.n. To break wind; to gabble, jabber.

تز *ṭaz*, | تس *ṭas*, } s.m. A pop, puff; flatus. H. (*ṭhas*). A slap, cuff, whack.

تستوس *ṭasṭūs*, s.m. Cracking, popping; discharge of firearms (as in a skirmish).

تسمس *ṭasmas*, a. Apathetic, dull, lazy.

تغ *ṭagh*, s.m. The pupil of the eye; the blue jay (*Coracias Bengalensis*). A creak, croak, grating sound.

تغر *ṭaghar*, s.m. A woollen carpet; felt; felt saddle cloth; old rag, clout, etc.

تغن *ṭaghan*, s.m. A coward, poltroon.

تغول *ṭaghawul*, v.a. To jar, grate, set on edge (as the teeth or nails).

تق *ṭaq*, s.m. A blow, rap, knock, whack, thump, etc. *ṭaq·kawul*, v.a. To bump, clash. *ṭaq·wahal*, v.a. To hit, strike, knock (as a nail, etc.).

تقول *ṭaqawul*, v.a. To censure, scold, reprove; to beat, batter, baste.

تك *ṭak*, s.m. Murrain, disease of cattle; a bang, slam; blow, thump, rap; a footfall, sound of feet.

تكا *ṭakā*, s.f. A footfall, sound of footsteps; explosion, sound of firearms.

تكاركي *ṭikārkai*, s.m. A plot of clear, hard, and level ground.

تكانه *ṭikāna*, s.f. Abode, lodging, residence, dwelling; boundary, limit, extent. H. (*ṭhikānā*).

تكاو *ṭikāo*, s.m. See تكانه.

تكتكانړي *ṭakṭakāṇrai*, s.m. Name of a game played by children; the clapper of a mill; a woodpecker.

تكر *ṭakar*, s.m. A jolt, push, shove. H.

تكړ *ṭukṛ*, s.m. A bit, morsel, piece. H. (*ṭukṛā*).

تكسري *ṭaksarai*, a. Mangy; a term of abuse. s.m. Murrain.

تككه *ṭakaka*, s.f. A cross bar of wood placed above the blade of a spade for the foot to rest upon.

تكلاستي *ṭaklāstai*, a. Active, nimble, smart, handy.

تكنده غرمه *ṭakanda·gharma*, | تكنړه غرمه *ṭakanṛa·gharma*, } s.f. Noon; midday; heat of noon or midday.

تكنړي *ṭakanṛai*, a. Obstinate, stubborn, restive.

تكور *ṭakor*, s.m. Fomentation, poultice. H.

تكول *ṭakawul*, v.a. To beat, bruise, hammer.

تكه *ṭaka*, s.f. Animosity, jealousy, hatred; thunderbolt; knuckle-bone. *ṭakah*, s.m. A species of ibex, or mountain goat.

تكي *ṭakai*, s.m. A dot, spot, speck; mark, streak; a bullock, horse, etc. with a spot on the forehead; appointed time or place; an atom, drop, molecule. *ṭika-ī*, s.f. A biscuit; wafer. H. (*tikiyā*); an orb, disk (as of the sun, etc.); a mark or butt for arrows; a loud laugh, guffaw. *pa-ṭakī*, ad. On the spot, at once, this minute.

تک *ṭag*, s.m. A cheat, impostor; assassin, robber. H. (*ṭhag*).

تکي *ṭagī*, s.f. Cheating, deceiving, robbery, theft.

تل *ṭal*, a. Close, dense, thick; full, replete, satiated. s.m. Division of a town or village; cluster of houses; a field, bed of flowers; closeness, denseness.

تم *ṭam*, s.m. Bark of a dog, growl of a wild beast.

تمتيل *ṭamṭīl*, s.m. A sandpiper, snippet.

تمک *ṭimak*, s.m. The cross-pole of a tent.

تنبل *ṭunbal*, v.a. To clean, pick (as the teeth); pluck, pick out (as thorns, etc.).

تند *ṭand*, a. Corpulent, fat, stout.

تنک *ṭang*, s.m. A creak, jar, twang, jingle. H. (*ḍankā*).

تنک‌تونک *ṭang-ṭūng*, s.m. Ding-dong, chime, notes of musical instruments.

تنکول *ṭangawul*, v.a. To jingle, clank, sound.

تنکه *ṭanga*, s.f. Name of a copper coin. H. (*ṭakā*). Money, wealth.

تنکيدل *ṭangedal*, v.n. To creak, jar, grate, twang.

توپ *ṭop*, s.m. A bound, jump, leap. H. (*ṭap*). A heap, pile, stack; excess, surplus.

توپک *ṭopak*, s.m. A musket, matchlock.

توپل *ṭopal*, s.m. The vertex, crown of the head.

توپۍ *ṭopa-ī*, s.f. A cap, hat, helmet; bowl or cup of a pipe. H. (*ṭopī*).

توته *ṭoṭa*, s.f. A bit, chip, fragment. A beggar's cup or tray. *ṭūṭa*, s.f. The hip, haunch. H. (*pūṭhā*).

توخ *ṭūk͟h*, s.m. Saliva, spittle.

توخه *ṭūk͟ha*, s.f. } Cough, expectoration.
توخي *ṭūk͟hai*, s.m. }

توخلي *ṭūk͟halai*, s.m. Hooping cough; croup. *ṭūk͟hala-ī*, s.f. Cap, head-covering, bonnet.

توخيدل *ṭūk͟hedal*, v.n. To cough, expectorate, spit.

توغ *ṭūg͟h*, a. Bent, bowed, stooping.

توقا *ṭoqā*, s.m. A grasshopper.

توقمار *ṭoqmār*, s.m. A buffoon, jester, clown.

توقه *ṭoqa*, s.f. Jest, joke, pleasantry, ridicule. A. (*ẓuḥka*).

توقي *ṭoqī*, s.m. A jester, buffoon, clown.

توک *ṭok*, a. Closely woven (as cloth). *ṭūk*, s.m. An atom, bit, particle. H.

توکيا *ṭokiyā*, s.f. A cleaver, bill-hook.

توکيدل *ṭūkedal*, v.n. To bud, grow, germinate, sprout. S. (*ṭūknā*).

توکرۍ *ṭokra-ī*, s.f. A basket. H. (*ṭokrī*).

توکي *ṭūkai*, s.m. A piece of cloth, length of cloth; piece, patch, repair. H.

تول *ṭol*, a. All, the whole, total. s.m. A party, flock, gang, drove.

تولتال *ṭolṭāl*, a. All, the whole, sum total.

تولکي *ṭolgai*, s.m. A party, small herd or flock.

تولول *ṭolawul*, v.a. To collect, gather, bring together.

تولي *ṭolai*, s.m. An assembly, party, company.

توليدل *ṭoledal*, v.n. To assemble, congregate, flock, herd or crowd together.

تونک *ṭong*, s.m. Irritation, provocation.

تونکاره *ṭongāra*, s.f. Insult, abuse, provocation, pecking. H. (*ṭungār*).

تيپر *ṭīpar*, s.m. A turnip.

تيت *ṭīṭ*, a. Bent, curved, crooked, bowed. *ṭīṭawul*, v.a. To bend, bow. *ṭīṭedal*, v.n. To be bent, bowed, inclined.

تيتاري *ṭīṭārai*, s.m. A plover, pewit, lapwing. H. (*ṭaṭīrī*).

تيتال *ṭīṭāl*, s.m. Cheat, imposture, fraud; evasion. P. (*ṭīṭāl*).

تيغ *ṭeg͟h*, s.m. A belch, eructation.

ټيک *ṭek*, s.m. The temple, side of the head.

ټيک *ṭīk*, s.m. } An ornament for the forehead;
ټيکه *ṭīka*, s.f. } a wafer of silver or gilt paper worn on the forehead. H. (*ṭīkā*).

ټيکاو *ṭīkāo*, s.m. Abode, lodging, residence. H. (*ṭhikānā*).

ټيل *ṭel*, s.m. A jostle, shove, push. H. (*ṭhel*).

ټيل ټال *ṭel·ṭāl*, s.m. Jostling; romping; dalliance.

ټينچي *ṭainchī*, s.m. A fop, beau, coxcomb, puppy.

ټينګ *ṭīng*, a. Close, compact, thick; coagulated, curdled; stiff, firm; tight, strong.

ث

ث *se*, The fourth letter of the Arabic alphabet, and the sixth of the Pukkhto. It is only found in words adopted from the Arabic. It is sometimes pronounced *th* as in the English *think*.

ثابت *sābit*, a. Proved, confirmed, established; firm, durable, stable, etc. A.

ثاني *sānī*, a. Second, the second. A.

ثبوت *sabūt*, s.m. Conviction, proof; firmness, stability. A.

ثنا *sanā*, s.f. Applause, praise, eulogium. A.

ثواب *sawāb*, s.m. A virtuous action; future reward of virtue. A.

څ

څ *dze*, or *dzīm*, The seventh letter of the Pukkhto alphabet. It is a soft form of ج, and is used instead of that letter in some words derived from the Persian and Hindi. It is also sometimes substituted for ز and س

څار *dzār*, s.m. An offering, sacrifice, victim.

څاله *dzāla*, s.f. A spider's web; bird's nest. S. (*jālā*).

څان *dzān*, s.m. Soul, life; mind, spirit; self; the privates; a lover, loved one. a. Beloved, dear. P. (*jān*).

څاندار *dzāndār*, s.m. Having life, an animal.

څانکندن *dzān·kandan*, s.m. Agony of death, the death-struggle. P. (*jān·kandan*).

څاي *dzāe*, s.m. Place, site, situation, station. P. (*jāe*). *dzāe·laral*, v.a. To fit, suit, become. *dzāe·nīwul*, v.a. To take up place or position, locate oneself; inhabit, colonize; take effect.

څبله *dzabla*, ad. Together, in company, one with another. *dzabla·bande*, Fold on fold, etc.

څز *dzaz*, s.m. A fizz, hiss, sputter.

څکه *dzaka*, ad. Because, hence, consequently, therefore, on this account. P. (*zirāki*).

څګر *dzigar*, s.m. The liver; heart, vitals; courage, mind, pluck. P. (*jigar*).

څل *dzal*, ad. Once, one time. *yo·dzal*, once. *dwah·dzala*, twice. *dre·dzala*, thrice. *las·dzala*, ten times, etc. *dzul*, s.m. Body clothes for a horse, or for cattle. H. (*jhul*).

څلوبۍ *dzaloba-ī*, s.f. A kind of sweetmeat. H. (*jalebī*).

څله *dzala*, s.f. Perplexity, distraction, hesitation.

څلکيدل *dzalkedal*, } v.n. To glitter, shine,
څليدل *dzaledal*, } sparkle, lighten. H. (*jhalak*).

څما *dzamā*, The genitive case singular of the first personal pronoun زه *zah*: Mine, of me.

څمل *dzamal*, v.a. To blink, wink (as in sunlight).

څمونږ *dzamūg*, } The genitive plural of the
څمونګ *dzamūng*, } first personal pronoun: Ours, of us.

څناور *dzanāwar*, s.m. An animal. P. (*jānwar*).

څنبل *dzanbal*, v.a. See څمل.

څنبول *dzanbawul*, v.a. To wag, shake; wink.

خنبيدل *dzanbedal*, v.n. To shake, totter, quiver; move, wag, writhe. P. (*junbīdan*).

خند *dzand*, s.m. Delay, procrastination.

خنگل *dzangal*, s.m. A wood; wilderness. S. (*jangal*).

خنړي *dzanṟai*, s.m. A boy, youth, schoolboy.

خني *dzane*, or *dzine*, pr. The indefinite pronoun; any, some, certain, few. Also خنِ *dzani* or *dzini*.

خوان *dzwān*, s.m. An adult, young man. a. Adolescent, youthful. S. (*jawān*).

خواني *dzwānī*, s.f. Youth, adolescence.

خواني مرګ *dzwānī-marg*, s.m. A form of curse; early or untimely death. P. (*jawānā-marg*).

خور *dzaur*, s.m. Oppression, violence; trouble, pain; grief, sorrow. A. (*jaur*).

خوړند *dzwaṟand*, a. Hanging, pendant.

خوز *dzoz*, s.m. Name of a plant, the camel's thorn (*Hedysarum alhagī*). P. (*jāj*).

خوزخانه *dzoz-khāna*, s.f. A hut made of camel's thorn, and used as a cool retreat in the hot weather.

خولنه *dzolana*, s.f. A chain, fetter. P. (*zawlānah*).

خولي *dzola-ī*, s.f. Havresack, bag, wallet. H. (*jholī*).

خوم *dzūm*, s.m. A son-in-law. S. (*jamāī*).

خومګي *dzūmgai*, s.m. A young son-in-law.

خوي *dzoe*, s.m. A son. P. (*zāe*).

خي *dzai*, s.m. Child, son, descendant. See زي.

خير *dzīr*, s.m. Contemplation, regard; look, survey, glance; a shrill sound, the highest note in music. P. (*jīl*). A kind of soft leather.

خيرمه *dzerma*, s.f. See زيرمه.

خيزمه *dzezma*, s.f. The eyelid.

خيل *dzel*, s.m. Ignorance, stupidity; obstinacy, perversity. A. (*jahl*). A line or string of buckets, etc. H. (*jel*).

ج

ج *jīm*, The eighth letter of the Pukkhto alphabet. It is sometimes substituted for the letters j, ژ, and ش.

جابر *jābir*, s.m. A despot, oppressor, tyrant. A.

جابه *jāba*, s.f. A leathern jar or pot with a spout, used by grocers to pour out oil, etc. H. (*jhābā*).

جادو *jādū*, s.m. Magic, conjuring. P.

جادوګر *jādū-gar*, s.m. A conjurer, juggler, magician.

جادوګري *jādū-garī*, s.f. Conjuring, sorcery, magic.

جادئي *jāḍa-ī*, s.f. A worn out old camel; a hag.

جار *jār*, s.m. Announcement, proclamation, notice. A. (*iẓhār*). A sacrifice, oblation, victim, offering. Evident, manifest. A. (*ẓāhir*).

جارباسل *jārbāsal*, v.a. To divert, turn aside, turn back; to vomit, spew. Def. See جاريستل.

جارچي *jārchī*, s.m. A crier, herald.

جارو *jārū*, s.m. A besom, broom, brush. H. (*jhāṟū*).

جاروتل *jārwatal*, v.n. To go back, return, revert.

جارول *jārawul*, v.a. To arrange or collect together the threads of the warp preparatory to weaving; to brush, sweep. H. (*jhāṟnā*).

جاري *jārī*, a. Current, flowing, proceeding. A.

جاريستل *jāryastal*, v.a. To vomit, spew; return, turn back. Def. See جارباسل.

جاړ *jāṟ*, s.m. Brambles, bushes, underwood; a brake, thicket; a purge, stool. H. (*jhāṟ*).

جاړه *jāṟa*, s.f. A bramble, bush, thorny bush.

جاسوس *jāsūs*, s.m. A detective, spy, emissary. A.

جاسوسي *jāsūsī*, s.f. Spying, duty of a detective.

جاكي *jākai*, a. Curdled, coagulated, clotted (as blood).

جاگير *jāgīr*, s.m. Land held in fief, a pension in land, land granted by government as a reward for military service, etc. P.

جال *jāl*, s.m. A net, sash. S. a. Counterfeit, forged. A. (*j'al*).

جاله *jāla*, s.f. A raft of timber or inflated hides; a bird's nest.

جالئي *jāla-ī*, s.f. A cobweb; the green vegetation in pools and watercourses; duckweed. S. (*jālā*).

جام *jām*, s.m. A bowl, cup, goblet. P.

جامبړه *jāmbṛa*, s.f. A coppice, brake, thicket.

جامه *jāma*, s.f. Garment, dress, robe; the jaw, the upper or lower jaw-bone. P.

جان *jān*, s.m. See ځان.

جانب *jānib*, s.m. Part, side. ad. Towards. A.

جانجي *jānjī*, s.m. A bridegroom's wedding guest or attendant.

جانور *jānwar*, s.m. See ځناور.

جاوجئي *jāwja-ī*, s.f. The hem, skirt, border, edging, etc. of a dress.

جاوله *jāwla*, s.f. Beeswax, fresh resin, gluten of wheat, milky sap of plants, etc.

جاويد *jāwīd*, s.m. } Endless, eternal. P.
جاويدان *jāwīdān*, }

جاويداني *jāwīdānī*, s.f. Eternity, immortality.

جاه *jāh*, s.m. Dignity, pomp, rank. P.

جاهل *jāhil*, a. Ignorant, barbarous, brutal. s.m. Fool, blockhead, ignoramus. A.

جاهلي *jāhilī*, s.f. Ignorance, stupidity.

جاي *jāe*, s.m. See ځاي.

جائداد *jā-edād*, s.m. Assets, effects, property. An assignment of land for the maintenance of troops. P.

جبر *jabr*, s.m. Force, oppression, violence. A.

جبه *jaba*, s.f. A bog, mere, marsh. H. (*jhābar*). *juba*, s.f. A frock, shirt; coat of mail. A.

جبين *jabīn*, s.m. The forehead. P.

جت *jat*, s.m. Name of a tribe located in the western parts of Afghanistan; they are largely engaged in trade.

جټ *jaṭ*, s.m. Name of a clan of Rajpūts settled in the Panjāb; they are entirely occupied in agriculture.

جثه *jussa*, s.f. Body, figure. A.

ججوره *jajūra*, s.f. The crop of a bird, maw, the first stomach of ruminants; double chin, dewlap. H. (*jhojh*).

ججوئي *jajū-ī*, s.f. Name of a plant, Anemone.

جخ *jakh*, s.m. Froth, foam. H. (*jhāg*). A midge, water-fly.

جخت *jukht*, a. Accurate, even, exact. P. (*juft*).

جد *jadd*, s.m. An ancestor, grandfather. A.

جدا *judā*, s.f. Apart, separate, distinct, different. P.

جدل *jadal*, s.f. Altercation, battle, strife. A.

جدول *jadwal*, s.m. Lines drawn on the sides of a page; marginal lines in a book. A.

جديد *jadīd*, a. Fresh, new. A.

جذام *juzām*, s.m. Leprosy. A.

جذب *jazb*, s.m. Absorption; imbibing, absorbing. A.

جذبه *jazba*, s.f. Fury, passion, rage. A.

جر *jar*, s.m. A gutter, drain; crack, fissure, cleft, etc. in the ground. P.

جراح *jarrāh*, s.m. A surgeon. A.

جرس *jaras*, s.m. A bell. A.

جرکانړي *jur-kānṛai*, s.m. To boot, surplus, over and above, into the bargain; profit, gain.

جرگتو *jirgatū*, s.m. Member of a Jirga.

جرگه *jirga*, s.f. An assembly, council, meeting, etc. of the heads of a village community, or the representatives of a clan, for consultation and deliberation on matters affecting the interests of the people they represent; a consultation.

جرم *jurm* or *jirm*, s.m. Crime, fault, sin. A.

جرمانه *jurmāna*, s.f. A fine, penalty.

جرموړه *jarmoṛa*, s.f. Name of an eruption of the skin; hives, nettlerash.

جرندهګري *jaranda-garai*, s.m. A miller.

جرنده *jaranda*, s.f. A mill for grinding corn, whether worked by cattle or water.

جرندئي *jaranda-ī*, s.f. A door bolt.

جره *jurrah*, s.m. A male falcon. A. See باز.

جريب *jarīb*, s.m. A measure of land equal to four kanāl. See كنال.

جريده *jarīdah*, a. Alone, solitary, unattended, unencumbered, travelling post-haste. A.

جړ *jaṛ*, s.m. Bubbling, oozing, trickling with a murmur (as water from a spring head). H. (*jhir-jhir*).

جړانګو *jaṛāngū*, s.m. Name of a tree (*Cassia fistula*).

جړاو *jaṛāo*, a. Jewelled. S.

جرجوري *jur-jūrai*, a. Trickling, murmuring, bubbling.

جړنګ *juṛang*, s.m. A creeping plant (as melons, etc.).

جړئي *jaṛa-ī*, s.f. Continued rain, shower, wet weather. H. (*jhaṛī*). The root of a herb used as a remedy for snake bites. S. (*jaṛī*).

جز *juz*, s.m. A part, portion, section; division of a book containing eight leaves. A. *juz*, p. Besides, except. P.

جزا *jazā*, s.f. Retaliation, requital, return; compensation, reward. A.

جزائل *jazā-el*, s.m. A rifle; long gun; swivel, wall piece, camel-gun. A.

جزائلچي *jazā-elchī*, s.m. A sharpshooter, marksman, rifleman.

جزبز *jizbiz*, s.m. A game played with knuckle bones. P.

جزبندي *juzbandī*, s.f. Binding of a book.

جزدان *juzdān*, s.m. Book-cover, bag for books.

جزيره *jazīra*, s.f. An island. A.

جزيه *jaziya*, s.f. A poll tax, capitation tax, levied by the Afghans on their subjects of another race and creed. A.

جس *jas*, s.m. Pewter. H. (*jast*).

جست *jast*, s.m. A bound, jump, leap, spring. P.

جستوجوي *just-o-jūe*, s.m. Enquiry, investigation, search. P.

جسته *jasta*, s.f. A kind of boot with high narrow heels. P.

جسر *jasr*, s.m. A large, strong camel. A. *jisr*, s.m. A bridge. A.

جسم *jism*, s.m. The body, living body. A.

جسه *jussa*, s.f. The human body. See جثه.

جشي *jashai*, s.m. Name of a prickly plant; the prickle of some kinds of grass.

جغ *jugh*, s.m. Yoke of a plough; yoke for oxen; a pair of oxen. S. (*jug*).

جغاغه *jaghāgha*, s.f. Name of a herb, caper spurge.

جغندر *jughandar*, s.m. Beetroot. P. (*chuqandar*).

جفا *jafā*, s.f. Oppression, violence, injustice. P.

جفاكار *jafākār*, s.m. A tyrant, oppressor.

جفاكاري *jafākārī*, s.f. Tyranny, oppression.

جفت *juft*, s.m. A couple, match, pair. P.

جفتك *juftak*, s.f. A kick with both hind legs.

جق جق *jaq-jaq*, s.m. Cackle of fowls; chatter, gabble.

جك *jak*, s.m. See جج.

جكړ *jakaṛ*, s.m. Gust of wind, wind and rain, drift of wind. H. (*jhakkar*).

جګړه *jagaṛa*, s.f. Altercation, strife, contention, wrangling. H. (*jhagṛa*).

جكناتي *jagnāta-ī*, s.f. A kind of fine cloth, muslin.

جل **jal,** s.m. A hedge of thorns round a house. A skylark. ***j-il*** or ***ja-al,*** s.f. A damsel, maid, virgin.

جلا ***jilā,*** s.f. Exile, separation. A. ***jilā-waṭan,*** s.m. Banishment, exile, emigration.

جلاب ***julāb,*** s.m. Cathartic, purge. A.

جلات ***jallāt,*** s.m. An executioner. A. (*jallād*).

جلاجل ***jalājil,*** s.m. A small bell; strings of them are fastened on the necks of cattle and the ankles of women.

جلار ***jalār,*** s.m. An irrigation wheel worked on the bank of a stream.

جلال ***jalāl,*** s.m. Majesty, splendour, glory, dignity, grandeur, state. A.

جلب ***jalab,*** s.m. A rein; attendance, retinue, escort. A. (*jilaw*).

جلبنگ ***jalbang,*** s.m. The stinging nettle (*Urtica interrupta*).

جلت ***jalt,*** a. Quick, active, brisk, fast; hasty, rash. P. (*jald*).

جلته ***jalata,*** s.f. A hamper, tall wicker basket.

جلتيا ***jaltiyā,*** s.f. Haste, speed, hurry, etc.

جلد ***jald,*** a. See جلت. ***jild,*** s.m. A book, volume, edition. A.

جلك ***jalak,*** s.m. A spindle, spinning reel.

جلناني ***jalnāna-ī,*** s.f. A kitchen, cook-house. P.

جلندري ***jalandara-ī,*** s.f. A whirligig.

جلوه ***jilwa,*** s.f. Adornment, splendour; nuptial meeting or feast; blandishment, coquetry. A.

جلي ***jala-ī,*** s.f. A scream, shriek.

جم ***jam,*** s.m. A cluster, group; clan, tribe; faction, party, society.

جماعت ***jamā'at,*** s.m. Assembly, congregation, crowd; mosque, house of prayer, meeting-house. A.

جمال ***jamāl,*** s.m. Beauty, elegance. A

جمالگوټه ***jamālgoṭa,*** s.f. A purgative nut, seed of *Croton tiglium*. A.

جمدر ***jamdar,*** s.m. Darnel, tares, wild oats. P.

جمعه ***jama'a,*** s.f. Assembly, congregation; sum total, amount, whole; plural number. A. (*jama'*). ***juma'a,*** s.f. Friday. A.

جمله ***jumla,*** s.f. Aggregate, whole, sum total. A.

جن ***j-in*** or ***ja-an,*** s.f. A damsel, maid. See جل. ***jinn,*** s.m. A demon, devil, one of the genii. A.

جناب ***janāb,*** s.m. Excellency, highness, majesty; dignity, power; margin, side; threshold. A.

جنازه ***janāza,*** s.f. A funeral. A.

جنبان ***junbān,*** a. Moving, stirring, shaking. P.

جنبش ***junbish,*** s.m. Agitation, movement. P.

جنبق ***junbaq,*** a. Close, clustered, massed.

جنبه ***janba,*** s.f. Party, faction, clan. A. (*jānib*).

جنت ***jannat,*** s.m. Paradise. A.

جنج ***janj,*** s.m. Bridegroom's party in a marriage procession or feast: party of men who accompany the bridegroom to fetch the bride home.

جنجال ***janjāl,*** s.m. Difficulty, bother, trouble; contention, strife, wrangling. S.

جنجنړ ***janjanr,*** s.m. Name of a kind of vetch.

جندره ***jandra,*** s.f. A padlock, instrument for drawing wire.

جنډه ***janḍa,*** s.f. Banner, ensign, standard, flag. H. (*jhanḍā*).

جنس ***jins,*** s.m. Genus, kind, species; gender; merchandise, goods, etc. A.

جنگ ***jang,*** s.m. Battle, combat, fight, war. P. ***jung,*** a. Collected, gathered, crumpled. s.m. A young camel. A collection, miscellany, assembly, gathering.

جنگه ***junga,*** s.f. Excess, surplus, boot, profit.

جنگي ***jangī,*** a. Warlike, brave. ***jangai,*** s.m. A grove, plantation, coppice. ***jungai,*** a. Collected, gathered (as cloth). s.m. A young camel.

جنوب ***junūb,*** s.m. The South. A.

جنون ***junūn***, s.m. Insanity, madness. A.

جني ***jina-ī***, s.f. A girl, daughter (not arrived at puberty); a virgin; a spinster.

جو ***jau***, s.m. Barley. P.

جواب ***jawāb***, s.m. Answer, reply; dismissal. A.

جوار ***jwār***, s.m. Maize, Indian corn (*Zea mays*). H. (*joār*). *narī-jwār*, s.m. Indian millet (*Holcus sorghum*).

جوارگر ***jūār-gar***, s.m. A gambler, gamester.

جواري ***jūārī***, s.f. Gambling, gaming. *jwārī*, s.m. See جوار.

جوال ***jowāl***, s.m. A sack, bag. P.

جوانوان ***jawānwān***, s.m. A kind of mustard or rape; the seeds yield an acrid oil, used as a cattle medicine, etc.

جواهر ***jawāhir***, s.m. A gem, jewel. A.

جوبه ***joba***, s.f. Emporium, market, mart. P.

جوټه ***jūṭa***, s.f. Leavings, refuse (as of food, etc.); base, false (as coins, gems, etc.). S. (*jhūṭhā*). *joṭah*, s.m. A buffalo calf.

جوټي ***jūṭa-ī***, s.f. Nodding, rocking (as in sleep); swaying, vibrating, swinging.

جودر ***jawdar***, s.m. See جمدر.

جور ***jaur***, s.m. See خور.

جوړ ***joṛ***, a. Healthy, strong, vigorous; prepared, arranged; right, correct. P. ad. Exactly, precisely, well.

جوړاب ***joṛāb***, s.m. Beauty, elegance, grace.

جوړښت ***joṛikkht***, s.m. Alliance, confederation, union; combination, junction.

جوړه ***joṛa***, s.f. A couple, set, pair; suit of clothes. H. (*joṛā*). Peace, amity, concord, truce.

جوز ***jauz***, s.m. A nut, kernel. A.

جوزه ***jauza***, s.f. A nutmeg.

جوس ***jawas***, s.m. Area, courtyard.

جوش ***josh***, s.m. Effervescence, ebullition; heat, rage; passion, lust. P.

جوكل ***jokal***, v.a. To weigh, measure. H. (*jokhnā*).

جولا ***jolā***, s.m. A weaver, spider. P. (*julāh*).

جولان ***jaulān***, s.m. Moving, wandering; capering, springing, lunging. P.

جولانگري ***jaulāngarī***, s.m. Cantering, galloping; exercising, lunging (a horse).

جوله ***jola***, s.f. See جهوله.

جولئ ***jola-ī***, s.f. See څولئ.

جونګړه ***jūngaṛa***, s.f. A hut, hovel, cabin, shed, hamlet. H. (*jhompṛā*).

جوني ***jūna-ī***, s.f. See جني.

جووه ***jowa***, s.f. A gutter, drain, water channel (for irrigating a field, etc.). P. (*jūe*).

جوهر ***jauhar***, s.m. A jewel, gem; essence, matter; virtue, work; the water or wavy marks on some kinds of steel.

جوهړه ***jūhaṛa***, s.f. A crease, pucker, wrinkle, furrow. H. (*jhūrī*).

جه ***jah***, a. Stubborn, refractory (as an animal); at bay, resisting. *ja-ja*, in. Words used to drive cattle.

جهاد ***jihād***, s.m. Crescentade, war with infidels. A.

جهاز ***jahāz***, s.m. A ship. P.

جهان ***jahān***, s.m. The world, universe; people. P.

جهت ***jihat***, s.m. Account, cause, reason; side, surface; form, manner, mode. A.

جهر ***jihr***, s.m. A kind of dance performed by men.

جهل ***jahl***, s.m. Ignorance, stupidity. A.

جهم جكړ ***jham-jakaṛ***, s.m. Wind and rain in gusts, drifts of wind and rain. H.

جهوله ***jhola***, s.f. Name of a disease; chlorosis, anæmia, splenitis.

جي ***jai***, s.m. A leather bag for water.

جيب ***jeb***, s.m. A pocket. A.

جيت *jeṭ*, s.m. Name of the second Hindu month, May–June; name of a tree, Egyptian Sesbania.

جينکي *jīnaka-ī*, s.f. A little girl, female child.

څ

څ *tse*, The ninth letter of the Pukkhto alphabet. It is a softened form of چ for which it is substituted in many words adopted from the Persian and Hindī. It is sometimes used instead of س and ش.

څاپيړه *tsāpeṛa*, s.f. A slap, blow, cuff. s. (*chapeṭā*).

څاڅکي *tsātskai*, s.m. A drop, minim, sprinkle.

څادر *tsādar*, s.m. A sheet, veil, mantle. H. (*chādar*).

څار *tsār*, s.m. Spying, scouting.

څارل *tsāral*, v.a. To spy, scout.

څاروي *tsārwai*, s.m. Cattle; a quadruped, beast, grazing animal. P. (*chārwā*).

څاره *tsāra*, s.f. Aid, help; cure, remedy. P. (*chāra*).

څاري *tsārī*, s.m. A scout, spy.

څاښت *tsākkht*, s.m. Forenoon, midtime between sunrise and noon; a meal taken at that time, breakfast. P. (*chāsht*).

څاښتي *tsākkhtī*, s.f. Breakfast, forenoon meal.

څاښکه *tsākkhaka*, s.f. A starling.

څاښي *tsākkhai*, s.m. Spinning rod, spindle.

څاک *tsāk*, s.m. Fissure, rent, slit; opening of a pocket; skirt or corner of a dress. P. (*chāk*).

څانګ *tsāng*, s.m. } Wing of a bird; branch
څانګه *tsānga*, s.f. } of a tree; pang, sharp pain.

څپ *tsap*, s.m. A winnowing tray made of reeds; winnowing. *tsap·wahal*, v.a. To winnow.

څپر *tsapar*, s.m. A thatch, thatched roof. H. (*chhappar*). A wooden frame used as a crusher to separate grain from husk.

څپرکي *tsaparkai*, s.m. A film, flake, pellicle, scale; thin sheet of water (as after rain).

څپري *tsaparai*, s.m. A puddle, pool. H. (*chhaprī*).

څپړ *tsapaṛ*, s.f. Pad of a camel's or elephant's foot; sound of soft footsteps. H. (*chhap*).

څپک *tsapak*, s.m. A hand's breadth, hand, palm. H. (*chappā*). A flake, pellicle, scale.

څپلاک *tsaplāk*, a. Crushed, squashed, pressed, squeezed. H. (*chhapākā*).

څپلي *tsapla-ī*, s.f. A sandal (of leather or grass). H. (*chappal*).

څپوټکي *tsapūṭkai*, s.m. An old cloth, kerchief, or duster tied over the head by women when grinding corn, sweeping the house, etc. H. (*chapoṭī*).

څپولي *tsapolai*, a. Entangled, knotted, matted (as the hair). H. (*chipatā*).

څپه *tsapah*, a. Inverted, upside down. *tsapa*, s.f. A wave, billow; blast, gust, puff, etc. of wind. H. (*chhappā*).

څپياکه *tsapiyāka*, s.f. A cow-dung cake (flat and dry), used as fuel.

څپيړه *tsapeṛah*, a. Grey, ash-coloured; pale. in. Coward! dastard! term of abuse. *tsapeṛa*, s.f. A slap with the open hand.

څپيدل *tsapedal*, v.n. To flutter, hover, flap the wings.

څټ *tsaṭ*, s.m. Nape, back of the neck.

څټک *tsaṭak*, s.m. A sledge hammer.

څټکي *tsaṭakai*, s.m. A small sledge hammer.

څټل *tsaṭal*, v.a. To lick, lap. H. (*chāṭnā*). *tsaṭal*, v.n. To be accumulated, collected, massed. s.m. Heap, mass; wholesale, by the lump. P. (*chastan*).

څټوټ *tsaṭwaṭ*, s.m. Apoplexy, sudden death.

ad. All at once, suddenly, instanter. H. (*chaṭ-paṭ*).

څټه *tsaṭa*, s.f. A sack; a sackful. H. (*chaṭ*).

څڅوبي *tsatsobai*, s.m. The coping or eaves of a roof or wall; a leaking or dropping of water.

څڅول *tsatsawul*, v.a. To pour by drops, drop, distil.

څڅيدل *tsatsedal*, v.n. To leak, trickle, drop, distil. P. (*shāshīdan*).

څخو *tsakho*, a. Some, few, somewhat, more or less. ad. Slightly, in some degree, somewhat.

څخه *tsakhah*, p. About, near, with, beside. ad. Together, altogether. P. (*chakh*).

څخيدل *tskhedal*, v.n. To crawl, creep, go on all fours (as a child). P. (*chakhīdan*).

څخيکول *tskhe-kawul*, v.a. To hop, skip.

څر *tsar*, s.m. Food, forage, pasture. S. (*char*).

څرپ *tsrap*, s.m. A flutter, flap; whirr.

څرپول *tsrapawul*, v.a. To flutter, flap the wings.

څرپيدل *tsrapedal*, v.n. To flounder, flap about (as a fish in shallow water).

څرخ *tsarkh*, s.m. A wheel; grindstone; revolution, turn, spin; chance, fortune; the heavens; a kind of falcon; a stab, puncture, prick. P. (*charkh*).

څرخه *tsarkha*, s.f. A reel; spinning wheel. P. (*charkha*).

څرخندوکي *tsarkhandūkai*, s.m. A teetotum, a boy's top.

څرخول *tsarkhawul*, v.a. To spin, reel, twirl, turn.

څرخيدل *tsarkhedal*, v.n. To revolve, spin, etc.

څرگند *tsargand*, a. Clear, evident, apparent, manifest, plain.

څرل *tsaral*, v.n. See څريدل.

څرمن *tsarman*, s.f. Hide, skin; leather. P. (*charm*).

څرمه *tsarma*, s.f. See څيلمه.

څروټکه *tsarwaṭka*, s.f. An ember, burning coal, live ashes.

څرول *tsarawul*, v.a. To graze, pasture cattle. P. (*charāndan* or *charānīdan*).

څريدل *tsaredal*, v.n. To graze, browse, crop. P. (*charīdan*).

څريکه *tsirika*, s.f. A prick, throb, lancing or shooting pain (as of a boil, etc.). P. (*charkh*). A spot, splash, stain (as of mud, etc.).

څړه *tsaṛah*, a. Alone, solitary; unmarried, single; light, unencumbered; simple. S. (*chhaṛā*). *tsaṛa-lār*, s.f. A footpath, bye road, track, etc. only practicable for one man at a time.

څړي *tsaṛa-ī*, s.f. A top knot, tuft or lock of hair on the crown of a shaven head.

څږي *tsagai*, s.m. The lungs, a lung.

څښاک *tskkhāk* or *tsakshāk*, s.m. Beverage, drink, liquor. *khwurāk-o-tskkhāk*, s.m. Aliment, food, victuals, meat and drink.

څښتن *tsakkhtan*, s.m. Owner, proprietor, lord, master, husband.

څښکو *tsakkhkū*, s.f. Name of a plant (*Cassia absus*): the seeds are used as a remedy in ophthalmia. P. (*chāksū* or *chākshū*).

څښکوړي *tsakkhkūṛai*, s.m. A small pipe, tube, nozzle, spout, etc.; child's penis.

څښل *tskkhal*, *tsakkhal*, or *tsakshal*, v.a. To drink, absorb, imbibe. P. (*chashīdan* or *chakānīdan*).

څک *tsak*, a. Stiff, unpliant, rigid. s.m. Lumbago. H. (*chik*).

څکل *tsakal*, v.a. To taste. S. (*chakhnā*) or P. (*chashīdan*).

څکنتون *tsakintūn*, } s.m. Flavour, taste, savour.
څکندن *tsakindan*, }

څکول *tskawul*, v.a. To cause to drink water (as cattle); to draw, lengthen, stretch.

څکوندل *tskūnḍal*, v.a. To pinch, tweak; squeeze, wring. P. (*chakāndan*).

څکه *tsaka*, s.f. Flavour, taste, relish; a precipice, cliff. *tsaka* or *tska*, ad. Then, therefore, thus.

څکي *tsakai*, s.m. A basket or safe suspended from the roof, to preserve the contents from cats, insects, etc. s. (*chhīkā*).

څکیدل *tskedal*, v.n. See څځیدل.

څلور *tsalor*, a. Four. P. (*chahār*).

څلورم *tsaloram*, a. Fourth.

څلوېښت *tsalwekkht* or *tsalweksht*, a. Forty. P. (*chahār·bīst*).

څلوېښتي *tsalwekkhtī*, s.f. The forty days of purification after childbirth; the fortieth day after the death of a person, when the relatives visit the grave, and feed the poor, etc.

څله *tsala*, ad. Why? wherefore? what for? P. (*charā*).

څلي *tsalai*, s.m. A ring for the finger or toe. H. (*chhallā*); a pile or heap of stones on the grave of a martyr (generally somebody murdered on the way side); a pillar of mud or masonry, as a boundary mark; a mound or platform from which to watch a field; a butt or mark for arrows; a temporary platform or shed.

څلېښ *tsalekkh*, | څلېښت *tsalekkht*, } s.m. Glue. P. (*saresh*).

څلېښناک *tsalekkhnāk*, a. Adhesive, glutinous, cohesive, clammy, viscous.

څم *tsam*, a. Flat, smooth, level, even.

څمڅۍ *tsamtsa-ī*, s.f. A spoon, ladle. P. (*chamcha*).

څملاستل *tsamlāstal*, | څملل *tsamlal*, } v.n. To lie down, recline, repose, lie flat.

څملول *tsamlawul*, v.a. To put to bed, put to rest.

څنډل *tsandal*, v.a. To agitate, shake, dust (as clothes), wave (as a sword). H. (*chhāntnā*).

څنډه *tsanda*, s.f. Brim, margin, edge; fringe, rim, verge, side.

څنګ *tsang*, s.m. The side, flank. *tsang·pa·tsang*, ad. Abreast, side by side.

څنګزن *tsangzan*, a. Top-heavy, tilted, lurched over.

څنګل *tsangal*, | څنګله *tsangala*, } s.f. The elbow; elbow joint; the forearm, cubit.

څنګه *tsanga*, ad. How? In what manner?

څو *tso*, a. Any, some, somewhat. P. (*chand*). ad. Till, until. P. (*chūn*). How many? how much? P. (*chand*).

څوارلس *tswārlas*, a. Fourteen.

څوباړي *tsobārai*, s.m. A flat piece of wood used to beat clothes in the process of washing. P. (*chobah*).

څوټ *tsot*, s.m. Attack, onset, foray, sortie; a blow, contusion, hurt. s. (*chot*).

څوڅ *tsūts*, s.m. A porpoise. s. (*sūs*).

څورب *tsorb*, a. Fat, corpulent, stout. P. (*charb*).

څورلي *tswarlai*, s.m. A chisel; a burglar's instrument for digging through a mud wall.

څوړ *tsor*, a. Crooked, wry, crumpled; emaciated, thin, withered (as a child badly nourished).

څوړي *tsorai*, s.m. A bullock, etc. with crumpled horns.

څوښۍ *tsūkkha-ī*, s.f. The penis of a boy; a nozzle, spout. P. (*choshak*).

څوک *tsok*, pr. Who? Which? Some, certain. Used only with reference to human beings.

څوکه *tsūka*, s.f. Apex, peak, tip, point, beak.

څوکۍ *tsoka-ī*, s.f. A guard, watch; place or station of a guard; tour of watching. H. (*chaukī*).

څول *tswal*, a. Tattered, torn, rent, worm-eaten. *tswal·tswal*, a. In rags, in tatters, in shreds.

خومبره tsombra, } ad. How much?
خومره tsomra,
خونبره tsonbra,

خونڅئي tsontsa-ī, s.f. See څڅئي.

خونړکه tsūnraka, } s.f. The tuft or curl of hair
خونړه tsunra, } left on the crown or temples of a shaven head. H. (chondā).

خوني tsone, ad. How much?

خوهره tsūhra, s.f. Hernia, rupture. H. (chūhrā).

خوي tsawai, s.m. Ambush, cover, ambuscade.

څه tsah, pr. What, any, some: what? P. (chi).

څېره tsihra, s.f. Face, countenance, visage. H. (chihrā).

څيخل tsekhal, v.a. To probe, prick, stab; cram, stuff. P. (sīkh, a probe).

څير tser, a. Like, similar, resembling.

څيره tsera, s.f. Picture, portrait, image, idol; effigy, scarecrow, grimace, P. (chehr).

څيريدل tsiredal, v.n. See شليدل.

څيړه tsira, s.f. A line, file, row; party, knot, troop.

څيز tsīz, s.m. A thing, item, article, object. P. (chīz).

څيلمه tselma, s.f. Border, margin, edge, side.

چ

چ che, or chīm, is the tenth letter of the Pukkhto alphabet. It is sounded like the ch in chair.

چابک chābuk, a. Active, quick, alert. s.m. A whip. P.

چابکي chābukī, s.f. Activity, dispatch, celerity.

چاپ chāp, s.m. Impression, stamp, print; a seal; an edition; flint lock (of a gun, etc.). H. (chāmp). a. Printed, stamped. H. (chhāp).

چاپلوس chāplūs, s.m. A flatterer, wheedler, toady. P. (chāplos).

چاپلوسي chāplūsī, s.f. Flattery, toadyism.

چاپه chāpa, s.f. A stamp, die, seal; a bundle of thorns of the ber bush, after the leaves have been shaken off. H. (chāp).

چاپي chāpī, s.f. Shampooing, pressing or squeezing the limbs. H. (chāmpī).

چاپير chāper, ad. All round, roundabout, around, on all sides. H. (chaupher).

چار chār, a. Four. P. s.m. Affair, business; remedy, cure. P.

چارخولک chār-khwalak, s.m. A cock's comb, wattle.

چاره chāra, s.f. Cure, help, remedy. P.

چاړا chāṛā, a. Stammering, stuttering; dumb, mute.

چاړه chāṛa, s.f. A long knife. H. (chhurā).

چاغ chāgh, a. Healthy, plump, vigorous; fat, stout, corpulent. P. (chāq).

چاک chāk, s.m. A fissure, rent, slit, chāk-kawul, v.a. To rend, split open, disembowel. Also چاق.

چاکر chākar, s.m. Servant, help, retainer. P.

چاکري chākarī, s.f. Attendance, service. P.

چاکو chākū, } s.m. A penknife. P.
چاقو chāqū, }

چاگل chāgul, s.m. A leather bottle for water. P. (chaghal).

چال chāl, s.m. Gait, motion, pace; bound, spring; custom, habit; manner, way; artifice, deceit, trick. S. Vomiting, spewing. H. (chhāl). chāl-kawul, v.a. To vomit, spew.

چالاک chālāk, a. Active, clever; dexterous, expert. P.

چالاکي chālākī, s.f. Activity, dexterity. P.

چاڼ chāṇ, a. Filtered, sifted, strained. H. (chhānā).

چاڼره chāṇra, s.f. Thatch, roofing of reeds,

twigs, etc. as a flooring for the earth of the roof. H. (*chhān*).

چانړي *chānṛī*, s.m. A dung-beetle.

چاوډ *chāwḍ*, a. Cracked, split. s.m. A fissure, rent.

چاوډل *chāwḍal*, v.n. To crack, split.

چاوډينک *chāwḍīnak*, a. Bold, pert, saucy (as a child).

چاول *chāwul*, s.m. A plummet. H. (*sākūl*).

چاه *chāh*, s.m. A well. P.

چايل *chāyal*, s.m. A mantle, veil of chintz.

چپ *chap*, a. The left hand, left side. P. *chip*, or *chup*, a. Silent. in. Silence! Hush! H.

چپاو *chapāo*, s.m. A foray, raid, surprise.

چپاول *chapāwul*, s.m. An advance guard of cavalry.

چپرډخ *chapardakh*, s.m. A game played by boys: ducks and drakes, pitch and toss.

چپروس *chaprūs*, a. See چاپلوس.

چپک *chapak*, a. Squint-eyed, squinting, askew. *chapake-starge*, Squinting eyes.

چپن *chapan*, s.m. A coat, frock. H. (*chapkan*).

چپه *chapah*, a. Inverted. P. *chapa*, s.f. A billow, wave; blast, puff, gust of wind; swoop of a hawk; height or crisis of a disease; an oar, paddle. H. See څپه.

چپئ *chapa-ī*, s.f. A kiss. H. (*pachchī*).

چت *chit*, a. Flattened, pressed, crushed, squashed. H. *chat*, s.m. Ceiling, roof. H. (*chhat*).

چتر *chatr*, s.m. Scar of a wound, bald spot on the head. H. (*chittī*).

چتري *chatrai*, a. Scarred, bald. s.m. Awning, canopy; umbrella. S. (*chhattar*).

چتئ *chita-ī*, s.f. A titmouse. H. (*chittī*).

چټ *chaṭ*, a. Bald-faced, beardless. s.m. A rake, debauchee, profligate, vagabond; thief, robber. P. (*chattah*).

چټ پټ *chaṭ-paṭ*, ad. Hastily, quickly. H.

چټاکئ *chiṭāka-ī*, s.f. Name of a weight equal to two ounces (Avoirdupois). H. (*chhaṭānk*).

چټکه *chiṭka*, s.f. A kind of red cotton cloth.

چټي *chaṭī*, s.f. Debauchery, profligacy.

چج *chaj*, s.m. A tray for winnowing corn, etc. P. (*chach*).

چجک *chajak*, s.m. The trigger of a gun.

چجه *chaja*, s.f. The poles projecting from the roof of a house; the side ribs of an ox, etc.; the crest or hood of a snake; stakes driven into the ground for catching fish. H. (*chhujjā*)

چخړبه *chakhṛaba*, s.f. Mud, slime, ground saturated with rain.

چخړه *chikhṛa*, s.f. See چخي.

چخن *chikhan*, a. Rheumy, mattery; filthy, dirty. P. (*chirk*).

چخه *chikha*, in. Away! Begone! Get out! P. (*chakhe*).

چخي *chikhai*, s.m. Mucus, rheum, matter from the nose or eyes, etc.

چر *char*, s.m. Chirp, twitter of a bird; chatter, prattle of children. A sand bank, mud deposited by a flood. H. *chur*, s.m. A gutter, furrow made by running water. *chari*, ad. See جري.

چراغ *chirāgh*, s.m. A light, lamp. P. Illumination.

چرب *charb*, a. See څورب.

چربي *charbī*, s.f. Fat, tallow, suet. P.

چرت *churt*, s.m. A doze, nap; nodding. H.

چرته *charta*, ad. Where; anywhere; ever.

چرچرئ *char-chara-ī*, s.f. A cracker, squib, firework.

چرخ *charkh*, s.m. See څرخ.

چرړه *chirṛa*, s.f. A rag, shred, tatter. H. (*chithṛā*).

چرس *chars*, s.m. A resinous product obtained from the flowers of the Indian hemp, and used as an intoxicating drug. H. (*charas*).

چرسي ***ch*arsī**, s.m. One addicted to the use of chars.

چرغ ***ch*ar*gh***, s.m. Name of a kind of hawk (*Falco sacer*). P. (*charkh*).

چرک ***ch*irk**, s.m. Dirt, filth; pus, matter. P.

چرکین ***ch*irkīn**, a. Dirty, filthy; purulent, mattery. P.

چرګ ***ch*irg**, s.m. A cock. a. Clever, shrewd, canny. Dappled, pied, spotted, mottled.

چرګبانګ ***ch*irg·bāng**, s.m. Cock-crow, daybreak. Also *chir·bāng*, or *char·bāng*.

چرګبرګ ***ch*rag·brag**, a. Piebald, spotted, streaked.

چرګک ***ch*irgak**, s.m. The hoopoe. Also called *mullā·chargak*.

چرګوړي ***ch*irgūṛai**, s.m. A chicken, pullet.

چرګي ***ch*argai**, s.m. An animal with a white face, or with a spot on the forehead. S. (*charkā*).

چرلندئ ***ch*urlanda-ī**, s.f. A humming-top.

چرلنډ ***ch*urlanḍ**, s.m. A blackguard, knave, rascal.

چرلول ***ch*urlawul**, v.a. To spin, turn, make revolve.

چرلئ ***ch*urla-ī**, s.f. A whirligig: a child's game in which walnuts are made to spin.

چرليدل ***ch*urledal**, v.n. To spin, revolve, whirl.

چرمباز ***ch*arambāz**, s.m. The outside bullock of two or more treading corn.

چرمینه ***ch*armīna**, s.f. Rope made of strips of raw hide. P.

چرې ***ch*are**, ad. Ever, at any time; anywhere; where. *chare·chare*, ad. Occasionally, sometimes, at times.

چریکار ***ch*arekār**, s.m. A farm servant, ploughman. The hair above the chin, imperial.

چړ ***ch*aṛ**, s.m. A sand bank or deposit left by a flood, bar in a river; a cascade, waterfall; a foot soldier's pike or staff; the bread of charity collected from house to house for the poor. ***ch*uṛ**, s.m. The heel of a door, the peg on which it revolves.

چړچه ***ch*aṛ*ch*a**, s.f. Dissipation, luxury, excess.

چړق ***ch*aṛaq**, s.m. A waterspout: sound of water splashing on the ground, splash, smash, crash

چړقاو ***ch*aṛqāo**, s.m. Sprinkling. H. (*chhirkāo*).

چړوکئ ***ch*aṛūka-ī**, s.f. A small knife, penknife.

چړي ***ch*aṛī**, s.m. A collector of the bread of charity.

چسپ ***ch*asp**, s.m. Cohesion, viscidity, stickiness. P.

چسپان ***ch*aspān**, a. Adhesive, sticky, viscous.

چسپول ***ch*aspawul**, v.a. To cement, glue, stick.

چسپیدل ***ch*aspedal**, v.n. To adhere, cleave to, stick. P. (*chaspīdan*).

چست ***ch*ust**, a. Active, quick; narrow, straight; tight, close-fitting (as a dress). P.

چستي ***ch*ustī**, s.f. Agility, activity, fleetness. P. ***ch*ustai**, s.m. Gut, tripe; rectum. P. (*chustā*).

چشم ***ch*a*sh*m**, s.m. The eye. P. (In comp. only.)

چشمک ***ch*a*sh*mak**, s.m. A wink, winking. P.

چشمکه ***ch*a*sh*maka**, s.f. An eye-glass. *chashmake*, pl. A pair of spectacles.

چشمه ***ch*a*sh*ma**, s.f. A spring, fountain; eye-glass. P.

چشي ***ch*i*sh*ai**, s.m. Name of a plant, the seed of which sticks to the fleece of sheep, etc., burdock.

چغ ***ch*a*gh*** or ***ch*i*gh***, s.m. Altercation, dispute; clamour, noise; shout, yell, scream. *chigh·chigh*, s.m. The cackle of fowls. *chagh·chugh*, s.m. Clamour, noise, tumult.

چغار ***ch*u*gh*ār**, s.m. Noise or song of birds; sound of a musical instrument.

چغاره *chighāra*, s.f. Clamour, outcry, noise.

چغر *chaghar*, s.m. A wall-eyed horse. P.

چغرو *chagharū*, s.m. An owl.

چغول *chaghawul*, v.a. To make a row, disturbance, noise.

چغيدل *chaghedal*, v.n. To dispute, haggle, wrangle.

چغزئ *chaghza-ī*, s.f. A kind of soft walnut. *chaghzī*, s.m. Whizz of an arrow passing through the air; crackling of wood when split.

چغک *chughuk*, s.m. A sparrow. P.

چغل *chughal*, s.m. Tell-tale, backbiter, sneak. P.

چغلي *chughlī*, s.f. Backbiting, tale-telling. P.

چغي *chughai*, s.m. A blinkard; seeing with the eyes half closed.

چف *chuf*, s.m. A breath, puff, blow (as of a charmer).

چقمق *chaqmaq*, s.m. The flint lock of a gun. T.

چقه *chuqa*, s.f. The cackle of fowls when angry; pecking, picking up grain, etc.

چک *chak*, s.m. A circular frame of wood or masonry, used as a foundation for wells; a disk. *chik*, s.m. Ropes used to yoke bullocks to a Persian wheel, traces.

چکچکه *chakchaka*, s.f. Clapping the hands by way of applause.

چکړ *chikaṛ*, s.m. Mire, mud, slosh. H. (*chikaṛ*).

چکس *chakas*, s.m. A perch, roost for birds (hawks particularly). H.

چکله *chikla*, s.f. A drop, dash, sprinkling, thimbleful.

چکلئ *chakla-ī*, s.f. The cog-wheel of a Persian irrigation wheel; a whirligig.

چکمه *chakma*, s.f. A stocking; boot. T.

چکوري *chikorai*, s.m. A newly-born calf.

چکه *chaka*, s.f. The palm, the hand; coagulated milk, curds. H. (*chakkā*), *chakah*, a. Practised, expert (as a thief). H. (*uchakkā*).

چکئ *chaka-ī*, s.f. Wafer, disk; biscuit, cake; lump, mass, clot; tail of the dumbah sheep.

چل *chal*, s.m. Artifice, deception, subterfuge, trick. S.

چلان *chalān*, s.m. Invoice, remittance, advice of despatch. S.

چلاو *chalāo*, s.m. Boiled rice. P.

چلباز *chalbāz*, s.m. A cheat, impostor, rogue.

چل چل *chal-chal*, s.m. Bustle, hurry, stir. S.

چل چلا *chal-chalā*, s.f. Bustle, stir, preparation of setting out on a journey. S.

چلر *chulur*, s.m. Blackguard, vagabond, rogue.

چلغوزي *chalghozai*, s.m. The pistachio nut; kernels of the pine seed. P.

چلقت *chalqat*, s.m. A thick padded coat for soldiers, a coat of mail.

چلکه *chalaka*, s.f. A wave, ripple, undulation.

چلم *chilam*, s.m. A tobacco bowl, smoking apparatus. H.

چلن *chalan*, s.m. Behaviour, custom, habit; currency. a. Current. S.

چلول *chalawul*, v.a. To start, set agoing; fire, shoot. H. (*chalānā*).

چله *chala*, s.f. A deluge, flood, stream, torrent. An ear-ring. H. (*chhaṛā*).

چلئ *chala-ī*, s.f. An ear of corn.

چليدل *chaledal*, v.n. To move, proceed, go, elapse, pass (as coin, etc.); flow; blow; stand, avail, succeed; walk, etc. H. (*chalnā*).

چم *cham*, s.m. See جم.

چمتاره *chamtāra*, s.f. A violin. H. (*chautārā*).

چم وخم *cham-o-kham*, s.m. A graceful gait, strut, waddle. P.

چمن *chaman*, s.m. A meadow, lawn, grass-plot. P.

چميار *chamyār*, s.m. A currier, tanner. P.

چنار *chinār*, s.m. Name of a tree, the plane tree (*Platanus orientalis*). P.

چنبيل *chanbel*, s.m. The jasmine. H.

چاچي *chinjai*, s.m. An insect, worm. H. (*chunna*). *chinjawul*, v.a. To disgust.

چاچيدل *chinjedal*, v.n. To be disgusted, nauseated, feel squeamish.

چند *chand*, a. Few, some, various, several; (in comp.) -times, -fold. ad. How many? How much? P.

چندنړ *chandanr*, s.m. Sandal wood. S.

چندنړهار *chandanr-hār*, s.m. A kind of necklace made of sandal-wood beads. S.

چندال *chandāl*, s.m. An abject, low, mean, or worthless fellow. S.

چنداول *chandāwal*, s.m. A rear guard of cavalry; the rear guard of an army; name of the Kazilbash troopers of Kabul. P.

چنغله *changhala*, s.f. A betrothed girl, bride elect.

چنغول *changhol*, s.m. A betrothed youth.

چنګ *chang*, s.m. A guitar, harp; a claw, the expanded hand. P.

چنګاښ *changākkh*, s.m. A crab, cray-fish. P. (*changār*).

چنګال *changāl*, } s.m. Claw, talon of bird,
چنګل *changul*, } the hand; the fingers. P.

changal, s.m. A measure of land equal to fifteen jarīb.

چنه *chana*, s.f. The short side of a house; mud wall of a house; side of a room. Barter, bargaining, haggling.

چنړاسه *chanrāsa*, } s.f. Mildew, mould.
چنړاشه *chanrāsha*, }

چنړچنړ *chanr-chanr*, } s.m. A sparrow,
چنړچنړک *chanr-chanrak*, } cock-sparrow.

چنړکاو *chanrkāw*, s.m. Sprinkling. H. (*chhirkāo*).

چنړل *chunral*, v.a. To crease, fold, plait; to select, sift, separate, pick. H. (*chunnā*).

چنړه *chanra*, s.f. Chick pea, vetch (*Cicer arietinum*). H. (*channā*). *chunra*, s.f. A fold, crease, pucker.

چوپاړ *chopāṛ*, } s.m. A summer-house,
چوپال *chopāl*, } arbour, temporary shed. S. (*chaupār*).

چوپل *chūpal*, v.a. To suck, chew (as mangoes, sugar-cane, etc.). S. (*chusnā*).

چوتي *chotai*, s.m. A clout or cloth worn between the legs to conceal the privates; ropes used in fastening a camel's load.

چوټي *choṭī*, s.m. A peak, mountain top; top-knot or crown-tuft (left on a shaven head). a. Dishevelled, unplaited, loose (as hair). H.

چوچي *chuchai*, s.m. A chicken, pullet. P.

چور *chūr*, a. Broken, bruised, shattered. S. s.m. Bit, atom, scrap; powder, filings, sawdust; sack, ruin, plunder. S.

چورنګ *chaurang*, s.m. Cutting off the four legs of an animal at one blow. S.

چوړي *chūṛai*, s.m. A menial servant, sweeper. H. (*chūhṛā*). *chaura-ī*, s.f. A fly flapper, generally made of horse-hair or the tail of the Tibet ox. H. (*chaunrī*).

چوړ *chawṛ*, a. Desolate, deserted, ruined. H. *chūṛ*, s.m. The heel or pivot on which a door revolves.

چوړه *chūṛa*, s.f. A bangle, bracelet. S. (*chūṛā*).

چوړيل *chūṛel*, s.m. Tar, pitch.

چوز *chūz*, s.m. A young or first year's hawk. P.

چوسار *chausār*, s.m. A file, rasp. H.

چوغي *chūghai*, a. Bowbacked, bent (from age or debility).

چوک *chūk*, s.m. Abatement, diminution, mitigation (as of anger, etc.); damage, loss, waste; error, miss, fault. H. *chauk*, s.m. A market, courtyard. H. *chok*, a. Seated, or squatted on all fours (as a camel, etc.).

چوکه *chūka*, s.f. A goad, prod, prick. H. (*chonkā*). A sharp, pricking, or stinging pain; dipping, moistening, sopping (as bread in milk, etc. at meals).

چوکي chauka-ī, s.f. A chair, stool; guard, watch; guard-house, station. H. (chaukī).

چوکيدار chaukīdār, s.m. Guard, watchman. H.

چول chawul, v.a. To split, rend, cleave asunder. chol, s.m. An arid tract, desert, waste. P. (chūl).

چولک cholak, s.m. Penis of a boy till circumcised. P.

چوم chūm or chom, s.m. A turf; clod of earth.

چونکي chūnkai, a. Indecent, obscene, shameless; impudent, bold, saucy.

چونگي chūngai, s.m. Duty, fee, tax, toll. H. (chūngī).

چونه chūna, s.f. Lime, mortar. S. (chūnā).

چوني chūnai, s.m. A dwarf, elf, pigmy; glazing on pottery, china; a gem, jewel, spark or bead.

چه chi, c. That, which; as, whereas; so, so that; whether, because. P.

چيتر chetar, s.m. Name of the twelfth Hindu month, March-April. S. (chait).

چيټي chīṭa-ī, s.f. A letter, note. H. (chiṭṭhī).

چيچړ chīchāṛ, s.m. A fold, crease, furrow, pucker, wrinkle.

چيچل chīchal, v.a. To bite, masticate, gnaw.

چيخل chīkhal, v.a. To goad, poke, punch.

چيرته cherta, ad. Where? See جرته.

چيره chīra, s.f. A turban with narrow twisted folds; maidenhead. S.

چير chīṛ, s.m. Gum, mucilage.

چيغه chīghā, s.f. A shout, scream, yell; clamour, noise, uproar. P. (chīkh).

چيلو chīlū, s.m. Name of a potherb.

چيلي chelai or chīlai, s.m. A kid, young goat. H. (chherī).

چيندخ chīndakh, s.m. A frog; bull frog.

چينگ chīng, a. Gaping, open, wide; straddled.

چينه chīna, s.f. A spring, fountain.

ح

ح he or ḥā, is the eleventh letter of the Pukkhto alphabet, and the sixth of the Arabic. It is only found in words adopted from the Arabic. It is sometimes replaced by ه, than which letter it has a different sound, being pronounced in the throat, and strongly aspirated.

حاجت ḥājat, s.m. Want, necessity, need. A.

حاجتمند ḥājatmand, } a. Needy, indigent. P.
حاجتمن ḥājatman, }

حاجي ḥājī, s.m. A pilgrim to Mecca: one who has made the pilgrimage to Mecca. A.

حاصل ḥāṣil, s.m. Produce, profit, result; corn, crops; duty, revenue; acquiring, collecting. A. ḥāṣil-laral, v.a. To produce, yield, give.

حاصلول ḥāṣilawul, v.a. To collect, acquire, gain.

حاصليدل ḥāṣiledal, v.n. To accrue, result, be gathered.

حاضر ḥāẓir, a. Present, ready, willing. A.

حاطه ḥāṭa, s.f. Enclosure, premises. A.

حافظ ḥāfiẓ, s.m. A blind man who has learnt the Quran by heart. Name of a Persian poet.

حاکم ḥākim, s.m. Commander, judge, master, ruler, governor. A.

حال ḥāl, s.m. Case, condition, state; affair, business, matter; now, present time. A.

حالت ḥālat, s.m. Case, condition, state.

حالي ḥālī, a. Modern, new, existent.

حامله ḥāmila, a. Pregnant, with young. A.

حبس ḥabs, s.m. Retention, imprisonment; prison; a prisoner. A.

حبشي ḥabshī, s.m. A Caffre, negro. A.

حبيب ḥabīb, s.m. A lover, friend. a. Beloved, dear. A.

حج ḥaj, s.m. Pilgrimage to Mecca. A.

حجاب *ḥijāb*, s.m. Bashfulness, modesty; curtain, veil. A.

حجام *ḥajjām*, s.m. A barber; cupper, phlebotomist. A.

حجامت *ḥajjāmat*, s.m. Shaving, cupping.

حجت *ḥujjat*, s.m. Argument, proof, reason; dispute, altercation. A.

حجتي *ḥujjatī*, a. Litigious, argumentative, quarrelsome. s.m. Wrangler, caviller, arguer

حجره *ḥujra*, s.f. A cell, chamber, closet. A. A public room or house in each quarter of a village, for the use of travellers and visitors, hostelry. A vestry, ward.

حد *ḥadd*, s.m. Boundary, limit; extent, extremity, degree; impediment; definition; starting post. A.

حديث *ḥadīs*, s.m. A tradition; the traditions and sayings of Muḥammad. A.

حذر *ḥazr*, s.m. Caution, prudence, fear. A.

حرارت *ḥarārat*, s.m. Fervour, heat, warmth. A.

حراست *ḥirāsat*, s.m. Care, watching, guarding. A.

حرام *ḥarām*, a. Forbidden, unlawful, wrong; sacred. A.

حرامي *ḥarāmī*, s.m. A bastard; robber, cheat; rogue, rascal. A.

حرص *ḥirṣ*, s.m. Greediness, ambition, avarice. A.

حرصناک *ḥirṣnāk*, a. Greedy, ambitious, covetous.

حرف *ḥarf*, s.m. A letter, particle, word. A.

حرکت *ḥarkat*, s.m. A short vowel. *ḥarakat*, s.m. Action, gesture, movement; impediment, obstacle, hindrance, prevention. A.

حرم *ḥaram*, a. Forbidden, sacred. s.m. The temple at Mecca; a sanctuary. *ḥarama*, s.f. A seraglio; concubine, wife. A.

حرمت *ḥurmat*, s.m. Chastity, honour; dignity, esteem, reverence. A.

حريان *ḥariyān*, a. See حيران.

حريف *ḥarīf*, s.m. A rival, enemy; partner, associate, friend. a. Clever, cunning; pleasant, agreeable. A.

حساب *ḥisāb*, s.m. Accounts; calculation, reckoning, account. A.

حسد *ḥasad*, s.m. Envy, jealousy, malice; emulation, ambition. A.

حسرت *ḥasrat*, s.m. Grief, sorrow, regret; desire, longing, yearning. A.

حسن *ḥasan*, a. Beautiful, good; a man's name. *ḥusn*, s.m. Beauty, elegance; goodness. A.

حسن‌حسين *ḥasan-ḥusen*, s.m. Name of a month, the Muḥarram.

حشر *ḥashr*, s.m. A concourse, meeting; resurrection of the dead. A.

حشمت *ḥashmat*, s.m. Dignity, pomp, state; train, retinue. A.

حصار *ḥiṣṣār*, s.m. Citadel, fortress. A. Enclosure, fence; besieging, surrounding.

حصه *ḥiṣṣa*, s.f. Division, part; lot, portion, share. A.

حضرت *ḥazrat*, s.m. Dignity, presence; highness, majesty, reverence, etc. (title of respect). A.

حضور *ḥuzūr*, s.m. Appearance, attendance, presence; your worship, etc. A.

حفاظت *ḥifāzat*, s.m. Care, custody; keeping, protection. A.

حق *ḥaqq*, s.m. Truth, right; equity, justice; portion, lot; the Deity. A. *ḥuq*, s.m. The sound of retching, vomiting.

حقا *ḥaqqā*, in. By God! Really! True! Indeed! A.

حقنه *ḥuqna*, s.f. A clyster; syringe. A.

حقير *ḥaqīr*, a. Contemptible, vile; lean, thin. A.

حقيقت *ḥaqīqat*, s.m. Truth; sincerity; explanation, narration, account. A.

حقيقي *ḥaqīqī*, a. Accurate, certain, real, true; own; just. A.

حكاك *ḥukāk*, s.m. A lapidary. A.

حكايت *ḥikāyat*, s.m. History, story, tale; narration. A.

حكم *ḥukm*, s.m. Command, decree, order, sentence; permission. A.

حكمت *ḥikmat*, s.m. Knowledge, wisdom; art, skill, cleverness; mystery, principle. A.

حكمتي *ḥikmatī*, a. Artful, clever, wise, skilful.

حكومت *ḥukūmat*, s.m. Authority, dominion, government, sovereignty. A.

حكيم *ḥakīm*, s.m. A doctor, physician; philosopher, sage. A.

حلال *ḥalāl*, a. Lawful, legal, right; clean, pure. A.

حلف *ḥalf*, s.m. An oath. A.

حلق *ḥalq*, s.m. The throat, windpipe. A.

حلقه *ḥalqa*, s.f. A circle, ring; knocker for a door; a fraternity, society. A.

حلوا *ḥalwā*, s.f. A kind of sweetmeat made of flour, butter and sugar. A.

حلوائي *ḥalwā-ī*, s.m. A confectioner.

حليم *ḥalīm*, a. Affable, gentle, tractable, mild. A.

حماقت *ḥimāqat*, s.m. Folly, ignorance, stupidity. A.

حمال *ḥammāl*, s.m. A porter, carrier. A.

حمام *ḥammām*, s.m. A Turkish bath, vapour bath. A.

حمايت *ḥimāyat*, s.m. Countenance, protection, support, defence, help, assistance. A.

حمايتي *ḥimāyatī*, s.m. Protector, patron, deliverer.

حمل *ḥaml*, s.m. A burden, load; pregnancy. A.

حمله *ḥamla*, s.f. Assault, attack, onset, charge. A.

حنا *ḥinnā*, s.f. See نكريزي.

حنظل *ḥanẓal*, s.m. See مرغوني.

حواله *ḥawāla*, s.f. Care, charge, custody, trust. A.

حور *ḥūr*, s.m. A boy of Paradise. A.

حوره *ḥūra*, s.f. A virgin of Paradise; black-eyed nymph. A.

حوصله *ḥauṣila*, s.f. Ambition, spirit, mettle; crop, maw, stomach. A.

حوض *ḥauẓ*, s.m. A cistern, tank, reservoir, vat. A.

حويلي *ḥawelai*, s.m. A dwelling, habitation, house; tenement, premises. A. Also *ḥawela-ī*, s.f.

حيا *ḥayā*, s.f. Bashfulness, modesty, shame. A.

حيات *ḥayāt*, s.m. Life. A.

حيران *ḥairān*, a. Astonished, amazed; perplexed, confounded. A.

حيراني *ḥairānī*, s.f. Amazement, confusion; perplexity, perturbation. A.

حيض *ḥaiẓ*, s.m. Menses, catamenia. A.

حيضه *ḥaiẓa*, s.f. A menstruous woman.

حيف *ḥaif*, s.m. Iniquity, oppression. a. Futile, useless. in. Alas! Ah! A.

حيله *ḥīla*, s.f. Artifice, pretence, deceit, trick. A.

حين *ḥīn*, s.m. Time, interval. A.

حيوان *ḥaiwān*, s.m. An animal, brute. A.

حيوانتوب *ḥaiwān-tob*, s.m. Brutality, savageness.

خ

خ *khe* is the twelfth letter of the Pukkhto alphabet, and the seventh of the Arabic. It is a guttural letter, and pronounced like the *ch* in the Scotch *loch*.

خاتم *khātim*, s.m. A seal; finger ring. A.

خاتمه *khātima*, s.f. Conclusion, end, finis. A.

خاته *khātah*, s.m. Ascent, rise; rising, ascending.

خادمه *khādama*, } s.f. Name of a kind of
خادمئ *khādama-ī*, } lizard with a bristly back.

خاده *khāda*, s.f. A grave-stone, tombstone; a pole or wooden tablet at the head of a grave.

خار *khār*, s.m. A thorn, bramble, prickle, thistle; a spike; the spur of a cock. P.

خارج *khārij*, a. Excluded, outcast, expelled. A.

خارجي *khāriji*, s.m. Name of a heretical sect amongst Moslems.

خارښت *khārakkht*, s.m. Itch, mange. P. (*khārisht*).

خارو *khāro*, s.f. A cock's comb, wattle. P. (*khār*).

خاشاک *khāshāk*, s.m. Rubbish, litter, refuse. P. Firewood, fuel. P.

خاش خاش *khāsh-khāsh*, s.m. Poppy seed. P.

خارک *khārak*, s.m. See چهارک.

خازه *khāza*, s.f. See خاده.

خاشه *khāsha*, s.f. A straw, splinter, bit, chip, etc.; name of a disease of the eye; mote in the eye.

خاشه کښ *khāsha-kakkh*, s.m. One who extracts motes from the eye; curer of the khāsha.

خاص *khāṣṣ*, a. Excellent, noble, pure; special, private, particular; peculiar, single, sole. A.

خاصه *khāṣṣa*, s.f. A kind of bread; a kind of muslin.

خاصيت *khāṣṣiyat*, s.m. Attribute, quality, temper, disposition, nature, property. A.

خاطر *khāṭir*, s.m. Heart, soul; inclination, propensity; account, sake; will, choice. A.

خاک *khāk*, s.m. Ashes, earth, dust. P.

خاکستر *khākistar*, s.f. Ashes. P.

خاکه *khāka*, s.f. Broken rice, etc., unfit for use; a fragment, particle of gems, etc.

خاگينه *khāgīna*, s.f. Omelet, dish of fried eggs. P.

خال *khāl*, s.m. A black spot, or mole on the skin; an artificial spot for ornament on the face, breasts, etc.

خالص *khāliṣ*, a. Genuine, pure, simple. A.

خالصه *khāliṣa*, s.f. Fallow land.

خالي *khālī*, a. Empty, vacant; unmixed, pure; mere, only; idle, unemployed. s.f. Saturday; the eleventh Afghan month corresponding with *ẕī-qa'da*. P.

خام *khām*, s.m. The horn end of a bow. A. See اوم.

خامتا *khāmtā*, s.f. A kind of coarse cotton cloth.

خاموش *khāmosh*, a. Mute, silent, still. P.

خان *khān*, s.m. A lord, prince; a title used by all Afghans and Pathans. T.

خانتما *khāntamā*, a. Proud, arrogant, vain.

خانه *khāna*, s.f. House, room, place. P.

خاندان *khāndān*, s.m. Family, household.

خانواده *khānawāda*, s.f. Family, house, tribe.

خانومان *khānomān*, s.m. Household (as house, family, servants, cattle, furniture, goods, chattels, fixings, etc.).

خاوره *khāwra*, s.f. Dust, earth, clay.

خاورين *khāwrīn*, a. Clayey, earthy, dusty.

خاوند *khāwand*, s.m. Master, owner, husband, lord, proprietor. P.

خايه *khāya*, s.f. Testicle. P.

خبث *khubṣ*, s.m. Envy, malice. A

خبر *khabar*, s.m. Advice, intelligence, news, report, rumour. A.

خبردار *khabar-dār*, a. Careful, cautious; aware, informed. A.

خبرگير *khabar-gīr*, s.m. A spy, informer; patron, protector.

خبرلوڅ *khabar-loṯs*, a. Eloquent, talkative.

خبرول *khabarawul*, v.a. To report, inform.

خبره *khabara*, s.f. Language, speech; affair, matter, thing.

خبريدل *khabaredal*, v.n. To be aware, acquainted, informed, etc.

خبيث *khabīṣ*, a. Impure, malignant, wicked. s.m. An evil spirit. A.

خپر *khapar*, s.f. Palm of the hand; sole of the foot.

خپسکي *khapaskai*, s.m. } The nightmare. A.
خپسه *khapasa*, s.f. } (*kābūs*).

خپل *khpul*, pr. Self, own. P. (*khūd*). *pa-khpul* or *pa-khpula*, ad. Spontaneously, of own accord. P. (*bā-khūd*).

خپلسر *khpul-sar*, a. Obstinate, self-opinionated.

خپلوالي *khpul-wālai*, s.m. Connection, relationship.

خپلول *khpulawul*, v.a. To adopt, appropriate, make one's own; win over, bias, sway, predispose.

خپلوي *khpulawī*, s.f. Connection, relationship, family, kindred, friendship.

خپليدل *khpuledal*, v.n. To be related, connected; to be biassed, influenced.

خپور *khpor*, a. Blown, blossomed, expanded (as a flower); dispersed, loose, scattered.

خپه *khapah*, a. Angry, offended, displeased, vexed. *khapa*, s.f. Suffocation, strangulation. P. (*khafa*). *khpah*, s.m. Tinder, touchwood.

خپگان *khapagān*, s.m. } Anger, rage, vexa-
خپگي *khapagī*, s.f. } tion.

خپي *khapī*, s.f. See کپي.

ختر *khatar*, s.m. See خطر.

ختل *khatal*, v.n. To ascend, mount, rise; issue. P. (*khāstan*, *khez-*).

ختم *khatm*, s.m. Conclusion, end; seal. a. Done, completed. A.

ختنه *khatna*, s.f. Circumcision. A. *khatana*, s.f. Rising, mounting, ascending.

خته *khata*, s.f. A shirt, shift.

خټ *khaṭ*, s.m. A hillock, knoll, mound; a low hill; bank of clouds. *kha-aṭ* or *khaṭ*, a. Muddy, turbid, miry. *khuṭ*, s.m. Effervescence, boiling, bubbling.

خټکيدل *khuṭkedal*, v.n. To bubble, boil, effervesce; to boil with rage, etc. H. (*khaṭaknā*).

خټبيل *khaṭbel* or *kha-aṭbel*, s.m. Dregs, lees, sediment, dross, precipitate.

خټک *khaṭak*, s.m. A kind of black-beetle. An unripe water melon used to make pickles. Name of a Pathan tribe settled in the low hills on the south of the Kabul river between Peshawar and Attak.

خټکي *khaṭakai*, s.m. A kind of melon of a green colour (peculiar to Afghanistan). *khuṭkai*, s.m. Ebullition, effervescence.

خټوله *khaṭola* or *kha-aṭola*, a. Muddy, turbid (as water).

خټه *khaṭa* or *kha-aṭa*, s.f. Mire, mud, slush, slime. *khuṭa*, s.f. Clay, marl.

خجل *khijjil*, a. Bashful, modest. A. (*khajal*).

خجونکو *khajūnko*, a. Capering, frisky, prancing; rebounding, skipping (as a ball or stone over the surface of water).

خڅوزه *khatsoza*, s.f. A bit, fragment, chip shred.

خڅه *khatsa*, p. See څخه.

خچر *khachar*, s.m. A mule. H. (*khachchar*).

خچن *khachan*, a. Dirty, rheumy. See چخن.

خچه *khacha*, s.f. The little finger; a bound, ricochet, rebound.

خداي *khudāe*, s.m. God, the Deity. P. (*khudā*). *khudā-ī*, s.f. Divinity, Godhead. P.

خدايا *khudāyā*, in. Oh God! P.

خدمت *khidmat*, s.m. Attendance, duty, service. A.

خدمتي *khidmatī*, a. Attendant, diligent, heedful.

خدمتگار *khidmat-gār*, s.m. A servant, attendant.

خدنگ *khadung*, s.m. Name of a tree, from the wood of which bows are made. A poplar tree. P.

خدل *khadal*, s.m. A large dog in good condition; a mastiff. a. Stout, burly, muscular.

خر *khar*, s.m. An ass, donkey. P. *kha-ar*, s.m. A snore. A.

خراب *kharāb*, a. Bad, depraved; spoiled, ruined; deserted, waste; abandoned, lost. A.

خرابي *kharābī*, s.f. Evil, mischief; destruction, ruin; waste.

خراج *khirāj*, s.m. Duty, revenue, rent, tax. A.

خراړه *kharāṛa*, s.f. Name of a bird; the sand grouse; a kind of skylark.

خراسان *khurāsān*, s.m. Name of a country. Afghanistan.

خراشكي *kharāshkai*, s.m. Phlegm, expectorated mucus, sputum. P. (*kharāsh*).

خربوزه *kharbūza*, s.f. A musk melon. P.

خربيشوي *kharbīshoe*, s.m. A boar, hog, pig.

خربټ *kharpaṭ*, s.m. A powder; a palmful to chuck into the mouth.

خربوڅه *kharpotsa*, s.f. Crawling on all fours (as a child).

خرټ *kharaṭ*, a. Fat, stout, plump.

خرته *kharatah*, s.m. Cheat, hypocrite, knave.

خرجدال *kharjadāl*, s.m. See خردجال.

خرجگجگلي *kharjagjagalai*, s.m. Name of a game played by boys.

خرجين *khurjin*, s.m. A bag, wallet, reticule. P.

خرڅ *kharts*, s.m. Expense, outlay; expenditure, means; price, fee, duty. A. (*kharch*).

خرڅوړي *khartsoṛai*, s.m. A rag, shred, tatter.

خرڅي *khartsī*, a. Extravagant, prodigal, lavish.

خرچ *khrach*, s.m. A crack, creak, crash, split; sound of splitting wood.

خرخاري *kharkhārai*, s.m. Ass's play, foolishness, nonsense; romping, boistering.

خرخښه *kharkhakkha*, s.f. Noise, tumult, discord, wrangling; a crowd, mob. P. (*kharkhasha*).

خرد *khurd*, a. Little, small. P.

خردجال *khardajāl*, s.m. Antichrist.

خردگ *khardag*, s.m. Name of a plant (*Salvia pumila*).

خرس *khirs*, s.m. A bear. P.

خرسند *khursand*, a. Contented, pleased, satisfied. P.

خرشن *kharshan*, s.m. Horse dung.

خرطوم *khartūm*, s.m. Proboscis of an elephant; dewlap of bulls, etc. A.

خرغينړي *khar-ghenṛai*, s.m. A toadstool, mushroom.

خرفه *khurfa*, s.f. Purslain. A.

خرقه *khirqa*, s.f. A patched garment, a kind of dress (worn by dervishes). A.

خُرکي *kha-arkai*, s.m. A snore, purr.

خرګي *khargai*, s.m. A young ass. *kha-argai*, s.m. A kind of grasshopper.

خرّم *khurram*, a. Cheerful, merry, joyful. P.

خرمن *khirman*, s.m. Harvest. P. Threshing floor.

خرمندي *kharmandai*, a. Tiny, small, wee, little.

خرمه *khurma*, s.f. A date (fruit and tree). P. (*khurmā*).

خرنار *kharnār*, s.m. Name of a plant, mullein (*Verbascum thapsus*).

خروار *kharwār*, s.m. An ass-load. P.

خروسک *kharosak*, s.m. A disease of the throat, quinsy.

خروش *kharosh*, s.m. Bustle, stir, tumult, noise. P.

خري *kharai*, s.m. A whitlow.

خريد *kharīd*, s.m. Purchase. P.

خريدار *kharīdār*, s.m. A purchaser. P.

خريړي *khareṛai*, s.m. Curds and whey; junket. *kha-areṛai*, s.m. A kind of edible mushroom.

خريز *khirīz*, s.m. Cotton stalks or stubble.

خريطه *kharīta*, s.f. Bag, packet, purse; letter bag, mail. P.

خريل *khrayal*, v.a. To shave. P. (*kharāshīdan*).

خړ *kha-ar*, a. Muddy, turbid; cloudy, obscure; drab, dust-coloured. *khur*, s.m. Sound of vomiting or retching, hawking. *khar*, s.m. A ravine, dry watercourse. See خوړ.

خړانګه *khrānga*, s.f. Bough or stem of a tree.

خرپ *khrap*, s.m. A crunch, crush, squash, smash.

خرتم *khartam*, s.m. See خرطوم.

خرس *khras*, s.m. Blow, clash, crash, slam.

خړل *kharal*, v.a. To dung, ease one's self, stool.

خړمت *kha-armat*, s.m. Snot, snivel, mucus of nose.

خړمور *kha-armor*, s.m. A kind of bustard, obārah.

خرند *kharand*, s.m. Stump of a tree, stubble.

خړوب *kharob*, a. Watered, saturated, irrigated (as a field).

خريس *khrīs*, a. Big, burly, great; stupid, heavy, dull. s.m. A lout, lubber.

خړين *khurīn*, a. Soft, sodden (as victuals), ripe, rotten (as fruit), festered (as a sore).

خزان *khizān*, s.m. Autumn. P.

خزانه *khazāna*, s.f. Treasury, store; magazine, granary; chamber of a gun.

خزله *khazala*, s.f. Litter, refuse, sweepings, etc.

خزنده *khazanda*, s.f. A reptile, insect, creeping thing. P.

خږ *khug*, a. Bruised, hurt, injured, pained. s.m. A bruise, cut, injury, wound; ailment, malady, disease. *khag*, s.m. Death rattle, gurgle in the throat.

خس *khas*, s.m. Litter, straw, dry grass, twigs, etc. P.

خسا *khsā*, a. See سخا.

خسمانه *khasmāna*, s.f. Protection, support; custody, ownership; housewifery, domestic economy. A. (*khaṣmāna*).

خسڼري *khasanrai*, s.m. A straw, mote, dry twig, etc.

خسي *khasī*, a. Castrated, gelt. s.m. A gelding, any castrated animal. A. (*khuṣṣī*). *khsai*, s.m. See سخي.

خسيل *khasīl*, s.m. Green corn used as fodder.

خشاک *khashāk*, s.m. Refuse, litter, rubbish; dry twigs, leaves, etc. P.

خشاوزه *khashāwza*, s.f. Orris root; root of the Iris or sweet flag. See سخاوزه.

خشت *khisht* or *khusht*, a. Damp, humid, moist, wet; drenched, dripping, reeking. *khusht-pusht*, a. Drenched to the skin, wet through, etc.

خشک *khushk*, a. Dry, arid, withered. P.

خشکه *khushka*, s.f. Plain boiled rice. P.

خشکي *khushkī*, s.f. Dryness, aridity; drought, dearth; dry land, travelling by land. P.

خشنود *khushnūd*, a. Contented, pleased. P.

خشي *khushai*, a. Crazy, demented, flighty; open, defenceless; unguarded, unprotected; without friends, etc. P. (*khushk* or *khush*).

خښ *khakkh*, a. Buried, interred, embedded.

خښتګ *khakkhtag*, خښتګي *khakkhtagai*, } s.m. A piece of cloth sewn into the fork of a pair of drawers or armpit of a coat. P. (*khash*, armpit).

خښته *khakkhta*, s.f. A brick. P. (*khisht*).

خښي *khakkhī*, s.m. Name applied to the Yusufzai tribe of Afghans. *khakkhai*, s.m. A male of the tribe. *khakkha-ī*, s.f. A female of the tribe.

خصلت *khaṣlat*, s.m. Nature, disposition; quality, virtue; custom, habit. A.

خصم *khaṣam*, s.m. A husband. A.

خصوصاً *khuṣūṣan*, ad. Especially, particularly. A.

خضر *khizr*, s.m. The prophet Elias. A.

خط *khaṭṭ*, s.m. Epistle, letter, note; writing; a line, lineament; down on the face, youthful beard. A.

خطا *khaṭā*, s.f. Error, fault, crime; mistake, miss. A.

خطاب *khiṭāb*, s.m. Address, title. A.

خطبه *khuṭba*, s.f. A sermon preached on Fridays in Muḥammadan places of worship for the welfare and prosperity of the reigning sovereign. A.

خطر *khaṭar*, s m. } Danger, fear, hazard, risk.
خطره *khaṭra*, s.f. } A.

خطرناك *khaṭar-nāk*, a. Dangerous, hazardous.

خطيب *khaṭīb*, s.m. A preacher. A.

خفقان *khafaqān*, s.m. Palpitation of the heart, breast-pang; vexation. A.

خگلن *khuglan*, s.m. Embers, hot ashes, hot cinders.

خل *khal*, s.m. Faith, hope, trust, belief.

خلات *khilāt*, s.m. A dress of honour, reward, present. A. (*khil'at*).

خلاص *khalāṣ*, a. Free, liberated; discharged, done. A.

خلاصه *khulāṣa*, s.f. Conclusion, inference, moral; abstract, summary. A.

خلاصي *khalāṣī*, s.f. Deliverance, freedom, release.

خلاف *khilāf*, s.m. Contradiction, opposition. a. Contrary, false. A.

خلاملا *khalā-malā*, a. Candid, frank, sincere.

خلبوري *khulborai*, s.m. A bung, cork, plug, spigot.

خلته *khalta*, s.f. A hamper (used by hill men). P. (*khalita*). See جلته.

خلش *khalish*, s.m. Interruption, hindrance; doubt, solicitude; suspicion. P.

خلط *khalṭ*, s.m. Confusion, mixture. *khilṭ*, s.m. One of the four humours of the human body. A.

خلق *khalq*, s.m. Creation, universe; mankind, people, the world. A. *khulq*, s.m. Nature, disposition, civility, politeness. A.

خلقت *khalqat*, s.m. Creation, people, the world. A.

خلقه *khalqa*, s.f. A coat, frock, gown. A.

خلل *khalal*, s.m. Defect, injury; interruption; prejudice. A.

خلوت *khilwat*, s.m. Privacy, retirement; closet, private chamber; private conference. A.

خله *khula*, s.f. The mouth; orifice, entrance.

خلي *khalai*, s.m. Bud, shoot, sprout. s. (*kalī*).

خم *kham*, s.m. A coil, twist; curl, ringlet. *khum*, s.m. An alembic, still, retort; jar, vase; boiler. P.

خمار *khumār*, a. Drunken, intoxicated; intoxicating, languishing (as the eyes). s.m. Headache, sickness after a debauch. P.

خمبه *khamba*, s.f. A kind of corn bin made of wattles, and plastered over with clay.

خمټ *khamaṭ*, a. Plump, chubby (as a baby).

خمچه *khamachah*, a. Little, short, small. *khamacha-guta*, s.f. The little finger. *khamache-pukkhta-ī*, s.f. The short ribs.

خمچي *khamache*, s.f. Coarsely ground millet or rice, broken rice; millet bread. H. (*kamāch*).

خمرئ *khumra-ī*, s.f. A drinking flask or cup; a small drum carried by beggars; a small mat of palm leaves used to pray upon. A.

خمسور *khamsor*, a. Familiar, free, unceremonious.

خمزري *khumazarai*, s.m. See شاپانگه.

خمن *khaman*, a. Bent, curved, crooked. P. (*kham*).

خمير *khamīr*, a. Fermented, leavened. A.

خميره *khamīra*, s.f. Dough, leaven, yeast, ferment.

خناق *khunāq*, s.m. A disease of the throat; quinsy. A. (*khunāq*).

خنجاره *khanjāra*, s.f. A kind of millet grain.

خنجر *khanjar*, s.m. A dagger. A.

خنجک *khinjak*, s.m. The mastic tree and fruit (*Pista Cabulica*).

خند *khand*, s.m. Name of a boy's game played with knuckle bones; marbles.

خندا *khandā*, s.f. A laugh; laughter. P. (*khandah*).

خندق *khandaq*, s.m. A ditch, moat, fosse. A.

خندل *khandal*, v.a. To laugh at, scoff, ridicule.

خندول *khandawul*, v.a. To cause to laugh.

خنده *khandah*, s.m. A pointer dog. Also *khandai*.

خندي *khundī*, a. Preserved, protected, kept; arranged, settled. *khundī-kawul*, v.a. To keep, preserve, take care of.

خنديدل *khandedal*, v.n. To giggle, laugh, titter. P. (*khandīdan*).

خنديل *khundiyal*, v.a. To keep, guard, protect, etc.

خند *khanḍ*, s.m. Stump of a tree.

خندن *khandan*, s.m. Zedoary (*Curcuma zerunbet*).

خنک *khunuk*, a. Cold, cool, chilly; temperate. P.

خنکي *khunukī*, s.f. Coldness, chilliness. P.

خو *khū*, s.m. Tinder, touchwood; a kind of sugar cane. H. *kho*, ad. Certainly, surely; then, at least.

خوا *khwā*, s.f. Margin, side, direction, quarter; nature, temperament; constitution, health; desire, wish.

خوار *khwār*, a. Poor, wretched; abject, mean; lean, thin; friendless, ruined. P.

خواري *khwārī*, s.f. Poverty, beggary, ruin; distress, etc.

خواره *khwārah*, s.m. Food, victuals.

خواست *khwāst*, s.m. Desire, wish; want, request. P.

خواښه *khwākkha*, s.f. Mother-in-law. P. (*khwāsh*).

خواله *khwāla*, s.f. Disclosing, revealing. *khwāla-wayal*, v.a. To disclose, reveal.

خوان *khwān*, s.m. } A tray, salver, platter. P.
خوانچه *khwāncha*, s.f. } A small tray.

dastar-khwān, s.m. A table-cloth, table-cover. P.

خواهش *khwāhish*, s.m. Desire, inclination, wish. P.

خوب *khob*, s.m. Sleep, slumber; a dream. P. (*khwāb*). *khūb*, a. Good, excellent; amiable, pleasant; fair, beautiful. P.

خوبي *khūbī*, s.f. Excellence, beauty, goodness. etc. P.

خوټه *khoṭa*, s.f. A testicle.

خوځول *khwadzawul*, v.a. To move, shift, remove, shake, agitate, wag.

خوځيدل *khwadzedal*, v.n. To move, shake, wag, stir.

خود *khūd*, pr. Self (in comp. only). P. *khod*, ad. See خو.

خودله *khūdala*, s.f. Bulrush, reed; the flower spike and down: the down is used as tinder.

خور *khor*, s.f. A sister. pl. *khwainde*. P. (*khwāhar*). *khor*, a. Open, expanded, blown (as a flower); dispersed, scattered; loose, dishevelled. *khwa-ar*, s.m. Scurf, scab, crust; bark, peel, rind, husk.

خوراک *khwurāk*, s.m. Food, victuals, diet, eatables. P.

خوراکي *khwurākī*, a. Edible, eatable, esculent.

خورځه *khordza*, s.f. Sister's daughter, niece.

خورجين *khūrjīn*, } s.m. Portmanteau, carpet-
خورجي *khūrjai*, } bag; a wallet, reticule. P.

خورجينه *khūrjīna*, s.f. A travelling-cap with flaps to cover the ears.

خورخل *khorkhal*, s.m. } Shears for shearing
خورخول *khorkhwal*, } sheep.

خورلنړه *khor-lanṛa*, s.f. A sister's daughter (used by a clan or tribe to designate the daughter of any member after marriage).

خورمه *khorma*, s.f. Incipient beard, down on the face.

خورندده *khwurindah*, a. Gluttonous, gormandizer. P.

خوروول *khwarawul*, v.a. To open, expand, loose, dishevel, spread out, disperse, scatter. *khūrawul*, To feed, supply with food.

خوري *khaura-ī*, s.f. Alum. *khawrai*, s.m. See خاوره.

خوريدل *khwaredal*, v.n. To expand, blossom, blow; to disperse, spread, scatter.

خورينګه *khorīnga*, s.f. Adopted sister, female friend.

خورينګي *khorīngai*, s.m. Sisterly love, friendship among women.

خوريي *khora-e*, s.m. Sister's son, nephew.

خوړ *khwaṛ*, s.m. Ravine, watercourse, dry bed of a river.

خوړل *khwuṛal*, v.a. To eat, feed; bite. P. (*khurdan*).

خوړول *khūṛawul* or *khwuṛawul*, v.a. To feed, victual, supply with food.

خوړه *khwaṛa*, s.f. Donation, gratuity, subscription; sandy bed of a ravine or dry watercourse.

خوږ *khog*, a. Sweet. *khūg*, a. See خږ. P. (*khūsh*).

خوږلوري *khog-lorai*, a. Sweetish, pleasant.

خوږه وله *khwaga-wala*, s.f. Liquorice root.

خوش *khūsh*, a. Agreeable, pleasant. P.

خشوي *khashoe*, s.m. See غشوي.

خوشه *khosha*, s.f. An ear of corn, bunch of grapes, spike of flowers, etc. P.

خوښ *khwakkh*, a. Delighted, pleased; pleasant, agreeable; charming, attractive. P. (*khūsh*).

خوښي *khwakkhī*, s.f. Will, pleasure, choice; delight, joy, gladness. P. (*khūshī*).

خوښينه *khwakkhīna*, s.f. See ښينه.

خوف *khof*, s.m. Fear, fright, alarm. A. (*khauf*).

خوګ *khūg*, s.m. A pig, hog. P. (*khūk*).

خول *khol*, s.m. A helmet, steel cap; case, sheath. H.

خوله *khwula*, s.f. A divorced wife who is taken back and received by the husband.

خولي *khwale*, s.f. (sing. obsolete) Perspiration, sweat. P. (*khwae*).

خولۍ *khola-ī*, s.f. A cap, skull-cap.

خون *khūn*, s.m. Murder, manslaughter; blood. P.

خوني *khūnī*, s.m. A murderer.

خوند *khwand*, s.m. Flavour, taste; pleasure, delight.

خوندناک *khwand-nāk*, a. Agreeable, pleasant.

خونه *khūna*, s.f. Chamber, room; court, hall, house; family, tribe. P. (*khāna*). *khawana*, s.f. Olive tree.

خوي *khoe*, s.m. Temper, disposition, nature; custom, habit, manner. P. (*kho*).

خويد *khwīd* or *khīd*, s.m. Green corn (used as fodder). P.

خوئيدل *khwa-edal*, v.n. To slip, slide, fall.

خيابان *khayābān*, s.m. An avenue; flower bed. P.

خيار *khiyār*, s.m. Choice, selection, trial. A.

خياط *khiyāṭ*, s.m. A tailor. A.

خيال *khiyāl*, s.m. Fancy, idea, thought; opinion, suspicion; delusion, vision. A.

خيانت *khiyānat*, s.m. Embezzlement, robbery of entrusted property; perfidy, treachery. A.

خيټه *kheṭa*, s.f. See ګيډه.

خيدک *khaidak*, s.m. Sour milk.

خير *khīr*, a. Enraged, angry; sorry, vexed. P. (*khīra*). *khair*, a. Good, well. s.m. Happiness, welfare; health, goodness; alms, charity. A.

خيرات *khairāt*, s.m. Alms, charity. A.

خيره *khīra*, s.f. Dirt, filth, pollution, ordure.

خيرن *khīran*, } a. Dirty, soiled, filthy, pol-
خيري *khīrai*, } luted.

خيز *khez*, s.m. Bounding, leaping, rising. P.

خيزول *khejawul*, v.a. To lift, elevate, raise, erect. P. (*khezāndan*).

خيږ *khīg*, s.m. The scab of a sore. S. (*khāj*).

خيښ *khekkh*, s.m. A kinsman, relation; wife's relations. P. (*khwesh*).

خيښي *khekkhī*, s.f. Relationship by marriage.

خيک *khīk*, s.m. A large inflated hide (used to cross rivers upon).

خيل *khel*, s.m. A clan, tribe; division of a clan, family. A.

خيل‌خانه *khel-khāna*, s.f. Clan, kindred.

خيم *khyam*, a. Coagulated, solidified, hardened (as the cheese, milk, etc.). A. (*qiyām*).

خيمه *khaima*, s.f. A tent, marquee. A.

د

د *dāl* is the thirteenth letter of the Pukkhto alphabet; it has a soft dental sound, and is often changed to ل in words derived from the Persian and Sanskrit.

دَ *da*, A particle, the sign of the Genitive case; it always precedes the word it governs, and is not affected by gender or number. It is sometimes used as the sign of the Ablative case instead of the particle له. Ex. دَ کلي نه *da kili na*, for له کلي نه *la kili na*, from the village.

دِ *di*, pr. 1. A form of the Genitive and Instrumental cases singular of the second personal pronoun تۀ *tah*, thou. Also written دي *de*. 2. A form of the Oblique cases singular of the proximate third personal pronoun دي *de*, he, she, it. 3. The sign of the third person in both numbers of the Imperative Mood.

دا *dā*, pr. One of the proximate demonstrative pronouns; this; that.

داب *dāb*, s.m. The large wooden axle of a Persian wheel; custom, manner; condition, situation. A.

دابه *dāba*, s.f. A quadruped, beast, brute; cattle. A.

داتکي *dātkai*, s.m. A plant used in dyeing (*Grislea tomentosa*). H. (*dhārī*).

داتوره *dātūra*, s.f. The thorn apple (*Datura fastuosa*). H. (*dhatūrā*).

داج *dāj*, s.m. Darkness, obscurity. A marriage portion: all that a wife takes with her to her husband. A. (*dahez*).

داخل *dākhil*, a. Entered, arrived. s.m. Arriving, entering. A.

داد *dād*, s.m. Equity, justice, law; revenge; (in comp.) given, bestowed. P.

دادا *dādā*, in. A term of affectionate address to a father or elder brother. Dear father! dear brother! H.

دار *dār*, s.m. Gallows, gibbet, stake. P. Dwelling, mansion. A. Master, owner, possessor, etc. (in comp.). P. A current, jet, spirt, stream. S. (*dhār*).

دارو *dārū*, s.m. Medicine, physic; gunpowder. H.

داروغه *dāroghah*, s.m. Overseer, superintendent, manager. P.

داره *dāra*, s.f. A stream, jet, spirt; cascade. S. (*dhār*).

دارىال *dāryāl*, s.m. A tambourine.

ډار *ḍār*, s.m. A band, company, gang (of

robbers). s. (*ḍāṛ*). A jaw tooth, grinder, molar. s. (*ḍāṛh*).

دارل *dāṛal*, v.a. To bite, lacerate, tear with the teeth (as a dog, etc.). To scold, reprove, snap at.

داره *dāṛa*, s.f. A foray, raid, surprise; cattle lifting; band, gang (of robbers); molar tooth.

داستان *dāstān*, s.m. A fable, story, tale. P.

داښت *dākkht*, s.m. A potter's furnace or oven. Durability, strength, endurance. P. (*dāsht*).

داغ *dāgh*, s.m. A spot, stain, blemish, mark; scar, cicatrix; brand, cautery. P.

داغي *dāghī*, a. Spotted, stained; scarred; cauterized; branded; blemished. P.

دال *dāl*, s.m. Pulse, lentils, vetches. S. a. Expressive, significant, typical (in comp.) A.

دالان *dālān*, s.m. Anteroom, hall, vestibule. P.

دام *dām*, s.m. A net, snare, trap. P.

دامن *dāman*, s.m. Border, skirt (of a garment, etc.); base or foot of a mountain. P.

دانا *dānā*, a. Learned, wise. s.m. A wise man. P.

داناي *dānā-ī*, s.f. Wisdom, knowledge. P.

دانست *dānist*, s.m. Knowledge, opinion. P.

دانش *dānish*, s.m. Intelligence, learning, science. P.

دانګ *dāng*, s.m. Name of a small coin; the sixth part of a دينار (*dīnār*).

دانه *dāna*, s.f. A berry; corn; grain, seed; pimple, boil; speck, granule. P. *dāna-dār*, a. Granular. *tora-dāna*, s.f. A boil, black head, furuncle; name of a black seed used in medicine.

داو *dāw*, s.m. Ambuscade, ambush; opportunity, power; time, turn, stroke (at play); stake, wager; cast or throw at dice, etc. P. H.

داي *dā-ī*, s.f. Nurse, midwife. P.

دائره *dā-ira*, s.f. A circle, orbit, ring; emblems, lines, symbols (used as amulets and charms). A.

دائم *dā-im*, a. Always, continual, perpetual. A.

دباره *dubāra*, ad. Again, second time. P.

دباغ *dabbāgh*, s.m. Currier, tanner. A.

دباغي *dabbāghī*, s.f. Business of a tanner.

دباندِ *dabāndi*, } ad. Outside, upon, on top,
دباندي *dabānde*, } above, over.

دباو *dabāw*, s.m. Authority, power, strength; subjection, pressure. H.

دبدبه *dabdaba*, s.m. Dignity, pomp, state. A.

دبلي *dablai*, s.m. A box, casket. H. (*ḍibbī*).

دبه *daba*, s.f. A jar or flagon made of untanned hide, and used to hold oil, butter, etc. H. (*ḍabbā*).

دبي *dabī*, s.f. Fruit ripened in straw or leaves, etc.

دپ *dap*, a. Deafened, stunned, stupefied.

دپاړ *dapāra*, } p. For, for the sake of, on
دپاره *dapāra*, } account of.

دپټه *dupaṭṭa*, s.f. A sheet of two breadths, used as a mantle or shawl. H

دجاج *dujāj*, s.m. Domestic fowl. A.

دختر *dukhtar*, s.f. Daughter, girl, virgin. P.

دخل *dakhl*, s.m. Access, entrance; intrusion, interference; produce, profit; advantage. A.

دخمه *dakhma*, s.f. Ambush, lair, cover.

دد *dad*, s.m. A beast of prey, rapacious animal. P.

در *dar*, s.m. A door. P *durr*, s.m. A pearl. A. *dar*, A particle used as a pronominal dative prefix of the second person with verbs and adverbs, without change for gender or number. Ex. *dar dzam* (I come to thee), *dar bāndi* (upon thee), etc.

دراز *darāz*, a. Extended, long. P.

درامد *darāmad*, s.m. Entrance. P.

دراني *durānī*, s.m. Name applied collectively to the western tribes of Afghans. P.

دراي *darā-ī*, s.f. A kind of red silk cloth. P.

درب *drab*, s.m. A bang, crash; roll, rumble. Name of a grass (*Agrostis linearis*). H. (*dūb*).

دربار *darbār*, s.m. A court, audience hall; levee. P.

درباري *darbārī*, a. Courtly. s.m. A courtier. P.

دربچه *darbacha*, s.f. See دریچه.

دربل *drabal*, v.a. To shake, press down (as flour, etc.). *drabal*, v.n. To subside, settle, sink, fall in, break down (as a roof, etc.); to crash, crumble.

دربلي *drabala-ī*, s.f. A tripod.

دربي *drabai*, s.m. A bang, crash, crumble, roll, rumble.

درپري *draparai*, s.m. Nettlerash, hives.

درج *darj*, s.m. A place for writing; written; a volume. A.

درجه *darja*, s.f. Degree, rank; step, stair. A.

درخته *drakhta*, s.f. A tree, shrub. P. (*darakht*).

درخواست *darkhwāst*, s.m. Appeal, demand; entreaty, request; desire, wish; proposal. P.

درد *dard*, s.m. Pain, ache, affliction; compassion, pity, sympathy. P. *durd*, s.m. Dregs, sediment. P.

دردمن *dardman*, a. Pained, afflicted, distressed. P.

درز *darz*, s.m. A crack, split, flaw; seam, suture; a rag, slip, strip, shred, etc. (of cloth). P.

درزي *darzī*, s.m. A tailor. P.

درس *dars*, s.m. A lesson, reading; lecture. A.

درست *drast*, a. All, whole, entire; fit, proper; just, true. ad. Entirely, wholly. P. (*durust*).

درسته *durasta*, s.f. Arms, armour, weapons.

درشت *durusht*, a. Rough, hard, harsh, stiff, rigid; fierce, surly, morose, stern. P.

درشتي *durushtī*, s.f. Asperity, roughness, severity, sternness, fierceness. P.

درشل *darshal*, s.f. The frame of a door.

درغل *darghal*, a. False, base (as coin, etc.). s.m. Cheat, liar, hypocrite; depravity, treachery, vice.

درغلول *darghalawul*, v.a. To cheat, deceive, mislead. H. (*warghalānā*).

درغول *darghol*, s.m. A gap, vent, sluice (as in a canal) to carry off the water of floods, etc.

درك *darak*, s.m. Mark, sign, trace; abode, place; entrance, passage; commencement; knowledge, understanding. A.

درکړ *drakaṛ*, s.f. Main spoke of a wheel; rim or felloe of a wheel.

درگاه *dargāh*, s.m. Court, palace; threshold; throne (divine); a shrine, sanctuary, mosque. P.

درگه *darga*, s.f. A copse, brake, thicket.

درلل *darlal*, v.a. } To have, own, possess,
درلول *darlawul*, } maintain, keep, retain.
See لرل.

درم *diram*, s.m. Money, specie; name of a coin; name of a weight. P. See درهم.

درمان *darmān*, s.m. Drug, medicine, remedy. P.

درمانده *darmāndah*, a. Distressed, destitute. P.

درماندگي *darmāndagī*, s.f. Adversity, distress; poverty, penury, misery. P.

درمند *dirmand*, s.m. A threshing-floor; garner; harvest heap. P. (*khirman*).

درميان *darmiyān*, a. Between, amidst, among. P.

درناوي *daranāwai*, s.m. Heaviness, solidity, weight; steadiness, constancy; courtesy, politeness, respect (to a superior).

درنده *darindah*, **a.** Rapacious, savage, fierce. **P.**

درنگ *drang*, s.m. Delay, procrastination, hesitation. **P.** (*dirang*).

درو *diraw*, s.m. Reaping, mowing, harvesting. **P.**

دروازه *darwāza*, s.f. Gate, entrance, door. **P.**

دروان *darwān*, s.m. A gatekeeper, porter. **P.**

درود *darūd*, s.m. Benediction, blessing. **P.**

دروزگر *darūz·gar*, s.m. A carpenter. **P.** (*darūd·gar*).

دروزه *drūza*, s.m. Stubble; shavings; chaff.

دروږ *darwag*, | درغوږ *darghwag*, } s.m. A cut, slit, or mark in the ears of cattle (for recognition).

دروغ *darogh*, s.m. A lie, falsehood, untruth. **P.**

دروغجن *daroghjan*, | دروغژن *daroghjan*, } a. False, lying. s.m. A liar.

درومل *drūmal*, v.n. To go, depart, set out, run, start.

درون *darūn*, a. In, within. **P.**

دروند *drūnd*, a. Heavy, weighty, ponderous.

دروه *droh*, s.m. Artifice, deceit, evasion, fraud; stratagem, feint (in war); hatred, malice, spite. **S.**

دروي *darwai*, s.m. Name of a reed from which mats are made (*Arundo karka*).

درويزګر *darwez·gar*, s.m. A beggar, mendicant.

درويزه *darweza*, s.f. Beggary, mendicancy. **P.** (*daryūza*).

درويشت *darwisht*, a. Twenty-three.

دره *dura*, s.f. A birch, scourge, cat of three tails. **A.** *dara*, s.f. A glen, valley; defile, gorge, hill pass. **P.**

درهم *dirham*, s.m. A drachm; name of a coin equal to the twentieth of a *dīnār*. **A.**

درهيسته *dar·hīsta*, ad. Towards or near thee or you.

در *dri*, | دري *dre*, } a. Three. **S.** (*tirī*).

دري *dara-ī*, s.f. A carpet. **H.** (*darī*).

درياب *daryāb*, s.m. River, sea, ocean. **P.** (*daryā*).

دريابي *daryābī*, a. Aquatic, of the sea.

دريافت *daryāft*, s.m. Enquiry, investigation; discovery, comprehension, understanding. **P.**

دريچه *darīcha*, s.f. A window, ventilator; air hole in a wall. **P.**

دريدل *daredal*, v.n. See ودريدل.

دري ښاخي *dre·kkhākhai*, s.m. A three-pronged pitchfork used to winnow corn.

دريغ *dregh*, s.m. Disinclination, repugnance; sigh, sorrow. **P.** (*daregh*).

دريغه *dregha*, s.m. Alas! Heigh ho! **P.** (*dareghā*).

دريه *darya*, s.f. See داريال.

دړزيدل *drazedal*, | دړکيدل *drakedal*, } v.n. To flutter, palpitate, bound, quiver. **H.** (*dhaṛaknā*).

دړه *daṛa*, s.f. A chip, splinter, fragment. **H.** *daṛe·daṛe*, a. Shattered, in atoms, bits, etc. *daṛa*, s.f. A stone or weight fixed to the lighter scale of a balance to equalize both sides. **H.** (*dhaṛā*). A ridge or bank of earth, high land, crest of a hill.

دړي *daṛa-ī*, s.f. A dry measure equal to four *ser* or eight pounds. **H.** (*dhaṛī*). A frontlet, ornament worn on the forehead by women. *daṛai*, s.m. A shelf, cupboard.

دزد *duzd*, s.m. A robber, thief. **P.**

دست *dast*, s.m. Purge, stool. Cubit, hand. **P.**

دستار *dastār*, s.m. A turban. **P.**

دستک *dastak*, s.m. Account book; passport, pass; summons, warrant. **P.**

دستکي *dastakai*, s.m. A small rafter placed over the large beams in a roof.

دستګله *dastgala*, s.f. A glove, mitten; gauntlet.

دستمايه *dastmāya*, s.f. The handle strap of a shield.

دستمبول *dastambol*, s.m. A musk melon.

دستور *dastūr*, s.m. Custom, fashion, usage; mode, manner, regulation. A clyster, enema. P.

دسته *dasta*, s.f. A handle; pestle; quire of paper; nosegay; bundle of 24 arrows; a bundle, handful; skein of thread or silk; division, brigade, etc. of an army. P.

دستي *dastī*, a. Manual, of the hand. ad. Quickly, immediately, sharply.

دسخط *dask͟hat*, s.m. Signature. P. (*dast-k͟hatt*).

دښت *dakkht*, s.m. Desert, wild, waste. P. (*dasht*).

دښمن *dukkhman*, s.m. An enemy, foe. P. (*dushman*).

دښمني *dukkhmanī*, } s.f. Enmity, hostility,
دښني *dukkhnī*, } hatred.

دعا *du'ā*, s.f. Benediction, blessing; prayer; imprecation, invocation. A.

دعوت *da'wat*, s.m. Convocation, invitation; entertainment, feast. A.

دعوه *da'wa*, s.f. Claim, plaint; accusation, action at law. A.

دغا *dag͟hā*, s.f. Deceit, imposture, treachery. P.

دغدغه *dag͟hdag͟ha*, s.f. Alarm, call to arms; tumult. A.

دغمه *dag͟hma*, s.f. A welt, weal, mark of a stripe.

دغه *dag͟hah*, pr. The proximate demonstrative pronoun: this, these. A. (*dik͟hah* or *dak*).

دف *daf*, s.m. A tambourine. P.

دفتر *daftar*, s.m. Record, register, roll; archives; a book; land, estate, registered share of land. P.

دفعه *daf'a*, s.f. Averting, repelling; time, turn; moment. A. (*dafa'*).

دفن *dafan*, s.m. Burial; funeral. A.

دق *diqq*, s.m. Trouble, vexation; hectic fever. A.

دقيقه *daqīqa*, s.f. A minute, moment; anything minute or subtle; a trifle, unimportant matter. A.

دل *dal*, s.m. Bruised or coarsely ground grain, grits. S. (*daliyā*). *dil*, s.m. The heart, soul; courage. P.

دلازاك *dalāzāk*, s.m. Name of a tribe who formerly held the Peshawar valley, whence they were ejected by the Afghans

دلال *dallāl*, s.m. A broker, agent, salesman; a pimp, go-between; horse dealer. A.

دلاور *dilāwar*, a. Brave, gallant, courageous. P.

دلاوري *dilāwarī*, s.f. Bravery, courage. P.

دلبار *dalbār*, s.m. See دربار.

دلبه *dalba*, s.f. A lure for hawks. A. (*talaba*).

دلته *dalta*, ad. Here, hither. P. (*dar īn jā*).

دلدل *daldal*, s.m. A quagmire, quicksand. H.

دلوه *dalwa*, s.f. A bucket, water-pail. A.

دلي *dala-ī*, s.f. A corn stack or rick. *dale*, ad. See دلته.

دليل *dalīl*, s.m. Demonstration, proof; director, guide. A.

دم *dam*, s.m. Breath, life; ambition, pride; moment, minute; edge of a sword; stewing over a slow fire. P. *dum*, s.m. Tail, end, extremity. P.

دماغ *dimāg͟h*, s.m. The brain. A.

دمامه *damāma*, s.f. A kettledrum. P.

دمبال *dumbāl*, ad. After, behind, in rear. P.

دمباله *dumbāla*, s.f. A rear guard. P.

دمچي *dumchī*, s.f. A crupper. P.

دمدمه *damdama*, s.f. A mound, bastion, redoubt. A.

دمړي *damṛa-ī*, s.f. The eighth part of a paisa. H.

دمه *dama*, s.f. Breath, respiration; rest, repose, ease; asthma; a pair of bellows. P.

دنبل *dunbal*, s.m. A boil, bubo. P.

دنبه *dunba*, }
دمبه *dumba*, } s.f. The fat-tailed sheep. P.

دند *dund*, s.m. Haze, mist, smoke; obscurity, darkness, gloom. H. (*dhundh*).

دندارو *dandārū*, s.m. A boil, carbuncle.

دندانه *dandāna*, s.f. Tooth of a saw or comb; a cascade, waterfall. P.

دندوکار *dandūkār*, s.m. Noise of thunder, roar of artillery, tumult; haze, smoke, etc.

دنکاچه *dunkācha*, s.f. See دوکانچه.

دنګ *dang*, a. Tall, high (in stature). s.m. A tall man; a jump, leap, vault, bound.

دنګل *dangal*, v.a. To jump, leap, bound.

دنګول *dangawul*, v.a. To make jump, leap, etc. (as a horse over a fence); to throw one off a wall, horse, etc.

دننه *danana*, p. In, within, inside. P. (*andarūn*).

دنیا *duniyā*, s.f. The world; people; wealth. A.

دوَ *dwa* or *do*, a. Two (in comp.). P. *daw*, s.m. See داو. *dau*, s.m. A run, race. *dau·kawul*, v.a. To run. P. (*daw*).

دوا *dawā*, s.f. Medicine, remedy; amulet, charm. A.

دوات *dawāt*, s.m. An inkstand. A.

دواړه *dwāṛah*, a. Both. Corr. of *dwah·wāṛah*.

دوبي *dūbai*, s.m. Summer, hot weather. *dobī*, s.m. A dyer, washerman. H. (*dhobī*).

دوپ *dūp*, s.m. Sunshine, glare, haze. S. (*dhūp*).

دوتر *dawtar*, s.m. Estate, hereditary, possession in land, fief. P. (*daftar*).

دود *dod*, s.m. Custom, fashion, way; dowry, property given with a bride; entertainment of a guest. a. Similar, like. ad. Likewise, similarly. *dūd*, s.m. Vapour, smoke. P.

دور *dūr*, a. Far, distant, remote. P. *daur*, s.m. Revolution, circular motion; age, cycle, period; time, turn. A.

دوران *daurān*, s.m. Time, age, cycle; vicissitude, fortune; turn, period, revolution. A.

دورمه *dūrma*, s.f. See دروي. H. (*durmā*). Pens for writing the oriental character, made from the reed stalk.

دوړه *dūṛa*, s.f. Dust, dry earth. S. (*dhūr*).

دوزخ *dozakh*, s.m. Hell. P.

دوزخي *dozakhī*, a. Infernal, hellish.

دوزه *dūza*, s.f. Bosh, folly, nonsense.

دوزي *dūzai*, s.m. A blockhead, booby, fool, simpleton, twaddler.

دوست *dost*, s.m. A friend; lover. P.

دوسه *dūsa*, s.f. A rush, forcible entry. H. (*dhasā*). *dusa·kawul*, v.a. To invade, rush into, force through, etc.

دوش *dosh*, s.m. The shoulder, back. ad. Last night. P.

دوشاله *doshāla*, s.f. A mantle or plaid made of two breadths of cloth sewn together. P.

دوشخانه *doshkhāna*, s.f. A vessel in which skins are placed preparatory to tanning. P.

دوشرل *dosharal*, s.m. A two-year-old goat, etc.

دوشنبه *doshanba*, s.f. Monday. P.

دوغ *dogh*, s.m. Butter-milk. P.

دوغښ *doghakkh*, s.m. See دوزخ.

دوک *dwak*, a. A two-year-old (colt, sheep, etc.). H. (*dok*). *dūk*, s.m. A bodkin, knitting pin; spindle. P.

دوکان *dūkān*, s.m. A shop, workshop. P.

دوکانچه *dūkāncha*, s.f. A platform, terrace; form, bench, settle (before a door or shop); seat or raised earth round a tree, etc.

دوکړه *dūkṛa*, s.f. A kind of kettledrum.

دوګانه *dogānah*, a. Double, twofold; a prayer with two genuflexions. P.

دولت *daulat*, s.m. Riches, wealth; fortune, property; empire, state; cause, effect, means. A.

دولتي *dolata-ī*, s.f. A kick with both hind legs.

دومي *dūmai*, s.m. } Cold, catarrh, influenza.
دومه *dūma*, s.f. }

دون *dūn*, a. Abject, base, ignoble, mean, vile. A.

دوند *dūnd*, s.m. See دند. H. (*dhundh*).

دونه *dūna*, s.f. A bonfire. H. (*dhūnī*).

دوني *dūne* or *dūnī*, ad. This much, to this extent.

دونړي *donṛa-ī* or *daunṛa-ī*, s.f. A milk pail. H. (*dohnī*).

دوه *dwah*, a. Two.

دوهي *dūha-ī*, s.f. Fireplace, chimney. H. (*dūhiyā*).

دوي *doe*, s.m. Custom, fashion, usage. *dwī*, pr. plural of دي *dai*, or *de*, This.

ده *dah*, pr. This. See دي. *dih*, s.m. A village. P. *dah*, in. A word used to drive or urge a horse.

دهات *dihāt*, s.m. The country. P.

دهان *dahān*, s.m. The mouth; orifice, aperture. P.

دهانه *dahāna*, s.f. Bridle bit, mouthpiece. P.

دهځ *dahadz*, s.m. Dowry, marriage portion, the property the wife carries with her to her husband. A. (*dahez*).

دهړه *dahṛa*, s.f. A jaw tooth, grinder, tusk.

دهشت *dahshat*, s.m. Alarm, fear, dread, terror. A.

دهقان *dihqān*, s.m. Peasant, villager; ploughman, farm servant. P.

دهليدل *dahaledal*, v.n. To fear, quake, tremble. H. (*dahalnā*).

دهمرده *dahmardah*, a. Bold, brave, strong. *dahmarda*, s.f. A lever.

دهور *dahor*, s.m. A weaver.

دهوس *dahūs*, s.m. Cuckold, term of abuse. A. (*daiyūs*).

دهه *daha*, s.f. The first ten days of Muḥarram; models of the tombs of Hasan and Husen carried about in procession during that time. P. (*dahā*).

دي *dai* or *de*, pr. This. Also written ده *dah*, دَ *da*, and دِ *di*. A. (*de* or *dī*).

ديار *diyār*, s.m. The cedar tree (*Cedrus deodara*).

ديارلس *diyārlas*, a. Thirteen.

ديانت *diyānat*, s.m. Honesty, probity; piety, virtue. A.

ديبا *debā*, s.f. Brocade. P.

ديباجه *debāja*, } s.f. Exordium, introduction, preface. A.
ديباچه *dībācha*, }

ديت *diyat*, s.m. Law of retaliation; price of blood, fine paid for murder, wounding, etc. A.

ديچکه *dechka*, s.f. A cauldron, stewpan, cooking pot. P. (*degcha*).

ديد *dīd*, s.m. Sight, show, spectacle. P.

ديدار *dīdār*, } s.m. Interview, sight, seeing. P.
ديدن *dīdan*, }

ديده *dīdah*, a. Seen, observed. *dīda*, s.f. The eye. P.

ديرش *dersh*, a. Thirty.

ديره *dera*, s.f. A dwelling, tent. H. (*derā*).

ديګ *deg*, s.m. A cauldron, boiler. P.

ديګچه *degcha*, s.f. Stewpan, saucepan. P.

دين *dīn*, s.m. Religion, faith. A.

دينار *dīnār*, s.m. Name of a coin, a ducat. The tenth part of a pice. A.

ديني *dīnī*, a. Religious; spiritual. A.

ديو *deo*, s.m. A demon, devil. P.

ديوال *dīwāl*, s.m. A wall. P. (*dīwār*).

ديوان *dīwān*, s.m. Divan, tribunal; steward, custodian; a book of poems, the rhymes of which end successively with every letter of the alphabet. P.

ديوانه *dīwānah*, a. Mad. See ليوني.

د

د *ḍāl* or *ḍe* is the fourteenth letter of the Pukkhto alphabet. It is similar in sound to the Sanskrit ड, and corresponds to the ڈ *ḍa* of the Hindūstānī.

داد *ḍād*, s.m. Comfort, consolation.

داده *ḍāḍa*, s.f. An unripe ear of corn; the ear of Indian corn roasted for food.

دار *ḍār*, s.m. Anxiety, fear; fright, terror. H. (*ḍar*).

داره *ḍāra*, s.f. Arbour, shed, hut of branches, etc.

داګ *ḍāg*, s.m. } داګه *ḍāga*, s.f. } Clear, dry and level ground; a patch of hard and bare ground.

دال *ḍāl*, s.m. A shield, buckler. H. (*ḍhāl*).

داندت *ḍānḍat*, s.m. A cotton carder's bow.

داندي *ḍānḍa-ī*, s.f. The beam of a balance; a pair of scales. H. (*ḍanḍī*). A blaze, conflagration.

دانګ *ḍāng*, s.m. A club, bludgeon, stick. H. Name of a copper coin, a penny.

دانګ لکي *ḍāng-laka-ī*, s.f. See توره آنه.

دانګوري *ḍāngora-ī*, s.f. A small club, baton.

دانګي *ḍānga-ī*, s.f. See تانګو.

دب *ḍab*, s.m. A slap, blow, thump. H. (*dhap*). An eddy, whirlpool; backwater, still water. Power, authority, strength. H. Fashion, shape; breeding, manners; mode, way. H. (*ḍhab*).

دبدبني *ḍabḍabanai*, a. Anxious, irresolute, wavering.

دبدوب *ḍabḍūb*, a. Apathetic, paralyzed, senseless.

دبره *ḍabara*, s.f. A pebble, stone, boulder.

دبلي *ḍabala-ī*, s.f. A mallet, pestle.

دبول *ḍabawul*, v.a. To beat, thrash, pommel.

دتي *ḍaṭai*, s.m. A brag, boaster, bully; term of abuse.

دچکه *ḍachka*, s.f. A trot; amble; jolt.

دد *ḍaḍ*, a. Empty, vacant, void; deep, bass, hoarse (sound).

ددوزه *ḍaḍūza*, s.f. Haze, smoke; flame and smoke.

دده *ḍaḍa*, s.f. The flank, side; edge, border; direction.

دران *ḍarān*, s.m. A bellow, low, bray (as of ox, ass, etc.).

درپل *ḍirpal*, s.m. A flatterer, parasite, toady.

درپلي *ḍirpalī*, s.f. Flattery, toadyism.

دره *ḍara*, s.f. Chip, splinter, fragment, shred, bit.

دز *ḍaz*, s.m. Bang, burst, explosion, report. A braggart, bully, blusterer.

دزدوز *ḍaz-ḍūz*, s.m. Report of firearms; a skirmish.

دغره *ḍaghara*, } دقره *ḍaqara*, } s.f. Butting, shoving, pushing; a butt, shove, push. H. (*ṭakkar*).

دک *ḍak*, a. Full, replete.

دکال *ḍukāl*, s.m. Dearth, famine, scarcity. H.

دکه *ḍaka*, s.f. A thrust, jolt, shove, push. H. (*dhakkā*). A clutch, grab, pounce, swoop. a. Pregnant, with young; full.

دکي *ḍakai* or *ḍikai*, s.m. A sapling, young tree; a dry stump or stalk; a twig, switch, stick, dry bush.

دګلاند *ḍuglānd*, s.m. Amble, jog, trot; ambling horse.

دګه *ḍaga*, s.f. The penis.

دګي *ḍagai*, s.m. A thin, lean, bony ox or horse, a rosinante. H. (*ḍaggā*).

دل *ḍal*, s.m. A kind of rake; cantonment, camp.

دله *ḍala*, s.f. Assembly, crowd, mob. S. (*ḍal*).

دم *ḍum*, s.m. Name of a tribe or caste of musicians and dancers. H. (*ḍom*).

دمامه *ḍamāma*, s.m. A drum; drumming. *ḍamāme-wahal*, v.a. To drum.

دمدوم *ḍamḍūm*, s.m. Rattle, roll, sound of a drum.

دنبره *ḍanbara*, s.f. Hornet, wasp. Name of a tree with thorny stems and dotted leaves; the black berries are used as pepper, and sticks are made from the branches.

دند *ḍanḍ*, s.m. A pool, pond, tank.

دنداره *ḍanḍāra*, s.f. A hornet, wasp; a stem, stalk, sprout (of herbs); stalk of leaves.

دندوكي *ḍanḍūkai*, s.m. A puddle, pool, tank.

دنگ *ḍang*, s.m. Melody, tune, modulation. H.

دنگر *ḍangar*, a. Thin, lean, scraggy. s.m. Cattle; a bullock, buffalo. H. (*ḍangar*).

دنگړي *ḍingara-ī*, دنگلي *ḍingala-ī*, s.f. A machine for drawing water from wells (by means of a lever pole, which is supported on a post, and has a bucket slung at one end and a weight fixed at the other). H. (*ḍhenklī*).

دو *ḍaw*, s.m. Flatus, emission of wind from behind.

دوب *ḍūb*, a. Drowned, immersed, sunk. H.

دوډه *ḍūḍa* or *ḍiwḍa*, s.f. The hip, haunch; hip joint.

دوډي *ḍoḍa-ī*, s.f. Bread; food. S. (*roṭī*).

دور *ḍūr*, s.m. Knitting. *ḍūr-kawul*, v.a. To knit. H. (*ḍor*).

دوزك *ḍūzak*, s.m. A brag, bully.

دوزه *ḍūza*, s.f. Chatter, prattle, nonsense; boasting, bragging, bluster, swagger.

دوغ *ḍūgh*, s.m. Expectoration, hawking, clearing the throat of phlegm.

دوغل *ḍoghal*, s.m. A cavity, hole, pit.

دول *ḍaul*, s.m. Manner, mode; dress, fashion. H. *ḍol*, s.m. A large drum; the cog-wheel of a Persian irrigation wheel; hopper, rim of a hand- or other mill. H. (*ḍhol*).

دولكي *ḍolkai*, s.m. A small drum.

دوله *ḍola*, s.f. A small bowl or basin; a cup, jar.

دولي *ḍola-ī*, s.f. A sedan chair or litter (carried by two men). H.

دومبك *ḍūmbak*, s.m. The rattle or roll of a drum.

دومبكي *ḍūmbakai*, s.m. A kettledrum, tambourine, gong, small drum.

ديډه *ḍīḍa*, s.f. A bung, plug, stopper; the piece of wood let into the hole of the lower stone of a handmill (to hold the iron pivot on which the upper one turns). *ḍeḍa*, s.f. A kind of ear-ring. H.

دير *ḍer*, a. Abundant, plenty, enough; many, much. H. (*ḍher*). *ḍer-wālai*, s.m. Abundance, plenty.

ديران *ḍerān*, s.m. A dunghill; a cloth worn by women during the menses.

ديره *ḍera*, s.f. A camp, tent, temporary lodging. H. (*ḍerā*).

ديري *ḍera-ī*, s.f. A hillock, mound, heap, pile. H. (*ḍherī*). *ḍerai*, s.m. A crowd, mob, multitude.

ديل *ḍīl*, s.m. Dress, mode, fashion; form, manner, shape; body, bulk, size. H. *ḍīl-ḍaul*, s.m. Appearance, dress, costume, fashion.

دينگ *ḍīng*, s.m. A crane, stork (*Ardea sp.*).

دينگ دينگي *ḍīng-ḍīngai*, s.m. Ding-dong, lullaby, song, chime, nursery rhyme.

ديوالي *ḍiwālai*, s.m. A bankrupt. H. (*ḍewāliyā*).

ديوټ *ḍiwaṭ*, s.m. A candlestick, lampstand. S.

ديود *ḍiwad*, s.m. A kind of perfumed candle used at weddings; a lamp-stand.

ديوه *ḍīwa*, s.f. A lamp. S. (*dīwā*).

ذ

ذ *zāl* is the fifteenth letter of the Pukkhto alphabet, and the ninth of the Arabic. It is only found in words adopted from the latter language.

ذات *ẕāt*, s.m. Essence, nature, soul; body, person, substance; breed, caste, race. A.

ذبحه *ẕabḥa*, s.f. Sacrifice, slaughter. A.

ذخيره *ẕakhīra*, s.f. Store, treasure; provisions, victuals. A.

ذره *ẕarra*, s.f. An atom, bit, jot, particle, little. A.

ذکر *ẕakar*, s.m. Membrum virile. A. *ẕikr*, s.m. Memory, recital, mention, relation. A.

ذلت *ẕillat*, s.m. Baseness, vileness, meanness. A.

ذليل *ẕalīl*, a. Abject, base, mean. A.

ذم *ẕam*, s.m. Blame, reproach. A.

ذمه *ẕimma*, s.f. Charge, trust; duty, responsibility, obligation. A.

ذوق *ẕauq*, s.m. Taste; delight, joy, pleasure. A.

ذهن *ẕihn*, s.m. Acumen, mind, sagacity, genius. A.

ذهين *ẕahīn*, a. Acute, sagacious, witty. A.

ر

ر *re* is the sixteenth letter of the Pukkhto alphabet; it has a soft, but clear and distinct, sound as the *r* in the word *rain*.

را *rā*, A particle used with verbs and adverbs as a pronominal dative prefix for the first person: me, us, to me, to us. Ex. *rākawul*, to give me; *rātsakha*, with me, etc.

راب *rāb*, s.m. Syrup. H.

رابري *rābrī*, s.f. Caudle, gruel, pap. H.

رابطه *rābiṭa*, s.f. Bond, connection, link. A.

رابيا *rābiyā*, s.f. A pair of leather sacks or bags for carrying water upon bullocks, camels, etc.

راپورِ *rāpori*, راپوري *rāpore*, } ad. On this side, here, hitherward, near me, us, etc.; up to me, or us.

راتګ *rātag*, s.m. Arrival, coming.

راتلل *rātlal*, v.n. To arrive, come. See راغلل.

راج *rāj*, s.m. Government, kingdom, reign, sway. S. A mason, builder, bricklayer. H.

راجا *rājā*, s.m. A title of Hindu potentates; king, prince, duke. S.

راحت *rāḥat*, s.m. Ease, quiet, repose, tranquility. A.

راړه *rāṛa*, s.f. See بروړه.

راز *rāz*, s.m. A secret, mystery. A.

رازدار *rāz-dār*, a. Trusty, faithful. s.m. A confidant.

رازق *rāziq*, s.m. The Deity; provider of daily wants. A.

راس *rās*, s.m. A bridle, leading-string, reins. H. Head; head of cattle. A.

راست *rāst*, a. Right, just, true; straight, level; right, right hand. P.

راستي *rāstī*, s.f. Fidelity, justice, loyalty. ad. Truly, indeed, really. P.

راشبيل *rāshbel*, s.m. A wooden shovel (used to winnow corn).

راشتلي *rāshtalai*, s.m. Refuse grain left on the ground after removal of the corn from the threshing floor.

راشکي *rāshakai*, s.m. A heap, lump, small mound.

راشه *rāsha*, s.f. A heap of grain, provisions, supplies; eminence, hillock, mound. *rāsha-darsha*, s.f. Visiting, acquaintance, intercourse.

راښکو *rākkhko*, s.m. A wire drawer; puller, drawer, strainer.

راضي *rāẓī*, a. Agreed, content, willing, satisfied. A.

راغ *rāgh*, s.m. A meadow, lawn; villa, summer-house; hill-side, declivity. P.

راغلل *rāghlal*, v.n. To arrive, come. (Not used in infin.) See راتلل.

راغه *rāghah*, s.m. Mountain skirt, hill-side.

رافضي, *rāfizī*, s.m. A heretic. A.

راقي, *rāqī*, s.f. Cornelian, red agate.

راکس, *rākis*, s.m. The centre one of a bevy of oxen treading out corn. *rākas*, s.m. Demon, devil. S.

راکول, *rākawul*, v.a. To give me, or us.

راګ, *rāg*, s.m. Music, song, tune. S.

رامزدګي, *rāmzadagī*, s.f. A crowbar, lever; roller.

راموسي, *rāmūsai*, s.m. The musk deer.

رانجونوني, *rānjūnūnai*, s.m. A box or case for rānjah.

رانجه, *rānjah*, s.m. Powdered antimony (applied to the edges of the eyelids as an ornament, and as a protection from excessive glare), collyrium.

رانده, *rāndah*, a. Driven out, rejected, expelled. P.

رانيول, *rānīwul*, v.a. To capture, seize, take.

راوړل, *rāwṛal*, v.a. To bear, bring, carry, fetch, etc. (only applied to inanimate objects). To bear, produce, bring forth, yield (as young fruit, etc.). P. (*āwurdan*).

راوستل, *rāwustal*, v.a. To lead, conduct, bring, fetch, etc. (only applied to animate objects). P. (*firistādan*).

راه, *rāh*, s.m. Road, way; manner (in comp.). P.

راهبټ, *rāhīt*, s.m. Head man of a village.

راهيسته, *rāhīsta*, ad. Here, hither, this way, near me, etc.

راي, *rāe*. s.m. Opinion, thought; counsel. P.

رب, *rabb*, s.m. The Deity. A. *rub*, s.m. Juice, syrup. P.

ربا, *ribā*, s.f. Usury. A. *ribā-khor*, s.m. An usurer.

رباب, *rabāb*, s.m. A rebeck, violin. P.

رباط, *rabāṭ*, s.m. Hostelry, inn, caravansary. A.

ربړ, *rabaṛ*, s.m. Bother, trouble, toil, labour. H.

ربړول, *rabṛawul*, v.a. To bother, worry, fatigue, drive about.

ربړيدل, *rabṛedal*, v.n. To labour, toil, trudge about, fatigue oneself, etc.

ربنړه, *rabanṛa*, s.f. Moonlight.

رپ, *rap*, s.m. A shelf, cupboard P. (*raf*).

رپک, *rapak*, s.m. A small shelf, bracket.

رپيدل, *rapedal*, v.n. To flutter, palpitate, quake, quiver, tremble, writhe, etc.

رت, *rat*, A particle used with adjectives to denote intensity (mostly of colour). Ex. *rat-tor*, a. Jet black. *rat-shin*, a. Bright green.

رتي, *rata-ī*, s.f. Name of a seed used as a weight (*Abrus precatorius*). S. (*rattī*).

رټ, *ra-aṭ*, s.m. A gush of tears, violent crying. a. Ample, capacious; loose, open, expanded.

رټل, *raṭal*, v.a. To reject, turn away, repel (as a visitor). To abuse, scold, taunt, reprove. H. (*raṭnā*).

رجرومه, *rajṛūma*, s.f. A collyrium box, case for powdered antimony. See رانجه.

رجوع, *rujū'*, s.f. Turning towards, return; bent, bias. A.

رچ, *rach*, s.m. A weaver's loom. H. (*rāchh*). *ruch*, s.m. Avidity, desire, pleasure (in eating). S. An ox that wounds itself by crossing the feet in walking.

رحلت, *rihlat*, s.m. Departure; death. A.

رحم, *rahm*, s.m. Compassion, kindness, mercy, pity. A. *riham*, s.m. The womb. A.

رحمان, *rahmān*, s.m. The Deity. a. Merciful. A.

رحمت, *rahmat*, s.m. Compassion, mercy, pity. A.

رخت, *rakht*, s.m. Apparel, furniture, goods, implements; a plough; tanned leather. P.

رخسار, *rukhsār*, s.m. The cheek, face. P.

رخصت, *rukhsat*, s.m. Discharge, leave, permission. A.

رخنه, *rakhna*, s.f. A cleft, fissure; hole, notch, fracture, flaw. P. See مخره.

رخه, *rakha*, s.f. Hatred, malice, spite.

رد *radd*, s.m. Refutation, rejection; rejoinder. A.

ردة *radda*, s.f. A layer, series, row; layer of bricks in a wall; work of a day (mason's). H. (*raddā*).

رديف *radīf*, s.m. Following in regular succession (as the letters of the alphabet), the rhyming word of a poem, a man riding behind another on the same horse, etc. A.

رړ *raḍ*, a. Ajar, open, wide open; amazed, confounded, petrified, stunned.

رړۍ *raṛa-ī*, s.f. Seed of a tree (*Melia sempervirens*).

رز *raz*, s.m. A vineyard. P.

رزق *rizq*, s.m. See روزي.

رژيدل *rażedal*, v.n. To cast off, moult, shed (as hair, horns, feathers, leaves, etc.); to be dispersed, shed, dropped, scattered. P. (*rekhtan, rez-*).

رس *ras*, s.m. Extract, juice, sap. S. Arriving (in comp. only). P.

رساله *risāla*, s.f. Mission; book; essay, letter; troop of horse. A.

رساليندي *rasālīndai*, s.m. An archer, bowman.

رسد *rasad*, s.m. Grain, provision, stores; supplies collected for an army. P.

رسم *rasam*, s.m. Custom, law; model, plan. A.

رسوا *ruswā*, a. Disgraced, dishonoured. P.

رسواي *ruswā-ī*, s.f. Ignominy, disgrace, dishonour.

رسول *rasūl*, s.m. A messenger, apostle; the prophet Muḥammad. A. *rasawul*, v.a. To send to, to convey to, conduct or lead to, etc.; make arrive. P. (*rasāndan*).

رسولي *rasawla-ī*, s.f. Bunion, corn, gall, wen; a cancer, diseased gland.

رسي *rasa-ī*, s.f. A cord, rope, string. S. (*rassī*).

رسيد *rasīd*, s.m. Arrival; acknowledgment, receipt. P.

رسيدل *rasedal*, v.n. To arrive, attain, reach, come up to, etc. P. (*rasīdan*).

رشته *rishta*, s.f. Line, series; connexion, relation. *rishta-dār*, s.m. Relation, kinsman. P.

رشک *rashk*, s.m. Envy, jealousy; malice, spite. P.

رشکي *rashakai*, s.m. A small mound, tumulus; heap, pile.

رشوت *rishwat*, s.m. A bribe. A.

رښتيا *rikkhtiyā*, a. True. s.f. Truth, veracity, reality. P. (*rāstī*).

رښتينتوب *rikkhtīn-tob*, s.m. Truthfulness, honesty, probity, righteousness.

رښتيني *rikkhtīnai*, | رښتوني *rikkhtūnai*, a. True, truthful, veracious; honest, upright, righteous.

رښکي *rikkhka-ī*, s.f. A band, fillet, ribbon, shred, slip, strip, fibre. P. (*resha*).

رضا *raẓā*, s.f. Assent, consent; pleasure, will. A.

رطوبت *ruṭūbat*, s.m. Humidity, wetness. A.

رعايت *ri'āyat*, s.m. Attention, favour; protection, kindness; indulgence, remission; honour, respect. A.

رعيت *ra'yat*, s.m. A subject, tenant. A.

رغبت *raghbat*, s.m. Avidity, desire, wish; pleasure; affection, esteem. A.

رغړول *rgharawul*, v.a. To trundle, roll (as a hoop, etc.). P. (*ghaltānīdan*).

رغړيدل *rgharedal*, v.n. To roll, wallow, tumble, toss (as an animal on the ground); to roll, trundle (as a stone down a slope). Def. in past ten. P. (*ghaltīdan*).

رغښتل *rghakkhtal*, v.n. See preceding word.

رغي *raghai*, s.m. A bowl, deep plate (as a soup plate); a deep and flat basket (in opposition to a shallow one).

رفتار *raftār*, s.m. Going, motion; gait, pace. P.

رفعه *raf'a*, s.f. Removing, repelling. A. *raf'a-daf'a*, s.f. Deciding, settling, finishing. A.

رفو, *rafū*, s.m. Darning, mending clothes; a darn. A.

رفيق, *rafīq*, s.m. Associate, comrade, friend. A.

رقص, *raqṣ*, s.m. A dance, dancing. A.

رقعه, *ruq'a*, s.f. A letter, note; bit, patch, piece. A.

رقم, *raqam*, s.m. A royal edict; kind, sort; mode, method; mark, sign. A.

رقيب, *raqīb*, s.m. Rival, enemy. A.

ركاب, *rikāb*, s.m. Stirrup; escort, train. A. A platter, salver, tray. P.

ركابي, *rikābī*, s.f. A plate, dish. P.

ركات, *rakāt*, s.m. A genuflexion, prostration (in prayer). A. (*rak'at*).

ركښ, *rakkkh*, s.m. Furrow, groove (as of a rifle); line, rut, track, scratch. P. (*rakh*).

ركن, *rukn*, s.m. A pillar, prop, support. A.

ركوع, *rukū'*, s.f. Bowing the head or body (in prayer). A.

ركيب, *rikeb*, s.m. A stirrup iron. P. (*rakīb*).

ركيبي, *rikebī*, s.f. See ركابي.

رګ, *rag*, s.m. A vein; tendon; nerve. P. *rag-wahal*, v.a. To inoculate; to bleed, let blood.

رګړي, *rigaṛai*, a. A child stinted in milk.

رګي, *ragai*, s.m. Consanguinity, blood relation; congenital or hereditary trait.

رمباړه, *rambāṛa*, s.f. A bellow, low (as of oxen).

رمبكي, *rambakai*, s.m. The bellow of a bull.

رمبه, *ramba*, s.f. A borer, centre-bit, auger. H. (*barmā*).

رمبي, *rambai*, s.m. A hoe, instrument for weeding; a cobbler's knife for cutting leather. H. (*ramba*).

رمز, *ramz*, s.m. A hint, nod, sign, wink. A.

رموز, *ramūz*, s.m. Enigma, riddle. A.

رمول, *ramawul*, v.a. To frighten, scare, terrify; to conduct or lead cattle (out to graze). H. (*ramnā*).

رمه, *ra-ama*, s.f. Mucus; muco-purulent matter from the bowels; any mucous discharge; dysentery. Also *r-ima*, and mostly used in the plural as *ra-ame* or *r-ime*. P. (*rim*). *ramma*, s.f. A herd, drove, or flock (of cattle, sheep, etc.). P.

رمي, *ra-amai* or *r-imai*, s.m. Dysentery, bowel complaint.

رميدل, *ramedal*, v.n. To be alarmed, terrified; to flock, herd together. P. (*ramīdan*).

رنځ, *randz*, s.m. Affliction, grief, pain; disgust, offence, vexation. P. (*ranj*).

رنځړه, *randzaṛah*, s.m. Pitch, tar; crude turpentine.

رنځور, *randzūr*, a. Afflicted, sick, pained; distressed, grieved; offended, vexed. P. (*ranjūr*).

رنځول, *randzawul*, v.a. To afflict, pain, vex, etc.

رنځيدل, *randzedal*, v.n. To fret, grieve, be hurt, pained, distressed. P. (*ranjīdan*).

رنجك, *ranjak*, s.m. Priming powder. H.

رند, *rind*, s.m. Debauchee, blackguard, rake. P.

رندار, *rundār*, s.f. See ورندار.

رنده, *randa*, s.f. A plane; carpenter's tool. P.

رنګ, *rang*, s.m. Colour; paint; kind, sort; manner, method, way. P.

رنګټ, *rangaṭ*, s.m. Crying, blubbering, weeping. H. (*rohaṭ*).

رنګړ, *ringaṛ*, a. } Beaten down, laid low,
رنګړي, *ringaṛai*, } levelled (as crops by wind and rain).

رنګي, *rangai*, a. Scanty, thin (as hair, crops, rain, etc.).

رنګين, *rangīn*, a. Coloured, painted; variegated, etc. P.

رنړا, *ranṛā*, s.f. Light, daylight, brilliancy, lustre, etc.

رو, *ro*, a. Easy, slow, soft, quiet. *ro-ro*, ad. Gently, slowly. *rū*, s.m. Face, surface. P.

روا *ranā*, a. Allowable, lawful, right, current, proper, etc. P. *rnā*, s.f. See ورا.

رواج *rināj*, s.m. Custom, usage, fashion. a. Customary, current, fashionable, saleable. A.

رواش *ranāsh*, s.m. Rhubarb; blanched leaf-stalk of the plant. P.

روان *ranān*, a. Current, flowing, moving, going. P. *runān*, a. See وران.

روانه *ranānah*, a. Despatched, departed. P. *ranāna*, s.f. A pass, passport. P.

رواني *ranānī*, s.m. Course, proceeding. P. *runānī*, s.f. See ورانی.

روايت *rināyat*, s.m. Fable, fiction, tale; history. A.

روبرو *rūbarū*, ad. Face to face, in front, opposite. P.

روپئي *rūpa-ī*, s.f. Name of a silver coin, rupee. S. (*rupiyā*).

روځ *rnadz*, s.f. A day, day, daytime. P. (*roz*).

روح *rūḥ*, s.m. Soul, spirit. A.

روخ *rokh* or *rūkh*, a. Fit, proper, ready; side, direction. P. (*rukh*).

روخي *rokhai*, s.m. Part, side (as of opponents).

رود *rod*, s.m. A river, stream. P.

رودل *randal*, v.a. To suck (as a child the breast). To mow, reap, cut (as corn, etc.).

رودنګ *rodang*, s.m. Madder (*Rubia tinctoria*). P.

روز *roz*, s.m. Day, daytime (in comp.). P.

روزګار *rozgār*, s.m. Employment, service; time, world. P.

روزمره *rozmarra*, ad. Always, daily, continually. P.

روزي *rozī*, s.f. Daily food, sustenance. P.

روژتي *rojatai*, s.m. A faster, keeper of Lent.

روژه *roja*, s.f. Fast, Lent. P. (*roza*).

رېږد *rūgd*, a. Habituated, accustomed; affluent, comfortable. A. (*raghd*).

روست *rost*, a. Decayed, carious, corrupt, rotten; fetid, putrid, stinking. Also وروست.

روستو *rūsto* or *rnusto*, ad. See وروستو.

روښان *rokkhān*, a. Bright, light, luminous; clear, manifest, conspicuous; glittering; radiant, refulgent. P. (*roshān*).

روښن *rokkhan*, a. Bright, light, shining. P. (*roshan*).

روښنائي *rokkhnā-ī*, s.f. Brightness, light. P. (*roshnā-ī*).

روضه *rauẓa*, s.f. Mausoleum, tomb, garden. A.

روغ *rogh*, a. Hale, healthy, sound, vigorous, well.

روغبړ *roghbar*, s.m. Shaking hands, asking after health; embracing.

روغن *roghan*, s.m. Grease, fat, tallow. P.

روغه *rogha*, s.f. Amity, peace; harmony, intercourse, friendship.

روک *rok*, s.m. Cash, ready money. S.

روګ *rog*, s.m. A strap, thong of a sandal, strap of a churning stick, etc.

روګه *rnuga*, s.f. See ورږه.

رومال *rūmāl*, s.m. A handkerchief; towel, napkin. P.

رون *rūn*, s.m. The thigh. H. (*rān*).

رونق *raunaq*, s.m. Beauty, elegance; order, symmetry; ornament, splendour. A.

رونړ *rūnr*, a. Bright, lustrous, radiant, shining.

روه *roh*, s.m. Name of an extensive tract occupied by the Eastern highlands of Afghanistan, between Kandahar on the west and the Indus on the east, Badakhshan on the north and Sind on the south.

روهيلي *rohīlai*, s.m. A Rohilla, native of Roh, so called by the people of Hindūstān; a highlander.

روي *ranai* or *rinai*, s.m. A ghost, goblin, demon; nightmare. *rūe*, s.m. Face, countenance, surface; cause, reason, sake. P.

رويت *rūyat*, s.m. Appearance, shape, etc. A.

رؤيدل *rū-edal*, v.n. To cavil, dispute, wrangle.

رهته *rahata*, s.f. Content, ease, tranquility. A. (*rāhat*).

رهټ *rahaṭ*, s.m. A wheel for drawing water, an irrigation wheel. H.

رهيل *rahel*, s.m. Reading desk, support for a book. P. (*raḥl*).

ري *rai*, s.m. Price current, rate, tariff.

ريا *riyā*, s.f. Dissimulation, evasion, hypocrisy. A. *rayā*, s.f. Braying of an ass.

رياست *riyāsat*, s.m. Command, dominion. A.

رياضت *riyāẓat*, s.m. Temperance, continence. A.

رياكار *riyā·kār*, s.m. A hypocrite. A.

ريبار *rebār*, s.m. A go-between, match-maker (between lovers or betrothed couples).

ريباري *rebārī*, s.f. Match-making, etc.

ريبدون *rebdūn*, s.m. Name of a tree (*Tecoma undulata*).

ريبل *rebal*, v.a. To mow, reap, cut (as corn, etc.).

ريچه *rīcha*, s.f. Young louse, nit, egg of a louse; a particle, jot, tittle. *rīche·rīche*, p. Atoms, particles, bits, etc.

ريخ *rīkh*, s.m. Dung of birds; loose stool, watery excrement of man or animals (as in diarrhœa). P.

ريخان *rīkhān*, a. Loose in the bowels, affected with diarrhœa, purged.

ريخي *rīkhai*, s.m. Dysentery, diarrhœa (in cattle). Tear, rent, slit (in clothes); a hole in a reservoir to let out the water.

ريدوان *redwān*, s.m. See ريبدون.

ريدي *redai*, s.m. Wild poppy; ragged robin; wild tulip.

ريزه *reza*, s.f. A bit, chip, filing, scrap, shred, etc. P.

ريږدول *regdawul*, v.a. To agitate, shake, move, etc.

ريږديدل *regdedal*, v.n. To flutter, shake, quiver, vibrate.

رئيس *ra-īs*, s.m. A chief, prince, lord. A.

ريش *rīsh*, s.m. The beard (in comp.). P.

ريشل *reshal*, v.a. To spin, twist. P. (*resha*, fibre).

ريښم *rekkham*, s.m. Silk. P. (*resham*).

ريښمين *rekkhmīn*, a. Silken, silky. P. (*reshmīn*).

ريښه *rekkha*, s.f. A fibre, shred, thread, yarn, strip, etc. P. (*resha*).

ريګ *reg*, s.m. Sand (in comp.). P.

ريم *rīm*, s.m. Matter, pus, rheum; dregs, dross. P.

ريمن *rīman*, a. Purulent, mattery, filthy, etc.

رينه *rīna*, s.f. A cobbler's awl. Also *nīra*.

ريودل *riyawdal*, v.a. To raise, elevate, lift.

ريوړي *rewṛa-ī*, s.f. A kind of sweetmeat. H. (*rewṛī*).

ريوند *rewand*, a. Sloping, slanting.

ړ

ړ *ṛe* or *ṛa* is the seventeenth letter of the Pukkhto alphabet. It has the same sound as the Sanskrit ड़ *ṛa*, or the Hindūstānī ڑ *ṛa*, with which it corresponds.

ړپ *ṛap*, s.m. Mucus, slimy discharge from the bowels (as in dysentery).

ړپول *ṛapawul*, v.a. To agitate, shake.

ړپيدل *ṛapedal*, v.n. To palpitate, writhe, quiver, tremble, wag, wave, move, etc.

ړت *ṛat*, a. Red, reddish. S. (*rat*). *ṛat·ghwāye*, s.m. A red bull. *ṛata·gīra*, s.f. A red beard.

ړقول *ṛaqawul*, v.a. To mix, mingle, stir up; to jostle, shove, shake: punch, thump.

ړنبي *ṛunbai*, a. See ورنبي.

ړندول *ṛandawul*, v.a. To blind, deprive of sight.

ړنديدل *ṛandedal*, v.n. To grow blind, become blind.

ړنګ *ṛang*, a. Broken up, destroyed, spoiled, razed; desolate, ruined, deserted.

ړواندي *ṛwānde*, p. See وواندي.

ړوند *ṛūnd*, a. Blind, sightless; dark, obscure.

ړي *ṛī*, m. A word used in driving cattle. *ṛai*, m. and *ṛa-ī*, f. A particle affixed to nouns as a sign of diminution. Ex. *kḥas*, s.m. A dry stick or straw. *kḥasaṛai*, s.m. A straw, splinter (such as gets blown into the eye). *kūza*, s.f. A water jar or gugglet. *kūza-ṛa-ī*, s.f. A small gugglet.

ز

ز *ze* is the eighteenth letter of the Pukkhto alphabet, and eleventh of the Arabic. It has no corresponding letter in the Sanskrit. It is often used instead of the letters ځ and ج, and sometimes also for ژ and ږ.

زاد *zād*, s.m. Food, provisions. A. a. Born (in comp.). P.

زار *zār*, a. Afflicted, lamenting. s.m. Lament, groan, complaint. P. See ځار *dzār*.

زاري *zārī*, s.f. Crying, lamenting, groaning. P.

زاړي *zāṛai*, s.m. A weanling, young of cattle, etc. after being weaned. a. Late, former; old, worn out. *zāṛa-ī*, s.f. A woman, cow, etc. whose milk has run dry; an animal out of milk.

زامن *zāman*, s.m. pl. of ځوي *dzoe*.

زانګو *zāngo*, s.f. A cradle, rocking chair, swing; rocking, swinging.

زانو *zānū*, s.m. The knee. P.

زانړه *zānṛa*, s.f. A crane, the Coolan (*Ardea courlan*).

زاهد *zāhid*, s.m. Hermit, monk, recluse. a. Religious, devout. A.

زاي *zāe*, s.m. See ځوي *dzoe*.

زباد *zbād*, a. Proved, tested, tried, verified. A. (*iṡbāt*).

زبان *zabān*, s.m. Dialect, language, speech; tongue. P.

زبر *zabar*, a. Above, superior; the vowel mark َ *a*. A.

زبردست *zabar-dast*, a. Oppressive, powerful, violent. P.

زبرګ *zburg*, s.m. Ancestor, elder; saint. a. Venerable, saintlike, reverend; great, large. P. (*buzurg*).

زبرګي *zburgī*, s.f. Eminence, greatness, superiority, etc.

زبون *zabūn*, a. Bad, evil, wicked; faulty, unlucky. P.

زبيښل *zbekkhal*, v.a. To suck, inhale, imbibe; to crumble, squash with the fingers (as bread, etc.).

زحمت *zaḥmat*, s.m. Affliction, trouble, pain. A.

زخم *zakhm*, s. A cut, wound, injury, sore, pain. A.

زخمي *zakhmī*, a. Wounded, hurt, pained, injured.

زخه *zakha*, s.f. A wart; excrescence on the bark of a tree. P.

زخيره *zakhīra*, s.f. See ذخيره.

زد *zad*, s.m. A blow, striking (in comp.). P.

زدايت *zdāyat*, s.m. Descent, family, race.

زدويل *zdoyal*, v.a. To grate, pare, rub, wear away; polish, scour, etc. P. (*zidāyīdan*).

زده *zdah*, a. Acquired, known, learned; remembered, recognized. P. (*āzmūdah*). *zadah*, a. Struck, beaten (in comp.); decayed, withered (as wood, etc.). P.

زر *zar*, s.m. Gold, money, riches. P. *spīn-zar*, s.m. Silver. *srah-zar*, s.m. Gold, pure gold. a. A thousand. P. (*hazār*). *za-ar* or *z-ir*, ad. Quickly, speedily, sharply. P. (*zūd*).

زراعت *zarā'at*, s.m. Agriculture, husbandry; crops, cultivation. A.

زربرخ *zarbarakh*, s.m. Talc, mica. A. (*abraq*).

زربيانگ *zarbiyāng*, s.m. Name of a currier's tool; a wooden scraper or muller for cleaning leather.

زردالو *zardālū*, s.m. An apricot. P.

زردكه *zardaka*, s.f. A carrot; name of a bird, yellow-hammer. P. (*zardak*).

زرغاله *zarghāla*, s.f. A lying-in or puerperal woman; the forty days after childbirth, puerperal state.

زرغون *zarghūn*, a. Green, verdant; sprouted, grown, germinated, fresh, new.

زركه *zarka*, s.f. Red-legged partridge, chikor.

زرگر *zar-gar*, s.m. A goldsmith. P.

زرگير *zar-gīr*, s.m. A thumbstall of leather (worn by archers, etc.).

زرني *zaranai*, s.m. A spy, scout, detective. *zarana-ī*, s.f. Peeping, spying; scouting, watching.

زرنيخ *zarnīkh*, s.m. Orpiment. P.

زرنړه *zaranṛa*, s.f. Mud, slime, ooze (as at bottom of pools, etc.). *zaranṛah*, s.m. See رنځړه.

زري *zarai*, s.m. A spy, scout; the sight (at the muzzle) of a gun. *zarī*, a. Golden, worked or woven with gold. P. *zare-zare*, a. Shattered, broken to atoms, etc. See ذره.

زرين *zarīn*, a. Golden. P.

زروكي *zarūkai*, s.m. A dress, garment; apparel, clothes; old rags, old clothes, etc.

زړه *zṛah*, s.m. Heart, mind, soul; courage, spirit; the heart. P. (*zahra*).

زړي *zaṛai*, } زنړي *zanṛai*, } s.m. A flat seed (as of melons, etc.) in opposition to round ones (called tukhm).

زږگي *ziggai*, s.m. See شيشكي.

زښت *zikkht*, a. Ugly, deformed; stern, severe. P. (*zisht*).

زعفران *z'afarān*, s.m. Saffron. A.

زغ *zagh*, s.m. See ژغ.

زغاښتل *zghākkhtal*, v.n. To run, flee. Def. in pres. ten. See زغليدل.

زغرد *zghard*, a. Fast, quick. ad. Quickly, fleetly.

زغره *zghara*, s.f. Chain armour, mail. P. (*zira*).

زغلول *zghalawul*, v.a. To drive, put to flight, make run, urge (as a horse).

زغليدل *zghaledal*, v.n. To run, flee. See زغاښتل. P. (*gurekhtan*).

زغمل *zghamal*, v.a. To bear, endure, undergo, sustain, suffer.

زغن *zaghan*, s.m. A kite. P.

زقوم *zaqūm*, s.m. Name of a plant, Indian cactus; it is said to form the diet of those condemned to hell. A.

زك *zik*, s.m. An inflated hide for crossing over rivers.

زكات } زكاة } زكوت } *zakāt*, s.m. Alms distributed according to the rules laid down in the Qurān. A.

زكام *zukām*, s.m. Catarrh, influenza, cold. A.

زكه *zaka*, c. See څكه. P. (*zirā ki*).

زكي *zakī*, a. Pious, continent. A.

زگ *zag*, s.m. Foam, froth, scum. H. (*jhāg*).

زگيروي *zgerwai*, s.m. A groan, moan, wail, whine.

زلزله *zalzala*, s.f. An earthquake. A.

زلفه *zulfa*, s.f. A curl, ringlet, lock of hair. P. (*zulf*).

زلفي *zulfa-ī*, s.f. A sword knot, tassel; door chain, staple, hook. P.

زلل *zalal*, s.m. Injury, loss, deficiency; blundering, erring; falling, stumbling. P.

زلمي *zalmai*, s.m. A youth, young man. A. (*talmīz*).

زلو *zallū*, s.m. A leech. P.

زليچه *zalīcha*, s.f. A rug, woollen carpet. P. (*qālīcha*).

زم *zam*, s.m. Hurt, injury, wound. P. (*zakhm*). *zam-zmolai*, a. Halt, helpless, crippled, maimed. Also *zam-zambolai*.

زمانه *zamāna*, s.f. Age, time; fortune; the world; the heavens. A. *zamāna-sāz*, s.m. A time server. P.

زمبور *zambūr*, s.m. See امبور.

زمرّد *zumurrud*, s.m. An emerald. P.

زمري *zmarai*, s.m. A tiger. Name of a plant, dwarf palm (*Chamærops Richiana*).

زمزم *zamzam*, s.m. Hagar's well at Mecca. A.

زمزمه *zamzama*, s.f. A concert; singing. A.

زمستان *zamistān*, s.m. Winter. P.

زمکه *zmaka*, s.f. Land, ground, earth, soil; the earth.

زموخ *zmokh*, a. } زموخت *zmokht*, } Astringent, binding, dry, rough (to the taste). P. (*zamukht*).

زمول *zmol*, a. } زمبول *zambol*, } Helpless, crippled, maimed, wounded, unable to move from wounds.

زمولي *zmolai*, a. } زمبولي *zambolai*, } Carried by the hands and legs (as a wounded man). See زم. (For *zam-bīwulai*.)

زمي *zma-ī*, s.f. Name of a plant that is burnt for the potash it yields (*Suæda fruticosa*).

زمين *zamīn*, s.m. The earth; ground, soil, land. P.

زميندار *zamīn-dār*, s.m. A farmer; peasant. P.

زميداري *zamīn-dārī*, s.f. Agriculture; husbandry; an estate, farm.

زن *zan*, s.f. A woman, wife. P.

زنا *zinā*, s.m. Adultery, fornication. P.

زناکار *zinā-kār*, s.m. An adulterer, fornicator.

زنانه *zanāna*, s.f. A woman, female; wife; the women's apartments. a. Feminine. P.

زنبق *zanbaq*, s.m. The tuberose (*Polianthes tuberosa*). Flowers embroidered on a dress. P.

زنبک *zunbuk*, s.m. Tassel, knot, rosette, flower.

زنبه *zunba*, s.f. Down or hair on the body.

زنځير *zandzīr*, s.m. A chain. P. (*zanjīr*).

زندان *zindān*, s.m. A prison, jail. P.

زندګاني *zindagānī*, } زندګي *zindagī*, } s.f. Existence, life; living, livelihood. P.

زنده *zindah*, a. Alive, living. P.

زندي *zunda-ī*, s.f. A halter, hangman's rope.

زندي *zunḍai*, s.m. A tassel, pendent. H. (*jhunḍ*).

زنزه *zanza*, s.f. A centipede.

زنکي *zanka-ī*, s.f. Cummin seed.

زنګ *zang*, s.m. Mould, rust. P. (*zangār*). Cymbal, bell (for the feet of dancing women). Name of a country, Zanguebar.

زنګل *zangal*, v.n. To hang, swing, wave, sway, etc. s.m. A forest, wood; wilderness. S. (*jangal*).

زنګول *zangawul*, v.a. To rock, swing, wave, etc.

زنګوله *zangūla*, s.f. A small bell, cymbal. P.

زنګون *zangūn*, s.m. The knee. P. (*zānū*). *zangūnah-starga*, s.f. The knee cap, knee pan.

زنګي *zangī*, s.m. An African, negro. P.

زنګيدل *zangedal*, v.n. To hang, swing, wave, vibrate.

زنل *zanal*, v.a. To imbed, insert, implant; strike, thrust, hit; stab, prick, impale. P. (*zadan, zan-*).

زنه *zana*, s.f. The chin; pit of the chin. P. (*zanakh*).

زنړغوزه *zanṛghoza*, s.f. A pine cone, fir cone; pine tree; seed of the edible pine. P. (*chalghoza*).

زنړي *zanṛai*, s.m. A flat seed (as of melons, etc.). A boy under the age of puberty; a school-boy.

زوال *zawāl*, s.m. Decline, wane, setting. A.

زوانکه *zarānaka*, s.f. Acne, pimples on the face of youths.

زود *zūd*, ad. Quick, quickly. P.

زودي *zūdī*, s.f. Alacrity, haste, quickness.

زور *zor*, s.m. Force, power, strength: effort, violence, vigour; weight. P. *zaur*, s.m. Anxiety, grief, sorrow, pain, trouble. A. (*jaur*). *zwar*, s.m. The vowel-point zabar.

زوراور *zorāwar*, a. Powerful, violent, strong. P.

زورل *zoral*, v.a. To vex, irritate; compel, force, coerce; to digest.

زوړ *zor*, a. Aged, ancient, old, worn out. P. (*zāl*).

زوزات *zauzāt*, } s.m. Children, issue, progeny, offspring. P. (*zah-wa-zād*).
زوزاد *zauzād*, }

زوږ *zwag*, s.m. Clamour, din, noise, sound.

زوښه *zūkkha*, s.f. A syrup or jelly prepared from ber or jujube berries.

زوغال *zūghāl*, s.m. Charcoal. P. (*zughāl*).

زوَلن *zawlan* or *ziwlan*, a. Purulent, suppurating, mattery.

زوم *zūm*, s.m. A son-in-law. S. (*jamā-ī*). *zwam*, a. Deficient, less, little; deducted, subtracted. ad. Rarely, seldom.

زومکي *zūmgai*, s.m. A son-in-law. S. (*jamā-ī*).

زومنه *zwamna*, s.f. Deficiency, loss.

زوول *zowul*, v.a. To bear, bring forth (as young). P. (*zādan*).

زوولي *zowulai*, a. Born, brought forth.

زوه *ziwa* or *zawa*, s.f. Matter, pus, ichor.

زوي *zoe*, s.m. A son.

زويرکي *zweryai*, s.m. See زګيروي.

زه *zah*, pr. I, the first person.

زهر *zahar*, s.m. Poison. P.

زهره *zahra*, s.f. Bile; the gall bladder; courage, heart, pluck. P.

زهګير *zahgīr*, s.m. The catch or notch at the end of a bow (to hold the bow-string).

زهوب *zahūb*, s.m. Matter, discharge (of a sore), pus.

زهي *zahe*, in. Bravo! Well done! Lo! P.

زهيدل *zahedal*, v.n. To decrease, waste, grow thin.

زهير *zahīr*, a. Reduced, weakened, thin (from sickness); melancholy, sad. A.

زي *zai*, s.m. Son, child, descendant (in comp.). P. Added to Afghan surnames it denotes the clan or tribe. Ex. *Yūsufzai*, s.m. A man of clan Yusuf. *Yūsufza-ī*, s.f. A Yusufzai woman. *Yūsufzī*, s.m. pl. The Yusufzais.

زيات *ziyāt*, a. Excessive, surplus, too much; more. A. (*ziyād*).

زياتي *ziyātī*, a. Excessive, great, more. A. (*ziyādatī*).

زيارت *ziyārat*, s.m. A shrine; tomb of a saint; visiting a shrine. A.

زيان *ziyān*, s.m. Damage, deficiency, loss; miscarriage, abortion. P.

زيانکار *ziyān-kār*, } a. Injurious, pernicious, noxious. P.
زياني *ziyānī*, }

زيب *zeb*, s.m. Beauty, elegance, ornament. P.

زيتونه *zaitūna*, s.f. The olive tree. A. (*zaitūn*).

زير *zer*, a. Below, under. The vowel point ـِ *i*. P.

زيراستر *zerāstar*, s.m. The lining of a dress. P.

زيرک *zīrak*, a. Acute, sagacious, penetrating, witty. P.

زيرکي *zīrakī*, s.f. Acumen, discernment, wit. P.

زيرمه *zerma*, s.f. Arrangement, preparation, disposal, setting in order.

زيري *zerai*, s.m. Glad tidings, good news.

زيريګر *zerai-gar*, } s.m. Bearer of glad tidings.
زيريګري *zerai-garai*, }

زيړ *ziyar*, a. Yellow. P. (*zard*). s.m. Brass.

زيړانکه *ziyarānaka*, s.f. The yellow wagtail.

زيړګله *ziyargula*, s.f. Name of a herb (*Callendula officinalis*).

زيړي *ziyaṛai*, s.m. Jaundice, icterus; yellowness.

زيږ *zīg*, a. Hard, rough, harsh, rigid, stiff; stern, austere, severe. P. (*zisht*).

زيږول *zegawul*, v.a. To beget, procreate, produce.

زيږيدل *zegedal*, v.n. To be born, begotten, brought forth. P. (*zā-idan*).

زيست *zīst*, s.m. Existence, life; employment. P.

زيله *zela*, s.f. A creeping plant; creeper, tendril.

زيم *zyam*, s.m. Humidity, moisture, dampness.

زيمناك *zyam-nāk*, a. Damp, humid, moist.

زين *zīn*, s.m. A saddle. P.

زينت *zīnat*, s.m. Beauty, elegance; dress, ornament. A.

زينه *zīna*, s.f. A ladder, steps. P.

زيور *zewar*, s.m. Jewels, ornaments. P.

ژ

ژ *je* is the nineteenth letter of the Pukkhto alphabet, and the fourteenth of the Persian, from which it is adopted. It has the sound of *s* in the word *pleasure*. By the Eastern Afghans it is sometimes used for ج or ږ, and by the Western tribes for ز.

ژامه *jāma*, s.f. The jaw, jaw-bone. P.

ژانه *jāna*, s.f. Adulation, flattery; coaxing.

ژاوله *jāwla*, s.f. Resin, pitch, wax, gum.

ژبه *jiba*, s.f. The tongue; language, speech; dialect. S. (*jībh*).

ژبونكي *jabūnkai*, s.m. Collar, cuff, frill, etc. (of a garment).

ژر *j-ir* or *ja-ar*, ad. Quickly, speedily. See زر *zir*.

ژرنده *jaranda*, s.f. A water mill. See جرنده.

ژړا *jaṛā*, s.f. Crying, sobbing, weeping. P. (*giriya*).

ژړل *jaṛal*, v.n. To weep, cry, sob, wail.

ژغند *jghanḍ*, s.m. A notch, nick, dent.

ژغ *jagh*, s.m. See جغ.

ژغورل *jghoral*, v.a. To keep, preserve, protect, guard, defend, nourish, support.

ژغوري *jghorai*, s.m. Protector, guardian, etc.

ژغونډي *jaghūnḍai*, s.m. The peg in a yoke (to prevent its slipping from the ox's neck).

ژلئ *jala-ī*, s.f. Hail. P. (*jāla*).

ژمي *jimai*, s.m. Winter, cold weather.

ژڼي *jaṇrai*, s.m. Catgut, bow-string, fiddle-string. A boy, lad, school-boy.

ژواك *jwāk*, s.m. Life, existence, being.

ژوبل *jobal*, a. Bruised, wounded, hurt.

ژور *jawar*, a. Deep, depressed, sunk.

ژورغالي *jawar-ghālai*, s.m. A pit or trench dug round the root of a tree (for water); a small pit made to hold a plant or sapling.

ژوره *jawara*, s.f. A leech.

ژوژ *jwaj*, s.m. See زوږ.

ژوند *jwand*, s.m. } Being, life, existence.
ژوندون *jwandūn*. }

ژوندي *jwandai*, a. Alive, living. P. (*zinda*).

ژوول *jowul*, } v.a. To chew, masticate; chew
ژويل *joyal*, } the cud. P. (*jāwīdan*).

ژئ *ja-ī*, s.f. Catgut, string of a bow or violin, etc. A water bag made of hide.

ږ

ږ *ge* is the twentieth letter of the Pukkhto alphabet, and peculiar to the Afghan language. By the Western tribes it is sounded like ژ, with which it is often interchanged. By the Eastern tribes it is pronounced as ګ, for which it is generally changed. In words introduced from Persian or Sanskrit, where this letter replaces ج, it has the sound of that letter or of *z* in *azure*.

ږدل *gdal*, v.a. To fix, place, put, set, lay. Def. in past ten. See كيښول. P. (*hīdan*).

ږدن *gdan*, s.m. A kind of millet. H. (*kodon*).

ږغ *gagh*, s.m. Noise, sound; accent, voice.

ږغورل *gghoral*, v.a. See ژغورل.

ږلئ *gala-ī*, s.f. Hail. See ژلئ.

ږمنځ *gamandz*, ږمنز *gamanz*, } s.f. A comb, hair comb.

ږو *go*, ad. A word used in comp. to denote oath or affirmation. Ex. *khudāe-go*, in. By God!

ږوند *grand*, s.m. See ژوند.

ږنږ *grag*, s.m. Noise, clamour, din, etc.

ږوي *gawai*, s.m. A being, creature, person. See وګړي.

ږيره *gīra*, s.f. The beard. P. (*rīsh*).

ږيري *gīrai*, a. Bearded, having a beard. *spīn-gīrai*, s.m. A white beard, grey beard, old man, elder. *rat-gīrai*, s.m. A red beard, one who dyes the beard with *nakrīza* (henna).

س

س *sīn* is the twenty-first letter of the Pukkhto alphabet, and the twelfth of the Arabic. It has the same sound as the English *s* in the word *song*, and in Pukkhto is sometimes, though wrongly, changed for the letters څ and ڇ.

سا *sā*, s.f. Breath, life, respiration, vital spark. S. (*sāns*).

سابق *sābiq*, a. Former, preceding. A.

سابون *sābūn*, s.m. Soap. A.

سابو *sābū*, s.m. Name of a grass from which mats are made (*Panicum Colonum*).

سابه *sābah*, s.m. Name of a grass (see preceding). Vegetables, greens.

ساپټ *sāpat*, ad. Completely, entirely, wholly.

ساتل *satal*, v.a. To keep, preserve; defend, protect, shelter; nourish, support.

ساتندوي *sātandoe*, ساتونكي *sātūnkai*, } s.m. Guardian, keeper, protector, etc.

ساتول *sātūl*, s.m. A chopper, cleaver; bill-hook.

ساحر *sāhir*, s.m. Magician, juggler, conjurer. A.

ساخت *sākht*, s.m. Make, construction; fabrication, pretence. P. A kind of leather, morocco leather.

ساختګي *sākhtagī*, s.f. Fabrication, pretence, sham.

ساخه *sākha*, s.f. A grating sound; calamity; judgment day. A. (*ṣākhat*).

ساد *sād*, a. Honest, good, trustworthy. S. (*sādh*).

سادو *sādū*, s.m. Imposter, knave, cheat.

ساده *sādah*, a. Plain, simple, unadorned; artless, candid, sincere; beardless; white. P.

سادين *sādīn*, s.m. Newly ploughed land, land prepared for sowing.

سار *sār*, s.m. Good news, glad tidings.

سارمه *sārma*, s.f. Name of a potherb.

سارنده *sārinda*, سارنګئ *sāringa-ī*, } s.f. A violin, guitar.

ساروان *sārwān*, s.m. A camel driver. P. (*sārbān*).

ساري *sārai*, a. Equal, par. s.m. A match, compeer, peer. P. (*sār*).

ساړه *sāra*, s.f. Cold weather; cold, frigidity.

ساز *sāz*, s.m. Accoutrements; apparatus, furniture; a musical instrument. P.

سازش *sāzish*, s.m. Confederacy, combination; plot, conspiracy. P.

سازنده *sāzindah*, s.m. Maker, performer. P.

ساعت *sā'at*, s.m. A minute, moment, hour. A.

ساعي *sā'ī*, a. Eager, earnest, zealous. A.

ساغر *sāg͟har*, s.m. A bowl, goblet. P.

ساغري *sāg͟harī*, s.m. The space between the tail and *anus* of a horse; a kind of leather, shagreen. P.

ساکن *sākin*, a. Quiet, tranquil, at rest. s.m. Resident, inhabitant. A.

ساګ *sāg*, s.m. Greens, potherbs, vegetables. S.

ساګینړي *sāgīnṛai*, s.m. A dish of rice and greens.

سالن *sālan*, s.m. Mixed or spiced food; flesh, fish, etc., eaten with rice or bread. H.

سالو *sālū*, s.m. A kind of red cloth of cotton. S.

ساله *sālah*, a. Aged (in comp. only); added to numeral adjectives, denotes age or years. Ex. *c͟hār-sālah*, a. Four years old. P.

سالیانه *sāliyānah*, a. Annual, yearly. P.

سامان *sāmān*, s.m. Apparatus, furniture, tools; arms, accoutrements. P.

سامانه *sāmāna*, s.f. Parade, pomp, state.

سامع *sāmiʻ*, s.m. A hearer. A.

سان *sān*, s.m. Muster, review of an army; calico; a grindstone, whetstone. P.

سانده *sānda*, s.f. Lament, wail.

ساندا *sānḍā*, s.m. Name of a kind of lizard with a thick tail. H.

سانګه *sānga*, s.f. A travelling party; a spear. S. A lament, wail; a bough, branch.

سانګي *sānga-ī*, s.f. A pitchfork.

سانړ *sānṛ*, s.m. A stallion, bull. S.

ساو *sāw*, s.m. Tax, tribute. *sāū*, a. Noble, well bred. P. (*s͟hāhū*).

ساونړ *sāwanṛ*, s.m. Name of the fourth Hindu month, July-August. S. (*sāwan*).

ساه *sāh*, s.m. Breath, vital spark, life. S. (*sāns*).

ساه‌لنډي *sāh-lanḍai*, a. Asthmatic. *sāh-lanḍī*, s.m. Asthma, dyspnœa, shortness of breath.

ساه‌ویسا *sāh-wīsā*, s.f. Belief, faith, trust, hope.

سایل *sāyil*, s.m. Asker, petitioner. A.

سایه *sāya*, s.f. Shade, shadow; apparition, spectre; shelter, protection; awning, canopy. P.

سب *sibb*, s.m. Reproach, reviling. A.

سبا *sabā*, s.m. Dawn, morning; morrow. A. (*ṣabāḥ*).

سبب *sabab*, s.m. Cause, motive, reason; means, instrument; affinity, connexion, relationship. A.

سبحان *subḥān*, s.m. Praising (God); the Deity. A. *subḥān-allah*, in. Good God! Oh God! A.

سبزه *sabza*, s.f. Herbage, verdure; incipient beard, bloom. *sabzah*, a. Grey, iron grey; sallow. P.

سبزي *sabzī*, s.f. Greens, vegetables. P.

سبق *sabaq*, s.m. A lecture, lesson, reading. A.

سبک *subuk*, a. See سپک.

سبوس *sabūs*, s.m. Bran, chaff. P.

سپارش *sipāris͟h*, s.m. Recommendation, intercession. P. (*sifāris͟h*).

سپارل *spāral*, v.a. To commit, consign, give in charge, intrust; recommend, etc. P. (*sipārīdan* or *sipurdan*).

سپاره *sipāra*, s.f. Name of a chapter in the Qurān (for *sīpāra*, thirty sections). P. *spāra*, s.f. An iron ploughshare.

سپاه *sipāh*, s.m. An army; a soldier. P.

سپاهي *spāhī*, s.m. A soldier. P.

سپر *spar*, s.m. A shield, buckler. P. (*sipar*).

سپرخي *sparḵ͟hai*, s.m. A packing needle, skewer, pin.

سپرد *sipurd*, s.m. Care, charge, keeping, trust. P.

سپرغه *sparg͟ha*, s.f. A well. (Raverty).

سپرلني *sparlanai*, s.m. Cavalier, horseman, rider.

سپرلي *sparlai*, s.m. The spring. *sparlī*, s.f. Riding, horse riding, equitation.

سپره *sapara*, s.f. Name of the second month of the Muḥammadan calendar. A. (*ṣafar*).

supra, s.f. The anus; a napkin, table-cloth. P. (*sufra*).

سپړل *spaṛal*, سپړدل *spaṛdal*, v.a. To undo, unclose, unfold, unravel, open out, etc.

سپږن *spagan*, a. Lousy, full of vermin, filthy.

سپږه *spaga*, s.f. A louse. P. (*sapash*).

سپک *spuk*, a. Light, flimsy; cheap; mean, trifling. P. (*subuk*).

سپلم *spalam*, s.m. See سپېرلم.

سپلمه *spalama*, s.f. A ring-dove.

سپلمي *spalma-ī*, s.f. Name of a plant (*Calotropis procera*, *Asclepias gigantca*), the mudar plant.

سپم *spam*, s.m. The eye of a needle; aperture, orifice, perforation. A. (*famm*).

سپند *sipand*, s.m. See سپېلني.

سپندخ *spandakh*, s.m. A large ball of worsted or cotton; a stuffed calf placed near a cow deprived of her own (to make her give milk).

سپنږسي *spanṛsai*, s.m. Cord, thread, twine, string.

سپوخځ *spokhadz*, سپوخځه *spokhadza*, s.f. Hypogastrium, belly below the navel, pubes, pelvis.

سپور *spor*, a. Dry, plain, unmixed, stale (as food). *spora-ḍoḍa-ī*, s.f. Dry bread. *spor*, a. Riding, mounted, seated upon. s.m. A horseman, cavalier. P. (*sawār*).

سپوږمي *spogma-ī*, s.f. Moon, moonlight.

سپوږي *spūṛrai*, s.m. Ringworm, porrigo.

سپه *sipah*, s.m. See سپاه.

سپهر *sipahr*, s.m. Celestial sphere, sky; fortune, time; the world. P. *sipahar*, s.m. Afternoon, the third watch. P.

سپي *spai*, s.m. A dog, hound.

سپيازه *spiyāza*, s.f. Abortion, miscarrying, dropping the young prematurely (applied to brutes only). a. Raw, unripe; useless, foolish.

سپېټه *sapeṭa*, ad. Never, positively, not a bit.

سپېځل *spedzal* or *spetsal*, v.a. To clean, clear, purify.

سپېځلي *spetsalai*, a. Spotless, clean, neat, spick-span.

سپيد *saped*, a. White. P. (*safed*).

سپيدار *spedār*, s.m. The white poplar tree. P. (*safedār*).

سپيده *sapeda*, s.f. White lead; dawn, day-break. P. (*safeda*).

سپيدي *sapedī*, s.f. Whiteness; dawn. P. (*safedī*).

سپېرکي *sperka-ī*, s.f. Lovage (the plant and seed). (*Ligusticum ajowan*).

سپېرلم *sperlam*, s.m. The grey-tailed fox; any quadruped (cattle) with a grey or white tail.

سپېره *sperah*, a. Grey, ashy, hoary; pale, colourless, ghastly.

سپېره‌کي *sperah-kai*, a. Pale, ashy, ghastly; coward.

سپېږمه *spegma*, s.f. The nostril.

سپېښته *spekkhta*, s.f. Membrane covering the stomach or heart; peritoneum, pericardium.

سپېلنی *spelanai*, s.m. Name of a plant, Syrian rue (*Peganum harmala*).

سپيمه *spiyama*, s.f. A bitch in heat seeking the dog.

سپين *spīn*, a. White, pure, fair, spotless.

سپېنګه *spenga*, s.f. See سپېږمه.

سپينه *spīna*, s.f. The tendon of the heel (*tendo Achillis*). Fat, suet, tallow.

ست *sat*, s.m. Invitation (to dinner), hospitality; civility, politeness. a. Flat, level; supine, straight on the back. H. (*chit*).

ستا *stā*, The genitive case singular of the second personal pronoun ته *tah*; of thee, thine.

ستار *sitār*, s.m. A guitar (of three strings), violin. P.

ستاره *stāra*, s.f. A star; a kind of firework. P. (*sitāra*). *stāra·prewatal*, v.n. To be unlucky, to have one's star in the descendant.

ستاسُ *stāsu*, } ستاسو *stāso*, } pl. of ستا. Yours, of you.

ستانه *stāna*, s.f. A threshold; house, family, race (of saints particularly). P. (*āstāna*).

ستايل *stāyal*, v.a. To laud, praise, glorify, extol. P. (*sitūdan*).

ستر *satr*, s.m. Veiling, covering, concealing; privates. A. *star*, a. Big, bulky, great, huge, strapping, etc.; deep, profound (as a well). P. (*saturg*).

سترغلي *starghalai*, s.m. The orbit; eyeball.

سترگه *starga*, s.f. The eye; a planet. (Diminutive of P. *sitāra*).

ستره *satra*, s.f. A curtain, mantle, veil.

ستري *satrai*, s.m. A cut crop as it lies on the field; pile of corn sheaves; heap, pile, mass. H. (*sathrāṅ*). *satrai·watrai*, a. Scattered, lying about (as leaves on the ground).

ستړي *staṛai*, a. Fatigued, weary, tired, fagged. P. (*siturdah*).

ستغ *stagh*, s.m. A bot, worm in the skin of cattle; a boil or abscess produced by the worm. a. Astringent, binding, rough to the taste; mean, sordid, avaricious.

ستل *satal*, s.m. A copper pail or bucket, cauldron. P.

ستم *sitam*, s.m. Oppression, violence, tyranny. P. *stam*, s.m. Forcing, straining; labour, travail. *stam·wahal*, v.a. To force, strain (as at stool, etc.).

ستن *stan*, s.f. A needle, pin; pillar, post. P. (*sitūn*).

ستنه *stana*, s.f. Return, retreat; retrenchment.

ستنول *stanawul*, v.a. To send back, return; to take back, retrench.

ستنيدل *stanedal*, v.n. To return, go back, retire.

ستوان *satwān*, s.m. Peasemeal, meal of parched corn, pulse, etc. S. (*sattū*).

ستوخ *stokh*, } ستوغ *stogh*, } a. Straight, difficult; bad, hateful. P. (*satakh*).

ستور *sutūr*, s.m. Cattle, beast of burden. P.

ستوري *storai*, s.m. A star. P. (*sitāra*).

ستوگه *stoga*, s.f. See استوگه.

ستومان *stomān*, a. Disgusted, vexed; repentant, sorry; fatigued, tired, fagged, weary.

ستون *stūn*, a. Returned, sent back; retrenched, withdrawn.

ستونول *stūnawul*, v.a. To send back, call back, recall; withdraw, retrench, subtract.

ستونيدل *stūnedal*, v.n. To return, come back; retire, etc.

ستوني *stūnai*, s.m. The larynx, *pomum Adami*.

ستوني ستغ *stūnī·stagh*, a. Supine; flat on the back.

ستيزه *steza*, s.f. Argument, controversy, dispute; quarrel, battle, conflict. P. (*siteza*). *sateza*, s.f. Table-land, flat ground on a hill side.

سټ *saṭ*, s.m. A cutler's block, a block of wood for fixing an anvil; a log, stump, root of a tree. An assault, sudden attack. The nape, back of the neck.

سټکوري *saṭkūrai*, a. Burnt, scorched, parched; dried up, withered, shrivelled; frost-bitten.

سجده *sijda*, s.f. Bowing the head and touching the ground with the forehead, prostration, adoration. A.

سجل *sijjil*, s.m. Bond, deed, register; decree of a judge; seal of a judge. The recording angel. A.

سچ *such*, a. Pure, genuine, real; candid, honest. S. Also سچه *suchah*.

سحار *saḥār*, } سحر *saḥr*, } s.m. Dawn, daybreak; morning, forenoon; morrow, to-morrow. A.

سحر ***siḥr***, s.m. Sorcery, magic, jugglery. A.

سحرگر ***siḥr·gar***, s.m. Magician, conjurer, sorcerer.

سخ ***sak͟h***, in. Excellent! Good! ad. The present year.

سخا ***sak͟hā***, s.f. } Munificence, generosity, liberality. A.
سخاوت ***sak͟hāwat***, s.m. }

سخا ***sk͟hā***, a. Putrid, rotten, stinking. H. (*ubsā*).

سخاوږه ***sk͟hāwaga***, s.f. Name of a medicinal root (*Kæmpferia galanga*); orris root, root of the Iris (*Iris Persica*).

سخت ***sak͟ht***, a. Hard, strong; difficult, troublesome; obdurate, violent; austere, stingy; cruel, harsh; painful, rigid, severe. P.

سختي ***sak͟htī***, s.f. Difficulty, trouble; violence, cruelty; austerity, severity, etc. P.

سخر ***sk͟har***, s.m. A father-in-law. P. (*k͟husar*). ***sak͟har***, s.m. A rock, boulder, stone.

سخره ***sak͟hara***, s.f. A rock, boulder, stone.

سخن ***suk͟hun***, s.m. Word, speech; affair, matter. P.

سخوښتن ***sk͟hwakkhtan***, s.m. Cinders, hot ashes.

سخوند ***sk͟hwand***, s.m. The cud. ***sk͟hwand·wahal***, v.a. To chew the cud.

سخوندر ***sk͟hwandar***, s.m. A young bullock, steer.

سخه ***sak͟ha***, s.f. Joy, delight, gladness, etc. (at the misfortune of another), crowing over an enemy.

سخي ***sak͟hī***, a. Munificent, generous, liberal. A. ***sk͟hai***, s.m. A calf, yearling calf.

سد ***sud***, s.m. Consciousness, intelligence; sensation, sense; memory. S. (*sudh*). ***sadd***, s.m. A barrier, wall. A.

سر ***sar***, s.m. The head; point, apex, summit, top. P. ***sirr***, s.m. A mystery, secret. A.

سراب ***sarāb***, s.m. Mirage, glare, vapour, resembling water at a distance (seen on desert plains). A. Mica, talc. A.

سراج ***sarrāj***, s.m. A saddler. A.

سراسر ***sarāsar***, a. All, the whole. ad. Wholly, entirely. P.

سراسري ***sarāsarī***, a. Brief, short, concise. P.

سراسیمه ***sarāsīmah***, a. Amazed, confounded. P.

سراغ ***surāg͟h***, s.m. Enquiry, search; mark, trace. P.

سرانه ***sarāna***, s.f. The upper bar of a doorway or frame.

سرانجام ***sarānjām***, s.m. Apparatus, utensils, materials; chattels, furniture, goods; ingredients, requisites; conclusion, accomplishment, end. P.

سرانداز ***sarāndāz***, s.m. The head piece of a bed; a carpet spread at the head of a room. P.

سراي ***srāe***, s.m. A caravansary, hospice, inn, hostelry; house. P. (*sarāe*).

سربانده ***sarbānda***, s.f. A patch of land, or portion of a field left unploughed or uncut. A rope used to fix the yoke of a plough.

سربانډه ***sarbānḍa***, s.f. Rope made of slips of raw hide; a rope for fastening the yoke of a plough.

سربسته ***sarbasta***, s.f. A cloth tied round the head by women when occupied with household duties, etc. P.

سرپ ***surup***, s.m. Lead. P. (*surb*). ***sirp*** or ***srup***, ad. Simply, purely, altogether, out and out, merely, etc. P. (*ṣirf*).

سرپوښ ***sarpokkh***, s.m. A cover, lid. P. (*sarposh*).

سرچشمه ***sarchashma***, s.f. A fountain, spring. P.

سرحد ***sarḥadd***, s.m. Boundary, frontier, limit. P.

سرخ ***surk͟h***, a. Red (in comp.). P. ***surk͟h·bād***, s.m. Name of a disease, erysipelas. P.

سرخچه ***surk͟hcha***, s.f. A red apricot. P.

سرخکه ***sark͟haka***, s.f. A starling; a kind of Mina (*Graculus roseus*).

سرخي ***surkhī***, s.f. Blight in corn, mildew; jaundice; brick dust; redness. P. ***surkha-ī***, s.f. A frill or fillet of cloth sewn on to the legs of women's trousers.

سرد ***sard***, a. Cold (in comp.). P.

سردار ***sardār***, s.m. Chief, principal, head. P.

سررشته ***sar-rishta***, s.f. Affinity, connection; office, employment; cord, rope. P.

سرژه ***sarja***, s.f. A species of mountain deer.

سرسام ***sarsām***, s.m. Delirium, frenzy. P.

سرسايه ***sarsāya***, s.f. Alms distributed on the conclusion of the Ramaẓān fast. A veil given by the father to a bride on the last day of the marriage festivities. P.

سرسري ***sarsarī***, a. Easy, facile. P.

سرشاهي ***sarshāhi***, s.f. Name of a weight equal to half an ounce.

سرشت ***sarisht***, s.m. Intellect, nature; temperament, disposition; complexion. P.

سرغنه ***sarghanah***, s.m. A chief, head man. P.

سرغوند ***sarghūnḍ***, s.m. A glandular tumour of the neck.

سرفه ***sarfa***, s.f. Advantage, gain, profit; frugal, sparing in expense; deficiency, default; forbearance. A. (*sarf*). ***surfa***, s.f. A cough. P.

سركار ***sarkār***, s.m. Government, court; province, district; superintendent. P.

سركښ ***sarkakkh***, a. Obstinate, rebellious, disobedient, perverse, etc. P. (*sarkash*).

سركښي ***sarkakkhi***, s.f. Obstinacy, rebellion, etc.

سركنډه ***sarkunḍa***, s.f. A cropped, cut, or trimmed head of hair; the hair cut short.

سركنډي ***sarkunḍai***, s.m. A man or boy with the hair trimmed or cut short.

سركوزي ***sarkūzai***, s.m. A pig, hog, swine.

سركول ***sarkol***, s.m. A mill-dam, weir.

سركه ***sirka***, s.f. Vinegar. P.

سركي ***sirka-ī***, s.f. Name of a scarlet insect, the scarlet fly.

سرگردان ***sargardān***, a. Bothered, confused, perplexed; wandering, at a loss, etc. P.

سرگرداني ***sargardānī***, s.f. Perplexity, trouble, worry.

سرگړي ***sargaṛai***, s.m. Name of a grass (*Apluda aristata*).

سرگشته ***sargashtah***, a. Amazed, astonished; giddy, flighty, wandering. P.

سرگله ***sargala***, s.f. A grazing tax, tax on cattle. P.

سرگين ***sargīn***, s.m. Cow-dung. P.

سرما ***sarmā***, s.f. Winter. P.

سرماتي ***sarmātai***, s.m. Coping, eaves of a wall.

سرمال ***sarmāl***, s.m. A rope used to fasten together the two halves of a bullock or camel load.

سرمايه ***sarmāya***, s.f. Capital, stock, store. P.

سرمه ***surma***, s.f. P. See رانجه.

سرنا ***sarnā***, } s.f. A clarion, flageolet. P.
سرناي ***sarnā-ī***, }

سرناچي ***surnāchī***, s.m. A flageolet player.

سرنامه ***sarnāma***, s.f. Superscription, address, title. P.

سرنگ ***surang***, s.m. A mine, tunnel, subterranean passage. S.

سرنگي ***surangai***, s.m. A burrow, little tunnel, etc. Diminutive of preceding word.

سرواښ ***sarwākkh***, s.m. A rope made of hair, and used to fasten cattle; a tether.

سروټكه ***sarwaṭka***, s.f. See سكروټه.

سرود ***sarod***, s.m. A song; music, melody. P.

سرودگر ***sarod-gar***, } s.m. A singer, musician. P.
سرودي ***sarodī***, }

سرور ***sarwar***, s.m. A chief, leader. P.

سروزنه ***sarwazana***, s.f. The hem in trousers, through which the waistband passes; a frill or fillet of cloth added to a pair of trousers.

سروه ***sarwa***, s.f. The cypress tree. P. (*sarw*).

سره ***sara***, s.f. Manure, offal, dung. ***sara***, ad. With, along with, together, in company.

سرده ور ***sarah-war***, a. Ample, broad, wide. See صور.

سریخ ***srīkh***, s.m. Name of a tree (*Mimosa seris*). S. (*siris*).

سریښ ***sarekkh***, s.m. See سلیښ.

سرین ***surīn***, s.m. The buttock. P.

سربنړ ***sarbanr***, s.m. Name of the eldest son of Kais (the great ancestor of the Afghans). His tribe. ***sarbanrai***, s.m. A male of the tribe.

سړپ ***srap***, s.m. The sound of splashing water; squash, smash, dash, etc. H. (*surap*).

سړه ***sarah***, a. Done, finished; free, liberated; alone, solitary; genuine, pure.

سړه بنړ ***sarah-banr***, s.m. See سربنړ.

سړه لرې ***sara-lire***, } s.f. Fever and ague.
سړه لوې ***sara-lawe***, }

سړی ***sarai***, s.m. A man, human being. ***sarī-tob***, s.m. Human nature, humanity.

سزا ***sazā***, s.f. Correction, punishment, retribution. P.

سزاوار ***sazāwār***, a. Deserving, fit, worthy; suitable, proper. P.

سزاول ***sazāwal***, s.m. Bailiff, tax-gatherer.

سږ ***sag***, ad. } This year, the current year.
سږکال ***sag-kāl***, }

سږمه ***sagma***, s.f. The nostril.

سږنی ***saganai***, a. This year's, of the present year.

سږی ***sagai***, s.m. The lung. P. (*shush*).

سسپار ***saspār***, s.m. A ploughshare.

سسپور ***saspor***, s.m. A mattock, hoe.

سست ***sust***, a. Indolent, lazy, negligent; feeble, slow, languid; loose, relaxed. P.

سستي ***sustī***, s.f. Idleness, laziness, etc. P.

سښا ***sakkhā***, s.f. Fizz, sputter, etc. (as of roasting meat).

سښسوره ***sakkhsora***, s.f. See مسپور.

سطح ***satah***, s.m. A surface, flat surface. A.

سعادت ***sa'ādat***, s.m. Felicity, happiness, good fortune. A.

سعیه ***sa'ya***, s.f. Endeavour, effort, purpose. A. (*sa'ī*).

سغ ***sagh***, s.m. See شغ.

سفر ***safar***, s.m. A journey, voyage. A.

سفوف ***safūf***, s.m. A powder. A.

سقاو ***saqqāw***, s.m. A water carrier. A.

سک ***sak***, a. Stiff, rigid. s.m. Lumbago, rheumatism. H. (*chik*).

سکاروی ***skārwai***, s.m. Pleurisy; rheumatism, sciatica.

سکالوه ***skālwah***, s.m. Conversation, discourse, talk, hum, buzz, murmur (of conversation).

سکانړ ***skānr***, a. Dark complexioned, ruddy, healthy, fresh, or agreeable complexion. s.m. A horse of a light bay colour.

سکروټه ***skarwata***, s.f. Embers, live coal.

سکړک ***sukruk***, a. Numbed, chilled, paralyzed with cold. ***sukrak***, s.m. Bread made of Indian corn or maize meal.

سکستل ***skustal***, v.a. To shear, clip (as sheep, etc.).

سکیښتل ***skakkhtal***, v.a. To cut, shape, design, cut out (as clothes). To clip, shear.

سکل ***skal***, v.a. See څښل.

سکنجبین ***sikanjabīn***, s.m. Oxymel; a drink made of lime-juice, honey and water. P.

سکندری ***skandara-ī***, s.f. A stumble, trip.

سکور ***skor***, s.m. Charcoal.

سکول ***skwal***, s.m. Shearing, clipping. ***skwal-kawul***, v.a. To shear, clip.

سکونت ***sukūnat***, s.m. Habitation, residence; quiet, rest, tranquility. A.

سکونداره ***skūndāra***, s.f. A pinch; pinching.

سکوندل ***skūndal***, v.a. To pinch, tweak.

سکوی ***skoe***, s.m. A stitch; sewing. Anxiety,

solicitude. *skoc·kanul*, v.a. To stitch, hem, sew.

سکویل *skoyal*, v.a. To rub, scrape, scratch (as the skin).

سکه *sika*, s.f. Lead; coin, impression, stamp; sterling, current. A. P. *sakah*, a. Related (of the same parents), full, own. S. (*sagā*). *ska*, ad. Because, therefore, then; as if, as it were.

سګ *sag*, s.m. A dog. P. *sag*, ad. See سر.

سګال *sigāl*, s.m. Suspicion, thought; calumny. P.

سګل *sugul*, s.f. A kind of buskin made of untanned leather, and worn by mountaineers as a protection for the legs from the snow.

سګلاو *sagalāw*, s.m. An otter. P. (*sagulāb*).

سګلۍ *sagala-ī*, s.f. See سلګۍ.

سګه *saga*, s.f. Capital, stock, store.

سل *sal* or *sil*, a. A hundred, one hundred, centum. P. (*ṣad*). *sill*, s.m. Consumption, phthisis, hectic fever. A.

سلاره *silāra*, s.f. A kind of striped cloth.

سلام *salām*, s.m. Salutation; peace, safety. A.

سلامت *salāmat*, s.m. Health, recovery; safety, salvation. A.

سلائي *salā-ī*, s.f. A bodkin, pin, skewer, pencil, etc. S. The upright pillar of a Persian wheel; a steel bodkin for applying antimony to the eyelids, etc.

سلت *salaṭ*, s.m. A shield, buckler.

سلسله *silsila*, s.f. Chain, series, succession; descent, lineage. A.

سلطان *sulṭān*, s.m. Emperor, sovereign, king. A.

سلطاني *sulṭānī*, a. Princely, royal. A.

سلطنت *sulṭanat*, s.m. Empire, sovereignty. A.

سلګۍ *salga-ī*, s.f. A sob, sigh, hiccough, sobbing cry.

سلوک *sulūk*, s.m. Behaviour, conduct, manner; intercourse, treatment, usage; attention, civility. A.

سله *sala*, s.f. A pig or mass of iron. H. (*sarī*).

سلي *salai*, s.m. An iron ring for the finger (worn as a charm against all kinds of calamities).

سليخ *salekh*, سليښ *salekkh*, s.m. Glue; birdlime; adhesiveness, cohesion, viscidity. P. (*saresh*).

سليقه *salīqa*, s.f. Disposition, nature; address, dexterity, method, etc. A.

سم *sum*, s.m. A hoof, whole hoof (as of a horse, etc.). *sam*, a. Even, flat, level, plane, straight. *samm*, s.m. Poison, venom. A. *sam*, s.m. An arrow. A. (*sahm*).

سماع *simā'*, s.f. Hearing, listening; a song, singing. A.

سمبالول *sambālanul*, v.a. To control, manage, moderate; to prop, support; protect, preserve; arrange, settle, put in order, etc. S. (*sambhālnā*).

سمت *simt*, s.m. Path, road, way; direction, quarter. A.

سمڅ *smats*, s.f. A cavern, cave. P. (*sumuj*).

سم دَلاسه *sam da lāsa*, ad. Straight from the hand, out of hand, forthwith, etc.

سمساره *samsāra*, s.f. A kind of lizard, iguana.

سمست *samist*, s.f. See سمڅ.

سمسور *samsor*, a., سمسوري *samsorai*, Come out, ripened, matured (as corn when in ear). s.m. A peer, equal, match, compeer.

سمن *saman*, s.m. Jasmine, lily of the valley. P.

سمند *samand*, a. Dun-coloured (horse). P.

سمندر *samandar*, s.m. A salamander. P.

سمندي *samandai*, s.m. A rat of a dun colour.

سمور *sumūr*, s.m. A marten, sable; sable skin. P.

سمه *sama*, s.f. A plateau, plain. Name of the Yūsufzai plain.

سن *san*, s.m. Age, year. A.

سنار *sunār*, s.m. A goldsmith. **s.**

سنامكي *sanā·makkī*, s.m. Senna leaves (*Cassia lanceolata*). Name of a stone, serpentine, porphyry. **H.**

سنبل *sunbul*, s.m. Hyacinth. **P.** Maidenhair fern.

سنت *sunnat*, s.m. Circumcision; the traditions of Muhammad; ordinance. **A.**

سنځل *sandzal*, v.a. To empty, bale, pour out. **P.** (*sanjīdan*).

سنج *sanj* (in comp.), A weigher. **P.** *sunj*, a. Empty, void, desolate, waste, deserted.

سنجاب *sanjāb*, s.m. Ermine. **P.**

سند *sannad*, s.m. Certificate, deed, diploma, document, grant, etc. **A.** *sind*, s.m. A river. The name of a country. **S.** (*sindh*).

سندان *sandān*, s.m. An anvil. **P.**

سندره *sandara*, s.f. A song; melody, song.

سنډا *sanḍā*, a. Burly, powerful, strong, stout. **S.**

سنډاسي *sanḍāsī*, s.m. A Hindu ascetic, devotee. **S.** (*sunyāsī*).

سنډه *sanḍah*, s.m. A bull buffalo. **S.** (*sānḍ*).

سنكيا *sankiyā*, s.f. Arsenic. **S.** (*sankhiyā*).

سنګ *sang*, s.m. A stone (in comp.). **P.**

سنګار *singār*, s.m. Decoration, dress, ornament, toilet. **S.**

سنګاوڼر *singāwaṉr*, s.m. A rudder, helm; barge pole, boat hook. **A.** (*sukkān*).

سنګر *sangar*, s.m. Barricade, stockade. **S.**

سنګزن *sangzan*, a. Lop-sided, top-heavy, lurched over, overbalanced.

سنګلاخ *sanglākh*, a. Stony, rocky; difficult, arduous. **P.**

سنګين *sangīn*, a. Heavy, weighty; solid, hard; important, serious, difficult; stony. s.m. A bayonet. **P.**

سني *sunnī*, s.m. An orthodox Muhammadan; one who believes in the equality of the four successors of Muhammad. a. Catholic, orthodox, true. **A.** *sunnī·tob*, s.m. Orthodoxy.

سنړ *saṉr*, The hemp plant (*Crotalaria juncea*); hemp. **S.** (*san*).

سو *sau*, a. A hundred. Only used with reference to more than one hundred. Ex. *sal* or *sil*, One hundred. *dre·sawa*, Three hundred. **S.**

سوا *siwā*, p. Except, besides, without. **A.**

سوال *sawāl*, s.m. Question, interrogation, proposition. **A.**

سوانګ *swāng*, s.m. Disguise, imitation, sham. **S.**

سوانګي *swāngai*, s.m. An actor, imitator.

سوټبوټ *sūṭ·būṭ*, a. Cross, surly, ill-natured; withered, dry; pure, simple; disagreeable, ugly; pinioned, tightened; all of a heap, by the run, etc.

سوټه *sūṭa*, s.f. Dung of cattle (as found on pastures), scybala. **A.** (*sudda*).

سوځول *swadzawul*, v.a. To burn, set on fire. **P.** (*sokhtāndan*, *sozān-*).

سوچه *sūchah*, a. Genuine, pure, prime, real. **S.**

سوخته *sokhtah*, a. Burnt (in comp.). **P.**

سود *sūd*, s.m. Gain, advantage; interest, profit. **P.**

سودا *saudā*, s.f. Commerce, trade, marketing, etc. **P.** Hypochondriasis, melancholy, madness; desire, love, ambition. **A.**

سوداګر *saudāgar*, s.m. A merchant, trader. **P.**

سودائي *saudā-ī*, a. Mad, melancholy, insane. **A.**

سوده *sūdah*, a. Abraded, frayed, rubbed, galled. **P.** Genuine, pure, simple; artless. **S.** (*sūdhā*). *sūda*, s.f. A stoppage, obstruction (of the bowels). **A.** (*sudda*). *sawda*, s.f. A basket, hamper; a wicker frame used as a dish cover, meat safe, etc.

سودر *sodar*, s.m. A boar, wild boar. **S.** (*sūkar*). a. Bald, bare-pated.

سور *sor*, s.m. Breadth, expanse, width. **H.** (*chauṛ*). *sor*, a. Riding, mounted. s.m. A cavalier, horseman. **P.** (*sawār*). *sūr*.

a. Red. f. *sra*. P. (*surkh*). *sūr*, s.m. Name of a tribe of Afghans.

سوراغزي *sūr-āghzai*, s.m. Name of a plant with red thorns (*Catha edulis*).

سورپلي *sūr-palai*, s.m. Name of a plant, the seed pod of which is covered with red prickles; cowitch (*Mucuna pruriens*); a kind of stinging nettle; a kind of grass with barbed spikes in the beard.

سورت *sūrat*, s.m. A chapter (of the Qurān). A.

سورسات *sūrsāt*, s.m. Provisions, stores, supplies, etc. (collected for a king, or an army on the march). P.

سورلکي *sūr-lakai*, s.m. Name of a bird with a red tail; stonechat, wheatear.

سورلنډ *sūrlanḍ*, s.m. A jackal.

سورلي *swarlī*, s.f. Riding; cavalcade, suite. P. (*sawārī*). *swarlai*, s.m. A chisel; burglar's tool, jemmy, pick.

سورمل *sūrmal*, s.m. Name of a grass with barbed spikes in the beard (*Apluda aristata*).

سورميږي *sūr-megai*, s.m. The red ant.

سوره *swara*, s.f. A daughter or slave girl given as the price of murder or blood, or in exchange for a wife or girl eloped with or abducted.

سوري *sūrai*, s.m. Aperture, orifice, hole, passage. P. (*sūrākh*). *sorai* or *siwrai*, s.m. Shadow, shade. *sūre*, s.f. (pl. of *sūra*, obsolete), A bawl, bellow, shout, scream.

سوريته *sūryata*, s.f. A female slave or bondwoman who has borne a child to her master; a concubine.

سوړ *soṛ*, a. Cold, frigid, frosty. P. (*sard*).

سوړبوئي *soṛ-bū-ī*, s.f. Stink, fœtor, stench.

سوړه *sūṛa*, s.f. A burrow, hole; aperture, orifice. P. (*sūrākh*).

سوړي *sūṛai*, s.m. A fissure, crack, cleft.

سوز *soz* (in comp.), Burning. P.

سوزاک *sozāk*, s.m. Gonorrhœa. P.

سوزش *sozish*, s.f. Burning, heat, fervour; inflammation; vexation.

سوزن *sozan*, s.m. A needle; pricker, pin. P.

سوزني *sozanī*, s.f. A quilt, counterpane, coverlet. P.

سوزه *sūza*, s.f. A fillet, patch, etc. in a dress; an adze.

سوسر *sūsar*, s.m. A porpoise. S. (*sūs*).

سوسن *sausan* or *sosan*, s.m. Name of a plant, the Chinese Iris, Daurian Lily; a purple or violet colour. A.

سوغ *sogh*, s.m. A sniff, snort, snuff; sound of blowing the nose. S. (*sūngh*). *sūgh*, s.m. A pinch of snuff, or anything taken between the finger and thumb.

سوغات *saughāt*, s.m. A curiosity, rarity, present. P.

سوغالي *soghālai*, s.m. A hare's form.

سوغن *sūghan*, a. Sniffling, snorting, snuffing. s.m. A sniveller.

سوغول *sūghawul*, v.a. To prod, poke, thrust.

سوغېدل *sūghedal*, v.n. To be pierced, stabbed, etc.

سوک *sūk*, s.m. The fist; a blow, cuff (with the fist); the stump of a tree.

سوکړ *sūkaṛ*, s.m. A tall, gaunt, thin, etc. man; a thin wiry beard.

سوکړک *sūkṛuk*, s.m. Bread made of Indian corn or maize.

سوکړه *sokṛah*, a. Dry, parched, withered. S. (*sūkhā*).

سوګند *saugand*, s.m. An oath. P.

سول *swal*, v.n. To burn, catch fire, ignite. Pr. *swadzī*. P. (*sokhtan*, *soz-*).

سولاغ *sūlāgh*, s.m. A hole, aperture, etc P. (*sūrākh*).

سولاغه *sūlāgha*, s.f. A water bucket; a strainer, colander.

سولول *sūlawul*, v.a. To rub, file, rasp, grate, abrade.

سولي *sūla-ī*, s.f. A gibbet, stake; a pole, juggler's pole. s. (*sūlī*).

سوليدل *sūledal*, v.n. To fray, chafe, fret, abrade, etc.

سوم *swam*, s.m. See سيم.

سونبه *sūnba*, s.m. A socket; heel of an arrow, axe, lance, etc.; a blacksmith's punch; a sponge staff, ramrod. H. (*sumbā*).

سوندر *swandar*, s.m. See سخوندر.

سونده *sūnda*, s.f. Jealousy, suspicion.

سوند *sūnd*, s.m. Dry ginger, s. (*sonṭh*). See شوند.

سوندک *sūndak*, s.m. The trunk or proboscis of an elephant. s. (*sūnd*).

سونګټ *sūngaṭ*, a. Burnt, scorched; withered.

سونګي *songai*, s.m. A pigmy, dwarf.

سونړ *sūnṛ*, s.m. See سوغ.

سونړول *sūnṛawul*, v.a. To blow the nose, snuff, snort.

سونړيدل *sūnṛedal*, v.n. To sniff, snuff, smell, etc.

سوور *swor*, a. Riding, mounted. s.m. A cavalier, horseman. P. (*sawār*).

سوره *sowa*, s.f. Name of a plant, sweet fennel (*Anethum sowa*). s. (*soā*).

سوه *swa*, s.f. A cloven hoof (as of oxen, sheep, etc.).

سوهاګن *sohāgan*, s.f. A favourite wife. s. See مېرونه.

سوهان *sohān*, s.m. A file, rasp. P.

سوي *sawai*, a. Consumed, burnt. *swai*, s.m. Burning, ardour; pain; compassion, pity.

سويشل *sweshal*, v.a. To milk. See لوشل.

سويه *soya*, s.f. } A hare. s. (*sasā*).
سوئي *so-e*, s.m. }

سه *sih*, a. Three (in comp.). P.

سهل *sahl*, a. Easy, facile. ad. Easily. A.

sahal, v.n. To bear, endure, suffer. s. (*sahnā*).

سهم *sahm*, s.f. Dread, awe, terror, fear. P.

سهوه *sahwa*, s.f. Mistake, error. A. (*sahw*).

سهه *saha*, s.f. Breath, life; respiration. Clothes line, clothes horse.

سهيدل *sahedal*, v.n. To endure, suffer. See سهل.

سهيل *suhel*, s.m. The star Canopus; the south. A.

سهيلي *sahelī*, s.f. A lady's maid, housemaid; a concubine, handmaid. s.

سياځه *siyādza*, s.f. A slab for grinding spices on; a cobbler's lapstone.

سياست *siyāsat*, s.m. Government; punishment. A.

سيال *siyāl*, s.m. An equal, peer; clansman, kin; like, resembling.

سيالي *siyālī*, s.f. Equality, purity, resemblance.

سياه *siyāh*, a. Black (in comp.). P.

سياهه *siyāha*, s.f. Muster, catalogue, register, etc.

سياهي *siyāhī*, s.f. Ink; blackness; register, list. P.

سيب *seb*, s.m. An apple. P.

سيپۍ *sīpa-ī*, s.f. A shell. H. (*sīpī*).

سيټ *set*, s.m. A banker, merchant. s. (*seṭh*).

سيځل *sedzal*, v.n. To burn, catch fire. See سول *swal*.

سيخ *sīkh*, s.m. A skewer, spit, ramrod. P.

سيخچه *sīkhcha*, s.f. A small skewer, etc.; a prong or bayonet fixed to a matchlock. P.

سيد *sayad*, s.m. A prince, lord; a descendant of Husain, the grandson of Muḥammad. A.

سير *sair*, s.m. Excursion, jaunt, picnic, recreation, walk. A. *ser*, s.m. Name of a weight equal to two pounds. H. *ser*, a. Satiated, full, replete, etc. (in comp.). P.

سيراب *serāb*, a. P. See خړوب.

سیرت *sīrat*, s.m. Manners, morals, conduct. A.

سیرلي *serlai*, s.m. A yearling kid.

سیرۍ *sera-ī*, s.f. Rent free land given to men of the religious classes, glebe; an estate, pension in land, fief.

سیزل *sezal*, } v.n. To burn, consume, kindle,
سیځل *sedzal*, } catch fire. P. (*sokhtan, soz-*).

سیسه *sīsa*, s.f. Lead. S. (*sīsā*).

سیکړه *saikṛa*, s.f. A hundred; a centum. S.

سیکل *sekal*, v.a. To foment, toast, warm. H. (*senknā*).

سیکن *sekan*, s.m. Aversion, antipathy, disgust; dislike, loathing (of food, etc.).

سیل *sail*, s.m. Walking, rambling; flowing, current; flood; flock of birds; shoal of fishes. A.

سیلاب *sailāb*, s.m. A current, torrent, flood; deluge, inundation. a. Abounding in water. P.

سیله *sela*, s.f. Partiality, friendship, affection. A. A javelin, pike; rapier, long sword. S.

سیلي *siyalai*, s.m. Rennet; the prepared stomach of a kid or lamb filled with coagulated milk. *siyala-ī*, s.f. Rope made of goat's hair, etc. *sīla-ī*, s.f. A slap, blow with the open hands. P. (*selī*). A dust storm, whirlwind; hurricane, tempest.

سیم *sīm*, s.m. Silver. P. Wire of any kind.

سیماب *sīmāb*, s.m. Quicksilver, mercury. P.

سیمرغ *sīmurgh*, s.m. A fabulous bird, griffin. P.

سیمک *sīmak*, s.m. A weaver's bodkin; knitting needle. P.

سیمه *sema*, s.f. A mare or ass in heat (seeking the male). *sīma*, s.f. Path, way, road; quarter, side, part.

سیمیا *sīmiyā*, s.f. Vermicelli. H. (*senwiyā*).

سیند *sīnd*, s.m. A river, sea. S. (*sindh*).

سینګار *sīngār*, s.m. See سنګار.

سینه *sīna*, s.f. Bosom, breast. P.

سیني *sīnī*, s.m. A tray, salver. P.

سیو *sew*, s.m. An apple. P.

سیوري *sewrai*, s.m. Shadow, shade.

ش

ش *shīn*, is the twenty-second letter of the Pukkhto alphabet. It has the sound of *sh* in English, and in Persian words introduced into Pukkhto is often changed to ښ.

شا *shā*, s.f. The back; the shoulders. P. (*shāna*).

شاباز *shābāz*, s.m. The bass string of a musical instrument; a royal falcon. P.

شاباش *shābāsh*, in. Bravo! well done! P.

شاپیانګه *shāpiyānga*, s.f. Name of a plant (*Withiana coagulans*).

شاپیټي *shāpeṭai*, s.m. A small shell found in hill streams and on mountain sides; a snail (*Achatina acicula*).

شاتر *shātar*, s.m. A groom, running footman.

شاتینګه *shā-ṭīnga*, s.f. The gizzard (of a fowl, etc.).

شادو *shādo*, s.m. A monkey. P. (*shādī*).

شاربل *shārbal*, v.a. To churn, stir about, etc. P. (*shor dādan* or *shorīdan*).

شاړ *shāṛ*, a. Rude, unmannered, boorish. Idle, out of work, unemployed; fallow, waste, uncultivated. s.m. A boor, bumpkin, clown, clodhopper.

شاش *shāsh*, s.m. Urine. P.

شاعر *shā'ir*, s.m. A poet. A.

شاګرد *shāgird*, s.m. An apprentice, pupil, disciple. P.

شال *shāl*, s.m. A shawl. S.

شالي *shāla-ī*, s.f. Rice plant, rice crop. S. (*shālī*).

شامت *shāmat*, s.m. Adversity, bad fortune. A.

شامل *shāmil*, a. Blended, comprised, united;

included, contained, ad. Together, along with. A.

شامي *shāma-ī*, s.f. A sepulchre, tomb, vault for dead bodies.

شاميانه *shāmiyāna*, s.f. Awning, canopy. P.

شان *shān*, s.m. Affair, business; condition, degree; dignity, state; constitution, nature. a. Like, resembling; used as an adjunct of similitude. Ex. *tor·shān*, a. Blackish; *spin·shān*, a. Whitish. ad. Like, as, similar, etc. P. (*sān*).

شانه *shāna*, s.f. A weaver's comb. P.

شاول *shāṛul*, s.m. A plummet, plumb-line. H. (*sāhūl*). P. (*shāqūl*).

شاولي واولي *shāṛlai·wāṛlai*, a. Careless, untidy; foolish, indiscreet; loose, dishevelled.

شاه *shāh*, s.m. A king; a title assumed by men of the *pīr* class. P.

شاهتره *shāhtara*, s.f. Name of a herb, common fumitory (*Fumaria officinalis.*). P.

شاهد *shāhid*, s.m. A witness. A.

شاهده *shāhida*, s.f. A sweetheart, mistress. P.

شاهدي *shāhidī*, s.f. Evidence, testimony. A.

شاهزاده *shāh·zādah*, s.m. A prince, king's son. P.

شاهزادي *shāh·zāda-ī*, s.f. A princess. P.

شاهي *shāhī*, a. Kingly, royal. s.f. Sovereignty, reign. P.

شاهين *shāhīn*, s.m. A kind of falcon. P.

شايان *shāyān*, a. Legal, worthy, suitable. P.

شايد *shāyad*, ad. Perhaps, possibly, perchance. P.

شب *shab*, s.m. Night (in comp.). P.

شب‌بو *shab·bo*, s.m. The tuberose lily (*Polianthes tuberosa*). P.

شبكه *shabaka*, s.f. A lattice, latticed window; a net, reticulated veil. P.

شبنم *shab·nam*, s.m. Dew; hoar frost. P.

شبه *shiba*, s.f. Agate, coral; a bead. P.

شبهه *shubha*, s.f. Uncertainty, doubt; suspicion; hesitation. A.

شپاړس *shpāṛas*, a. Sixteen.

شپږ *shpag*, a. Six. P. (*shash*).

شپشتي *shpishtai*, s.m. The spoke of a wheel.

شپنغوده *shpan·ghoda*, s.f. Name of a bird, the shepherd's deceiver, lapwing, pewit.

شپنكي *shpankai*, s.m. A shepherd boy.

شپني *shpanī*, s.f. Shepherd life, tending sheep.

شپول *shpol*, s.m. A sheep cot, sheep pen, or fold; a thorn hedge; halo round the moon.

شپون *shpūn*, s.m. A shepherd. P. (*shubān*).

شپه *shpa*, s.f. Night. P. (*shab*).

شپيته *shpetah*, a. Sixty.

شپيتي *shpetai*, s.m. A wedge to cleave wood with.

شپيشتي *shpeshtai*, s.m. A wedge; a kind of clover. P. (*supust*).

شپيشتري *shpeshtarai*, s.m. A kind of trefoil or vetch (*Medicago denticulata*).

شپيلي *shpela-ī*, s.f. A tube, pipe, barrel of a gun; fife, flute, whistle; hollow reed; blowpipe. *shpelai*, s.m. Whistling, a whistle. *shpelai ghaṛaṛul*, v.a. To whistle.

شتاب *shitāb*, s.m. Haste, quickness, speed. a. Hasty, quick, rash. P.

شتاه *shatāh*, a. Artful, cunning; immodest, lewd. A.

شتاهه *shatāha*, s.f. A lewd, wanton, etc. woman.

شترلړ *shuturlar*, s.m. The bar or beam that prevents the ropes of a Persian wheel (on which are fastened the water pots) from coming in contact with each other.

شتركه *shuturaka*, s.f. A cascade; spurt, jet, gush (of water).

شتري *shuturī*, s.f. Name of a kind of cloth made of camel's hair. P.

شته *shta*, A form of the third person singular and plural, present tense of the auxiliary verb يم *yam*, I am; there is, there are. P. (*hast*).

شتي *shata-ī*, s.f. A barbed arrow; the spike or ear of maize after the grain has been removed; the green mould on old walls; the green scum on stagnant pools.

شتل *shaṭal*, a. Lazy, indolent. See شدل.

شجاع *shujā'*, a. Brave, bold, courageous. A.

شجاعت *shujā'at*, s.m. Bravery, courage. A.

شجره *shajara*, s.f. List of saints; genealogical table. A.

شڅرلي *shatsurlai*, s.m. A chisel.

شخ *shakh*, a. Hard, rough, tough, rigid, stiff. P.

شخړه *shkhaṛa*, s.f. Gibberish, nonsense, twaddle, trash; crowd, mob, multitude.

شخوده *shakhūdah*, a. Clawed, scratched. P.

شخول *shkhwal*, s.m. Din, tumult, noise; rumble, murmur, rustle.

شخولي *shkhwalai*, s.m. A quiver for arrows.

شخوند *shkhwand*, s.m. The cud. *shkhwand-wahana*, s.f. Chewing the cud, ruminating. *shkhwand-wahunkai*, s.m. A ruminant, an animal that chews the cud. See سخوندر *skhwandar*.

شدت *shiddat*, s.m. Force, violence, vehemence. A.

شدني *shudanī*, a. Possible, practicable, probable. P.

شدياره *shudyāra*, s.f. Land ploughed and made ready for sowing. P. (*shudkār*).

شديد *shadīd*, a. Difficult; acute, intense; vehement, violent. A.

شدل *shaḍal*, a. Indolent, lazy, slow; unbleached or unwashed cloth.

شر *sharr*, s.m. Villany, wickedness, depravity, evil. A. *shir*, s.m. Pitter-patter, sound of falling rain; the whizz of an arrow passing through the air.

شراب *sharāb*, s.m. Wine, spirits. A.

شرارت *sharārat*, s.m. Depravity, villany, wickedness. A.

شراکت *shirākat*, s.m. Partnership, fellowship. A.

شربت *sharbat*, s.m. Sherbet, beverage, drink. P.

شرحه *sharḥa*, s.f. Commentary, explanation; allowance, pay, rate. A.

شرشاي *sharshā-ī*, s.f. See سرشاهي.

شرط *sharṭ*, s.m. Agreement, bargain; stipulation, condition; bet, wager; mark, sign. A.

شرطي *sharṭī*, a. Conditional; a bargainer, better. A.

شرعه *shar'a*, s.f. Muḥammadan law; equity, law. A.

شرعي *shar'a-ī*, a. According to law, legal. A.

شرغشي *sharghashai*, s.m. Name of a reed from the stalks of which stools, baskets, etc. are made (*Saccharum sara* and *S. spontaneum*).

شرغه *sharghah*, a. A horse with a white forehead, or with white eyes.

شرک *shirk*, s.m. Infidelity, paganism; company, society, partnership. A.

شرکت *shirkat*, s.m. Partnership. A.

شرم *sharm*, s.m. Bashfulness, modesty, shame. P.

شرمښ *sharmakkh*, s.m. A wolf.

شرمناک *sharm-nāk*, a. Bashful, modest, unassuming. P.

شرمنده *sharmindah*, a. Ashamed, disgraced, shamed. P.

شرمندگي *sharmindagī*, s.f. Disgrace, shame. P.

شرمول *sharmawul*, v.a. To disgrace, shame, dishonour; to rape, ravish.

شرميدل *sharmedal*, v.n. To blush, be modest, be abashed, ashamed, etc.

شروع *shurū'*, s.f. Beginning, commencement. A.

شري *sharai*, s.m. The measles; a rash on the body of infants; tooth-rash. A. (*sharā*).

شرير *sharīr*, a. Wicked, depraved, vicious. A.

شريعت *sharī'at*, s.m. Muḥammadan law; equity, justice, law. A.

شريف *sharīf*, a. Noble, eminent. A.

شريفه *sharīfa*, s.f. The eave of a roof; projecting ledge of a wall.

شريک *sharīk*, s.m. Accomplice, ally; comrade, partner. A.

شړته *sharata*, s.f. See شړهته.

شړشم *sharsham*, s.m. Mustard (the plant and seed). P. (*sarshaf*). S. (*sarson*).

شړل *sharal*, v.a. To eject, depose, turn out, drive away. A. (*shārid*).

شړنگ *shrang*, s.m. A jingle, clink, chink; chime, ring, echo.

شړنگول *shrangawul*, v.a. To jingle, ring, etc.

شړنگيدل *shrangedal*, v.n. To chime, jingle, ring, tinkle, etc. P. (*charangīdan*).

شړونکي *sharūnkai*, | a. Deposed, expelled,
شړوني *sharūnai*, | ejected.

شړهته *sharhata*, s.f. A barleycorn, grain of barley; a particle, bit, small quantity.

شړهيدل *sharhedal*, v.n. To crumble, decay, decompose, rot, become sodden, etc. H. (*sarnā*).

شړئ *shara-ī*, s.f. A blanket. A. (*sh'ar*).

شست *shast*, s.m. The space between the thumb and forefinger; a thumbstall (used by archers); aim, sight (as of a gun or arrow). P.

شستئ *shasta-ī*, s.f. Name of a plant (*Chrysanthemum Indicum*).

ششت *shasht*, s.m. A mirror attached to a ring and worn on the thumb by women.

ششني *shashanai*, | s.m. The neigh of a
ششڼړي *shashanrai*, | horse.

ششڼريدل *shashanredal*, v.n. To neigh.

شعر *shi'r*, s.m. Poetry, verse. A.

شعله *shu'la*, s.f. A blaze, flame. A.

شعور *shu'ūr*, s.m. Intellect, reason, knowledge. A.

شغ *shagh*, s.m. Whizz, whirr (as of a bullet or bird passing through the air), etc.

شغال *shaghāl*, s.m. A jackal. P.

شغرب‌مغرب *shaghrib-maghrib*, s.m. East and west. A. (*mashriq-maghrib*).

شغل *shughl*, s.m. Employment, occupation. A.

شغله *shughla*, s.f. See شعله.

شفا *shifā*, s.f. Cure, recovery; remedy. A.

شفاعت *shafā'at*, s.m. Entreaty, intercession, recommendation. A.

شفتالو *shaftālū*, s.m. A peach. P.

شفق *shafaq*, s.m. Twilight, dusk. A.

شفقت *shafaqat*, s.m. Clemency, compassion, kindness, mercy. A.

شک *shakk*, s.m. Doubt, suspicion; hesitation, uncertainty. A.

شکار *shkār*, s.m. Alkali, potash.

شکال *shkāl*, s.m. Hobbles for the fore feet of a horse. See شکيل.

شکايت *shikāyat*, s.m. Complaint, accusation. A.

شکر *shukr*, s.m. Gratitude, thanks. A.

شکرانه *shukrāna*, s.f. Gratitude, thanks; premium, fee, payment for service done. P.

شکره *shakara*, s.f. Sugar. P. (*shakar*).

شکري *shikrai*, s.m. A kind of falcon or hawk. P. (*shikrah*). *shkarai*, s.m. A flat basket of a circular shape. H. (*sikhar*).

شکست *shikast*, a. Broken, fractured; dispersed, worsted, beaten. P.

شکل *shakl*, s.m. Appearance, figure, form, etc. A.

شکلي *shaklai*, s.m. The end or tail of a turban.

شکم *shikam*, s.m. The belly (in comp.). P.

شکمن *shakk-man*, a. Doubtful, dubious, suspicious.

شکنجه *shikandza*, s.f. A press, vice; bookbinder's press; stocks for the legs; rack, pillory; torture. P. (*shikanja*).

شكور *shkor*, } s.m. A flat basket. H. (*sikhar*).
شكير *shker*, }

شكونړ *shkūnr*, s.m. A porcupine.

شكيل *shkel*, s.m. P. (*shikil* or *shigil*). See شكال.

شګاره *shigāra*, s.f. A pregnant woman or animal.

شګري *shigrai*, s.m. A priming horn, powder horn.

شګلن *shiglan*, a. Sandy, gravelly.

شګوفه *shigūfa*, s.f. A bud, blossom. P.

شګه *shiga*, s.f. Sand, gravel.

شل *shall*, a. Paralyzed, palsied. P. *shal*, s.m. A pike, javelin, spear. P. *shil*, a. Twenty, a score.

شلانده *shlānda*, s.f. A toad, frog.

شلټ *shalaṭ*, a. See شل.

شلخي *shalkhai*, s.m. Name of a pot-herb; common dock (*Rumex acutus*).

شلغم *shalgham*, s.m. A turnip. P.

شلك *shilik*, s.m. A discharge, salvo, round, volley, salute, boom of a gun. A. (*shalakh*).

شلم *shilam*, a. Twentieth.

شلوار *shalwār*, s.m. Trousers, pants. P.

شلول *shlawul*, v.a. To tear, rend, split, break, burst. H. (*chīrnā*).

شلوم *shlom*, s.m. } See شوملي.
شلونبي *shlonbe*, s.f. }

شليته *shalīta*, s.f. A large sack or net for baggage, etc. (when loaded on cattle). P.

شليدل *shledal*, v.n. To burst, tear, split, break, etc. H. (*chirnā*).

شمار *shumār*, s.m. Counting, reckoning. P.

شمارل *shmāral*, v.a. To count. See شميرل.

شمال *shimāl*, s.m. The North. *shamāl*, North wind. A.

شمځي *shamdza-ī*, s.f. Spine, backbone.

شمشتي *shamshata-ī*, s.f. A tortoise.

شمشير *shamsher*, s.m. A sword. P.

شمعه *sham'a*, s.f. A candle, lamp. A.

شمكلي *shamkalai*, s.m. The unwoven end of a web or warp (used as a duster, etc.).

شمكور *shamkor*, a. Night-blind, nyctalopic. s.m. One who is subject to night-blindness. P. (*shab-kor*).

شمكوري *shamkorī*, s.f. Night-blindness, nyctalopia.

شمكي *shamkai*, s.m. Name of a plant used in medicine; vervain.

شمله *shamla*, s.f. The end of a turban; a shawl or sash for the waist.

شموخه *shamūkha*, s.f. Name of a grass and its seed (*Panicum frumentaceum*). P. (*shāmākh*).

شمه *shama*, s.m. An atom, jot, particle; odour, perfume. A.

شميرل *shmeral*, v.a. To count, compute, reckon. P. (*shumārīdan*).

شناخت *shnākht*, s.m. Acquaintance, recognition, knowledge. P. (*shinākht*).

شناز *shināz*, s.m. An inflated hide, used to cross rivers upon. P. (*shinā*, swimming).

شنبه *shanbah*, s.m. Saturday. P.

شنده *shandah*, a. Desperate, inconceivable, incredible, impossible.

شنډ *shanḍ*, a. Barren, sterile, unproductive, unfruitful. H. (*sanḍhar*).

شنډي *shanḍa-ī*, s.f. Name of a tree (*Melia sempervirens*); evergreen bead-tree.

شنګرپ *shingrip*, s.m. Cinnabar, vermillion. P. (*shangarf*).

شنګړي *shingṛa-ī*, s.f. Tower, keep, hornwork of a fort; a mould for casting pottery, etc.

شنل *shanal*, v.a. To explore, look, search, try, sound, etc. P. (*shāndan*, to comb).

شنوا *shinwā*, a. Hearing. P. (*shinudan*).

شنه *shna*, Feminine of شين, which see.

شني *shnai*, s.m. Name of a tree and its fruit (*Pistacia Kabulica*), the mastic tree.

شنيدل *shanedal*, v.n. To flutter, writhe, quiver, wriggle, shake, etc.

شو *sho* or *shaw*, s.m. See شب.

شوپا *shopā*, a. Uncircumcised; term of abuse.

شوپرک *sho·parak*, s.m. A bat. P. (*shab·para*).

شوتل *shotal*, s.m. Name of a trefoil (*Trifolium repens*). P. (*shaftal*). Name of a pot-herb (*Malva parviflora*), marsh-mallow.

شوخ *shokh*, a. Cheerful, humorous; playful, mischievous; insolent, pert; wanton, saucy. P.

شوخون *sho·khūn*, s.m. A night attack, surprise. P. (*shab·khūn*).

شوخي *shokhī*, s.f. Fun, mischief, frolic; coquetry, lewdness, wantonness. P.

شوده *shaudah*, s.m. Milk.

شور *shor*, s.m. Cry, noise, riot. P.

شوړه *shoṛa*, s.f. The beard of grasses; a wisp of grass or straw used as a plug or bung.

شوشک *shūshk*, s.m. The curve of an arch.

شوشئ *shūsha-ī*, s.f. A firebrand, torch. P. (*shūsha*).

شوق *shauq*, s.m. Desire, inclination; fondness, love; gaiety, cheerfulness; curiosity. A.

شوقدر *sho·qadar*, s.m. Name of a festival on the 14th of the month *sh'abān* (*shabi·barāt*). P. (*shab·qadr*).

شوک *shūk*, a. Plucked, robbed, stripped, etc.
shūk·pūk, a. Plucked bare, bare as a bone.

شوکاڼري *shokāṇrai*, s.m. A flat stone used to bake cakes upon; soapstone, firestone (used for the vent hole of a furnace, etc.).

شوکت *shaukat*, s.m. Dignity, pomp, state. A.

شوکور *sho·kor*, a. See شمکور.

شوکول *shūkawul*, v.a. To pluck, pick, cull; to rob, strip, tear off, etc. P. (*shūkhūdan*).

شوکه *shūka*, s.f. Plundering, robbing, stripping (as passengers on the roads). The beak of a bird.

شوګه *shūga*, s.f. A kind of rice.

شوګير *sho·gīr*, a. Watching by night, vigilant; a night watch, vigil. P. (*shab·gīr*).

شوګيري *sho·gīrī*, s.f. Watching at night, awake all night, etc.

شول *shwal*, v.n. To be, become, exist. P. (*shudan*).

شولخ *sholakh*, s.m. The skin of the tongue.

شولګره *sholgara*, s.f. A rice field, a rice swamp.

شوله *shola*, s.f. The rice plant. P. (*shālī*).
shūla, s.f. The colic. S. (*sūl*).

شوم *shūm*, a. Miserly, stingy; unfortunate, vile; hungry, faint. A.

شوملي *shomle*, s.f. (pl. of *shomla*, obsolete), Buttermilk, curds and whey.

شومه *shūma*, s.f. The watch between midnight and daylight; food taken at that hour; food given to the friends of a deceased person on the night of the funeral. P.

شومي *shūmī*, s.f. Hunger, faintness; stingyness, niggardliness; misfortune, etc. A.

شونټئ *shonṭa-ī*, s.f. A pine torch, slips of resinous pine wood used as torches, matches, etc.

شونډ *shūnḍ*, s.m. The lip. S. (*honṭh*).

شونډپاره *shūnḍ·pāra*, s.f. Hare lip.

شونډک *shūnḍak*, s.m. The proboscis of an elephant.

شونډه *shūnḍa*, s.f. The lip.

شوه *shawa*, s.f. Name of a tree, the sisoo (*Dalbergia sisoo*).

شوي *shoe*, s.m. Coarse cotton cloth.

شها *shahā*, s.f. A mistress, sweetheart. A.

شهاب *shihāb*, s.m. A meteor, falling star. A.
shahāb, s.m. Milk and water. A.

شهتير *shahtīr*, s.m. A rafter, beam. P.

شهد *shahd*, s.m. Honey. P.

شهده shuhdak, s.m. A blackguard, debauchee, rake, libertine, profligate. H. (shuhdā).

شهرت shuhrat, s.m. Fame, renown; divulging, celebrating, publishing. A.

شهلا shahlā, a. Hazel-eyed. A.

شهند shahand, s.m. A kind of falcon.

شهوت shahwat, s.m. Lust, concupiscence. A.

شهوتناك shahwat-nāk, شهوتي shahwatī, } a. Lascivious, lewd, lustful; lust exciting. A.

شهيد shahīd, s.m. A martyr, witness. a. Killed. A.

شهين shahīn, s.m. A kind of Falcon; a camel gun, a wall piece, carronade. P. The beam of a balance.

شي shai, s.m. An article, item, thing. A.

شيبره shebara, s.f. A continued fever.

شيبه shebah, s.m. A downpour, heavy shower (of rain).

شيخ shekh, s.m. A chief, prelate; venerable old man; a title given to converts to Islam. A.

شيدا shaidā, a. Love mad; in love. P.

شير sher, s.m. A lion, tiger. P. shīr, s.m. Milk (in comp.). P.

شيرازه shīrāza, s.f. The stitching at the back of a book; the curtain or wall of a fort. P.

شيرخشت shīr-khisht, s.m. A kind of manna. P.

شيرخط sher-khaṭ, s.m. Heads and tails, pitch and toss, tossing money for play.

شيره shīra, s.f. Batter, pap. P.

شيرين shīrīn, a. Sweet; affable, gentle, pleasant, etc. (in comp.). P.

شيشك shīshk, s.m. Name of a plant (*Lithospermum arvense*).

شيشكي shīshkai, s.m. A hedgehog. P. (chizak).

شيشه shīsha, s.f. A mirror, looking glass. P.

شيطان shaiṭān, s.m. The devil, Satan. A.

شيطاني shaiṭānī, s.f. Devilry, wickedness.

شيعه shī'ah, s.m. A follower of the sect of 'Ali; a heretic, infidel; sectarian. A.

شيله shela, s.f. A ravine, gully, watercourse; dry bed of a river.

شين shīn, a. Green, verdant; fresh, clear; blue, azure (as the sky). f. shna.

شيني shīnai, s.m. A whitlow; a tick, dog-louse.

شيوه shewa, s.f. Declivity, slope, slant. P. (sheba). Business, profession, trade; custom, habit; toilet, decoration; coquetry.

ښ

ښ kkhīn or kshīn, called also kheshīn, is the twenty-third letter of the Pukkhto alphabet. It is a combined form of خ and ش and corresponds in sound with the Hindi ख or ष. By the Yusufzais and Eastern Afghans generally, it is pronounced as kkh, and by the Khaṭaks and Western tribes as ksh. It is very often substituted for ش in words introduced from the Persian.

ښاپيرك kkhāperak, s.m. A bat. P. (shab parak).

ښاپيري kkhāperai, s.m. A fairy; the king of the fairies. P. (shāh-parī).

ښاخ kkhākh, s.m. Branch or bough of a tree; the branch or arm of a river, etc. P. (shākh).

ښاخي kkhākha-ī, s.f. A pitchfork, prong.

ښاد kkhād, a. Delighted, happy, pleased, gay, etc. P. (shād).

ښادان kkhādān, ښادمن kkhād-man, } a. Joyous, happy, gay.

ښادي kkhādī, s.f. Delight, joy, happiness, pleasure, etc. P. (shādī).

ښاديانه kkhādiyāna, s.f. Festivity, music, song; rejoicing. P. (shādiyāna).

ښارك kkhārak, s.m. The piece of wood (in the mouth of the upper millstone) through which the iron axle of a hand-mill passes; a piece of wood in the mouth of a churning jar or bottle for the passage of the churn stick.

ښرگ *kkhārag*, s.m. The jugular vein. P. (*shāh-rag*).

ښاروني *kkhārūna-ī*, s.f. A starling.

ښاغل *kkhāghal*, v.a. To gratify, please, content; to choose, like, prefer.

ښامار *kkhāmār*, s.m. King of serpents, a dragon. P. (*shāh-mār*).

ښانک *kkhānak*, s.m. A kneading dish, trencher, a wooden platter. P. (*shānak*).

ښانگه *kkhānga*, s.f. The lower limb, thigh and leg, inferior extremity.

ښانگه ور *kkhānga-war*, a. Long-legged, spindle-shanked.

ښايست *kkhāyast*, s.m. Beauty, comeliness, elegance, grace; worthiness, propriety, fitness. Also *kkhāyast-wālai*.

ښايسته *kkhāyastah*, a. Handsome, beautiful, comely; worthy, fit, proper; well, good. P. (*shā-īstah*).

ښائي *kkhā-ī*, ad. May be, perhaps, possibly, probably. P. (*shāyad*).

ښپه *kkhpa*, s.f. The foot.

ښتري *kkhatrī*, s.m. A Hindu trader or shopkeeper. S. (*khatrī* or *kshatri*).

ښتگري *kkhatgarai*, s.m. The ankle, ankle joint; fetlock, fetlock joint.

ښځونک *kkhadzonak*, s.m. Hermaphrodite, effeminate man.

ښځه *kkhadza* or *kkhidza*, s.f. Woman. wife. a. Female, feminine, feminine gender. A. (*zauja*).

ښخ *kkhakh*, a. Hard, rigid, inflexible, stiff. P. (*shakh*). a. Buried, etc. See خښ.

ښرا *kkharā*, s.f. A curse. See ښيره.

ښروه *kkharawa*, s.f. The yew tree (*Taxus baccata*). The castor oil tree (*Ricinus communis*). A. (*khuroa'*).

ښكار *kkhkār*, s.m. Chase, hunting, sport; game, prey; plunder. P. (*shikār*).

ښكاره *kkhkārah*, a. Clear, manifest, apparent, visible, evident. P. (*āshkār*).

ښكاري *kkhkārī*, s.m. A hunter. fowler, sportsman; a robber. P. (*shikārī*).

ښكالوه *kkhkālwah*, s.m. Conversation, discussion; buzz, hum, murmur (of talking).

ښكته *kkhkata*, ad. Down, below, under. *kkhkatanai*, a. Inferior, lower, under.

ښكر *kkhkar*, s.m. A horn, antler; powder horn.

ښكري *kkhkarai*, s.m. A flat round basket. See شكري *shkarai*.

ښكل *kkhkul*, s.m. A kiss. *kkhkul-kawul*, v.a. To kiss. *kkhkal*, v.a. To draw, pull, tighten; to pen, write; endure, suffer; flay, remove, strip. See كښل.

ښكلول *kkhkulawul*, v.a. To kiss.

ښكلي *kkhkulai*, a. Kissed; handsome, pretty; comely, elegant; agreeable, pleasant. *kkhkalai*, a. Drawn, tight, tense; written; suffered, endured, etc.

ښكنځل *kkhkandzal*, s.m. Abuse, vituperation. P. *kkhkandzal* or *kkhkandzal-kawul*, v.a. To abuse, call bad names, etc. P. (*shikanjīdan*).

ښكول *kkhakawul*, v.a. To move, shake, loosen; slide, slip; push, thrust. *kkhkawul*, v.a. To cause to draw, extract, etc. See ښكل *kkhkal*.

ښكيدل *kkhakedal*, v.n. To fall, glide, slip, slide.

ښكيل *kkhkel*, s.m. A hobble, tether, fetter for the feet of cattle (to prevent their straying); cheat, fraud, imposition, trick. See شكيل.

ښكيه *kkhkiya*, ad. See ښكته.

ښلونه *kkhalūna*, s.f. A whitlow, abscess, boil.

ښندل *kkhandal*, v.a. To bestow, contribute, give, dispense, spend, etc.

ښنزه *kkhanza*, s.f. A boil, abscess, pustule.

ښنګري *kkhangarai*, s.m. Ankle, ankle-joint; fetlock; a cloven hoof.

ښنه *kkhna*, s.f. The hip bone (*os ilium*).

ښوڅه *kkhūtsa*, s.f. Nettlerash, hives.

ښور *kkhor*, s.m. Nest or hive of ants, bees, or wasps, etc.

ښورن *kkhoran*, a. Barren, sterile; nitrous, saline (as land).

ښوروا *kkhorwā*, s.f. Soup, broth. P. (*shorbā*).

ښورول *kkhorawul*, v.a. To move, agitate, rock, wave to and fro, etc.

ښوره *kkhora*, s.f. Nitre, saltpetre. P. (*shora*) *kkhora-nāk*, a. Barren, sterile, full of nitre.

ښوريدل *kkhoredal*, v.n. To move, undulate, vibrate, wave, swing. P. (*shorīdan*).

ښونه *kkhona*, s.f. The olive tree.

ښوول *kkhowul*, v.a. To show, indicate. See ښيل.

ښوي *kkhwai*, a. Slippery, smooth.

ښوهول *kkhwahawul*, } v.a. To slide, slip, or
ښويول *kkhwayawul*, } push along (on a smooth surface).

ښوئيدل *kkhwa-edal*, v.n. To slip, slide, glide, fall down. Also ښوهيدل *kkhwahedal*. P. (*shāfīdan*).

ښه *kkhah* or *kshah*, a. Good, proper, well; healthy, sound; fair, pleasant, etc. in. Well! Good! P. (*khūb*).

ښهر *kkhahr*, s.m. A town, city. P. (*shahr*).

ښي *kkhai* or *kshai*, a. Right, right hand, etc.

ښيره *kkhera* or *kshera*, s.f. Curse, malediction, imprecation, denunciation.

ښيښه *kkhīkkha*, s.f. A bottle, glass, phial. P. (*shīsha*).

ښيګړه *kkhegaṛa*, s.f. Excellence, goodness; value, worth; profit, advantage, benefit.

ښيل *kkhayal*, v.a. To show, point out; teach, instruct. P. (*nishāndan*). Def. in past ten. See ښوول. *kkhayal*, v.a. To reject, repudiate, turn off (as a disobedient son, etc.); to arm, equip oneself. P. (*shāyīdan*).

ښينه *kkhīna*, s.f. Sister-in-law, wife's sister.

ص

ص *ṣwād* is the fourteenth letter of the Arabic and the twenty-fourth of the Pukkhto alphabet. It is generally pronounced like س, and is only found in words adopted from the Arabic.

صاحب *ṣāḥib*, s.m. Master, lord; owner, possessor. A.

صادر *ṣādir*, a. Happened, issued, produced, passed, etc. A.

صاف *ṣāf*, a. Clean, pure, candid, frank, etc. A.

صافي *ṣāfī*, s.f. A filter, strainer.

صبا *ṣabā*, s.m. Morning, dawn; to-morrow; the morning breeze. A. (*ṣabāḥ*).

صبح *ṣubḥ*, s.f. Morning, daybreak, dawn. A.

صبر *ṣabr*, s.m. Endurance, patience. A.

صحاف *ṣaḥḥāf*, s.m. A bookbinder; bookseller. A.

صحبت *ṣuḥbat*, s.m. Companionship, society, picnic, dinner party, company; cohabitation; coition. A.

صحت *ṣiḥḥat*, s.m. Health, integrity, perfection. A.

صحرا *ṣaḥrā*, s.f. A desert, wilderness. A.

صحي *ṣaḥī*, a. Accurate, true, just, certain, perfect, entire. A. (*ṣaḥīḥ*).

صداقت *ṣadāqat*, s.m. Sincerity, truthfulness, candour, friendship. A.

صدقه *ṣadqa*, s.f. Alms, propitiatory offerings, sacrifice. A.

صديق *ṣadīq*, a. Faithful, true, sincere, just. A.

صراف *ṣarrāf*, s.m. A banker, money lender. A.

صرف *ṣirf*, ad. Only, alone; simply, merely,

etc. A. *ṣarf*, s.m. Excess, gain, increase; expense, expenditure, waste. A.

صرفه *ṣarfa*, s.f. Expense, expending; profit, profusion; surplus; waste. A.

صف *ṣaff*, s.m. A line, file, rank, row; series, order, etc. A.

صفا *ṣafā*, a. Clean, clear, pure. A.

صفائی *ṣafā-ī*, s.f. Purity, cleanness; innocence. A.

صفت *ṣifat*, s.m. Attribute, quality; commendation, praise; description; an adjective. A.

صفحه *ṣafḥa*, s.f. Page of a book; face, surface. A.

صفره *ṣafara*, s.f. Name of the second month of the Muhammadan calendar. A. (*ṣafar*).

صلحه *ṣulḥa*, s.f. Concord, peace; reconciliation, truce, treaty, armistice. A. (*ṣulḥ*).

صلوة *ṣalūt*, } s.m. Benediction, prayer; mercy or compassion of God. A.
صلات *ṣalāt*, }

صندل *ṣandal*, s.m. Sandal wood. A.

صندوق *ṣandūq*, s.m. A box, trunk, chest, casket. A.

صندوقچه *ṣandūqcha*, s.f. Casket, small box.

صنوبر *ṣanobar*, s.m. A fir, pine, conifer. A.

صواب *ṣawāb*, s.m. Virtuous action; rectitude, right. A.

صوبه *ṣūba*, s.f. A province, division of a country. A. *ṣūba-dār*, s.m. Viceroy, provincial governor.

صورت *ṣūrat*, s.m. Appearance, form, face; portrait, countenance; manner; case, condition, state; body, person; the privates. A.

صوفي *ṣūfī*, a. Pious, devout; intelligent, wise. s.m. A philosopher, members of the Sūfī sect. A.

صياد *ṣayād*, s.m. A hunter, fowler, sportsman. A.

صيد *ṣaid*, s.m. Game, prey. A.

صيقل *ṣaiqal*, s.m. Cleaning, polishing, scouring, furbishing; a polisher, etc. A.

صيقلگر *ṣaiqal-gar*, s.m. A polisher of swords, knives, etc.

ض

ض *dwād* or *ẓād*, is the fifteenth letter of the Arabic, and the twenty-fifth of the Pukkhto alphabet. It is pronounced like ز, and is only found in words from the Arabic, in which language it has the sound of *d* or *dh*.

ضابط *ẓābiṭ*, s.m. Master, ruler, governor. A.

ضابطه *ẓābiṭa*, s.f. Canon law, rule, regulation. A.

ضامن *ẓāmin*, s.m. Security, sponsor, bail, bond. A.

ضامني *ẓāminī*, s.f. Surety, bail, security.

ضايعه *ẓāy'a*, s.f. Loss, detriment, injury. *ẓāy'ah*, a. Lost, destroyed, spoiled, perished; fruitless, abortive. A. (*ẓāī'*).

ضبط *ẓabṭ*, s.m. Confiscation; check, control. a. Confiscated, seized. A.

ضحى *ẓuḥā*, s.m. Forenoon, between sunrise and noon; a prayer repeated at that time. A.

ضد *ẓidd*, s.m. Contrary, opposite; enemy, rival; opposition, contrariety. A.

ضرب *ẓarb*, s.m. A blow, thump; coining; stamp; violence; emphasis (in speech). A.

ضرر *ẓarar*, s.m. Damage, detriment, injury; loss, ruin; affliction, distress. A.

ضرور *ẓarūr*, a. Expedient, necessary; urgent, unavoidable. A.

ضرورت *ẓarūrat*, s.m. Necessity, exigence, want; compulsion, force. A.

ضعف *ẓu'f*, s.m. Debility, weakness. A.

ضعيف *ẓa'īf*, a. Weak, feeble, infirm. A.

ضلعه *ẓil'a*, s.f. A district, division of a province. A.

ضماد *ẓamād*, s.m. Embrocation, plaster. A.

ضمانت *ẓamānat*, s.m. Security, bail, surety. A.

ضيافت *ẓiyāfat*, s.m. Banquet, entertainment, feast; invitation, hospitality. A.

ط

ط *ṭoe* is the sixteenth letter of the Arabic and the twenty-sixth of the Pukkhto alphabet. It is only found in words adopted from the Arabic, and has a sound stronger than ت, for which it is sometimes changed.

طابوت *ṭābūt*, s.m. A coffin, bier. A.

طاعت *ṭā'at*, s.m. Obedience, devotion. A.

طاق *ṭāq*, s.m. An arch, cupola; alcove, shelf. a. Odd, singular, unique, not even. A. *juft-o-ṭāq*, s.m. Odd and even (the game).

طاقچه *ṭāqcha*, s.f. A niche, recess, shelf.

طاقت *ṭāqat*, s.m. Ability, force, power, strength. A.

طاقي *ṭāqī*, a. Arched, arching.

طالب *ṭālib*, s.m. An enquirer, seeker; student. Asking, demanding. A.

طالع *ṭāli'*, s.m. Appearing, rising (as the sun). A. *ṭāli'-man*, a. Fortunate, prosperous.

طائفه *ṭā-ifa*, s.f. People, nation, race, tribe; party, band, troop; suite, equipage. A.

طب *ṭibb*, s.m. Medicine, magic. A.

طبابت *ṭibābat*, s.m. The practice of medicine. A.

طباق *ṭabāq*, s.m. A kneading dish or platter. A.

طبعه *ṭab'a*, s.f. Disposition, temperament, nature, quality. A. (*ṭab'*).

طبق *ṭabaq*, s.m. A dish, plate; leaf; disk; cover; a layer; gold leaf. A.

طبقه *ṭabqa*, s.f. A floor, stage, story; class, order; degree, rank; a shelf, recess. A.

طبل *ṭabl*, s.m. A drum. A.

طبله *ṭabla*, s.f. A small tambourine, small drum; a wooden platter or tray for fruit, etc. A.

طبيب *ṭabīb*, s.m. A physician. A.

طبيبي *ṭabībī*, s.f. Profession of a physician, physic. A.

طبيعت *ṭabī'at*, s.m. Nature, disposition, temper; constitution, health; property, quality, essence. A.

طبيله *ṭabela*, s.f. A stable. A.

طرب *ṭrab*, s.m. Hilarity, mirth, joy. A.

طرحه *ṭarḥa*, s.f. Manner, mode. A. (*ṭaraḥ*).

طرز *ṭarz*, s.m. Fashion, mode, manner. A.

طرف *ṭaraf*, s.m. Side, direction, quarter. A. *ṭaraf-dār*, s.m. A follower, partizan. a. Partial, prejudicial. *ṭaraf-dārī*, s.f. Favour, assistance; prejudice.

طرفين *ṭarafain*, s.m. Both sides, both parties. A.

طريقه *ṭarīqa*, s.f. Path, way; manner, mode; religion, rite; sect, party; custom, habit. A.

طعام *ṭa'ām*, s.m. Food, victuals; eating. A.

طعامبه *ṭa'āmba*, s.f. Food, victuals.

طعنه *ṭa'na*, s.f. Reproach, disgrace, reproof; scoffing, reviling, taunting. A. (*ṭa'n*).

طغيان *ṭughiyān*, s.m. Rebellion, sedition; perverseness, insolence. *ṭughiyānī*, s.f. Excess, overflowing, flood. A.

طفل *ṭifl*, s.m. Babe, infant. A. *ṭiflī* or *ṭufūliyat*, s.m. Infancy, childhood. A.

طفيل *ṭufail*, s.m. Sponger, parasite, glutton. A. ad. Through, by means of, by agency of. A.

طلا *ṭilā*, s.f. Gold; name of a gold coin, ducat. A.

طلاق *ṭalāq*, s.m. Divorce, repudiation. A.

طلائي *ṭilā-ī*, a. Golden, covered with gold. A.

طلب *ṭalab*, s.m. Demand, desire, request; call, summons; enquiry, search; pay, salary. A. *ṭalab-dār*, s.m. A creditor; dunning, demanding. *ṭalab-gār*, s.m. A seeker.

enquirer. a. Desirous. *ṭalab-nāma*, s.f. A summons, citation.

طلبه *ṭalaba*, s.f. A lure, call, etc. for hawks, etc.

طلسم *ṭilism*, s.m. Amulet, charm, spell, talisman; marvel, wonder, prodigy. A.

طمعه *ṭam'a*, s.f. Avidity; desire, longing; avarice, greediness, covetousness. A. (*ṭam'*).

طناب *ṭanāb*, s.m. Tent rope, clothes line, cord, etc. A.

طور *ṭaur*, s.m. Manner, mode; condition, state. A.

طوفان *ṭūfān*, s.m. Deluge; inundation; tempest, storm, hurricane. A. *ṭūfānī*, a. Boisterous, stormy; quarrelsome.

طوق *ṭauq*, s.m. Yoke, collar; necklace; ring for the neck. A.

طول *ṭūl*, s.m. Length. a. Long, lasting. A.

طومار *ṭūmār*, s.m. A book, volume. A.

طهارت *ṭahārat*, s.m. Purity, cleanliness; sanctity; purification. A.

طي *ṭai*, s.m. Folding, rolling up. A.

ظ

ظ *zoe* is the seventeenth letter of the Arabic and the twenty-seventh of the Pukkhto alphabet. It is only found in words from the Arabic.

ظالم *ẓālim*, s.m. Oppressor, tyrant. a. Cruel, oppressive, tyrannical. A.

ظاهر *ẓāhir*, a. Manifest, apparent, evident, clear; outward appearance.

ظاهرا *ẓāhirā*, ظاهراً *ẓāhiran*, ad. Outwardly, apparently, publicly, openly, evidently. A.

ظاهري *ẓāhirī*, a. Outward, external, apparent. A.

ظرافت *ẓarāfat*, s.m. Elegance; politeness; wit, humour; polish. A.

ظرف *ẓarf*, s.m. A vase, vessel, jar.

ظريف *ẓarīf*, a. Witty, jocose; ingenious, clever; elegant, polished, polite. A.

ظفر *ẓafar*, s.m. Victory, triumph. A.

ظلم *ẓulm*, s.m. Oppression, injustice, cruelty, tyranny. A.

ظلمت *ẓulmat*, s.m. Obscurity, darkness, A.

ظن *ẓann*, s.m. Idea, thought, opinion; suspicion, jealousy. A.

ظني *ẓannī*, a. Supposed; suspected. A.

ظهر *ẓuhr*, s.m. Mid-day; the time just after the sun has passed the meridian. A.

ع

ع *'ain* is the eighteenth letter of the Arabic and the twenty-eighth of the Pukkhto alphabet. It is a very weak guttural aspirate, articulated by compression of the muscles of the fauces. It varies in sound according to the vowel point by which it is "moved," and in this work is represented by ' placed above and before the vowel by which it is "moved," as *'a*, *'i*, *'u*, etc. It is only found in words derived from the Arabic, and is sometimes replaced by ا.

عابد *'ābid*, s.m. A devotee, votary. A.

عاجز *'ājiz*, a. Humble, helpless; hopeless, dejected; exhausted, weak; impotent, powerless. A.

عاجزي *'ājizī*, s.m. Weakness; helplessness; humility.

عادت *'ādat*, s.m. Custom, usage, habit. A. *'ādatī*, a. Habituated, accustomed, inured, addicted.

عادل *'ādil*, a. Just, upright, impartial. A.

عارف *'ārif*, a. Devout, holy; wise, ingenious. A.

عاريت *'āriyat*, s.m. Borrowing, lending (what is itself to be returned). A. *'āriyatī*, a. Borrowed; lent.

عاشق *'āshiq*, s.m. A lover. A. *'āshiqī*, s.f. Amour, love, courtship.

عاشوره *'āshūra*, s.f. The first ten days of the month Muḥarram. A.

عاصي *'āṣī*, s.m. A sinner, rebel. A.

عافيت *'āfiyat*, s.m. Health, safety. A.

عاقبت *'āqibat*, s.m. Conclusion, end; futurity, the future. ad. After all, finally, at last. A.

عاقل *'āqil*, a. Sensible, wise. A.

عالم *'ālam*, s.m. The world, universe; people, mankind, creation; time, state. A. *'ālim*, a. Learned, knowing, wise. A.

عالي *'ālī*, a. Eminent, high, sublime. A.

عام *'āmm*, a. Common, general, public. s.m. The vulgar, public, common people. A.

عامّي *'āmmī*, s.m. A layman; one of the public.

عامل *'āmil*, s.m. Revenue collector, governor, ruler, finance minister. A.

عائد *'ā-id*, a. Happening, occurring; reverting, returning (as money, etc.). A.

عبادت *'ibādat*, s.m. Adoration, divine worship. A.

عبارت *'ibārat*, s.m. Meaning, signification; phrase, style, speech. A.

عبث *'abas̱*, a. Vain, useless, absurd, idle. ad. In vain, uselessly. A.

عبرت *'ibrat*, s.m. Example, warning. A.

عبور *'ubūr*, s.m. A ferry, ford; crossing, passing over. A.

عتاب *'itāb*, s.m. Anger, displeasure, rebuke, reproach, reprimand. A.

عجائب *'ajā-ib*, a. Wonderful, astonishing. s.m. Wonders, curiosities. A.

عجب *'ajab*, } a. Wonderful, rare, curious. A.
عجيب *'ajīb*, }

عجز *'ajz*, s.m. Impotence, weakness, helplessness; meekness, humility, submission. A.

عدالت *'adālat*, s.m. A court of justice; equity, justice; law. A.

عداوت *'adāwat*, s.m. Animosity, enmity, hostility, hatred, strife. A.

عدد *'adad*, s.m. Number; item. A.

عدل *'adl*, s.m. Justice, equity. A.

عدم *'adam*, s.m. Nonexistence, nonentity; nothing; privation. A.

عدول *'udūl*, s.m. Refusing, declining. A.

عذاب *'aẕāb*, s.m. Anguish, torment, pain; torture, punishment. A.

عذر *'uẕr*, s.m. Apology, excuse. A. *'uẕr-khwāh*, s.m. Apologist; condoler, sympathizer. P. *'uẕr-khwāhī*, s.f. Apology, excuse; condolence, sympathy. P.

عرس *'urs*, s.m. Oblations, offerings (to a saint); a marriage feast. A.

عرش *'arsh*, s.m. Firmament; roof; throne. A.

عرصه *'arṣa*, s.f. Area, space; interval, while, time; a plain. A.

عرض *'arẓ*, s.m. Petition, request, representation. A. *'arẓ-begī*, s.m. An officer who presents petitions, letters, etc. (in native courts). T. *'arẓ-dāsht*, s.m. Statement, written petition. P. *'arẓ-dār*, s.m. A petitioner. P. *'araẓ*, s.m. An accident, casualty; muster of troops. A.

عرضي *'arẓī*, s.f. A memorial, petition; letter from an inferior. A.

عرف *'urf*, a. Known as, alias, commonly called; the late; proper, equitable; goodness, merit; confession. A.

عرفي *'urfī*, a. Notorious, well-known, public. A.

عرق *'araq*, s.m. Essence, juice; spirit; sap; sweat. A.

عروس *'arūs*, s.f. Bride, spouse. A. *'arūsī*, s.f. Marriage, wedding. A.

عزت *'izzat*, s.m. Grandeur, power; glory; honour, respect. A.

عزلت *'azlat*, s.m. Retirement (from office), dismissal, discharge. A.

عزلتي *'azlatī*, s.m. A hermit, recluse. A.

عزلي *'azlī*, s.f. Abdication, retirement. A.

عزم *'azm*, s.m. Purpose, intention, design. A.

عزيز *'azīz*, a. Dear, beloved, precious. s.m. An esteemed or honoured friend; great man, saint; a nephew; a king of Egypt (the title). A.

عزيزگلي *'azīz·galī*, عزيزولي *'azīz·walī*, } s.m. Relationship between nephew and uncles.

عزيزي *'azīzī*, s.f. Esteem, respect, friendship.

عسل *'asl*, s.m. Honey. A.

عشر *'ushr*, s.m. Tithe, tenth part. A.

عشرت *'ashrat*, s.m. Enjoyment, pleasure, delight; society, pleasant intercourse, etc. A.

عشق *'ishq*, s.m. Affection, love. A. *'ishq·bāz*, a. Amorous, gallant. P. *'ishq·bāzī*, s.f. Love-making, gallantry. P.

عصا *'aṣā*, s.f. A club, mace, baton, staff. A.

عطا *'aṭā*, s.f. A gift, present; giving. A.

عطار *'aṭṭār*, s.m. A perfumer. A.

عطر *'aṭr*, s.m. Perfume, fragrance, essence. A.

عظيم *'aẓīm*, a. Great, huge, immense; high in dignity. A.

عفريت *'ifrīt*, s.m. Demon, spectre, ghost. A.

عقب *'aqab*, ad. After, behind, in rear. A.

عقد *'aqd*, s.m. Agreement, compact, contract; knot; marriage knot; necklace, collar. A.

عقل *'aql*, s.m. Reason, sense; intellect, wisdom; opinion, understanding. A. *'aql·man*, a. Intelligent, wise. P. *'aql·manī*, s.f. Wisdom, intelligence. P.

عقلي *'aqlī*, a. Judicious, rational, sensible, reasonable. A.

عقوبت *'uqūbat*, s.m. Punishment, torture. A.

عقيده *'aqīda*, s.f. Belief, faith, tenet. A.

عكس *'aks*, s.m. Contrary, opposite; reflection, inversion; image, shadow. A.

علاج *'ilāj*, s.m. Cure, remedy; medicine. A.

علاقه *'ilāqa*, s.f. Relation, connection, interest; commerce, correspondence, intercourse. A.

علامت *'alāmat*, s.m. Mark, sign, symptom; emblem, ensign, escutcheon. A.

علاوه *'alāwa*, ad. Besides, in addition. A.

علت *'illat*, s.m. Cause, pretence; dirt, filth; defect, disease. A.

علف *'alaf*, s.m. Grass, hay, fodder. A.

علم *'ilm*, s.m. Knowledge, science. A.

علماء *'ulamā*, s.m. The learned, scholars, wise. A.

علمي *'ilmī*, a. Learned, scientific. A.

علي *'alī*, a. Eminent, high, noble. A. *'alī bau·bau*, s.m. A bogy, goblin, scarecrow.

عليحده *'alaiḥidah*, a. Apart, separate, distinct. A.

عليم *'alīm*, a. Learned, wise. A.

عمارت *'imārat*, s.m. Building, edifice; habitation, fortification. A.

عمده *'umdah*, a. Great, noble; choice, excellent. A.

عمر *'umr*, s.m. Age, lifetime. A.

عمل *'amal*, s.m. Action, operation, effect; work, practice. A.

عمله *'amala*, s.f. Officials, staff, subordinates. A.

عملي *'amalī*, a. Practical, artificial. A.

عناب *'unnāb*, s.m. Jujube fruit and tree. A.

عناد *'inād*, s.m. Obstinacy, perverseness, stubbornness. A. *'inādī*, a. Stubborn, obstinate, etc.

عنايت *'ināyat*, s.m. Favour, gift, present. A.

عنقا *'unqā*, s.f. The phœnix. A.

عنقريب *'anqarīb*, ad. Nearly, shortly, soon. A.

عنكبوت *'ankabūt*, s.m. A spider. A.

عود *'ūd*, s.m. Aloes wood; incense. A.

عورت *'aurat*, s.m. The private parts. A.

عورته *'aurata*, s.f. A woman, wife.

عوض *'iwaz*, s.m. Retribution, recompense, reward; exchange. A.

عهد *'ahd*, s.m. Compact, contract; promise, treaty; conjuncture, season, time; reign, life-time; oath, vow. A.

عهده *'uhda*, s.f. Commission, obligation, agreement; appointment, office, post. A.

عيال *'ayāl*, s.m. Family, children; household, domestics, etc. A.

عيان *'ayān*, a. Clear, visible, manifest. A.

عيب *'aib*, s.m. Blemish, defect, vice; disgrace, fault, sin. A. *'aib·nāk*, a. Defective, faulty.

عيد *'īd*, s.m. Festival, holy day; Easter. A.

عيش *'aish*, s.m. Enjoyment, delight, pleasure. A. *'aish·o·'ashrat*, s.m. Jollity, enjoyment. A.

عين *'ain*, a. Exact, just, very, real, etc. s.m. The eye; sight; essence. A.

عينكه *'ainaka*, s.f. An eyeglass, spectacles. A. (*'ainak*).

غ

غ *ghain*, is the nineteenth letter of the Arabic, and the twenty-ninth of the Pukkhto alphabet. It is a guttural letter, and is pronounced by a compression of the fauces at the time of articulation. It is sometimes used instead of ق, and is itself sometimes replaced by ګ.

غاب *ghāb*, s.m. A dish, plate. T. (*qāb*).

غار *ghār*, s.m. A cave, cavern, pit. A.

غارت *ghārat*, s.m. Devastation, plunder, sack. A.

غارمه *ghārmah*, s.m. Sun's rays; heat of the sun; noonday heat. P. (*garma*).

غاري *ghārai*, s.m. A glutton.

غاړه *ghāṛa*, s.f. The throat, fauces; coast, shore; border, bank, margin; neck of a bottle or jar; joke, pleasantry, fun. *ghāṛa·ghara-ī*, s.f. Embracing, hugging. a. Connected, joined together.

غازي *ghāzī*, s.m. Champion, hero, warrior (for the faith), crescentader. A.

غاښ *ghākkh*, s.m. A tooth.

غاښور *ghākkhawar*, s.m. Having large teeth; a kind of harrow or rake.

غاښي *ghākkhai*, s.m. A prong, pitchfork; crest or ridge of a mountain, pass over a mountain.

غافل *ghāfil*, a. Careless, negligent, thoughtless. A.

غالب *ghālib*, s.m. A form, mould. A. (*qālib*). *ghālib*, a. Excelling, overcoming, superior. ad. Most likely.

غالبوزه *ghālbūza*, s.f. A hornet, wasp.

غال وبول *ghāl·o·būl*, غال وغول *ghāl·o·ghūl*, } s.m. Clamour, uproar, noise, din.

غالي *ghāla-ī*, غاليچه *ghālīcha*, } s.f. A rug, small carpet. A.

غانده *ghāndah*, a. Disagreeable, offensive, loathsome, stinking. P. (*gandah*).

غاو *ghāw*, s.m. Noise, din, uproar, tumult.

غاوچي *ghāwchī*, s.m. Doorkeeper, porter.

غائب *ghā-ib*, a. Absent, invisible, concealed. A.

غايت *ghāyat*, a. Very, chiefly, extremely. s.m. Extremity, end; filth, ordure, dirt. A.

غبار *ghubār*, s.m. Dust, haze, obscurity, vapour; impurity, foulness. A.

غبرګ *ghbarg*, a. Double, duplex, twofold.

غبغب *ghab·ghab*, s.m. Dewlap, double-chin. P.

غپ *ghap*, s.m. Bark, yelp, snap (of a dog).

غپل *ghapal*, v.a. To bark, snap, yelp, etc.

غپه *ghupa*, s.f. A dip, dive, plunge.

غټ ghaṭ, a. Big, bulky, large, stout, great, etc.; great in rank, power, etc. H. (kaṭṭā).

غټي ghaṭai, s.m. A block, lump, mass, etc.

غڅکي ghuṭskai, s.m. A bullock, ox, bull.

غچ ghach, s.m. Hatred, malice, spite, envy. Noise, sound of walking in mud, etc. H.

غچي ghachī, s.f. Scissors. See بياتي

غدر ghadr, s.m. Villany, deceit, perfidy. A.

غذا ghizā, s.m. Aliment, food, diet. A.

غر ghar, s.m. Mountain, hill. S. (gir). ghur, s.m. Bronchocele, goitre. gha-ar, s.m. Leap, bound, jump. Rattle (as of wheels).

غرا gharā, s.f. Peal, roar, boom, thunder; roaring, thundering (noise).

غراره gharāra, s.f. A large sack. A.

غرانډه gharānḍa, s.f. A blaze, flame.

غربت ghurbat, s.m. Emigration, travelling; exile, separation from friends. A.

غربه gharaba, s.f. A cannon, gun.

غربي gharabbai, s.m. Boom, report (of a cannon). A buckle, breastplate, clasp.

غرپ ghurap, s.m. A gulp. P.

غرپش ghurpish, s.m. Din, clamour, noise, row.

غرڅني ghartsanai, a. Mountain, highland, of the hills.

غرڅه ghartsah, a. A hill goat; inhabitant of the hills, highland (animal).

غرزنگ ghurzang, s.m. A bound, leap. P.

غرض gharaz, s.m. Aim, object, design, purpose; business, meaning, interest, occasion, use, want; spite, selfishness, hatred. ad. In fine, in short, in a word.

غرغړه gharghaṛa, s.f. Gurgling; a gurgle. A. A blaze, flame, fire.

غرغشت gharghusht, s.m. Romping, frolic, fun, sport; a play amongst women. ghurghusht, s.m. Name of the third son of Kais. ghurghushtī, s.m. The Ghurghushtis, clan or tribe of Ghurghusht.

غرغشتي gharghashtī, s.f. A kind of peach (Amygdalus Persicus).

غرق gharq, a. Drowned, sunk, immersed. A.

غرقاب gharqāb, s.m. A whirlpool, vortex. P.

غركمانه ghur-kamāna, s.f. A pellet bow. P. (golā). P. (kamān).

غرگي ghargai, s.m. Boulder, rock; stone, pebble; hillock, mound.

غرمه gharma, s.f. Noon, mid-day, hottest part of the day. ṭakanḍa-, ṭakanṛa-, or ṭakana-ī-gharma, s.f. Exactly noon, hottest time of the day.

غرند ghrand, s.m. The neck, throat, windpipe. P. (gardan).

غرندي ghrandai, s.m. The hollow over the collar bone.

غرنگ gharang, s.m. The creaking of a wheel.

غرنيكه ghur-nīkah, s.m. A great grandfather.

غروب ghurūb, s.m. The west; setting (of the sun). A.

غرور ghurūr, s.m. Pride, vanity. A.

غروړي ghurūṛai, s.m. A node, tumour.

غره gharah, a. Haughty, arrogant, proud, vain; deceived, misled; cross, stern. A. ghara, s.f. Backside, podex. ghurra, s.f. First day of the moon; whiteness. A.

غري gharai, s.m. The throat. See غرند.

غرياښه ghuryākkha, s.f. } A button hole, loop.
غرياښي ghuryākkhai, s.m. } See پلواښه.

غريب gharīb, a. Meek, humble; poor; foreign, strange. A.

غريدل gharedal, v.n. To chatter, gabble, jabber; to bellow, roar; peal, boom, thunder.

غريز gharīz, s.m. Clemency, forbearance. P.

غريو gharew, s.m. Noise, hum, murmur; lamentation, groaning, weeping. P.

غړانگه ghaṛānga, s.f. A shout, scream, yell; a long neck. ghaṛānga-war, a. Long-necked.

غرڅكي ghuruṭskai, s.m. A spark. See بڅري.

غرل *gharal*, v.a. To plait, spin, twist, roll; to fold, roll up, envelop. See غښتل.

غرنب *ghurunb*, s.m. Boom, peal, roar, thunder, etc.

غرنبل *ghranbal*, v.n. } To bellow, roar, low; to peal, thunder, boom.
غرنبيدل *ghranbedal*, }

غرند *gharand*, a. Lax, loose; frail, soft, weak; idle, lazy, negligent; tardy, slow; cautious, stealthy, sly.

غروندي *gharwandai*, s.f. A dog collar, halter, tether for horses; a loop, slip knot; the loop in the letters ت, ډ, ړ.

غري *gharai*, s.m. A kind of coarse bread given to the poor; the calf of the leg.

غريدل *gharedal*, v.n. To growl, snarl; to grate, jar (upon the ear); to blow, wheeze, breathe roughly.

غز *ghaz*, s.m. The Tamarisk tree (*Tamarix Indica*).

غزا *ghazā*, s.f. War against infidels, crescentade. in. Astonishing! A.

غزار *ghuzār*, a. Dropped, fallen, upset.

غزل *ghazal*, s.m. An ode, love song. A.

غزول *ghazawul*, v.a. To lay flat, lay down, prostrate, stretch out (as the arm, leg, etc.).

غزيدل *ghazedal*, v.n. To lie down, lie flat, recline, etc. Also *gazedal*.

غږ *ghag*, s.m. Noise, sound, voice, etc.

غږول *ghagawul*, v.a. To sound, make a noise, etc.

غږيدل *ghagedal*, v.n. To sound, resound, vibrate, etc.

غسل *ghusl*, s.m. Ablution, bathing. A.

غشايه *ghushāyah*, s.m. pl. of غشوئي.

غشو *ghasho*, s.m. A curry comb.

غشوئي *ghushoe*, s.m. Dung of cows and buffaloes.

غشي *ghashai*, s.m. An arrow; spoke of a wheel; pole or shaft of a cart, plough, etc. a. Direct, swift, straight.

غښتل *ghakkhtal*, v.a. To plait, twist; roll, fold, envelop. Def. in pres. ten. See غرل.

غصب *ghasab*, } s.m. Compulsion, force; oppression, violence; plunder; passion, vengeance, wrath. A.
غضب *ghazab*, }

غصه *ghussa*, s.f. Anger, passion. A.

غفلت *ghaflat*, s.m. Negligence, carelessness. A.

غفور *ghafūr*, a. Merciful, forgiving. A.

غل *ghal*, s.m. A thief, robber. *ghul*, s.m. Dung, excrement, fæces.

غلا *ghlā*, s.f. Robbery, theft. A.

غلاف *ghilāf*, s.m. A case, cover, sheath. A.

غلام *ghulām*, s.m. A slave. A.

غلانزه *ghulānza*, s.f. Udder, mammary gland.

غلبله *ghalbala*, s.f. Noise, uproar, tumult.

غلبه *ghalaba*, s.f. Advantage, superiority; assault; prevalence; strength. A.

غلبيل *ghalbel*, s.m. A colander, sieve; sifting, winnowing. P. (*ghirbāl*).

غلت *ghulat*, s.m. Cheat, trick, deceit (at play). *ghulatī*, s.f. Swindling, cheating.

غلط *ghalat*, s.m. Error, mistake. a. Wrong, mistaken. A.

غلغله *ghulghula*, s.f. Tumult, row, disturbance, etc. P.

غلوزه *ghlawza*, s.f. A honey bee. See لوزه.

غلول *ghulawul*, v.n. To deceive, dupe, mislead. H. (*war-ghūlānā*).

غله *ghalla*, s.f. Corn, grain. A.

غلي *ghalai*, a. Concealed, hidden; silent, still; sneaking, stealthy. *ghulai*, s.m. A whirlpool, eddy, vortex; a bubble.

غليم *ghalīm*, s.m. A robber; enemy. A. (*ghanīm*). *ghalīmī*, s.f. Animosity, hatred, enmity.

غم *gham*, s.m. Anxiety, sorrow, grief. A. *gham-jan*, a. Grieved, sorrowful.

غمّاز *ghammāz*, s.m. Informer, tale-bearer. A. *ghammāzī*, s.f. Backbiting, tale-bearing.

غماشه *ghamāsha*, s.f. A gnat, mosquito.

غمبه *ghumba*, s.f. A gland, bubo, tumour.

غمزه *ghamza*, s.f. A wink, glance; ogling. A.

غمي *ghamai*, s.m. The stone of a ring; a seal; ferule of a knife handle, etc.

غميدل *ghamedal*, v.n. To fret, chafe, worry; to be overcome, subdued, conquered.

غنا *ghanā*, s.f. Riches, wealth. A.

غانچه *ghuncha*, s.f. A bud, sprout; a bunch. P.

غندِ *ghundi*, a. See غوندِ.

غندل *ghandal*, s.f. A sprout, shoot; young shoots of mustard and other plants used as pot-herbs. *ghandal*, v.a. To disparage, run down, find fault with; to dislike, disapprove, disrelish.

غنداري *ghundārai*, s.m. A noose, snare for birds (formed of a hair loop fixed to a lump of clay); a phlegmon, carbuncle; a disease in cows, etc.

غندايه *ghundāyah*, s.m. A lad, youth, stripling; a boor, clodhopper, country bumpkin.

غندهاري *ghundhārai*, s.m. See غنداري.

غنزاښه *ghunzākkha*, s.f. A kind of sweet cake made of flour and sugar, fried in butter.

غنزاښي *ghunzākkhai*, s.m. An instrument for separating the seeds of cotton from the fibre.

غنم *ghanam*, s.m. Wheat. P. (*gandum*).

غنه *ghanna*, s.f. A thorny bush, branch of a thorny tree. pl. *ghane*, Thorns, bramble.

غني *ghanī*, a. Wealthy, rich. A.

غنيمت *ghanīmat*, s.m. Plunder; abundance; good fortune, boon. A.

غنړه *ghanra*, s.f. A kind of spider, the tarantula (*Lycosa tarantula*).

غو *gho*, s.m. Copulation, coition.

غوا *ghwā*, s.f. A cow. S. and P. (*gāw*).

غوارودوني *ghwārūdūnai*, s.m. A kind of lizard, the iguana.

غواښکي *ghwākkhkai*, s.m. The notch in the head of an arrow.

غوباري *ghobārai*, s.m. A horsefly, gadfly.

غوبل *ghobal*, s.m. Treading out corn by driving cattle over it; threshing.

غوبني *ghobanī*, s.f. Cowherding, tending cattle.

غوبه *ghobah*, s.m. A cowherd, grazier of cows.

غوپه *ghopa*, s.f. A dive, dip, plunge; dipping, submersion, immersion.

غوټ *ghūṭ*, a. Docked, clipped, cut short.

غوټه *ghoṭa*, s.f. A dip, dive, plunge; dipping, immersion; a clutch, snatch, swoop; a fit, paroxyism, convulsion. A. (*ghoṭā*). *ghūṭa*, s.f. An articulation, joint, knot; band, strap; group, party (of horsemen).

غوټي *ghūṭai*, a. Docked, cropped, cut short. s.m. A horse with a docked tail, dog with cut ears, man with an amputated limb, tree with the boughs cut off, etc. *ghūṭa-ī*, s.f. A rose-bud, a bud; a globule, drop, bubble; a button, knot, jewelled flower, etc.

غوجل *ghojal*, s.f. A cow-shed, cow-pen.

غوڅ *ghwats*, a. Cut, divided, incised.

غوچه *ghūcha*, in. Ho! Hallo! I say!

غور *ghaur*, s.m. Reflection, thought, meditation, care, attention. A.

غورزول *ghwarzawul*, v.a. To fling, pitch, project; to cast off, throw away.

غورزيدل *ghwarzedal*, v.n. To palpitate, toss, flutter, bound, etc.

غوره *ghūrah*, s.m. A cotton pod; unripe dates or grapes. P. *ghwarah*, a. Choice, good, excellent, preferable. P. (*gawārah*).

غوړ *ghwaṛ*, s.m. Fat, grease, suet. a. Oily, greasy, fatty, unctuous.

غوړاسکي *ghwaṛāskai*, s.m. Name of a shrub (*Dodonæa Burmanniana*).

غوړپكه *ghorpaka*, s.f. Calamity, accident; event, occurrence; cry of distress.

غوړول *ghwaṛawul*, v.a. To unclose, open (the

eyes); distend, inflate, spread. ghwaṛawul, v.a. To anoint, grease, oil, lubricate, etc.

غوري ghwaṛī, s.m. Butter, grease, tallow, ghī.

غوريدل ghwaṛedal, v.n. To germinate, sprout, grow, expand, spread, open, unfold, etc.

غوريژه ghwaṛeja, s.f. Name of a plant (*Indigofera Gerardiana*).

غوز ghoz, s.m. The fat of the kidneys; flatus, wind from the belly. P.

غوزكركي ghozakarkai, s.m. A dung beetle.

غوزه ghoza, s.f. Pod, capsule, cocoon, shell, etc. P. (ghoja).

غوزي ghūzai, s.m. Bosom, embrace, arms; armful; lap. P. (āghosh). ghozai, s.m. A kind of black beetle.

غوږ ghwag, s.m. The ear; screw of a violin. P. (gosh).

غوږي ghwagai, s.m. A floodgate, lock, sluice; the horn end of a bow; key of a violin; streak of sunlight through clouds.

غوشاك ghoshāk, s.m. Fresh cowdung.

غوښت ghokkht, s.m. Italian millet (*Panicum Italicum*). Desire, request, want, wish. P. (khwāst).

غوښتل ghokkhtal, v.a. To solicit, request, desire, wish, want. P. (khwāstan, khwāh-).

غوښه ghwakkha, s.f. Flesh, meat. P. (gosht). ghwakkha-war, a. Fleshy, stout, plump.

غوښي ghokkhai, s.m. See غوري.

غوغا ghoghā, s.f. Clamour, din, noise, etc. P.

غول ghūl, s.m. An imaginary demon of the woods, man-wolf, loup-garou. A. ghol, s.m. Party, crowd, gang; corps, troop, company; flock, flight (of birds). H. (gol).

غولونكي gholawunkai, s.m. A stye on the eyelid.

غوله كمانه ghola-kamāna, s.f. See غركمانه.

غولي gholai, s.m. Area, yard, court. ghola-ī, s.f. A small party, gang; small flock (of birds).

غوند ghūnd, a. Alike, similar.

غوندِ ghūndi, } ad. As if, as it were, just as,
غوندي ghūnde, } etc.

غوندي ghūndai, s.m. A bag, pannier or sack of goat's hair (for carrying loads upon camels, bullocks, etc.). s. (gon).

غونډ ghūnḍ, a. Round, globular, circular; plump, squat; lumpy. s.m. A bubo.

غونډري ghūnḍurai, s.m. A ball, globe, anything circular or round, a lump.

غونډكي ghūnḍaka-ī, s.f. Any round projection, knob, or mass; *mons veneris*.

غونډه ghūnḍa, s.f. A hillock, small detached hill, a mound; lump of dough; boulder, pebble, etc.

غونډهاري ghūnḍhārai, s.m. See عنداري.

غونډي ghūnḍai, a. Dumpy, low, squat, dwarf, short; a venomous spider, tarantula. ghūnḍa-ī, s.f. A low mound, hillock; a dumpy or short woman, etc.

غونزيدل ghūnzedal, v.n. To creep, crawl.

غونه ghūna, s.f. The hair of the skin; pores of the skin; colour of the skin. ghūna-zīgedal, v.n. To roughen (as the skin from cold, etc.), to stand on end (as the hair, etc.), to horripilate.

غوول ghowul, v.a. To copulate, have sexual intercourse. P. (gādan). Def. in pres. ten. See غيل.

غوئيلنګ ghwa-e-lang, s.m. The rope passed between the hind legs of a bullock to fix the packsaddle; a crupper.

غوئيمنډ ghwa-e-manḍ, s.m. Stampede of oxen or cattle; footmarks of a herd of cattle; a rush, bolt, stampede. a. Trodden, trampled, crushed (under foot)

غوئيمه ghwa-e-ma, s.f. A cow or buffalo ready for, or seeking the male.

غوئي ghwa-e, s.m. A bull; bullock, ox.

غه ghah, pr. See هغه.

غيب *ghaib*, a. Absent, invisible, concealed. A.

غيبت *ghibat*, s.m. Slander, detraction, calumny. A. *ghaibat*, s.m. Absence, invisibility. A.

غير *ghair*, a. Different, strange, foreign. ad. Except, unless. s.m. A stranger. In composition it denotes negation. A.

غيرت *ghairat*, s.m. Modesty, bashfulness; self-respect; honour, courage; emulation, jealousy, enmity. A. *ghairat-man*, a. or *ghairat-nāk*, a. Bashful; jealous; emulous, etc.

غيره *ghyara*, s.f. The wild donkey, wild ass.

غيږ *ghey*, s.m. The arms, embrace, bosom; an armful; the lap; a wallet. P. (*āghosh*).

غيل *ghayal*, v.a. To copulate. Def. in past ten. See غوول. P. (*gā-īdan*). *ghīl*, s.m. A grove, wood, forest. A.

غيله *ghela*, s.f. A herd or flock of goats and sheep. P. (*galla*).

غيږ *ghenr*, s.m. The penis of a man or beast; *membrum virile*. P. (*ker*).

ف

ف *fe* is the twentieth letter of the Arabic, and thirtieth of the Pukkhto alphabet. It is frequently changed for پ.

فاتحه *fātiha*, s.f. Commencement, exordium; the beginning of the first chapter of the Qurān; it is repeated when praying for the souls of the dead. A.

فاجر *fājir*, s.m. Adulterer, fornicator. A.

فاحش *fāhish*, a. Indecent, obscene. A.

فارسي *fārsī*, a. Persian. P.

فارغ *fārigh*, a. Disengaged, at leisure. A.

فاسد *fāsid*, a. Depraved, vicious. A.

فاسق *fāsiq*, a. Impious, sinful; fornicator. A.

فاش *fāsh*, a. Apparent, manifest. P.

فاصله *fāṣila*, s.f. Interval, space. A.

فاضل *fāẓil*, a. Abundant; excellent; learned. A.

فاعل *fā'il*, s.m. Agent, actor; doing, making. A.

فاقه *fāqa*, s.f. Starvation; poverty, want. A.

فال *fāl*, s.m. Augury, omen; diet, regimen. A.

فالتو *fāltū*, a. Spare, surplus. H.

فالوده *fālūda*, s.f. Name of a sweetmeat; a kind of flummery. P.

فانوس *fānūs*, s.m. A lantern; shade for a lamp. P.

فاني *fānī*, a. Transitory, inconstant. A.

فائده *fā-ida*, s.f. Advantage, benefit, profit. A.

فتحه *fatha*, s.f. Conquest, victory. A.

فتراك *fitrāk*, s.m. Saddle straps; cords fixed to a saddle and used to tie game, etc., to. P.

فتنه *fitna*, s.f. Disturbance, hostility; sedition, strife. A.

فتور *futūr*, s.m. Anarchy, strife, quarrel. A.

فتوي *fatwā*, s.f. Decree, sentence, judgment. A.

فتيله *fatīla*, A match, wick. A.

فدا *fidā*, s.f. Ransom, sacrifice. A.

فراخ *farākh*, a. Ample, spacious; abundant, cheap; wide, expanded. P.

فرار *farār*, a. Absconding, flight. *farārī*, s.m. A deserter, runaway. A.

فراست *firāsat*, s.m. Sagacity, penetration. A.

فراش *farāsh*, s.m. Valet, bed-maker, chamberlain; carpet spreader. A.

فراغت *firāghat*, s.m. Ease, leisure, repose. A.

فراق *firāq*, s.m. Absence, separation. A.

فراموش *farāmosh*, a. Forgotten. P.

فراوان *farāwān*, a. Abundant, much. P.

فرحت *farhat*, s.m. Pleasure, joy. A.

فرد *fard*, s.m. A list, catalogue, roll; sheet (of paper); individual, one, single. A.

فردا *fardā*, s.f. Morrow, to-morrow. P.

فرزند *farzand*, s.m. A child, issue, progeny. P.

فرسخ *farsakh*, } s.m. A league, parasang;
فرسنگ *farsang*, } four miles. P.

فرش *farsh*, s.m. Flooring, pavement; carpeting; bedding; matting, etc. A.

فرښته *firikkhta*, s.m. An angel. P. (*firishta*).

فرصت *furṣat*, s.m. Ease, convenience, leisure; occasion, opportunity, rest. A.

فرض *farz*, s.m. Divine command; obligation, duty, indispensable duty. A.

فرق *farq*, s.m. Difference, distinction. A.

فرقه *firqa*, s.f. A class, tribe, set, sect. A.

فرمان *farmān*, s.m. Command, order; edict, grant, patent. P.

فرمايل *farmāyal*, v.a. To command, order, direct. P. (*farmūdan*).

فرنگي *farangī*, a. European, Frank. P. *farangai*, s.m. A European.

فرياد *faryād*, s.m. Complaint, cry for redress, exclamation, lament. P.

فريب *fareb*, s.m. Deception, trick; fraud, deceit. P.

فريبي *farebī*, a. Impostor, cheat. P.

فريفته *fareftah*, a. Infatuated, charmed, enamoured. P.

فريوان *frewan*, a. See فراوان.

فساد *fasād*, s.m. Mutiny, rebellion; disturbance, tumult, riot. A. *fasādī*, a. Rebellious, mutinous, seditious, etc.

فسق *fisq*, s.m. Adultery; obscenity; iniquity, sin. A.

فصل *faṣl*, s.m. Crop, harvest; time, season; section, chapter. A.

فصيح *faṣīḥ*, a. Eloquent, fluent (in speech). A.

فصيل *faṣīl*, s.m. Breastwork, parapet. A.

فضل *fazl*, s.m. Excellence, virtue; increase, gain; favour, gift, grace. A.

فضول *fuẓūl*, a Redundant, exuberant; excessive, extravagant. A. *fuẓūlī*, s.f. Excess, redundance, extravagance.

فطر *fiṭr*, s.m. Breaking (a fast). A. *'īdu-l-fiṭr*, s.m. The festival held on the termination of the Ramaẓān. A.

فطرت *fiṭrat*, s.m. Cunning, sagacity; alms distributed on the *'īdu-l-fiṭr*. A.

فعل *f'il*, s.m. Operation, action, work; a verb. A.

فغان *fighān*, s.m. Complaint, lament, wail. in. Alas! P.

فقر *faqr*, s.m. Poverty, beggary. A.

فقط *faqaṭ*, ad. Merely, simply, only. A.

فقيه *fiqha*, s.f. Theology, jurisprudence. A. (*fiqh*).

فقيه *faqīh*, s.m. A theologian. A.

فقير *faqīr*, s.m. A beggar, mendicant (religious). A. *faqīrī*, s.f. Beggary, poverty; life of a faqīr.

فكر *fikr*, s.m. Reflection, thought; idea, notion; care, concern; anxiety, solicitude. A.

فلان *falān*, s.m. Penis, *membrum virile*. P.

فلانكي *falānkai*, } s.m. A certain one, so and
فلاني *falānai*, } so, such a thing, etc. A. (*falāna*).

فلك *falak*, s.m. The heavens, sky; destiny, fate, fortune. A.

فليته *falīta*, s.f. See فتيله.

فليل *fulel*, s.m. A kind of scented hair oil.

فن *fann*, s.m. Science, skill, art. A.

فنا *fanā*, s.f. Frailty, mortality. a. Frail, mortal. A.

فواره *fawāra*, s.f. A jet, spout, fountain, spring. A.

فوت *faut*, s.m. Death. A. *fautī*, a. Dead.

فوج *fauj*, s.m. An army. A.

فوفنا *fū-fanā*, a. Annihilated, destroyed, utterly destroyed, exterminated.

فهرست *fihrist*, s.m. Index; list, inventory. P.

فيصله *faiṣala*, s.f. Decision, decree; sentence, settlement. A. *faiṣal*, a. Decided, settled.

فيض *faiẓ*, s.m. Abundance, plenty; bounty, favour, grace. A.

فيل *fīl*, s.m. An elephant. P.

ق

ق *qāf*, is the twenty-first letter of the Arabic, and the thirty-first of the Pukkhto alphabet. With few exceptions it is only found in words from the Arabic.

قاب *qāb*, s.m. A kneading trough; platter, dish, salver. A.

قابض *qābiẓ*, a. Astringent; seizing, taking. A.

قابل *qābil*, a. Able, clever, skilful, worthy; possible, sufficient. A.

قابله *qābila*, s.f. A midwife.

قابو *qābū*, s.m. Authority, command; will, power; opportunity, possession. T.

قاتر *qātir*, s.m. A mule. P.

قاتل *qātil*, a. Deadly, killing, mortal. s.m. An assassin, murderer. A.

قاتي *qātī*, s.f. See قحط.

قادر *qādir*, a. Powerful, potent. A.

قادري *qādirai*, a. Curtailed, docked, cut off. *qādara-ī*, s.f. A kind of frock or gown worn by the Afghans.

قارغه *qārghah*, s.m. A crow, rook.

قاري *qārī*, s.m. A reader of the Qurān. A.

قاري درياب *qārī-dariyāb*, } s.m. The ocean, sea.
قالي درياب *qālī-dariyāb*, } A. (*q'ari-daryā*).

قاشوغه *qāshogha*, s.f. A ladle, spoon. P.

قاصد *qāṣid*, s.m. Courier, messenger, postman. A.

قاصر *qāṣir*, a. Defective, impotent; deficient, failing. A.

قاضي *qāẓī*, s.m. A judge, lawgiver. A.

قاعده *qā'ida*, s.f. Rule, system; custom, manner. A.

قاغه *qāgha*, s.f. A crow, jackdaw, chough. S. (*kāgā*).

قافله *qāfila*, s.f. A caravan, travelling party. A.

قال *qāl*, s.m. A word, saying, speech. A. *qīl-o-qāl*, s.m. Dispute, altercation, controversy. A.

قالب *qālib*, s.m. A mould, cast; form, figure, bust, model; the body. A.

قالي *qālī*, s.f. } A carpet, woollen carpet. P.
قالين *qālīn*, s.m. }

قاليچه *qālīcha*, s.f. A rug, drugget, small carpet. P.

قام *qām*, s.m. Family, tribe. See قوم.

قامت *qāmat*, s.m. Stature; figure, form. A.

قانع *qān'i*, a. Satisfied, contented. A.

قانون *qānūn*, s.m. Canon, regulation, statute, rule. A.

قائزه *qā-iza*, s.f. A watering bridle; bit of a bridle. A. (*qā-izī*).

قائل *qā-il*, a. Convinced, acknowledging. A.

قائم *qā-im*, a. Firm, fixed, stable, erect. A.

قبا *qabā*, s.f. A frock, gown, jacket; a quilted coat; cover for a book. A.

قباحت *qabāḥat*, a. Deformity; dishonesty, wrong. A.

قبر *qabar*, s.m. A grave, tomb. A.

قبض *qabẓ*, s.m. Contraction; costiveness; astringency; receipt; tax, tribute. A.

قبضه *qabẓa*, s.f. Handle (of a sword, etc.); grip, grasp; possession. A.

قبل *qabl*, First, foremost. ad. Previously, before. A. *qabal*, a. Besieged, invested, surrounded. A. *qibal*, s.m. Power; plenty; presence; on the part of, in respect of. A.

قبله *qibla*, s.f. In front, opposite; altar, temple; worship; father. A.

قبول *qabūl*, s.m. Assent, consent; approbation, favourable reception. a. Accepted, approved, consented. A. A holster.

قبولي *qabūlai*, s.m. A holster, pistol case for saddle. A. (*qubūr*).

قبه *qubba*, s.f. An arch, dome, vault. A.

قبيله *qabīla*, s.f. A family; tribe; wife. A.

قت *qat*, s.m. A fold, layer, plait. *qat-pa-qat*, Fold on fold, layer on layer.

قتار *qatār*, s.m. A line, file, rank, row, series, order. A. (*qaṭār*).

قتاري *qatārai*, s.m. Contention, squabble, foolish talk; a wrangler.

قتره *qatra*, s.f. A drop, minim. A. (*qaṭra*).

قتغ *qatagh*, s.m. Meat, fish, soup, etc., eaten with bread to give it a relish; made dish, entrée. P.

قتال *qitāl*, s.m. Battle, slaughter. A.

قتل *qatl*, s.m. Slaughter, homicide, murder. A.

قتي *qutai*, s.m. A ball for play (made of leather or cotton). *quta-ī*, s.f. A dimple on the cheek. *qutta-ī*, s.f. A powder flask (made of untanned leather). S. (*kuppī*).

قجري *qajarī*, s.f. A kind of saddle cloth made of thick felt (it covers the saddle and the horse's fore and hind quarters as well). P.

قچر *qachar*, s.m. A mule. a. Obstinate, perverse. H. (*khachchar*). s.m. A sneak, knave, rogue, cheat.

قچي *qichai*, s.m. A band, gang, party.

قحط *qaḥt*, s.m. Famine, scarcity, dearth. A.

قد *qadd*, s.m. Height, stature. A.

قدر *qadr*, s.m. Value, worth, price; dignity, importance; degree, measure; quantity, size; destiny, fate. A.

قدرت *qudrat*, s.m. Authority, power; omnipotence. A.

قدرتي *qudratī*, a. Divine. A.

قدغن *qadaghan*, قتغن *qataghan*, } s.m. Prohibition, injunction. P.

قدم *qadam*, s.m. Footstep, pace. A.

قديم *qadīm*, a. Ancient, old. A.

قر *qur*, s.m. Rumbling sound in the bowels. *qur-qur*, s.m. Borborygmus. A. (*qarāqar*).

قرابت *qarābat*, s.m. Affinity, kinship, relationship; vicinity, proximity. A.

قرات *qirāt*, s.m. Reading, pronunciation. A.

قرار *qarār*, s.m. Rest, quiet, tranquility; stability, firmness, agreement, engagement; patience, waiting. a. Firm, stable; quiet, tranquil. A.

قراري *qarārī*, s.f. Firmness, stability; rest, ease. a. Firm, stable, quiet, etc.

قران *qurān*, s.m. Name of the book of the Arabian prophet Muḥammad; also called *furqān*.

قراول *qarāval*, s.m. Advance guard of an army; picquet, vidette, sentinel. T.

قربان *qurbān*, s.m. Sacrifice, oblation, victim; a quiver. A.

قربت *qurbat*, s.m. Relationship; proximity. A.

قرت *qurut*, s.m. A kind of very hard cheese; a ball of compressed and dried curds. *qurut-kānrai*, s.m. A pebble of nodular limestone (so named from the resemblance to a nodule or ball of *qurut*). H. (*kankar*).

قرص *qurṣ*, s.m. An orb, disc; the sun; name of an ornament for the neck (of women).

قرض *qarẓ*, s.m. A debt; loan. A

قرط *qurṭ*, s.m. A gulp, draught. A.

قرعه *qur'a*, s.f. Lot, wager, drawing lots. A.

قرق *qurq*, s.m. Confiscation, embargo, seizure. A.

قرقره *qarqara*, s.f. A plume of feathers for the head (generally of crane's feathers). A. (*qarqarā*, a crane).

قرقري *qarqarai*, s.m. The gripes in a horse.

قرغيچن *qarghechan*, قرقيچن *qarqechan*, } a. Benumbed, chilled, doubled up with cold, etc.

قرمساق *qurramsāq*, s.m. Cuckold; pimp; a term of abuse. T.

قرن *qarn*, s.m. A conjunction of the planets; a century. A.

قرنا *qarnā*, s.f. Clarion, trumpet, horn. A.

قريب *qarīb*, a. Close, near; akin, relative. A.

قرينه *qarīna*, s.f. Analogy, context, likeness, similarity, tenour. A.

قز *qaz*, s.m. Raw silk. P.

قزاق *qazzāq*, s.m. A cossack, robber. T.

قسب *qasab*, s.m. Red silk; small turban.

قسط *qist*, s.m. Instalment, portion, tax. A.

قسم *qism*, s.m. Kind, species, sort; division, part. A. *qasam*, s.m. An oath. A.

قسمت *qismat*, s.m. Destiny, fate, lot; distribution, share; division, portion. A.

قشلاق *qishlāq*, s.m. A hamlet, village; winter quarters of the nomade tribes of western and northern Afghanistan. T. The summer quarters are termed *īlāq*. T.

قصاب *qaṣṣāb*, s.m. A butcher. A.

قصاص *qiṣāṣ*, s.m. The law of retaliation (as eye for eye, blood for blood, etc.). A.

قصد *qaṣd*, s.m. Intention, purpose, aim, wish. A.

قصداً *qaṣdan*, ad. Purposely, intentionally. A.

قصر *qaṣr*, s.m. Defect, diminution. A.

قصور *quṣūr*, s.m. Defect, failure, omission, want; error, fault; crime, sin. A.

قصه *qiṣṣa*, s.f. Story, tale; relation, narration; dispute, quarrel. A.

قصيده *qaṣīda*, s.f. An ode, poem. A.

قضا *qazā*, s.f. Fate, destiny; death, fatality; order, decree, judgment; praying at the appointed time; saying a prayer after the appointed time has passed. A.

قضيه *qaziya*, s.f. Contention, litigation, quarrel; calamity, misfortune; death; declaration, proposition. A.

قطب *qutb*, s.m. North pole; Polar star; axis or spindle of a millstone; axis. A.

قطعي *qat'aī*, a. Incontestible, true, fact. ad. Really, truly, fully. A.

قفس *qafas*, } s.m. A cage; latticework. A.
قفص *qafaṣ*, }

قفل *qufl*, s.m. See قلف. A.

قلا *qalā*, s.f. See قلعه.

قلاب *qullāb*, s.m. A hood for the head of a hawk. A.

قلابه *qulāba*, s.f. A hook, hinge, staple. A.

قلار *qalār*, a. Resting, quiet. See قرار.

قلاش *qalāsh*, a. Cunning, crafty, shrewd.

قلبه *qulba*, s.f. A plough. A.

قلپ *qalp*, a. Adulterated, alloyed; counterfeit (as coin, etc.). A. (*qalb*).

قلعه *qil'a*, s.f. Castle, fort; royal residence. A.

قلعي *qil'aī*, s.f. Tin; solder. A.

قلف *qulf*, s.m. A lock; bolt.

قلم *qalam*, s.m. A pen, reed; graft; cutting of a plant. A.

قلنج *qulinj*, s.m. The colic. A.

قلندر *qalandar*, s.m. A hermit, anchorite, ascetic; a monk who has abandoned the world, family, friends, etc. P.

قلنگ *qulang*, s.m. Revenue, tax.

قمار *qimār*, s.m. Dice, gambling with dice. A. *qimār-bāz*, s.m. A gambler.

قماش *qamāsh*, s.m. Manners, foibles; goods, chattels. A.

قمچي *qamchī*, s.f. A horsewhip. T.

قمر *qamar*, s.m. The moon. A.

قمري *qumrī*, s.f. A turtle dove. A.

قميص *qamīṣ*, s.m. Chemise, shirt. A.

قنات *qanāt*, s.m. Walls of a tent; canvas walls used to enclose a space about a tent. A. *qanāt*, s.m. Confectionery, sweetmeats. A. (*qanād*).

قناعت *qanā'at*, s.m. Contentment, tranquility; abstinence. A.

قنج *qanj*, s.m. Deceit, imposture, trick. A.

قند *qand*, s.m. Sugar candy, sugar. A.

قنديل *qandīl*, s.m. Chandelier, lamp. A.

قواعد *quwā'id*, s.m. Regulations, rules; military exercise, drill. A.

قوام *qiwām*, s.m. Essence, extract, syrup. A. *qiwāmī*, a. Ropy, thick, syrupy.

قوت *qūt*, Victuals, aliment, food; subsistence, livelihood. A. *qūt-lā-yamūt*, s.m. Sufficient to sustain life. A. *quwat*, s.m. Strength, vigour; power, authority; faculty, virtue. A.

قوچ *qūj*, s.m. A fighting ram. P.

قوچق *qūchaq*, a. Fat, stout, lusty. T.

قوده *qawda*, s.f. A handful, a gripful.

قورمه *qorma*, s.f. A dish of meat stewed up with spices and fruits. T.

قول *qaul*, s.m. Word, saying; contract, promise; agreement, consent. A.

قوم *qaum*, s.m. Nation, people, family, sect, tribe. A

قوي *qawī*, a. Powerful, strong, vigorous; solid, firm, stable. A.

قهر *qahr*, s.m. Anger, passion, rage; vengeance, fury; severity, punishment. A.

قهرژن *qahr-jan*, } a. Irascible, passionate,
قهرناک *qahr-nāk*, } wrathful, furious.

قهقهه *qahqaha*, s.f. Loud laughter. A.

قي *qai*, s.m. Spewing, vomiting. A.

قياس *qiyās*, s.m. Consideration, judgment, opinion, thought; guess, supposition. A.

قيامت *qiyāmat*, s.m. The last day; resurrection; calamity. a. Wonderful, marvellous. A.

قيد *qaid*, s.m. Bondage, imprisonment; fetter, obstacle; obligation, compact. A.

قيدي *qaidī*, s.m. Prisoner, captive.

قيزه *qaiza*, s.f. See قائزه.

قيل *qīl*, s.m. A word, speech, saying. A.

قيمت *qīmat*, s.m. Price, value. A. *qīmatī*, a. High-priced, expensive; valuable.

قيمه *qīma*, s.f. Minced meat. A.

قينچي *qainchī*, s.f. Scissors. T.

ک

ک *kāf* is the twenty-second letter of the Arabic and the thirty-second of the Pukkhto alphabet. It is pronounced like the English *k*, and is sometimes interchanged with ق.

ک *ka* is a form of the third person singular and plural of the present tense of the verb کول *kawul*, to do. It is also used as an abbreviated form for که *ka*, and نو که *nu ka*, which are forms of the imperfect and past tenses, and the imperative mood of that verb. See following word.

کا *kā* is a form of the third person singular and plural of the present tenses, and imperative mood of the verb کول *kawul*, to do.

کابين *kābīn*, s.m. A marriage portion or settlement, wife's portion, dowry. P.

کاتک *kātak*, s.m. Name of the seventh Hindu month: October-November. S. (*kātik*).

کاته *kātah*, s.m. A glance, look; looking.

کاپور *kāpūr*, s.m. Camphor. A. (*kāfūr*).

کاتب *kātib*, s.m. A scribe, writer. A.

کاټي *kāṭī*, s.f. A wooden saddle; stocks for criminals. S. (*kāṭhī*).

کاختي *kākhtī*, s.f. Famine, scarcity, dearth. A. (*qaht*).

کاذب *kāzib*, s.m. A liar. a. False. A.

کار *kār*, s.m. Business, profession; action, affair; labour, work. P. *pa-kār*, a. Necessary, useful; required, wanted.

کارد *kārd*, s.m. A knife. P.

کاربښت *kārikkht*, s.m. A wine-press; a vat in which grapes are pressed.

کاروان *kārwān*, s.m. Caravan, travelling party. P.

کاره *kāra*, s.f. A deep basket made of cane or reeds; a kind of millet (*Paspalum kora*).

کاري *kārī*, a. Effectual, efficacious. P.

کاريز *kārez*, s.m. An aqueduct; subterranean canal for irrigating fields. P.

کاريزه *kāriza*, s.f. Name of a plant, safflower (*Carthamus oxyacantha*). P. (*khāriza*).

کاریگر *kārī-gar*, s.m. Artificer, mechanic, workman; skilful workman. P.

کاړ *kāṛ*, ⎫
کانړ *kāṇṛ*, ⎭ s.m. Coarse sand, gravel, shingle.

کاړه *kāṛa*, s.f. Caudle, posset, curdled milk.

کاز *kāz*, s.m. Shears, scissors; den of a wild beast; a cavern or cave used by shepherds as a shelter for their flocks. P. *kāz*, s.m. A wild goose. T. (*qāz*).

کاږل *kāgal*, v.a. To draw, extract, pull out; to write, delineate, sketch. Def. in past ten. See کښل.

کاسب *kāsib*, s.m. Mechanic, artist, artificer. A.

کاسه *kāsa*, s.f. A bowl, cup, goblet. A. *ṣhna-kāsa*, s.f. A rainbow.

کاسیر *kāsīr*, s.m. Adulterer, fornicator. *kāsīrī*, s.f. Adultery, fornication.

کاش *kāsh*, s.m. Pommel or bow of a saddle; a small holster or saddle bag.

کاشکي *kāshke*, in. God grant! Would to God! P.

کاشي *kāshī*, s.m. A glazed tile or brick. P. *kāshī-gar*, s.m. Maker of glazed pottery. P. *kāshīn*, s.m. Glazed pottery. P.

کاغ *kāgh*, a. Cunning, clever, acute.

کاغذ *kāghaz*, s.m. Paper. P. *kāghazī*, s.f. A kind of thin skinned lime. a. Delicate, soft, thin; written, printed; documentary.

کافر *kāfir*, s.m. Unbeliever, infidel. A. *kāfirī*, Name of a people inhabiting Kafiristan, a country of Hindu Kush to the north of Kabul. *kāfirai*, s.m. A man Kafir. *kāfira-ī*, s.f. A Kafir woman.

کافي *kāfi*, a. Enough, sufficient; competent, able. A.

کاک *kāk*, s.m. A biscuit, a hard cake of bread, etc. baked upon heated stones. P.

کاکا *kākā*, s.m. Paternal uncle; term of respectful address to a senior. H. Elder brother. P.

کاکړ *kākaṛ*, s.m. Name of an Afghan clan.

کاکل *kākul*, s.m. A curl, lock, ringlet. P.

کاکنج *kākanj*, s.m. Name of a kind of millet (*Panicum Italicum*).

کاکي *kāka-ī*, s.f. Paternal uncle's wife. H.

کال *kāl*, s.m. A year. P. (*sāl*). *sag-kāl*, This year. *paros-kāl* or *parosag-kāl*, Last year. *waṛam-kāl*, Year before last. *lā-waṛam-kāl*, Three years ago.

کالبوت *kālbūt*, s.m. Human body; heart; form, figure, mould, model. P. (*kālbud*).

کالخواهي *kālkhwāhī*, s.f. Good will, good wishes; approbation, choice. P. (*khair-khwāhī*).

کالکوچ *kālkūch*, s.m. A bend, turn, curve, twist.

کالکوچن *kālkūchan*, a. Bent, curved, distorted.

کالکوچکه *kālkūchaka*, s.f. A bend, turn, swerve (as of a hunted hare, fox, etc.).

کالکنډي *kālkunḍai*, s.m. A kind of small edible melon that grows wild.

کالکه *kālaka*, s.f. Cotton in the pod; the cotton plant. *kālak-cho*, s.m. Dry stalks of the cotton plant (used as fuel).

کالي *kālai*, s.m. Article, instrument, tool; garment, dress; ornament, jewel. pl. *kālī*, Apparatus, tools; furniture, clothes, jewelry, etc. P. (*kālā*).

کام *kām*, s.m. Desire, wish. P. *kām-nā-kām*, ad. Willing or unwilling, nolens volens.

کامبوري *kāmbūrai*, s.m. Dry mustard stalks after threshing out the seed.

کامبیله *kāmbela*, s.f. Name of a tree (*Rottlera tinctoria*). H. (*kamīla*).

کامل *kāmil*, a. Complete, perfect; learned. A.

کامیاب *kāmyāb*, a. Prosperous, successful. P. *kāmyābī*, s.f. Prosperity, success.

کان *kān*, s.m. A mine, quarry. P. *kān*, s.m. Reed, rush, bullrush (*Panicum spicatum* and *Juncus effusus*).

كانتي ***kānṭa-ī***, s.f. Book-board, pasteboard.

كانجنړ ***kānjanṛ***, s.m. Part of a Persian wheel; the large beam that rests on the side walls, ·· l fixes the central upright pillar of the wheel.

كانڊِ ***kāndi***, } A form of the third person
كاندي ***kānde***, } singular and plural of the present tense of the verb كول *kawul*, to do.

كانګه ***kānga***, s.f. Gripes, tenesmus, tormina; violent straining at stool without ejection of matter. H. (*kānkhā*).

كانګي ***kāngai***, s.m. Echo, reverberation.

كانه ***kāna***, s.f. Calamity, disaster; business, affair; border, margin; frame, edging; a quill feather; upper part of the face. ***kānah***, a. Stupid, ignorant, foolish; decayed, rotten at the core. S. (*kānā*).

كاني ***kānī***, a. Mineral, fossil. P. ***kānai***, a. Blind of one eye. S. (*kānā*). ***kānaī***, s.f. Whiskers, hair at the temples; a reed, straw, cane, etc. (used by weavers to spread the warp upon).

كاڼري ***kāṇrai***, s.m. A stone. P. (*kān*).

كاواك ***kāwāk***, a. Demented, insane; awkward, clumsy; hollow, useless; thoughtless; acting as one deprived of self-control.

كاه ***kāh***, s.m. Straw, stubble. P. ***kāh·gil***, s.m. Plaster of mud and straw for walls. P.

كاهښت ***kāhakkht***, s.m. Mange, itch; grating or setting the teeth on edge.

كاهل ***kāhil***, a. Indolent, lazy, slow. A. ***kāhilī***, s.f. Apathy, indolence, neglect.

كاهن ***kāhin***, s.m. Astrologer, magician. A. ***kāhinī***, s.f. Astrology, magic, sorcery.

كب ***kab***, s.m. A fish.

كباب ***kabāb***, s.m. Roasted meat. P. ***kabābī***, s.m. A cook.

كبر ***kibr***, s.m. Arrogance, pride. A. ***kibr·jan***, a. Arrogant, haughty, proud.

كبره ***kbara***, s.f. Name of a plant (*Capparis spinosa*). H. (*kabar*).

كبك ***kabk***, s.m. A partridge. P.

كبل ***kabal***, s.m. Cause, motive, reason. ***kabl***, s.m. Name of a grass (*Agrostis linearis*).

كبلي ***kablai***, s.m. A fawn, young gazelle; sandpiper, snippet; curlew.

كبي ***kabī***, s.f. A halter for a horse; a rope passed over the head and through the mouth, instead of a headstall and bit.

كبير ***kabīr***, a. Great, large; senior, full-grown. A.

كپري ***kaparai***, s.m. The skull. S. (*khoprī*).

كپړۍ ***kupṛa-ī***, s.f. A powder flask of leather, a leathern jar or bottle. S. (*kuppī*).

كپي ***kapī***, s.f. See كبي. ***kupa-ī***, s.f. See كپړۍ.

كت ***kat***, s.m. Catechu. H. (*kath*). ***kat***, s.m. A pile, heap; line, series, row.

كتاب ***kitāb***, s.m. A book. A. ***kitābī***, a. Written; learned, well read.

كتل ***katal***, v.n. To look, see, view. H. (*taknā*).

كته ***kata***, s.f. A pack-saddle or pad for bullocks, donkeys, etc.

كتي پتي ***kitī-pitī***, s.f. Gibberish, nonsense. a. Confused, jumbled (as speech).

كتي لعل ***kutī·l'al***, s.m. Name of a plant (*Withiana somniferum*).

كټ ***kaṭ***, s.m. A cot, bed, bedstead. S. (*khaṭ*). ***kaṭ·kai***, s.m. A small bed, settle, cot. ***kaṭ·oṭai***, s.m. A child's bed, cradle.

كټ وټ ***kaṭ·waṭ***, a. See كڼ.

كټوري ***kaṭorai***, s.m. A brass bowl, metal cup. H. (*kaṭorā*).

كټوۍ ***kaṭwa-ī***, s.f. An earthenware cooking pot.

كټه ***kaṭah***, a. Big, bulky, large. H. (*kaṭṭā*).

كټي ***kaṭai***, s.m. A buffalo calf; the straw of pulse (used as fodder).

كثرت *kasrat*, s.m. Abundance, excess. A.

كثير *kasīr*, a. Abundant, excessive. A.

کڅوړه *katsora*, s.f. A bag, purse, reticule, wallet.

کڅوک *katswak*, s.m. Mild small-pox, chicken-pox.

كجاوه *kajāwa*, s.f. A camel-litter. P.

کجک *kajak*, s.m. Hammer or cock of a gun; a curl or lock of hair worn on the forehead by females.

کجل *kajal*, s.m. Soot, lamp-black. S.

کچ *kach*, s.m. Measurement; fault, flaw, error. a. Diminutive, small, less, little. H. (*kachchā*). *kuch*, s.m. Butter.

کچکول *kachkol*, s.m. A bowl or trough of wood used by mendicants to collect contributions in. P.

کچماچو *kachmāchū*, s.m. Name of a plant (*Solanum nigrum*), deadly nightshade.

کچنۍ *kachana-ī*, s.f. Courtezan, whore, dancing girl. H. (*kanchanī*). *kuchinai*, a. Small, diminutive, puny.

کچوټي *kachotai*, a. Diminutive, tiny, wee.

کچه *kachah*, a. Crude, immature, raw; silly, inexperienced; clay-built, slight. H. (*kachchā*).

کدائي *kadā-ī*, s.f. A kind of frock, long coat, gown.

کدخدا *kad·khudā*, s.m. Head man of a village or family; married man, master. P. *kad-khudā-ī*, s.f. Marriage, the office of *kad-khudā*.

كدو *kadū*, s.m. Pumpkin, bottle-gourd. P.

کډله *kadala*, s.f. A cabin, hut, hovel (of reeds, etc.); a hole, pit.

کډه *kada*, s.f. Family, household; migration, flitting, change of residence.

کدهل *kadhal*, s.m. Land prepared for sowing rice in.

کډۍ *kada-ī*, s.f. A pit, hole; ditch, trench; the hole under a loom for the weaver's feet when at work.

کر *kar*, s.m. Agriculture, farming; tilling, ploughing, and sowing. P. *ka-ar*, s.m. Thin, watery excrement, looseness of the bowels.

کراسته *krāsta*, s.f. Felt, a thick woollen fabric (unwoven).

كرام *kirām*, a. Venerable, noble, great. A.

كرامت *kirāmat*, s.m. Excellence, nobleness; miracle. A.

كراهت *kirāhat*, s.m. Aversion, disgust. A.

کراهه *kirāha*, s.f. Hire, rent, fare. P. (*kirāya*).

کربوړي *karborai*, s.m. A kind of lizard; chameleon.

کرپ *krap*, s.m. A munch, crunch.

کرپندوکي *krapandūkai*, } s.m. Cartilage,
کرپندي *krapandai*, } gristle.

کرپول *krapawul*, v.a. To crunch, munch; bite, champ, gnaw.

کرت *karat*, s.m. One time, stroke, turn, go. A. *yo·karat*, Once. *dre·karata*, Thrice, etc. *karāt·marāt*, Often, frequently, etc. A.

کرتب *kartab*, s.m. Action, business; practice, exercise; skill; horse exercise. S

کرتوت *kartūt*, s.m. Work, business, action. S.

کرته *kurta*, s.f. A coat, jacket, tunic. P.

کرټ *kruṭ*, ad. At all, not at all, never, by no means, not in the least.

کرچ *krach*, s.m. An old hawk or falcon (one fully trained). *krach*, s.m. Sound of a crunch, crash, squash, etc.

کرچوني *krachūnai*, } s.m. Cartilage, gristle.
کرچي *krachai*, }

کرچي *krichī*, s.f. Name of a plant (*Anthemis nobilis*).

کرخت *karakht*, a. Austere, rigid, rough, hard. P.

کردار *kirdār*, s.m. Conduct, action, deed. P.

کرړي *kirṛai*, s.m. A cricket. *kariṛī*, s.m. Name of an Afghan tribe, also called کرلاڼري.

کرسي *kursī*, s.f. Chair, seat, throne; firmament, heaven. P. *kursī-nāma*, s.f. Genealogical tree; list of precedence.

کرښمه *karakkhma*, s.f. Amorous look, wink, ogle, leer. P. (*karashma*).

کرښنه *karakkhna*, s.f. Carving, drawing, painting, engraving.

کرښه *karkkha*, s.f. A line, streak, scrawl, scratch, furrow.

کرغ *kurugh*, s.m. A meadow, pasture.

کرک *karak*, s.m. A snipe, woodcock. P. *kark*, s.m. Rhinoceros, rhinoceros hide. P. (*karg*). *krak*, s.m. A furrow, rut, scratch.

کرکنډه *karkanḍa*, s.f. A rolling stone; landslip on a hill-side; rock or stone hurled down a hill upon an enemy.

کرکڼ *karkanṛ*, s.m. A brake, copse, thicket.

کرکڼه *karkanṛa*, s.f. A bramble, brier, thorny bush; the jujube tree (*Zizyphus vulgaris*).

کرکه *kraka*, s.f. Aversion, disgust. A. (*ikrāh*).

کرل *karal*, v.a. To till, plough and sow. P. (*kāshtan-kār*).

کرلاڼري *karlāṇṛī*, s.m. Name of a tribe of Afghans located in Bājawar.

کرم *karam*, s.m. Clemency, kindness. A. *kirm*, s.m. A worm. P.

کرمنګ *kurmang*, s.m. Pheasant, wild fowl.

کرنډۍ *karanḍa-ī*, s.f. A trowel. H. (*karnī*).

کروړ *karoṛ*, a. Ten millions; a crore. S.

کروړه *karoṛa*, s.f. A whip, scourge. H. (*koṛā*). *karwaṛa*, s.f. Blackberry bush and fruit (*Rubus vulgaris*).

کروسند *krosand*, a. Dry, withered (as wood).

کروه *kroh*, s.m. A coss; a measure of distance nearly equal to two miles. P.

کره *karah*, a. Genuine, pure; candid, sincere. s. (*kharā*). *kara*, s.f. Spade, hoe. *kara*, ad. With, along with. See سره.

کرهډ *kurhaḍ*, s.m. Name of a plant used as a pot-herb (*Chenopedium album*).

کرۍ *kara-ī*, s.f. A fetter, ring, buckle, link, staple; beam, rafter. H. (*kaṛī*). *kara-ī*, ad. All, the whole, the entire (day or night). *kara-ī-wradz*, All day. *kara-ī-shpa*, All night. *kure*, in. Begone! Get out! Away! (to a dog).

کریاب *kariyāb*, a. Disengaged, idle, unused; clogged, hampered, hindered, obstructed; distressed, helpless, tired.

کریابي *kariyābī*, s.f. Obstruction, hindrance, impediment, bar, hitch, etc.

کریړه *kiriṛa*, s.f. Name of a plant (*Capparis aphylla*). S. (*karīl*). Weeds, grass, etc., collected from a ploughed field.

کریړي *kiriṛai*, s.m. Name of a tree (*Salvadora Persica*).

کریز *kurīz*, s.m. Moulting (of birds). P.

کریم *karīm*, a. Merciful, gracious, bountiful. A.

کریهه *kreha*, s.f. See کراهه.

کریه *karīh*, a. Abominable, detestable; dirty, filthy. A. *karya*, s.f. Injunction, charge, command.

کړ *kuṛ*, s.m. A gurgle, bubbling sound; cackle or cluck of a hen.

کړاونه *kaṛāwna*, s.f. See کنړاوه.

کربیزن *kurbezan*, a. Snotty-nosed, sniveller.

کربیزي *karbeze*, s.f. (pl. of *karbeza*, obsolete) Snot, mucus from the nose.

کړپ *kṛap*, s.m. See کرپ.

کړټي *kṛaṭai*, s.m. A crease, furrow, crumple, pucker, wrinkle.

کړشپ *kaṛshap*, a. Toothless, old. *kaṛshapai* s.m. A toothless old man.

کړکړي *kuṛkuṛai*, s.m. A turtle dove.

کړکه *kuṛuka*, s.f. A clucking hen; a sitting or hatching hen.

كركي *kurka-ī*, s.f. A kind of bird trap made of a horn bow and catgut, a gin, springe. *kirka-ī*, s.f. A wicket, window, loophole; gate. H. (*khirkī*).

كړل *kṛal*, v.a. To do, perform, execute, etc. P. (*kardan*).

كړم *karam*, a. Maimed, halt, crippled, lame.

كړميزي *karmeze*, s.f. Snot. See كربيزي.

كړوسي *karwasai*, s.m. A great grandson.

كړه *krah*, s.m. Act, deed; doing, making.

كړه وړه *kṛah-wṛah*, s.m. Beauty, grace; neatness, tidiness, spruceness; arrangement, order.

كړهي *karahai*, s.m. A caldron, boiler (metal); an iron cooking pot. S. (*karāhī*). *kurhai*, s.m. Name of a corn measure, the fourth part of an اوږي *ogai*.

كړڅي *karetsa-ī*, s.f. A ladle, iron spoon. H. (*karchhī*).

كړيدل *karedal*, v.a. To be parched, scorched, dried; to be reduced, emaciated; to waste, wither, pine, droop (through sickness or grief). H. (*kurhnā*).

كړينګ *krīng*, a. Awry, distorted, crooked, twisted. *krīng-prīng*, a. All awry, all askew.

كږدي *kigda-ī*, s.f. A tent made of coarse camlet, or goat's hair cloth (used by nomad Afghans).

كږل *kagal*, v.a. To disapprove, to dislike; find fault with, disparage, run down. P. (*kaj*).

كږلي *kagalai*, a. Calamitous, unlucky; unwelcome.

كږليچ *kaglech*, s.m. A bend, crook, turn.

كس *kas*, s.m. Human being, individual, person; anyone, a man. P. *kas*, s.m. A ravine, gully, dry course of a torrent, passage cut by floods. H. *kus*, s.m. Vulva, vagina. P.

كسب *kasb*, s.m. Trade, occupation, employment. A.

كسبت *kisbat*, s.m. An instrument case; huntsman's bag for balls, powder, etc., etc.; a bag or case in which barbers, surgeons, etc., keep their tools. A.

كستيج *kustīj*, s.m. The hole in the hem of a pair of drawers, etc., through which the string passes.

كسكر *kaskar*, a. Burnt, dry, arid, scorched; contracted, shrivelled; withered, frost bitten.

كسل *kasal*, v.a. To see, look. See كتل.

كسوري *kasūrai*, a. Broken spirited, distressed, unequal to, impotent.

كسي *kasai*, s.m. The pupil of the eye.

كشاله *kashāla*, s.f. Dragging, trailing, pulling, etc.

كشپ *kashp*, s.m. A tortoise. P. (*kashaf*).

كشته *kishta*, s.f. A kind of dried plum, used in medicine, and by goldsmiths to clean their metals with. P. *kushta*, s.f. A sublimate of mercury. P. *kushtah*, a. Killed, slain; slaked (as lime, etc.). P.

كشر *kashr*, a. Junior, younger; cadet, subaltern; less, minor.

كشكچي *kishikchī*, s.m. Watchman, guard, porter. P.

كشمالو *kashmālū*, s.m. Name of a plant, holy basil (*Ocymum sanctum*).

كشور *kishor*, s.m. The manis or pangolin, scaly ant-eater (*Manis crassicaudata*). *kishwar*, s.m. Country, region, climate. P.

كشي *kashai*, s.m. An only son. *kasha-ī*, s.f. Bar or pig iron; a hoe, mattock. H. (*kasī*).

كښ *kakkh*, s.m. A draw, pull; inhalation, whiff, inspiration; suck. P. (*kash*).

كښت *kikkht*, s.m. A crop, sown field, growing crop. P. (*kisht*). *kukkht*, s.m. A defile, gorge, gap in the hills. (Raverty.)

كښل ***kakshal*** or ***kkshal***, v.a. To draw out, extricate, extract, pull, pluck out; to write, draw, sketch, etc. Def. in pres. ten. See كاږل. P. (*kashīdan*). ***kkshul***, s.m. A kiss.

كښلول ***kkshulawul***, v.a. To kiss.

كښلي ***kkshulai***, a. Comely, fair, handsome, pretty; kissed.

كښول ***kakshawul*** or ***kkshawul***, v.a. To cause to extract, draw, etc. To cause to write, etc. See كښل.

كښه ***kakkha***, s.f. Brace, tightener, puller.

كښي ***kakkhai***, s.m. A watchman, guard (over cattle, crops, etc.). P. (*kashak*). ***kkshe***, p. In, within. ***pa-kkshe***, ad. Inside, within.

كښيباسل ***kkshebāsal***, v.a. To insert, introduce, implant, stick in, stuff in, etc. Def. in past ten. See كښييستل ***kksheyastal***.

كښيده ***kakkheda***, s.f. A kind of needlework, embroidery. P. (*kashīda*).

كښيږدل ***kkshegdal***, v.a. To place, set, put down, arrange, dispose, etc. Def. in past ten. See كښيښول.

كښيكښل ***kkshekkshal***, v.a. To shampoo (or ښكيښكل ***kkhkekkhkal***).

كښيناستل ***kkshenāstal***, v.n. To sit, settle, be seated. P. (*nishastan*).

كښينول ***kkshenawul***, v.a. To seat, settle, instal, fix, set down, etc.

كښيوتل ***kkshewatal***, v.n. To fall into, drop into, enter, descend into, etc.

كښييستل ***kksheyastal***, v.a. To insert, introduce, etc. Def. in pres. ten. See كښيباسل ***kkshebāsal***.

كعبه ***k'aba***, s.f. The temple at Mecca. A.

كفارت ***kifārat***, s.m. Expiation, atonement, penance. A.

كفايت ***kifāyat***, s.m. Enough, sufficiency; economy, thrift. A.

كفر ***kufr***, s.m. Blasphemy, infidelity, paganism. A.

كفن ***kafan***, s.m. Winding sheet, shroud. A.

كك ***kak***, s.m. A splinter, straw; treacle, syrup.

ككرۍ ***kakara-ī***, s.f. The skull. ***kakarai***, s.m. A pup, puppy dog.

ككړ ***kakaṛ***, a. Defiled, polluted, stained; a spiritless man. f. ***kakaṛa***, Raped, ravished; a whore, strumpet.

ككوي ***kakawai***, s.m. Name of a bird.

ككوړه ***kakoṛa***, s.f. Name of a plant, bitter gourd.

ككوړي ***kakoṛai***, s.m. A kind of biscuit, round cake baked on heated stones; a disk.

كل ***kal***, a. Bald, scald headed. P. ***kal***, s.m. Oilcake. S. (*khal*). ***kull***, a. All, universal; amount, total. A.

كلال ***kulāl***, s.m. A potter. P.

كلام ***kalām***, s.m. A word, speech; conversation, talk. A.

كلان ***kalān***, a. Elder, great; large. P.

كلت ***kulat***, s.m. Name of a grain, seed of (*Dolichos biflorus*). S. (*kulthī*).

كلك ***klak***, a. Firm, hard; stiff, rigid, etc. P. (*karakht*).

كلكل ***kalkal***, s.m. Wrangling, quarrelling. H.

كلمه ***kulma***, s.f. An entrail, gut; sausage. A. (*qulmā*). ***kalima***, s.f. A word, speech; the Muhammadan belief or creed. A.

كلنك ***kulang***, s.m. A long-legged fowl; a crane, heron. P. A pick, pickaxe; a bow; hammer of a gun; dower, furniture of every description which a bride brings to her husband.

كلني ***kalanai***, Added to words in composition, denotes the age. Ex. ***pīndzah-kalanai***, a. Five years old.

كلوټ ***kaloṭ***, a. Dark, dark-complexioned.

كلوښه ***kalokkhta***, s.f. A wisp of straw, floss of silk, curl, tuft, bundle, etc.

كله ***kula***, ad. Ever, at any time, sometime;

when? since when? *kala-kala*, Now and then, occasionally, sometimes. *kala-shū-lā-kala*, Since when? how long? *kala*, s.f. The head. P.

كلي *kilai*, s.m. A village. A. (*qil'a*). *kalai*, a. Short-horned, without horns. P. (*kal*). *kala-ī*, s.f. Bunion, callosity, corn. *killī*, s.f. A key. H. *kullī*, s.f. A gargle, gargling. H.

كم *kam*, a. Deficient, less, little, seldom, scanty (in comp.). P. *kum* or *kam*, pr. What? which? See كوم.

كمال *kamāl*, s.m. Perfection, excellence; completion. a. Complete, perfect. A.

كمان *kamān*, s.m. A bow. *kamān-gar*, s.m. A bow-maker. P.

كمانچه *kamāncha*, s.f. Bow of a violin. P.

كماٸي *kamā-ī*, s.f. Earning, gain, profit, wages. H.

كمبلي *kambala-ī*, s.f. A butterfly.

كمر *kamar*, s.f. A cliff, precipice; steep bank; ridge of a hill, etc.; the waist, loins. P. *kamar-kīsa*, s.f. A waist belt with powder flask, etc., etc. *komar-band*, s.m. A girdle, waist-belt. P.

كمري *kamarī*, a. Relating to the loins, lumbar; weak in the loins (as a horse).

كمك *kumak*, s.m. Aid, help; reserve of an army. T. *kumakī*, a. Auxiliary. s.m. Assistant, helper.

كمند *kamand*, s.m. A ladder of ropes; halter, lasso, noose; a tethering rope; ringlet or long curl. P.

كمنړ *kamanr*, a. Faded, withered, decayed.

كمنړيدل *kamanredal*, v.n. To droop, decay, wither, fade, etc. H. (*kumlānā*).

كموده *kamoda*, s.f. A dish of rice boiled with ghee, and flavoured with spices.

كميس *kamīs*, s.m. A shirt. See قميص.

كمين *kamīn*, a. Mean; defective; humble, poor. s.m. A village serf. P.; an ambuscade. A.

كمينه *kamīnah*, a. Humble, meek; abject, base; mean, ignoble. P. *kamīnī*, s.f. Humility, meekness; baseness.

كن *kan* (in comp.), Digger, digging. P. *kun* (in comp.), Actor, doer; doing, acting. P.

كناټي *kunāṭai*, s.m. Buttock, rump. *kunāṭa-war*, a. Broad-buttocked, large rumped.

كنار *kinār*, s.m. Side, edge; bosom, embrace. P.

كنال *kanāl*, s.m. A land measure equal to twenty *marla*; the fourth part of a *jarīb*.

كنايت *kināyat*, s.m. } Allusion, hint, meta-
كنايه *kināya*, s.f. } phor, sign. A.

كنتكين *kantkīn*, a. Made of thread.

كنج *kunj*, s.m. A corner, nook; grove, bower. P.

كنجك *kunjak*, s.m. } A cowrie, small shell
كنجكه *kunjaka*, s.f. } (used as money).
(*Cypræa moneta*).

كنجوغه *kanjogha*, s.f. Saddle straps, cords attached to a saddle (used to tie game, etc.).

كنجي *kunja-ī*, s.f. A key. H. (*kunjī*). A small water jar or ewer (of pottery).

كند *kand*, s.m. A gorge, ravine, dry watercourse, excavation. P. *kind*, s.m. A tattered and patched garment worn by dervishes. *kund*, a. Blunt. P.

كنداغ *kundāgh*, s.m. The stock of a gun. P. (*kunda*).

كندره *kandara*, s.f. A fissure, chasm; gully, watercourse, ravine; broken or ravine cut ground. S. (*kandarā*).

كندل *kandal*, v.a. To dig, excavate. P. (*kandan*).

كندو *kandū*, s.m. A corn bin.

كنده *kanda*, s.f. A gully, ravine, watercourse (cut by floods). P. *kunda*, s.f. Block, log; stock of a gun, ploughshare, etc. P.

كندي *kandai*, s.m. A potsherd, bit of broken pottery; a division, or quarter of a village, parish ward. s. (*khanḍ*). *kunḍī*, s.f. Calendering (cloth). H.

كند *kanḍ*, s.m. Sugar candy. s. (*khanḍ*). Gum. s. (*gond*). *kunḍ*, s.m. A widower.

كندا *kunḍā*, a. Harelipped, having a broken horn.

كنداس *kunḍās*, s.m. A man who has lost, or broken his front teeth; a toothless old man.

كندال *kanḍāl*, s.m A cup, bowl, basin, etc. (of pottery).

كندتون *kunḍtūn*, s.m. Widowhood.

كندر *kanḍar*, s.m. Ruins of a house or village, broken and decayed walls, ruins; a place haunted by demons. H. (*khanḍar*).

كندك *kanḍak*, s.m. A herd of deer, flock of goats or sheep; a piece of bread.

كندوكپر *kanḍ-o-kapaṛ*, a. Shattered, smashed, broken to bits, cut to pieces, etc.

كندلئي *kanḍala-ī*, s.f. Name of a plant (*Bryonia grandis*). A prickly seed that sticks to the fleece of sheep.

كندو *kanḍaw*, s.m. A notch, dent, gap; dip in a hill, gap in a wall, notch in wood, etc. a. Dented, notched. H. (*khanḍā*).

كندول *kanḍol*, كندولي *kanḍolai*, s.m. See كندال.

كنده *kanḍa*, s.f. The spring or source of a river. *kunḍa*, s.f. A widow. A hook, fish hook, hook of a door, etc. H. (*kunḍā*).

كندئي *kunḍa-ī*, s.f. See كنړئي.

كنزل *kanzal*, v.a. See ښكنځل.

كنزله *kunzala*, s.f. Sesame, the plant and seed (*Sesamum orientale*). P. (*kunjad*).

كنزګوته *kanza-gūta*, s.f. The third or ring finger.

كنستل *kanastal*, v.a. To dig, excavate.

كنف *kanaf*, s.m. Brink, edge, margin. A.

كنګال *kangāl*, a. Poor, friendless. s.

كنګخر *kangalkhaṛ*, s.m. Rubbish, sticks, straw, etc. carried down by floods, drift wood.

كنګر *kangar*, s.m. Pumice stone. H. (*khangar*).

كنګره *kangura*, s.f. A pinnacle, turret; battlement, parapet; niched or loopholed wall; porthole; the plume of a helmet; ornaments on a crown. P.

كنګري *kangarai*, s.m. A puppy. See كوتري.

كنګس *kangas*, s.m. A trip, stumble.

كنګل *kangal*, a. Congealed, frozen; compact, solid, dense. s.m. Ice.

كنګو *kangū*, s.m. Saffron.

كنل *kanal*, v.a., كنودل *kanawdal*, To dig. See كندل.

كنه *kana*, s.f. A dog tick, sheep louse, large tick. The border of a garment, edge of a shawl. P.

كنيزه *kanīza*, s.f. A female servant, housemaid; a concubine. P. (*kanīz*).

كنړ *kanṛ*, s.m. Mucus from the nose, snot.

كنړاوه *kanṛāwa*, s.f. A clog, patten. H. (*kharāṅw*).

كنړه *kanṛa*, c. If not, of course, otherwise, then.

كنړي *kanṛai*, s.m. The warp (in weaving). *kanṛa-ī*, s.f. A wooden cup or bowl.

كواره *kawāra*, s.f. A pannier or basket, used to carry fruit, etc. in. H. (*gaṅwārā*).

كوب *kūb*, s.m. A hump, hunch. a. Humped. s. (*kub*).

كوبي *kūbai*, s.m. A hunch-back, humped ox or camel, etc. One of the pieces or stops of wood, in the horizontal wheel of a Persian wheel, which catches the cogs of the smaller wheel.

كوپ *kūp*, a. Bowed, stooping, bent, crooked in the back (as from old age).

كوپله *kopla*, s.f. A lark, skylark.

كوت *kaṅt*, a. Contracted, drawn in, pinched, tucked in, shrunk (as the belly from hunger).

كوتان *kotān*, s.m. A pelican.

كوتاه *kotāh*, a. Brief, short (in comp.). P.

كوتره *kautara*, s.m. A pigeon. P. (*kabūtar*).

كوتري *kūtrai*, s.m. A pup, puppy dog. H. (*kutrū*).

كوتک *kotak*, s.m. Bludgeon, club; a pestle. H. (*kūtak*). The back of the head, occiput.

كوتل *kotal*, s.m. A pass over a mountain. P. A led horse. H. *kūtal*, v.a. To cut up, disjoint, divide. H. (*kāṭnā*).

كوتي *kwatai*, s.m. A dimple on the cheek or chin.

كوتي لال *kūtī-lāl*, s.m. See كتي لعل.

كوټ *koṭ*, s.m. A castle, fort, stronghold, hill fort. S.

كوټخه *koṭakha*, s.f. A cap made to cover the forehead and ears, a travelling cap; a mouthpiece or nosebag for cattle.

كوټل *kūṭal*, v.a. To pound, bruise; cudgel, beat, thrash, wallop. H. (*kūṭnā*).

كوټوال *koṭwāl*, s.m. The chief constable of a village or town. H.

كوټه *koṭa*, s.f. A mansion, large house; a chamber room. H. (*koṭhā*). *kūṭah*, s.m. A dog. H. (*kuttā*)

كوټئ *koṭa-ī*, s.f. A factory, warehouse, bank. H. (*koṭhī*). *koṭai*, s.m. The head. *kūṭai*, s.m. An ass colt, a young donkey. H. (*khotrā*).

كوثر *kauṣar*, s.m. Name of a well in Paradise. Name of a disease, tetanus, lockjaw; stroke of the wind, or of cold.

كوڅه *kūtsa*, s.f. A lane, street. P. (*kūcha*).

كوڅئ *kotsa-ī*, s.f. See كونڅئ.

كوچ *kūch* or *koch*, s.m. Migration, a march. P. *kochi*, s.m. A nomade.

كوچت *kūchaṭ*, a. Small, little, young. P. (*kūchak*). *kūchaṭ-wālai*, s.m. Smallness; childhood.

كوچمال *kūchmāl*, s.m. The leader of a march; conductor of a caravan.

كوچي *kūchai*, s.m. The tendon of the heel (*Tendo Achillis*). H. (*khūnch*). *kūchai*, s.m. An ass colt. *kocha-ī*, s.f. A cloak made of felt. *kochī*, s.m. A nomade.

كودالئ *kūdāla-ī*, s.f. A hoe, mattock. S. (*kudālī*).

كودري *kawdarai*, s.m. A potsherd.

كودک *kodak*, s.m. A boy, youth. P.

كودله *kodala*, s.f. Hut, cabin, hovel.

كودن *kawdan*, a. Silly, foolish, imbecile. A.

كودي *kodai*, s.m. A pot, pipkin; potsherd.

كوديک *kawdīk*, s.m. A cooking pot, earthen pot.

كوډ *koḍ*, s.m. A shell, charm. S. (*gaḍh*).

كوډه *koḍa*, s.f. Sorcery, enchantment; jugglery. *koḍ-gar*, s.m. A sorcerer, magician, conjurer.

كوډئ *kawḍa-ī*, s.f. A cowrie. S. (*kauṛī*). *kūḍa-ī*, s.f. A shed, arbor, temporary hut made of boughs and leaves. H. (*kūṭī*).

كور *kor*, s.m. A house, dwelling, habitation; wife, family. H. (*ghar*). *kwar*, s.m. A wild grape tree, vine. *kor*, a. Blind. P. Border, margin, side. H.

كوربه *korbah*, s.m. Landlord, master of house; host, paterfamilias.

كورته *kūrta*, s.f. A coat, jacket, frock. H.

كورغندل *korghundal*, s.m. Indian cactus, prickly pear.

كوركمان *kūrkamān*, s.m. Turmeric.

كورمانه *kormāna*, s.f. Domestic economy, housewifery, keeping house.

كوروالي *kor-wālai*, s.m. Marital duty, intercourse between husband and wife.

كوره *korah*, a. New, unused. H. (*korā*).

كوري *korai*, s.m. Net for carrying grass, forage, etc. H. (*khārā*). *kūrī*, in. Away! Get out!

كوړ *koṛ*, s.m. Leprosy. S. (*koṛh*).

كوړمه *koṛma*, s.f. Family, household, wife.

كوره *kora*, s.f. A hole made in the ground for playing at marbles. H.

كوري *kūrai*, s.m. A measure of corn equal to the fourth part of an اوري *ogai*. H. (*kurā*). *korī*, s.m. A leper. a. Leprous. s. (*korhī*).

كوز *kūz*, a. Below, under; low, lower

كوزكتل *kūz-katal*, v.a. To look down, be sick at stomach, feel nausea.

كوزغالي *kūz-ghālai*, s.m. A dog's basin or eating dish.

كوزه *kūza*, s.f. A gugglet, long-necked water jar.

كوژدن *kojdan*, } s.f. Betrothal, marriage engagement. See غوښتل.
كوژدنه *kojdana*, }

كوژه *koja*, s.f. Eating the fast, not keeping the روژه.

كوږ *kog*, a. Bent, crooked, askew. P. (*kaj*).

كوږل *kwagal*, v.a. To endeavour, strive.

كوږووږ *kog-wog*, a. Very crooked, all awry.

كوس *kūs*, s.m. A large drum. P.

كوښښ *kokkhikkh*, s.m. Endeavour, application, zeal. P. (*koshish*).

كوښلي *kūkkhalai*, a. See كښلي *kkshulai*.

كوښه *kokkha*, A kind of slipper. P. (*kaush*).

كوك *kūk*, s.m. Crying, sobbing. S.

كوكري *kūkarai*, s.m. A puppy dog. S.

كوكړي *kokarai*, s.m. A biscuit, bun. See ككوړي.

كوكنار *koknār*, s.m. The poppy plant; the capsule. P.

كوكه *kūka*, s.f. See كوك.

كوكوړي *kokorai*, s.m. A large bannock or cake of bread baked upon heated stones.

كوكۍ *kūka-ī*, s.f. Name of a tree (*Rhamnus virgatus*). *kokai*, s.m. A boy, lad, child. *koka-ī*, s.f. The cheek, side of the face; a little girl, female child.

كول *kawul*, v.a. To do, act, perform. *kūl*, a. Cotemporary, peer, of the same age. *kol*, s.m. A pond; a ford, shallow water. A. (*qūl*). *kol*, s.m. See كهول.

كولك *kolak*, s.m. The brow above the forehead; a hole in the roof by way of chimney.

كولنډ *koland*, s.m. A piece of stick used to tether cattle, etc. by the neck or foot; a log of wood attached to the neck of cattle to prevent their straying.

كولي *kolai*, s m. A helmet, hat. P. (*kulāh*).

كوليار *koliyār*, s.m. Name of a tree (*Bauhinea variegata*). H. (*kachnār*).

كوم *kūm*, pr. What? which? that which. P. (*kudām*).

كومك *komak*, s.m. Aid, help. See كمك.

كومي *kūmai*, s.m. The palate; cleft in the palate.

كونتر *kawntar*, s.m. A pigeon. See كوتر.

كونټي *kūntai*, s.m. A shepherd's crook; a stick with a crook at the end.

كونځۍ *kontsa-ī*, s.f. The braided or plaited hair at the back of the head of women.

كونسټ *kūnsat*, a. Contracted, shrunk, shrivelled. s.m. Foundation, base, root; stock or stump (as of a tree).

كونكي *kawunkai*, s.m. Actor, agent, doer, performer. *konkai*, a. (for *kamkai*), Diminutive, small.

كونګري *kūngarai*, s.m. A puppy dog.

كونه *kūna*, s.f. Backside, podex, anus. P. (*kun*). *kūna-starkai*, s.m. A clout, child's napkin.

كوني *kūnī*, s.m. } A catamite.
كونيكي *kūnīgai*, s.f. }

كوني *kūnai*, s.m. A dog louse, dog tick. Mortar, lime, whitewash.

كوني كبر *kūnī-kabar*, s.m. A crab.

كوڼ *kūnr*, a. Deaf. P. (*kar*). *konr*, s.m. A tick, dog louse.

كوه *koh*, s.m. Mountain, hill (in comp.). P.

كوهستان *kohistān*, s.m. Mountain country,

highlands. P. Name of the highland tract north of Swat.

کوحي *kūhai*, s.m. A well. S. (*kūā*).

کوئي *koe*, s.m. Itching, titillation.

کوښل *kwakkhal*, v.a. To write. Def. in pres. ten. See کارل.

کوئي کبر *koe-kabar*, s.m. See کوني کبر.

کويلي *koyilai*, } s.m. Pot-scrapings, burnt
کويني *koyinai*, } part of victuals at the bottom of a pot. H. (*khurchan*).

که *ki*, c. If, as, that. P.

کهاره *kahāra*, s.f. A pannier. See کواره.

کهاړه *kahāṛa*, s.f. A ring of rope, straw, etc. used as a target for arrows.

کهالي *kahālī*, s.f. Indolence, laziness; yawning, gaping, stretching. A. (*kāhilī*).

کهتر *kihtar*, a. Junior, minor, less, small. P.

کهربا *kahrubā*, s.f. Amber. P.

کهند *kuhand*, a. Ancient, old. P. (*kuhan*).

کهول *kahol*, s.m. Family, house, tribe.

کهه *kaha*, s.f. Itching; nausea.

کهي *kahai*, s.m. A reed, rush; a kind of clay, ochre. *kaha-ī*, s.f. A pickaxe; axle of a water mill; a ditch, trench.

کيجم *kejam*, s.m. A saddle cloth of felt.

کيدل *kedal*, v.n. To be, to become.

کير *kīr*, s.m. Rice and milk cooked together. S. (*khīr*). *ker*, s.m. *Penis virilis*. P.

کيړي *kīrṛai*, s.m. A mole cricket.

کيرئي *kīra-ī*, s.f. The felloe or rim of a wheel.

کيړ *keṛ*, s.m. A screen or wattling made of the twigs of the tamarisk tree; a hedge, paling, etc. of tamarisk twigs.

کيړه *keṛa*, s.f. An iron ring in a plough; twigs or saplings (generally of the tamarisk tree) used in forming the roof of a house. H. (*keṛā*).

کيږدل *kegdal*, v.a. (For کښيږدل or ښکيږدل.) To set, place, put, etc. Def. in past ten. See کيښول.

کيس *kais*, s.m. The name of the great ancestor of the Afghans. He had three sons named Saṛabanṛ, Batanṛ, and Ghurghusht, to whom are traced in three great divisions all the different tribes of Afghans.

کيش *kesh*, s.m. Faith, religion, belief; manner, quality. P. Damask, diaper. H. (*khīs*).

کيښودل *kekkhodal*, } v.a. To place, put, set,
کيښول *kekkhawul*, } etc. Def. in pres. ten.
کيښوول *kekkhowul*, } See کيږدل.

کيښئي *kīkkha-ī*, s.f. A worm, mite, insect.

کيف *kaif*, s.m. Intoxication. A. *kaifī*, a. Intoxicated; intoxicating. s.m. A drunkard, sot.

کيفيت *kaifiyat*, s.m. Condition, state; statement, account; description, remark. A.

کيک *kaik*, s.m. A flea. P.

کيکر *kīkar*, s.m. Acacia tree. H.

کيل *kīl*, s.m. Furrow, rut, track, scratch. H. (*līk*).

کيلک *kīlak*, s.m. A hobble or fetter for the feet of a horse; a cord or tassel used to tie the scabbard to the sword handle.

کيمخت *kīmukht*, s.m. Shagreen; leather prepared from the hide of the horse or ass.

کيميا *kīmiyā*, s.f. Alchemy, chemistry. A.

کيناستل *kenāstal*, v.n. To sit, sit down, settle, subside. (For ښکيناستل or کښيناستل.)

کيند *kind*, s.m. A tattered and patched garment worn by dervishes.

کينول *kenawul*, v.a. To seat, instal, set. (For ښکينول or کښينول.)

کينه *kīna*, s.f. Malice, spite, rancour. P. *kīnawar*, a. Spiteful, revengeful, malicious.

کينړ *kīnṛ*, a. The left hand, left side, left.

گ

گ *gāf*. This letter being unknown in the Arabic is called the Persian kāf. It is the twenty-sixth letter of the Persian, and the thirty-third of the Pukkhto alphabet. It always has the sound of *g* hard as in *gun*. By the Yusufzais and Eastern Afghans it is very generally substituted for ږ *g*.

گاټلۍ *gāṭla-ī*, s.f. A bundle, package. H. (*gaṭhrī*).

گاټۍ *gāṭa-ī*, s.f. A small flat pebble, or bit of pottery set at the bottom of a pipe bowl, to prevent the tobacco getting into the stem. *gāṭai*, s.m. A round pebble, or pellet of dried clay, used to shoot from a sling.

گاډۍ *gāḍa-ī*, s.f. A cart, waggon. H. (*gāṛī*).

گاډيره *gāḍera*, s.f. Mixed grain, meal of pulses, corn, etc. mixed together; bread of mixed meal.

گازره *gāzara*, s.f. A carrot. S. (*gājar*).

گاگره *gāgra*, s.f. Granite amygdaloid, trap-rock.

گالل *gālal*, v.a. To keep, preserve; watch over, care for; to finish, complete.

گام *gām*, s.m. A pace, step. P.

گانده *gāndah*, s.m. Future, coming time. P. (*āyanda*).

گانډۍ *gānḍa-ī*, s.f. The pole or shaft by which a Persian wheel is set in motion, and to which the bullocks are yoked. H. (*gādhi*).

گانګوړه *gānguṛa*, s.f. Snivelling, snuffling, speaking through the nose.

گانړه *gāṉṛa*, s.f. Pawn, pledge; jewel, ornament, trinket. S. (*gahnā*.)

گانړۍ *gāṉṛa-ī*, s.f. An oil press. H. *ghānī*).

گاودم *gāwdum*, a. Tapering, like a cow's tail. P.

گاوز *gāwuz*, s.m. Stag, elk. P. (*gawaz*).

گاولي *gāwlai*, s.m. A kind of sandal or slipper made of leather. [*mesh*).

گاوميښ *gāwmekkh*, s.m. A buffalo. P. (*gāw-*

گاونډ *gāwanḍ*, a. Neighbouring, next door.

گاونډي *gāwanḍai*, s.m. A neighbour, parishioner, fellow townsman. S. (*gāoṅtī*).

گاه *gāh*, s.m. Time; place (in comp.). P.

گاهر *gāhar*, s.m. A drove of oxen, herd of cows.

گاهو *gāhū*, s.m. Drover, cattle driver.

گاهي *gāhe*, ad. Ever, anytime; once, sometime. P. *gāhe-gāhe*, ad. At times, sometimes, occasionally. P. *gāhī*, s.f. A deep wound or sore.

گايل *gāyal*, a. Wounded. H. (*ghāyal*).

گبر *gabr*, s.m. A fire worshipper, Zoroastrian. P.

گبينه *gabīna*, s.f. Honey; honeycomb. P. (*angabīn*).

گپه *gapa*, s.f. Chatter, prattle, talk. H. (*gap*). A lump or handful of mud.

گپي *gapī*, s.f. A cord used as halter, bit and bridle of rope.

گتکه *gatka*, s.f. Fencing foil. H. (*gadkā*).

گتمه *gutma*, s.f. A button hole or loop; a thimble, thumbstall of leather.

گټ *gaṭ*, s.m A boulder, rock, stone; a dark and heavy cloud. *guṭ*, s.m. A corner, angle, recess; a hole dug in a wall by burglars.

گټل *gaṭal*, v.a. To acquire, realize, gain; to win, succeed, gain the victory, etc. P. (*yāftan*).

گټمۍ *guṭma-ī*, s.f. A thimble.

گټه *gaṭa*, s.f. A pebble, stone; advantage, gain, profit.

گټۍ *giṭa-ī*, s.f. A potsherd, bit of stone; gravel, shingle; urinary calculus, stone in the bladder. *giṭai*, s.m. Pebble, small stone. H. (*gīṭī*).

گټين *giṭin*, a. Stony, pebbly, gravelly, shingly.

گځاري *gadzārai*, s.m. Refuse, chaff, stubble.

گڅ *gats*, a. Left, the left side.

گڅي *gatsai*, a. Left-handed.

گچ *gach*, s.m. Lime, cement, mortar. H.

گداي *gadāe*, s.m. A beggar, mendicant. P. (*gadā*). *gadā-ī*, s.f. Begging; beggary, poverty. P.

گدل *gdal*, v.a. To place, set. P. (*hīdan*). See يدل.

گډ *ga-aḍ*, s.m. A ram, sheep. H. (*gāḍar*). *gaḍ*, a. Mixed, compounded, blended. *guḍ*, a. Halt, lame, crippled, maimed.

گدړ *gidaṛ*, s.m. A jackal. H. (*gīdaṛ*).

گډندي *gaḍandai*, s.m. A dancer.

گډوډ *gaḍ-waḍ*, a. Higgledy-piggledy, confused, entangled, jumbled. H. (*gaḍ-maḍ*).

گډوري *gaḍūrai*, s.m. A lamb.

گدوزي *gadozai*, s.m. A span, the space between thumb and forefinger.

گډول *gaḍawul*, v.a. To mix, compound, combine, etc.; to make dance.

گډون *gaḍūn*, s.m. Intercourse; mixture. Name of a Pathan tribe located on the southern slopes of the Mahaban mountain.

گډه *ga-aḍa*, s.f. An ewe, sheep.

گډهل *gaḍhal*, s.m. A bucket, tub, pail.

گډي *guḍa-ī*, s.f. A lame woman; a doll. H. (*guḍḍā*). *guḍai*, s.m. A lame man, etc. *gaḍa-ī*, s.f. A cushion, pad. H. (*gaddī*).

گډيدل *gaḍedal*, v.n. To dance; to be mixed, confused, blended, etc.

گډيدنه *gaḍedana*, s.f. Dancing; mixing, blending.

گډيدونکي *gaḍedūnkai*, } s.m. A dancer; mixer.
گډيدوني *gaḍedūnai*, }

گډيره *gaḍera*, s.f. Mixture; intercourse.

گډيکه *gaḍeka*, s.f. The support of a spinning wheel; the crutch at the side of a sandal.

گذار *guẕār*, s.m. A blow, stroke; pass, turn, round, etc. P.

گذر *guẕar*, s.m. A ferry, ford, passage. P.

گذران *guẕrān*, s.m. Employment, living, livelihood. P.

گړ *ga-aṛ*, s.m. Rumble, rattle, clatter, etc. (as of wheels).

گر *gar* (in comp.), added to words denotes -doer, -maker, -performer. P.

گران *grān*, a. Important, momentous; heavy, weighty; dear, precious; difficult, hard. P. (*girān*). *grānī*, s.f. Dearth, scarcity, dearness of provisions, etc.

گرت *grut*, s.m. Interdigital space (hand or foot); angle between the trunk and branch of a tree. *grut-niwul*, v.a. To hold between the finger and thumb (as a pen, arrow, etc.).

گرد *gird*, a. Circular, round. P. *girdāgird*, a. Round about, all round, on all sides. P. *gard*, s.m. Dust; the globe; fortune. P.

گرداب *girdāb*, s.m. A whirlpool. P.

گردن *gardan*, s.m. The neck. P.

گردني *gardanī*, s.f. A horse cloth. P.

گردون *gardūn*, s.m. A wheel; firmament, heavens; destiny, fortune; a chariot. P.

گردي ليچي *gardai-lechai*, s.m. The arm above the elbow; humerus.

گرز *garz*, s.m. Dust. P. (*gard*). *gurz* or *gruz*, s.m. A battle-axe, club, mace. P.

گرزندي *garzandai*, } s.m. A reel, spindle; whirligig.
گرزني *garzanai*, }

گرزول *garzawul* or *girzawul*, v.a. To turn, change about, turn round, wheel, twirl, etc.

گرزيدل *garzedal* or *girzedal*, v.n. To revolve, spin, turn about, wander, meander, walk about, etc. P. (*gardidan*).

گرول *gargal*, v.a. To scratch, claw, scrape (with the nails).

گرکنډه *garkanḍa*, s.f. See ګرکنډه.

گړکي *ga-aṛkai*, s.m. The rattle or rumble of wheels.

گرگ *garg*, s.m. Mange, itch, scab. *gurg*, s.m. A wolf. P.

گرگره *gurgura*, s.f. Name of a tree yielding an edible fruit or berry (*Reptonia buxifolia*).

گرګس *gargas*, s.m. A vulture. P. (*kargas*). *gargas*, s.m. The cavity of the chest, thorax.

ګرګه *garga*, s.f. A log, block, stump of a tree.

گرم *garm*, a. Hot, warm; active, zealous; fiery, virulent; eager, intent; crowded, thronged. P. *gram*, a. Confuted, convicted; censured, rebuked. *guram*, s.m. A clump of trees; anxiety, mental distress, perturbation.

ګرمکه *garmaka*, s.f. A heat spot, vesicle, pustule. pl. *garmake*, Prickly heat (*Lichen tropicus*).

گرمه *garmah*, s.m. A kind of melon. P.

گرمي *garmī*, s.f. Heat, warmth, etc.; the venereal disease. P.

ګرنډه *garanḍa*, s.f. Name of a shrub and its fruit (*Carissa spinarum*). H. (*karaundā*).

ګرو *graw*, s.m. Pawn, pledge. P. (*girau*).

ګرول *garawul*, v.a. To scratch, claw, scrape (with the nails).

ګرولبي *grolbai*, s.m. Phlegm, mucus or pus from the lungs.

ګروه *griwa*, s.f. The collar bone, neck above the collar bone; collar of a garment; button-loop. P. (*girebān*). *guroh*, s.m. A band, troop; people, tribe; party, sect. P.

ګروهيدل *grohedal*, To admire, follow; be attracted, captivated; flock to; to fear, respect, revere. P. (*girwīdan*).

ګريوان *girewān*, s.m. Collar of a garment; the neck. P. (*girebān*).

ګريوه *grewa*, s.f. See ګروه *griwa*.

ګړ *gaṛ*, A castle, fort. S. (*gaṛh*).

ګړدۍ *gaṛda-ī*, s.f. The whirl of a spindle.

ګرنج *granj*, s.m. A clink, jingle, ring (of money), tinkle (of a bell), etc. *guṛanj*, s.m. A low voice, whisper.

ګړندي *gaṛandai*, a. Quick, hasty, precipitate, rash; nimble, swift, fast.

ګړنګ *gaṛang*, s.m. Abyss, crater; cavity, shaft, pit. *gṛang*, s.m. Mucus from the nose, snot.

ګړوبي *guṛobai*, s.m. Sherbet, eau sucré, sugar and water.

ګړونج *gaṛwanj*, s.m. A frame or stand for water jars; a stand, stage, platform. S. (*ghaṛwanchā*).

ګړه *guṛa*, s.f. Raw sugar, brown sugar. S. (*guṛ*).

ګړۍ *gaṛa-ī*, s.f. A measure of time, about twenty-four minutes; a clock, watch. S. (*ghaṛī*). A pond, pool. H. (*gaṛhā*). A fort, castle. S. (*gaṛhī*).

ګز *gaz*, s.m. A yard measure; a ramrod. P.

ګزک *gazak*, a. Festered, sloughed, suppurated, mortified (a wound); nipped with cold. P. s.m. Corruption, decay.

ګزن *guzan*, s.m. Palsy, paralysis. *guzanwahalai*, a. Palsied, paralysed.

ګږ *gag*, a. Dappled, mottled; hybrid, mongrel.

ګستاخ *gustākh*, a. Insolent, impertinent, rude, saucy, pert. P. *gustākhī*, s.f. Impertinence, assurance, pertness, etc.

ګسه *gasa*, s.f. Rebound, recoil, ricochet; blow, dig, stroke, poke.

ګسيا *gasiyā*, a. Abraded, rubbed, frayed. S. (*ghasā*).

ګښت *gakkht*, s.m. Patrolling, walking round, strolling, wandering. P. (*gasht*).

ګفتار *guftār*, s.m. Discourse, conversation. P.

ګفتګوي *guft-goe*, s.m. Conversation, talk, etc. P.

ګګر *gagar*, a. Brawny, muscular, stout, strong.

ګګروځه *gagaṛodza*, s.f. A shiver, tremble.

ګګشتو *gugushtū*, s.m. A turtle dove, ring-dove. H. (*ghūghū*).

ګل *gul*, s.m. A rose; a flower in general. P. A disease of the eye, albugo. Monday. *gil*, s.m. Clay, earth. P.

ګلاب *gulāb*, s.m. Rosewater. P. *gulābai*, s.m. A barber.

ګلخن *gulkhan*, s.m. A flat slab of stone used

for the flooring of a Turkish bath; a furnace, stove. P.

كلستان *gulistān*, ⎫ s.m. A rose bed, flower
كلشن *gulshan*, ⎭ garden. P.

كلو *gulu*, s.m. The throat, neck. P. *gilau*, s.m. Name of a plant, called also *kulmakalai* (*Mimosa scandens*). H. (*gilau*).

كله *gila*, s.f. Complaint, lament, grumble. P. *gila-man*, a. Complaining, grumbling. P. *galla*, s.f. A herd, flock. P.

كلئ *gala-ī*, s.f. Hail. See برلئ.

كم *gum*, a. Lost, missing, wanting. P.

كمارل *gumāral*, v.a. To consign, entrust, give in charge, commit. P. (*gumārīdan*, *gumāshtan*).

كماشته *gumāshtah*, s.m. Agent, factor. P.

كمان *gumān*, s.m. Doubt, suspicion; imagination, fancy; thought, supposition. P.

كمراه *gumrāh*, a. Erring, astray. P.

كمنز *gamanz*, s.f. A comb. See برمنز.

كناه *gunāh*, s.m. Crime, fault, sin. P.

كنبته *gunbata*, s.f. An arch, dome, cupola, vault. P. (*gumbad*).

كنج *ganj*, s.m. A granary, market; treasure, store. P.

كنجي *ganjai*, a. Bald, scald headed; a vulture. H. (*ganjā*).

كنجيفه *ganjīfa*, s.f. A pack of cards; game at cards. P.

كند *gand*, s.m. A patchwork garment worn by dervishes. *gind*, s.m. A ball for play. s. (*gend*). *gund*, a. Equal, level, even, on a par; peer, compeer, match. *gundi*, ad. By chance, perhaps, possibly.

كندنه *gandana*, s.f. A leek (*Allium porrum*). P.

كنده *gandah*, a. Fœtid, stinking. P. *gundah*, a. Coarse, thick. P.

كڼد *ganḍ*, s.m. Edging of a garment; an ornamental collar worn by women; edging of clay round a millstone. s. (*ganḍā*). A patchwork coat worn by dervishes.

كڼدل *ganḍal*, v.a. To hem, sew, stitch, baste, etc. P. (*nigandan*).

كڼدولي *ganḍolai*, s.m. A short sleeved shift or jacket worn by women.

كڼدهير *ganḍher*, s.m. Name of a plant (*Rhazzia stricta*).

كڼدهيرئ *ganḍhera-ī*, s.f. A joint or segment of sugar cane (cut for convenience of chewing). s. (*ganḍerī*).

كڼدي *gunḍī*, s.f. Collar of a dress; edging of a garment; a button loop, button. H. (*ghunḍī*). *gunḍai*, s.m. Refuse ears of corn, straw, etc. left on the threshing-floor. *gunḍe*, ad. By chance, possibly, perhaps.

كڼديري *ganḍerai*, s.m. The oleander or rose bay (*Nerium odorum*).

كنزه *gunza*, s.f. A crease, crumple, pucker, wrinkle; a comb.

كنس *gans*, a. Stunned, stupefied, deafened. P.

كنكپ *gankap*, s.m. A cut-purse, pickpocket. H. (*gaṭh-kaṭā*).

كنك *gung*, a. Dumb, mute. P.

كنكري *gungrī*, s.m. Boiled grain of pulse, wheat, etc. Grain steeped in water. s. (*ghūngnī*).

كنكري *gingarai*, s.m. A small bell for the feet of pigeons, hawks, etc. H. (*ghūngrū*).

كنكس *gangas*, s.m. A bend, swerve, turn, twist; narcissus, daffodil.

كنكوسي *gangosai*, s.m. Rumour, report; hum, murmur, whisper; sound of footsteps, talking, etc.

كنه *gunah*, s.m. Sin, crime, fault. P. *gunah-gār*, s.m. A sinner, culprit. *gunah-gārī*, s.f. Sinfulness, guiltiness, criminality. P. *ganna*, s.f. The sugar cane. H. (*gannā*).

كنهر *gunhar*, s.m. Name of a pot-herb (*Amarantus polygamus*).

گنړ *ganṛ*, a. Close, dense, thick, crowded; cloudy. S. (*ghan*).

گنړل *ganṛal*, v.a. To count, reckon; to consider, know. P. (*angārdan*).

گنړني *ganṛanai*, s.m. The womb.

گنړه *ganṛa*, ad. As if, as though; know, reckon.

گواښ *gwākkh*, s.m. Arbitration, mediation; compromise, settlement.

گواښګرندي *gwākkh-grandai*, s.m. Intercessor, mediator; negotiator, arbitrator.

گواښل *gwākkhal*, گواښېدل *gwākkhedal*, v.n. To pick a quarrel, peck at, irritate, prepare to quarrel; chide, reproach, blame. To mediate, parley, compromise, settle a quarrel. P. (*gawājidan*).

گواندي *gawāndai*, s.m. A neighbour. H.

گواه *gawāh*, s.m. A witness. P.

گواهي *gawāhī*, s.f. Evidence, testimony. P. *gawāhī-lal*, v.a. To testify, give evidence. *gawāhī-lūnai*, s.m. A witness, testifier.

گوپ *gūp*, s.m. The evening star, Venus; a bank of clouds.

گوته *gūta*, s.f. A finger, toe.

گوټ *gūṭ*, s.m. A corner, angle, nook; a hole dug in a wall by burglars. *gūṭ-mātawul*, v.a. To break into a house through a hole in the wall (as burglars).

گوجر *gūjar*, s.m. A grazier, cowherd. Name of a tribe of Rājpūts dwelling amongst the Eastern Afghans, and mostly occupied as cattle breeders and graziers. S.

گوجي *gūjai*, s.m. A small fresh-water shell; a fir cone.

گودر *gūdar*, s.f. Ford, ferry, passage. P. (*guzar*).

گوډ *goḍ*, s.m. Weeding, thinning plants. S. (*khod*). *goḍ-kawul*, v.a. To weed.

گوډا *gūḍā*, s.m. A doll, puppet. H.

گوډي *gūḍai*, s.m. A pouch; ear of Indian corn before the grain is formed. *gūḍa-ī*, s.f. A doll, puppet.

گور *gor*, s.m. A grave, tomb. P. *gor-kan*, s.m. A grave-digger. P. *gūr*, a. See گنړ.

گوراگور *gorāgor*, a. Fast, quick.

گورستان *goristān*, s.m. A graveyard. P.

گورکښ *gor-kakkh*, s.m. Name of an animal found in graveyards, Indian badger.

گورل *goral*, v.a. To see, look, inspect, view, etc. P. (*girāndan*). Def. in past tenses. See کتل.

گورم *goram*, s.m. A drove of buffaloes.

گوروان *gorwān*, s.m. A drover, grazier, cattle driver.

گوره‌خر *gorah-khar*, s.m. The wild ass. P. (*gorkhar*).

گورهنده *gorhanda*, s.f. Rough uneven ground; ravine, chasm, pit, fissure.

گوړئ *gūṛa-ī*, s.f. Juice or sap of trees.

گوشي *goshī*, s.f. Capitation tax on cattle.

گوښه *gokkha*, s.f. Corner, angle, nook; privacy, retirement; aside, side; cell, closet. P. (*gosha*).

گوگړ *gogaṛ*, s.m. Sulphur. P. (*gogird*). *gūgaṛ*, a. Aged, old, worn out (man or beast).

گوگل *gogal*, s.m. Cavity of the chest, thorax. *gūgal*, s.m. Name of a gum resin, Indian bdellium. S. *gogil*, s.m. Sulphur. P. (*gogird*).

گوله *gola*, s.f. A mouthful, morsel.

گولئ *gola-ī*, s.f. A ball, bullet, pill. H. (*golī*).

گوماندو *gūmāndū*, s.m. Mushroom, toadstool.

گونځه *gūndza*, s.f. A crease, wrinkle. See گنزه.

گونګټ *gūngaṭ*, s.m. A dung beetle.

گونګو *gūngū*, s.m. The yellow crocus, saffron.

گونګي *gūngai*, s.m. An owl.

گونه *gūna*, s.f. Colour, face, figure, form; kind, species. P.

گونړ *gūnṛ*, s.m. A weevil, insect in corn. H. (*ghun*).

گوهاټه *gohāṭa*, A stack of cowdung (dried and stored for use as fuel).

گوهار *gūhār*, s.m. A drove of oxen or buffaloes.

گوهر *gauhar* or *gūhar*, s.m. A pearl, gem; essence, nature, substance, disposition; intellect, wisdom; lustre of a gem or metal. P.

گوي *goe*, s.m. Dry cowdung; a ball. P.

گويا *goyā*, ad. As if, thus, as one would say, etc. P.

گه *gah*, s.m. Time, place. See گاه.

گهواره *gahwāra*, s.f. A cradle, swing. P.

گهور *gahūr*, a. Dense, shady, umbrageous.

گهي *gahe*, ad. Ever. See گاهي.

گهيځ *gahīdz*, s.m. Dawn, morning.

گياه *giyāh*, s.m. Grass, herbage, weeds. P.

گيدي *gedī*, a. Stupid. P. *gedī-khar*, s.m. Stupid ass.

گيډه *geḍa*, s.f. Belly, abdomen.

گيډي *geḍai*, s.m. A load of wood, grass, etc., for the head. *geḍa-ī*, s.f. A small sheaf of corn, a bundle of grass, faggot of sticks, etc.

گير *gīr*, a. Caught, seized, captured, taken; (in comp.) conqueror, taker, seizer. P. *ger*, a. Surrounded, besieged, enclosed. H. (*gher*).

گيړکه *gīṛaka*, s.f. A magpie.

گيسو *gesū*, A curl, ringlet. P.

گيندي *genḍai*, s.m. A rhinoceros; a shield of rhinoceros hide. S. (*gainḍā*).

گيڼرني *geṇranai*, s.m. The womb.

گيول *gayawul*, } v.a. To interlace, intertwine,
گيېل *gayayul*, } wattle, net.

ل

ل *lām* is the twenty-third letter of the Arabic, and the thirty-fourth of the Pukkhto alphabet. It is often substituted for the letters ں and ر in words from the Hindi and Persian.

لا *lā*, ad. Even, yet, still, hitherto, otherwise, unless. A particle prefixed to words to denote privation or negation, and equivalent to the English prefixes *im-*, *in-*, *un-*, etc., and the affix *-less*. A.

لابه *lāba*, s.f. Jest, irony, ridicule. P.

لاپه *lāpa*, s.f. Boasting, bragging. P. (*lāf*). *lāp-shap*, a. Proud, arrogant; bragging, boasting.

لات *lāt*, s.m. Name of an idol of the ancient Arabians.

لاټو *lāṭū*, s.m. A shrike, butcher bird; a humming-top; a whip-top. H.

لاجبر *lājbar*, s.m. Lapis lazuli. P. (*lājward*).

لاچي *lāchī*, s.f. Cardamums. H. (*ilāchī*).

لاډو *lāḍū*, s.m. A kind of sweetmeat. H. (*laḍḍū*). A humming-top. H. (*laṭṭū*).

لار *lār*, s.f. A road, way, path. P. (*rāh*).

لارغه *lārghah*, s.m. Delay, procrastination; lateness, slowness. ad. Ago, formerly. *lire-lārghah*, ad. Long ago, of yore; long since.

لاړل *lāṛal*, v.n. To go, depart, set out. Def. in pres. ten. See تلل *tlal*. P. (*rāh-raftan*).

لاړه *lāṛa*, s.f. Saliva, spittle. S. (*lār*).

لازم *lāzim*, a. Necessary, urgent; proper, suitable. A.

لاس *lās*, s.m. The hand; the arm. P. (*dast*).

لاسته *lāsta*, s.f. Direction, side, quarter.

لاستي *lāstai*, s.m. Handle, haft, hilt.

لاشوره *lāshora*, s.f. Name of a tree and its fruit (*Cordia Myxa*). H. (*lāsoṛa*).

لاښ *lākhsh*, s.m. A corpse, carcase. P. (*lāsh*).

لاغر *lāghar*, a. Weak, thin, lean. P.

لافه *lāfa*, s.f. See لاپه.

لاک *lāk*, s.m. Gum lac; sealing wax. S. (*lākh*).

لاکن *lākan*, a. Waxed; covered with wax. *lākin*, c. But, etc. See ليکن.

لاګ *lāg*, s.m. Dealings on credit with a tradesman.

لاګي *lāgī*, s.f. Trade, commerce. s.m. A dealer, customer.

لال *lāl*, a. Red; dumb. P. s.m. A ruby. P. (*l'al*).

لالا *lālā*, in. Master! Sir! H.

لالن *lālan*, s.m. A lover, sweetheart. S.

لاله *lāla*, s.f. A tulip. P. *lāla·gul*, s.m. The corn-poppy.

لالي *lālai*, a. Dear, beloved, darling.

لانبو *lānbo*, s.f. Swimming. *lānbo·zan*, s.m. A swimmer.

لاندِ *lāndi*, لاندي *lānde*, } ad. Below, under, beneath, down. *lānde·bānde*, ad. Upside down, topsy-turvy, tumbled, jumbled.

لاندي *lāndai*, s.m. Salt meat, sun-dried meat.

لانډي *lānḍa-ī*, s.f. A kind of snake, *amphisbœna*.

لانديس *lānḍes*, s.m. Name of a tree and its fruit (*Cassia fistula*).

لانګه *lānga*, s.f. The cord at the foot of a bed, which is used to brace up or tighten the netting. The name of a tree from the wood of which arrows are made.

لانړه *lānṛa*, s.f. Name of a plant (*Salsola kali*); it is burnt for the potash it yields. Spittle, saliva. See لاړه.

لانوده *lānwdah*, a. Wet, damp. Pl. of لوند.

لاونړ *lāwanṛ*, s.m. Caudle, posset.

لاهو *lāhū*, a. Flooded, swept away by a flood, floated down by a river, etc.

لاهه *lāha*, s.f. Alluvium, mud, mire, muddy deposit left by floods.

لاي *lāe*, s.m. Mire, mud. See preceding word.

لائق *lā-iq*, a. Becoming, fit, suitable; proper, deserving, worthy; capable, qualified, expedient. A.

لب *lab*, s.m. The lip; brim, edge; bank, margin; coast, shore. P.

لباس *libās*, s.m. Apparel, clothes, dress; garb. A.

لپ څت *lap·tsaṭ*, a. Fertile, fruitful (as land).

لپړ *lapaṛ*, a. Coarsely ground, gritty, unevenly mixed, clogged, clotty, lumpy (as food); thick stalks, stringy fibres, etc. mixed with pot-herbs; stiff, stark.

لپه *lapa*, s.f. The palm held to receive a thing; a handful, palmful. *lapakai*, s.m. The quantity containable in both hands held together. H. (*lapkā*).

لت پت *lat·pat*, a. Soiled, polluted, splashed; trampled, trodden down, etc.

لتاړه *latāṛah*, a. Trodden, trampled; spoiled, ruined.

لته *lata*, s.f. A kick. H. (*lāt*).

لټ *laṭ*, s.m. An axle; axle of a Persian wheel, weaver's loom, etc. A fishing stake, bird springe. a. Dull, indolent, lazy, listless. s.m. A lubber, lazy brute.

لټ پټ *laṭ·paṭ*, a. Tangled, tumbled, confused; soiled, stained; trampled, trodden.

لټول *laṭawul*, v.a. To examine, seek, search, rummage, turn over, investigate, look into, etc. H. (*ṭaṭolnā*).

لټه پير *laṭa·per*, s.m. Romping, frolicking, playing pranks, playing roughly, boisterous play.

لحاف *lihāf*, s.f. A coverlet, quilt. A.

لحد *lahad*, s.m. The niche in the side of a grave for the reception of a dead body. A.

لحظه *lahza*, s.f. A moment; glance, look. A.

لد *lid*, s.m. Horse dung. H. (*lid*).

لدن *ladan*, لدون *ladūn*, } s.m. Inspiration. *'ilm-i-ladūn*, s.m. Inspired knowledge, inherent wisdom. A.

لډر *laḍar*, s.m. A dealer in old clothes, rags, etc. a. Imbecile, foolish, stupid.

لذت *lizzat*, s.m. Flavour, taste; delight, enjoyment. A. (*lazzat*).

لذيذ *laziz*, a. Pleasant, savoury. A.

لر *lar*, a. Lower, inferior; subordinate, minor;

conquered, subdued. p. Under, below, beneath. *lar·taraf*, s.m. The losing side, lower side. *liri*, ad. Far, far off, off, away. P. (*dūr*)

لرغون *larghūni*, ad. Already, ere now, before, long since, long ago.

لرغوني *larghūnai*, a. Former, pristine, old. *larghūne*, ad. Long ago, formerly, anciently, of old.

لرگي *largai*, s.m. A stick, staff; timber, wood. H. (*lakṛī*). *liragai*, s.m. The lobe of the ear.

لرل *laral*, v.a. To own, have, possess. P. (*dāshtan, dār-*).

لره *lura*, A particle used as the sign of the dative case; to, unto, near, with, at; for, for the sake of.

لري *larai*, s.m. The small intestines; bowel, gut. Defeat, discomfiture, loss. *lire*, ad. Off, away; far, far off, distant.

لړ *laṛ*, s.m. A row, bead, string, thread (as of beads, pearls, pots, etc.). H. [(*larza*).

لړزه *laṛza*, s.f. A shake, tremor, quiver. P.

لړزيدل *laṛzedal*, v.n. To tremble, shake, shiver, quiver. P. (*larzīdan*).

لړل *laṛal*, v.a. To mix, stir, stir up, combine, stir about. H. (*lahrānā*).

لړم *laṛam*, s.m. A scorpion.

لړمون *laṛmūn*, s.m. The bowels, the internals, the heart, liver, lungs, etc. P. (*darūn*).

لړمه *laṛama*, s.f. Nettlerash, hives, urticaria.

لړوڅټو *laṛo·tsaṭo*, a. Mean, low, vulgar. s.m. A rascal, blackguard, scoundrel, vagabond.

لړه *laṛa* or *la-ara*, s.f. Fog, mist, vapour.

لږ *la-ag* or *lag*, a. Small, little, less; few, scarce. *la-ag·der*, a. More or less, somewhat, a little, few, some.

لږکوټي *la-agkūṭī*, ad. Little; somewhat, few; scantily, slightly.

لس *las*, a. Ten. S. (*das*). *lasam*, a. Tenth.

لستوڼي *lastūṇrai*, s.m. Sleeve of a dress.

لسته *lasta*, s.f. Handle, hilt. P. (*dasta*).

لسره *lasara*, ad. Never, not at all, not a bit.

لشمكه *lashmaka*, } s.f. Artful, intriguing,
لشمكي *lashmaka-ī*, } cunning, deceitful (woman); wanton, lewd, shameless (woman).

لشه *lasha*, s.f. Spike, prickle, bristle; sting of an insect; beard or spike of corn, grasses, etc. P. (*nesh*).

لښته *lakkhta*, s.f. A twig, switch, rod, cane.

لښتي *lakkhtai*, s.m. A brook, rivulet, linn, stream. *lakkhta-ī*, s.f. A dancing girl; ear-drop, pendant (of gold or silver). Name of a plant, the root of which is used as a charm by wounded persons to protect them from the evil wishes of their enemies, who, it is believed, by eating some of the root and then breathing upon a wounded man can prevent the healing of his wound, until some of their own spittle be applied to it; visitors to a wounded man are therefore requested to spit on a bit of the root, which is then passed over the wounds. The root is commonly found mixed with those of the madder plant (*majīṭ* or *rodang*) as sold in the shops.

لښكر *lakkhkar*, s.m. An army, multitude. P. (*lashkar*).

لښكي *lakkhke*, ad. Little. See لكوټي.

لطافت *latāfat*, s.m. Delicacy, elegance; humour, wit, facetiousness. A.

لطف *lutf*, s.m. Courtesy, gentleness, kindness. A.

لطيف *latīf*, a. Elegant, delicate; agreeable, pleasant; courteous, kind, gracious. A.

لطيفه *latīfa*, s.f. A joke, witticism. A.

لعاب *lu'āb*, s.m. Mucilage. A.

لعل *l'al*, s.m. A ruby. P.

لعن *l'an*, s.m. Cursing, damning. A.

لعنت *l'anat*, s.m. Anathema, curse, malediction. A. *l'anatī*, a. Damned, cursed, execrated. A.

لغت *lug͟hat*, s.m. Dialect, phraseology; dictionary; word. A.

لغته *lag͟hata*, s.f. A kick. P. (*lagad*).

لغړ *lag͟haṛ*, a. Bare, stripped, naked; poor, destitute. *lūṯs-lag͟haṛ*, a. Bare as a bone, stark naked.

لغز *lag͟hz*, s.m. A slip, slide, stumble. P, *lug͟hz*, s.m. Enigma, riddle. A.

لغوي *lug͟hawī*, a. Linguistic, literal meaning of a word. A.

لفافه *lifāfa*, s.f. Cover, envelope, wrapper. A.

لفظ *lafz̤*, s.m. A word, saying. A.

لقب *laqab*, s.m. Surname, title; nickname. A.

لقمه *luqma*, s.f. A morsel, mouthful. A.

لقوه *luqwa*, s.f. Spasmodic distortion of the face; paralysis of the facial nerve. A.

لقه *luqah*, s.m. A bully, brag.

لک *lak*, a. Stiff. rigid, straight; punctured, bored, pierced. s.m. A lac, a hundred thousand. S.

لکړه *lakaṛa*, s.f. A beam, rafter; pole, staff; barge pole; boat hook. H. (*lakaṛ*).

لکوټي *lakūṭe*, or *lakūṭī*, ad. A little, somewhat, slightly, not much. See لږکوټي.

لکوړي *lakoṛai*, s.m. Name of a fruit.

لکه *laka*, s.f. A blemish, blot, spot, stain; the tail (of bird or beast). ad. Like, so, as, thus.

لکه‌لمي *laka-lamai*, s.m. The rump bone, tail bone, coccyx.

لکي *laka-ī*, s.f. The tail (of bird or beast); a meteor, falling or shooting star.

لګړ *lagaṛ*, s.m. A kind of hawk. H.

لګنړ *lagaṉṟ*, s.m. A washing basin. P. (*lagan*).

لګول *lagawul*, v.a. To attach, fix, join; ascribe, impose, add; place, put, set; employ, engage, use; set to work, etc. H. (*lagānā*).

لګيا *lagiyā*, a. Applied, attached, placed; employed, occupied; intent.

لګيدل *lagedal*, v.n. To adjoin, reach, touch, apply; happen, befall, occur, begin; be occupied, employed, etc. H. (*lagnā*).

لال *lal*, a. Dumb, mute, speechless. P. (*lāl*).

لل *lal*, v.a. To utter, pronounce, say, express. Only used with a few words as, *ganāhī-lal*, v.a. To give evidence, testify, bear witness, etc. *salām-lal*, v.a. To say salām, pay respects.

للم *lalam*, a. Arid, dry, unirrigated (land).

للمي *lalamī*, s.m. Crops entirely dependent on the rains for water, unirrigated crops.

للئي *lala-ī*, s.f. Lullaby, hushaby. *lala-ī-lalos͟ha*, Hushaby baby, words intoned to put a child to sleep.

للون *lalūn*, s.m. Weeding, thinning (a field or garden).

لم *lam*, s.m. Tail, end, extremity; fat tail of the Afghan sheep. P. (*dum*). *lamawar*, a. Fat tailed, having a fat tail.

لمبړ *lumbaṛ*, s.m. A fox. H. (*lūmbaṛ*).

لمبل *lambal*, v.a. To bathe, wash, clean, purify.

لمبه *lamba*, s.f. A blaze, flame.

لمبيدل *lambedal*, v.n. To wash, bathe.

لمڅي *lamtsai*, s.m. Felt. P. (*namad*).

لمسول *lamsawul*, v.a. To incite, instigate. urge, prompt, tempt. A. (*lams*).

لمسون *lamsūn*, s.m. Instigation, prompting.

لمغړئي *lamg͟haṛa-ī*, s.f. Contortion, writhe, twist; device, trick, wile; shamming, malingering.

لمن *laman*, s.m. Border, hem, skirt; margin, edge, verge. P. (*dāman*).

لمور *lamawar*, a. Fat tailed (as Afghan sheep).

لنبل *lanbal*, v.a. To bathe. See لمبل.

لنده *linda*, s.f. A bow.

لندي *lindai*, s.m. An archer, bowman. *linda-ī*, s.f. A small bow used by carpenters to work a drill or *barma*; the bow of a fiddle; one of the bones of the forearm; the outer bone of the leg; the hamstrings; any bent or arched twig; guard of a sword; a jet, spout, spurt of water.

لند *lanḍ*, a. Brief, short.

لنده *lanḍah*, s.f. Lower end of the spine, sacrum.

لندي *lanḍa-ī*, s.f. A kind of poetry or verse, with seven or eight syllables to the line. A kind of snake, the head and tail of which are like each other (*amphisbæna*).

لنګ *lang*, a. Lame, crippled. P. *lung*, s.m. A cloth worn over the loins and hips when bathing; a clout worn between the thighs. P.

لنګټي *lingaṭa-ī*, s.f. Name of a herb (*Heliotropum orientale*).

لنګر *langar*, s.m. An anchor; almshouse, kitchen. P.

لنګري *langarai*, s.m. A shallow metal dish, in which dough is kneaded; a deep bowl of metal or pottery in which snuff, spices, etc. are pounded; mortar. H. (*langrī*).

لنګور *langor*, s.m. A span between the thumb and forefinger.

لنګه *langa*, a. Puerperal, childbed; a puerperal woman, a woman for forty days after childbirth; an animal about to drop its young; an animal suckling its young; a bird hatching or sitting on eggs; with young, breeding, pregnant. *langa·kkhadza*, A puerperal woman. *langa·ghwā*, A milch cow. *langa·chirga*, A brood hen. *langa*, s.f. A brace. See لانګه.

لنګي *lunga-ī*, s.f. A scarf, sash (used as a headdress, or waist-band, or worn as a sash over the shoulders). P. (*lūngī*).

لنګېدل *langedal*, v.n. To litter, drop young. P. (*langīdan*).

لو *lū*, s.m. Smoke. P. (*dūd*). *lau*, s.m. Reaping, mowing. P. (*dirau*).

لواړ *lwāṛ*, a. Coarse, thick; rough, uneven; boorish, clownish; rude, unpolished.

لواطة *liwāṭat*, s.m. Sodomy. A.

لوال *liwāl*, a. Hungry, peckish; longing, yearning; inclined, hankering. A. (*luwāh*)

لواور *lawā·or*, s.m. A sickle, scythe. See لور *lor*.

لوبان *lobān*, s.m. Benzoin. A.

لوبه *loba*, s.f. Play, fun, frolic, game. A. (*l'ab*).

لوبيا *lobiyā*. A kind of bean (*Dolichos sinensis*).

لوټ *lūṭ*, s.m. Booty, plunder, spoil. S.

لوټه *lūṭa*, s.f. A clod, clod of earth. H. (*londā*).

لوټکي *loṭkai*, s.m. A pot, pipkin (of the kind used on Persian wheels). H. (*loṭā*). A small pillar of baked clay, three of which are used to form a tripod for the support of the iron dish on which cakes of bread are baked.

لوڅ *lūts*, a. Bare, naked, nude. P. (*luch*). *lūts·lapaṛ*, or *lūts·pūts*, a. Stark naked, bare as a bone, without a shred.

لوڅک *lūtsak*, لوچک *lūchak*, a. Alone, destitute, friendless; profligate, vagabond, libertine; having little hair on the body (as a dog, etc.).

لوڅه پوڅه *lotsa·potsa*, s.f. Rolling and tumbling (as a baby on its back); rolling on the ground (as a dog, horse, etc.). H. (*loṭ·poṭ*).

لوح *lauḥ*, s.m. A board or tablet used by schoolboys to write upon. A.

لوحه *loḥa*, s.f. A ruler, or scale of iron for drawing lines.

لوخړه *lūkhaṛa*, s.f. A blaze, flame. S. (*lūkh*).

لوخه *lūkha*, s.f. Bulrush (*Pencillaria spicata*); soft rush (*Juncus effusus*). P.

لودل *lawdal*, v.a. To say, express. See لل. Particularly applied to giving evidence, paying respects, etc. P. (*lāwīdan*).

لودي *lodī*, s.m. Name of an Afghan tribe, famous as having furnished emperors of Hindostan.

لور *lor*, s.m. A sickle, scythe. Direction, side. *lūr*, s.f. A daughter. P. (*dukhtar*).

لورايه *larwarāya*, ad. From afar, a long way off. (For لهورايه *la rwarāya*.)

لوري *lorai*, s.m. Direction, quarter, side.

لور *lawar*, s.m. A bludgeon, club, baton; a wooden pestle. s. (*loṛhā*). *lwaṛ*, a. Elevated, raised, high; upland, rising, hilly, etc. (ground). *lwaṛa·jawaṛa·zmaka*, High and low-, up and down-, undulating-, uneven-, or broken ground.

لوړول *lwaṛawul*, v.a. To detach, divide, separate, part, sever.

لوړيدل *lwaṛedal*, v.n. To part, separate, fall away.

لوزه *lauza*, s.f. A honey bee.

لوږه *lwuga*, s.f. Hunger. s. (*bhūkh*).

لوږي *lwugai*, a. Hungry, famished. s. (*bhūkhā*).

لوستل *lwustal* or *lūstal*, v.a. To read, learn. P. (*nabistan*, to write).

لوستل *lawastal*, v.a. To bale, empty; disperse, scatter, strew, daub, dash, besmear. Irr. pres. *lawanī*. Past, *lawast*.

لوشل *lwashal*, v.a. To milk (as a cow, etc.). P. (*doshīdan*).

لوښتل *lwukkhtal*, v.n. To part, separate, diverge, fall away, abscond. Def. in pres. ten. See لوړيدل.

لوښي *lokkhai*, s.m. A basin, pan, pot, etc. s. (*lokhar*). Nature, temperament, quality.

لوغزه *lwaghza*, s.f. A milch cow, goat, etc.

لوغړن *lūgharan*, a. Charred, smoked, smoke stained.

لوغونه *lawaghūna*, s.f. A milk pail.

لوګري *lau·garai*, s.m. A reaper, mower.

لوګي *lūgai*, s.m. Smoke, vapour, steam.

لوليه *lūlapah*, a. Burnt to ashes, scorched.

لولو *lolo*, s.m. An ornament for the arm or turban.

لولول *lwulawul*, v.a. To cause to read, to teach or learn by reading.

لوله *lola*, s.f. A ball or skein of thread; roll of paper, cloth, etc. P.

لولي *lolai*, s.m. A dancing boy. *lola-ī*, s.f. A dancing girl, prostitute. P. (*lūlī*).

لوم *lūm*, s.m. A net, noose, snare. P. (*dām*). s. (*lūm*).

لومكه *lūmaka*, } s.f. A noose, snare; a bird
لومه *lūma*, } trap of horse-hair nooses.

لون *laun*, s.m. Colour, hue; kind, species. s.

لونبړ *lūnbaṛ*, s.m. A fox. See لمبړ.

لوند *lūnd*, a. (f. *lamda*) Damp, moist, wet. P. (*nam*).

لونډ *lawanḍ*, s.m. A bachelor; widower; adventurer, vagabond, rake. P. (*lawind*).

لونګ *lawang*, s.m. A clove. s. (*laung*). *laung*, s.m. Posset, caudle, boiled milk and sugar.

لونه *lūna*, s.f. An abscess, boil.

لوهار *lohār*, s.m. A blacksmith. s.

لوهاني *lohānī*, s.m. Name of an Afghan tribe, principally occupied as carriers of merchandise between Hindustan and Turkistan. (For *rawānī*, by which name they are sometimes called.)

لوي *loe*, a. Great, large; corpulent, stout; chief, superior; full grown; great in office, rank, etc.

لويدل *lwedal*, v.n. To fall, slip, slide; drop down, fall down, tumble down, etc.

لويشت *lwesht*, s.f. A span between the thumb and little finger. P. (*bilisht*).

لويشتنک *lweshtinak*, } s.m. A pigmy, dwarf;
لويشتينک *lweshtīnak*, } small span; precocious child.

لويګنده *lweganda*, s.f. The temple, space between the ear and eye; fontanelle of an infant.

لوينه *lwina*, s.f. A net or snare for birds.

لوېرند *lwegand*, s.m. A sponger, parasite, toady.

له *la*, A preposition governing the ablative

case; from. A preposition or affix governing the dative case; to, unto.

لبري *lahaṛai*, s.m. A beam, rafter.

ليلپاند *lahlapānd*, a. Scorched, charred. See لولپه.

لياقت *liyāqat*, s.m. Capacity, fitness; ability, skill; merit, worth. A.

ليتي *leṭa-ī*, s.f. Batter, paste, pap. H. (*leṭī*). *leṭai*, s.m. Hard clay, marl.

ليچ *lech*, s.m. Ophthalmia, disease of the eyes.

ليچن *lechan*, a. Blear-eyed.

ليچه *lecha*, s.f. The cubit, forearm.

ليچي *lecha-ī*, s.f. The trotters of a sheep, etc.

ليدل *līdal*, v.a. To see, look, perceive. P. (*dīdan*). Irr. Pres. (*wīnī*). Past, *līdah*.

ليده *līdah*, s.m. Seeing, sight, vision. P. (*dīdah*).

ليره *līra*, s.f. A shred or strip of cloth. H. (*līr*).

ليرئي *lera-ī*, s.f. Narrow ridge or edge of a hill.

ليزم *lezam*, a. Confuted, abashed.

ليږدل *legdal*, v.a. To march, set out, pack up and depart.

ليږدول *legdawul*, v.a. To load and move off, march.

ليږل *legal*, v.a. To send, despatch, transmit.

ليښل *lekkhal*, v.a. To load, lade; march, set out. Def in pres. ten. See ليږدل.

ليک *līk*, s.m. A line, mark, ruled line; furrow, rut, scrawl, wheel track. H

ليکل *līkal*, v.a. To write. H. (*likhnā*).

ليکن *lekin*, c. But, yet, moreover. A.

ليکه *līka*, s.f. A line, furrow. See ليک.

ليمه *lema*, s.f. The pupil of the eye; the eye.

ليندہ *līnda*, s.f. A bow.

ليندي *līndai*, s.m. A bow. See لندی.

ليندہ *lendah*, a. Bald; scald headed.

لينگي *lengai*, s.m. The leg.

ليو *lew*, s.m. Plaster, mud plaster. H.

ليوال *lewāl*, a. Hungry. s.m. Appetite, hunger. See لوال.

ليور *lewar*, s.m. Husband's brother. S. (*dewar*).

ليوني *lewanai*, a. Demented, mad. P. (*dīwānah*).

ليوهل *lewahal*, v.a. To plaster, daub, smear.

ليوه *lewah*, s.m. A wolf.

ليه *liyah*, a. Useless, worthless; uncontrolled, dissolute; wanton, lewd. Covered, veiled; noble, exalted. A. *liya*, s.f. The tamarisk tree. ad. Merely, simply, only.

م

م *mīm* is the twenty-fourth letter of the Arabic, and the thirty-fifth of the Pukkhto alphabet. It is a labial letter, and is sounded like the English *m*. In words where it is followed by ب it is sometimes changed to ن, as لنبه *lanba* for لمبه *lamba*, flame. Prefixed to the imperative of a verb it denotes prohibition, being in place of the particle مه *ma*, as مکوه for مه کوه *makawa*, don't. It is added to the cardinal numbers to form the ordinals, as لس *las*, ten—لسم *lasam*, tenth.

مِ *mi*, A form of the genitive and instrumental cases, singular number, of the first personal pronoun زه *zah*, I. Also written مي *me*.

ما *mā*, The instrumental case and inflected form of the first personal pronoun زه.

مابوب *mābūb*, a. Beloved. See محبوب.

ماپښين *māpakkhīn* or *māpakshīn*, s.m. Afternoon; afternoon prayers. P. (*namāz-peshīn*).

مات *māt*, a. Broken, cracked; beaten, dispersed; torn, lacerated. P.

ماتول *mātawul*, v.a. To break, burst open, smash; to break in upon, disperse, beat, etc.

ماته *māta*, s.f. Prey, quarry. S. (*mārā*).

ماتيدل *mātedal*, v.n. To break, burst, crack.

ماتس *māṭus*, s.m. A bump, swelling (from a blow).

ماچي *māche*, s.f. (pl. of *mācha*) Vermicelli.

ماخستن *mākhustan*, s.m. Bedtime, evening; bedtime prayers. P. (*namāz-khuftan*).

ماده *māda*, s.f. Article, clause; matter, subject. A. (*mādda*). *māda*, s.f. Female. a. Feminine. P.

ماديان *mādiyān*, s.f. A mare. P.

مادين *mādīn*, s.f. A female. P.

مار *mār*, s.m. A serpent, snake. P.

مارج *mārij*, s.m. A flame of fire. A.

مارجري *mār-jaṛai*, s.m. Name of a bulbous root used as a remedy for snake bites.

مارغه *mārghah*, s.m. Pl. of مرغه which see.

ماري هاري *māṛe-hāṛe*, in. Exclamation of complaint, dear me! oh dear!

مازدگر *māzdigar*, s.m. Afternoon; evening; afternoon prayers. P. (*namāz dīgar*).

مازو *māzū*, s.m. A gallnut. P.

ماسپښين *māspakkhīn*, s.m. See ماپښين.

ماسته *māstah*, s.m. Curds, curds and whey.

ماښختن *māskhutan*, s.m. See ماخستن.

ماسوا *mā-siwā*, ad. Besides, moreover. A.

ماسه *māsa*, s.f. Name of a weight equal to twelve grains. H.

ماسي *māsa-ī*, s.f. Leather socks worn inside the shoes, and not removed in the house.

ماش *māsh*, s.m. Name of a kind of pulse or bean (*Phascolus Max*). S. *girgirah-māsh*, s.m. Bean meal.

ماشله *māshala*, } s.f. A skein, hank of thread
ماشوره *māshoṛa*, } or silk.

ماشوق *māshūq*, s.m. A lover. See معشوق.

ماشوم *māshūm*, s.m. An infant. See معصوم.

ماشي *māshai*, s.m. A musquito, gnat.

ماښام *mākkhām* or *mākshām*, s.m. Evening. P. (*namāz shām*).

ماغزه *māghzah*, s.m. The brains (pl. of مغز which see).

ماکو *mākū*, s.m. A weaver's shuttle. S. (*mākho*). Name of an Afghan clan.

مال *māl*, s.m. Property, wealth; effects, goods; cattle, merchandise. A. *māl* (in comp.), Rubbing, rubber. P. *ma-āl*, s.m. End, issue. A. *khair-ma-āl*, s.m. A happy issue.

مالدار *māl-dār*, a. Wealthy, rich in cattle, etc. Owner of cattle; cattle grazier.

مالت *mālat*, s.m. A division, quarter, parish, ward. A. (*muhalla*).

مالش *mālish*, s.m. Polishing, rubbing, friction. P.

مالک *mālik*, s.m. Master, owner, proprietor. P.

مالکندي *mālkunḍa-ī*, } s.f. Name of a plant,
مالکنړي *mālkunṛa-ī*, } caltrops (*Tribulus terrestris*).

مالگه *mālga*, s.f. Salt.

مالگبه *mālgbah*, s.m. Collector of salt, drysalter.

مالگين *mālgīn*, a. Salt, saline.

مالگينړي *mālgīnṛai*, s.m. A game played by boys.

مالوچ *mālūch*, s.m. Picked cotton, carded cotton

ماله *māla*, s.f. A weaver's brush; clod crusher; rubber. P.

ماما *māmā*, s.m. Maternal uncle. S.

مامن *māman*, Place of security, asylum. P.

مامور *māmūr*, a. Established, ordered, fixed. S.

مامولکه *māmūlaka*, s.f. A water-wagtail. A. (*māmolā*).

ماموي *māmū-ī*, s.f. A dried apricot, with the kernel preserved inside it.

مامي *māmī*, s.f. Aunt, maternal uncle's wife.

مانجي *mānji*, s.m. A marriage guest of the bridegroom. H. (*mānjhā*, wedding feast).

ماندره *mandara*, s.f. A tent rope; a heart string, one of the *cordæ tendineæ*.

مانده *māndah*, a. Weary, fatigued, tired. P. *mānda*, s.f. A heart string, tendinous cord of the heart.

ماندينه *māndīna*, s.f. A female. P. (*mādīn*).

مانع *mān'i*, s.m. Forbidder, preventer; obstacle, hindrance. A.

مانگي *māngai*, | s.m. A boatman, sailor. H.
مانړگي *mānṛgai*, | (*mānjhī*).

مانموله *mānmola*, s.f. Name of a pot-herb.

مانه *māna*, | s.f. Blame, complaint; mur-
مانړه *mānṛa*, | mur, lament.

مانړو *mānṛū*, s.m. A kind of wild sloe or plum, the name of a herb used in medicine.

مانړي *mānṛai*, s.m. Estrangement, misunderstanding; umbrage, pique. *mānṛa-ī*, s.f. Edifice, building; pile, storied house.

مانړيگر *mānṛī·gar*, a. Annoyed, piqued, displeased, estranged.

ماولي *māwlai*, s.m. The piece of wood in the centre of the upper millstone, through which the pivot of the lower one passes.

ماه *māh*, s.m. The moon (in comp.); month. P.

ماهي *māhai*, s.m. A fish. P. (*māhī*).

مائچي *mā-iche*, s.f. Vermicelli. See ماچي.

مائل *mā-il*, s.m. Propensity, inclination, tendency. A.

مائلان *mā-ilān*, a. Partial, biassed, inclined. A.

مايه *māya*, s.f. Capital, stock; leaven, ferment; rennet. P. *māyah*, s.m. A double humped camel. P.

مباح *mubāḥ*, s.m. An indifferent action, an action neither ordained nor prohibited in the law. A.

مبادا *mabādā*, in. God forbid! lest! be it not! P.

مبارك *mubārak*, a. Fortunate, happy; holy. in. Hail! welcome! A. *mubārakī*, s.f. Congratulation, happiness. A.

مبالغه *mubāligha*, s.f. Hyperbole, exaggeration. A.

مبتدي *mubtadī*, s.m. Tyro, novice, beginner; beginning. A.

مبتلا *mubtilā*, a. Captivated, fascinated; involved in trouble, distracted. A.

مبلغ *mublagh*, s.m. A sum, ready money; much, many. A.

مبهم *mubham*, a. Ambiguous, occult, unknown, secret. A.

متره *matra*, s.f. Posset, sillabub, curdled milk; dregs, sediment, refuse. *matrah*, a. Rare, scarce.

متصل *mutaṣṣil*, a. Contiguous, close, adjoining. A.

متعلق *mut'alliq*, a. Concerning, relative; belonging to. A.

متفرق *mutafarriq*, a. Separate, distinct; dispersed. A.

متفق *mutaffiq*, a. United, agreeing; accomplice. A.

متل *matal*, s.m. Proverb, adage; fable, saying. A. (*maṣal*).

متن *matan*, s.m. Middle or text of a book. A.

متوجه *mutawajjah*, a. Facing, turning; attending, favouring. A.

متولي *mutawallī*, s.m. Superintendent or treasurer (of a mosque). A

مته *matah*, s.m. A wild boar

متيازه *mitiyāza*, s.f. Urine. S. (*mūt*).

مټ *ma-aṭ*, s.m. The arm; fore limb of an animal.

مټ *maṭ*, s.m. Celerity, dispatch; deep dust on a road; a kind of earthenware pot. *muṭ*, s.m. The fist, closed hand. H. (*muṭh*).

مټاك *maṭāk*, s.f. A walnut with a hard shell.

مټاكه *maṭāka*, s.f. A bump, swelling from the sting of a bee, etc.; nettlerash; ball of a pellet-bow; kind of hard walnut.

مټر *muṭar*, s.m. Dolt, fool, piss-a-bed. S. (*mūtr*).

مټكي *maṭkai*, s.m. Bracelet, ornament for the arm. A large earthen jar. H. (*maṭkā*).

مټه *maṭa*, s.f. Clay, marl, greasy earth. S. (*maṭṭī*). *maṭah*, a. Lazy, stubborn, obstinate.

متي *muṭai*, s.m. The fist; handle, hilt. s. (*muṭhī*). *muṭa-ī*, s.f. A bow for cleaning cotton; the club with which it is worked. Handle of a plough, hilt of a sword, etc.

متياي *miṭiyā-ī*, s.f. A sweetmeat; confectionery. H. (*miṭhā-ī*).

متيز *maṭīz*, s.m. A man who has eloped with another's wife or daughter.

متيزه *maṭīza*, s.f. A woman who has eloped with a man to whom she is not married; elopement, running away (of lovers).

مثال *misāl*, s.m. Metaphor, allegory; likeness, simile, parable, saying. A.

مثقال *misqāl*, s.m Name of a weight equal to fifty-four grains (troy). A.

مثل *masal*, s.m. A proverb. See متل.

مثلاً *maslan*, ad. For example; *e.g.*; *i.e.*; *viz.* A

مجاور *mujāwar*, s.m. A verger, sweeper at a mosque or shrine. A.

مجرا *mujrā*, s.f. Premium, allowance; deduction, retrenchment. A.

مجرب *mujarrab*, a. Proved, tried; skilled, expert. A.

مجرد *mujarrad*, a. Alone, single; unmarried. A.

مجرم *mujrim*, a. Sinful, criminal. s.m. A culprit. A.

مجلس *majlis*, s.m. Assembly, congregation; meeting, party. A.

مجمر *majmir*, s.m. A chafing dish, incense dish. A.

مجمل *mujmal*, s.m. Abstract, summary. A.

مجنون *majnūn*, a. Insane, love mad. P.

مڅوڅكي *matsotskai*, s.m. See مچچكي.

مچ *mach*, s.m. A fly; the sight at the muzzle of a gun.

مچچكي *machichkai*, s.m. Name of a plant used in medicine.

مچک *machak*, s.m. A shepherd's crook.

مچمچي *machmachai*, s.m. A honey bee.

مچلوغزه *machaloghza*, } s.f. A sling (for throw-
مچوغنه *machoghana*, } ing stones).

مچه *macha*, s.f. A kiss. H. (*machhī*).

مچي *macha-ī*, s.f. A bee.

محافظت *muhāfizat*, s.m. Custody, care, protection. A.

محال *mahāl*, a. Absurd, impossible. A.

محبت *muhabbat*, s.m. Affection, love. A.

محبوب *mahbūb*, a. Loved, beloved. A.

محتاج *muhtāj*, a. Needy, indigent, necessitous. A.

محتسب *muhtassib*, s.m. A censor. A. An official who parades the streets armed with a thong, sees that the faithful duly perform their prayers and repeat the belief, etc. A.

محراب *mihrāb*, s.m. The alcove or closet in a mosque, in which the priest, facing Mecca, performs prayers before the congregation. A.

محرم *muharram*, a. Sacred, forbidden. A.

محرمه *muharrama*, s.f. Name of the first month of the Muhammadan calendar.

محروم *mahrūm*, a. Forbidden, prohibited; deprived, excluded. A.

محصول *mahsūl*, s.m. Custom, excise, duty, tax.

محض *mahz*, a. Pure, simple. ad. Purely, solely. A.

محفوظ *mahfūz*, a. Secure, protected. A.

محکم *muhkam*, a. Firm, strong, secure. ad. Firmly. A.

محکمه *muhkama*, s.f. A court of justice. A.

محل *mahall*, s.m. Place, house, abode; time. A.

محله *muhalla*, s.f. A district, parish, ward; place, building, edifice. A.

محمد *muhammad*, a. Praised. s.m. Name of the Arabian prophet. A.

محنت *mihnat*, s m. Labour, toil, trouble; wages, hire; affliction, difficulty, misfortune. A.

مخ *makh*, s.m. Face, front, surface; civility, kindness, courtesy. S. (*mukh*). *makhā-makh*, ad. Face to face, opposite.

مخالف *mukhālif*, a. Adverse, opposed, contrary. A.

مخالفت *mukhālafat*, s.m. Opposition, contrariety. A.

مخبر *mukhbir*, s.m. A spy, reporter, informer. A.

مختار *mukhtār*, s.m. A free agent, attorney. a. Absolute, independent; chosen, selected. A.

مختصر *mukhtaṣar*, a. Abridged. s.m. Compendium, abstract, epitome. A.

مختلف *mukhtalif*, a. Discordant, diverse. A.

مخسره *makhsara*, s.f. Jesting, joking. See مسخره.

مخرني *makhranai*, s.m. A kind of plum, apricot.

مخفي *mukhfī*, a. Secret, concealed, hidden. A.

مخلص *mukhliṣ*, a. Sincere, true (friend). A. *mukhlaṣ*, s.m. Asylum, refuge. A.

مخلوط *makhlūṭ*, a. Mixed, combined, confused. A.

مخلوق *makhlūq*, s.m. Creature, created being. a. Created. A.

مخور *makhawar*, a. Polite, courteous, civil, kind.

مخه *mukha*, s.f. A butt for arrows, archery butt. *makha*, s.f. Direction, side, way.

مخي *makhai*. a. Equal, even, par. s.m. Compeer, peer, equal, clansman.

مدار *madār*, s.m. Affability, complaisance, favour, politeness, kindness. A. (*mudārā*).

مدام *mudām*, ad. Always, continually, ever. A.

مدت *muddat*, s.m. Time, space, long time. A.

مدد *madad*, s.m. Aid, help, succour. A.

مدرس *mudarris*, s.m. Professor, teacher, head of a college. A.

مدرسه *madrassa*, s.f. College, university, school. A.

مدعا *muddʿā*, s.f. Desire, wish; object, view. A.

مدعي *muddaʿī*, s.m. A plaintiff, claimant, prosecutor; enemy. A. *muddaʿī-alaiki*, s.m. A defendant. A.

مذكور *mazkūr*, a. Aforesaid, mentioned. s.m. Discourse, mention, conversation. A.

مذمت *mazamat*, s.m. Abuse, contempt. A.

مذهب *mazhab*, s.m. Religion, sect. A.

مذي *maza-ī*, s.f. Mucus from urethra or vagina. A.

مراد *murād*, s.m. Desire, wish; purport, design. A.

مرانده *marānda*, s.f. A tent rope. See مانده.

مراوه *mrāwa*, s.f. The part of a Persian wheel which supports one of the troughs.

مربي *murabbī*, s.m. Tutor; guardian; patron. A.

مرت *murt*, s.m. A kind of wormwood; a powder applied to the private parts of infants.

مرتبه *martaba*, s.f. Degree, office, rank; class, order; time, turn. A.

مرتد *murtadd*, s.m. Apostate, renegade. A.

مرجان *marjān*, s.m. Coral. P.

مرجيونړه *marjīwanṛah*, s.m. Coral diver, pearl diver. S. (*marjīyā*).

مرچ *mrach*, s.f. Pepper. S. (*mirch*). *sra-mrach*, s.f. Red pepper, capsicum.

مرد *mard*, s.m. A man; a male. P.

مردار *murdār*, a. Polluted, filthy, foul; ugly. s.m. Carrion, offal, pollution. P.

مردانه *mardānah*, a. Manly, brave. P.

مردرو *mard-rau*, s.m. Parapet, breastwork. P.

مردك *mardak*, s.m. A ball, cannon ball.

مردكه *mardaka*, s.f. } A bullet, pellet, bolus;
مردكي *mardakai*, s.m. } a marble, pebble.

مردم *mardum*, s.m. Man, mankind; people, the world. P.

مردود *mardūd*, a. Outcast, reprobate, rejected. A.

مرده *murdah*, a. Dead. s.m. A corpse. P.

مردي *mardī*, s.f. Manliness, bravery; virility, semen. P.

مرسته *mrasta*, s.f. Partiality, favour; help, aid, assistance.

مرسل *mursal*, s.m. Messenger; prophet. A.

مرسله *mursila*, s.f. Epistle, missive. A.

مرشد *murshid*, s.m. Guide, teacher, director (religious); monitor, instructor. A.

مرصع *muraṣṣa'*, a. Jewelled, gilt. A.

مرض *maraẓ*, s.m. Disease, sickness. A.

مرضي *marẓī*, s.f. Will, pleasure. A. *maraẓī*, a. Sick, diseased. A.

مرغ *mragh*, s.m. A large stone used in the exercise of "putting the stone."

مرغچچي *marghachichai*, s.m. Name of a grain used to make necklaces, etc.; Job's tears, seeds of *Coix lachryma*.

مرغړي *margharai*, s.m. A tumour, glandular swelling.

مرغلره *marghalara*, s.f. A pearl.

مرغمي *marghumai*, s.m. A kid. See ورغومي.

مرغه *marghah* (pl. *mārghah*), s.m. A bird. P. (*murgh*). *margha*, s.f. A kind of grass (*Milium filiforme*). P. (*margh*).

مرغۍ *margha-ī*, s.f. A little bird, any small bird.

مرکنډۍ *markanḍa-ī*, s.f. The throat, neck; windpipe and gullet.

مرگ *marg*, s.m. Death, decease, demise. P.

مرگوټي *margoṭai*. s.m. Paroxysm of death, death struggle, death.

مرله *marla*, s.f. A land measure equal to four and a half yards square.

مروت *marwat*, s.m. A coil, twist; screw. *marwat*, s.m. Name of a district between the Indus and Sulaiman mountains; name of the tribe inhabiting Marwat. *muruwat*, s.m. Urbanity, generosity; fortitude, manliness. A.

مرور *marawar*, a. Displeased, offended, piqued.

مروري *marorī*, s.f. Name of a plant (*Helicteres isora*). H.

مروړ *maroṛ*, s.m. Convolution, turn, twist. H.

مرونډۍ *marwanḍa-ī*, s.m. Name of a shrub (*Vitex negundo*).

مرهم *marham*, s.m. A plaster, ointment, salve. A.

مرۍ *mara-ī*, s.f. The neck, throat, gullet and windpipe; a bead; a charm.

مريد *murīd*, s.m. Disciple, follower. A.

مريض *marīẓ*, a. Diseased, sick. A.

مرينړه *marīnṛa*, s.f. Patch of a field left uncut, work left unfinished.

مرئي *mra-e*, s.m. A slave, bondsman.

مړ *muṛ*, a. Dead, lifeless, defunct. P. (*murd*). *muṛ·kawul*, v.a. To kill, deprive of life, put out (as fire, etc.).

مړام *mṛām*, } a. Decayed, withered, faded.
مړاو *mṛāw*, }

مړانه *maṛāna*, s.f. Bravery, heroism, manliness. P. (*mardānah*).

مړځپن *maṛtsapan*, a. Faded, withered, decayed.

مړد *maṛd*, s.m. A saint, religious guide.

مړشومه *muṛ·shūma*, s.f. Food sent by friends and relatives to the house of a deceased person on the day of death

مړز *mṛaz*, s.f. A quail.

مړغونه *maṛaghūna*, s.f. Bitter apple, colocynth (*Citrullus Colocynthis*).

مړغېچن *maṛghechan*, a. Faded, withered; frost bitten, nipped by cold. See مړځپن

مړل *mṛal*, v.n. To die. P. (*murdan*).

مړني *maṛanai*, a. Brave, daring, manly. s.m. A hero. P. (*mardānah*).

مړوښه *maṛokkha*, s.f. A married woman, woman under coverture, wife.

مړوند *maṛwand*, s.m. The wrist, wrist joint.

مړه *maṛah*, } in. Man! Sir! Master! Sirrah!
مړي *maṛai*, } P. (*mard*).

مړی *muṛai*, a. Dead, lifeless. s.m. A corpse,

dead body. *maṛa-ī*, s.f. A morsel, mouthful.

مزاج *mizāj*, s.m. Constitution, temperament, habit, disposition, temper, nature. A.

مزاخ *mazākh*, s.m. A joke, jest; ridicule. A.

مزد *muzd*, s.m. Hire, salary, wages; perquisite, premium; corn taken by a miller as the price of grinding. P. *mazdah*, s.m. A miller.

مزدگري *muzd garai*, s.m. A miller.

مزدور *mazdūr*, s.m. A labourer, workman. P. *mazdūrī*, s.f. Labour, work; hire, wages. P.

مزري *mzarai*; s.m. A leopard, panther; tiger.

مزکه *mzaka*, s.f. Earth, ground, land, soil.

مزل *mazal*, s.m. A stage. See منزل.

مزه *maza*, s.f. Flavour, relish, taste; delight, enjoyment, pleasure. P. (*mazā*).

مزي *mazai*, a. Powerful, strong. s.m. Cord, twine, thread, string; edging or piping of a dress.

مږ *mag*, s.m. A ram. S. (*mekh*).

مږک *magak*, s.m. A rat.

مږل *magal*, v.a. To rub. Def. in past ten. See مښل.

مږه *magah*, s.m. A rat. P. (*mūsh*).

مږه کوري *magah-kūrai*, s.m. A mouse, young rat.

مس *mis*, s.m. Copper. P. *mas*, s.m. A cup for collecting lamp-black.

مسافر *musāfir*, s.m. A traveller, stranger. A.

مست *mast*, a. Drunk, intoxicated; proud, wayward; wanton, sensual. P.

مستک *mastak*, s.m. Name of a weed, darnel, tares. Name of a resin, mastick. A. (*maṣṭakī*).

مسجد *masjid*, s.m. A mosque, house of prayer. A.

مسحه *masha*, s.f. Anointing; wiping. A. (*masḥ*).

مسخراچي *maskharāchī*, s.m. A buffoon, jester, clown. T.

مسخره *maskhara*, s.f. Drollery, jesting. P.

مسرف *musrif*, a. Prodigal, extravagant. A.

مسکن *maskan*, s.m. Abode, dwelling. A.

مسکي *maskai*, s.m. Laughing, smiling; simper, smile. H. (*muskān*).

مسل *musal*, v.n. To simper, smile.

مسله *masala*, s.f. Proposition, question; a precept of Muḥammad. A.

مسند *masnad*, s.m. A throne. A.

مسواک *miswāk*, s.m. A toothbrush. A.

مسئ *masa-ī*, s.f. An ornament for the head.

مسيدل *musedal*, v.n. To simper, smirk, smile.

مسين *misīn*, a. Made of copper or brass, brazen. P.

مسينه *misīna*, s.f. A set of copper pots and pans.

مشابه *mushābih*, a. Resembling, like. A.

مشابهت *mushābihat*, s.m. Resemblance, likeness, conformity. A.

مشاته *mushāta*, s.f. An ugly face, cross look.

مشاد *mushād*, a. Ugly, cross-looking.

مشال *mashāl*, s.m. A torch. A. (*mash'al*).

مشت *musht*, s.m. A fist, closed hand. P.

مشته *mushta*, s.f. A cotton carder's beetle or club.

مشر *mashar*, a. Elder, senior, chief.

مشرف *musharraf*, a. Honoured, exalted. A.

مشرق *mashriq*, s.m. The east. A.

مشرک *mushrik*, s.m. An infidel. A.

مشغول *mashghūl*, a. Busy, occupied, employed. A.

مشغولا *mashghūlā*, s.f. Business, occupation; pastime, recreation.

مشفق *mushfiq*, s.m. Friend, companion. a. Kind, merciful, obliging. A.

مشق *mashq*, s.m. Copy, exercise, example. A.

مشقاب *mashqāb*, s.m. A trencher, kneading dish. T.

مشقت *mushaqqat*, s.m. Labour, pains, trouble, toil. A.

مشک ***mashk***, s.m. A leather sac for holding water. P. ***mushk***, s.m. Musk. P.

مشکار ***mushkār***, s.m. A falconer; chief huntsman. P. (***mīr-shikār***).

مشکل ***mushkil***, a. Difficult. A.

مشکندي ***mushkunḍa-ī***, s.f. A pod or bag of musk.

مشکنړه ***mashkanṛa***, s.f. A glass bead.

مشکي ***mushkai***, a. Musk-coloured, dark brown.

مشکین ***mushkīn***, a. Musky, smelling of musk.

مشوانړي ***mashwānṛa-ī***, s.f. An inkstand. H. (***misiyānī***). ***mashwānṛī***, s.m. Name of an Afghan clan.

مشورت ***mashwarat***, s.m. Consultation, counsel, advice. A.

مشه ***masha***, s.f. The priming pan of a gun.

مشهور ***mashhūr***, a. Notorious, celebrated, famous, well known, published. A.

مښل ***mukkhal***, v.a. To rub, polish; anoint, lubricate. Irr. Pres. ***mugi***. Past, ***mukkhah***. P. (***mushtan***).

مښوکه ***makkhūka***, s.f. Beak, bill of a bird.

مصاله ***maṣāla***, s.f. Spice, seasoning. A. (***maṣālah***).

مصرف ***maṣraf***, s.m. Cost, expenditure. A. ***muṣrif***, a. Prodigal, extravagant. A.

مصروف ***maṣrūf***, a. Expended; changed. A.

مصلحت ***maṣlahat***, s.m. Advice, consultation, counsel; convenience, expedience. A.

مصلا ***muṣallā***, s.f. A carpet used to pray on. A.

مصیبت ***muṣībat***, s.m. Adversity, calamity, disaster, misfortune. A.

مضبوط ***mazbūṭ***, a. Firm, fixed, strong. A.

مضر ***muẓirr***, a. Hurtful, pernicious. A.

مضمون ***mazmūn***, s.m. Meaning, sense. A.

مطابق ***muṭābiq***, a. Agreeable, conformable, suitable. A.

مطالعه ***muṭāl'a***, s.f. Contemplation, consideration; reading, study. A.

مطبوع ***maṭbū'***, a. Acceptable, worthy; innate, natural. A.

مطرب ***muṭrib***, s.m. A musician. A.

مطلب ***maṭlab***, s.m. Desire, wish; aim, object; meaning, purport. A.

مطلق ***muṭlaq***, a. Absolute, supreme. ad. Entirely, wholly, altogether. A.

مطلوب ***maṭlūb***, a. Wanted, required. A.

مظلوم ***maẓlūm***, a. Injured, oppressed; mild, gentle. A.

معاش ***m'āsh***, s.m. Living, livelihood, subsistence. A. ***m'āsharat***, s.m. Conversation, society, living together. A.

معاف ***mu'āf***, a. Absolved, exempted, forgiven. A. ***mu'āfī***, s.f. Exemption, immunity; rent free lands. A.

معالجه ***mu'ālija***, s.f. Cure, remedy; healing. A.

معاملت ***mu'āmalat***, s.m. } Affair, transaction,
معامله ***mu'āmala***, s.f. } business. A.

معتبر ***mu'tabar***, a. Trustworthy, reputable, confidential, respectable. A.

معتدل ***mu'tadil***, a. Temperate, moderate. A.

معتقد ***m'utaqid***, s.m. A believer, faithful person. a. Confiding, believing, trusting. A.

معتکف ***m'utakif***, a. Devout, pious. A.

معجزه ***m'ujiza***, s.f. A miracle. A. (***m'ujiz***).

معجون ***m'ajūn***, s.m. Confection, electuary. A.

معدوم ***m'adūm***, a. Abolished, non-existent. A.

معده ***m'ida***, s.f. Stomach. A.

معذور ***m'azūr***, a. Excused, disappointed. A.

معرفت ***m'arifat***, s.m. Knowledge; account. cause, reason. p. By, through, by means of. A.

معرکه ***m'arika***, s.f. Assembly or convocation of arbitrators to settle disputes between warring tribes. A.

معروف ***m'arūf***, a. Known. A.

معشوق ***m'ashūq***, s.m. A loved man; lover. A. ***m'ashūqa***, s.f. A mistress, sweetheart.

معصوم ***m'aṣūm***, s.m. An infant, babe. a. Innocent, simple; defended, preserved. A.

معطل *m'attal*, a. Idle, neglected, unemployed; suspended from office, disengaged. A.

معقول *m'aqūl*, a. Just, proper, reasonable. A.

معلوم *m'alūm*, a. Known; notorious, distinguished; apparent, evident. A.

معمار *m'imār*, s.m. A builder; mason. A.

معمور *m'amūr*, a. Full, stocked; cultivated; happy. A.

معمول *m'amūl*, a. Customary, practised. A.

معنا *m'anā*, } s.f. Meaning, signification,
معني *m'anī*, } sense. A.

معهود *m'ahūd*, a. Agreed, determined, fixed, promised. A.

معين *mu'aiyan*, a. Appointed, established, certified, fixed. A.

مغاك *mughāk*, s.m. A pit. P.

مغانه *mghāna*, s.f. The groin, inside of thigh.

مغرب *maghrib*, s.m. The west. A.

مغرور *maghrūr*, a. Arrogant, proud, haughty. A.

مغز *maghz*, s.m. Brain, marrow, pith. P.

مغزن *maghzan*, a. Powerful, strong.

مغزي *maghzī*, s.f. Border, edging. P.

مغلوب *maghlūb*, a. Conquered, overcome. A.

مغيلان *mughīlān*, s.m. Acacia tree. A.

مفاجات *mafājāt*, s.m. Sudden death. A.

مفارقت *mufāriqat*, s.m. Absence, separation. A.

مفاصله *mafāṣila*, s.f. Interval, distance. A.

مفت *muft*, ad. Gratis, for nothing. A.

مفتاح *miftāḥ*, s.m. A key. A.

مفتي *muftī*, s.m. A lawgiver, chief justice. A.

مفرد *mufrad*, a. Alone, solitary, single. s.m. The singular number. A.

مفسد *mufsid*, s.m. Rebel, seditious person; evildoer, mischief maker. A.

مفصل *mufaṣṣal*, a. Detailed, distinct; full, ample. ad. Fully, distinctly. A.

مفلس *muflis*, a. Destitute, poor.

مفيد *mufīd*, a. Profitable, salutary. A.

مقابل *muqābil*, a. Confronting, opposite; comparing, matching, equalling. A.

مقابله *muqābala*, s.f. Comparison, matching, opposition, contending. A.

مقاتله *muqātala*, s.f. Slaughter, carnage. A.

مقال *maqāl*, s.m. Speech, discourse, talk. A.

مقام *muqām*, s.m. Abode, dwelling; mansion, place; stage, resting place. A.

مقبره *maqbara*, s.f. A tomb, sepulchre, mausoleum. A.

مقبول *maqbūl*, a. Acceptable, agreeable; accepted. A.

مقتدي *muqtadi*, s.m. Imitator, follower. A.

مقتول *maqtūl*, a. Killed, slain. A.

مقدار *miqdār*, s.m. Measure, quantity. A.

مقدس *muqaddas*, a. Consecrated, holy. A.

مقدم *muqaddam*, a. Prior, antecedent; chief, leader. A.

مقدمه *muqaddama*, s.f. Preamble, preface; affair, matter, business; cause (in law). A.

مقدور *maqdūr*, s.m. Ability, power, possibility. A.

مقرر *muqarrar*, a. Fixed, established, certain; unquestionable, infallible. ad. Certainly, positively. A.

مقسوم *maqsūm*, a. Distributed, divided. A.

مقصد *maqṣad*, s.m. Design, purpose, wish, aim. A.

مقعد *maq'ad*, s.m. The hips; anus, podex. A.

مقل *muql*, s.m. Fruit of the dwarf palm. A.

مقوي *muqawwī*, a. Strengthening, tonic. A.

مقيش *muqqaish*, s.m. Brocade. A.

مقيم *muqīm*, a. Constant, fixed, stable. s.m. Resident, dweller, lodger. A.

مكار *makkār*, a. Deceitful, insidious. s.m. Cheat, hypocrite, impostor. A.

مكاري *makkārī*, s.f. Hypocrisy, imposture, roguery. A.

مكان *makān*, s.m. Place, station. A.

مكتب *maktab*, s.m. A school. A.

مکر ***makr***, s.m. Deceit, evasion, fraud. A.

مکرر ***mukarrar***, a. Repeated, reiterated. A.

مکروه ***makrūh***, a. Odious, hateful, disgusting. A.

مکنړه ***makanṛa***, s.f. The wooden catch which fixes the upright pillar of a Persian wheel to the cross-beam.

مکيز ***makez***, s.m. Pretence, coquetry.

مګر ***magar***, c. Except, but, otherwise, only, moreover, unless. P. s.m. A crocodile, alligator. S.

مګهر ***maghar***, s.m. A stone used in a game like pitch and toss, ducks and drakes, etc.; a stone used in the exercise of "putting the stone."

مل ***mal***, s.m. Associate, comrade, chum. S. (*mel*).

ملا ***mlā***, s.f. The loins, waist. ***mullā***, s.m. Schoolmaster, doctor, scholar, learned man. A.

ملاتړ ***mlā·taṛ***, s.m. Armed retainer, henchman; mercenary soldier; reserve of an army; aid, succour, support. a. Armed, accoutred, having the loins girded.

ملاچرګک ***mullā·chargak***, s.m. The hoopoe.

ملاح ***mallāḥ***, s.m. Boatman, sailor. A.

ملاحظه ***mulāḥaza***, s.f. Consideration, contemplation, notice, regard; looking at. A.

ملازم ***mulāzim***, s.m. Attendant, servant. a. Attentive, diligent. A.

ملاست ***mlāst***, a. Reclining, lying down.

ملاستل ***mlāstal***, v.n. To recline. See څملاستل.

ملاقات ***mulāqāt***, s.m. Interview, meeting; visiting. A.

ملال ***malāl***, a. Dejected, sad; drooping, faded. s.m. Languor; grief, sadness. A.

ملامت ***malāmat***, s.m. Blame, censure, rebuke. a. Reproved, censured. A. ***malāmatī***, a. Reprehensible, blameable. A.

ملتوي ***multawī***, a. Protracted, delayed. s.f. Delay, procrastination. P.

ملخ ***mlakh***, s.m. A locust. P. (*malakh*).

ملعون ***mala'ūn***, a. Cursed, execrated. A.

ملخوزه ***malkhoza***, s.f. Name of a potherb, fenugreek (*Trigonella fœnugræcum*).

ملک ***mulk***, s.m. Country, kingdom, region. A. ***malik***, s.m. Chief, master, king. A. ***milk***, s.m. Possession, property, right. A. ***malak***, s.m. An angel. A.

ملکه ***malaka***, s.f. An angel. ***malika***, s.f. Queen, empress, mistress, wife of a *malik*.

ملکي ***malikī***, s.f. Office or duty of malik. ***mulkī***, a. Civil, political, relating to the country or empire. ***milkī***, s.m. A farmer, landholder. A.

ملګري ***mal·garai***, s.m. Associate, comrade, chum.

ملګرتیا ***malgar·tiyā***, ملګيري ***malgīrī***, } s.f. Friendship, companionship, association, etc.

ململ ***malmal***, s.m. Muslin. H.

ملمع ***malmah***, a. Enamelled, glazed, gilded; coated, covered. A. (*mulamm'ā*).

ملنډه ***malanḍa***, s.f. A joke, jest.

ملنډي ***malanḍai***, s.m. Buffoon, jester, clown

ملنګ ***malang***, s.m. An ascetic, hermit. H.

ملنګان ***malangān***, s.m. Name of a grass (*Cyperus elatus*). H. (*malanga*).

ملو ***malaw***, s.m. A sac or bag in which loads are packed previous to loading.

ملوب ***malob***, s.m. Blood and water.

ملوک ***malūk***, a. Delicate, handsome.

ملول ***malūl***, a. Faded; sad. See ملال.

ملونه ***mlūna***, s.f. Bridle, reins and bit. P. (*dahāna*).

مله ***mala***, s.f. Name of a grass.

ملهم ***malham***, s.m. Ointment, salve. P. (*marham*).

ملي ***malai***, a. Emasculated, castrated (by crushing the testicles). H. (*malā*).

مليا ***miliyā***, a. Encountering, meeting. S. (*milā*).

ممانعت *mumāni'at*, s.m. Prohibition, hindrance. A.

ممانړه *mamān̲r̲a*, s.f. Name of a tree (*Sageretia oppositifolia*).

ممتاز *mumtāz*, a. Eminent, illustrious, exalted. A.

ممريز *mamrez*, s.m. A spur. P. (*mahmez*).

ممکن *mumkin*, a. Possible. A.

مملکت *mumlakat*, s.m. Empire, dominion. A.

مملوک *mamlūk*, a. Possessed, in one's power. s.m. A Mameluke, captive, slave. A.

من *man*, s.m. Name of a weight. The *man* of Tabriz, used in Western Afghanistan, is equal to eight pounds (avoirdupois); that of Peshawur is equal to eighty pounds. A.

منا *manā*, s.f. A raised platform or stage for watching a field from.

منات *manāt*, s.m. Name of an idol of the ancient Arabians. A.

مناجات *munājāt*, s.m. Prayers, supplications. A.

منادي *munādī*, s.f. Proclamation. A.

مناره *munāra*, s.f. A minaret, turret. A.

مناسب *munāsib*, a. Convenient, proper, fit. A.

مناسبت *munāsabat*, s.m. Expediency, propriety, fitness; comparison, connexion, relation. A.

منافق *munāfiq*, s.m. Atheist, heretic; hypocrite; enemy. A.

منال *manāl*, s.m. Substance, wealth. A.

منبر *minbar*, }
ممبر *mimbar*, } s.m. A pulpit. A.

منت *minnat*, s.m. Entreaty, supplication, obligation, favour. A.

منتر *mantar*, s.m. Charm, spell, philter. S.

منتظر *muntaẓir*, a. Expecting, looking for. A.

منځ *mand̲z̲*, s.m. Centre, middle. ad. Between, atwixt.

منځگري *mand̲z̲-garai*, s.m. Mediator, go-between.

منځوي *mand̲z̲wai*, a. Central, medial.

منج *manj*, s.m. A bed, bedstead. S. (*manjā*). *munj*, s.m. Name of a grass from which ropes are made (*Saccharum munja*). S. (*mūnj*).

منجقي *manjaqai*, s.m. Clitoris.

منجله *manjala*, }
منجيله *manjīla*, } s.f. A ring of grass or rags, used as a stand for round bottomed vessels, or as a pad for the head to support a load, etc.

منحصر *munhaṣir*, a. Besieged, surrounded. A.

من *man*, }
مند *mand*, } m. A possessive particle added to nouns and adjectives to denote endowment or possession. P.

مندانړو *mandān̲r̲ū*, s.m. A churning stick; rolling pin. H. (*manthanī*). Name of a plant.

مندري *mandrai*, a. Short, squat, little. H. (*mandarā*). *mundarai*, s.m. An ear-ring. H. (*mundrā*).

مندنړ *mandan̲r̲*. See مندنړ.

منډړ *manḍaṛ*, s.m. The withers of a horse, etc. H. (*mondhā*). Mustard seed.

منډ *manḍ*, s.m. Footprint, footmark; footstep; the stump of a tree.

منډر *munḍar*, s.m. The stump of a tree.

منډر *manḍar*, }
منډن *manḍan*, }
منډنړ *manḍan̲r̲*, } s.m. Name of one of the two great divisions of the Yūsufzai tribe, located on the Sama or Yūsufzai plain.

منډل *manḍal*, v.a. To cram, stuff, thrust, or force in; to knead the limbs, shampoo.

منډړ *manḍaṛ*, s.m. An arbour; porch, verandah, shed, H. (*manḍṛā*).

منډوس *manḍos*, s.m. A play ball. A cloth tied over the head and under the chin; a small turban. H. (*munḍāsā*).

منډه *manḍa*, s.f. A pace, step; race, run, course. *manḍa-wahal*, v.a. To stamp with the foot. *manḍe-wahal*, v.a. To run, race.

منډهي *manḍha-ī*, s.f. A market. H. (*manḍī*).

منډي *munḍai*, s.m. The innermost of two

bullocks treading corn, or working a Persian wheel. A pollard, or lopped tree; a man who has lost a limb; a short, squat person.

منزل **manzil**, s.m. A day's journey, stage. A.

منزلت **manzilat**, s.m. Dignity, rank. A.

منسوخ **munsū<u>kh</u>**, a. Abolished, cancelled. A.

منشا **man<u>sh</u>ā**, s.f. Beginning, origin, source. A. **mun<u>sh</u>ā**, s.f. Intention, meaning, wish. A.

منشي **mun<u>sh</u>ī**, s.m. Secretary, writer, clerk. A.

منصب **manṣab**, s.m. Dignity, office. A.

منصف **munṣif**, s.m. Arbitrator, judge, umpire. a. Equitable, just. A. **munṣifī**, s.f. Arbitration, judgment; decision, justice. A.

منظور **manẓūr**, a. Approved, accepted, chosen; seen, looked at. A.

منعه **man'a**, s.f. Refusal, prohibition. A. (*mana'*).

منكر **munkir**, s.m. Denying, rejecting. A.

منگ **mung**, pr. We. See مونږ.

منگار **mangār**, s.m. A viper. See منگور.

منگاره **mangāra**, s.f. A scratch with the nails.

منگر **mangar**, c. But, etc. See مگر. s.m. Name of the eighth Hindu month, October-November. S. (*aghan*).

منگري **mangarai**, s.m. A viper, a small venomous snake.

منگز **mangaz**, s.f. A hair comb, a comb.

منگل **mangul**, s.f. The hand, claw, paw.

منگنړ **manga<u>nr</u>**, s.m. A bug.

منگور **mangor**, s.m. A viper. See منگري.

منگه **munga**, pr. One of the plural oblique forms of the first personal pronoun زه; us.

منگي **mangai**, s.m. An earthenware pitcher for water. **mangoṭai**, s.m. A small pitcher.

منل **manal**, v.a. To obey, submit, yield, comply, attend; accept, believe, agree, confess. S. (*mānnā*).

منه **manah**, s.m. An arbour, shed (of boughs and leaves).

مني **manai**, s.m. Autumn, autumn harvest. **manī**, s.f. Semen, sperma genitale. A. Egoism, egotism. P. **munai**, s.m. A sage; a devout, pious, or holy man. S. (*munī*).

منړه **ma<u>nr</u>a**, s.f. An apple.

مو **mo**, pr. A form of the genitive and instrumental cases plural of the second personal pronoun تۀ. **mū**, pr. A form of the genitive and instrumental cases plural of the first personal pronoun زه. **mū**, s.m. Fat, grease, tallow, suet. The hair (in comp.). P.

مواجب **muwājib**, s.m. Pension, salary. A.

موره **muwara**, s.f. An instrument for cleaning cotton.

مواس **muwās**, s.m. Backbiter, tell-tale; rebel, mischief maker. **mawās**, s.m. Asylum, protection, refuge. H.

موافق **muwāfiq**, a. Apt, agreeing, conformable, like, consonant, suitable. A.

موافقت **muwāfaqat**, s.m. Analogy, conformity, etc.

موت **maut**, s.m. Death. A.

موټ **moṭ**, s.m. Name of a pulse (*Phaseolus aconitifolius*). H. (*moṭh*). **mūṭ**, s.m. The hand closed, fist; a handful; handle, hilt. S. (*muṭh*).

موج **mauj**, s.m. A wave, billow. A.

موجب **mūjib**, s.m. Cause, motive, reason. A.

موجود **maujūd**, Present; existing. A.

موچنړه **mo<u>ch</u>a<u>nr</u>a**, s.m. A cobbler's wife; a shoe.

موچي **mo<u>ch</u>ī**, s.m. A cobbler, leather worker. H.

موده **mūda**, s.f. Appointed time, season.

موذن **muwazzin**, s.m. Public crier to prayers. A.

موذي **mūẕī**, a. Pernicious, hurtful, noxious. A.

مور **mor**, s.m. A mother. (pl. *mainde*). P. (*mādar*). **mor**, s.m. A peacock. S. **mor**, s.m. An ant. P.

موراني **morāna-ī**, s.f. Ferule of a knife handle.

مورچنگ **mor<u>ch</u>ang**, s.m. A Jew's harp. P.

مورچه *morcha*, s.f. A battery, redoubt; rust. P.

مورګني *mor·ganai*, s.m. A relative by the mother's side.

مورګه *morga*, s.f. Brim, edge, rim, margin, border, etc.

مورني *moranai*, a. Of the same mother by different fathers.

موروث *maurūs*, a. Hereditary. A.

موري *mora-ī*, s.f. A drain, gutter, waterpipe. H. (*morī*).

موړ *moṛ*, a. Sated, satisfied, surfeited; comfortable, well off, in easy circumstances.

موړه *moṛa*, s.f. A pad, cushion for the back of a baggage animal. A stool. H. (*moṛhā*).

موز *mauz*, s.m. A plantain. A.

موزه *moza*, s.f. A boot; a stocking. P.

موږ *mūg*, pr. A plural form of the first personal pronoun زه. Also written منګ.

موږي *moyai*, s.m. A peg, stake, tent peg.

موسم *mosim* or *mausim*, s.m. Season, time. A.

موسي *mosa-ī*, s.f. A stone used in a game like pitch and toss.

موش *mūsh*, s.m. A rat; a mouse. P.

موصوف *mauṣūf*, a. Described; celebrated, praised. A.

موضع *mauz'a*, s.f. District, place, village. A.

موقع *mauq'a*, s.f. Contingency, occurrence; proper, fit, suitable. A.

موقوف *mauqūf*, a. Deferred, postponed; relinquished, stopped; dependent. A.

موک *mok*, s.m. A bribe.

مولا *maulā*, s.m. God; judge, lord, master. A.

مولي *molai*, s.m. A wooden pestle; stump of a tree. *mūla-ī*, s.f. A radish. S. (*mūlī*).

موم *mom* or *mūm*, s.m. Wax. P.

مومن *momin*, a. Believing, orthodox, faithful. A.

موميائي *momyā-ī*, s.f. Name of a waxy substance found in caves, and used as a remedy for fractures, bruises, and sprains; mummy wax. P.

موندره *mūndra*, s.f. A ring, ear-ring, finger ring. S. (*mūndrī*).

موندل *mūndal*, v.a. To find, get, obtain, procure, gain, acquire, etc.

موندي *mūndai*, s.m. A goat or ram with short ears or horns, or without horns.

مونډ *mūnḍ*, s.m. Root of a tree, germ of a plant; source, origin, cause; germ, nucleus, radix.

مونز *mūnz*, s.m. Prayer. See نمونځ.

مونګ *mūng*, pr. See منګ or موږ.

مونړي *mūnrai*, s.m. A plug of rags, etc. used to stop the hole of a cistern or tank.

مويښي *marekkhe*, s.f. (pl.). Hemorrhoids, piles; *pruritus ani*.

مه *ma*, ad. of prohibition used with the imperative mood; no, don't.

مهار *muhār*, s.m. A bridle, reins; the nose peg and string by which a camel is led. P.

مهال *mahāl*, s.m. Delay, respite, pause. A.

مهتابي *mahtāba-ī*, s.f. A kind of firework. P.

مهتر *mihtar*, s.m. A chief, prince; a groom. P.

مهتمم *muhtammim*, s.m. A superintendent, factor. a. Thoughtful, anxious. A.

مهجور *mahjūr*, a. Forsaken, left; separated, cut off. A.

مهر *mahr*, s.m. Marriage portion, settlement. A. *muhr*, s.m. A seal; gold coin equal to sixteen rupees. P. *mihr*, s.m. Affection, kindness. P.

مهرباش *mihrbāsh*, } a. Indulgent, friendly,
مهربان *mihrbān*, } kind, favouring. P.

مهربانګي *mihrbāngī*, } s.f. Favour, friendliness,
مهرباني *mihrbānī*, } kindness. P.

مهرکن *muhr·kan*, s.m. A seal engraver. P.

مهره *muhra*, s.f. A shell; a rubber for smoothing paper, etc. P.

مهري *muhrī*, a. Sealed, stamped. s.f. A gutter, drain, waterpipe. P.

مهلت *muhlat*, s. Deferring, retarding; laziness, indolence; leisure, time. A.

مهلك *muhlik*, a. Deadly, killing, mortal. A.

مهم *muhimm*, a. Important, momentous. s.m. Risk, hazard, danger. A.

مهمان *mihmān*, s.m. A guest, stranger. P.

مهماني *mihmānī*, s.f. Hospitality, entertainment.

مهمند *muhmand*, s.m. Name of an Afghan tribe.

مهميزه *mahmeza*, s.f. A spur. P. (*mahmez*).

مهنړه *mahanṛah*, s.m. A boatman, sailor.

مهي *mahai*, s.m. A fish. P. (*mahī*). *mahe*, s.f. (pl.). A kind of pulse (*Phaseolus max*).

مهيرګه *maherga*, s.f. Epilepsy. See ميرګي.

مهين *mahīn*, a. Fine, subtle, thin. P.

مهينه *mahīnah*, a. Foregoing, preceding, prior; elder, first-born; early sown crops. ad. Before, ere now, previously.

مي *me*, pr. A form of the genitive and instrumental cases singular of the first personal pronoun زه. See مِ. *mai*, s.m. Wine, spirits. P.

ميا *miyā*, s.m. Title of a religious class; a friar; master, sir. H. (*miyān*).

مياشت *myāsht*, s.f. A month; new moon.

ميان *miyān*, s.m. The loins, middle, waist; sheath, scabbard. p. Between, betwixt. P.

ميانه *miyāna*, s.f. Name of the eleventh Afghan month, between the festivals of Ramazān and Qurbān. P. *miyānah*, a. Middling, medium, medial. P.

ميتل *mītul*, v.a. To piss, make water.

ميچ *mech*, s.m. Measure, scale; measurement, reckoning. P. *mech-kawul*, v.a. To measure.

ميچن *mechan*, s.f. A handmill. A. (*mījan*).

ميخ *mekh*, s.m. A bolt, peg, tent peg. P.

ميخچو *mekhchū*, s.m. A nail, pin, spigot.

ميدان *maidān*, s.m. Area, field, plain; field of battle; parade ground; race-course. P.

ميده *maidah*, s.m. Meal, flour, fine meal. P.

مير *mīr*, s.m. Chief, leader; a title given to Sayads. P.

ميرات *mīrāt*, } s.m. Heritage, patrimony. A.
ميراث *mīrāṣ*, }

ميراثي *mīrāṣī*, a. Inherited, hereditary. s.m. Name applied to a class of bards, improvisatores, or singers.

ميرڅمن *mīrtsaman*, a. Deceitful, false, lying; hateful, vile, odious.

ميرڅي *mīrtsī*, s.f. Woe, distress, trouble; malice, spite, enmity; pique, umbrage.

ميرخاني *mīrkhāna-ī*, s.f. A kind of turban; a kind of fine cloth. P.

ميرزا *mīrzā*, s.m. Grandee, noble, prince; title given to a secretary or scribe. P.

ميرسنګ *mīr-sang*, s.m. A conch, a large shell used as a trumpet by hammām keepers, to announce the opening of the baths. S. (*sankh*).

ميرګنج *mīr-ganj*, s.m. A kind of vulture; the royal vulture. P.

ميرګي *mergai*, s.m. Epilepsy. H. (*mirgī*).

ميرمن *merman*, s.f. Lady, matron, madam, mistress, hostess.

ميره *maira*, s.f. Mother-in-law, stepmother. S. (*maibhā*). A desert, open plain.

ميړه *meṛah*, s.m. Husband, lord, master, owner.

ميز *mez*, s.m. A table. P. *mezmān*, s.m. A guest. P.

ميزان *mīzān*, s.m. Balance, pair of scales; metre, measure; addition. P.

ميزر *maizar*, s.m. A veil of fine muslin worn by women.

ميزري *maizarai*, } s.m. The dwarf palm
ميځري *maidzarai*, } (*Chamærops Richiana*).

میږ *meg*, s.f. An ewe. P. (*mesh*).

میږتون *megatūn*, s.m. An ant's nest.

میږي *megai*, s.m. An ant, the black ant.

مُیسّر *muyassar*, a. Procurable, obtainable. A.

میشت *mesht*, a. Settled, abiding, residing.

میشته *meshta*, s.f. Abode, residence, dwelling. A. (*m'aīshat*). *meshta-kawul*, v.a. To inhabit, colonize.

میښ *mekkh*, s.m. A bull buffalo, buffalo. S. (*mahish*).

میښبه *mekkhbah*, s.m. A buffalo grazier; owner of buffaloes.

میښمیښ *mīkkhmīkkh*, a. Sick at stomach, nauseated; disappointed, chagrined.

میعاد *miy'ād*, s.m. Time or place of a promise.

میل *mīl*, s.m. A bodkin, needle, skewer; the barrel of a gun; a horse that stands on its hind legs. P. *mail*, s.m. Dirt, rust, scum. S. *mai-l*, s.m. Partiality, desire, fondness, inclination. A.

میلان *mai-lān*, a. Inclined, partial, biassed, bent on. A.

میلمستیا *melmastiyā*, s.f. Hospitality, entertainment.

میلمه *melmah*, s.m. A guest, visitor. P. (*mezmān*).

میلو *melū*, s.m. A bear. H. (*mallū*).

میله *mela*, s.f. A fair; picnic; concourse of people gathered together for religious or commercial purposes. S. (*melā*).

میمي *meme*, in. The bleating of sheep, kids, etc.; the call of a child for the mother's breast. S.

مین *mayan*, a. Fond of, loving, in love. s.m. A lover. A. (*mail*).

مینا *maīnā*, s.f. Name of a bird (*Graculus Indicus*).

مینځ *myandz*, a. Midst. See منځ.

مینځل *mīndzal*, v.a. To wash. P. (*mīsīdan*). See وینځل.

میاجور *mīnjawar*, s.m. A sweeper at a mosque or shrine. A. (*mujāwir*).

میندہ *mīndah*, s.m. A male kept for breeding purposes; bull, ram, etc.

مینه *mīna*, s.f. Affection, love; partiality, regard. *mena*, s.f. Building, habitation, house.

میو *miyaw*, s.m. The mew of a cat.

میوه *mewa*, s.f. Fruit in general; raisins. P.

مئ *ma-ī*, s.f. Name of a kind of pulse (*Phaseolus radiatus*).

ن

ن *nūn* is the twenty-fifth letter of the Arabic, and the thirty-sixth of the Pukkhto alphabet. It is a dental letter, and has the sound of the English *n*. It is added to some nouns to transform them to adjectives, as پم *pam*, mange; پمن *paman*, mangy. Added to the Aorist and Future tenses of verbs it denotes certainty or belief, as کوي *kawī* (he does), کوين *kawīna* (he surely does). It is also used as an adverbial prefix of negation instead of نه *na*, as منل *manal* (to obey), نمنل *namanal* (to disobey).

نا *nā*, No, not; a negative particle prefixed to nouns, participles, and adjectives, has the same meaning as the English prefixes *dis-*, *in-*, *un-*, etc. as ناپاک *nāpāk* (unclean), ناقلار *nāqalār* (discomposed), ناراست *nārāst* (unfair), etc.

ناب *nāb*, a. Pure, genuine. P.

ناپړ *nābaṛ*, ناپړ *nāpaṛ*, } a. Clumsy, sturdy, stout; huge, gigantic, immense.

ناتار *nātār*, s.m. Plunder, devastation, destruction.

ناتكي *nātka-ī*, s.f. Individuality, oneness, unity.

ناجو *nājū*, s.m. A pine, fir tree. P.

ناڅاپه *nāt͟sāpa*, ad. Suddenly, unawares.

ناچ *nāc͟h*, s.m. A dance. S.

ناخن *nāk͟hun*, s.m. A nail (of finger or toe). P.

ناخنه *nāk͟huna*, s.f. A disease of the eye, pterygium. P.

نادان *nādān*, a. Ignorant, simple. P. *nādānī*, s.f. Ignorance, stupidity.

نادر *nādir*, a. Exquisite, choice, rare. A.

نار *nār*, s.m. A shoot, sprout. Fire, hell. A. A pomegranate. P.

نارنج *nāranj*, s.m. An orange. P.

نارو *nārū*, s.m. Guinea worm, dracunculus. H.

ناره *nāra*, s.f. A shout, call. See نعره.

نارينه *nārīnah*, a. Male, masculine; manly, bold, brave. P. (*narīnah*).

ناري *nārai*, s.m. Food, refreshment. See نهاري.

ناړ *nāṛ*, s.m. A shoot, sprout; stalk, stem, stubble. H.

ناړه *nāṛa*, s.f. Stalk or stem of a grass or herb.

ناړي *nāṛai*, s.m. Rope made of strips of raw hide.

ناز *nāz*, s.m. Blandishment, coquetry; elegance, gracefulness; fondling, soothing; consequential airs, pride. P.

نازک *nāzak*, a. Delicate, elegant; fragile, tender; light, thin. P.

نازکه *nāzaka*, s.f. A doll; mistress.

نازل *nāzil*, a. Descending, alighting, dismounting; befalling, occurring. A.

نازله *nāzila*, s.f. Calamity, misfortune. A.

نازنين *nāznīn*, a. Delicate, lovely. P.

نازول *nāzawul*, v.a. To fondle, pamper, spoil (as a child).

نازيدل *nāzedal*, v.n. To coquet, assume consequential airs.

ناست *nāst*, a. Seated, sitting.

ناسره *nāsarah*, a. Alloyed, counterfeit, impure; false (as coin), etc. P.

ناسوت *nāsūt*, s.m. Humanity, human nature. A.

ناسور *nāsūr*, s.m. Sinus, fistula. A.

ناسولت *nāsolat*, a. Uncircumcised. A. (*nāsunnat*).

ناشپاتي *nās͟hpātai*, s.m. A pear. P.

ناشته *nās͟hta*, s.f. Breakfast, luncheon. P. (*nās͟htā*).

ناښنده *nāk͟khanda*, } s.f. Impropriety, wrong.
ناښنه *nāk͟khana*, }

ناصح *nāṣiḥ*, s.m. Adviser, counsellor, monitor. A.

ناطق *nāṭiq*, s.m. Speaking, a speaker. A.

ناظر *nāẓir*, s.m. Observing, seeing; inspector, supervisor; an officer in judicial courts, sheriff. A.

ناظم *nāẓim*, s.m. Governor, ruler; arranger, composer. A.

ناغه *nāg͟ha*, s.m. Mulct, fine, poundage; respite, adjournment. *nāg͟hah*, a. Vacant, empty, void; unemployed, out of use. T.

ناف *nāf*, s.m. The navel. P.

نافه *nāfa*, s.f. A musk pod. P.

نافع *nāfi'*, a. Advantageous, profitable, useful. A.

ناقص *nāqiṣ*, a. Deficient, imperfect. A.

ناقل *nāqil*, s.m. A reciter, reporter. A.

ناک *nāk*, s.m. A pear. P. m. A particle added to nouns to denote endowment or possession, and corresponding with the English affix *-ful*, as *g͟ham·nāk* (woeful), *qahr·nāk* (wrathful), *s͟harm·nāk* (bashful). etc.

ناکاره *nākāra*, a. Useless. See نکاره.

ناکه *nāka*, s.f. An alligator. S. (*nākā*).

ناګاه *nāgāh*, ad. Suddenly, unawares, unexpectedly, all at once. P.

ناګمان *nāgumān*, } a. Abrupt, sudden, unexpected. ad. Unawares, by surprise. P.
ناګهان *nāgahān*, }

نال *nāl*, s.m. A horse shoe. See نعل.

نالش *nālis͟h*, s.m. Complaint, lament, growl, grumble. P.

نالہ **nāla**, s.f. A canal, stream, rivulet; gutter, drain, watercourse; weeping, lamentation. P.

نالي **nālī**, s.f. A quilt, etc. See نهالي.

نام **nām**, s.m. Name (in comp.). P.

ناموس **nāmūs**, s.m. Renown, fame, reputation; disgrace; female part of a family. A.

نامہ **nāma**, s.f. Book, letter; treatise, writing. P.

نامور **nāmwar**, | نامير **nāmer**, } a. Celebrated, famous, renowned. P.

نان **nān**, s.m. Baked or leavened bread. P.

نانگہ **nānga**, s.f. A blackberry.

نانوائي **nānwā-ī**, s.m. A baker. P.

ناور **nāwar**, s.m. A reservoir, pond, tank, cistern.

ناوک **nāwak**, s.m. An arrow; tube, pipe; bee's sting. P.

ناوکي **nāwaka-ī**, s.f. A doll, plaything. **nāwakai**, s.m. An arrow; name of a plant (*Jasminum revolutum*).

ناوہ **nāwa**, s.f. A canal, gutter; a tube, pipe; a long barrelled gun.

ناوې **nāwe**, s.f. A bride.

ناويات **nāwiyāt**, a. Rare, choice, matchless, peerless.

ناويت **nāwiyat**, s.m. Honeymoon, bridal state.

نائي **nā-ī**, s.m. A barber. S. **nāe**, s.m. A reed, pipe; flute. P.

نائب **nā-ib**, s.m. Deputy, lieutenant. A.

نايک **nāyak**, s.m. Chief, leader, master, patron. S.

نايڼړہ **nāyaṇṛa**, s.f. A barber's wife.

نبات **nabāt**, s.m. Sugar. P. A herb, grass. A.

نبض **nabẓ**, s.m. The pulse (at the wrist). A.

نبي **nabī**, s.m. A prophet. A. **nabūwat**, s.m. Prophecy, prophetship. A.

نتکي **natka-ī**, s.f. A small ring worn in the nose by women. H.

نتل **natal**, v.a. To despoil, plunder, sack, ravage, etc.

نتہ **nata**, s.f. A ring worn in the nose by women; the peg of wood in a camel's nose. S. (*nath*).

نتيجہ **natīja**, s.f. Consequence, result, issue; reward, retribution. A.

نټ **naṭ**, s.m. Name of a caste of Indians who are jugglers, tumblers, ropedancers, etc. A cheat, rogue, knave. S.

نثار **nis̤ār**, a. Scattering, strewing. A.

نجات **najāt**, s.m. Escape, flight; salvation. A.

نجار **najjār**, s.m. A carpenter. A.

نجاست **najāsat**, s.m. Filth, impurity, dirt, offal. A.

نجتل **njatal**, v.a. To implant, imbed, stick into, thrust. Irr. Pres. *njanī*; Past, *njātah*.

نجس **najis**, a. Nasty, dirty; filthy, foul. A. **najas**, s.m. Dirt, dung, filth, ordure. A.

نجوم **nujūm**, s.m. Astrology, astronomy. A. **najūmī**, s.m. Astrologer, fortune-teller. A.

نجيب **najīb**, s.m. A kind of soldier, guardsman. a. Noble, excellent. A. **najīb-zādah**, s.m. A nobleman.

نڅا **natsā**, s.f. Waving, shaking; bounding, dancing. S. (*nachā*).

نڅي **natsa-ī**, s.f. Cord, twine. See انڅي.

نچور **nichor**, s.m. A squeeze, wring. H.

نچوړول **nichoṛawul**, v.a. To squeeze, wring, rinse.

نچہ **nacha**, s.f. A weaver's reel; tube of a smoking apparatus or ḥuqqa. P. (*necha*).

نخالص **nakhālaṣ**, a. Genuine, pure, unmixed. A. (*nikhālaṣ*).

نخرہ **nakhra**, s.f. Coquetry, pretence, artifice; trick, sham; joke, pleasantry. P. A hole, fissure, crevice. See رخنہ.

نخرہباز **nakhra-bāz**, s.m. An affected person. **nakhra-bāza**, s.f. A coquette. P.

نخښ **nukhakkh**, s.m. A flesh-hook, an iron hook used to draw meat out of a pot.

نخښہ **nakhkkha**, s.f. A plan, chart. See نقشہ.

نخل *nakhl*, s.f. A date tree, palm tree. A.
nakhlistān, s.m. A palm or date grove.

نخوت *nakhwat*, s.m. Pomp, pride. A.

نخود *nukhūd*, s.m. A kind of pulse (*Cicer arietinum*). P.

ندا *nidā*, s.f. Voice, sound; call, shout. A.

نداپ *naddāp*, } s.m. A cotton carder, cotton
نداف *naddāf*, } dresser. A.

ندامت *nadāmat*, s.m. Contrition, regret. A.

ندرور *ndror*, s.f., pl. *ndrende*, Sister-in-law, husband's sister. S. (*nand*).

نديم *nadīm*, s.m. A courtier; intimate friend. A.

نذر *nazr*, s.m. A gift, present, offering. A.

نذرانه *nazrāna*, s.f. A present offered or received when people of rank meet, or pay their respects to a prince; tribute; fees paid to Government for grants of land, office, etc. A.

نر *nar*, a. Male, masculine; manly, bold. P.

نرخ *nirkh*, s.m. Tariff, price current, rate. P.

نرسوي *narsiwai*, s.m. A kind of wild pomegranate. a. Sunburnt, scorched by the sun.

نرکښ *narkakkh*, s.m. A mountain ram; leader of a herd.

نرکوښ *narkokkh*, s.m. A fish-hook; a hook used to gather fruit from the tree. See مخښ.

نرگس *nargis*, s.m. The narcissus. P.

نرلوخ *narlūkh*, s.m. The bulrush. See لوخه.

نرم *narm*, a. Soft, tender; easy, gentle, silly. P.

نرمۍ *narma-ī*, s.f. The lobe of the ear.
narmī, s.f. Softness; mildness; silliness. P.

نرناحق *nar-nāhaqq*, ad. Entirely unjust, altogether wrongfully, without cause, illegally. P. (*bar-nāhaqq*).

نري *narai*, a. Fine, narrow, thin, slender.

نړا *naṛā*, s.f. A bellow, bray, roar, low, shout. A. (*n'ara*).

نړل *naṛal*, v.a. To bray, roar, bellow; call, shout.

نړول *naṛawul*, v.a. To raze, demolish, knock down, level, overthrow (as walls, etc.).

نړۍ *naṛa-ī*, s.f. World, universe, globe.

نړېدل *naṛedal*, v.n. To crumble, fall down, tumble, fall to ruin, subside (as walls, etc.).

نزاکت *nazākat*, s.m. Delicacy, neatness, elegance. P.

نزله *nazla*, s.f. Defluxion of humours; catarrh. A.

نزدي *nizde*, } ad. Close, near, adjacent, con-
نژدي *nijde*, } tiguous. P. (*nizd*).

نژديکي *nijdeki*, s.m. Closeness, nearness, contiguity.

نږي *ngai*, s.m. A sneeze.

نږور *ngor*, s.f., pl. *ngende*, Son's wife, daughter-in-law.

نس *nas*, s.m. Abdomen, belly; concupiscence, lust; a sinew, tendon; nerve, vein. A.

نسب *nasab*, s.m. Genealogy, lineage. A.

نسبت *nisbat*, s.m. Affinity, relation; reference, respecting, regarding. A.

نسخه *nuskha*, s.f. Prescription, recipe; exemplar, copy, model; book, letter, writing. A.

نسرين *nasrīn*, s.m. A wild rose. P.

نسغ *nasagh*, s.m. Boring, piercing (as the nose, ears, etc.). A. Order; execution, torture. P. (*nasaq*).

نسکور *naskor*, a. Inverted, upside down.

نسل *nasal* or *nasl*, s.m. Breed, descent, family, origin, pedigree, race. A.

نسوار *naswār*, s.m. Snuff. S. (*nās*).

نسيم *nasīm*, s.m. A breeze, gentle air, zephyr. A.

نسيه *nasiya*, s.f. Credit, money promised. P.

نشان *nishān*, s.m. A mark, sign; scar; butt; family arms; ensign, standard. P.

نشتر *nishtar*, s.m. A lancet. P.

نشته **nishta**, Negative form of شته, Is not. P. (*nest*).

نشست **nishast**, s.m. Sitting, seated (in comp.). P.

نشم **nashm**, s.m. Deceit, craft, artfulness; lewdness, wantonness, extravagance, luxury.

نشمي **nashmī**, a. Luxurious, extravagant; lewd, wanton; crafty, artful.

نشه **nasha**, s.f. Intoxication. A. (*nashā*).

نشيب **nasheb**, s.m. Declivity; hollow. P.

نښان **nikkhān**, s.m. Mark, sign. See نشان.

نښاني **nikkhānī**, s.f. A keepsake, token, sign.

نښتر **nakkhtar**, s.m. A pine tree, conifer.

نښتل **nkkhatal** or **nkshatal**, v.n. To hitch, catch, stick, be caught, entrapped; to cling, cleave to, etc. P. (*nishākhtan*, *nashtidan*).

نښتيځل **nakkhtedzal**, v.a. To squeeze, wring, strain.

نښلول **nkkhlawul**, v.a. To obstruct, catch, stop, jam, hitch, entrap.

نښه **nakkha** or **naksha**, s.f. Mark, sign, token; emblem, device; banner, flag, standard; target, butt. A. (*naqsha*).

نصب **naṣb**, s.m. Fixing, establishing, planting. A.

نصف **niṣf**, a. Half. A.

نصيب **naṣīb**, s.m. Destiny, fate, lot. A.

نصيحت **naṣīhat**, s.m. Admonition, counsel, advice. A.

نطفه **nutfa**, s.f. Seed, sperm; semen. A.

نظام **niẓām**, s.m. Arrangement, order; custom, habit, constitution; sovereign, ruler. A.

نظر **naẓar**, s.m. Sight, vision; look, glance; regard, observation. A.

نظم **naẓm**, s.m. Poetry, verse. A.

نعره **n'ara**, s.f. Bawl, shout, call; noise, clamour. A.

نعل **n'al**, s.m. A horse shoe; ferrule of a scabbard. A

نعمت **n'imat**, s.m. Favour, benefit; delight, joy; affluence, ease, wealth. A.

نغاره **naghāra**, s.f. A kettle-drum. A. (*naqāra*).

نغاړل **nghāṛal**, v.a. To fold, envelop, wrap, roll up.

نغري **ngharai**, s.m. A fireplace.

نغړدل **nghaṛdal**, v.a. To swallow, gulp.

نغښتل **nghakkhtal**, v.a. To fold, wrap, roll, etc. Def. in pres. ten. See نغاړل.

نغلاند **naghlānd**, a. Hungry.

نغم **nagham**, s.m. A mine, tunnel. P.

نغمه **naghma**, s.f. Melody, music, song. A.

نغوتل **nghwatal**, v.a. To attend, listen, give ear, etc. Irr. Pres. *nghwagī*. Past, *nghwat*.

نغوښيدل **nghwakkhedal**, v.n. To crawl, creep.

نغي **nughai**, s.m. Brand, scar, cicatrix; cutting off the nose, ears, etc.

نفاق **nifāq**, s.m. Enmity, disagreement; hypocrisy, fallacy. A.

نفر **nafar**, s.m. A person, individual; servant, groom. A.

نفرت **nafrat**, s.m. Abomination, aversion; flight, terror. A.

نفرين **nafrīn**, s.m. Malediction. curse, imprecation. P. Detestation, aversion. A.

نفس **nafas**, s.m. Respiration, breath; moment, minute. A. **nafs**, s.m. Spirit, substance, soul; sensuality, concupiscence; lust, desire; envy, pride; vice; gravity; sperm; penis. A.

نفساني **nafsānī**, a. Carnal, sensual, lustful; luxurious. A.

نفعه **naf'a**, s.f. Profit, advantage, gain. A. (*nafa'*).

نفقه **nafaqa**, s.f. Necessary expenses of living (food, clothing, and lodging). A.

نقاب **niqāb**, s.m. A veil. A.

نقاش **naqqāsh**, s.m. A draftsman, sculptor, painter; carver, engraver. A.

نقب **naqb**, s.m. Tunnel, mine. gallery;

burrow; excavation. A. *naqb·zan*, s.m. A miner, excavator; burglar. *naqb·zanī*, s.f. Tunneling; housebreaking by digging through the walls.

نقد *naqd*, s.m. Cash, ready money. A.

نقره *nuqra*, s.f. Silver. A.

نقش *naqsh*, s.m. Carving, painting, embroidering, etc. A.

نقشه *naqsha*, s.f. Map, pattern, model, plan, etc. A.

نقصان *nuqṣān*, s.m. Blemish, defect; injury, loss, damage, etc. A.

نقطه *nuqṭa*, s.f. A spot, dot, point. A.

نقل *naql*, s.m. Fable, anecdote; history, tale; copying, imitating, transcribing; copy; change of place, migration. A.

نكاح *nikāḥ*, s.m. Marriage, matrimony, wedlock. A.

نكاره *nakārah*, a. Useless, worthless; invalid. P.

نكته *nukta*, s.f. A subtle point, mystical meaning. A.

نكريزه *nakrīza*, s.f. Name of a plant (*Lawsonia inermis*), the henna plant. pl. *nakrīze*, Henna leaves; the dye obtained from them.

نكس *nakas*, a. Abject, mean; friendless, poor. P. (*nākas*).

نكير *nakīr*, s.m. Name of an angel. *Munkir Nakīr*, The names of two angels who examine the spirits of the dead in the grave. A.

نگار *nigār*, s.m. Effigy, picture, idol. P.

نگاه *nigāh*, s.m. A look, glance, sight; observing, watching; custody, care. P. *nigāh·bān*, s.m. Guard, keeper. P.

نكښي *ngakkhai*, s.m. A plaited lock of hair on the temple or forehead (of women).

نګوبي *ngūbai*, s.m. Pommel of a saddle.

نګولي *ngolai*, s.m. Meat, fish, etc., eaten with bread or rice as a relish, a made dish, entrée.

نګون *nigūn*, a. Inverted; hanging downwards. P.

نل *nal*, s.m. A reed; tube, pipe, spout. S.

نله *nala*, s.f. Urinary passage, urethra. S. (*nalā*).

نم *nam*, a. Damp, moist, wet. P. *nam*, a. The ninth. P. (*nuhum*).

نماز *namāz*, s.m. Prayer. See نمونځ.

نمازل *nmāzal*, v.a. } To rear, sustain, support,
نمانځل *nmāndzal*, } bring up, cherish, nourish; to pamper, spoil. P. (*nawāzidan*).

نماښام *nmākkhām*, s.m. Evening. See ماښام.

نمد *namad*, s.m. Felt, unwoven woollen stuff. P.

نمر *nmar*, s.m. The sun, sunshine.

نمري *nmarī*, s.m. (pl.) Clothes, garments, dress.

نمړ *numaṛ*, ad. Before, formerly. a. Prior, first; fixed, determined; betrothed, engaged; promised, pledged; bespoken.

نمړي *numaṛai*, a. Former, preceding, etc. *nmaṛa-ī*, s.f. A morsel. See نوړۍ.

نمسي *nmasai*, s.m. A grandson. P. (*nawāsa*). *nmasa-ī*, s.f. A granddaughter. P. (*nawāsī*).

نمك *namak*, s.m. Salt (in comp.). P.

نمله *numla*, s.f. A felt pad for a saddle. P. (*namda*).

نمود *namūd*, s.m. Guide, index; display, show. P.

نمودار *namūdār*, a. Conspicuous, famed, noted. s.m. Specimen, model, sample; proof; index. P.

نمونځ *nmūndz*, s.m. Prayer. P. (*namāz*).

نمونه *namūna*, s.f. Pattern, specimen, sample. P.

نن *nan*, ad. To-day. *nan·wradz*, This day, to-day. *nan·shpa*, This night, to-night. *nan·ṣabā*, To-day or to-morrow, in these days, in a day or two.

ننباسل *nanabāsal*, v.a. To insert, etc. Def. in past ten. See ننيستل.

ننداره *nandāra*, s.f. Sight, spectacle, show; glance, look, inspection. P. (*namūdārī*).

ننډرور *nandror*, s.f. Husband's sister. See ندرور.

ننزړه *nanzaṛah*, s.m. Tar, pitch.

ننکه *nanaka*, s.f. A vesicle, pustule.

ننکۍ *nanaka-ī*, s.f. Small pox.

ننګ *nang*, s.m. Honour, reputation; disgrace. P. *nang-o-nāmūs*, Honour, disgrace. P.

ننګو *nangū*, s.m. A span; the space between the thumb and forefinger.

ننګيالي *nang-yālai*, a. Honourable, reputable.

ننني *nananai*, a. Hodiernal, of to-day.

ننواته *nananwātah*, s.m. Entrance, admission: refuge, shelter, asylum.

ننوتل *nananwatal*, v.n. To enter, go in, intrude; to take refuge, seek protection from another.

ننه *nana*, ad. Inside, within.

ننيستل *nanayastal*, v.a. To insert, introduce, draw in, retract, conduct, or lead in, etc. Def. in pres. ten. See ننباسل.

نو *naw*, s.m. Moisture, dampness. P. (*nam*). *nau*, a. Fresh, new, young. P. *nū*, s.m. The navel.

نواب *nawāb*, s.m. A chief, governor of a province. A.

نواحي *nawāḥī*, s.f. Environs; territories. A.

نواره *nawāra*, s.f. Cultivation, habitation, population.

نوار *niwāṛ*, s.m. Broad tape. H.

نواړي *niwāṛai*, s.m. The tape or lacing of a pair of trousers; the hem in which the tape passes.

نواز *nawāz* (in comp.), Cherishing. P.

نوازش *nawāzish*, s.m. Favour, patronage. P.

نوبت *nobat* or *naubat*, s.m. Period, time, turn; opportunity, occasion; accident; occurrence; degree, pitch; keeping watch; relieving guard; musical instruments sounded at the gate of a great man's house, or at the market place, etc., at fixed intervals. A.

نوبهار *nau-bahār*, s.m. Spring, early spring. P.

نوخۍ *nūtsa-ī*, s.f. Pliers, forceps, pincers. H. (*nochī*).

نور *nor*, a. Other, another, different, more. ad. Besides, moreover, also, likewise. H. (*aur*). *nūr*, s.m. Light, splendour. P. *nwar*, s.m. The sun. See نمر.

نوراني *nūrānī*, a. Bright, light, clear. P.

نوروز *nau-roz*, s.m. New year's day of the Persian calendar. P.

نوري *nwarī*, s.m. Old clothes. See نمري.

نوړز *nwaṛaz*, s.f. A quail.

نوړۍ *nwaṛa-ī*, s.f. A mouthful, morsel; food. P. (*nihārī*).

نوريدل *nwaṛedal*, v.n. To peel, excoriate, strip off.

نوږد *nogd*, نوږي *nogai*, s.m. Genus, kind, source, origin. A. (*nau'*).

نوس *naus* or *naws*, s.m. Spirit, soul; self; lust, sensuality. A. (*nafs*).

نوسي *nwasai*, s.m. Grandson. See نمسي.

نوعه *nau'a*, s.f. Species, kind; manner, mode. A.

نوک *nūk*, s.m. A nail (toe or finger); claw (of an animal or bird). S. (*nakh*).

نوکاره *nūkāra*, s.f. A scratch, claw, scrape; clawing, scratching.

نوکر *naukar*, s.m. A servant. P. *nokarī*, s.f. Service.

نول *nūl*, s.m. Grief, sorrow, affliction. P. (*nāla*).

نولس *nolas*, a. Nineteen. *nolasam*, a. Nineteenth.

نولي *nolai*, s.m. A weasel, mongoose. S. (*newlā*).

نوليدل *nūledal*, v.n. To fret, pine, grieve, sorrow.

نوم *nūm*, s.m. Name; reputation, fame;

honour, character. s. (*nām*). *nūm*, s.m. The name.

نوماندي *nūmāndai*, a. Named, called, yclept.

نومد *nūmd*, a. Damp, wet. See لوند.

نومړي *nūmaṛai*, a. Named, called; famed, celebrated; eminent, great.

نوميد *naumed*, a. Hopeless, without hope. P.

نوند *nūnd*, a. Damp, wet. See نومد.

نونكۍ *nūnaka-ī*, s.f. A furuncle, boil, pustule. See ننكۍ.

نوي *nawai*, a. New, fresh; unused; young; late, modern. P. (*nau*). *nawai*, s.m. The inside one of a drove of oxen treading corn. *nawe*, a. Ninety. *nūe*, s.f. Mother's brother, maternal uncle.

نه *nuh*, a. Nine. *na*, ad. Nay, no. Negative particle. Neither, nor, not

نهاد *nihād*, s.m. Habit, nature, quality. P.

نهار *nahār*, a. Fasting. P.

نهاري *nahārai*, s.m. Breakfast, luncheon, forenoon meal, refreshment. P.

نهال *nihāl*, s.m. A sapling, shoot, sprout, seedling. P.

نهالي *nihālī*, s.f. A cushion, mattress; quilt, coverlet; sapling, seedling, sucker.

نهان *nihān*, a. Concealed, hidden. P.

نهايت *nihāyat*, a. Extreme, excessive. ad. Extremely. s.m. Extremity, limit; excess. A.

نهر *nahr*, s.m. A canal, stream, rivulet. A. *nahar*, a. Fasting, unfed. P.

نهنګ *nahang*, s.m. A whale, leviathan, crocodile. P.

نهوه *nahwa*, s.f. Refusing food, fasting.

نهه *naha*, s.f. Tuesday.

نهيه *nahiya*, s.f. Prohibition; interdict. A. (*nahī*).

ني *nai*, s.m. A reed, tube; flute, pipe. P.

نيا *niyā*, s.f. A grandmother.

نياز *niyāz*, s.m. Petition, supplication; indigence, poverty; a thing dedicated. P. *niyāz-man*, a. Indigent, suppliant. *niyāzī*, s.m. Lover, friend. Name of a Pathan tribe.

نياګانه *niyāgāna*, s.f. A mother's family or relations.

نيام *niyām*, s.m. Sheath, scabbard; bandage for a broken limb; plough tail or handle. P. (*miyān*).

نياو *niyāw*, s.m. Right, equity, justice. S.

نيايه *niyāyah*, s.m. Maternal uncle.

نيبو *nību*, s.m. A lemon, citron. S.

نيت *niyat*, s.m. Purpose, intention, design; will, desire, wish. A.

نيټه *neṭa*, s.f. Bargain, contract; promise, engagement; appointed time; season.

نيرنګ *nairang*, s.m. Deceit, evasion, fraud; magic, sorcery; miracle, novelty. P.

نيره *nīra*, s.f. A cobbler's awl.

نيز *nīz*, s.m. Deluge, inundation, flood; drift wood, rubbish, etc. carried by floods. ad. Also, again, likewise. P.

نيزه *neza*, s.f. A spear, lance. P.

نيستي *nestī*, s.f. Non-existence. P.

نيشتر *neshtar*, s.m. A lancet, fleam. See نشتر.

نيښ *nekkh*, s.m. A prickle; sting of an insect; puncture, prick; tusk of a camel, dog, etc. P. (*nesh*).

نېغ *negh*, a. Straight, stiff, upright, erect.

نيک *nek*, a. Moral, honest; good; lucky. P. *nayak*, s.m. See نايک.

نيکوکار *nekokār*, a. Righteous, honest, moral. P.

نيکه *nīkah*, s.m. Paternal grandfather, ancestor.

نيكي *nekī*, s.f. Piety, virtue, goodness, morality. P.

نيل *nīl*, s.m. Indigo; blue. S.

نيلاب *nīlāb*, s.m. The river Indus. Name of a town on the Indus below Attak.

نيلم *nīlam*, s.m. A sapphire. S.

نيلي *nīlai*, s.m. A grey horse. P.

نیم *nīm*, a. Half. P. *nīma-khwā*, a. Immature, crude, unripe; changeable, fluctuating; bootless, unavailing.

نیمایه *nīmāyah*, s.m. A half, one-half.

نیمبولئ *nīmbola-ī*, s.f. A necklace of gold and glass beads (worn by women). H.

نیمتنی *nīmtanai*, s.m. A vest, waistcoat, jacket.

نیمگړی *nīmgiṛai*, a. Unfinished, incomplete.

نیمچه *nīmcha*, s.f. A short sleeved fur coat. *nīmchah*, a. Hybrid, mongrel. s.m. Name applied to certain tribes of Kafiristanis who have become converts to Islām.

نیمی *nīmai*, s.m. A half, moiety.

نینزکه *nenzaka*, s.f. See نازکه.

نینکه *nenaka*, s.f. Name of a bird, the tomtit.

نینی *nīne*, s.f. (pl.) Parched grain.

نیوز *niyūz*, s.m. Flood, torrent, inundation. *niyūz-wṛai*, a. Drift wood, rubbish carried by floods.

نیول *nīwul*, v.a. To catch, lay hold of, take, capture, seize. Irr. Pres. *nisī*. Past, *nīwah*.

ڼ

ڼ or نړ *ṛūn*, This compound letter is peculiar to the Pukkhto alphabet, of which it is the thirty-seventh in number. It has a peculiar sound formed by a combined pronunciation of the component letters; the sound of the *n* is nasal, and that of the *r* full and rolling as pronounced by a Frenchman. By some tribes this letter is pronounced as *n* doubled or emphatic, as *rannā* for *ranrā*, *gann* for *ganr*, etc. This letter does not occur at the commencement of any word in the Pukkhto language.

و

و *wāw*, is the twenty-sixth letter of the Arabic and the thirty-eighth of the Pukkhto alphabet. As a consonant it has the sound of *w*, and is sometimes interchanged with ب. As a vowel it has the sound of *o*-, *ū*-, and *au*, as is explained in the Grammar.

وَ *wa*, c. A copulative conjunction used to connect words and sentences; and, also. P. A particle used as the sign of the vocative case. A particle used with signs of the dative case.

وُ *wu*, A particle prefixed to the aorist, future, and perfect tenses, and imperative mood of verbs; it corresponds to the ب similarly used in the Persian, and like that letter is also sometimes rejected as redundant.

وِ *wi*, An abbreviated form of the third person singular, perfect tense of the verb ویل *wayal*, To speak.

وابسته *wābastah*, a. Related, connected, bound. s.m. An adherent, dependant. P.

واپس *wāpas*, ad. Again, back, return. P.

واته *wātah*, s.m. Exit, issue, coming out.

واټ *wāṭ*, s.f. A road, path. S. (*bāṭ*).

واټن *wāṭan*, s.m. Distance, interval, space.

واج *wāj*, s.m. Barter, exchange, trading in kind.

واجب *wājib*, a. Expedient, fit, necessary, proper; worthy, just, reasonable. A.

واحد *wāḥid*, a. One, single, sole. A.

واخ *wākh*, in. Alas! sorrow! woe!

واده *wādah*, s.m. Marriage, wedding; marriage festival. *wāda*, s.f. Agreement, promise, vow. A. (*w'ada*).

وار *wār*, s.m. Turn, time, period. P. A blow, stroke; attack, assault. H. Leisure, rest. S. *wār*, A particle added to nouns to denote similitude or endowment. P.

وارث *wāris*, s.m. Heir, owner, lord. A.

واريزه *wārīza*, s.f. Intermittent fever.

وارة *wāṛah*, a. All, the whole. ad. Wholly.

واز *wāz*, a. Open, ajar, gaping. P. Fat, blubber.

وازده *wāzda*, } s.f. Fat, blubber.
وازگه *wāzga*, }

وازه *wāza*, s.f. A fathom, stretch of both arms extended; stride of a horse.

واژگون *wāžgūn*, a. Inverted, upside-down. P.

واسطه *wāsṭa*, s.f. Account, cause, sake, reason. A. *wāsiṭa*, s.f. Agency, medium, means. A.

واسيكه *wāsīka*, ad. Immediately, now, at once.

واښ *wākkh*, s.m. } Rope or cordage made of
واښکي *wākkhkai*, } goat's or camel's hair.

واښه *wākkhah*, s.m. Fodder, grass, hay; herbage, pasture.

واصل *wāṣil*, a. Arrived, met; coupled, joined. A.

واعظ *wā'iẓ*, s.m. Preacher, lecturer. A.

واف *wāf*, s.m. Nightingale; songster. P.

واقع *wāq'i*, s.m. Befalling, happening, occurring; appearing. A.

واقعه *wāq'ia*, s.f. Event, occurrence, incident.

واقعي *wāq'ī*, a. Proper, right, true. ad. Truly, actually, really. A.

واقف *wāqif*, a. Acquainted, conversant. A.

واک *wāk*, s.m. Authority, command; choice, will; power, force. P.

واگه *wāga*, s.f. A bridle, rein. H. (*bāg*).

وال *wāl*, } A particle added to nouns to denote
والا *wālā*, } resident, inhabitant; agent, owner, keeper, etc. H. Ex. *buner-wāl*, A resident of Buner. *hotī-wālā*, A townsman of Hoti.

والا *wālā*, a. Dignified, sublime, high. A. s.f. A kind of silk, sarcenet. P.

والد *wālid*, s.m. A father. A.

والده *wālida*, s.f. A mother. A.

والدين *wālidain*, s.m. Both parents. A.

واله *wāla*, s.f. Rivulet, canal, stream.

والي *wālī*, s.m. A chief, ruler, prince. A. *wālai*, s.m. An earring. S. (*bālī*). *wālai*, m. A particle affixed to nouns and adjectives to denote endowment or possession, as, *plan* (wide), *plan-wālai* (wideness). H. (*wālā*).

وام *wām*, s.m. Debt, credit, loan; borrowing, lending. P.

وانړه *wānṛa*, s.f. A pile of grain mixed with the husk and chaff as trodden out on the threshing floor, a pile of grain, husk and chaff before winnowing.

واورا *wāwrā*, s.f. A kind of vulture.

واوره *wāwra*, s.f. A flake of snow. pl. *wāwre*, Snow. P. (*barf*).

واويلا *wāwailā*, s.f. Wail, lament, bewailing. A.

واه *wāh*, in. Bravo! well done! excellent. P.

واهمه *wāhima*, s.f. Fancy, imagination. A.

واي *wāe*, in. Alas! woe! woe to you! A.

وبا *wabā*, s.f. Plague, pestilence, epidemic, disease. A.

وبال *wabāl*, s.m. Sin, crime, fault. A.

وبلته *wabulta*, } ad. Together, one with
وبله *wabla*, } another.

وبله باندي *wabla-bānde*, ad. One above another, before and behind, in layers, in folds, together, etc.

وپار *wapār*, s.m. Trade, traffic, commerce. S. (*baipār*).

وپاري *wapārī*, s.m. A merchant, trader.

وت *wat*, s.m. Interval, gap; gorge, defile; pass. *wit*, a. See ويت.

وتر *watar*, a. Watered, saturated, irrigated (field). *witar*, s.m. A voluntary prayer not enjoined by the *farẓ* nor the *sunnat*.

وتراوي *watrāwī*, a. Unaccented, without harmony (as poetry).

وتل *watal*, v.n. To issue, emerge, come out, go forth; to exude, ooze.

وته *waṭa*, s.f. Discount, exchange; defect, deficiency; injury, blemish. H. (*baṭṭā*).

وجاړ *wujāṛ*, a. Desolate, ruined, waste. H. (*ujāṛ*).

وجاړي *wujāṛai*, s.m. Wilderness, desert, wild.

وجل *wajal*, وجلل *wajlal*, v.a. To kill, slay, put to death. Irr. Pres. *wajnī*. Past, *wājah*.

وجود *wujūd*, s.m. Body, being, substance; penis. A.

وجه *waja*, s.f. Nape, occiput, depression at the back of the neck. *wuja*, s.f. A nerve, vein, tendon, sinew.

وجهه *wajha*, s.f. Cause, reason; manner, way; appearance, visage. A.

وڅکه *wutska*, s.f. A raisin; a kind of raisin without pips.

وچ *wuch*, a. Arid, dry; parched, withered; sapless; without milk, etc.

وچکول *wuchkūl*, وچکولي *wuchkūlai*, A castrated ram, wether.

وچکي *wuchaka-ī*, s.f. A burning fever.

وچولي *wuchwulai*, s.m. The forehead, brow.

وحش *waḥsh*, s.m. A wild beast. A.

وحشت *waḥshat*, s.m. Fear, fright; solitude, desert, wild, waste. A.

وحشي *waḥshī*, a. Fierce, savage, ferocious, wild. A.

وخ *wakh*, in. Ugh! Oh! Heigh ho!

وخت *wakht*, s.m. Time, season. A. (*waqt*).

وداع *widā'*, s.m. Adieu, farewell. A.

ودان *wadān*, a. Cultivated, inhabited; peopled, prosperous. *wadānī*, s.f. Prosperity, plenty; cultivation, population. P. (*ābādān*).

ودانول *wadānawul*, v.a. To cultivate, populate, people, colonize.

ودانيدل *wadānedal*, v.n. To flourish, prosper.

ودرول *wudrawul*, v.a. To erect, set up, pitch (as a tent, etc.); prop, support; to stop, stay, halt.

ودريدل *wudredal*, v.n. To stand, stand up, stand still; arise, get up; stay, abide, halt, stop.

ودول *wadawul*, v.a. To marry, give in marriage, take in marriage.

واديدل *wadedal*, v.n. To be married, taken or given in marriage.

وډ *waḍ*, a. Fallow land, land from which the crop has been gathered.

ور *war*, s.m. A door, gate. P. (*dar*). *war*, m. A particle added to nouns to denote possession or endowment, as *dzān* (life), *dzānwar* (an animal). P. *war*, The pronominal dative affix, singular, of the third personal pronoun, as *war-dza*, go to him.

ورا *wrā*, s.f. A marriage procession; party of women who conduct the bride to the house of the bridegroom. S. (*barāt*). *warā*, ad. Afar, far off, yonder; beyond, besides. A.

ورابانړي *wrā-bānṛai*, s.m. A male member of the *wrā*, or marriage procession; guest at a wedding feast.

وراثت *wirās̱at*, s.m. Heritage, heirship. A.

وراځه *wrādza*, s.f. A species of louse which infests camels, sheep, dogs, etc.

وراره *wrārah*, s.m. Brother's son, nephew. *wrāra*, s.f. A woman whose brother is dead.

وراشه *wrāsha*, s.f. Language, dialect. H. (*bhāshā*).

وران *wrān*, a. Destroyed, ruined, spoiled; desolate, deserted, waste. P. (*wairān*). *wrānī*, s.f. Desolation, ruin; spoiling, ruining.

ورايه *warāya*, ad. Far, far away; beyond, yonder. *la-warāya*, From afar.

وربوز *wurbūz*, s.m. The snout, muzzle.

ورتګ *wartag*, s.m. Outset, departure, exit.

ورتلل *waratlal*, v.n. See ورغلل.

ورتول *wratawul*, v.a. To fry, grill, roast, broil.

ورتيدل *wratedal*, v.n. To fret; be broiled, fried.

ورت *wrat*, s.m. A gush or flood of tears.

ورځ *wradz*, s.f. A day; daytime. P. (*roz*).

ورځي *wardzane*, } ad. Outside, without (the
ورچني *warchane*, } house).

ورځه *wrudza*, s.f. The eyebrow.

ورخ *warkh*, s.m. } A small hole or passage in
ورخه *warkha*, s.f. } the side of a watercourse to let out the water for irrigation of fields, etc.

ورخاړي *warkhārai*, s.m. Name of a pot-herb, purslain (*Portulaca oleracea*). A disease of goats and sheep, murrain.

ورخته *warkhata*, ad. Firstly, in the first place.

ورخړه *warkhara*, s.f. Rubbish, litter, sweepings.

ورد *wird*, s.m. Reading the Qurān at certain fixed times; daily use, practice, task. A.

ورزيدل *warzedal*, v.n. To fly (as a bird).

ورژل *warjal*, v.a. To chop, mince. Pres. *warjanī*. Past, *wārjah*.

ورژي *wrije*, s.f. (pl.) Rice (the grain). A. (*aruz*).

ورږ *wrag*, s.m. Mane of a horse, etc.

ورږه *wraga*, s.f. A flea. *wargah*, s.m. Biestings, the first milk after calving or kidding.

ورستو *wrusto*, ad. After, behind, astern.

ورستول *warustawul*, v.a. To send. See آستول.

ورسته *wrustah*, s.m. The rear, stern.

ورستي *wrustai*, } a. Hinder, posterior, rear,
ورستني *wrustanai*, } hindmost, rearmost, backmost.

ورستيدل *wrastedal*, v.n. To decay, rot, putrefy, stink.

ورسركول *warsarkawul*, v.a. To give freely or liberally.

ورشو *warsho*, s.f. A grass plot, lawn, meadow.

ورطه *warta*, s.f. A labyrinth, maze; whirlpool, vortex. A.

ورغاړي *warghārai*, s.m. A paste of butter and flour used to anoint newborn babes and puerperal women with.

ورغلل *waraghlal*, } v.n. To arrive at, go to,
ورتلل *waratlal*, } set out to, depart. Irr. Pres. *wardzam*. Past, *warāghlam*. See راتلل and راغلل.

ورغومي *warghūmai*, s.m. A young kid.

ورغوي *warghawai*, s.m. The palm, sole.

ورق *waraq*, s.m. A card, leaf of a book. A.

ورک *wruk*, a. Lost, mislaid; wasted.

ورکړل *warkral*, } v.a. To give, present, be-
ورکول *warkawul*, } stow, grant (to another).

ورکول *wrukawul*, v.a. To lose, mislay; squander, waste. H. (*lukānā*).

ورکه *wruka*, s.f. Deprivation, loss; wasting.

ورکيدل *wrukedal*, v.n. To be lost, to wander, stray; to be mislaid, forgotten.

ورګ *warg*, s.m. The fleece of a sheep. *wrag*, s.m. The mane of a horse, etc.

ورله *warla*, a. Big with young, pregnant.

ورم *waram*, s.m. Swelling, tumour. a. Swelled, tumefied, inflated. A.

ورمارګه *warmārgah*, } s.m. An eruption of boils
ورماګه *warmāgah*, } on the face (of children).

ورمېږ *warmeg*, s.m. The nape, the neck.

ورندار *wrandār*, s.f. Brother's wife, sister-in-law.

وَرنيکه *wa-arnīkah*, s.m. A great grandfather on the father's side; an ancestor.

ورو *wro*, ad. Gently, slowly.

وروځه *wrūdza*, s.f. The eyebrow. See ورځه.

ورور *wror*, s.m. A brother. P. (*barādar*). *wrorī*, s.f. Fraternity, brotherhood.

وروست *wrost*, a. Rotten, putrid, decayed.

ورول *warawul*, v.a. To tear, rend, lacerate.

ورون *wrūn*, s.m. The thigh. P. (*rān*).

ورهول *warhawul*, v.a. To liberate, release, set free, save. P. (*rahānīdan*).

ورهيدل *warhedal*, v.n. To escape, become free. P. (*rahīdan*).

وري *wrai*, s.m. A lamb. P. (*barra*). *warai*,

s.m. A bundle or load for the head; one of the packs of a camel's or bullock's load.

وريت *wrīt*, a. Broiled, grilled, roasted, fried.

وريځ *waryadz*,
وريځه *waryadza*, } s.f. A cloud.

وريدل *waredal*, v.n. To tear, be torn, rent, etc.

وريدل *waredal*, v.n. To rain, drizzle, shower.

وريره *wrera*, s.f. Brother's daughter, niece.

وريشل *wreshal*, v.a. To spin, twist.

وريښم *wrekkham*, s.m. Silk. P. (*resham*).

وړنيزه *wra-eza*, s.f. Bridesmaid, female guest at a wedding.

وړ *wa-ar*, a. Successful, victorious, winning. P. (*burd*). H. (*war*). *waṛ*, s.m. Scab, crust of a sore; miscellany, mass, bits of gold and silver mixed together. *wuṛ*, a. Small. P. (*khurd*). See ووړ.

وړاندِ *wṛāndi*,
وړاندې *wṛānde*, } ad. Ahead, in front, before, foremost.

وړاندې *wṛāndai*, a. Prior, preceding, foremost. s.m. The front, bow, prow, advance, van.

وړاندينی *wṛāndīnai*, a. Foremost, prior, first.

وړانه *wa-aṛāna*, Success, winning, gaining. *wa-aṛāna-pa-aṛāna*, Winning and losing.

وړل *wṛal*, v.a. To bear, support, carry, convey, remove, take away; endure, put up with, etc. (only used with reference to inanimate objects). Def. in past ten. See يوسل. P. (*burdan*).

وړم *waṛam*, ad. Last but one (applied only to times and seasons). *waṛam-kāl*, The year before last. *waṛama-shpa*, The night before last. *lā-waṛama-wradz*, Three days ago.

وړمبې *wṛumbe*, ad. Firstly, in the first place.

وړمبی *wṛumbai*,
وړمبنی *wṛumbanai*, } a. First, principal, foremost, chief.

ووړکی *wṛūkai*, a. Tiny, small, wee.

ووړول *wuṛawul*, v.a. To powder, pulverize, grind, triturate.

ووړنبې *wṛūnbe*, ad. See وړمبې.

ووړه *wuṛah*, s.m. Flour, meal, powder.

وړی *wuṛai*, s.m. Summer. *wṛai*, ad. Removed, carried away; borne, endured. *waṛa-ī*, s.f. Wool, fleece. *ūṛai*, m. A particle affixed to nouns to denote smallness, as *chirg* (a cock), *chirgūṛai* (a cock chicken).

وز *wuz*, s.m. A he-goat; mountain goat. P. (*buz*).

وزر *wazr* or *wazar*, s.m. The wing of a bird or insect; fin of a fish. P. (*bāzū*).

وزګار *wuzgār*, a. Unemployed, unused, unoccupied; idle, inactive, at leisure.

وزګری *wuzgarai*, s.m. A young goat.

وزمه *wazma*, s.f. The charge of a gun.

وزن *wazn*, s.m. Measure, weight; metre (of verse); esteem, reputation. A.

وزير *wazīr*, s.m. A minister of state, prime minister. A.

وزيري *wazīrī*, s.f. The office of Wazīr. s.m. Name of a Pathan tribe, the Wazīrīs.

وزيمه *wazema*, s.f. An ewe or goat seeking the male, in heat.

وژل *wajal*,
وژلل *wajlal*, } v.a. To kill, slay. See وجلل.

وژه *wuja*, s.f. A nerve, vein, sinew.

وږم *wagm*, s.m.
وږمه *wagma*, s.f. } Breath, vapour, exhalation, steam.

وږمکۍ *wagmaka-ī*,
وږمۍ *wagma-ī*, } s.f. The moon.

وږی *wugai*, a. Hungry, famished. *wagai*, s.m. An ear of corn, grasses, etc.

وس *was*, s.m. Endeavour, attempt, trial; ability, power, force; advantage; opportunity; authority. S. (*bas*).

وسته *wasta*, s.f. A pond, pool.

وسک *waska*,
وسکه *waska*, } ad. As, as if, as it were. Finally, then, therefore.

وسله *wasla*, s.f. Arms, accoutrements, weapons; tools, implements. A. (*silāh*).

وسمه *wasma*, s.f. Leaves of the Indigo plant, used as a dye for the hair. A.

وسواس *wiswās*, s.m. Apprehension, suspense, doubt, hesitation; distraction of mind; temptation of the devil. A. *wiswāsī*, a. Apprehensive, distracted; perplexing, causing doubt or suspense.

وسوسه *waswasa*, s.f. Temptation; suspense. A.

وسه *wasa*, s.f. A summer shower, summer rain.

وسيله *wasīla*, s.f. Affinity, conjuncture, cause, medium, means; prop, support, patronage. A. *wasīla-dār*, s.m. Client, defendant.

وشته *washta*, s.f. A joke, jest; joking.

وښتي *wakkhte*, s.f. (pl.) An inferior kind of rice.

وښخور *wakkhkhor*, s.m. An herbivorous animal, grass eater.

وښکل *wukkhkal*, v.a. To pull. See وکښل.

وښي *wakkhai*, s.m. A bracelet.

وصال *wiṣāl*, s.m. Meeting, interview; death. A.

وصف *waṣf*, s.m. Encomium, praise. A.

وصول *wuṣūl*, s.m. Arrival, acquisition; juncture. A.

وصيت *waṣiyat*, s.m. A will, making a will; precept, mandate. A.

وضو *wuẓū*, s.m. A form of purification by ablution before prayer. A.

وطن *waṭan*, s.m. Birthplace, home, native country. A.

وطواط *waṭwāṭ*, s.m. A kind of swallow; a bat; a languid man, timid man. A.

وطي *waṭī*, s.f. Copulation, coition. A.

وظيفه *waẓīfa*, s.f. Pension, stipend, salary; religious duty, task. A.

وعظ *w'aẓ*, s.m. Sermon, lecture; admonition. A.

وغه *wagha*, s.f. A long red worm; a kind of intestinal worm.

وغيره *waghaira*, ad. And so forth, and the rest, et cetera, etc.

وفا *wafā*, s.f. Fidelity, sincerity. A.

وقار *wiqār*, s.m. Dignity, estimation; constancy, steadiness; mildness, modesty; honour, reputation. A.

وقت *waqt*, s.m. Time, season. A.

وقف *waqf*, s.m. Endowment, foundation, legacy for pious purposes. A.

وقوف *wuqūf*, s.m. Sense, understanding; experience, information. A.

وکښل *wukkshal*, v.a. To draw. See کښل.

وکيل *wakīl*, s.m. Attorney, agent; delegate. A. *wakālat*, s.m. Commission, embassy, agency. A.

وګړي *wagaṛai*, s.m. A creature, man, human being.

ول *wal*, s.m. A coil, curl, twist, etc. H. (*bal*). *wul*, A particle added to nouns and adjectives to form the infinitive mood of active verbs. *wal*, s.m. Cheapness. See ويل *wel*.

ولاړ *walāṛ*, a. Erect, upright, standing.

ولاړي *walāṛi*, } ad. A short time, brief interval,
ولاړې *walāre*, } somewhat, slightly.

ولايت *wilāyat*, s.m. Abroad, foreign country. A. *wilāyatī*, s.m. A foreigner. a. Foreign.

ولل *wlal*, v.a. To wash.

وله *wala*, s.f. A canal, watercourse, stream; a cane, reed; willow tree. *wula*, s.f. Root of a plant. *wlah*, s.m. Washing. *wala*, p. To, unto; sign of the dative case.

ولِ *wali*, } ad. But, besides, yet, however. A.
ولې *wale*, } (*walek*). Why? wherefore?

ولي *walī*, s.m. Lord, prince, master. A. *wilī*, a. Melted. See ويلي.

وليشت *wlesht*, s.m. A span. See لويشت.

وند *wand*, s.m. A bank, dyke, embankment. P. (*band*).

وندر *wandar*, s.m. A tethering rope with

several loops for the feet of goats, sheep, etc.

وندني *wandanai*, s.m. A bandage, binder, wisp of straw used to tie up a sheaf of corn, etc.

وندیار *wandyār*, s.f. Brother's wife. See ورندار.

وند *wand*, s.m. A field, estate, farm, parcel of land.

ونده *wanda*, s.f. Division, portion, quota, share.

ونگره *wangara*, s.f. Pond, pool, lake.

ونه *wana*, s.f. A tree, shrub.

وو *wo*, s.m. Air, wind; rheumatism. P. (*bād*).

وودل *wūdal*, v.a. To weave, plait, braid.

وودہ *wūdah*, a. Asleep, sleeping.

ووړ *woṛ*, a. Diminutive, minute, small, wee.

ووړکي *woṛkai* or *woṛukai*, s.m. A little one, child.

ووړوکي *woṛūkai*, a. Minute, tiny, very small.

ووته *wūna*, s.f. A kind of Damascened sword.

وهل *wahal*, v.a. To beat, hit, strike, wallop, baste.

وهلندي *wahlandai*, a. Wavy, tortuous, meandering, serpentine, winding.

وهم *wahm*, s.m. Idea, fancy, conjecture; anxiety, dread. A. *wahmī*, a. Fanciful, flighty, etc.

وهوه *wahwah*, in. Bravo! well done!

وهویله *wahwaila*, s.f. Lament. See واویلا.

وهیر *waher*, a. Forgotten.

ویاړ *wiyāṛ*, s.m. Vanity, conceit; envy, jealousy.

ویاړل *wiyāṛal*, v.a. To boast, exult, chuckle.

ویت *wīt*, a. Ajar, open, gaping; pert, saucy; mischievous, wanton.

ویتکي *wītakai*, s.m. A mischievous, pert, precocious, forward, etc. child.

ویته *wīta*, s.f. Impudence, precocity, pertness, etc.

ویخ *wekh*, s.m. Root of a tree; foundation, root; origin, source. P. (*bekh*).

ویر *wīr* or *vīr*, s.m. Mourning, lamentation; beating the breast. P. *wīr-jalai* or *wīra-jalai*, s.m. A mourner, lamenter.

ویران *wairān*, a. Desolate, ruined, waste. P. *wairāna*, s.f. A desert, wilderness, solitude. *wairānī*, s.f. Desolation, ruin. P.

ویره *wera*, s.f. Fear, fright, alarm. *werawul*, v.a. To frighten, terrify, alarm.

ویریدل *weredal*, v.n. To fear, be afraid.

ویړ *wīṛ*, a. Open, distended, spread out, expanded.

ویړول *wīṛawul*, v.a. To strew, spread out, scatter, etc.

ویړیدل *wīṛedal*, v.n. To expand, open out, blossom, etc.

ویړیا *weṛiyā*, ad. Free, gratis, for nothing.

ویزار *wīzār*, a. Angry, displeased, chagrined, vexed. P. (*bezār*). *wīzārī*, s.f. Anger, displeasure.

ویسا *wīsā*, s.f. Faith, belief; trust, reliance.

ویساک *wīsāk* or *waisāk*, s.m. Name of the first Hindu month, April-May. S. (*baisākh*).

ویش *wesh*, s.m. Division, distribution; lot, share.

ویشتل *wīshtal*, v.a. To cast, hurl, throw; discharge, propel, shoot. Pres. *wuli*. Past, *wīsht*.

ویشل *weshal*, v.a. To distribute, divide, allot; sift, separate.

ویشله *weshala*, s.f. A kind of unleavened bread, a pancake.

ویښ *wīkkh*, a. Awake, waking, vigilant.

ویښته *wekkhtah*, s.m. Hair, a hair.

ویل *wayal*, v.a. To say, speak, talk, tell. *wel*, s.m. Cheapness, low price. H. (*wārā*).

ویلني *welanai*, s.m. Herb mint, peppermint. P. (*pūdīna*).

ویله *wela*, s.f. A brook, small stream, rivulet.

ويلي *wilī*, a. Fused, melted; liquefied, thawed. H. (*pighlā*).

وينا *wainā*, s.f. A lament, wail; dirge, funeral song; conversation, speech, talk.

وينځل *wīndzal*, v.a. To wash, cleanse, purify.

وينځه *wīndza*, s.f. A bondmaid, slave girl.

وينه *wainah*, s.m. The white ant.

ويني *wīne*, s.f. (pl.) Blood.

ويي *wayai*, s.m. A word, saying; talk, speech.

ه

ه *hā* or *he* is the twenty-seventh letter of the Arabic and the thirty-ninth of the Pukkhto alphabet. It is sometimes substituted for ح, and by some hill tribes is used instead of خ and ښ. At the end of a word it is either "perceptible" or aspirated (*hāe-ẓāhir*), or it is "imperceptible" or unsounded (*hāe-khafī*). Words ending in the former are of the masculine gender, and those ending in the latter are of the feminine. *Hāe-khafī* is added to nouns, adjectives, etc. ending in a consonant for the formation of their feminines. Adjectives ending in *hāe-ẓāhir* form their feminines by changing it to *hāe-khafī*, and this letter itself is often dropped and replaced by the short vowel َ (*zabar*), especially in poetry. At the end of Arabic words it is generally written with a couple of dots over it (ة) and pronounced as ت.

ها *hā*, s.f. An egg (of bird, insect, reptile, etc.); the testicle. *hā*, ad. Aye, yes. See هو. *hā*, in. Lo! Behold!

هاتڼره *hātaṛa*, s.f. An elephant. S. (*hāthnī*).

هاتي *hātī*, s.m. An elephant. S. (*hāthī*).

هادي *hādī*, s.m. Director, leader, guide. A.

هار *hār*, s.m. Necklace, garland, wreath; herd, flock, drove (of cattle). S. *hār*, A particle affixed to nouns denoting sound, to form their plurals, as *shrang* (a jingle), *shrangahār*.

هاړ *hāṛ*, s.m. Name of the third Hindu month, June-July. S. (*asāṛh*).

هاړهوړه *hāṛa-hūṛa*, s.f. Clamour, noise, tumult.

هارې *hāre*, s.f. (pl.) Entreating, coaxing, wheedling.

هاله *hāla*, s.f. A halo or circle round the moon. P. *hāla*, ad. Then, at that time.

هامون *hāmūn*, s.m. A desert, plain. P.

هانډۍ *hānḍa-ī*, s.f. A cooking pot, stewpan. S. (*hānḍī*). *hānḍa-i-wāl*, s.m. A messmate, pot companion. H.

هاها *hāhā*, s.f. Laughter, laughing loudly. A.

هاهو *hāhū*, s.m. Noise, din, tumult; fame, report, rumour. H. (*hūhā*).

هاي *hāe*, in. Alas! Woe! S. *hāe-hāe*, Alas, alas! Dear, oh dear! *hāe-hāe*, Ah me! Woe, woe! *hā-ī*, pr. See following word.

هايه *hāyah*, pr. An emphatic form of the proximate demonstrative pronoun; this, this very.

هبته *habatah*, a. Worthless, useless, spoiled. A. (*habaṭah*).

هبه *hiba*, s.f. A bequest, gift. A.

هبه‌دبه *haba-daba*, s.f. Name of a disease, croup.

هپ‌دپ *hap-dap*, a. Hasty, quick, rash. ad. Suddenly, all of a heap, quickly. H. (*hap-jhap*).

هپه *hapa*, s.f. Help, succour, rescue; reprisal, foray, raid, incursion.

هته *hata*, s.f. Beam of a weaver's loom; the cubit, forearm.

هتيات *hatiyāt*, s.m. Foresight, caution, care. A. (*iḥtiyāt*).

هتيار *hatiyār*, s.m. Apparatus, arms; implement, tool. S. (*hathyār*).

هټ *haṭ*, s.m. Obstinacy, perversity, stubbornness. s. a. Erect, standing; stationary, stock-still.

هټال *haṭāl*, a. Prevented, stopped, driven back, repelled, hindered. H.

هټالول *haṭālawul*, v.a. To hinder, prevent, repel, push back, etc. H. (*haṭānā*).

هټکي *haṭkai*, s.m. Hiccough. H. (*hichkī*).

هټه *haṭah*, a. Active, stout, vigorous. H. (*haṭā*).

هټي *haṭa-ī*, s.f. A chandler's shop, market. s.

هجر *hijr*, s.m. Absence, separation. A.

هجران *hijrān*, s.m. Separation (from friends, etc.).

هجرت *hijrat*, s.m. Flight; the flight of Muḥammad from Mecca to Medina; the date or era of that event. *hijrī*, s.f. The Muḥammadan era. A.

هجره *hujra*, s.f. A kind of inn or hostelry for the reception of travellers and visitors, free of expense; there is always one of these buildings in each quarter of a village amongst the Yusufzais and Eastern Afghans generally. The *hujra* is also used as a town-hall and vestry-room; also as a club or place of common resort for the men of the quarter in which it is situated.

هجړي *hijṛai*, s.m. An eunuch, hermaphrodite. H. (*hijṛā*).

هجګي *hijgī*, s.f. Spelling. A. (*hajī*).

هڅ *huts*, a. Infatuated, mad. H. (*huch*).

هڅه *hatsa*, s.f. Labour, trouble, toil; desire, inclination, wish.

هيچ *hich*, ad. Nothing. See هيچ.

هدايت *hidāyat*, s.m. Guidance, direction. A.

هدف *hadaf*, s.m. A butt, target, mark. A.

هدهد *hudhud*, s.m. The hoopoe. A.

هديره *hadera*, s.f. Area, enclosure; graveyard.

هديه *hadiya*, s.f. A present to a teacher, schooling fee. A.

هډ *haḍ*, s.m. A bone; centre or hard part of fruit, etc. s. (*haḍḍī*). Ancestry, lineage; greatness, nobility.

هډو *haḍo*, ad. Never, not at all, no such thing. in. I say! a term of familiarity or affection.

هډور *haḍawar*, a. Bony, strong.

هډوکي *haḍūkai*, s.m. A bone, stone of fruit.

هډي *haḍai*, s.m. Bone spavin; a node; tongue bone; tonsil. s. (*haḍḍā*).

هر *har*, s.m. A rogue, wag. s. *har*, s.m. Bray of an ass. *har*, a. Every, each, any (in comp.). P. *har-wakht*, Each time. *hara-wradz*, Every day.

هراس *hirās*, s.m. Fear, terror. P.

هراول *harāwul*, s.m. Advanced guard of an army. T.

هراند *harānd*, a. Fearful, timid.

هرتال *hartāl*, s.m. Orpiment. s.

هرټ *haraṭ*, s.m. A Persian wheel for drawing water from a well. H.

هرځائي *hardzā-ī*, s.m. Vagabond, wanderer, rascal.

هرج *harj*, s.m. Interruption, delay; tumult, sedition. A.

هرزه *harzah*, a. Nonsensical, frivolous. *harza*, s.f. A trifle, bagatelle, absurdity. P.

هرکاره *harkārah*, s.m. A courier, messenger; emissary, spy; man of all work. P. *harkāra*, s.f. An iron spoon, a large ladle.

هرګاه *hargāh*, ad. Whenever, wherever. P.

هرګز *hargiz*, ad. Ever, never. P.

هرګوره *hargora*, ad. At least, at all events, by all means; wholly, altogether, entirely.

هرئ *hira-ī*, s.f. Excuse, pretence, shift, plea. A. (*hīla*).

هريړه *hareṛa*, s.f. Name of a nut used in medicine, and as a dye, myrobalan (*Terminalia chebula*).

هرپي *harpa-ī*, s.f. A casket, small box.

هزاره *hazārah*, s.m. Name of a Tartar tribe

who possess the hill country between Kabul and Herat.

هزم *hazm*, s.m. Digestion. A. (*haẕm*).

هژدات *hajdāt*, s.m. Bell metal, bronze, brass. S. (*ajdhāt*).

هسار *hisār*, s.m. A castle, fort. A. (*ḥiṣār*). Difficulty, embarrassment. a. Enclosed, surrounded. besieged.

هسارول *hisārawul*, v.a. To enclose, surround, besiege; stop, prevent, keep.

هساريدل *hisāredal*, v.n. To be besieged, enclosed, etc., to stick, stop, be stuck, clogged, etc.

هسپه *haspa*, s.f. Erysipelas; quinsy; purpura. *haspa·buṭai*, s.m. Name of a plant used as a remedy for *haspa* (*Indigofera sp.*).

هستي *hastī*, s.f. Being, existence. P.

هسک *hask*, a. High, lofty, tall. p. Above, aloft. *hisk*, s.m. Lottery, hazard, chance; drawing lots, lot.

هسِ *hasi*, } ad. As, thus, in like manner,
هسې *hase*, } likewise, therefore.

هښمه *hakkhma*, s.f. An April shower, a spring shower soon passing away (of rain).

هغومبره *haghombra*, ad. So much, that much.

هغه *haghah*, pr. The third personal pronoun; he, she, it. The remote demonstrative pronoun; that. A. (*haẕā*).

هفته *hafta*, s.f. A week. P.

هکڼبکڼ *hak·pak*, a. Aghast, confounded, confused. H. (*hakkā·bakkā*).

هګۍ *haga-ī*, s.f. An egg. See ها.

هل *hal*, s.m. Handle of a plough; a plough. S.

هلاک *halāk*, s.m. Perdition, ruin, death. a. Dead, killed; annihilated, lost, ruined. A.

هلاکت *halākat*, s.m. Perdition, death.

هلاکي *halākī*, s.f. Ruination, destruction. A.

هلال *hilāl*, s.m. The new moon; the first and last two or three days of the moon. A. *halāl*, a. Lawful, etc. See حلال.

هلاهل *halāhal*, s.m. Deadly poison. S.

هلته *halta*, ad. } There, yonder, thither, in
هلته کي *halta·ke*, } that place, over there.

هلک *halak*, s.m. A boy, lad, youth. a. Small, little; slight, mean; debased, cheap; easy, soft; silly, useless. H. (*halkā*).

هلکت *halakat*, s.m. } Boyhood, youth.
هلکوالي *halak·wālai*, }

هلکينه *halkīna*, s.f. Infancy, childhood.

هلم *halam*, s.m. Cress, watercress (*Lepidum sativum*). H. (*hālim*).

هلواک *halwāk*, a. Fast, swift, quick, fleet, rapid.

هله *halla*, s.f. Charge, attack, onset, assault; riot, uproar, tumult. A. *hala*, ad. Then, at that time.

هلي *hale*, ad. Here, hither, in this place.

هم *hum*, c. Also, even, likewise. P. (*ham*) (in comp.). Together, with, same, equal, etc. as *hum·kār*, s.m. A fellow workman. *hum·wazn*, Of equal weight. *hamm*, s.m. Solicitude, anxiety, care. A.

هماي *humāe*, s.m. Phœnix, bird of happy omen. P. (*humā*).

همّت *himmat*, s.m. Bravery, courage; resolution, spirit. A.

همّتناک *himmat·nāk*, } Resolute, daring, bold,
همّتي *himmatī*, a. } courageous.

همراه *hamrāh*, s.m. Companion, fellow-traveller. p. Along with, together. P.

همسا *hamsā*, s.f. A mace, stick. See امسا.

همګي *hamagī*, } a. All, the whole. P.
همه *hamah*, }

همياني *hamiyāna-ī*, s.f. A purse. P.

هميشه *hamesha*, a. Perpetually, always. P.

هنج *hanj*, s.m } Assafœtida. S. (*heng*).
هنجه *hinja*, s.f. }

هند *hind*, s.m. India, Hindustan.

هنداره *hindāra*, s.f. A mirror, looking glass.

هندكو *hindko*, s.f. The language of the Indians.

هندكي *hindka-ī*, s.m. The Indians; name of an Indian tribe (converts to Islam), settled in parts of the Peshawar valley and surrounding hills. *hindkai*, s.m. An Indian (Mussulman). *hindka-ī*, s.f. An Indian woman.

هندو *hindū*, s.m. A Hindu; a pagan, idolater.

هندوبار *hindūbār*, s.m. A place where Hindus dwell or meet; dealings with a Hindu.

هندوستان *hindūstān*, s.m. India, Upper India, the country of the Hindus.

هندوګی *hindūgai*, s.m. A term of abuse. A Hindu grocer, grain dealer.

هندوانه *hindwāna*, s.f. A water melon. P.

هندواړۍ *hindwāṛra-ī*, } s.f. A Hindu woman.
هندوه *hindawa*, }

هنډه *hunḍah*, s.m. A wolf. H. *hanḍa*, s.f. Ambition, desire, wish; fancy; want. *hinḍah*, s.m. A stallion, bull, male kept for breeding purposes.

هنډئي *hunḍa-ī*, s.f. Bill of exchange, money order. S. (*hunḍī*).

هنر *hunar*, s.m. Art, skill; virtue, quality. P. *hunar-man*, a. Clever, ingenious. P

هنس *hans*, s.m. A goose, swan. S. (*hāns*).

هنګام *hangām*, s.m. Period, time, season. P.

هنګامه *hangāma*, s.f. Mob, crowd, assembly; uproar, riot, tumult; assault, onset. P.

هنوز *hanoz*, ad. Yet, hitherto, still. P.

هنړ *hanṛ*, s.m. Neigh of a horse, bray of an ass.

هنړهنړيدل *hanṛ-hanṛedal*, v.n. To neigh, bray. H. (*hinhinhānā*).

هو *ho*, ad. Aye, yea, yes. S. (*hān*). in. Halloa! ho! S. Hurrah! An exclamation used when rushing on an enemy in battle.

هوا *hawā*, s.f. Wind, atmosphere, air; lust, desire; affection, love; pride, conceit. A. *hawā*, in. Dear me! Ah! Alas! See هاي.

هوار *hawār*, a. Even, smooth; level, flat; fit, proper; gentle, docile. P. (*hamwār*).

هوباره *hūbārah*, s.m. A kind of bustard. A.

هوبهو *hūbahū*, ad. Exactly, perfectly, quite. A.

هوده *hūda*, s.f. Charming, exorcising, mesmerising (by breathing). Appointment, office, post, business. A. (*'uhda*). *hauda*, s.f. A litter or sedan used by women when they travel; a seat or stage placed on the back of an elephant. A.

هوډ *hoḍ*, s.m. The contrary, opposite.

هوډه *hoḍa*, s.f. Perversity, obstinacy.

هوډي *hoḍai*, a. Stubborn, perverse, wayward; opposed, opposite. s.m. Name of a hill opposite Attak (on the Indus), on the top of which are some Buddhist ruins.

هور *hor*, s.m. Time, season. Fire. A deer.

هورِ *hūri*, } ad. There, thither, over there.
هوري *hūre*, }

هوږه *hūga*, s.f. Garlic.

هوس *hawas*, s.m. Lust, concupiscence; ambition, desire; curiosity. A. *hawas-nāk*, a. Sensual, ambitious, etc.

هوسا *hosā*, a. Refreshed, recruited; untired, unwearied; idle, lazy. P. (*hoshā*). *hosā-kawul*, v.a. To recruit, rest, refresh, repair, refit, etc.

هوسي *hosai*, s.m. A deer, gazelle. P. (*āhū*).

هوښ *hokkh*, s.m. Sense, understanding; mind, soul; judgment. P. (*hosh*).

هوښيار *hokkhyār*, a. Intelligent, sensible, wise; cautious, discreet, prudent.

هوښيارتيا *hokkhyār-tiyā*, } Intelligence, discretion, prudence.
هوښياري *hokkhyārī*, s.f. }

هوک *hūk*, a. Flooded, inundated, sunk.

هوكلۍ *hokla-ī*, s.f. A large wooden pestle.

هوكه *haukah*, a. Fatigued, tired, weary.

هوكي *hokai*, s.m. Assent, consent, saying "yes"; consent of parents to marriage of a daughter.

هول *hūl*, s.m. Bolt or bar of a door. *haul*,

s.m. Horror, fear, terror. A. *haul·nāk*, a. Terrible, awful, dismal, fearful.

هومره *homra*, } ad. So much, that much,
هونبره *honbra*, } this much.

هونړا *honṛā*, s.f. A kind of trap for catching birds; the perch placed over the trap.

هوي *hūe*, in. Alas! See هاي.

هويدا *hawidā*, a. Evident, manifest, clear. P.

هويه *hoya*, s.f. An egg.

هه *hah*, in. Indeed! Really! Oh ho! Halloa!

هي *hai*, in. Alas! Dear me! *hai·hai*, in. What a pity! Dear me! Wonderful! Strange!

هيات *hayāt*, s.m. Form, aspect, visage, face. A.

هيبت *haibat*, s.m. Panic, terror, awe. A. *haibat·nāk*, a. Terrific, awe-inspiring, fearful.

هيڅ *hets*, ad. Nothing, nought, none. P. (*hech*). *hets·tsok*, Nobody. *hets·shai*, Nothing.

هيچر *hechari*, } ad. Never, at no time.
هيچري *hechare*, }

هيچرته *hecharta*, ad. Nowhere.

هير *her*, a. Forgotten, omitted, lost to memory.

هيړوي *heṛrai*, s.m. A sheep of the long-tailed breed. H. (*bheṛā*).

هيرقطار *hīr·qaṭār*, s.m. Indian file, one behind the other, filing along.

هير *heṛ*, s.m. Time, season, period. H. (*pher*).

هيره *heṛa*, s.f. Turn, time. ad. Once, one time. *yawa·heṛa*, Once. *dwa·heṛa*, Twice, etc.

هيري *heṛai*, s.m. A sheep. See هيړوي.

هيز *hīz*, s.m. Hermaphrodite. P.

هيزګي *hezgī*, s.f. Spelling. See هجګي.

هيسته *hīsta*, ad. Here, hither. *rāhīsta*, Near me. *darhīsta*, Near thee. *warhīsta*, Near him, her, it, etc.

هيښ *hekkh*, a. Amazed, confounded, perplexed.

هيضه *haiẓa*, s.f. Cholera morbus. A.

هيغ *hegh*, a. Stiff, straight. See نيغ.

هيكل *haikal*, s.m. An ornament for the neck; face, figure, form, person; palace, temple. A.

هيل *hel*, s.m. Cardamoms. A. (*elā*).

هيله *hīla*, s.f. Subterfuge, trick. See حيله.

هيلۍ *hīla-ī*, s.m. A duck, water fowl.

هينګ *heng*, s.m. A groan, moan, sigh.

هيواد *hewād*, s.m. Country, region, clime.

هيون *hayūn*, s.m. A horse; camel. P.

هيهات *haihāt*, a. Lamenting, wailing. A. in. Alas! Begone!

ي

ي *yā* or *ye* is the twenty-eighth letter of the Arabic and the fortieth and last of the Pukkhto alphabet. When used as a consonant it has the sound of *y*, if moved by a vowel (*mutaḥarrik*), and of the French *e* or English *ey* (as in *they*), if quiescent or unmoved (*sākin*). When used as a vowel it has the sound of ī (*yāe·m'arūf*), or *e* (*yāe·majhūl*) if preceded by the short vowel *kasra* ـِ, and of the diphthong *ai*, if preceded by the short vowel *fatha* ـَ (*yāe·sākin·māqabl·i·maftūḥ*), as is explained in the Grammar. *Yāe·m'arūf*, preceded by *hamza* ـٔ has the sound of *a-ī* (*yāe·m'arūf māqabl·i·hamza·i·khafī·i·maksūr*), and is the termination of a number of feminine nouns, both in the singular and plural. In Pukkhto the vowel sounds *yāe·m'arūf* (ī), *yāe·majhūl* (*e*), and *yāe·m'arūf māqabl·i·hamza* (*a-ī*) are often dropped and replaced by the short vowel *kasra* ـِ.

يا *yā*, c. Either, or, whether. P. in. Oh! Vocative particle. Oh! Halloa! A.

ياب *yāb* (in comp.), Finding, obtaining. P. *kam·yāb*, a. Scarce. P.

يابو *yābū*, s.m. A pony. H.

ياد *yād*, s.m. Recollection, memory. P. *yādawul*, v.a. To remind, mention, call to mind. *yādedal*, v.n. To recollect, remember, recur.

يار *yār*, s.m. Paramour, lover, friend; comrade, companion, assistant. P. *yārī*, s.f. Friendship.

ياستي *yāsta-ī*, You are; a form of the second person plural present tense of the defective verb *yam*, I am.

ياسمين *yāsamīn*, s.m. Jasmine. P.

ياغي *yāghī*, a. Mutinous, rebellious. s.m. A rebel, mutineer. A. (*bāghī*).

ياغيگړ *yāghī·gaṛ*, s.m. A mutineer, rebel. *yāghī·gaṛī*, s.f. Mutiny, rebellion; sedition, revolt.

يافت *yāft*, s.m. Earnings, perquisites. P.

ياقوت *yāqūt*, s.m. A ruby. A.

يال *yāl*, s.m. The mane of a horse, etc. P.

ياور *yāwar*, a. Aiding, helping, friendly. s.m. Coadjutor, assistant; companion, friend. P. *yāwarī*, s.f. Help, succour, aid.

ياوره *yāwara*, s.f. A big-bellied mare, ass, etc.

ياوه *yāwah*, a. Vain, absurd, futile; ruined, lost. P. *yāwa·goe*, s.m. A talker of nonsense.

ياهو *yāhū*, s.m. Jehovah. A.

يبل *yabl*, a. Barefooted. See ابل.

يتيم *yatīm*, s.m. An orphan. A.

يخ *yakh*, a. Cold, frigid; cooled, damped; satiated; slaked, subsided. s.m. Cold; ice. P.

يخني *yakhnī*, s.f. Coldness, frigidity, chilliness; cold, chill; gravy, jelly. P.

يراق *yarāq*, s.m. Arms, accoutrements, weapons. T.

يرړي *yarṛai*, s.m. A sheep. See هيرړي.

يرز *yarz*, s.m. Ability, skill, fitness, capacity; merit, worth; propriety, expediency; consistency, congruity.

يرزن *yarzan*, a. Expedient, fit, worthy, suitable.

يرغمال *yarghamāl*, s.m. A hostage. P.

يرغه *yarghah*, a. Ambling. s.m. An ambler, an ambling horse or mule; a horse or mule with the ears slit. P.

يرمن *yar·man*, a. Timid, timorous, nervous, fearing, shy.

يره *yara*, s.f. Fear, fright. ad. Really, truly, yes, indeed, verily. P. (*āre*).

يزد *yazd*, / يزدان *yazdān*, } s.m. God. P.

يږ *yag*, s.m. A bear.

يږه *yaga*, s.f. A she-bear. A kind of ulcer.

يساول *yasāwul*, s.m. A mace-bearer; equerry, mounted attendant on a man of rank. P.

يستل *yastal*, v.a. To eject, expel, pick out, extract, produce, etc. Def. in pres. ten. See باسل.

يشم *yashm*, s.m. Jasper, jade, agate. P.

يشند *yashand*, a. Boiling, effervescing.

يشنا *yashnā*, s.f. Ebullition, effervescence.

يشول *yashawul*, v.a. To boil, cook, stew.

يشيدل *yashedal*, v.n. To boil, bubble, ferment, effervesce. P. (*joshīdan*). See ايشيدل.

يښل *yakkhal*, v.a. To put, place, set, deposit, etc. P. (*shāndan*). Applied to inanimate objects. Def. in pres. ten. See ږدل.

يښودل *yakkhodal*, / يښول *yakkhawul*, } v.a. To place, put, set. See ايښودل.

يښي *yakkhai*, a. Placed, put, set.

يعني *y'ane*, ad. Namely, that is to say, viz., i.e. A.

يغما *yaghma*, s.f. Plunder, booty, spoil. P.

يقين *yaqīn*, a. Certain, sure, true, real. ad. Certainly, surely, truly. A. *yaqīnī*, s.f. Reality, certainty. a. Certain, sure, real.

يقيناً *yaqīnan*, ad. Assuredly, certainly. A.

يک *yak*, a. One (in comp. only). P. *yak·dil*, a. Of one mind, unanimous. *yak·lakhta*, ad. All at once, suddenly.

يکلنگه *yak·linga*, s.f. A lever used to draw water from a well. P. See ډنگلئ.

يكشمبه *yak·shamba*, s.f. Sunday. P.

يك‌لائي *yak·lā-ī*, s.f. A mantle of a single layer of cloth. P.

يكه *yakah*, a. Unique, single, alone, sole; a one-horse chaise. P.

يكي *yakī*, s.f. Name of a small copper coin.

يگان *yagān*, a. Single, unique. P.

يگانگي *yagānagī*, s.f. Singleness, uniqueness; unanimity, concord, unity. P.

يگانه *yagānah*, a. Single, sole; unanimous, agreed. P.

يگه *yaga*, s.f. A kind of corroding ulcer; a disease affecting the tail of a horse, melanosis; cancer; a she-bear. See يږه.

يل *yal*, s.m. Hero, champion. P.

يلغر *yalghar*, s.m. Foray, raid, incursion. A.

يله *yalah*, a. Free, liberated; wandering, vagabond. *yala*, s.f. A bog, marsh, morass.

يم *yam*, s.m. The ocean, sea. A. *yam*, I am, the first person singular present tense of the defective verb "to be" (inf. wanting).

ينگ *yang*, s.m. Conduct, behaviour; manner, mode, way.

يو *yo*, a. One; a, an. P. (*yak*).

يواځي *yawādzai*, a. Alone, single, solitary. ad. Separately, alone, apart.

يواد *yawād*, s.m. Country, region. See هيواد.

يور *yor*, s.f. Husband's brother's wife. pl. *yūure*.

يورش *yūrish*, s.m. Assault, charge; invasion. P.

يوز *yūz*, s.m. A lynx; panther. P.

يوسپزي *yūsupzī*, s.m. Name of a powerful clan of Afghans, the Yūsufzais.

يوستوي *yawastawai*, a. Single, without fold or lining (as a garment).

يوسفزي *yūsufzī*, s.m. See يوسپزي.

يوسل *yosal*, v.a. To bear, carry, support, put up with, endure (applied only to inanimate objects). Irr. Pres. *yosī*. Past, *yowar*. See وړل.

يوم *yūm*, s.m. A shovel, spade (with a bar of wood fixed above the blade as a rest for the foot in shoving it into the ground). *yaum*, s.m. A day. A.

يون *yūn*, s.m. Pace, step; gait, carriage, custom, habit; moving, passing.

يوه *yawa*, } s.f. A plough. *yawe* or *yiwe*, pl.
يويه *yoya*, } Ploughing, tilling.

ييښل *yekkhal*, v.a. To put, set. See ښېل.

ييم *yīm*, s.m. A shovel. See يوم *yūm*.

يه *ya*, ad. No, not. P.

ي *e*, A form of the Genitive and Instrumental cases, singular and plural of the third personal pronoun هغه, His, hers, its, theirs, etc. He, she, it, they.

END OF PART I.

PART II.

ENGLISH AND PUKSHTO.

PART II.

ENGLISH AND PUKSHTO.

ABBREVIATIONS.

a. adjective; ad. adverb; c. conjunction; in. interjection; p. preposition; pr. pronoun; s. substantive; v.a. verb active; v.n. verb neuter; *k. kawul*; *ked. kedal.*

Aback, ad. *biyarta, wrusto, pastana.*

Abaisance, s. *salām, sijda, t'azīm.*

Abandon, v.a. *pregdal, prekkhodal, prekkhawul, preyakkhal*; *tark k.*

Abandoned, a *prekkhodalai, preyakkhai* or *prikkhai.*

Abandonment, s. *prekkhodana, prekkhawuna.*

Abase, v.a. *spukawul.*

Abased, v.n. *spukedal.* a. *spukawulai, spukedalai.*

Abasement, s. *spuk-wālai, spukedana.*

Abash, v.a. *sharmawul.*

Abashed, v.n. *sharmedal.* a. *sharmsār, sharmindah*; *pakkhemān*; *sharmedalai.*

Abate, v.a. *kamawul, leg k.* v.n. *kamedal, leg ked.*

Abatement, s. *kamedina, kam-wālai, kamtiyā, legedena, la-ag-wālai*; *chūk.*

Abbreviate, v.a. *landawul.*

Abbreviation, s. *land-wālai.*

Abdicate, v.a. *tark k. pregdal.* (Abandon.)

Abdicator, s. *tark kawūnkai, prekkhodūnkai, tārik.*

Abdomen, s. *geda, kheṭa.* (hypogastrium) *spokhdza, spokhz.* (hypochondrium) *tishai, ḍaḍa.*

Abet, v.a. *madad warkawul, pushtī k.*; *lamsawul.*

Abetment, s. *madad, pushtī, komak*; *lamsūn.*

Abettor, s. *madad-, pushtī-, komak-,* etc. *warkawūnkai*; *lamsūnai.*

Abide, v.n. *osedal, āstedal, pātedal, pātai ked. wudaredal.*

Abject, a. *khwār, dūn, sperah-kai, sperah-makh.*

Abjectness, s. *khwārī, tabāhī.*

Ability, s. *qābiliyat, ṭāqat, was, yarz*; *qābiltob.*

Abjure, v.a. *munkiredal.*

Able, a. *qābil, tuwānā.* v.n. *shwul, tuwānedal.* v.a. *tāqat-, zor-, wāk-, was-,* etc. *laral.*

Ablution, s. *ghusl.* (ceremonial) *āwdas, wazū, taimūm* or *tebūn.*

Abode, s. *dzāe, astoga, astogna, ṭīkāo, mīshta, kor, makān, kilai, deṛa, borjal.*

Abolish, v.a. *bandawul, mauqūf-, man'a-, mansūkh-,* etc. *k.*

Abominable, a. *bad, palīt, nā-pāk, stūkh, murdār.*

Abominate, v.a. *bad manal, chinjawul, kraka ākhistal, nafrat k., ghandal, kagal.*

Abort, v.a. *geḍa, ghurzawul, ziyān k.*

Abortion, s. *da geḍe ziyān.* (in animals) *piyāza.*

Abortive, a. *be-fā-ida, 'abas, bāṭil, nā-kār.*

Above, p. *pās, dapāsa, bānde, dabānde, porta, pakūrta.*

Abound, v.n. *wadānedal, ziyātedal, ḍeredal.*

About, p. *chāpera, chauper*; *dapāra, bābat*; *nizde* or *nijde, qarīb, tsakha* or *khatsa*; *lagiyā, mashghūl*; *pa andāz, pa ḥisāb.*

Abrade, v.a. *sūlawul, garawul, gargal, gasiyā k.* v.n. *sūledal, blodal, blosedal, gasiyā, ked.*

Abrasion, s. *sūda, blos, gasiyā*; *blosedana, sūledana.*

Abreast, ad. *barābar, tsang pa tsang.*

Abroad, ad. *bahar* or *bāhir, pa pradī mulk* (or *dzāe*) *kkhke.*

Abrupt, a. *gaṛandai, za-ar* or *zir, jalt*; *zig, lwāṛ.* s. *ḍoghal, kand, gaṛang, kamar.*

Abruptly, ad. *nā-tsāpa, nā-gūmān, nāgāh, sam da lāsa.*

Abscess, s. *kharai, kkhanza, shīnai, nanaka-ī, kkhlūna, lūna.*

Abscond, v.n. *puṭedal, takkhtedal, firārī ked.*

Absence, s. *biyal-tūn, judā-ī, hijrān*; *nisht-wālai, ghair ḥāzirī.*

Absent, a. *ghā-ib, nishtah, ghair ḥāzir*; *biyal, judā*; *ghāfil, be-khūd, pa fikr kkshe ḍūb.*

Absolve, v.a. *pulawul, bakkhal* or *bakhkkhal.*

Absolved, a. *bakkhalai, pulawulai, khalāṣ, m'uāf.*

Absolute, a. *pūrah, sarāsar, amānī, tamām, ṭol, muṭlaq*; *khpul-sar* or *khapsar, wāk-dār, mukhtār.*

Absolutely, ad. *amānī, sarāsarī, tamāmī.*

Absolution, s. *bakkhana, khalāṣī, pul* (or *pa-al*), *najāt.*

Absorb, v.a. *tskkhal* or *tskal* or *skal, wuchawul.*

Absorbed, v.n. *wuchedal, jazb ked.*

Abstain, v.a. *parhez-, pāl-,* etc. *k.* *lās-, dzān-,* etc. *būsal—yastal, lās-, dzān-,* etc. *sātal.*

Abstemious, a. *parhez-gār, kam-khwurāk, pārsā.*

Abstinence, s. *pāl, parhez*; *roja*; *pārsā-ī.*

Abstract, s. *mujmal, khulāṣa.* v.a. *bāsal—yistal, kāgal—kkhkal*; *biyalawul, judā k.*

Abstruse, a. *bārīk, narai, puṭ*; *grān, mushkil.*

Absurd, a. *'abas, be-hūdah, wuch pucha, yāwah, khushai, prat, harzah.*

Absurdity, s. *be-hūdagī, be-wūqūfī, kam-'aqlī.*

Abundance, s. *ḍer-wālai, wadānī, ābādī, frewānī, ziyāt-wālai.*

Abundant, a. *ḍer, ziyāt, frewān, ṭal.*

Abuse, s. *kkhkandzal* or *kanzal, peghor.* v.a. *kkhkandzal* or *kanzal, kanzal-, ruswā-,* etc. *k.* *peghor warkawul*; *bad sulūkī-, be-hurmatī-,* etc. *k.*

Abusive, a. *jiba-war, kanzal kawūnkai.*

Abyss, s. *gaṛang, kanda, ḍoghal, jawara.*

Accede, v.a. *manal, qabūlawul.*

Accent, s. *lahja, qirāt, ẓarb, ghag, makhraj.*

Accept, v.a. *manal, qabūlawul*; *ākhistal*; *khwakkhawul, pasandawul, kkhah gaṇṛal.*

Acceptable, a. khwakkh, ghwarah. v.n. pasandedal, khwakkhedal, qabūledal.

Access, s. dakhl; rāsha darsha, nanawātah.

Accession, s. khātah, khatana.

Accident, s. āfat, wāq'ia, ḥādis̤a, balā.

Accidental, a. qaẓā-ī, qismatī.

Acclamation, s. zwag zūg, hāhū, chīgha; āparīn, shābāsh.

Accommodate, v.a. dzāyawul; khidmat k. altsawral, hawārawul.

Accommodation, s. dzāe; khidmat.

Accompany, v.n. malgarai ked.; khatsa tlal.

Accomplice, s. mal, malgarai, sharīk, yār.

Accomplish, v.a. tamāmawul, pūrah k. pa dzāe rāwṛal; kawul, kṛal.

Accomplished, a. tamām shawai or -kaṛai, pūrah; qābil, pohānd, hunar-man, kāmil.

Accomplishment, s. tamāmī, anjām, taiyārī; hunar, qābil-tob, kāmil-tob.

Accord, s. rogha, joṛa, pukhulā-tob, āshtī; barābarī, nisbat. (of own-) pa khpul. (of one-) yak jihat, yak dil, yo shān. v.n. yak sān- or yo shān-, barābar-, etc. ked. lagedal.

According to, p. pa—sara. (-custom) pa dastūr sara.

Accordingly, ad. la de na, dzaka.

Accost, v.a. pukkhtedal, salām k. pukkhtana k. wayal, khabare k. nāre wahal.

Account, v.a. ganṛal, pohedal, shmeral. s. ḥisāb, shumār; qiṣṣa, bayān, naql, taẕkira; dzawāb or jawāb, khabara.

Accountable, a. ẓāmin; tāwān- or dzawāb warkawūnkai.

Accoutre, v.a. mlā taṛal, drasta- or wasla āghostal.

Accrue, v.n. ḥāsiledal, paidā ked.; khatal.

Accumulate, v.a. gaṭal, ṭolawul, yodzāe-, jam'a-, ambār-, etc. k. v.n. ṭoledal, jam'a, yodzāe-, etc. ked.

Accuracy, s. rikkhtīn-tob, rikkhtīnī, jukht-wālai.

Accurate, a. rikkhtīnai, sūchah; jukht, barābar, rikkhtiyā.

Accusation, s. tuhmat or tomat, d'awa, malāmat, peghor, tor.

Accuse, v.a. d'awa-, faryād-, etc. k. tuhmat taṛal or -wayal or -pore k. peghor warkawul, tor pore k.

Accuser, s. d'awa- or tor pore kawūnkai, mudda'ī.

Accustom, v.a. āmokhtah-, 'ādat-, etc. k. rugdawul.

Ache, s. dard, khūg, randz, zakhm. v.n. khūgedal, dardedal.

Acid, a. trīw. (f.) tarwa.

Acidity, s. trīw-tob, trīw-wālai.

Acknowledge, v.a. manal. v.n. qā-iledal.

Acknowledgment, s. manūn, qabūl; ḥujjat, rasīd; shukrāna.

Acorn, s. kwarai.

Acquaint, v.a. khabarawul, pohawul, āgāh k.

Acquaintance, s. pejand-galī, āshnā-ī; āshnāe. pejāndah. (f.) āshnāya, pejandala.

Acquainted, v.n. khabaredal, pohedal, āgāh-, wāqif-, etc. ked.

Acquire, v.a. gaṭal, mūndal, paidā-, ḥāṣil-, sagah-, etc. k.

Acquit, v.a. pulawul, bakkhal, wa-aṛ k.

Acrid, a. trīkh. (f.) tarkha.

Acridity, s. trīkh-wālai, trīkh-tob.

Across, ad. pore, pore ghāṛe.

Act, v.a. kawul, kṛal, pāzah-, 'amal-, etc. k.

Action, s. kār, kṛah, 'amal, ḥarkat, pāzah, chār.

Active, a. chālāk, chust, takṛah, tund, tez.

Actively, ad. pa chālākī sara.

Activity, s. chālākī, chustī, tund-wālai.

Actor, s. kawūnkai, kṛūnai, fā'il, 'āmil. (in a play) naṭ, pekkhe-gar, toq-mār, swāng kawūnkai or swāngai.

Actually, ad. *rikkhtiyā, pa wāq'i, qaṭ'aī.*

Acute, a. *tez, terah, sakht; hokkhyār, pohind.*

Acuteness, s. *tez-wālai, terah-tob, sakhtiyā; hokkhyār-tiyā, hokkhyārī, pohind-wālai.*

Adage, s. *matal, miṣl, miṣāl.*

Adapt, v.a. *joṛawul, dzāyawul, hawārawul, atsawral, samawul, drust-, barābar-,* etc. *k.*

Add, v.a. *joṛawul, lagawul, gaḍawul.*

Addition, s. *mīzān, ḥisāb; joṛawūna, gaḍawūna.*

Additional, a. *ziyāt, nor, bul.*

Addle, a. *skhā, gandah, wrost.*

Address, v.a. *sawāl-, tapahūs* or *tapos-,* etc. *k. wayal, pukkhtedal; sar-nāma likal* or *kāgal—kkhkal, darkhwāst k. salām k.*

Adept, s. *ustāẓ, kārī-gar, pokh, pūrah, hunarman.*

Adequate, a. *bas, pūrah, kāfī.*

Adhere, v.n. *lagedal, nkkhatal, chaspedal; grohedal.* v.a. *laman niwul, tāb'i-dārī k.*

Adherent, s. *tāb'i-dār, mlā-taṛ, ṭaraf-dār, para-dār, wābastah; charekār, hamsāyah, faqīr.* a. *slekkh-nāk, bokkht, chaspān; nkkhatai, lagedilai.*

Adhesion, s. *pewastagī; chasp; nkkhatūn.*

Adhesive, a. *slekkh-nāk, bokkht, barwai, chaspān.*

Adieu, s. *da khudāe pa amān, salām.*

Adjourn, v.a. *nāgha-, barkhwāst-, mauqūf-,* etc. *k.*

Adjust, v.a. *tartīb-, durust-, barābar-,* etc. *k. samawul, joṛawul, atsawral, hawārawul; pūrah-, faiṣal-, ārāstah-,* etc. *k.*

Admirable, a. *nādir, 'ajīb, gharīb.*

Admire, v.n. *grohedal.* v.a. *kkhah gaṇral, stāyal.*

Admission, s. *dakhl, nanawātah, rāsha dar-sha; manana, qabūledana.*

Admit, v.a. *dakhl-* or *lār warkawul; manal, qabūlawul.*

Admonish, v.a. *pand-, naṣīḥat-, tambīh-,* etc. *k. malāmatawūl, ṭaqawul, traṭal, raṭal.*

Adopt, v.a. *khwakkhawul, pasandawul, ikhtiyārawul; ākhistal.*

Adore, v.a. *parastī-, 'ibādat-, sijda-,* etc. *k.*

Adorn, v.a. *psolawul, singārawul, sāzawul, kkhewa k. kkhāyastah k. joṛawul.*

Adulation, s. *khūshāmad, chāplūsī, ḍirpalī.*

Adulator, s. *khushāmad-gar, chāplūs, ḍirpal.*

Adult, s. *dzawān, zalmai, zalmoṭai, bāligh.*

Adulterate, v.a. *gaḍawul, nāsarah k.*

Adulteration, s. *gaḍūn, qalp-wālai.*

Adulterer, s. *kāsir, zanā-kār.*

Adultery, s. *kāsīrī, zanā.*

Advance, v.n. *wrānde tlal* or *-ked.* s. *por, qarẓ, peshgī; taraqqī; gūndah.*

Advantage, s. *kkhegaṛa, gatta, sūd, fā-ida, bih-būdī, naf'a; barai, ghalaba, fatḥa, wa-aṛ-wālai.*

Advantageous, a. *sūd-man, ghwarah, kkhah.*

Adventure, s. *kār, chal, chār, wāq'ia.*

Adventurer, s. *lawand, gashtai; chaṭ, lūtsak.*

Adversary, s. *dukkhman, mudda'ī.*

Adversity, s. *tangī, tangsiyā, kam-bakhtī, bad-bakhtī, sakhtī, shāmat; dukkhmani, mukhālifat, kharkhasha.*

Advice, s. *maṣlaḥat, mashwarat, pand, ṣalāḥ, naṣīḥat; khabar, iṭṭilā'a.*

Advise, v.a. *pand-, naṣīḥat-,* etc. *-warkawul; maṣlaḥat kawul; khabarawul.*

Advisable, a. *munāsib, lāzim, lā-iq, ghwarah.*

Advocate, s. *wakīl, mukhtār.*

Adze, s. *tarkkhadza, tesha, sūza.*

Afar, ad. *lire, la warāya.*

Affable, a. *ḥalīm, mihrbān, makhawar, khush sulūk, khush-goe.*

Affair, s. *kār, khabara, chār, muqaddama, mu'āmala, amr.*

Affect, v.a. *kār-, aṣr-, 'amal-, pāzah-, tāṣīr-,* etc. *k.* (feign) *bāna-, makr-,* etc. *k.*

Affectation, s. *nāz, nakhra, makez, nakhra-bāzī; bahānā, chal, fareb, makr, ḥīla.*

Affected, a. *chal-bāz, makr-jan, bahānā-khor, farebī, ḥīla-bāz; nakhra-bāz.*

Affection, s. *mīna, maḥabbat, 'ishq, mihr, tapāk; mayan-tob, khwā khogī, ulfat.*

Affectionate, a. *mayan, mihrbān, khwā khogai.*

Affinity, s. *nisbat, 'alāqa; khpel-walī, rishta-dārī, ragai, wābastagī, sar-rishta.*

Affirm, v.a. *wayal, iqrār, k. lal* or *lawdal, gawāhī lal*

Affirmation, s. *qaul, lafẕ, qarār, iqrār, is̱bāt.*

Afflict, v.a. *āzārawul, zaḥīrawul, randzawul.*

Afflicted, a. *randzūr, gham-jan, dard-man.*

Affliction, s. *randz, gham, dard, āzār, paskhāk* or *pakhsāk, mirtsī, sakhtī.*

Afford, v.a. *warkawul, khartsawul, da warka-wulo ṭāqat laral.* v.n. *shwal, kedal, tu-wānedal.*

Affront, s. *khwā-badī, mānṛai; spuk-tiyā, be-'izzatī.*

Afoot, a. *palai, pa kkhpo, piyādah.*

Afraid, v.n. *weredal* or *yeredal.* (in animals) *tarahedal, bugnedal.*

After, p. *pas, b'ad, wrusto.* (year after year) *kāl pa kāl.* (-to-morrow) *pas sabā.* (following-) *pase.* a. *wrustai, wrustanai, wrustīnai, pasīnah.*

After all, ad. *ākhir.*

After-birth, s. *prewān.* (caul) *obanṛa.*

Afternoon s. *dwah-pahār.* (early) *pekkhīn, māspekkhīn.* (late) *dīgar, māzdīgar.*

Afterwards, ad. *pas, ākhir, biyā, b'ad.*

Again, ad. *biyā, dubāra, bul heṛ, bula plā, bul wār.* (-and again) *biyā biyā, wār pa wār.*

Agape, a. *chīng, wīt, wāz.*

Age, s. *'umr, san.* (era) *daur, daurān, dahr, zamāna.* (old-) *zoṛ-tiyā, zoṛ-wālai.*

Aged, a. *zoṛ, buḍā.* (-man) *spīn-gīrai.* (-woman) *spīn-sara.*

Agent, s. *peshkār, nā-ib, wakīl, dīwān, kārdār.*

Aggravate, v.a. *pārawul, ṭaqawul, raṭal; batar k. ziyātawul.*

Aggregate, s. *ṭol, ṭol-ṭāl, jumla, wāṛah.*

Aghast, a. *hak-pak, ḥaq-ḥairān.*

Agile, a. *chālāk, gaṛandai, tak-lāstai, jalt.*

Agility, s. *chālākī, chustī, sam-dastī.*

Agitate, v.a. *tsanḍal, khwadzawul, laṛal, kkhorawul, shanawul.*

Agitated, v.n. *rapedal, khwadzedal; eshedal; kkhoredal.* a. *tsanḍalai, laṛalai.*

Agitation, s. *laṛza, rapedana; eshnā, josh.*

Ago, ad. *pakhwā, larghūne.* (long-) *lārghah, līre lārghah.*

Agony, s. *dzān-kandan; 'azāb, dard.*

Agree, v.a. *manal qabūlawul, iqrār k. rogha-, joṛa-,* etc. *k. hokai wayal,* or *k.* v.n. *pakhulā-, rāẕī-, yo zṛak-, yo jihat-.* etc. *ked.*

Agreeable, a. *khwakkh, pīrzo, khwand-nāk, kkhah, kkhāghalai, manẕūr, ghwarah.*

Agreeably, ad. *pa mūjib, pa ḥukm sara; khwand sara, khwakkhī sara.*

Agreement, s. *joṛa, rogha; sharṭ, wāda, lafẕ, qaul, qarār; neṭa, taṛa, oe.*

Agriculture, s. *kar, īwe* or *yawe, zamīn-dārī, baz-garī, zirā'at, dihqānī, charekārī.*

Agriculturist, s. *kar-kawūnkai, zamīndār, kikkht-gar, dihqān, charekār, baz-gar.*

Ague, s. *saṛa taba, saṛa lawe* or *saṛa lare, wāreza.*

Ah! in. *wā-ī! wūe! ākhkkh! wākhkkhe! hāe! wāh! wāwailā! daregha!*

Ahead, ad. *wṛānde, pa makh kkshe.*

Aid, s. *kumak, madad, pushtī, yāwarī.*

Ailing, a. *randzūr, nā-joṛ, nā-rogh, bīmār, māndah.*

Ailment, s. *randz, nā-joṛ-tiyā, nā-rogh-tiyā, bīmārī, maraẕ, māndagī, dard, āzār.*

Aim, s. *niyat, maṭlab, qaṣd, gharaẕ, irāda; naẕar; nakkha, tsalai, mukha.* v.a. *niyat-, qaṣd-,* etc. *k. naẕar taṛal* or *lagawul.*

Air, s. *bād, hawā.* (musical-) *badala, wazn, trang, sarod.* (assumed-) *nāz, nakhra, shokh.* (mien) *wajha, tsihra, ḍaul, chāl, chalan, ṣūrat.*

Alarm, *khof, yera* or *wera, tars, bāk*; *dagh-dagha, hāhū, ghāl-o-ghūl, shor-shaghab, zway-zūg, hāṛa-hūṛa, chagh-chugh, ghoghā.* v.a. *werawul, tarhawul*; *baidār-, khabar-dār-,* etc. *k. ḍamāma-, naghāra-, ḍolkai-,* etc. *wahal.*

Alarming, a. *khawf-nāk, tars-nāk, haibat-nāk.*

Alas! in. *hāe-hāe! wāe-wāe! armān dai!*

Alchemy, s. *kīmiyā.*

Alchemist, s. *kīmiyā-gar.*

Alert, a. *baidār, khabar-dār, hokkhyār*; *chā-lāk, chust, tak-lāstai.*

Alertness, s. *baidārī, hokkhyār-tiyā*; *chālākī.*

Alias, a. *nūmāndai, nūmedah, 'urf.*

Alien, a. *pradai, begānah, gharīb.*

Alight, v.n. *kūzedal, nāziledal.*

Alike, a. *gund, barābar, yo-shān, yo-rang, siyāl, makhai.*

Aliment, s. *tskkhāk-khwurāk, ṭa'ām, shūma.*

Alimentary, a. *khwurākī, da khwuṛalu.*

Alive, a. *jwandai, baidār.*

Alkali. s, *kkhora, shkār.*

All, a. *ṭol, wāṛah, amānī, kul.* (-day) *kara-ī wradz.* (-night) *kara-ī shpa.* (at-) ad. *kruṭ, la sara.*

Allay, v.a. *kamawul, saṛawul, la-agawul.*

Allegiance, s. *tāb'i-dārī.*

Allegory, s. *misl, misāl, matal.*

Alliance, s. *joṛa, para, janba, joṛikkht*; *khpul-awī, khweshī.*

Alligator, s. *nahang, nāka.*

Allot, v.a. *weshal, hisk āchawul.*

Allotment, s. *wesh, brakha, hisk, wanḍ, paṭai.*

Allow, v.a. *manal, qabūlawul*; *pregdal—pre-kkhodal*; *rawā laral*; *bakkhal, kkhandal*; *ijāzat-, ḥukm,* etc. *warkawul.*

Allowance, s. *mawājib, tankhwāh rizq.* (in weight) *daṛa, ṭūṭankai.*

Allure, v.a. *ghulawul, darghalawul, fareftah-, mayan-,* etc. *k.*

Allurement, s. *fareftagī, ghuledana, mīna.*

Alluvium, s. *lāha, khatta, chīqaṛ.*

Ally, s. *mal, malgarai, yār*; *kumakī, sharīk.*

Almighty (the), *khudāe ta'ālā, ḥaqq ta'ālā.*

Almond, s. *bādām.*

Almonry, s. *langar, langar-khāna.*

Almost, ad. *nijde, qarīb.*

Alms, s. *khairāt, zakāt, ṣadqa, sarsāya, qurbānī*; *shukrāna.* (-house) *langar-khāna.*

Aloft, p. *pās, porta, bar.*

Alone, a. *yawādzai, tsaṛah, biyal, tanhā.*

Aloud, a. *pa ūchat āwāz sara.*

Alphabet, s. *paṭa-ī.*

Already, ad. *lā, os, la wṛūnbī na, larghūne.*

Also, c. *hum, aw, wa, o.*

Altar, s. *da qurbānī dzāe* or *-dunkācha.*

Alter, v.a. *badlawul.* v.n. *āwukkhtal, bad-ledal, girzedal.*

Alteration, s. *badal, tabdīl*; *girzedina.*

Altercation, s. *jagṛa, takrār, kharkhakkha, qīl-o-qāl, steza, qaẓiya, qatārai.*

Alternative, s. *chāra*; *wāk, ikhtiyār.*

Although, c. *agarchi, siwā, la de na, ziyāt la de na, sara la de.*

Altogether, ad. *amānī, sarāsar, bilkul, ṭol-ṭāl, wāṛah, srup.* (in comp.) *tak-, ṭap-.* Ex. *tak spīn* (altogether white), *ṭap rūnd* (altogether blind).

Alum, s. *khāwra-ī, spīna khāwra.*

Always, ad. *mudām, har-kala, hamesha, tal, tar tala.*

Amalgam, s. *qala-ī.*

Amass, v.a. *gaṭal, ṭolawul*; *yo-dzāyawul.*

Amaze, v.a. *hariyānawul, rabṛawul, sar-gardān-, hekkh-, sarāsīmah-,* etc. *k.*

Ambassador, s. *āstodzai, elchī.*

Amber, s. *kah rubā.*

Ambergris, s. *'ambar.*
Ambiguous, a. *shakk·dār, shakk·man.*
Ambition, s. *himmat, zṛah, tam'a, dam*
Amble, s. *yargha.* v.n. *pa yargho tlal.*
Ambuscade, s. } *puṭ·gana-ī, pasūnai, tsawai,*
Ambush, s. } *dakhma, kamīn.*
Amen, ad. *āmīn, hase di wī.*
Amenable, a. *eman, pos, narm; da qābū lāndi; da tāwān pīrzo.*
Amend, v.n. *raghedal, joṛedal.*
Amendment, s. *kkhegaṛa, raghedana.*
Amends, s. *tāwān, badal, nāgha, būnga.*
Amiable, a. *nek, mihrbān, ḥalīm.*
Amicable, a. *nek·khwāh, khair·khwāh.*
Amidst, p. *pa mandz kkhke.*
Amiss, a. *khaṭā, ghalat; bad, nā·sāz, nā·lā·iq, nā·munāsib.*
Amity, s. *rogha, joṛa, dostī, āshtī.*
Ammoniac, s. (gum-) *ṣamāgh, oshāq.* (sal-) *noshādar.*
Ammunition, s. *da jang kālī, -sāmān, -asbāb; dārū mardak; golā bārūt.*
Amongst, p. *pa mandz kkshe* or *kkhke.*
Amorous, a. *mayan, 'āshiq.*
Amount, s. *mablagh, jam'a, jumla, kul, ṭol·ṭāl, wāṛah.*
Amour, s. *āshnā-ī, yārī, 'āshiqī, 'ishq·bāzī.*
Ample, a. *arat, plan, psorawar, sara·war; ḍer.*
Amplify, v.a. *artawul, planawul; ḍerawul, ziyātawul.*
Amputate, v.a. *prekawul* or *prekṛal.*
Amulet, s. *t'awīz, tāwītak, amel, dawā.*
Amusement, s. *tamāsha, nandāra, loba.*
Analogy, s. *miṣāl; nisbat.*
Anarchy, s. *patna, balwā, yāghī·garī.*
Anathema, s. *kkhera, l'anat* or *n'alat.*
Ancestor, s. *nīkah, plār nīkah.*
Ancestry, s. *peṛa-ī, aṣl, pusht, rag, noga.*
Anchor, s. *langar.*
Anchorite, s. *zāhid, qalandar, gokkha·nishīn.*
Ancient, a. *zoṛ, pakhwānai, kuhand.*

Anciently, ad. *pakhwā, lire larghūna-ī.*
Ancients, s. *pakhwānī 'ālam* or *-khalq.*
And, c. *aw, wa, o.*
Anecdote, s. *qiṣṣa, naql, riwāyat, khabara.*
Anew, ad. *biyā, niwī.*
Angel, s. *pirikkhtah, malak.*
Anger, s. *qahr, ghuṣṣa, ghaẓab, khapagī.*
Angle, s. *gūṭ, grut, dwa·kkhākha.*
Angry, a. *khapah, bṛoṣ.* v.n. *khapah ked.*
Anguish, s. *'aẕāb; swai.*
Angular, a. *kog, kṛīng, gūṭlai, kālkūchan.*
Animal, s. *dzanāwar, ḥaiwān.* a. *dzān·dār, gawai, wagaṛai.*
Animation, s. *jwand, jwandūn, dzān, sā; baidārī, chālākī; khush·hālī.*
Animosity, s. *kīna, dukkhnī, 'adāwat, badī, ṭaka, khuṣūmat, bughẓ.*
Ankle, s. *kkhangarai, kkhatgarai; gīṭa-ī.*
Annals, s. *tawārīkh, akhbār; shajara.*
Annex, v.a. *lagawul, taṛal, joṛawul; lāndi k. ākhistal.*
Annihilation, s. *nā·būdī, halākat, fū·fanā.*
Announce, v.a. *khabarawul, wayal; tsargand-, kkhkārah-,* etc. *k. munādī k. jār wahul.*
Annoy, v.a. *pārawul, zoral, rabṛawul khapah k.*
Annual, a. *kālanai, har kālah.*
Annually, ad. *kāl pa kāl.*
Annul, v.a. *bandawul, man'a-, mauqūf-, mansūkh-,* etc. *k.*
Annular, a. *ghūnḍ* or *ghūnḍ·man, tsarkhan, tsalai.*
Anoint, v.a. *ghwaṛawul, mugal—mukkhal.*
Anomalous, a. *be·tartīb.*
Another, a. *bul, nor, bul tsok, nor tsok, bul tsa, nor tsa, bul yo, nor yo.*
Answer, s. *dzawāb, pāsukh.* v.a. *dzawāb-, tāwān-,* etc. *warkawul.*
Ant, s. *megai, mor.* (black-) *tor megai.* (red-)

sūr megai. (white-) *oenah.* (-hill) *megatūn kkhor.*

Antagonist, s. *dukkhman, muqābil; raqīb, belak; dzawāb, makhai.*

Antecedent, a. *pakhwānai, wṛūnbanai, pekkhīn.*

Antechamber, s. *dālān, dihlīz, mandaw.*

Antelope, s. *osai, chikārah.*

Anterior, a. *wṛāndīnai, pukhwānai, wṛūnbanai, pekkhīn.*

Anticipation, s. *pesh·dastī, pesh·bandī.*

Antidote, s. *tiriyāk, 'ilāj.*

Antimony, s. *rānjih, surma, kuhl.* (-box) *rānjṛūma, ranjūnūna.* (-bodkin) *salā-ī.*

Antipathy, s. *kraka.* (to food) *sekan.*

Anvil, s. *sandān, palk; tsaṭ.*

Anxiety, s. *gham, andekkhnā, wiswās, fikr; gram.*

Anxious, a. *gham·jan, andekkh·man, wiswāsī, fikr·man; gram·nāk.*

Anus, s. *kunna, supra.* (prolapsus ani) *būra-ī.* (pruritus ani) *mawekkhe.*

Any, a. *tsok, tsa.*

Apart, a. *biyal, judā, yawādzai.*

Apartment, s. *khūna, koṭa, dzāe.*

Apathetic, a. *be·parwā, be·khabar, kāhil; laṭ, shaṭal* or *shalaṭ, sust, ṭas mas.*

Aperture, s. *sūṛa, khula, spam* or *swam.*

Apex, s. *sar, peza, pitska, tsūka.*

Apologize, v.a. *'uẕr ghokkhtal; minnat k.*

Apoplexy, s. *tsaṭ waṭ, sakta.*

Apostatize, v.a. *īmān-, dīn-,* etc. *bāelal.* v.n. *dīn-, īmān-,* etc. *na jārwatal.*

Apostle, s. *rasūl, astādzai, paighāmbar.*

Apothecary, s. *pansārai.*

Apparatus, s. *sāz, sāmān, kālī, asbāb.*

Apparel, s. *āghūstan, pokkhāk; jāme, zaṛūkī, kālī, nwarī.*

Apparent, a. *tsargand, kkhkārah, bartser, awtsār, bewrah, ẓāhir* or *jār.*

Apparently, ad. *bartseran, pa jār, ẓāhiran.*

Appeal, v.a. *ghokkhtal, minnat-, sawāl-,* etc. *k.*

Appear, v.n. *tsargandedal, kkhkārah-, bartser-,* etc. *ked.; m'alūmedal.*

Appearance, s. *ṣūrat, wajha, tsihra, rang, shakl.*

Appease, v.a. *saṛawul, pukhulā-, raẓā-,* etc. *k.*

Appetite, s. *ishtihā, lwaga, khwā, liwāl·tob, zṛah; raghbat, shahwat, mīna.*

Applaud, v.a. *stāyal, shābāshī-, āparīn-,* etc. *k.*

Applause, s. *shābāshī, stāyana.*

Apple, s. *mawra, seb.* (crab-) *māwrā.* (-of eye) *lema, kasai, bātor, torai.* (Adam's-) *stūnai.*

Applicable, a. *munāsib, sazāwār, durust, jukht, joṛ.*

Application, s. *mihnat, kokkhikkh, lagiyā·tob; 'arẓ, sawāl, darkhwāst.*

Apply, v.a. *lagawul, pore taṛal; sawāl-, 'arz-, darkhwāst-,* etc. *k.* v.n. *barābar-, jukht-,* etc. *lagedal; joṛedal, lagedal.*

Appoint, v.a. *kkhkenawul* or *kenawul, muqarrar k. wulāṛawul, wudrawul.* (-a time) *wāda k. neṭa taṛal.*

Appointment, s. *dzāe, 'uhda; lafẓ, sharṭ; wāda, neṭa, taṛa.*

Appraise, v.a. *bai'a-, qīmat-, nirkh-,* etc. *taṛal.*

Apprehend, v.a. *nīwul, giriftār k.* v.n. *pohedal, m'alūmedal; weredal, andekkhedal, wiswāsī ked.*

Apprehension, s. *nīwah, giriftārī, gīr; poha, khiyāl; khawf, andekkhnā, wiswās, wera.*

Apprentice, s. *shāgird.*

Apprize, v.a. *khabarawul, āgāh k.*

Approach, v.n. *nijde kedal.*

Approbation, s. } *pasand, khwakkh, pīrzo,*
Approval, } *raẓā, manẓūrī, qabūlī.*

Appropriate, v.a. *khpulawul, dzān ta ākhistal, rānīwul, lānde k.*

Approve, v.a. *khwakkhawul, manẓūr-, pasand-,* etc. *k., manal, qabūlawul, kkhāghal.*

Apricot, s. *zardālū, makhranai.* (preserved-) *khubānī.* (dried-) *kishta, ashāṛai, māmū-ī.*

April, s. *wīsāk* or *baisāk*. (-shower) *wasa*.
Apropos, a. *jukht, joṛ, barābar*.
Apt, a. *munāsib*; *qābil, lā-iq*; *kārī-gar*.
Aqua-fortis, s. *tez āb*.
Aquatic, a. *ābī, dariyābī*.
Aqueduct, s. *nāla, wāla, lakhtai, nāwa, pūl*; *tarnāo*; *kārez*; *tarai*.
Arable, a. *sūdīn, shudiyār*; *da kar, da karalo*.
Arbitrary, a. *zorāwar, khapsar* or *khpul-sar*.
Arbitrate, v.a. *gwākkhal* or *gwākkhedal*; *gwākkh-grandai-, jirga-, munṣifī-, inṣāf-, 'adālat-*, etc. *k*.
Arbitration, s. *gwākkh, jirga, munṣifī, m'arika*.
Arbitrator, s. *jirgatū, gwākkh-grandai, munṣif*.
Arbour, s. *chopāl, jūngaṛa, tsapar, manah, dāṛa, kūḍala, kūḍa-ī*.
Arch, s. *qubba, gunbata, ṭāq, mihrāb, kamān*.
Archer, s. *līndai, līnda-kakkh, ghash-lāstai, rasā-līndai, kamān-kakkh, tīr-andāz, bar-kakkh*.
Archery, s. *kamān-kakkhī, tīr-andāzī*.
Architect, s. *rāj, m'imār, joṛawūnkai*.
Archives, s. *daftar, shajara, tawārīkh*.
Ardent, a. *tod, garm*; *tund, tez*; *mast*.
Ardour, s. *tod-wālai, todūkha, garmī*; *tezī, tund-wālai*; *mastī, tapāk*.
Arduous, a. *sakht, grān, mushkil, drūnd*.
Area, s. *maidān, sama, zmaka*; *angawr, gholai, jawas*.
Argument, s. *bahs, hujjat, munāzara, dalīl, wāsṭa*.
Arid, a. *wuch, sawai, sokṛah, sokhtah*; (as land) *chol, lallam*; *tosand*.
Aridity, s. *wuch-wālai, khushkī, sokhtagī*.
Arise, v.n. *pātsedal, khatal, walāṛedal, porta ked.*; *wudredal*.
Aristocracy, s. *khān-khwānīn, khānawādah khalq, firqa da ghaṭo khalqo*.
Aristocrat, s. *khānawādah saṛai, da ghaṭ-*, or *da loe kor-*, etc. *saṛai*.

Arm, s. *lās*. (above elbow) *gardai-lechai, torgharai, mett*. (below elbow) *tsangal, lecha* or *letsa*. (cubit bone) *līnda-ī*.
Arm, v.a. *mlā taṛal, wasla-, drasta-*, etc. *āghostal*; *dzān sambālawul*.
Armistice, s. *rogha, joṛa*; *gwākkh*.
Armful, s. *ghūzai, gheg*.
Armour, s. (chain) *zghara, zira*. (steel) *j'aba, baktar, jaushan*. (clad in) *zghar-yālai, baktar-*, etc. *āghostai, zira-, baktar-*, etc. *pokkh*.
Armpit, s. *trakh, tkharg, aṛkh, baghal*.
Arms, s. *wasla, drasta, da jang kālī, -sāz, -asbāb*, or *-hatiyār*.
Army, s. *lakkhkar, fauj*.
Aromatic, a. *khūshbū-dār, bū-ī-nāk*.
Around, ad. *chāpera, khwā o shā, girdā gird, chār chāpera*.
Arouse, v.a. *wikkhawul, pātsawul, baidārawul*.
Arrange, v.a. *sambālawul, tartīb k., tanḍal, atsawral, lagawul, joṛawul, khundiyal*.
Arrangement, s. *tartīb, dzerma, bandobast, khundī-tob, joṛikkht*.
Array, s. *para, tsīṛa, para-bandi, ṣaff, qaṭār*; *libāṣ, āghūstan, pokkhāk, zaṛūkī*. v.a. *poslal, pokkhal, āghostawul, zaṛūkī āghostal*; *para-*, etc. *taṛal* or *wudrawul*.
Arrears, s. *bāqī, pātī*.
Arrest, v.a. *nīwul, giriftār-, gīr-, band-, qaid-*, etc. *k*.
Arrival, s. *rātag, rātah, rasedah, dakhl, āmad, rātlina, rasedana*.
Arrive, v.n. *rātlal—rāghlal, rasedal*.
Arrogance, s. *kibr, bād, maghrūrī, khāntamā, gustākhī*.
Arrogant, a. *kibr-jan, bādī, maghrūr, gharah, gustākh*.
Arrow, s. *ghashai, tīr*. (-flight) *tīr-partāb, tīr-ras*. (wing place of-) *par-khāna*. (blunt-) *toqa, tuqqa*. (barbed-) *shata-ī*. (iron tip of-) *tūbrai*. (shaft of-) *lānga*.

tila-ī. (notch of-) ghwākkhkai. (wing of-) banra, wazar.

Arsenal, s. silāḥ-khāna, jabba-khāna.

Arsenic, s. senkiyā, hartāl.

Art, s. hunar, ḥikmat, chal; kasb, pesha, ṣan'at, ustādī, pand, kārī-garī, dast-kārī.

Artery, s. rag. (of the pulse) nabẓ.

Artful, a. ḥikmatī, hunar-man; farebī, chal-bāz, chalwalai, ḥīla-bāz.

Article, s. kālai, shai, tsīz.

Artifice, s. chal, ḥīla, bāna, fareb, ṭagī, makr, palma, lamghaṛa-ī, hirā-ī.

Artificer, s. kasb-gar, kārī-gar, pesha-war.

Artificial, a. jūṭah, nāsarah, naqlī; kasbī, hunarī; joṛ kaṛai, sākhtah.

Artillery, s. top-khāna.

Artisan, s. See Artificer.

Artist, s. ustād, kārī-gar, hunar-man; naqqāsh.

Artless, a. sādah-dil, rikkhtūnai, karah.

As, c. laka, hase. (-if) laka chi, ganre.

Ascarides, s. kīkkhai, chinjai.

Ascend, v.n. khatal, porta ked., pātsedal.

Ascent, s. khātah, khatana; taraqqa-ī, lwaṛa.

Ascertain, v.a. m'alūmawul, zdah-, taḥqīq-, etc. k.

Ascetic, s. zāhid, faqīr; malang, darwesh, qalandar.

Ascribe, v.a. nisbat lagawul, pore taṛal, pore k.

Ashamed, a. sharmindah, sharmsār, pakkhe-mān. v.n. sharmedal, pakkhemān ked.

Ashes, s. īre, khākistar. (hot-) skhwakkhtan, khoglan. (cold-) saṛe īre.

Aside, ad. biyal, pa ḍaḍe, pa trats.

Ask, v.a. pukkhtedal, ghokkhtal, sawāl-, tapos-, pukkhtinna-, pursān-, etc. k.

Aslant, a. trats, tratskan, sangzan, kṛīng; shewah, sar-dzawar, sar-lwaṛ, pa rewand.

Asleep, a. ūdih, bīdih, khob-wṛai.

Aspect, s. makh, ṣūrat, tsiḥra, rang, shakl, rūe.

Asperity, s. zīg-wālai, lwāṛ-tiyā, zmokh-tiyā.

Asperse, v.a. peghor warkawul, tor pore k., tuhmat wayal, ghandal, kagal.

Aspire, v.a. tam'a-, ārzū-, umed-, etc. laral.

Ass, s. khar. (-colt) bachrai, kūṭai, kūchai. (wild-) gorkhar, ghyarah. (-load) kharwār. (-play) khar-mastī, khar-khāṛai, khar-tīza.

Assafœtida, s. hanj, hanja.

Assail, v.a. halla-, dāṛa-, tsoṭ-, yūrush, etc. k.

Assassin, s. qātil, khūnī, marg kawūnkai.

Assassinate, v.a. wajal or wajlal, meṛ k., khūn-, marg-, etc. k.

Assault, s. halla, guzār, tsoṭ, yūrush.

Assemble, v.a. ṭolawul, yo-dzāe-, jam'a-, etc. k. v.n. ṭoledal, yo-dzāe-, jam'a-, etc. ked.

Assembly, s. ṭolai, majlis, ḍala, jam'iyat; jirga.

Assent, s. raẓā, qabūl, hokai, oe.

Assert, v.a. wayal, lal or lawdal.

Assertion, s. wayai, wayana, khabara, lafẓ, lana, qaul, d'awa.

Assessment, s. kkhkewaṭ, māliya, bāj, ikhrāj.

Assiduity, s. kokshiksh or kokkhikkh, miḥnat, sa'ī, tapāk.

Assiduous, a. miḥnatī, sā'ī, kokkhikkhī.

Assign, v.a. neṭa taṛal, muqarrar k.; barāt warkawul.

Assimilation, s. gundī-tob, makhī-tob, hum-shaklī, hum-rangī.

Assist, v.a. komak-, madad-, mrasta-, pushtī-, etc. k., lās warkawul or nīwul.

Assize, s. 'adālat, maḥkama; nirkh, rai.

Associate, s. mal, malgirai, āshnāe, yār; rafīq, sharīk. v.a. malgīrī k.; yārī-, āshnā-ī-, etc. k.; kilai k.; ṣuḥbat k.; sharīkī k.

Association, s. malgīrī, malgir-tiyā, sharīkī.

Assort, v.a. chunral, atsanral, tartīb k.

Assortment, s. tartīb, chinda.

Assume, v.a. ākhistal, ikhtiyār-, d'awa-, etc.

k. (airs) *nāz-, nakhra-,* etc. *k.* v.n. *nāzedal.*

Assumption, s. *khpel-sarī, zorāwarī, bādī-tob, kibr; wāk, ikhtiyār; ākhistana.*

Assurance, s. *bāwar, i'tibār, sā-wīsā, yaqīn, tawwakul; gustākhī, be bākī.*

Assuredly, ad. *be-shakk, be shubha, albatta.*

Asthma, s. *sāh-* or *sā landī, kotāh sākī.*

Asthmatic, a. *sāh landai, kotāh sāhi.*

Astonish, v.a. *hariyānawul, rabrawul, hekkh-, sargardān-, hak-pak-,* etc. *k.*

Astonishing, a. *'ajab, 'ajībah, 'ajūbah.*

Astonishment, s. *hariyānī* or *hairānī.*

Astray, a. *wruk, gumrāh, be lār.*

Astringent, a. *qābiz, ṭīng, klak, zmokht, stagh.*

Astrologer, s. *rammāl, najūmī.*

Astrology, s. *ramal, 'ilm da nujūm.*

Asunder, ad. *biyal, judā.*

Asylum, s. *āsra, panāh, nanawātah, aman.*

At, p. *pa, pa kkhke.* (-home) *pa kor kkhke.* (-least) *hargora, lkho.* (-once) *yak lakhta, pa ṭikī.* (-last) *ākhir.* (-length) *bāre.* (-me) *rā bānde.* (-most) *pa hadda.* (-all times) *har wakht, har kala.* (-how much) *pa tsomra.* (-all) *hado, bekhī.* (-present) *pa dā sā'at* or *-wakht* or *-mahal.* (-hand) *nijde, khatsa* or *tsakha.* (-first) *wrūnbe, awwal.* (-all events) *khwāh nā khwāh.* (-times) *kala kala.* (-sight) *pa līdah, pa kātah.* (-night) *pa shpak.*

Atheism, s. *ilhād, inkār, zindīqī, gumrāhī.*

Atheist, s. *mulhid, zindīq, munkir da khudāe.*

Athlete, s. *pahlawān, kaṭah.*

Athletic, a. *pahlawān, kaṭah, zor-man.*

Atmosphere, s. *bād, hawā.*

Atom, s. *pūṭai, pītsānrai, ṭoṭai, zarra, chūr, reza, shama, dara.*

Atone, v.a. *tāwān-, badal-, 'iwaz-,* etc. *warkawul; kafārat k. dzār-, ṣadqa-, qurbān-,* etc. *k.*

Atrocious, a. *bad sakht, bashpar.*

Atrophy, s. *narai randz, kaṛedana, wuchklak-wālai.*

Attach, v.a. *lagawul, taṛal, pore k., khpulawul, pewastak-, grohedak-,* etc. *k.*

Attachment, s. *pewastūn, taṛūn, band; mīna, mayan-tob, mahabbat, grohedana.*

Attack, v.a. *halla-, hamla-, guzār-, tsoṭ-, dāṛa dopa-, kappa dapa-, yūrush-,* etc. *k.*

Attain, v.a. *mūndal, biyā-mūndal; gaṭal, paidā-, hāsil-,* etc. *k.* v.n. *rasedal, shwal.*

Attainable, a. *mūndūnai, shwūnai, da mūndalo.*

Attainment, s. *gāṭak, biyā-mūnd; mūndena, rasedana.*

Attempt, s. *qaṣd, āzmekkht, zor, kokkhikkh, was, s'aī.*

Attend, v.a. *āwredal, ghwag bāsal—yastal* or *-gdal—ikkhodal, nghwatal, ghaur-, fikr-,* etc. *k.; khabar ākhistal, khidmat-, madār-,* etc. *k.* v.n. *malgarai ked. hāzir osedal*

Attendance, s. *khidmat, nokrī.*

Attendant, s. *khidmat-gār, nokar, mulāzim; mal, malgirai; mlā-taṛ, jilaw-dār, nafar.*

Attention, s. *lihāz, fikr, s'aī, kokkhikkh, baidārī, khabar-dārī, hokkhyārī.* (to a guest) *melmastiyā, mezmānī, madār, makh.*

Attentive, a. *hokkhyār, baidār, khabar-dār.*

Attest, v.a. *gawāhī lal* or *lawdal, shāhidī warkawul* or *lal.*

Attestation, s. *gawāhī, shāhidī; gawāhī lana* or *warkawūna.*

Attire, v.a. *zarūkī-, nwarī-, pokkhāk-, libās-, jāme-,* etc. *āghostal; poslal, āghostawul.*

Attitude, s. *wajha, ḍaul, ṣūrat, shān, hāl.*

Attorney, s. *wakīl, mukhtār.*

Attract, v.a. *rākāgal—rākkhkal; grohedak-, fareftah-,* etc. *k. ghulawul; mayan k.*

Attracted, a. *rākkhkalai; grohedalai,* etc. v.n. *grohedal, mayan ked.*

Attraction, s. *rākkhkana, kakkhikkh; mīna, mayan-tob; dil-barī; dil-farebī; grohedana.*

Attribute, s. *khūe, khaṣlat, ṣifat, khāṣṣiyat.*

Audacious, a. *be bāk, nā·tars: be adab, gustākh.*

Audacity, s. *be bākī; be adabī.*

Audience, s. *majlis, dalbār; àwredūnkī, sām'iān.*

Auditor, s. *āwredūnkai, sām'i.* (of accounts) *muḥāsib, ḥisāb kawūnkai.*

Augment, v.a. *ziyātawul, ḍerawul.*

Augmentation, s. *ziyāt·wālai, ḍer·wālai; ziyātedena, ḍeredana.*

Augur, s. *pāl-* or *fāl katūnkai, fāl bīn, fālī, fāl yastūnkai.*

Augury, s. *fāl katena, fāl yastena, fāl bīnī.*

August, a. *ghaṭ, loe.* (the month) *bādro.*

Aunt, s. (father's or mother's sister) *tror.* (father's brother's wife) *tandor, tandyāra, kāka-ī.* (mother's brother's wife) *māma-ī.*

Auspicious, a. *iqbāl·man, bakhtawar, nek·bakht, mubārak.*

Austere, a. *sakht, zīg; trīw, zmokht; sūṭ. sūṭ·būṭ.*

Authentic, a. *rikkhtiyā, rikkhtīnai, taḥqīq.*

Author, s. *muṣannif, kitāb kkhkawūnkai; joṛawūnkai, kawūnkai, wayūnkai,* etc.

Authority, s. *wāk, ikhtiyār, was; maqdūr, zor, qudrat, ḥukūmat; ḥukm, farmān, sanad.*

Authorize, v.a. *ḥukm-, wāk-, ikhtiyār-,* etc. *warkawul.*

Autumn, s. *manai, khizān, kharīf.*

Auxiliary, a. *komakī, madad·gār, janba·dār.*

Avail, v.a. *fā-ida-, naf'a-,* etc. *rasawul.* v.n. *chaledal, pakār ked.* or *-rātlal.*

Avarice, s. *ḥirṣ, tam'a, bakhīlī.*

Avaricious, a. *bakhīl, ḥirṣ·nāk, ḥāriṣ, tām'i.*

Avaunt, in. *lire sha! biyarta sha!*

Avenge, v.a. *badal-, qiṣāṣ-, tāwān-,* etc. *ākhistal.*

Averse, a. *nā·rāẓ, mukhālif, khwā bad.*

Aversion, s. *kraka, chinjedana, kagana, ghandana.*

Avert, v.a. *man'a-, daf'a-,* etc. *k., girzawul, jārbāsal,—jāryastal.*

Avidity, s. *tam'a, liwāl·tob, shauq, raghbat.*

Avocation, s. *kār, kasb, pesha.*

Avoid, v.a. *parhez k., dzān sātal.*

Await, v.n. *muntaẓir osedal, wudredal, pātedal.*

Awake, a. *wīkkh, baidār.* v.n. *wīkkhedal, pātsedal, baidār ked.*

Aware, a. *khabar, āgāh, wāqif; zdah.*

Away, ad. *lire.* in. *lire sha, biyarta sha.*

Awe, s. *khof, wera* or *yera, tars, bāk, haibat, tor.*

Awful, a. *khawf-, tars-, sahm-,* etc. *-nāk,* etc.

Awhile, ad. *drang sā'at, la-ag sā'at.*

Awkward, a. *kāwāk; lwāṛ.*

Awl, s. *nīra* or *rīna.*

Awning, s. *chatrai, siwrai, shāmiyāna, sāewān.*

Awry, ad. *pa trats, krīng prīng, kog wog.*

Axe, s. *tabar.* (battle-) *tabar·zīn, gurz.*

Axis, s. *quṭb, ghashai.*

Axle, s. *laṭ, tīrak, tsākkhai.*

Aye, ad. *ho, āre, kkhah.*

Azure, a. *shīn.*

B.

Babble, v.a. *bak bak-, baṛ baṛ-,* etc. *k.* v.n. *ṭaredal.*

Babbler, s. *bak bakai, baṛ baṛai, ūnai, ṭarai.*

Babe, s. *bachai, tankai, tandai, m'aṣūm* or *māshūm, tai rawai, pa-ī rawdūnkai, wṛūkai.*

Bachelor, s. *lawand, tsaṛah, mujarrad.*

Back, s. *shā.* ad. *biyarta, biyā, wrusto, pastana, pas.* (behind one's-) *pase shā.*

Back, v.n. (go-) *pastana-, wrusto-, biyarta-,* etc. *ked., stūnedal* or *stanedal.* v.a. (aid) *panāh-, komak-, pushtī-,* etc. *-warkawul, ḍaḍa lagawul.*

Backbite, v.a. *chughlī-, ghībat-, ghammāzī-,* etc. *k.*

Backbiter, s. *chughlkhor, ghibat karūnkai, marās, ghammāz.*

Backbone, s. *mlā tīr, shamdza-ī.*

Backdoor, s. *da chane war, da kor da shā war.*

Backside, s. *kunātai, kunnā-ghara, dumbāla; wrustai, shā.*

Backward, a. *nā-rāz, laṭ, ṭas mas, nā-rāst; sust, pasīnah.* ad. *wrusto, pastana, biyarta.*

Backwards, ad. *pa biyarta, wrusto.* a. *naskor, arawulai, apūṭak.*

Bad, a. *bad, nā-kārah, kharāb, nā-sarah.*

Badge, s. *nakkha* or *nakhkkha, nikkhān, togh, 'alāmat.*

Badger, s. *tor-lamai, gor-kakkh*

Badly, ad. *va bad shān sara.*

Badness, s. *kharābī, badī, 'aib.*

Baffle, v.a. *rabṛawul, ghulawul, wār khaṭā k., be fā-ida-, 'abas-,* etc. *k.*

Bag, s. *taila-ī, dzola-ī.* (clothes-) *katsoṛa, būtskha, buqcha.* (money-) *hamiyānī, badra.* (letter-) *kharīta.* (grain-) *tsaṭa, ghūndai.* (tent-) *gharāra.* (trinket-) *butskhakai.* (leather-) *bana-ī, gūḍai.* (ammunition-) *kīsa, kisbat.* (leather water-) *mashk, chāgul.* (leather air-) *shināz, zik, jai.* (baggage-) *malaw.*

Baggage, s. *asbāb, rakht, sāmān, partal.*

Bail, s. *ẓāminī, ẓamānat.* (the person) *ẓāmin.* (to give-) *ẓamānat-, ẓāmin warkawul.* (to take-) *ẓamānat-, ẓāmin ākhistal.*

Bailiff, s. *muḥaṣṣil, patwārī, kārdār, sazawal.*

Bait, v.a. *tsar-, wākkhah-, khwāṛah-,* etc. *warkawul; bāolī warkawul; nahārai-, tāmba* or *ta'ām-, khwurāk-,* etc. *warkawul.*

Bake, v.a. *pa tanūr kkhke pakhawul; kaṛawul, wrītawul.*

Baker, s. *nānwā-ī, nān paz.*

Balance, s. *tala, tarāzū.* (the beam) *ḍānḍa-ī.* (the scale) *pela.* (the tongue) *jiba.* (of an account) *bāqī.* v.a. *talal, jokal; bāqī pūrah k., ḥisāb barābar k.*

Balcony, s. *bālā-khāna.*

Bald, a. (from age) *kal.* (from disease) *ganjai, sudar, lendah, chatrai, pa-akhai.*

Bale, s. *anḍai, panḍ, peṭai.* (of grass) *geḍai.* v.a. *sandzal, toyawul, lawastal.*

Baleful, a. *bad, muẓirr, tāwānī, ziyānī.*

Balk, v.a. *wār khaṭā k., 'abas k., wrānawul.*

Ball, s. *vanḍos, panḍoskai, manḍos; gola-ī, mardakai; ghunḍūrai; nāch, gaḍedena.*

Ballad, s. *sandara, lanḍa-ī, chār-bait, ghazal, ṭapa, miṣr'a, stāyana.*

Ballast, s. *langar*

Ballot, v.a. *qur'a-, kish-, pecha-,* etc. *āchawul.*

Balustrade, s. *kangura.*

Bamboo, s. *bans.*

Band, s. *paṛk, ṭolai, ṭolgai, ghol, tamba; firqa, janba; khel, cham.*

Bandage, s. *paṭa-ī, band, taṛūnai.* (for the head) *sar-pechak, sar-taṛūnai, tsapūṭkai, sar-basta.* (for clothes) *tanra-ī.* (a child's-) *seznī.*

Bandbox, s. *tawang.*

Banditti, s. *ghlah, shūk-mār, dāṛ, tāṛ, qaẓāk.*

Bandy, v.a. *radd badal k., qīl-o-qāl k., chaghawul.* a. *kog.* (-legged) *kage kkhpe.*

Bane, s. *zahr; nuqṣān, tāwān, ziyān.*

Baneful, a. *zahr-dār; nuqṣānī, muẓirr, moẓī,* etc.

Bang, v.a. *ṭakawul, wahal, ṭak-, ḍaz-, ṭas-,* etc. *wahal.*

Bangle, s. *bāhū, wakkhai, chūrā, karai, ma-aṭkai.*

Banish, v.a. *sharal, be waṭan-, jilā waṭan-,* etc. *k.*

Bank, s. *pūla, wand, band.* (river-) *ghāṛa.* (high-) *kamar.* (opposite-) *pore ghāṛa.* (-of clouds) *gūp, kha-aṭ.* (for money) *khizāna, koṭa-ī.*

Banker, s. *ṣarrāf, khizānchī, seṭ.*

Bankrupt, s. *nā-dār, dewāliyā, tabāh, khwār.*

Banner, s. *nakkha, janḍa, bairaq, tūgh.*

Bannock, s. (plain) *tsapaṭa-ī, kakoṛa.* (oiled-) *weshala.* (buttered-) *parāṭa, lūcha.* (sweet-) *amrasa.*

Banquet, s. *ẕiyāfat, melmastiyā, mihmānī.*

Banter, v.a. *ṭoqa-, washta-, maskhara-,* etc. *k.*

Bar, s. (cross-) *hūl.* (upright-) *aṛam, aṛamai.* v.a. *bandawul, hūl-, aṛam-,* etc. *lagawul.*

Barbarian, s. *dzangalī, jāhil, baṇr-māṇrū.*

Barbarity, s. *be raḥmī, dzangalī-tob, jāhil-tob.*

Barbarous, a. *be raḥm; jāhil, dzaban, lwāṛ.*

Barbed, a. *shata-ī* or *biyak larūnkai.*

Barber, s. *nā-ī, gulāba-ī.*

Barberry, s. *korai, karwara, zirishk.*

Bard, s. *mīrāṣī, ḍum, shā'ir.*

Bare, a. *barbanḍ* or *barmanḍ, lūts; ta-ash, khālī.* (-faced) *be makh, be ḥayā, be sharm, be parda.* (-footed) *abl, pkkhe-able.* (-headed) *sar-tor.* (-backed) *lūts, barbanḍ.*

Barley, ad. *surup, ta-ash, khālī, faqaṭ, ṣirf.*

Bargain, s. *sharṭ, w'ada, iqrār, lafẓ, neṭa, taṛa, 'ahd.* v.a. *sharṭ-,* etc. *k.* or *taṛal, saudā-, bai'a-,* etc. *k., chana wahal.*

Barge, s. *beṛa-ī, kishta-ī.* (-pole) *singāwaṇr.*

Bark, s. (tree-) *paṭ, poṭ, poṭakh, postakai, khwar.* (dog's-) *ghap, ghapā, ghāp.* v.a. *poṭ-,* etc. *kāgal—kkhkal* or *-bāsal—yastal; ghapal, ghap wahal.* v.n. *ghapedal.*

Barley, s. *orbūshe.* (a grain of-) *orbūsha.* (husk of-) *sharhata.* (-bread) *orbūshīna.* (-gruel) *oghra.* (-grits) *dal, bata.*

Barm, s. *khamīra, toma* or *tomna, māya.*

Barn, s. *khirman, dīrmand, ambār-khāna.*

Barrack, s. *spāhī-khāna, urdū, ḍal.*

Barrel, s. *nal, nalī, shpela-ī.* (-bellied) *gagar, geḍa-war, kheṭa-war.*

Barren, a. (animal or tree) *shanḍa.* (land) *ḍāg, ūjāṛ, shāṛ.* (saline) *kkhoran.* (sandy) *shīglan, shigloṛa-ī.*

Barrenness, s. *shanḍ-wālai, shanḍ-tob.*

Barricade, s. *sangar, bāṛa, kūtsa-bandī.*

Barrier, s. *pūla, brīd* or *brīt, ḥadd.*

Barter, s. *adal-badal, plor, chana, saudā, lāgī, pīral-ploral, rākṛah-warkṛah.* v.a. *adal-badal-, plor-,* etc. *k., chana wahul.*

Base, a. *palīt, murdār, dūn, ḥarāmī, bad-ẕāt, kam-aṣl, be nog.* (-coin) *nā-sarah, jūṭah.*

Base, Basis, s. *āra, wekh, kūnsaṭ, būnsaṭ bunyād, pāya, pkkha, sar.*

Baseness, s. *dūnī, ḥarāmī-tob, bad-ẕātī,* etc.

Bashful, a. *sharm-nāk, ḥayā-nāk* or *ḥayā-dār, ghairat-nāk* or *ghairat-man.*

Basin, s. (of wood) *kanḍai* or *kaṇrai, būgh.* (of pottery) *kanḍol, kanḍolai.* (kneading-) *kkhānak.* (beggar's-) *kachkol.* (wash-hand-) *tasht, lagan.* (dog's-) *chaṭ.*

Bask, v.a. *pitāo-, nwar-, or-,* etc. *ta kkhke-nāstal.*

Basket, s. *ṭokra-ī.* (flat-) *shkarai* or *shkorai* or *shker, kkhkarai.* (fruit-) *kawāra, kāra.* (winnowing-) *chaj, tsap.* (safe-) *tsakai.* (clothes-) *tawang.* (bread-) *sawada.* (withy-) *keṛa.*

Bass, a. *bog, ḍaḍ.*

Bastard, s. *ḥarāmī, ḥarām-zādah, khaṭā-zowulai.*

Baste, v.a. *wahal, ṭakawul, kūṭal, atsaṇral.* (sew) *ganḍal, pezal, bezal.*

Bastion, s. *bruj, morcha, damdama.*

Bat, s. *kkhāperak, shaparak.*

Batch, s. *gundī; nughd, ẕāt.*

Bath, s. (cold-) *ghusl.* (vapour-) *ḥammām.*

Bathe, v.a. *ghusl k., lanbal.* v.n. *lanbedal.*

Baton, s. *amsā, lawaṛ, koṭak.*

Battalion, s. *palṭan.*

Batter, v.a. *wahal, ṭakawul, kūṭal, naṛawul, daṛ-daṛ-, chūr-chūr-, kanḍ-kapar-,* etc. *k.*

Battery, s. *morcha, damdama.*

Battle, s. *jang.* (-array) *tsīṛa, para-basta, ṣaff-taṛak.*

Battlement, s. *kangura.*

Bawl, v.a. *naṛal, chighawul, nāre-, chighe-,* etc. *wahul.*

Bay, a. *sūr*. (at-) *jah*. (to stand at-) *jah ked*.
Bayonet, s. *sikhcha, sangīn*.
Be, v.n. *kedal, shwal, osedal*.
Beach, s. *ghāra*.
Beacon, s. *nakkha, nikkhān, munāra, tsalai*.
Bead, s. (stone) *mara-ī*. (glass) *mashkaura*. (jet) *shaba*.
Beak, s. *makkhūka, tsūka, shūka*.
Beam, s. *bensh, lakara, lakarai, patera, barga*.
Bean, s. *lobiyā*.
Bear, s. *yag, melū, khirs*.
Bear, v.a. *wral, rāwral; zghamal, petsal*. v.n. *sahal, sahedal*. (-young) *zegedal, zowul*.
Beard, s. *gīra, rīsh*. (of grasses) *banbal, lasha, shora*. (grey-) *spīn·gīrai*. (-less) *chat*.
Bearer, s. *wrūnkai; zghamūnkai*, etc.
Beast, s. *dzanāwar, hairān*. (wild-) *wahsh*. (-of prey) *dad*. (-of burthen) *bār·kakkh, sutūr*. (quadruped) *tsārwai, dāba*.
Beastliness, s. *gandagī, palītī, murdārī; hairān·tob, dangar·tob*.
Beastly, a. *gandah, palīt, murdār*.
Beat, v.a. *wahal, takawul, kūtal; pa-ar-, māt-, lāndi-*, etc. *k*., *barai mūndal* or *gatal*.
Beaten, a. *wahalai, takawulai, kūtalai; pa-ar, māt*.
Beater, s. *wahūnkai*, etc.; *pa-ar-*, etc. *kawūnkai, wa-ar, barai mūndūnkai* or *gatūnkai*.
Beating, s. *wahal, wahana, kūtana, kūtal, takawul, takawūna; pa-ar kawūna*, etc.
Beau, s. *tatai, tainchī, bānkiyā, daulī*.
Beautiful, a. *kkhāyastah, kkhkulai, khūb sūrat, pa-ī-* or *pej·makhai*.
Beautify, v.a. *kkhāyastah k., kkhāyast warkawul, andzorawul*. (-oneself) *singār-, kkhewa-*, etc. *k*.
Beauty, s. *kkhāyast, kkhāyast·wālai, jorūb, krah·wrah, pa-ī makh·tob*.

Because, c. *dzaka, ska, la de na, la kubla*.
Beckon, v.a. *ishārat k., lās tsandal*.
Become, v.n. *shwal, kedal, osedal; pīrzo-, lā-iq-, munāsib-*, etc. *ked*.
Bed, s. *bechānra*. (-stead) *kat, pālang, manj*. (-coverlet) *brastan, lihāf*. (-mattress) *tolā-ī, nihālī, taltak*. (-cushion) *bālikkhī, bālin, bālikkhtak*. (-sheet) *tsādar, pālang pokkh*. (-time) *mākhustan* or *māskhutan*. (-ridden) a. *zmol, zam·zambolai* or *zam·zmolai*.
Bee, s. *macha-ī*. (honey-) *ghlauza* or *lauza, mach·machai*. (black-) *baurā*. (-hive) *gabīna, garbīnai, kkhor*.
Beet, s. *chughandar* or *chuqandar*.
Beetle, s. *gūngat, ghozai, ghozakarkai, khaatak, chānrī*. (mallet) *dabalai, baghdar, tsobārai*.
Befall, v.n. *nāziledal, prewatal, rasedal, wāq'i ked*.
Before, p. *pakhwā, wrūnbe, wrānde, qabl, dwrānde, makh kkhke*.
Beforehand, ad. *awwal, wrūnbe, peshtar*.
Beg, v.a. *gadā-ī k., khair ghokkhtal; minnat-, sawāl-*, etc. *k*.
Beget, v.a. *zegawul, zowul, blārbawul, dakawul, paidā k., shigāra k*.
Beggar, s. *gadāe, paqīr, muflis, kangāl, nestman, khwār*.
Beggary, s. *gadā-ī, gadā·tob, paqīrī, khwārī*.
Begin, v.a. *shurū'-, ibtidā-, darak-*, etc. *k*.
Beginner, s. *shurū' kawūnkai, mubtadī*.
Begone, in. *dza! lire sha! wruk sha! chikhe!*
Behalf, s. *wāsita, khātir, dapāra, pa haqq*.
Behave, v.a. *sulūk k*. v.n. *chaledal, ramedal*.
Behaviour, s. *chāl, chalan, tarīqa, sulūk*.
Behind, p. *wrusto, dumbāl, pastana, pa shā*.
Behold, in. *gora! wu·gora! wu wina!*
Behove, v.n. *lāzim-, wājib-, munāsib-*, etc. *ked*.
Belch, s. *agramai, argai, dakār, tegh*. v.a. *agramai-*, etc. *bāsal—yastal* or *-k*.
Belief, s. *bāwar, i'tibār; īmān, dīn*.

Believe, v.a. *bāwar-*, etc. *k.* or *laral*; *īmān-*, etc. *rāwṛal.*
Believer, s. *bāwar kawūnkai*; *īmān-dār*, *mūmin*, *m'utaqid.*
Bell, s. *zangola*, *zang*, *jaras*, *janganrari*, *julājil.*
Belle, s. *nādira*, *nāznīna*, *pa-ī makha.*
Bellow, v.a. *naṛal*, *naṛā-*, *nāre-*, etc. *wahal.* v.n. *ghuṛunbedal*, *ghurchedal.*
Bellows, s. *bana-ī*, *pūgar.*
Belly, s. *geḍa*, *kheṭa*; *nas.* (-ache) *kānga.* (-fretting) *qur-qurai.*
Belong, v.n. *lagedal*, *nisbat ked.*, *kedal.*
Beloved, a. *maḥbūb*, *mayan.*
Below, ad. *kkhkata*, *kkhkiya*, *lānde*, *kūz*, *lar.*
Belt, s. *tasma*, *rog*, *band.* (waist-) *kamar-kīsa.* (sword-) *paṭa.* (shoulder-, ornamental) *banda-ī.*
Bench, s. *takhta*, *dunkācha.*
Bend, v.a. *ṭīṭawul*, *kagawul.* v.n. *ṭīṭedal*, *kagedal*, *kālkūch-*, *kaglech-*, etc. *ked.*
Beneath, p. *lānde*, *dalānde*, *kkshata*, *kkshiya.*
Benediction, s. *du'ā*, *du'ā da khair*, *tabarruk.*
Benefactor, s. *da n'imatūno bakkhūnkai*, *kkhegaṛa kawūnkai*, *khairāt warkawūnkai.*
Beneficent, a. *bakkhana kawūnkai*, *faiẓ-*, or *-n'imat rasawūnkai.*
Beneficial, a. *kkhah*, *fā-ida-*, *sūd-*, *naf'a-*, etc. *-man.*
Benefit, s. *kkhegaṛa*, *gaṭa*, *sūd*, *bihbūd*, *fā-ida.*
Benevolent, s. *sakhī*, *sakhāwatī*, *khairātī*, *mihrbān.*
Bent, a. *ṭīṭ*, *kog.*
Benumbed, a. *qaṛqechan*, *maṛghechan*, *ūdah.*
Bequeath, v.a. *hiba-*, *mīrāt-*, etc. *k.*
Bequest, s. *mīrāṡ* or *mīrāt*, *hiba*, *tarka.*
Bereave, v.a. *ākhistal*, *shūkawul*, *lūṭs k.*
Berry, s. *dāna.*
Beseech, v.a. *minnat-*, *d'uā-*, etc. *k.*
Beside, ad. *tsakha* or *khatsa*, *nizhde*, *pa tsang*, *pa aṛakh*, *pa ḍaḍe.*
Besides, p. *siwā*, *ziyāt*, *'alāwa*, *nor.*
Besiege, v.a. *ḥiṣārawul* or *īsārawul*, *ger k.*
Bespeak, v.a. *numaṛ k.*
Best, a. *ghwarah*, *ḍer kkhah*, *la ṭolo na kkhak.*
Bestow, v.a. *bakkhal*, *warkawul*, *kkhandal.*
Bet, v.a. *sharṭ taṛal.*
Betimes, ad. *wakhtī.*
Betray, v.a. *ghulawul*, *ṭagī-*, *pudūlī-*, etc. *k.*, *parda porta k.*, *khwāla wayal.*
Betroth, v.a. *koẑdan k.*
Betrothal, s. *koẑdan*, *koẑdana*, *koẑda.*
Betrothed, a. (-youth) *changhol.* (-maid) *changhala.*
Better, a. *ghwarah*, *awlātar*, *bihtar.*
Between, ad. *pa mandz* (or *myandz*) *kkshe.*
Beverage, s. *sharbat*, *tskkhāk.*
Bevy, s. *sail*, *ghol*; *paṛk*, *ṭolai*; *khel.*
Bewail, v.a. *wāwailā-*, *ẓārī-*, *faryād-*, etc. *k.* (-the dead) *wīr k.*, *wainā wayal.*
Beware, v.n. *pohedal*, *khabar-dār-*, *hokkhyār-*, *baidār-*, *āgāh-*, etc. *osedal* or *ked.* v.a. *parhez-*, *pahm-*, etc. *k.*
Bewilder, v.a. *ḥariyānawul*, *rabṛawul*, *sargardānawul*, *hekkh-*, *hak-pak-*, *hak-ḥairān-*, etc. *k.*
Bewitch, v.a. *naẓar lagawul*, *siwrai āchawul*, *koḍ k.*, *ghulawul*, *fareftah-*, *mayan-*, etc. *k.*
Beyond, p. *pore*, *lire*, *hagha khwā*, *pore ghāṛa*, *bāhar*, *warā* or *warāya.*
Bias, s. *khwā*, *mīna*, *zṛeh*, *mrasta*, *rujū'a.* v.a. *khwā girzawul*, *lamsawul*, *ma-il-*, *ma-ilān-*, *grohedah*, etc. *k.*
Bible, s. *kitāb.* (Pentateuch) *tauret.* (Psalms) *zabūr.* (Gospels) *anjīl.* (Muhammad's) *qurān*, *furqān.*
Bicker, v.a. *chighawul*, *raṭal*, *traṭal*, *dāṛal*, *qaẓiya-*, *jagṛa-*, etc. *k.*
Bier, s. *tābūt*, *da muṛī takhta.*
Biestings, s. *wargah.*
Big, s. *loe*, *ghaṭ*, *kaṭah*, *star.*
Bile, s. *trīkhai*, *zahra*, *ṣafrā.*

Bilious, a. *ṣafrā-ī.*

Bill, s. (bird's) *makkhūka.* (account) *ḥisāb.* (note) *ḥujjat, tamassuk.* (-of exchange) *hunḍa-ī.* (-of sale) *qibāla, bai'a·nāma.*

Bind, v.a. *taṛal, lagawul, joṛawul.* (a book) *juz·* or *jild·bandī k.*

Binder, s. *taṛūnkai, taṛūnai.* (in comp.) *-band.*

Binding, s. *taṛūn, wandanai.* (book-) *jild·bandī.*

Biography, s. *tazkira, riwāyat.*

Bird, s. *marghah, marghai.* (-catcher) *mashkār, kkhkārī.* (-lime) *slekkh.* (-net) *dām, ḍaba-ī, jāl, dwa·gaza.* (-noose) *ghunḍārai, lwīna, lūma, lūmaka.* (-springe) *laṭ, talaka, kuṛka-ī.* (-trap) *paṛka, honrā.*

Birth, s. *zowah, zowūna, zegedeh, zegedina, tawallud, paidā-ish.* (-place) *waṭan, da paidā-ikkht dzāe.* (-day) *da tawallud wradz.* (-right) *ḥaqq da mashari.*

Biscuit, s. *kak, kakoṛa.* (sweet-) *amrasa.*

Bit, s. *ṭoṭa, ṭoṭai, khatsosa.* (of food) *nwaṛa-ī, ṭūk.* (of a horse) *mlūna, qā-iza, dahana.*

Bitch, s. *spa-ī.* (-in heat) *spayama* or *spa-ema.*

Bite, v.a. *chīchal, khwuṛal, dāṛal, chak lagawul.*

Bitter, a. *trīkh, talkh.*

Bittern, s. *baglai, kablai.*

Bitterness, s. *trīkh·wālai, trīkh·tob, trīkh·tiyā.*

Bitumen, s. *qafr ul yahūd.*

Black, a. *tor.* (jet-) *tek tor.*

Blacken, v.a. *torawul.* v.n. *toredal.*

Blackguard, s. *charlanḍ, chaṭ, chulur, bad·m'ash, laṛalai, ḥarāmī, lūch lawanḍ, laṛo tsaṭo, kachar.*

Blackish, a. *tor·shān.*

Blackmail, s. *bunga.*

Blacksmith, s. *lohār, āhangar.*

Bladder, s. *pūkanra-ī.*

Blade, s. *palka, tegh.* (of grass) *khalai.* (of scissors) *para, pal.* (of plough) *pāla, saspāra.*

Blame, s. *malāmat, 'aib, taqṣīr, quṣūr, wabāl, gunāh.* v.a. *malāmatawul, raṭal, traṭal.*

Blameable, a. *malāmatī, taqṣīrī, gunah·gār.*

Blameless, a. *be gunāh, be quṣūr, be malāmat.*

Blamelessly, ad. *nā·ḥaqq, be sabab, be gunāh,* etc.

Bland, a. *post, narm, khog, mulā-im.*

Blandishment, s. *nāz, nakhra, karashma, makez; kkhewa, singār, ḍaul.*

Blank, a. *ta·ash* or *t·ish, khālī, spīn, sūdah.*

Blanket, s. *shaṛa-ī, krāsta.*

Blaspheme, v.a. *kufr wayal.*

Blast, s. (breath) *pūk, pūkai.* (wind) *sila-ī, jakaṛ, chapa.* (sound) *bāng, āwāz, ghag.*

Blast, v.a. *ālwūzawul, fanā k., barbādawul, wrukawul; kkhere k.*

Blaze, s. *lūkhaṛa, lanba, bāmbaṛra, ḍūnḍa-ī, baṛānḍa, ghaṛānḍa.* v.a. *lūkhaṛa-,* etc. *k.*

Bleach, v.a. *spīnawul, spetsal.*

Bleak, a. *soṛ, yakh.*

Blear, a. *objan, dund, khīran, lechan, zawlan.*

Bleat, v.a. *bregan-, me me-,* etc. *k.* v.n. *bāngedal.*

Bleed, v.n. *wīnedal, wīne bahedal.* v.a. *rag wahal, wīne bāsal—yāstal.*

Blemish, s. *'aib, quṣūr, dāgh, tor, rakhna.*

Bless, v.a. *d'uā-, tabarruk-,* etc. *k., barakat warkawul.*

Blessing, s. *d'uā, da khair, barakat, tabarruk.*

Blight, s. *torka-ī, surkha-ī.*

Blind, a. *ṛūnd.* (stone-) *ṭap ṛūnd.* (night-) *shamkor* or *shokor.* v.a. *ṛandawul, nā·bīnā k.* v.n. *ṛandedal.*

Blindfold, v.a. *starge puṭawul.* (-cattle) *kholai taṛal.* (-hawks) *ṭopa-ī pasarawul.*

Blindness, s. *ṛūnd·wālai, ṛund·tiyā.* (night-) *shamkor·tiyā.*

Blink, v.a. *starge wahal, dzezme rapawul, dzanbal* or *dzamal.*

Blister, s. *tanrāka, pūla-ī, maṭāka.*

Blithe, a. *kkhād, khūsh·dil, khandā·rūe.*

Bloat, v.a. *paṛsawul.* v.n. *paṛsedal.*

Block, s. *tsaṭ, mūnḍ, garga, kunda.*

Blockade, v.a. *ḥiṣārawul* or *ïsārawul, bandawul.*

Blockhead, s. *gedī-khar, khar, pūhaṛ, dūzai.*

Blood, s. *wīne.* (-shed) *khūn.* (breed) *ẕāt, rag, aṣl, nog.* (-stained) *pa wino habatah.*

Bloom, v.n. *ṭūkedal, zarghūnedal, ghwaredal.*

Blossom, s. *ghūṭa-ī, gul.* v.n. *khwaredal, spaṛedal, spaṛdai ked., ghwaredal,* etc.

Blot, s. *laka, ṭakai, dāgh; 'aib, nāmūs, tor.*

Blow, s. *guzār.* (of fist) *gasa, ḍab, ṣūk, ṭas.* (of breath) *pūk, pūkai.* (of wind) *sīla-ī.*

Blow, v.a. (a fire) *pūkal, pūk wahul.* (as wind) v.n. *ālwatal, chaledal.* (as a flower) *ṭūkedal, ghwaredal, spaṛedal, spaṛdai ked.* (a bugle) v.a. *ghagawul.* (-out) *muṛ-, soṛ-,* etc. *k.* (-down) *ringaṛai k.*

Bludgeon, s. *koṭak, lawaṛ, ḍāng.*

Blue, a. *shīn-, nīl-, āsmānī-,* etc. *-rang.*

Blunder, s. *khaṭā.* v.a. *khaṭā k.*

Blunderbuss, s. *gharābīn, ṣaff-shikan.*

Blunt, a. *pa-ats* or *p-uts.* (-ness) s. *pa-ats-wālai.*

Blur, s. *dāgh, 'aib, tor, laka, ṭakai.*

Blurt, v.a. *parda prānatal, khwāla wayal.*

Blush, v.n. *sharmedal.*

Bluster, v.a. *lāp wahul, ṭar-ṭar k., dam wahal.*

Blusterer, s. *lāpak, ṭarai, dūzak, ḍaz.*

Boar, s. *sarkūzai, kharbishoe, khūg.* (wild-) *soḍar, matah.*

Board, s. *takhta.* (writing-) *lauḥ, paṭa-ī.* (food) *tskkhāk khwurāk.*

Boast, v.a. *lāp-, lāpa-, dam-,* etc. *wahal* or *k.*

Boasting, s. *lāpa, lāp shāp, dam.*

Boat, s. *beṛa-ī, kishta-ī.* (bridge of-) *pul, jisr.* (-man) *mānrgai, mahaurak, mallāḥ.*

Bodkin, s. *salā-ī, sīkhcha, stan, dūk.*

Body, s. *tan, jussa, ṣūrat, wujūd, jism.* (in comp.) *andām.* (of men, etc.) *ṭolai, ṭolgai, ghol, paṛk, khel, tanba, firqa.*

Bog, s. *bokkht, bokkhtenna, yala, taramna, palanda.*

Boil, v.a. *eshawul* or *yashawul, khūṭ k.* v.n. *eshedal* or *yashedal, khūṭ ked.*

Boil, s. *dāna, nanaka-ī.* (blackhead-) *tora-dāna.* (acne-) *dzwānaka.* (heat-) *garmaka.* (whitlow) *kharai, shīnai.* (carbuncle) *kkhandza.* (abscess) *kkhalūna, lūna*

Boiler, s. *khum, kaṛahai, deg, dechka.*

Boiling, s. *eshnā, khūṭkai; yashānd* or *eshānd.*

Boisterous, a. *tund, tez, mast.*

Bold, a. *maṛanai, zṛeh-war, tūrzan, bahādur, dilāwar, be bāk; gustākh, chūnkai, wītak.*

Boldness, s. *maṛāna, zṛah-war-tob, tūrzan-tob, bahādurī, maṛanī-tob, be bākī; gustākhī, shokhī, chūnkī-tob, be makh-tob, be ḥayā-tob.*

Bolster, s. *bālakkht, bālīn, takya.*

Bolt, s. *hūl, mekhchū, bala-ī, jaranda-ī, aṛamai.*

Bond, s. *band, dzolana, dzel, kaṛa-ī, zandzīr.* (note) *ḥujjat, tamassuk.* (union) *pewand, band, jorikkht.* (blood) *ragai, khpulawī, rishta, wābastagī.* (compact) *wāda, taṛūn, taṛa, bandanr, lafẓ.*

Bondage, s. *qaid, band, bandī-tob; bandagī, ghulāmī, mra-e-tob.*

Bondmaid, s. *wīndza, kanīza, barda.*

Bondman, s. *mra-e, ghulām.*

Bondsman, s. *ẓāmin, yarghamāl* or *yarghamal.*

Bone, s. *haḍ, haḍūkai.*

Bonfire, s. *dūna, alāo, ḍānḍa-ī.*

Bonny, a. *kkhāyastah, kkhkulai, pa-ī-makhai* or *pej-makhai, pa-ī-makh.*

Bony, a. *haḍawar.*

Booby, s. *sādah-dil, pūhaṛ, gedī-khar, kam-'aql.*

Book, s. *kitāb.* (bound-) *jild.* (unbound-) *juz.* (-stand) *rahel.* (in comp.) *-nāma.* (-binding) *juz-* or *jild-bandī.* (-boards) *kānta-ī.* (-binder) *jild-gar, ṣaḥḥāf.*

Boon, s. ghanīmat, n'imat, barakat, bakht; in'ām, bakhkhshikhsh, bakkhana. a. khūsh-dil, kkhād, khandā-rūe, khūsh-ṭab'a.

Boor, s. ganwār, ghunḍāyah, lnāṛ, pūhaṛ, dzaban.

Boot, s. moza, chakma. (for women) jasta. (to-) ad. pa gaṭe, pa weṛiyā, pa ziyāt, junga.

Booth, s. tsapar, kūḍala, mana, jūngaṛa.

Bootless, a. 'abas, be fā-ida, nīma-khwā, nīmgaṛai.

Booty, s. lūṭ, gaṭa, shūka, tāla, ghārat.

Borax, s. tankār.

Border, s. ḥadd, brīd, pūla; ghāṛa, morga; tsanḍa, tsalma, ja-ī, laman.

Bore, v.a. barma-, sūrai-, etc. k., sīkhal. petsal.

Born, a. zowulai, zegedalai, paidā shawai. (in comp.) -zādah, -zai, -dzoe.

Born, v.n. zegedal, zowul, paidā ked.

Borrow, v.a. por-, qarz-, etc. ākhistal. (a thing to be returned) 'āriyat-ākhistal.

Borrower, s. porawuṛai, qarz-dār.

Bosom, s. (embrace) gheg, ghūzai. (chest) ṭaṭar. (breast) sīna.

Both, a. dwāṛah, dwah-wāṛah.

Bottle, s. kkhīkkha.

Bottom, s. wekh, tal, mūnḍ; kūnsaṭ, būnsaṭ.

Bottomless, a. be pāyān, nā-pāyāw or nā-pāyāb.

Bough, s. tsānga, khrānga, lakkhta. (large-) kkhākh, khanḍ, ṭāl.

Bound, v.a. dangal, ṭop wahul, traplal. v.n. trapedal, ghwurzedal. (ricochet) v.a. tīndak wahal. (limit) v.a. pūla-, brīd-, ḥadd-, etc. ṭaral.

Boundary, s. pūla, ḥadd, brīd.

Boundless, a. be ḥadda, be anda, be shāna, be nihāyata, be qiyāsa.

Bountiful, a. sakhī, sakhāwatī, faiz-rasān, kkhandana-, bakkhana-, etc. kawūnkai.

Bounty, s. sakhāwat, sakhī-tob, bakkhana.

Bow, s. salām, adab; ṭiṭ-wālai.

Bow, s. līnda, līnda-ī, kamān. (-string) ja-ī. (middle of-) mūṭai. (horn of-) ghwagai, khām. (notch of-) zih-gīr. (-for practice) darwesha-ī. (pellet-) ghur-kamāna. (pellet-cup) pāṭa-ī. (bar of cup) panjakai. (-of a fiddle) kamāncha. (rain-) da būḍa-ī ṭāl, sara-shna kāsa. (to bend a-) v.a. ja-ī bānde k. (to unbend a-) v.a. ja-ī kūzawul. (-maker) kamān-gar.

Bow, v.a. ṭīṭawul. v.n. ṭīṭedal.

Bowels, s. laṛmānah, kulme. (of ruminants) lirrai.

Bower, s. chopāl, jūngaṛa, tsapar, dzodz-khāna.

Bowl, s. (pottery) kanḍol, kanḍolai. (glazed-) zarghūn-kanḍol. (china-) chūna-ī or chīna-ī. (wooden-) kāsa, pīna, kunṛa-ī or kunḍa-ī. (metal-) kaṭorai.

Box, s. ṣandūq, ṣandūqcha. (clothes-) taunṛa-ī. (band-) tawang. (trinket-) haṛpa-ī. (pill-) dablai. (in comp.) -dān. (blow) tsapeṛa ṭas.

Boy, s. halak, woṛkai. (school-) janṛai. (plough-) ghunḍāyah. (dancing-) lakkhtai, lolai.

Boyhood, s. halak-wālai, wṛūk-wālai, janṛī-tob.

Brace, s. taṛūn, tanṛa-ī, wandanai; lānga, piyāṛma, kakkha; joṛa, juft, qulba.

Brace, v.a. klakawul, tangawul, ṭīngawul, kāgal—kkhkal.

Bracelet, s. (above elbow) ma-aṭkai, bāzū-band. (below elbow) bāhū, bangṛai. (at wrist) kangaṇṛ, kaṛai, wakkhai, gajrai.

Bracket, s. darai, raf; pushta, aṛam.

Brackish, a. mālgīn, kkhora-nāk; triw.

Braid, v.a. odal.

Brain, s. maghzah.

Brake, s. karkanṛa, jāṛa, jāmbṛa.

Bramble, s. karkanṛa, jāṛa; aghzai, ghana.

Bran, s. *sūṛī, būṭ-sūṛī, gadzārī.*

Branch, s. *kkhākh, tsānga, khanḍ.* (family-) *kor, naṣl, pusht, aliwād.*

Brand, v.a. *dāghawul, nughai gdal—īkkhodal*; *tor-, tuhmat-,* etc. *pore k., makh-torai k.*

Brandish, v.a. *tsanḍawul.*

Brass, s. *ziyaṛ.*

Brave, a. *maṛanai, zṛeh-war, tūrzan, bahādur, takṛah, mazbūṭ, dilāwar.*

Bravery, s. *maṛūna, mardī, zṛah-war-tob,* etc.

Bravo, in. *shābāsh! āprīn!*

Brawl, v.a. *jagṛa-, qaẓiya-,* etc. *k., chighawul.*

Brawler, s. *jagṛāū, takrārī, jang-yālai.*

Bray, v.n. *hinredal.*

Breach, s. *chāwd, tsāk, darz*; *kanḍaw, chwanḍ.*

Bread, s. *ḍoḍa-ī.* (leavened-) *khamīra.* (unleavened-) *patīra.* (barley-) *orbūshīna.* (maize-) *sūkṛak.* (millet-) *khamacha, piyātsa.* (mixed meal-) *rāṛa, broṛa.* (dry-) *spora ḍoḍa-ī.* (-of charity) *gharai, chaṛ.*

Breadth, s. *plan-wālai, arat-wālai, sor* or *psor.*

Break, v.a. *mātawul.* (-to atoms) *chūr-char-, daṛ-daṛ-, kanḍ-kapaṛ-, māt-guḍ-,* etc. *k.*

Breakfast, s. *nārai* or *nahārai, nāshta, tsākkhtī.* (-during Lent) *pesh-manai* or *-namai* or *-lamai.*

Breast, s. *sīna.* (nipple) *tai.* (-band) *tapor.*

Breastplate, s. *chaprās.*

Breastwork, s. *sangar, mard-raw, faṣīl.*

Breath, s. *sā* or *sāh, dam* or *dama.*

Breathe, v.a. *sā-, dam-,* etc. *ākhistal* or *rākāgal—rākkhkal.* (-upon) *damawul, dam k.*

Breeches, s. *parṭūg, shalwār.*

Breed, s. *aṣl, naṣl, ẕāt, rag-rīkkha, nogai, zād-zawzāt, rang.*

Breed, v.a. *pālal, parwaral*; *zegawul, naṣl-paidā k.* v.n. *langedal, zegedal*; *blārbedal, warla ked.*

Breeding, s. *pālinna, parwarish*; *tarbiyat, t'alīm*; *langa, blārba, warla, ḍaka.*

Breeze, s. *hawā, bād, bādūkai, wagma.*

Brethren, s. *wrūṇrah, 'azīzān.*

Brevity, s. *lanḍ-wālai, lanḍ-tiyā.*

Bribe, s. *baḍa, rishwat, mok.*

Brick, s. *khakkhta.* (-bat) *ṭoṭa, roṛa.* (-dust) *surkhī.* (-kiln) *paja.* (-layer) *kullāl.*

Bridal, a. *nāweyat.*

Bride, s. *nāwe.* (bride's maid) *wrā-bāṇra-ī, wre-aza* or *wreyaza, mānja-ī.* (bride's female servant) *īnga.*

Bridegroom, s. *zalmai.* (bridegroom's man) *wrā-bāṇrai, jānjī, mānjī.*

Bridge, s. *pul.* (-of nose) *tindoṛai, tanbeza* or *tambūzai* or *tambūzak.* (of fiddle) *ṭaṭū, khargai.* (to make a-) v.a. *pul taṛal.*

Bridle, s. *wāga, mlūna*; *jalab* or *jalaw.* (of cord) *gapī, pā-ī.* (camel's-) *pezwān.*

Brief, a. *lanḍ, kotāh.*

Brigade, s. *tuman, dasta.*

Brigand, s. *ghal, shūk-mār, qazzāq.*

Bright, a. *rūṇr, rokkhān, tāb-nāk*; *spīn, shīn.*

Brighten, v.a. *rūṇrawul, spīnawul, pākawul, rokkhān k.* v.n. *rūṇredal, dzaledal* or *dzal ked. brekkhedal*; *spīnedal, shīn-, pāk-,* etc. *ked.*

Brightness, s. *raṇrā, brekkhnā, rokkhnā-ī.*

Brim, s. *morga, ghāṛa, tsanḍa.*

Brimstone, s. *gogar* or *gogil.*

Brindled, a. *brag, gag, chrag-brag, ablaq.*

Briny, s. *mālgīn.* (brine) *mālgīna oba.*

Bring, v.a. (-animate objects) *rāwustal.* (-inanimate objects) *rāwṛal.* (-forth young) *langedal.* (-off) *bachawul.* (-up) *pālal, parwaral.* (-under) *lānde k.*

Brink, s. *ghāṛa, morga, tsanḍa, ḍaḍa.*

Brisk, a. *chust, chālāk, takṛah, tund, gaṛandai.*

Bristle, v.a. (as the hair or skin) *wekkhtak-, ghūnā-,* etc. *-zigedal* or *walāṛedal.* s. *da sarkūzī wekkhtak.*

Brittle, a. *nāzuk, mātedūnai, narai, spuk.*

Broad, a. *plan, arat, sara-war* or *psora-war.*

Broadcloth, s. *banāt.*

Broadness, s. *plan·wālai, arat·wālai, sor* or *psor.*

Brocade, s. *kimkhwāb, zar·baft, muqqaish.*

Broil, v.a. *wrītawul, kabābawul, teyal, talawul.*

Broken, a. *māt.* (-to bits) *māt·guḍ, kanḍ·kapaṛ, char·chūr, daṛ·daṛ.*

Broker, s. *dallāl.*

Bronchocele, s. *ghur.*

Brood, s. *zawzād* or *zauzāt, alwād, bachī.*

Brood, v.n. *ghamedal, nūledal, kaṛedal*; *fikr·man-, andekh·man-, wiswāsī-,* etc. *ked.* (sit on eggs) *kuṛkedal, kuṛaka ked.*

Brook, s. *lakkhtai, nahar, arākh, walla, khwaṛ.* (dry bed of-) *kanda, kas, shela.*

Broom, s. *jārū.*

Broth, s. *kkhorwā.*

Brother, s. *wror.* (elder-) *mashar wror.* (younger-) *kishar wror.* (middle-) *mandz·wai wror.* (foster-) *da tī-* or *da to wror.* (full-) *sakah wror.* (half-) *nā·sakah wror.* (-in-law) *awkkhai.* (husband's-) *lewar.* (-hood) *wrorī, wror·walī, wror·galwī, wror·wālai.*

Brow, s. *wuchwulai* or *wucharlai, tandai, kolak.* (-of a hill) *kamar, tarai.*

Brown, a. *mushkai, bor, kha-aṛ.* (light-) *sperah.* (dark-) *sūr·bor.*

Browse, v.a. *powul.* (tend at-) *piyāyāl.* v.n. *tsaredal.*

Bruise, v.a. *blodal, sūlawul, dzabal*; *kuṭal, ṭakawul.* (-grain) *dal k.*

Brush, s. (weaver's-) *māla.* (fox's-) *lakai.* v.a. *jārū k.* (-clothes) *tsanḍal.*

Brushwood, s. *dzangal, jāṛ, jāmbṛa.*

Brutal, a. *be dard, be raḥm, sakht·dil, dzaban, ḥaiwānī.*

Brute, s. *ḥaiwān, dad, dzanāwar.*

Bubble, s. *bulbula* or *burbura, ghulai, jalh.* v.n. *eshedal, khūṭ ked., khūtsedal.*

Bubo, s. *ghumba, ghunḍāṛai, stagh.*

Buck, s. *osai.* (-rabbit) *soe.*

Bucket, s. *boka, taghārai, satal*; *dalwa, gaḍhal*; *solāgha.*

Buckle, s. *kara-ī, gharabbai.*

Buckler, s. *ḍāl, sipar.* (-handle) *lāstai, mūṭai.* (-cushion) *gaḍai.* (-boss) *patrai.*

Bud, s. *ghūṭa-ī.* (leaf-) *ghandal.* v.n. *ṭūkedal. ghwaredal, zarghūnedal.* v.a. *red-, qalam-,* etc. *k.*

Buffalo, s. *mekkh, gāwmekkh.* f. *mekkha.* (young-) *katai.* (two-year-old-) *joṭah.* (bull-) *sanḍah.*

Buffoon, s. *ṭoqī, ṭoq·mār, washtī, washt·mār, malanḍai, maskharāchī, pekkhe·gar.*

Buffoonery, s. *ṭoqa, washta, malanḍa, maskhara.*

Bug, s. *mungawr, kaṭmal.* (tree-) *khasak.*

Bugbear, s. *bāgū, bagalolai, bau.*

Bugle, s. *turai.* (Bugler) *turī·mār.*

Build, v.a. *joṛawul.*

Building, s. *kandar, mānra-ī, koṭa, kor.*

Bulb, s. *ghūṭa, ghūṭa-ī.* (garlic-) *palai.*

Bulk, s. *ghaṭ·wālai, loe·wālai.*

Bulky, a. *ghaṭ, loe, nāpaṛ, star, khrīs, gagar.*

Bull, s. *hinḍah* or *minḍah.* (-calf) *skhai.*

Bullet, s. *mardaka* or *mardak, gola-ī.*

Bullion, s. *srah·zar, spīn·zar.*

Bullock, s. *ghwayai* or *ghwa-e ghutskai, dangar.* (steer) *zāṛai, skhwandarkoṭai, skhwandar.*

Bully, s. *ẓālim, zorāwar, luqah, ḍaz, zorūnkai.*

Bulrush, s. *lūkha, kahai, nal, baḍagāl.*

Bump, s. *pārsob, māṭūs, maṭāka, ghūnḍa, pūpaka, punḍ.*

Bunch, s. *ghoṭai, ghūncha, khosha.*

Bundle, s. *gāṭlai, peṭai, geḍai, panḍa, panḍūkai.* (-of hay) *beda, kalokkhta.*

Bung, s. *būja, ḍiḍa, khulborai, shora.*

Buoyant, a. *spuk, pāyāwai.*

Bur, s. *jishai, kandala-ī.*

Burden, s. *bār.* v.a. *bār āchawul* or *k.*; *legdawul.*

Burdensome, a. *drūna, grān, sakht.*

Burglar, s. *ghal, kandar-* or *gūṭ mātanūnkai.*

Burglary, s. *ghlā, kandar-* or *gūṭ mātanūna.* (to commit-) v.a. *kandar-* or *gūṭ mātanul* or *k., naqb-zanī k.*

Burial, s. *khakkhanūna, khakkhedina.* (service) *janāza.* (-ground) *goristān, qabristān.*

Burlesque, s. *toqa, malanda, mazākh.*

Burn, v.a. *swadzawul, sedzawul; balawul.* v.n. *swal, sedzal, baledal.*

Burning, s. *swai; sedzana; baledana; balawūna.*

Burnish, v.a. *rūnrawul, dzalkawul, rokkhān-, ṣaiqal-, ṣāf-, pāk-, brekkh-nāk-,* etc. *k.*

Burrow, v.a. *sūrai-* or *sūra-, ghār-, surang-,* etc. *k.,* or *kanawdal,* or *kanal,* or *kanastal.*

Burst, v.n. *chāwdal, prak chāwdal, shledal, tsīredal, chāq ked.* (-into) *dūsa k.* (-out) *mātedal.* (-upon) *rā-māt ked.*

Bury, v.a. *khakkhawul.*

Bush, s. *būṭai, jāra, ḍakai.*

Bushel, s. *ogai.* (a quarter-) *kurai.*

Business, s. *kār, kasb, pesha, shewa.*

Buskin, s. *sugul; mōsa-ī.*

Bustard, s. *tsūrai, kha-aṛ-mor, ḥūbārah, tughdarī.*

Bustle, s. *chal-chalā, hatsa, tag-o-dau, tagā-pū.*

Busy, a. *lagiyā, mashghūl.*

But, c. *lekin, mangar, wale, balki, siwā.*

Butcher, s. *qaṣṣāb.* v.a. *ḥalālawul; wajlal* or *wajal, qatl-, marg-, khūn-, muṛ-,* etc. *k.*

Butt, s. *nakkha, mukha.* (-with the head) *ṭakar, ḍaghara* or *ḍaqara.* v.a. *ṭakar-,* etc. *wahal.*

Butter, s. *kuch.* (preserved-) *ghwaṛī.*

Butterfly, s. *parakai, tārūgai, kambala-ī, bāmbīlakai.*

Buttermilk, s. *shomle* or *shlombe.* (sour-) *tarwe.*

Buttock, s. *kūnāṭai, surīn.*

Button, s. *ghoṭai.* (-loop) *tanra-ī, gūtma, palwākhā, ghaṛāsha.*

Buttress, s. *pushtī, aṛam.*

Buxom, a. *takṛah, chāg, tāzah, khandā-rūe.*

Buy, v.a. *pīral* or *pīrawdal, pa baiʻe ākhistal.*

Buzz, v.n. *bonredal.*

Buzzing, s. *bonr, bonrkai, bonredana.*

By, p. *pa.* (-day) *pa wradzi.* (-thousands) *pa zirgūno.* (-hundreds) *pa ṣawūno.* (-all means) *pa har shān.* (-degrees) *pa ro ro, pa qalār.* (-no means) *pa hets shān, hechare, hado.* (-and-bye) *pa drang, drang sāʻat pas.* This preposition is often followed by *sara* (with), as *pa har shān sara,* by all means, etc.

C.

Cabal, s. *janba, para, gundī.*

Cabbage, s. *gobī, karamkala.*

Cabin, s. *koṭa; jūngaṛa, kuḍala, tsapar.*

Cable, s. *da beṛa-ī biyāsta* or *-pa-aṛai* or *-rasa-ī.*

Cactus, s. *ṭohaṛ, zaqūm, qūrghandal.*

Cackle, v.a. *jak-jak-, chagh-chugh-,* etc. *k., chūqa wahal.*

Cadaverous, a. *sperah.*

Cadence, s. *wazn, āwāz, ghag, trang, badala.*

Cage, s. *pinjra, qafas.*

Cajole, v.a. *ghulawul, ṭagal.*

Calamitous, a. *bad-* or *kam-bakht, bad-naṣīb, balā-nāk, āfatī, ghaẓab-nāk.*

Calamity, s. *balā, āfat, nāzila, muṣībat.*

Calcine, v.a. *kushtah-, īre-,* etc. *k.*

Calculate, v.a. *shmāral,* or *shmeral, ḥisābawul, ganral.*

Calculation, s. *ḥiṣāb, shumār* or *shmerah, andāza.*

Caldron, s. *khum, deg, satal; degchai, kaṛahai.*

Calendar, s. *patra, taqwīm.*
Calender, v.a. *batī-, kundī-, chāp-*, etc. *k.*
Calf, s. *bachai, chikorai.* (bull-) *skhai.* (buffalo-) *kaṭai.* (camel-) *jūngai, botai.* (stuffed-) *spandakh.* (-of leg) *paṛkai, gharai.*
Calico, s. *chīṭ.*
Calk, v.a. *chānd-, darz-*, etc. *-bandī k.*
Call, s. *bāng, nāra.* (-for dogs) *tū·tū.* (-for cattle) *ṛī·ṛī.* (-for cats) *pa-ash·pa-ash.* (-for hawks) *qū·qū.* (-to drive cattle) *ta-arya·ta-arya.* (-to encourage dogs) *tap·tap.* (-to encourage fighting rams, etc.) *jig·jig, ḍrich·ḍrich.*
Call, v.a. *nāra wahal, bāng wayal, ghag k.* (summon) *balal, ṭalab k.* (name) *wayal, nūm ākhistal; nūm kegdal—kekkhodal* or *kkhkegdal*, etc. (-to mind) *yādawul.* (-back) *stūnawul* or *stanawul.* (-bad names) *kanzal k., kkhkandzal* or *kanzal.*
Called, a. *nūmāndai, nūmedah.*
Calling, s. *kār, kasb, pesha.*
Callous, a. *sakht, klak; be dard, be parwā.*
Callousness, s. *sakhtī, klak·wālai; be dardī.*
Calm, a. *āsūdah, karār, ārām, band, walāṛ.* v.a. *walāṛawul, sarawul, ārām warkawul.* s. *qalār·tiyā-* or *walāṛ·tiyā da bād.*
Calmly, ad. *pa qalār sara, pa ro ro.*
Calmness, s. *ārām-, qalār-, walāṛ-*, etc. *-tiyā; rāḥat, ṭāṭob.*
Calumniate, v.a. *tuhmat-* or *tūmat-, tor-*, etc. *-pore k., peghor warkawul, ghībat k.*
Calumny, s. *tuhmat, tor, peghor, ghībat.*
Camel, s. *ūkkh, shutur.* (young-) *jūng* or *jūngai, botai.* (rutting-) *baṛbaṛai.* (-driver) *sarwān, ūkkhbah.* (-saddle) *kata, pālān.* (-litter) *kajāwa.* (-bridle) *peswān.* (-nose peg) *nata.*
Camp, s. *ḍera, muqām; urdū, ḍal.*
Campaign, s. *jang, ghazā, jihād; sama, maidān.*
Camphor, s. *kāfūr.*
Can, v.n. *shwal, tuwānedal.* s. *loṭkai.*
Canal, s. *nāla, wāla.* (small-) *lakkhtai.*
Cancel, v.a. *wrānawul, man'a k., bāṭil k.*
Cancer, s. *yaga, rasawla-ī, kkhandza, nāsūr.*
Candid, a. *rikkhtīnai, spīn, sūchah, ṣāf.*
Candidate, s. *umed·wār.*
Candle, s. *bāta-ī.* (-stick) *ḍīwaṭ.*
Candour, s. *rikkhtīn·tob, spīn·wālai, ṣafā-ī.*
Cane, s. *bet.* (sugar-) *ganai.* (-for eating) *ponḍa.* (-for the mill) *khū.*
Canister, s. *dablai, kaṛpa-ī, ṣandūqcha.*
Cannibal, s. *saṛī-* or *ādam·khor, khūnāṛai.*
Cannon, s. *top, topa.* (-ball) *golā, gola-ī.*
Canoe, s. *kishta-ī.*
Canon, s. *qānūn, ā-īn, dastūr.*
Canopy, s. *chatr, sāewān, shāmiyāna, siwrai.*
Cant, s. *makr, riyā.* (-word) *takiya kalām.*
Canton, s. *tapa, cham, jam, khel.*
Cantonment, s. *urdū, ḍal, chāwṇra-ī.*
Canvas, s. *biyasta-ī, ṭapṛa.*
Cap, s. *ṭopa-ī, khola-ī.* (padded-) *ṭūkhala-ī.* (-with ear flaps) *koṭakha, khūrjīna.*
Capable, a. *qābil, tuwānā, shwūnkai.*
Capacious, a. *art, jawar, kushād.*
Capacity, s. *tuwān, qābiliyat, qābil·tob, idrāk; art·wālai, dzāe.*
Capital, s. *aṣl, māya, panga, saga.* a. *aṣlī, awwal, wṛūnbanai; da marg lā-iq* or *-sazāwār.*
Capsicum, s. *srek·mrich.*
Caprice, s. *khiyāl, wahm.*
Capricious, a. *khiyālī, wahmī, nā·qalār.*
Captious, a. *ḥujjatī, takrārī, jang·yālai.*
Captivate, v.a. *ghulawul, farestah-, mayan-, koḍ-*, etc. *k.*
Captive, s. *qaidī, bandī.*
Captivity, s. *qaid, band.*
Capture, v.a. *nīwal, ākhistal, giriftār k.*
Caracole, v.a. *top-, khartīza-, kharchaka-*, etc. *-wahal.*

Caravan, s. *kārwān, qāfila, sānga.*
Caravansary, s. *srāe, kārwān·srāe, rabāṭ.*
Caraway, s. *zīra, sperkai.*
Carbuncle, s. *kkhandza, dandārū, ghunḍārai.*
Carcass, s. *muṛai, lāsh.*
Card, s. *pāṇṛa, pata.* (playing-) *tās, ganjīfa.*
Card, v.a. *alājī-, tonbiyā-,* etc. *k.*
Cardamom, s. *ilāchī, hel.*
Carder, s. (cotton-) *alāj*; *nandāp* or *naddāf.* (his bow) *līnda.* (the beam) *ḍānḍat.* (the cord) *ja-ī.* (the beetle) *ḍabalai.* (the staff) *chūka.* (the comb) *alājī.*
Care, v.a. *fikr-, parwā-, ghaur-,* etc. *k., andekkhnā-, gham-,* etc. *k., khāṭir-, makh-, mulāḥiza-,* etc. *k., khabar·dārī-, tsoka-ī-,* etc. *k., sātana-, khundī-,* etc. *k.*
Career, s. *daur, daurān*; *manḍa, zghākkht.*
Careful, a. *khabar·dār, hokkhyār*; *fikr·man.*
Carefulness, s. *khabar·dārī, hokkhyār·tiyā.*
Careless, a. *be khabar, be parwā, be fikr, be gham, ghāfil, shānlai·nāwlai.*
Caress, v.a. *nāzawul, nāz-, mīna-, dilāsa-,* etc. *k.*
Carious, a. *chinjan, wrost, skhā, sharkedalai.*
Carnage, s. *qatl, marg, khūn.*
Carnal, a. *nafsānī, shahwat·nāk, mast.*
Carnivorous, a. *ghwakkha·khor.* (-animal) *dad.*
Carol, v.a. *stāyal.* s. *stāyana.*
Carouse, v.a. *bad·masti k., sharāb tskkhal* or *tskal*; *nasha k.*
Carpenter, s. *tarkāṇr, darūz·gar.*
Carpet, s. *farsh*; *ghāla-ī, ghālīcha.* (cover for a-) *chāndānī.* (praying-) *sajjāda, muṣalla.*
Carriage, s. *gāḍa-ī*; *bār·bardārī, bār·kakkh*; *yūn, chāl, raftār*; *ḍaul, wajha.*
Carrier, s. *wṛūnkai*; *bār·kakkh, bār·bardār*; *harkārah, ḥammāl.*
Carrion, s. *murdār.*
Carrot, s. *gāzara, zardaka.*
Carry, v.a. *wṛal, rāwṛal.*
Cart, s. *gāḍa-ī, irāba.* (-man) *gāḍ-ī·wān.*
Cartilage, s. *krachai, krachūnai, krapandūkai.* (-of the nose) *tandwai, tīndorai.*
Carve, v.a. *kanal* or *kanastal.* (-meat) *kūtal.*
Cascade, s. *tsādar, dāra, tandūra.*
Case, s. *lifāfa, pokkh, ghilāf.* (sword-) *tekai, teka, miyān*; *kisbat, kīsa*; *ṣandūqcha, karpa-ī*; *ḥāl, ḥālat.*
Casement, s. *kaṛka-ī.*
Cash, s. *naghd* or *naqd, rok.*
Casket, s. *dabalai, karpa-ī, ṣandūqcha.*
Cast, v.a. *wishtal, āchawul, ghurzawul, lawastal.*
Cast, s. *kālbūt, ghālab* or *qālib.* (at play) *daw, guzār.*
Caste, s. *rang, zāt, aṣl, qām* or *qaum, nog.*
Castle, s. *koṭ, qil'a, gaṛa-ī.*
Castor-oil, s. *da arhanḍo tel.*
Castrate, v.a. *khaṣṣī-, ākhtah-, malai-,* etc. *k.*
Casual, a. *qismatī, naṣībī, nā·gahān, nā·gūmān.*
Casualty, s. *āfat, kāna, nāzila.*
Cat, s. *pisho.* (tom-) *barghūṭ* or *narghūṭ.* (wild-) *pish·pṛāng.* (young-) *pishongaṛai.*
Catalogue, s. *siyāha.* (of men) *asāmī.*
Cataract, s. *dāra, tsādar.* (of the eye) *parda, dund.*
Catarrh, s. *zukām, dūmai, sāṛa, yakhnī, nazla.*
Catastrophe, s. *balā, āfat, muṣībat, kāna.*
Catch, v.a. *niwul, ākhistal, giriftār k.*
Catechize, v.a. *sawāl-, pukkhtena-,* etc. *k.*
Caterpillar, s. *pīsha-ī, chinjai.*
Catgut, s. *ja-ī, jaṇrai.*
Cattle, s. *tsārwai, ḍangar, māl, dāba.*
Caudle, s. *matar, lāwaṇr, kaṛa.*
Caught, v.n. *nkkhatal.* a. *nkkhatai.*
Caul, s. *obaṇra, da bachī parda.*
Cause, s. *sabab, jihat, kabl, bā-iṣ, wāsta*; *muqaddama.*

Cauterize, v.a. *dāghawul, dāgh lagawul.*
Cautious, a. *khabar-dār, hokkhyār, baidār.*
Cavalcade, s. *sparli* or *swarli*; *jilaw.*
Cavalier, s. *spor* or *swor.*
Cavalry, s. *swāreh, risāla.*
Cave, s. *smats* or *samist, ghār, kāz.*
Cavity, s. *doghal, ṭūbkai, jawara, kanda.*
Cease, v.a. *pregdal—prekkhodal—prekkhawul.* v.n. *ākhiredal, tamāmedal.*
Ceaseless, a. *mudāmī, dā-im.*
Cedar, s. *diyār.*
Cede, v.a. *pregdal, spāral, warkawul*; *manal.*
Ceiling, s. *chat, bām, tsapar.*
Celebrate, v.a. *stāyal.* (-a day) *manal.*
Celebrated, a. *nūm-war, nām-dār, nāmer, mashhūr.*
Celebration, s. *stāyana*; *manena.*
Celestial, a. *āsmānī, jannatī.*
Celibacy, s. *lawanḍ-tob, tsaṛah-wālai.*
Cell, s. *khūna, koṭa*; *gokkha, hujra.*
Cellar, s. *tah-khāna.*
Cement, s. *salekkh.* (mortar) *kūnai, gach.*
Cemetery, s. *maqbara, rauza*; *qabristān, goristān, hadera.* (-of saints) *ziyārat, dargāh.*
Censer, s. *mujmir.*
Censor, s. *muhtasib.*
Censure, v.a. *malāmat k., ṭaqawul, raṭal, traṭal.* (-oneself) *gram k.*
Cent, s. *sil.* (per-) *saikaṛa, pa sil, sil pase.*
Centipede, s. *zanza.*
Central, a. *miyānah, mandzai* or *mandzwai.*
Centre, s. *mandz* or *myandz.*
Centuple, a. *sil-bragh, sil-chand.*
Century, s. *sil-kāl.*
Cerate, s. *malham, paha, mom-roghan.*
Ceremony, s. *madār, khātir, makh, adab, taklīf, dastūr, rasm.*
Certain, a. *yaqīn, tahqīq, ṣahīh, muqarrar.* (-one) *palānkai* or *falānai.*
Certainly, ad. *be shakk, albatta, rikkhtiyā.*
Certainty, s. *yaqīnī, zbād, tahqīqī, ișbāt.*
Certificate, s. *sanad, chīṭa-ī, kāghaz.*
Certify, v.a. *yaqīn-, zbād-, ṣābit-, tahqīq-,* etc. *k.*; *khabar-, āgāh-,* etc. *k.*
Chafe, v.a. *blodal, sūlawul, mugal—mukkhal.* v.n. *blosedal, sūledal, sūdah ked.* (grieve) *ghamedal, sūledal, kaṛedal.*
Chaff, s. *būs, proṛ, sūrī.* (of rice) *khamache.* (of corn, etc.) *drūze, gadzāre.*
Chagrin, s. *randz, khapagān, nūl, gram.*
Chain, s. *zandzīr.* (-link) *kara-ī.*
Chair, s. *kursī, chaukī*; *kaṭkai, peṛa-ī.*
Chalk, s. *spīna-khāwra.*
Challenge, v.a. *jang gokkhtal*; *d'awa-,* etc. *k.* v.n. *gwākkhedal.*
Challenger, s. *mudd'a-ī*; *jang joe*; *gwākkhkai.*
Chamber, s. *koṭa, khūna.*
Chameleon, s. *karboṛai, tsarmakkhkai.*
Champ, v.a. *krapawul, chīchal.*
Champaign, s. *maidān, sama, ṣahrā.*
Champion, s. *pahlwān, tūrzan, bahādur.*
Chance, s. *naṣīb, qismat*; *wār, puk*; *daw.* v.n. *nāziledal, prewatal, wāqi'a ked.*
Change, v.a. *badlawul.* (-money) *māṭawul.* v.n. *badledal, āwukkhtal, girzedal.*
Changeable, a. *nā-pāedār, nā-qalār*; *khūshai, nīma-khwā.*
Channel, s. *lār*; *nāla, rūd-khāna, lakkhtai.*
Chant, v.a. *sarod-, sandera-, badala-,* etc. *wayal.*
Chaos, s. *tor-tam, ẓulmat.*
Chapter, s. *bāb, faṣl.* (of Qurān) *sūra.*
Character, s. *khoe, khaṣlat*; *ṣifat, khāṣṣiyat*; *nūm, nāmūs*; *bashanj, pat.*
Charcoal, s. *skor.* (pl. *skārah*). (live-) *sarwaṭka* or *skarwaṭa.*
Charge, s. *amānat, spārah, sipurd, hawāla.* (order) *hukm, kariya, farmān.* (price) *bai'a, qīmat.* (expense) *kharts.* (onset) *halla, tsoṭ, guzār, brīd.* (advice) *maṣlahat.* (prohibitory) *qadaghan.*

Charge, v.a. *spāral, amānat-*, etc. *k.* (order) *farmāyal, ḥukm-*, etc. *narkawul.* (accuse) *d'awa k., tuhmat-, tor-*, etc., *-pore k.* (attack) *halla-*, etc. *k.* (load) *ḍakawul.* (enjoin) *tākīd-*, etc. *k., pohawul.* (in accounts) *kharts līkal.*

Charger, s. *jangī ās*; *tabākh, ghāb* or *qāb, tasht.*

Charitable, a. *sakhī, khairātī, sakhāwatī.*

Charity, s. *khairāt*; *zakāt, ṣadqa, sarsāya.*

Charm, s. *t'awīz.* (kind of) *mara-ī, tāwītak, amel, dawā, ṭilism.* (for snakes, etc.) *pāṛ.* (juggle) *mantar, koḍa, jādū, siḥr, hūda.*

Charm, v.a. *hūda-, dam-*, etc. *k.*; *pāṛawul*; *jādū-*, etc. *k., fareftah k., ghulawul.*

Charmer, s. *jādū·gar, koḍ·gar, siḥr·gar.* (snake-) *pāṛū.* (mistress) *dil·bar, dil·rubā, nāznīna.*

Charming, a. *kkhāyistah, khwakkh, khwand·nāk.*

Chart, s. *nakhkkha* or *naqsha.*

Charter, s. *sanad, 'ahd·nāma, iqrār·nāma.*

Chase, s. *kkhkār, ṣaid*; *pairawī, manḍa.* v.a. *kkhkār k., takkhtawul, zghalawul, pase manḍe·wahal.*

Chasm, s. *ḍoghal, ṭūbkai, gorhanda, gaṛang*; *kanda, chāwd, jawara.*

Chaste, a. *pāk·laman, neko·kār, pākīzah, pāk.*

Chat, v.a. *kitī·pitī khabare k.*

Chatter, v.a. *bak·bak-, ṭar·ṭar-, chiṛ·chiṛ-*, etc. *k.*

Chattels, s. *asbāb, kālī, sāmān, māl, bar·bast.*

Cheap, a. *arzān, wal* or *wel, spuk.*

Cheapness, s. *arzān·tiyā, wel·wālai.*

Cheat, s. *ṭag, farebī, darghal, sādū, makār, chal·bāz, chal·walai*; *ṭagī, droh, chal, makr.*

Cheat, v.a. *ṭagal, ṭagī-, fareb-, chal·bāzī-, darghalī-*, etc. *k., drohawul.*

Check, v.a. *aṭālawul, ḥiṣārawul, man'a k., sambālawul, nkkhlawul, wudrawul.*

Cheek, s. *angai, anangai, koka-ī, bārkho.*

Cheer, s. *chigha, nāra*; *ārām, khwakkhī*; *'aish, khwand, maza*; *kkhādī*; *melmastiyā.*

Cheer, v.a. *chighe-*, etc. *wahal*; *tasallī-, dilāsa-*, etc. *k.*

Cheerful, a. *khwakkh, khush·hāl, kkhād, kkhādān, kkhād·man, khandā·rūe.*

Cheerless, a. *be dil, be ārām*; *khwār, lūts.*

Cheese, s. *panīr.* (soft-) *bagoṛa, potsa.* (hard-) *qurut.*

Chequer, v.a. *brag-, gag-, rangīn-, chrag·brag-*, etc. *k.*

Cherish, v.a. *pālal, parwaral, nmāndzal*; *sātal, jghoral, khundiyal.*

Cherisher, a. *pālūnkai, parwarūnkai.* (in comp.) *parwar.*

Chess, s. *shatranj.* (-board) *bisāṭ.* (king) *shāh.* (queen) *wazīr.* (castle) *rukh.* (knight) *asp.* (bishop) *pīl.* (pawn) *piyādah.* (check) *kisht.* (checkmate) *māt.* (-player) *shatranj·bāz.*

Chest, s. *ṭaṭar, sīna.* (the cavity) *gargas, gogal.* (clothes-, etc.) *tawṉra-ī, ṣandūq.*

Chestnut, s. *banj, banj·pāṛ.* a. *surang.*

Chew, v.a. *chīchal, jowul, krapawul.* (the cud) *shkhwand k.*, or *-wahal*, or *-māṭawul.*

Chicken, s. *chirgūṛai, chūchai.* (-pox) *katswak.*

Chide, v.a. *raṭal, traṭal, peghorawul, dāṛal.*

Chief, a. *mashar, awwal, wṛūnbai.* s. *sardār, arbāb, khān, malik, ra-is, sarghanah, rāhīṭ.*

Chiefly, ad. *akṣar, wṛūnbe, awwalan.*

Chiefship, s. *khānī, sardārī, malikī.*

Child, s. *bachai, woṛkai, wṛūkai, māshūm*; *farzand, tūng.*

Childbirth, s. *langa, lang·wālai, langa·tob.*

Childhood, s. *halak·wālai, wṛūk·wālai, halkat, halkīna.*

Childish, a. *halak·shān*; *nā·dān.*

Childless, a. *lā·walad, be zawzāt, be farzand.* (by death) *būr.*

Chill, a. *soṛ, yakh.* s. *sāṛeh, yakhnī.*

Chilliness, s. *soṛ·wālai, yakhnī, sāṛeh.*

Chime, v.a. *tarāne wayal, trangawul, tāl wahal.* v.n. *trangedal, granjedal.* s. *trang, tāl, tarāna.*

Chimney, s. *lū-kakkh, da lūgī sūrai.*

Chin, s. *zina, zanakh, zanakh-dān.* (double-) *ghab-ghab, jajūra.*

Chink, s. *chānd, darz, rakhna, chāq.* (sound) *shrang, granj.* v.n. *shrangedal, granjedal.*

Chintz, s. *chīt.*

Chip, s. *tota, totkai, tūtankai, tarāza.*

Chipped, a. *būrai.*

Chirp, v.a. *chaur-chaur-, chir-chir-,* etc. *k.*

Chisel, s. *tswarlai, kkhatsulai* or *shatsurlai.*

Choice, a. *ghwarah, kkhah, khāss.* s. *wāk, ikhtiyār*; *khwakkh, pasand, razā.*

Choke, v.a. *khapah k., mara-ī khapa k.* v.n. *khapah ked*

Cholera, s. *wabā.*

Choose, v.a. *khwakkhawul, chunral, latawul, anrawul, kkhāghal, pasand k.*

Chop, v.a. *kūtal, warjal, tota-tota-, bja-,* etc. *k.*

Christ, s. *hazrat 'īsā, rūh-ullah.*

Christian, s. *'īsānī, naṣārā*; *tarsā.*

Christianity, s. *'īsānī mazhab* or *-dīn.*

Chronic, a. *der-pā, multanī.*

Chronicle, s. *tawārīkh*; *akhbār*; *roz-nāma.*

Chuckle, v.n. *khandedal, musedal.* (over enemy) v.a. *sakha k., wiyāral.* (as a fowl) *chugh-chugh k.*

Chum, s. *mal, malgarai*; *handa-ī-wāl*; *hujra-wāl.*

Church, s. *masjid, jumā'at.*

Churl, s. *ganār, dihqān, ghundāyah*; *lwār*; *bakhīl, shūm.*

Churn, v.a. *shārbal.*

Churning, s. *shārbal.* (-stick) *mandānrū.* (-tie) *barangai.* (-strap) *rog, tasma.* (-dish) *donra-ī.* (-cover) *bargholai.*

Cinder, s. (cold-) *skor.* (hot-) *skarwata, khuglan, skhwakkhtan.*

Cinnabar, s. *shingrap.*

Cinnamon, s. *dārchīnī.*

Circle, s. *tsarkh, churlai, chambar, dā-ira.*

Circuit, s. *daur, daurān*; *gakkht.*

Circular, a. *ghūnd* or *ghūnd-man, tsarkhai.*

Circulate, v.a. *chalawul, girzawul, jārī k.* v.n. *chaledal, girzedal, jārī ked.*

Circumcision, s. *sunnat, khatna.*

Circumspect, a. *hokkhyār, baidār, khabar dār, pokh.*

Circumstance, s. *hālat, hāl*; *khabara.*

Circus, s. *jaulān-gāh.*

Cistern, s. *hauz, baha-ī, talāo, dand.*

Citadel, s. *qil'a, kot, gara-ī, arg, bālā-hiṣār.*

Cite, v.a. *balal, talab k.*; *yādawal.*

Citizen, s. *kkhahr-wāl*; *daftarī.*

Citron, s. *nīmbū, triw nāranj.*

City, s. *kkhahr.*

Civil, a. *mulkī, dīwānī*; *makhawar, sulūkī, mihrbān.* (-court) *mulkī 'adālat.* (-war) *patna, khāna-jangī.* (-power) *'adālat.*

Civilian, s. *'āmmī*; *kasb-gar*; *ahl da qalam.*

Civility, s. *makhawarī, makh-tob, madār, adab, nek-sulūk, mihrbāngī.*

Civilize, v.a. *ābādawul, kkhāyastah-, ārāstah-,* etc. *k.* *sarī-tob chalawul.*

Claim, v.a. *d'awa-, darkhwāst-,* etc. *k.*

Claimant, s. *mudd'aī, dād-khwāh, d'awa-dār.*

Clammy, a. *bokkht, slekkht-nāk, barnai, chaspān.*

Clamour, s. *zwag-zwūg, shor-shaghab, ghoghā.*

Clamp, s. *patrai.*

Clan, s. *qām, khel, firqa, ulūs, tabar, cham.*

Clandestine, a. *put, pinham, ghalai.*

Clangour, s. *shrang, granj, trang.*

Clap, v.a. (the hands) *tāl wahal*; *shābāsh k.*

Clapper, s. *tak-takānrai, jiba, spai.*

Clarify, v.a. *pāk-, pākīzah-, spīn-, ṣāf-,* etc. *k.*

Clarion, s. *sarnāe.* (-player) *surnāchī.*

Clash, v.a. *blodal, takar-, daka-,* etc. *khwural.* v.n. *blosedal.*

Clasp, v.a. pa ghegi nīwul; bargrandī k.

Class, s. aṣl, ẕāt, rang, nogai; ṭolai, cham, khel; darja, pāya.

Classification, s. tartīb, dzerma.

Clatter, v.a. tranganwul, shranganwul, granjanwul.

Clause, s. faṣl; sharṯ.

Clavicle, s. grewa.

Claw, s. changāl, mangul, panja, nūk. v.a. panja-, etc. wahul, nūkāra k.

Clay, s. maṭa- or maṭīna khāwra, khaṭa.

Clayey, a. maṭīn, khāwrīn.

Clean, a. pāk, pākīzah, ṣāf, spīn. v.a. pāk-, etc. k.

Clear, a. pāk, ṣaf; tsargand, kkhkārah, bartser, awtsār, bewrah; yalah, āzād, khalāṣ. v.a. spetsal, pākawul, spīn-, etc. k. tsargand-, etc. k. yalah-, etc. k. (-the throat) ghāṛa tāza k.

Clearness, s. pāk-wālai; tsargand-wālai, etc.

Cleave, v.a. chawul. (asunder) chaurang k. prekawul. (-to) v.n. nkkhatal, lagedal, chaspedal.

Cleaver, s. ṭoqiyā, sātūl; prekawūnai.

Cleft, s. chāwd, chāq, wat, darz; kandaw, kand.

Clemency, s. ḥalīmī, shafaqat, raḥmat.

Clement, a. ḥalīm, mulā-im, raḥīm, narm.

Clergy, s. pādriyān, mullāyān, bāmbanrān.

Clerk, s. kātib, līkūnkai, kkhkawūnkai.

Clever, a. hokkhyār, pohānd, pokh; hunrman, kārī-gar, qābil; kāgh, chirg.

Client, s. d'awa-gar, mudd'a-ī.

Cliff, s. kamar, tsaka, lākkh.

Climate, s. āb-o-hawā, hiwād, iqlīm.

Climb, v.n. khatal.

Climber, s. khatūnai. (plant) bel.

Cling, v.n. nkkhatal, chaspedal, lagedal.

Clink, v.n. shrangedal, granjedal.

Clip, v.a. (hair, etc.) skustal, kaṭeyal. (cloth, etc.) skakkhtal. (dock) ghūṭ k. or -prekawul. (hair of head) sar-kunḍai k.

Cloak, s. bārāna-ī; chogha, baraka. (felt-) kosai. (fur-) postīn. (blanket-) junga kiṛī shaṛa-ī.

Clock, s. gaṛī, sā'at

Clod, s. lūṭa, chūm, gapa.

Clog, s. kanrāwa; haṭāl, nkkhata, bār. v.a. haṭālawul, kariyābawul, nkkhlawul.

Close, v.a. bandawul, joṛawul, lagawul, pewand k.; tamāmawul, khatm k. (a door) pore k. (a book) ṭapawul or ṭap wahal.

Close, s. ākhir, khatm; bāra, shpol, haḍera.

Close, a. nijdai; tang; pewastah; bakhīl, shūm; ṭīng, tat, ganr. (as cloth) ṭok. (as stars) jambaq. (-cut) ghūṭ, lanḍ.

Closeness, s. nijdekī; tang-wālai; pewastagī; bakhīlī, shūm-wālai; ṭīng-wālai.

Closet, s. ḥujra, khūna; gūṭ, gokkha.

Cloth, s. karbās, khāmtā; alwān, chīṭ, etc. (woollen woven-) paṭū, baraka, shaṛa-ī, pashmīna, etc. (woollen unwoven-) krāsta, lamtsai, kosai, namada, etc. (broadcloth) banāt.

Clothe, v.a. āghustawul, pokkhal, poslal; āghostal.

Clothes, s. zaṛūkī, nwarī or nmarī, pokkhāk, āghostan, libās, jāme. (swaddling-) oranrai.

Cloud, s. waryadz.

Clout, s. chīrra, khartsoṛai, ṭaghar. (loin-) lung, chotai, taṛāqa-ī. (child's-) kūnastarkai; taṛūnai.

Clove, s. lawang. (-necklace) lawang-hāṛ.

Cloven, a. (cleft) chāwd, chāq. (-hoof) swa.

Clover, s. speshtarai, shautal, speshtai.

Clown, s. ṭoq-mār, malanḍai, pekkhe-gar, maskharāchī; gawār, pūhaṛ, kāwāk, shāṛ.

Cloy, v.a. sekan k., kraka ākhistal.

Club, s. amsā, koṭak, lawaṛ, ḍāng. (society) cham, ṣuḥbat, jumā'at.

Cluck, v.a. kuṛ-kuṛ k.

Clue, s. bilga or balga, darak.

Clumsy, a. kāwāk, bad-wajha, bad-ḍaul.

Cluster, s. *wagai, khosha*; *ganr, ṭolai.*
Clutch, v.a. *pa mūṭ nīwul, ghoṭa-, chapa-*, etc. *nīwul* or *wakal.*
Coagulate, v.a. *ṭīngawul, klakawul, tomna-, māya-*, etc. *k.* v.n. *kangal-, khyam-*, etc. *ked.*
Coalesce, v.n. *gaḍedal, yo·dzāe ked.*
Coarse, a. *lwāṛ, ghaṭ.*
Coast, s. *ghāṛa, duḍa, tselma.*
Coat, s. *kurta, kudā-ī, khalqa, qādara-ī, landa-ī, andraka.* (-for rain) *bārāna-ī.* (-of mail) *zghara, zira.*
Coax, v.a. *dam-, dam·dilāsa-, jāna-*, etc. *k., jigī·jigī-, hāṛe·hāṛe-*, etc. *k.*
Cobbler, s. *mochī, tsamyār.*
Cobweb, s. *jāla-ī.*
Cock, s. *chirg.* (game-) *panḍāw·chirg.* (-of a gun) *pāe, kajak.* (-crow) *charbāng* or *chirg·bāng.*
Cockade, s. *jogha, tūgh, zunbuk.*
Code, s. *shar'a.* (Afghan-) *pukkhtūn·walī.*
Co-equal, a. *siyāl, makhai, gund.*
Coerce, v.a. *zoral, lānde k.*
Coeval, a. *hum·dzolai, hum·'umr.*
Coffer, s. *khizāna.*
Coffin, s. *tābūt.*
Cog, v.a. *chāplūsī-, ḍirpalī-*, etc. *k., ghulawul.* (of a wheel) s. *būṛai.*
Cohabit, v.a. *kilai-, kor-*, etc. *k., kor·wālai k.*
Cohesive, a. *bokkht, barwai, slekkht·nāk.*
Coil, s. *pech, tāo, wal.*
Coin, s. *sika, paisa, naghd* or *naqd.* (counterfeit-) *jūṭah, nā·sarah.*
Coincide, v.n. *jukht-, barābar-, joṛ-*, etc. *lagedal.*
Cold, a. *soṛ, yakh.* s. *sūṛa, yakhnī*; *zukām, dūmai, nazla.*
Colic, s. *bād·gola, sūda, shwala.*
Collapse, v.n. *drabal, alwal·prewatal.*
Collar, s. *grewān.* (-of a dress) *grewa.* (neck-) *ṭauq.* (dog-) *ghowaṛandai.*

Colleague, s. *mal, malgarai.*
Collect, v.a. *ṭolawul, gaṭal, jam'a k., laṭawul.*
College, s. *madrassa, maktab.*
Collision, s. *ḍika, ṭakaṛ*; *blos, blosedana.*
Colloquial, s. *da 'āmmiyāno jiba, wrāsha.*
Collusion, s. *joṛikkht, ṭagī, sāzish.*
Collyrium, s. *rānjah, surma, kuhal.* (-case) *rānjaṛūma.* (-bodkin) *salā-ī.*
Colocynth, s. *maṛaghūnai, tarkha kakora.*
Colonize, v.a. *ābādawul, wadānawul.*
Colony, s. *bānḍa, nawa-ī*; *ābādī, wadānī.*
Colour, s. *rang, laun.* v.a. *rangawul.*
Coloured, a. *rangīn, rang kaṛai.*
Colours, s. *nakkha, janḍa, bairaq, togh.*
Colt, s. *bihānr.* (two-year-old-) *dwak.*
Column, s. *tsalai, munār, stan* or *sitūn.*
Comb, s. *gamanz* or *mangaz*; *shāna.* (honey-) *gabīna.* (cock's-) *chār·khwaluk.* (curry-) *ghasho.*
Combat, s. *jang, muqaddama.*
Combatant, s. *jangī, mlā·taṛ, tūrzan.*
Combine, v.a. *joṛawul*; *gaḍawul, laṛal.*
Come, v.n. *rātlal—rāghlal, rasedal.*
Comedy, s. *malanḍa, pekkha, ṭoqa, swāng.*
Comely, a. *kkhkulai, kkhāyastah, pa-ī·makhai.*
Comet, s. *da jārū storai.*
Comfort, s. *ārām, mor·tiyā, ārām·tiyā*; *dilāsa, tasallī, ḍāḍ, khwā·khogī.*
Coming, a. *gāndah, āyandah.*
Command, s. *hukm, kariya, farmān, amr*; *wāk, was, qābū*; *farz.* v.a. *farmāyil, hukm-*, etc. *k.*
Commander, s. *hākim, sardār, sar·guroh.*
Commence, v.a. *ibtidā-, shur'ū-, darak-*, etc. *k.*
Commend, v.a. *stāyal, sipārish k.*
Commendation, s. *stāyana, sipārish.*
Commerce, s. *saudāgarī, wapār, lāgī, rākṛah·warkṛah.*
Commissary, s. *dāroghah*; *ūstādzai.*
Commission, s. *sunad, 'uhda*; *parwāna, farmān*; *kār.*

Commit, v.a. *spāral, pāslawul, gumāral, ḥawāla-*, etc. *k.*; *kawul, kṛal.* (-adultery) *zinā-, kāsīrī-*, etc. *k.* (-robbery) *ghlā k.*

Committee, s. *jirga, m'arika, majlis.*

Commodious, a. *dzāe-war, munāsib, lā-iq, pīrzo.*

Commodity, s. *māl, jins, saudā.*

Common, a. *'āmm, jārī, chalan.* s. *maidān, panḍ-ghālai, ḍāga, ṭikārkai; borjal.*

Commonly, ad. *aksar, ziyātī.*

Community, s. *cham* or *jam, khel, ulūs; rāsha-darsha, gāwanḍī-tob, malgar-tiyā.*

Compact, a. *ganr* or *gūr, tat, ṭing.* (-cloth) *toq.* (-crops) *ṭal.* s. *wāda, lafz, taṛa, neṭa.*

Companion, s. *mal, malgarai; āshnāe, rafīq.*

Company, s. *majlis; ṭolai, paṛk, ghol; malgīrī, āshnā-ī; melmastiyā, ṣuḥbat.*

Comparison, s. *muqābala, misāl, nisbat.*

Compass, s. *qibla-numāe; chāper, gakkht; ḥadd, dzāe.* (reach) *partāb.* v.a. *ḥiṣārawul* or *isārawul.*

Compasses, s. *parkār.*

Compassion, s. *dard, raḥm, zṛah-swai, tars.*

Compatible, a. *munāsib, pīrzo; barābar.*

Compel, v.a. *zorel, lānde k.*

Compensate, v.a. *tāwān-, nāgha-, badal-*, etc. *warkawul.*

Competence, s. *kifāyat, rozī.*

Competent, a. *qābil, lā-iq.*

Competition, s. *muqābala.*

Complacent, a. *ḥalīm, post, narm, makhawar.*

Complainant, s. *mudd'a-ī, faryādī, d'awagar; gila-man.*

Complaint, s. *nālish, māna, gila, faryād.*

Complaisance, s. *mākh-tob, makhawarī, narmī, mihrbāngī.*

Complete, a. *pūrah, tamām, khatm, kāmil; bashpaṛ, amānī.*

Complex, a. *gaḍ-waḍ; grān, mushkil.*

Complexion, s. *da tsihre rang, charda, mizāj.* (dark-) *kalof.*

Compliment, s. *madār, adab, salām, makh.*

Comply, v.a. *manal, qubūlawul.* v.n. *rāẓī ked.*

Compose, v.a. *joṛawul; tartīb-, ārāstah-*, etc. *k.*; *saṛawul; līkal, kāgal-kkhkal.*

Composition, s. *gaḍūn, gaḍedena, gaḍa.*

Compound, v.a. *gaḍawul.* a. *gaḍ.*

Comprehend, v.n. *pohedal.*

Comprehension, s. *poh, pahm, fikr.*

Compress, v.a. *chit k., drabawul.*

Comprise, v.a. *shāmil-, yo-dzāe-*, etc. *k.*

Compute, v.a. *ganral, shmeral, ḥisābawul.*

Comrade, s. *mal, malgarai, yār.*

Concave, a. *jawar, doghal.*

Conceal, v.a. *puṭawul, pokkhal, ghalai k.*

Concealment, s. *puṭ-wālai, puṭedina, ghalītob.*

Concede, v.a. *manal, qabūlawul, bakkhal.*

Conceit, s. *khpul-sarī, bād, wiyāṛ, kibr.*

Conceited, a. *bādī, khpul-sar, kibr-jan.*

Conceivable, a. *shwūnkai.*

Conceive, v.n. *pohedal.* v.a. *fikr-, qiyās-*, etc. *k.*; *blārbedal, ḍakedal.*

Conception, s. *poh, pahm, fikr, qiyās, khiyāl; blārbedina, blārba-wālai, umed, ḍaka.*

Concern, s. *kār, m'amala; gham, fikr, parwā; andekkhnā, wisnās.*

Concerned, a. *gham-jan, fikr-man; wisnāsī, andekka-nāk.*

Concerning, p. *bābat, ḥaqq.*

Concert, s. *ittipāq; malgar-ṭiyā; zamzama.*

Conciliate, v.a. *pakhulā k., grūkkhal.*

Concise, a. *lanḍ, kotāh.*

Conclude, v.a. *tamāmawul, ākhir-, khatm-*, etc. *k., khalāṣawul; m'alūmawul, ganral.* v.n. *pohedal.*

Concord, s. *rogha, joṛa, āshtī, ashtoka.*

Concourse, s. *ṭolai, jumā'at, ganr-'ālam.*

Concubine, s. *wīndza, 'aurata, sūryata.*

Concupiscence, s. *nas, mastī, shahwat.*

Concur, v.n. *yo-jihat-, yo-zṛah-, rāẓī-*, etc. *ked.*

Concussion, s. *ṭakar, ḍaka.*

Condemn, v.a. *bad manal, man'a k.*; *gunāh-, wabāl-, taqṣīr-*, etc. *ṣābitawul* or *dzāyawul.*

Condescend, v.a. *mihrbāngī-, makh-, mulāḥiza-, madār-*, etc. *k.*

Condiment, s. *masāla.*

Condition, s. *ḥāl, ḥālat, ṣūrat, yang, shān*; *wāda, neṭa, lafẓ, sharṭ.*

Condole, v.a. *lās·nīwah k.*; *pātiḥa wayal, khwā·khogī k., pokkhal.*

Conduct, s. *chāl·chal, chalan, ṭarīqa*, etc.; *badraga*; *sulūk, madār, makh.*

Conduct, v.a. *badraga k., botlal—bīwul*; *rāwustal, rawānawul, chalawul.*

Confection, s. *ḥalwā, miṭiyā-ī, qanāt, shīrīnī.*

Confederacy, s. *para, janba, gundī.*

Confederate, s. *para·dār, janba·dār*; *mal.*

Conference, s. *jirga, maṣlaḥat, sawāl·dzawāb.*

Confess, v.a. *manal, khwāla wayal.* v.n. *qā-iledal.*

Confidence, s. *bāwar, yaqīn, sāwisā, khal, i'tibār.*

Confine, v.a. *band-, qaid-, ḥiṣār* or *isār-*, etc. *k.*

Confirm, v.a. *rikkhtiyā-, zbād-, ṣābit-, taḥqīq-*, etc. *k.*

Confiscate, v.a. *nāgha-, ẓabṭ-, qurugh-*, etc. *k.*

Confluence, s. *gaḍedana.*

Conform, v.n. *yo·shān-, yo·ḍaul-, yo·makh-, yo·zṛah-*, etc. *ked.*

Confound, v.a. *gaḍ·waḍawul, laṛal, shārbal*; *ḥariyānawul, rabṛawul, sargardānawul, pareshān-, hak·pak-, hekkh-, huts-*, etc. *k.*

Confront, v.a. *makhā·makh-, muqābala-*, etc. *k.*

Confute, v.a. *lā·dzawāb-, gram-, radd-*, etc. *k.*

Congeal, v.n. *ṭīngedal, kangal ked.*; *khyam ked.*

Congratulate, v.a. *mubārakī k.* or *wayal.*

Congregation, s. *ṭolai, jamā'at, majlis.*

Conjecture, s. *gūmān, 'aql, khiyāl.*

Conjugal, a. *da tsakkhtan aw da kkhadze, da wādah kaṛai aw da wadedali.*

Conjunction, s. *pewand, joṛ, taṛūn.*

Conjuncture, s. *wakht, neṭa, nobat, ṭāng.*

Conjure, v.a. *qasam-, saugand-*, etc. *warkawul*; *jādū-, koḍa-*, etc. *k.*

Conjurer, s. *jādū·gar, koḍ·gar, siḥr·gar*

Connect, v.a. *joṛawul, lagawul, taṛal.*

Connexion, s. *joṛ, band, taṛūn*; *nisbat*; *ragai, khpolwī, khekkhī.* (carnal-) *gho, ghowūna kor·wālai.*

Connive, v.a. *starge puṭawul.*

Connubial, a. See Conjugal.

Conquer, v.a. *barai k.*, or *-mūndal, pa-aṛ k.*, etc.

Conquest, s. *barai, wa-aṛa, wa-aṛāna.*

Conscience, s. *īmān, diyānat*; *rikkhtīn·tob.*

Conscious, a. *khabar·dār, baidār, hokkhyār.*

Consecrate, v.a. *niyāz-, khairāt-*, etc. *k.*, or *-manal.*

Consent, s. *raẓā, qabūl, hokai, oe.*

Consequence, s. *natīja*; *pāzah.*

Consequently, ad. *dzaka, tro.*

Consider, v.a. *fikr-, pahm-, qiyās-*, etc. *k.*. *andekkhnā-, hosh-*, etc. *k.*; *ganral.* v.n. *pohedal.*

Considerable, a. *loe, grān*; *ḍer*; *drund.*

Consign, v.a. *spāral, pāslawul, gumāral, ḥawāla k.*; *āstawul, legal.*

Consignment, s. *spārina, ḥawāla*; *asbāb, jins.*

Consist, v.n. *joṛedal, osedal, kedal, shwal.*

Consistent, a. *joṛ, sam*; *klak, ṭīng.*

Console, v.a. *tasallī-, dilāsā-, ḍāḍ-*, etc. *warkawul.*

Consort, s. *tsakkhtan, meṛah*; *kkhadza, artīna.* v.a. *kilai-, kor-, rozgār-, khasamāna-*, etc. *k.*; *yārī-, āshnā-ī-, malgīrī-*, etc. *k.*

Conspicuous, a. *tsargand, kkhkārah, mashhūr.*

Conspirator, s. *yāghī·gar, mufsid, pasātī.*

Conspire, v.a. *sāzish-, badī-*, etc. *k.*

Constant, a. *pāedār, qā-im.*

Constantly, ad. *har·wakht, har·sā'at.*

Consternation, s. *ḥariyānī, sargardānī*; *khof, yara, bāk, tor, tars, trahā.*
Constipation, s. *qabẓ, qabẓiyat.*
Constituent, a. *aṣlī, ẕātī.*
Constitute, v.a. *joṛawul, wudrawul, paidā-, muqarrar-*, etc. *k., walāṛawul.*
Constitution, s. *mizāj, ṭab'a, khwā.*
Constrain, v.a. *zoral, sambālawul, ṭīngawul.*
Construct, v.a. *joṛawul, binā k.*
Consul, s. *wakīl, mukhtār.*
Consult, v.a. *jirga-, maṣlaḥat-, mashwarat-*, etc. *k.*
Consume, v.a. *ṣarf-, talaf-, kharts-*, etc. *k.*
Consummate, a. *pūrah, pokh, kāmil.*
Consumption, s. *kharts, ṣarfa*; *narai-randz, dīqq, sill.*
Contact, s. *joṛ, lagedena*; *blos, blosedana.* (to come in-) v.n. *blosedal, jangedal, lagedal.*
Contagion, s. *wabā*; *gazak.*
Contain, v.a. *dzāyawul.* v.n. *dzāedal.*
Contaminate, v.a. *palīt-, nā-pāk-, skhā-, kakaṛ-, gazak-*, etc. *k.*
Contemn, v.a. *spuk ganṛal.*
Contemplate, v.a. *ghaur-, fikr-*, etc. *k.*; *nandāra-, tamāsha-*, etc. *k.*
Contemporary, s. *ham-dzolai, hum-wakht, kūl.*
Contemptible, a. *spek, dūn, khushai.*
Contemptuous, a. *kibr-jan, bādī, be makh.*
Contend, v.a. *jagṛa-, qaẓiya-, takrār-*, etc. *k.*
Content, a. *rāẓī, moṛ.* s. *raẓā, moṛ-tiyā.*
Context, s. *matan, 'ibārat, maẓmūn.*
Contiguous, a. *nijdai, pewastah.*
Continent, a. *parhez-gār, pāk-laman.* s. *zmaka, barr, wucha.*
Contingent, a. *mauqūf*; *'āriẓī.*
Continual, a. *pāedār, jārī, dā-im, pāyindah.*
Continuance, s. *pāedārī, mudāmī, dā-imī.*
Continue, v.n. *pāedal, osedal, pitedal.*
Contortion, s. *tāo, pech, wal, kālkūchaka.*
Contour, s. *mekh, gūna, tsihra, shakl, ḍaul.*
Contract, s. *wāda, neta, bandaṇr, lafẓ*; *teka.*
Contract, v.a. *tangawul, kāgal—kkhkal.* (a promise) *wāda-, neṭa-*, etc. *taṛal* or *k.* (a debt) *por ākhistal.* (a marriage) *wādah k., nikāḥ ekhel.* v.n. *kawt ked.*
Contradict, v.a. *khilāf wayal, radd-, darogh-jan-, hoḍ-*, etc. *k.*
Contrary, a. *khilāf, mukhālif, hoḍai.* s. *'aks, hoḍ.*
Contrast, v.a. *makhā-makh-, muqābala-*, etc. *k.*
Contrite, a. *tauba-gār, pakkhemān.*
Contrive, v.a. *band-, tadbīr-, ḥikmat-*, etc. *taṛal.*
Control, v.a. *sambālawul, qābū-, lānde-*, etc. *k., was chalawul.*
Controversy, s. *jagṛa, qaẓiya, radd-badal, baḥs, ḥujjat, steza.*
Contumacy, s. *sarkakkhī, yāghī-garī.*
Contumely, s. *peghor, kkhkandzal, spuk-tiyā.*
Contusion, s. *blos, māṭūs, pūpaka, khūg, jobal.*
Convene, v.a. *ṭolawul, yo-dzāe k., balal.*
Convenient, a. *joṛ, pīrzo, khwakkh.*
Convention, s. *jirga, majlis, m'arika*; *wāda, taṛa, bandaṇr, neṭa.*
Conversant, a. *wāqif, āmokhtah, khabar-dār.*
Converse, v.a. *khabare k., sawāl-dzawāb k.*
Convert, v.a. *badlawul*; *murīd-, mutaqid-*, etc. *k.*
Convex, a. *ghūnḍ, gunbatī.*
Convey, v.a. (things) *āstawul, wṛel, legal.* (animals) *botlel—biwul, rāwustal.*
Convict, s. *qaidī, bandī.*
Convict, v.a. *gunāh-*, etc. *ẕbād k.* or *s̱ābit k.*
Convince, v.a. *qā-il k., gram k.*
Convivial, a. *khūsh-hāl, kkhād, khandā-rūe, melmah-dost.*
Convoke, v.a. *balal, ṭalab k., ṭolawul.*
Convoy, s. *badraga* or *badraqa.*
Convulsion, s. *ghoṭa, parghaz*; *balwā.*
Cook, v.a. *pakhawul.* s. *bāwarchī* or *babarchī*
Cool, a. *soṛ, yakh*; *be parwā*; *mānrai-gar.*

Cool, v.a. *saṛawul, yaḵẖawul.* v.n. *saṛedal.*

Coolness, s. *sāṛa, soṛ·wālai, yaḵẖnī.* (pique) *marawar·tiyā, marawar·tob, mānṛai.*

Coop, s. (of leather) *daba.* (-maker) *dabbāg͟h.*

Coping, s. *tsatsobai, bala-ī, parc͟haṭai, sarmātai, s͟harīfa.*

Copious, a. *ḍer, frewān.*

Copper, s. *tāmba.*

Copse, s. *jangai, darga, g͟hīl.*

Copulate, v.a. *g͟hayal—g͟howul, kor·wālai-, g͟ho-, jimā'a-,* etc. *k.*

Copy, s. *naql, namūna, nusḵẖa*; *mas͟hq.*

Coquetry, s. *nāz, naḵẖra, makez, karas͟hma.*

Coral, s. *marjān.* (-diver) *marjīwanṛah.*

Cord, s. (thick-) *biyāsta, pa-aṛai, rasa-ī.* (thin-) *muzai, tār, spanṛsai.* (hair-) *antsa-ī, siyala-ī, wākkhkai.* (palm leaf-) *būnṛ.*

Core, s. *māg͟hzah, zṛeh, zaṛai.*

Coriander, s. *ḍaniya.*

Cork, s. (bung) *būja, ḍīḍa, ḵẖulborai.*

Cormorant, s. *kotān.* (glutton) *g͟hārai.*

Corn, s. *g͟hala, dāna.* (green-) *ḵẖwīd, ḵẖasīl.* (-stubble) *drūza.* (mowed-) *satrai.* (-sheaf) *geḍa-ī.* (-stack) *dala-ī.* (-bin) *kandū, koṭa-ī, ḵẖamba.* (-straw) *nāṛ.* (-broken straw) *būs.* (-treading floor) *dirmand, ḵẖirman.* (pile of trodden-) *wānṛa.* (of the foot) *baura-ī, rasaula-ī, kila-ī, meḵẖ.*

Corner, s. *gūṭ, gokkha*; *daḵẖma.*

Corporeal, a. *jismānī.*

Corpse, s. *muṛai, lās͟h, murdah.*

Corpulent, a. *tsorb, peraṛ, g͟haṭ, punḍ.*

Correct, a. *joṛ, juḵẖt, durust, barābar, sam, rikkhtiyā, kkhah.*

Correspond, v.n. *joṛ-, sam-, barābar-,* etc. *lagedel, maḵẖai ked.* v.a. *c͟hīṭa-ī-, kāg͟haz-,* etc. *līkal* or *kāgal—kkhkal* or *legal.*

Corroborate, v.a. *rikkhtiyā-, zbād-, ṣubūt-,* etc. *k.*

Corrode, v.a. *zang ḵẖwuṛal.* v.n. *zang ked.*

Corrupt, v.a. *bonṛawul, palītawul, kakaṛawul, sḵẖā-, wrost-,* etc. *k.*

Cost, s. *bai'a, ḵẖarts, qīmat*; *tāwān, nuqṣān.*

Costive, a. *qābiẓ, ṭing, klak.*

Costiveness, s. *qabẓ, qabẓiyat.*

Costly, a. *qīmat·nāk, grān·bahā.*

Costume, s. *jāma, libās.*

Cot, s. *kaṭkai, kaṭoṭai.*

Cottage, s. *kaḍala, jūngaṛa*

Cotton, s. *mālūc͟h.* (-plant) *punba, kālaka.* (-seed) *pundāna.* (-stubble) *ḵẖirīz, ḵẖaṛand.* (-stalks) *banbe·c͟ho, kālak·c͟ho.* (-pod) *g͟hoza.* (-picker) *panḍol·gar.* (his share) *panḍolī.* (-dresser) *naddāp, alāj.* (his mallet) *ḍabalai.* (his bow) *ḍānḍaṭ.* (his gin) *alājī.* (carded-) *pāg͟hunda.* (roll of-) *pūnṛa-ī.* (skein of-) *mās͟hoṛa.* (-thread) *tonbiyā, aṭa.* (-reel) *aṭeran.*

Cough, s. *ṭūḵẖai, ṭuḵẖa, ṭūḵẖ·ṭūḵẖ.* (hooping-) *pūḵẖalai, tora·g͟hāṛa, haba·ḍaba.* v.n. *ṭūḵẖedal.*

Council, s. *jirga, m'arika*; *dalbār, majlis.*

Counsel, s. *pand, naṣīhat*; *maṣlahat, tadbīr, mas͟hwarat*; *wakīl.*

Count, v.a. *s͟hmeral, ḥisāb k.*; *ganṛal.*

Countenance, s. *maḵẖ, tsihra, bas͟hra*; *mihrbāngī, mrasta, mulāḥiẓa.*

Counterfeit, a. *jūṭah, nā·sarah.* v.a. *bāna-, palma-, c͟hal-, ṭagī-,* etc. *k.*

Counterpane, s. *bṛasten, taltak.*

Counterpart, s. *joṛa, pala, maḵẖai, dzawāb.*

Country, s. *mulk, hewād.* (own-) *waṭan.* (foreign-) *wilāyat.* (-man, etc.) *waṭanī.*

County, s. *pargana, tapa.*

Couple, s. *joṛa, qulba, juft*; *dwah.*

Courage, s. *maṛāna, mardī, zṛeh, nar·tob, dilāwarī, tūrzan·tob, dzwān·mardī, himmat.*

Courageous, a. *maṛanai, zṛeh·war, dilāwar, turzan, himmat·nāk.*

Courier, s. *qāṣid, c͟hapar, āstādzai.*

Course, s. *zghākkht, manḍa*; *daur, daurān*; *yūn, chāl*; *lār*; *maidān*. (of-) ad. *albatta, be·shakk*.

Court, s. *dalbār, daulat·khāna*. (civil-) *'adālat, maḥkama*. (-yard) *gholai, anganr·janas*.

Court, v.a. *ghokkhtal*; *mīna-, 'ishq·bāzī-*, etc. *k*.

Courteous, a. *makhawar, mihrbān, nek·khoe*.

Courtesan, s. *kachana-ī, lola-ī*.

Courtesy, s. *makh, mulāḥiza, adab, nek·sulūk*.

Courtier, s. *dilbārī*.

Courtship, s. *'ishq·bāzī, mīna, kkhpa·ārtūn, changhal·bāzī*.

Cousin, s. (father's brother's child) m. *tarbūr*; f. *tarla*. (mother's brother's child) *da māmā dzoe* or *lūr*.

Covenant, s. *wāda, taṛa, bandanr, 'ahd, qaul*.

Cover, s. *sar·pokkh, tekai, lifāfa*. (dish-) *bargholai*. (basket-) *kāra, sawada*.

Cover, v.a. *puṭawul, pokkhal*.

Covering, s. *pokkh, pokkhikkh, libās*; *miyān*.

Covet, v.a. *ṭam'a-, ḥirṣ-*, etc. *k*.

Covetous, a. *ṭam'a·jan, ḥirṣ·nāk, liwāl*.

Covey, s. *sail, ghol*.

Cow, s. *ghwā*. (-in heat) *ghwa-ema*. (milch-) *langa-*, or *pa-ī·wara ghwā*. (dry-) *zāṛa-ī*. (-pen) *ghojal*. (herd of-) *gohār*. (-dung) *ghoshoe*. (-dung fuel) *tsapiyāka*. (-dung stack) *gohāṭa*. (-keeper) *ghobah*.

Coward, s. *nā·mard, tuzan, kaṛū, sperkai, sperah·makh, taghan*.

Coy, a. *yer·man, sharm·sār, sharm·nāk, stāra prewatai*.

Crab, s. *kūnī·kabar, changākh*. (-louse) *baṛora*.

Crack, s. *chāwd, darz, daṛa, rakhna*. (sound) *ḍaz, ṭas, trāk, khrach, ṭaq*.

Crack, v.n. *chāwdal, darz-*, etc. *ked*. v.a. *ḍaz-*, etc. *k*., or *wahal*.

Crackle, v.n. *tsir·tsir-, sakkhā-*, etc. *ked*.

Cradle, s. *kaṭkai*; *zāngo, gahwāra*.

Craft, s. *kār, kasb, pesha*; *fareb, chal, ḥīla*.

Craftsman, s. *kārī·gar, kasb·gar, pesha·war*.

Crafty, a. *chal·bāz, ḥīla·bāz, ṭag·bāz, farebī*.

Crag, s. *tsūka, kamar, garang*.

Cram, v.a. *manḍal, ḍakawul*.

Cramp, s. *brekkh, tāo*.

Crane, s. *ḍing, zānrai, kulang*.

Crash, s. *khrach, khṛap, khṛas, drab*. v.n. *drabal, naṛedal*.

Crater, s. *garang, tortam, ḍoghal, kūhai*.

Crave, v.a. *ghokkhtal, minnat-, khwāst-*, etc. *k*.

Crawl, v.n. *tskhedal* or *tskedal, pa kharpotso tlal, ghūndzedal*.

Crazy, a. *lewanai, khushai, saudā-ī*.

Creak, v.n. *chingedal, trangedal*.

Cream, s. *perawai*.

Crease, s. *jūhaṛa, kṛaṭai, chīchaṛ, gundza*. v.a. *chunral, jung k., jūhaṛa-*, etc. *k*.

Create, v.a. *paidā k., joṛawul*.

Creation, s. *duniyā, naṛa-ī, khalq, makhlūq*.

Creator, s. *khāliq, paidā kawūnkai*.

Creature, s. *bandah, wagaṛai, ganai*; *ḥaiwān, dzanāwar*; *makhlūq*.

Credit, s. *por, qarẓ*; *nasiyah*; *bāwar, yaqīn, i'tibār*. v.a. *bāwar-*, etc. *k*. (buy on-) *pa por-*, etc. *ākhistal*.

Creditable, a. *mu'tabar*; *ākhistal*.

Creditor, s. *porawuṛai*.

Creed, s. *īmān, dīn, maẕhab*; *kalima*.

Creep, v.n. See Crawl.

Creeper, s. *bel*; *dzela, jurang*.

Crescent, s. *myāsht, hilāl*.

Cress, s. *halam, tezak, tartezak*.

Crest, s. (bird's-) *chār·khwalai* or *chār·khwalak*; *zūnḍai*. (snake's-) *chaja*. (-of a hill) *kamar, ghākkhai*; *tsūka, peza*. (-of a helmet) *ṭurra, tāj*.

Crevice, s. *sūrai, chāwd, darz, daṛa*.

Crew, s. *ghol, ṭolai*; *dala*. (ship's-) *jahāzī*.

Cricket, s. *kirṛai, karboṛaī.*
Crier, s. *jārchī, munādī karūnkai.* (-to prayers) *mu-azzin, mullā·bāng wayūnkai.*
Crime, s. *gunāh, wabāl, taqṣīr, khaṭā, bazah, jurm.*
Crimson, a. *arghawānī, lāl, sūr.*
Cringe, v.a. *chāpalūsī-, ḍirpali-, khūshāmad-,* etc. *k.*
Cripple, a. *guḍ, kaṛam, zam·zmolai, shall, sukṛuk.* v.a. *guḍ-,* etc. *k.*
Crisis, s. *sā'at, ṭāng, nobat*; *kamāl.*
Critic, s. *ḥarf·gīr, 'aib·joe.*
Crockery, s. *lokkhī·largī, kaṭwī·kanḍolī.*
Crocodile, s. *magar, nahang.*
Crook, s. *kūnḍa.* (shepherd's-) *kūnṭai, aṛām-kai, machak.*
Crooked, a. *kog, kṛing, tsoṛ, ṭīṭ, kālkūch.*
Crop, s. *faṣl.* (bird's-) *jajūra, ḥauṣila.* v.a. *tsaral*; *shūkawul*; *ghūṭ k.*
Cross, v.n. (-over) *pore watel* or *-tlal.* v.a. *lānde·bānde-, ore·pore-,* etc. *k.* (-breed) *rag gaḍawul.*
Cross, a. *sūṭ·būṭ, mānṛai·gar, marawar, khapah.* (-breed) *dwah·ragah.*
Crouch, v.n. *ghilai ked., peṭedal.* (cringe).
Crow, s. *qāghah* or *qārghah.*
Crow, v.a. (-over rival) *sakha-, wiyāṛ-,* etc. *k.*
Crowd, s. *ganṛ·'ālam, ḍala, lakhkar.*
Crown, s. *tāj, khol.* (-of head) *ṭaṭar, ṭopal.*
Crude, a. *ūm, khām, kachah, nīmgaṛai, nīma·khwā, ūmghalan.*
Cruel, a. *ẓālim, be·raḥm, kānṛai·zṛah, sakht.*
Crumb, s. *ṭoṭai, pūṭai, chūr, reza.*
Crupper, s. (horse's-) *dumchī.* (bullock's-) *ghwa-e lang, piyāṛma.*
Crush, v.a. *chīt·pīt-, tsaplāk-,* etc. *k., da kkhpo·lānde k., paz wahal.*
Crust, s. *poṭ.* (scab) *khwar, waṛ, khig.*
Crutch, s. *ṭāpoṛa.* (-of a sandal) *gaḍeka.*
Cry, v.a. *jaṛal.* (-violently) *pa raṭ·raṭ jaṛal.* (call) *naṛal, nāre wahul, bāng wayal.*
Cry, s. *jaṛā*; *nāra, bāng.*
Crystal, s. *bilaur*; *qalam*; *gach.*
Cubit, s. *tsangal, lecha, kata.*
Cuckold, s. *dahūs, bagharai.*
Cucumber, s. *bādrang, tara, tarai.*
Cud, s. *shkhwand.* (-of hawks, etc.) *par muhra.*
Cuddle, v.n. *ghāṛa·ghaṛa-ī ked.*
Cudgel, s. *koṭak, ḍāng, lawaṛ.* v.a. *kūṭal, wahul, ṭakawul.*
Cuff, s. *tsapeṛa, ḍab, ṭas.* (-of a coat) *las-tūnṛai, piyākhla.*
Cuirass, s. *bakhtar, jaushan.*
Culinary, a. *pakhalai.*
Cull, v.a. *shūkawul*; *chunṛal.*
Culpable, a. *malāmati, taqṣīri.*
Culprit, s. *gunāh·gār, taqṣīrī.*
Cultivate, v.a. *ābādawul, wadānawul*; *kar-, īwe* or *yawe-,* etc. *k.*
Cultivation, s. *ābādī, wadānī*; *kar, īwe* or *yawe, zarā'at.*
Cultivator, s. *zamīndār, kikkhī·gar.* (hired-) *dihqān, charekār.*
Cumin, s. *zīra, zanka-ī.*
Cunning, a. *chal·bāz, farebī*; *kāgh, chirg.* s. *hunar, ḥikmat.*
Cup, s. (metal-) *kaṭorai, jām.* (pottery-) *kanḍol* or *kanḍolai.* (wooden-) *kunṛa-ī* or *kunḍa-ī, kāsa.* (china-) *piyāla, kāsa.*
Cupidity, s. *shahwat, mastī, naus*; *ḥirṣ.*
Cupola, s. *gunbat.*
Cupping-horn, s. *kkhkar.* (to cup) v.a. *kkhkar lagawul.*
Cur, s. *spai, kūtrai*; *qachar, lawanḍ.*
Curb, s. *kaṛa, zandzīra.* v.a. *sambālawul, qābū k.*
Curd, s. *mästeh, chaka*; *posta, matra, kha-areṛai.*
Curdle, v.a. *tomna-, māya-, ṭing-,* etc. *k.*
Cure, v.a. *joṛawul, raghawul.* s. *'ilāj, ragha-wūna.*

Curious, a. *'ajīb, nādir*; *ghwag·tsār.*
Curl, s. *wal, zulf, tsūnra.*
Current, a. *jārī, chalan, rawā.* s. *chalānda, dāra.*
Currier, s. *tsamyār, dabbāgh.*
Curry, v.a. *kaṛāṛa k.* (tan) *dabbāghī k.* (-favour) *chāplūsī-, ḍirpalī-*, etc. *k.*
Curse, v.a. *kkhere-, l'anat-, bad·d'uā-*, etc. *k.* s. *kkhera*, etc.; *balā, āfat, wabāl, ghazab,*
Curtain, s. *parda, satra.* (-of a fort) *shīrāza.*
Curve, s. *ṭīṭa, kālkūch, kag·lech, wal, pech.*
Cushion, s. *bālikkhtak, balikkht·goṭai.*
Custody, s. *amānat, ḥawāla*; *qaid, band*; *sātena, ĵghorana, khundī·tob.*
Custom, s. *dastūr, rasm, chāl, 'ādat, dod, rawāj.* (tax) *māliyā, khirāj, tāwān, bāj.* (-house) *tsoka-ī, ṭānra.* (-collector) *muḥaṣṣil, bāj·dār.*
Cut, s. *tsīra, parhār.* (-purse) *gan·kap.* a. *tsīralai, ghwuts, jobal.*
Cut, v.a. *tsīral.* (-off) *prekawul* or *prekṛal.* (-out clothes, etc.) *skakkhtal.* (wound) *ĵobalawul, ghwutsawul.* (-short) *ghūṭ prekawul, lanḍ k.*
Cutler, s. *āhan·gar, ṣaiqal·gar, lohār.*
Cycle, s. *dour, daurān, tsarkh, zamāna.*
Cylinder, s. *nal, shpelai.*
Cymbal, s. *zang, zangūla, jalājal.*
Cypress, s. *sarwa, ṣanobar.*

D.

Dab, v.a. *tapal.*
Daddy, s. *bābū, dādā.*
Daffodil, s. *nargis, kangas.*
Dagger, s. *chāṛa, bihbūdī, pesh·qabza.*
Daily, ad. *rozmarra, har·roza, hara·wradz.*
Dainty, a. *khūsh·khwurak*; *khwand·nāk, maza·dār, tuḥfa.*
Dale, s. *dara.*
Dalliance, s. *nāz·o·nakhra, 'ishq·bāzī, 'āshiqī·m'ashūqī*; *dirang, lārghah, sustī, mulṭawī.*
Damage, s. *tāwān, nuqṣān, ziyān, troṭ.*
Dame, s. *merman, bībī, korbana.*
Damn, v.a. *kkhere-, l'anat-, bad·d'uā-*, etc. *k., peṭī·mū k., gūna wrukawul.*
Damnable, a. *l'anatī, lā-iq da kkhero.*
Damp, a. *lūnd, tar, nam·nāk, zyam·nāk, ob·jan.*
Damsel, s. *peghla, jina-ī.* (betrothed-) *changhala.*
Dance, s. *gaḍeda*; *nāch*; *atanr, jihr.* v.n. *gaḍedal.* v.a. *nāch k. atanr-*, etc. *-āchawul.*
Dancer, s. *gaḍedūnkai, gaḍandai.* (rope-) *bāzī·gar, naṭ.*
Dangerous, a. *khaṭar·nāk.*
Dangle, v.n. *dzwaṛandedal, awezānd ked.*
Dapple, a. *brag, gag.*
Dare, v.n. *gwākkhedal.* v.a. *jah k., gwākkhawul.*
Dark, a. *tor, tārīk.* (-complexion) *kaloṭ.*
Darkness, s. *tyāra, tārīkī*; *tortam, ẓulmat.*
Darling, s. *mayan, m'ashūq, dzān.*
Darn, v.a. *bezal* or *pezal, ganḍal*; *rafū k.*
Dart, s. *shalgai, barcha, bala.* (iron) *sela.*
Dash, v.a. *wīshtal.* (-in pieces) *chūr·chūr-, ṭoṭe·ṭoṭe-, pūṭī·pūṭī-*, etc. *k.* (-water) *lawastal, toyawul.*
Dastard, s. *nā·mard, tizan, kaṛū.*
Date, s. *tārīkh.* (fruit) *khajūra.*
Daub, v.a. *lewawul, akheṛal, akhāṛa k.*
Daughter, s. *lūr.* (-in law) *ngor.* (step-) *parkaṭa-ī, banza-ī.* (brother's-) *wrera.* (sister's-) *khordza.*
Dauntless, a. *be·bāk, zṛeh·war.*
Day, s. *wradz.* (to-) *nan.* (of to-) *nananai.* (-by day) *wradz pa wradz.* (every-) *hara wradz.* (-book) *roznāma.* (-light) *rawṛā wradz.* (-dawn) *chirg·bāng, ṣabā, sapede.* (by-) *da wradzi.* (-star) *starga.* (all the-) *kara-ī wradz.*

Dazzle, v.n. *brekkhedal, dzaldal, dzal ked.*

Dead, a. *muṛ, muṛai.* (-as a tree) *mṛām* or *mṛāw.*

Deadly, a. *qātil.*

Deaf, a. *kūnṛ.* (-as a post) *ṭap kūnṛ.*

Deafness, s. *kūnṛ-wālai.*

Deal, v.a. *weshal, brakha k.*; *wapār-, lāgī-,* etc. *k.*; *lār-, rozgār-, lāg-,* etc. *k.* s. *da nakkhtar largai.*

Dealer, s. *wapārī, lāgī*; *saudāgar, parāchah, ṭaṭār.* (Hindu-) *banṛiyah, katrī, hindū.*

Dealing, s. *wapār, lāg, sūd-saudā*; *kārobār, rozgār, lār, 'alāqa.*

Dear, a. *mayan*; *grān.* (-me!) *hāe-hāe!* (my-) *dzāna, dzamā dzān!*

Dearth, s. *kākhtī, matrah, tangsiyā, ḍukāl.*

Death, s. *ajal, marg, qaẓā.* (early-) *dzwānī-marg.* (sudden-) *tsaṭ-waṭ*; *mufājāt.*

Debase, v.a. *spekawul, kamawul, leggawul*; *be rūe-, be mekh-,* etc. *k.*; *jūṭah-,* etc. *k.*

Debate, v.a. *baḥṣ k.*

Debauch, s. *bad-mastī.*

Debauchee, s. *lawanḍ, kāsīr, bad-'amalī, chaṭ.*

Debauchery, s. *lawanḍ-tob, charcha, kāsīrī.*

Debility, s. *nā-tuwānī, kamzor-tiyā, māndagī.*

Debt, s. *por, qarẓ.*

Debtor, s. *porawuṛai, qarẓ-dār.*

Decant, v.a. *toyawul.* v.n. *toyedal* or *to-edal.*

Decay, v.n. *mṛāmedal, wrostedal, sharhedal*; *skhā ked.*

Deceitful, a. *chal-bāz, ṭag-bāz, farebī, droh-ūnai.*

Deceive, v.a. *ṭagal, ghulawul, ṭagī-, fareb-,* etc. *k.*

December, s. *poh* or *po.*

Decent, a. *joṛ, kkhah*; *munāsib, lā-iq.*

Decide, v.a. *faiṣal k.*

Decidedly, ad. *be-shakk.*

Decisive, a. *pūrah, kāfī-shāfī.*

Declaration, s. *iẓhār*; *gawāhī, shāhidī.*

Declare, v.a. *wayal, lawdal* or *lal.*

Decline, v.n. *prewatal, zawāl ked.*; *lā-ag-, kam-,* etc. *ked.* v.a. *inkār k.*

Declivity, s. *jawara, tahana, rewand.*

Decompose, v.n. *wrostedal, skhā ked., shaṛhedal.*

Decorate, v.a. *joṛawul*; *andzorawul, singār-awul, kkhāyistah-, ārāstah-,* etc. *k.*; *postal, kkhewa k.*

Decorous, a. *joṛ, munāsib, kkhāyistah.*

Decoy, v.a. *ghulawul, ṭagawul.*

Decrease, s. *kam-tiyā, legwālai.* v.n. *kamedal, la-ag ked.*

Decree, s. *ḥukm, fatwā.*

Decrepit, a. *ṭap, khwār, zoṛ, kamzor.*

Dedicate, v.a. *niyāz-, ṣadqa-,* etc. *k.*

Deduct, v.a. *mujra ākhistal, stanawul, zwam k.*

Deed, s. *kār, kṛah, 'amal*; *sanad, qabāla.* (-of gift) *hiba-nāma.*

Deep, a. *ḍoghal, star, jawar, kand*; *pokh, hokkhyār.*

Deer, s. *osai.* (young-) *kablai.*

Deface, v.a. *wrānawul, habata k., kharāb k.*

Defame, v.a. *ruswā-, bad-nām-,* etc. *k., ghandal*; *tuhmat-, tor-,* etc. *pore k.*

Default, s. *khaṭā, taqṣīr.*

Defeat, v.a. *māt k., pa-aṛ k.*; *man'a k.*

Defection, s. *jārwātah*; *yāghī-garī.*

Defenceless, a. *lā-chār*; *be-panāh, khushai, ḍāga-ḍagalai.*

Defend, v.a. *bachawul, panāh k., ṣātal, gālal, jghoral, khundī k., madad k.*; *'uẓr-, dzawāb-,* etc. *k.*

Defendant, s. *asāmī, muddā-'alaih.*

Defender, s. *sātandoe, jghorai, bachawūnkai, panāh-, khundī-,* etc. *-kawūnkai.*

Defer, v.a. *lārghah-, dirangī-, sustī-,* etc. *k.*

Deference, s. *makh, mulāḥiẓa, madārā, liḥāẓ*: *bāwar, i'tibār.*

Deficient, a. *kam, leg*; *waṭah, troṭ, zwam.*

Defile, s. *tanga-ī, darra.*

Defile, v.a. *palītawul, kakaṛawul, nā-pāk-, murdār-*, etc. *k.*

Define, v.a. *pūla-, brīd-, ḥadd-*, etc. *ṭaṛal*; *m'anā bayānawul.*

Definite, a. *muqarrar.*

Deflower, v.a. *bikr shlawul*, or *mātawul.*

Deformed, a. *bad-shakl*, or *-ḍaul*, or *-rang.*

Defraud, v.a. *drohawul, ṭagal, ghulawul.*

Defray, v.a. *kharts pūrah k., khejawul.*

Defy, v.a. *jang ghokkhtal, gwākkhal, d'awa k.*

Degenerate, a. *spuk, nā-kār, khwār, kam-aṣl.*

Degrade, v.a. *spekawul, makh-tor k.*

Degree, s. *pāya, dzāe, darja, martaba*; *qadr, ḥadd, andāza.*

Dejected, a. *gham-jan, dil-gīr, malāl, nūl-jan.*

Deign, v.a. *manal, qabūlawul, rawā-laral.*

Deism, s. *sūfī-garī.*

Deist, s. *sūfī.*

Deity, s. *khudāe, allah, rabb.*

Delay, v.a. *drangī-, lārghah-, dzanḍ-, sustī-, multawī-*, etc. *k.*

Delegate, s. *astādzai, wakīl*; *nā-ib, peshkār.* v.a. *āstawul, legal, rawānawul*; *spāral, ḥawāla k.*

Deleterious, a. *tāwānī, nuqṣānī, muẓirr.*

Deliberate, v.a. *fikr-, ghaur-, andekkhnā-*, etc. *k., maṣlaḥat-, tadbīr-, mashwarat-*, etc. *k.*

Delicacy, s. *bārīkī, narai-wālai*; *nāzakī, kkhkulī-tob*; *khwand, maza.*

Delicate, a. *narai, bārīk*; *nāzuk, kkhkulai.*

Delicious, a. *khwand-nāk, maza-dār.*

Delight, s. *kkhādī, khwand, khūsh-ḥālī, khwakkhī.* (-over enemy) *sakha, wiyāṛ.*

Delighted, a. *kkhād, khūsh-ḥāl, khwakkh.*

Delineate, v.a. *kāgal—kkhkal, līkal.*

Delirious, a. *be-khūd, be-hokkh.*

Delirium, s. *be-khūdī, be-hokkhī, haẓiyān.*

Deliver, v.a. *spāral, ḥawāla k.*; *warkawul*; *khalāṣawul, āzādawul, yalah k*; *bachawul*; *wurhawul*; *bayānawul, wayal.*

Deliverance, s. *khalāṣī, āzādī, yalah-wālai.*

Delude, v.a. *ghulawul, farestah k.*

Deluge, s. *sailāb, nīz* or *nyūz, chala, ṭughiyānī.* v.a. *gharqawul, ḍūbawul.*

Delusion, s. *khām-khiyāl, fareb, khaṭā.*

Demand, v.a. *d'awa k., ghokkhtal.*

Demeanour, s. *yūn, wajha, chāl-chalan.*

Demesne, s. *daftar, zmeka, wanḍ, ada-ī.*

Demolish, v.a. *naṛawul, wujāṛawul, wrānawul, nā-būd-, tālā-, kharāb-*, etc. *k.*

Demon, s. *dew, perai, rawai, ghūl.* (possessed of a-) *paṭ nīwulai.*

Demonstrate, v.a. *tsargandawul, bartser-, kkhkārah-*, etc. *k., kkhayal—kkhowul*; *zbād-, iṣbāt-*, etc. *k., dalīl rāwṛal.*

Demur, v.a. *drangī-, multawī-*, etc. *k.*; *andekkh-, shakk-, gumān-*, etc. *laral.*

Demure, a. *ghalai, ghaṛand*; *drūnd, sūṭ.*

Den, s. *ghār, kūz*; *ghālai.*

Denial, s. *inkār, nahiya, munkir-tob*; *ibā.*

Denizen, s. *astogūnkai, osedūnkai.*

Denote, v.a. *kkhayal—kkhowul, kkhkārah k., bayānawul.*

Denounce, v.a. *ghandal, kagal, ruswā k., bad-nāmawul, malāmatawul, raṭal.*

Dense, a. *ganr, gūr.* (-crops) *ṭal, tat.* (-cloth) *ṭok.* (-liquids) *ṭing.*

Dent, s. *jghanḍ, kanḍaw, wat.*

Denude, v.a. *barbanḍawul, poṭ-, tsarman-*, etc. *-kāgal—kkhkal* or *-bāsal—yastal.*

Deny, v.a. *inkār k.* v.n. *munkiredal.*

Depart, v.n. *tlal—lāṛal, lwukkhtal, rawānedal, drūmal*; *legdal—lekkhal.*

Departure, s. *tah, tlana, legdana, rawānagī, wartag, pand.*

Depend, v.n. *dzwaṛandedal, āwezānd ked.*; *āsra-, umed-*, etc. *laral*; *mauqūf-*, etc. *ked.*

Dependant, a. *dzwaṛanḍ*; *mauqūf.*

Dependence, s. *āsra, umed, takiya, bāwar*; *i'tibār*; *'alāqa*; *tāb'i-dārī.*

Dependent, s. *hamsāyah, tāb'i-dār.*

Deplore, v.a. *afsos-, tartāb-, gila-*, etc. *k.*

Deponent, s. *gawāhī lūnaī, shāhid.*

Deportment, s. *yūn, chāl, chalan, taur.*

Depose, v.a. *gawāhī-, shāhidī-*, etc. *lal* or *lawdal*; *sharal*; *mauqūf k.*

Deposit, s. *amānat*; *graw.* v.a. *gdal* or *īgdal, yakkhodal* or *īkkhodal, yakkhawul* or *īkkhawul*; *spāral*; *amānat kegdal*, etc.

Deposition, s. *gawāhī, shāhidī.*

Depository, s. *ambār·khāna, koṭī.*

Depraved, a. *bad, kharāb, nā·kār, tabāh.*

Deprecate, v.a. *minnat-, d'uā-*, etc. *k., panāh-, 'uzr-*, etc. *-ghokkhtal.*

Depreciate, v.a. *spukawul, kamawul, la-agawul*; *kagal, ghandal, spuk ganral.*

Depredation, s. *lūṭ, nātah, tālā, tākht, tārāj.*

Depress, v.a. *lānde k., ghamawul*; *ṭīṭawul.*

Depression, s. *gham, khapagān, dil·tangī, da zṛeh nūl*; *ḍoghal, jawar, tahna, jawar·tiyā.*

Deprive, v.a. *ākhistal, shūkawul, man'a k.*

Depth, s. *jawar·tiyā, star·wālai.*

Deputation, s. *jirga, m'arika, astādzī.*

Depute, v.a. *jirga-*, etc. *āstawul* or *legdal*; *wakīl, wudrawul.*

Deputy, s. *nā-ib, wakīl*; *jirgatū, astādzai.*

Derision, s. *ṭoqa, khandā, pekkha.*

Derive, v.a. *mūndal, gaṭal, paidā k.*

Derogate, v.a. *ghandal, kagal, spukawul.*

Derogatory, a. *spek, ruswā, nā·kār, nāsāzā.*

Descant, v.a. *bayānawul, wayal.*

Descend, v.n. *kūzedal, nāziledal, prewatal.*

Descendant, s. *alwād, zawzād, nasl, zurriyāt.*

Descent, s. *kūzedana, prewātah, nazūl*; *jawar, tahna*; *aṣl, zāt, peṛa-ī.*

Describe, v.a. *bayānawul, kkhayal—kkhowul.*

Description, s. *bayān, naql*; *ṣūrat, shān*; *rang.* -

Desert, s. *ḥaqq, qadr, saẓāwārī, lā-iq·wālai.*

Desert, s. *ṣaḥrā, maidān, maira, dakkht, chol, bāyābān.* a. *wairān, wujāṛ, ta-ash, dzangal.*

Desert, v.a. *pregdal, prekkhodal, prekkhawul, prekkhal, tark k.* v.n. *takkhtedal, puṭedal.*

Deserted, a. *wairān, ghair·ābād, khushai, ṛang, sunj*; *prekkhodai, prīkkhai, tark·kaṛai.*

Deserter, s. *takkhtedūnkai.*

Deserve, v.a. *ḥaqq laral.* v.n. *lā-iq-, wājib-, saẓāwār-, qābil-*, etc. *-ked.*

Design, s. *niyat, rūkh, qaṣd, irāda*; *mudd'ā, matlab*; *band, chal*; *nakhkkha* or *naqsha.*

Design, v.a. *niyat-*, etc. *taṛal* or *laral*; *joṛawul.*

Desirable, a. *khwakkh, pīrzo, ghwarah.*

Desire, s. *ghokkht, armān, ārzū, murād, hanḍa, hatsa, khwakkhī.* (carnal) *naus, shahwat.*

Desire, v.a. *ghokkhtal, armān-*, etc. *laral· farmāyal.*

Desolate, a. *wairān, wujāṛ, ṛang, sunj, chauṛ*, v.a. *wairānawul, wujāṛawul, tālā-*, etc. *k.*

Despair, s. *nā·umedī*; *gham, nūl.*

Desperate, a. *be·bāk, lewanai.*

Despise, v.a. *spuk ganral, bad manal, kagal.*

Despot, s. *ẓālim, zorāwar, khpul·sar.*

Despotism, s. *ẓulm, zorāwarī, zabardastī.*

Destination, s. *borjal, ṭikāo, mazal.*

Destiny, s. *naṣīb, qismat, taqdīr, bakht*; *ajal.*

Destitute, a. *khwār, lā·chār, be·kas, muflis.*

Destroy, v.a. *wrānawul, habatah-, halāk-. tālā-, kharāb-, nā·būd-, fanā-*, etc. *k.*

Destruction, s. *halākat, kharābī, wrānī*, etc.

Destructive, a. *muẓirr, ziyānī, tāwānī.*

Desultory, a. *be·tartīb, nā·qalār, be·sar.*

Detach, v.a. *biyalawul, judā k., lwuṛawul.*

Detached, v.n. *biyaledal, lwukkhtal, judā ked.*

Detachment, s. *ghol, dasta, ṭolai, ta'ināt.*

Detail, v.a. *biyal·biyal-, judā·judā-, mufaṣṣal-*, etc. *-wayal* or *-bayānawul* or *-likal.*

Detain, v.a. *man'a k., aṭālawul*; *khundiyal, sātal*; *stūnawul*; *bandawul, qaid k.*

Deter, v.a. *yerawul* or *werawul.*

Determination, s. *qaṣd, niyat*; *ḥukm, amr.*
Detest, v.a. *bad manal* or *-ganṛal, kagal, chinjawul, kraka ākhistal.*
Detract, v.a. *ghandal, chughlī-, ghībat-*, etc. *k. tor pore k., spukawul*; *kamawul, leggawul.*
Detriment, s. *tāwān, ziyān, nuqṣān, khalal, budrī, troṭ.*
Devastate, v.a. *natal, wrānī-, lūṭ-, tālā-, pacmālī-, tākht·tārāj-, chaur-*, etc. *k.*
Develop, v.a. *ziyātawul, wadānawul.*
Deviate, v.n. *girzedal, āwukkhtal, gharedal, gumrāh ked.* v.a. *girzawūl.*
Device, s. *band, tadbīr, ḥikmat, chal*; *nakkha.*
Devil, s. *shaiṭān*; *dew, rawai.*
Devious, a. *kag·lech, kālkūchan.*
Devise, v.a. *band taṛal, tadbīr-*, etc. *k.* (give) *bakkhal, kiba k.*
Devolve, v.n. *rasedal, prewatal, lāzim ked.*
Devote, v.a. *ṣadqa-, qurbān-*, etc. *k.*; *niyāz-*, etc. *manal* or *k.*; *bakkhal, wudrawul.*
Devotee, s. *zāhid, muttaqud.*
Devotion, s. *'ibādat, bandagī*; *nmūndz*; *mashghūlā shughl, lagiyā.*
Devout, a. *nek, m'utakif, nmāndz·guzār.*
Dew, s. *pa-arkha.*
Dewlap, s. *jajūra*; *ghab·ghab, ghuṭ·yālai, gharai.*
Dexterous, a. *chālāk, tak·lāstai.*
Dialect, s. *jiba, wrāsha.*
Dialogue, s. *sawāl·dzawāb, khabare.*
Diamond, s. *almās.*
Diaphragm, s. *prīnr, parda (da geḍe).*
Diarrhœa, s. *bahedana da dastūno.* (to have-) v.a. *rīkh wahul.* (having-) a. *rīkhan.*
Diary, s. *roz·nāma.*
Dice, s. *qimār.*
Dictionary, s. *lughat.*
Die, v.n. *mṛal, muṛ ked.*
Diet, s. *khwurāk*; *pāl·parhez.*
Difference, s. *biyal·tūn* or *biyal·wālai, farq.*
Different, a. *biyal, bul, judā.*
Difficult, a. *sakht, grān, mushkil.*
Difficulty, s. *sakhtiyā, grān·tiyā, tangsiyā.*
Diffidence, s. *wiswās, andekkhnā*; *yara, wahm*; *stāra*; *shakk, shubha.*
Diffuse, v.a. *khwarawul.*
Dig, v.a. *kandal* or *kanal, kanawdal, kanastal.*
Digest, v.a. *hazm k.*
Dignity, s. *pāya, martaba*; *qadr, 'izzat.*
Dike, s. *kanda, kāha-ī*; *khandaq*; *pūla, wand.*
Dilapidate, v.n. *naṛedal, wrānedal.*
Dilate, v.a. *planawul, arat k., ūgdawul.* v.n. *ghwaredal, planedal, paṛsedal.*
Dilatory, a. *sust, laṭ, drang, nā·rāst.*
Dilemma, s. *balā, nkkhatai, sākha.*
Diligent, a. *miḥnatī, kokshiksh kawūnkai, sā'ī.*
Dilute, v.a. *makhīn-, narai-*, etc. *k.*
Dim, a. *dund.*
Diminish, v.a. *kamawul, landawul, legg k.*
Diminutive, a. *pūṭai, wṛūkai, waṛkoṭai, kuchanai, kachoṭai, kharmandai, woṛ, legg.*
Dimple, s. *kwata-ī*; *ta-apai.*
Din, s. *ghāw, zwag·zūg, shor.*
Dinner, s. *tsakkhtī*; *ḍoḍa-ī*; *khwurāk.*
Dint, s. *zor, quwwat.*
Dip, v.a. *ḍubawul, gharqawul, ghoṭa-, ghūpa-*, etc. *-warkawul -wahal* or *-khwuṛal.* (-as bread in soup, etc.) *chūka k.*
Diploma, s. *sanad.*
Dire, a. *bashpaṛ, sakht*; *haibat·nāk.*
Direct, a. *sam, negh, barābar.*
Direct, v.a. *kkhayal—kkhowul*; *farmāyal, ḥukm-chalawul*; *naẓar lagawul*; *sar·nāma līkal*, or *-kāgal—kkhkal.*
Direction, s. *lorai, khwā, rūkh, makh, palaw*; *sar·nāma, nakkha*; *farwān, ḥukm.*
Directly, ad. *pa ṭakī, pā de sā'at, sam da lāsa.*
Director, s. *kkhowūnkai*; *kār kawūnkai*; *pīr-*
Dirge, s. *wīr* or *vīr, wainā.*
Dirt, s. *khīra, palītī, rash.*
Dirty, a. *khīran, khichan, palīt.*

Dis-, the particle of negation, is expressed by the prefixes *be-*, *nā-*, *lā-*, *bad-*, etc.

Disable, v.a. *lā-chār-*, *nā-tuwān-*, *be-tāqat-*, *be-maqdūr-*, *'ājiz-*, etc. *k.*

Disadvantage, s. *tāwān*, *ziyān*, *nuqsān*.

Disadvantageous, a. *'abas*, *be-fā-idah*.

Disaffected, a. *yāghī*, *sar-kakkh*, *nā-rāz*.

Disagree, v.n. *nā-rāz-*, *mukhālif-*, etc. *ked.*

Disagreeable, a. *kagalai*, *bad*, *ghāndah*.

Disagreement, s. *jagṛa*, *steza*, *poṭ*.

Disappear, v.n. *puṭedal*, *wrukedal*, *ghā-ib ked.*

Disappoint, v.a. *nā-umed k.*

Disappointed, a. *nā-umed*, *malāl*; *mikkh-mikkh.*

Disapprove, v.a. *bad-manal*, *kagal*, *ghandal.*

Disaster, s. *āfat*, *bad-balā*, *randz*, *musībat.*

Disastrous, a. *bad-* or *kam-bakht.*

Disbelieve, v.a. *na-manal*, *bāwar na-kawul.*

Discard, v.a. *sharal*; *liri k.*

Discern, v.a. *pejandal*, *m'alūmawul*; *katal*, *goral*, *lidal.*

Discerning, a. *hokkhyār*, *pohānd.*

Discernment, s. *poh*, *'aql.*

Discharge, v.a. *khalāsawul*, *ta-ashawul*; *lire-*, *biyarta-*, etc. *k.*, *dzawāb warkawul*; *ghurzawul*, *wishtal*; *purah k.*, *pa dzāe k.*

Discharge, s. *khalāsī*, *dzawāb.* (explosion) *ḍaz*, *shilak.* (-from debt, etc.) *rāzī-nāma*, *faisal-nāma.*

Disciple, s. *murīd*, *shāgird*, *tālib.* (-of Christ) *hawārī.*

Discipline, s. *ā-īn*, *qā'ida*, *dastūr.*

Disciplined, a. *āmokhtah*, *el.*

Disclose, v.a. *prānital tsargandawul*, *kkhkā-rah-*, *bartser-*, etc. *k.*, *parda porta k.*, *khwūla wayal*, *spekkhta āṛawul*, *pudūlī k.*

Discolour, v.n. *bad-rang-*, *dāghī-*, etc. *-ked.*

Discomfit, v.a. *lānde-*, *pa-ar-*, *māt-*, etc. *k.*

Discompose, v.a. *rabṛawul*, *hariyānawul*; *wrānawul*, *kharāb-*, *gaḍ-waḍ-*, *be-tartīb-*, etc. *k.*, *wār-khatā k.*

Disconsolate, a. *gham-nāk*, *nūl-jan*, *dil-tang.*

Discontented, a. *nā-rāz*, *be-sabr.*

Discontinue, v.a. *pregdal—prekkhodal*, *pre-kkhawul*, *prekkhal*, *tark k.*

Discord, s. *patna*, *pasāt*; *sākha.*

Discordant, a. *nā-sāz*, *be-tāng.*

Discover, v.a. *m'alūmawul*, *pejandal*; *tsar-gandawul*, *kkhkārah-*, *bartser-*, etc. *k.*; *kkhayal—kkhowul*; *mūndal*, *biyā-mūndal.*

Discount, s. *troṭ*, *waṭa.*

Discourage, v.a. *yerawul*, *zṛah chīngawul.*

Discourse, s. *khabare*, *qīl-o-qāl*, *gangosai*, *kkhkālwa*, *wayana.*

Discreet, a. *hokkhyār*, *pohānd*, *pokh.*

Discuss, v.a. *bahs k.*

Disease, s. *bīmārī*, *maraz*, *āzār*, *nājoṛ-tiyā*, *nārogh-tiyā*, *randz.*

Diseased, a. *bīmār*, *marīz*, *nājoṛ*, *nārogh*, *randzūr*, *āzārī.*

Disembark, v.a. *kūzawul.* v.n. *kūzedal.*

Disengage, v.a. *āzādawul*, *khalāsawul*, *yalah k.*, *prānital*, *spaṛdal.*

Disfigure, v.a. *bad rangawul*, *wrānawul.*

Disgorge, v.a. *jārbāsal—jāryastal.*

Disgrace, v.a. *bad-nām-*, *ruswā-*, *makh-tor-*, *be-nang-*, *be-makh-*, etc. *k.*, *sharmawul.*

Disgraceful, a. *bad*, *nā-kkhanai*, *nā-lā-iq.*

Disguise, s. *bāna*, *libās*, *swāng.*

Disgust, s. *kraka.*

Disgusted, v.n. *chinjedal.*

Dish, s. (wooden-) *pīna.* (brass-) *tālai.* (iron-) *tabakhai.* (pottery-) *taba-ī*, *taghā-rai.* (china-) *rikabī.* (chafing-) *majmir.* (-of stone for baking on) *shokāurai.* (-of made food) *sālan*, *qatagh*, *ngolai.*

Dishearten, v.a. *zṛah chīngawul*, *nā-umed k.*

Dishevelled, a. *spaṛdalai*; *shāwlai-wāwlai.*

Dishonest, a. *be-īmān*, *nā-rāst.*

Dishonour, s. *be-'izzatī*, *bad-nāmī*, *makh-torī.*

Disjoint, v.a. *kūtal*, *band prekawul*, *bja k.*

Disk, s. *chakai*, *tsarkhai*, *qurs.*

Dislike, v.a. *bad manal, chinjawul, kagal, kraka ākhistal, ghandal.*

Dislocate, v.a. *be·dzāe k.*

Dismal, a. *khof·nāk, andekkh·nāk, tars·nāk; tor, tārīk; gham·jan, malāl.*

Dismantle, v.a. *naṛawul, wrānawul, shūkawul, barbanḍawul, spaṛdal.*

Dismay, s. *wera* or *yera, khof, tor, bāk.*

Dismiss, v.a. *rukhṣat k., dzawāb warkawul, lire-, biyarta-,* etc. *k.*

Dismount, v.n. *kūzedal.*

Disobedient, a. *yāghī, sar·kakkh.*

Disoblige, v.a. *wezār-, khapah-, randzūr-,* etc. *k., kaṛawul.*

Disobliging, a. *be·makh, be·muruwwat.*

Disorder, s. *be·tartībi, gaḍ·waḍ·tob, be·band·obastī.* v.a. *gaḍ·waḍ k.*

Disown, v.n. *munkiredal.*

Disparage, v.a. *spukawul, kogal, ghandal, tor pore k., ghībat k.*

Dispatch, v.a. *āstawul, legdal, legal; chalawul, rawānawul.*

Dispatch, s. *talwāṛ, tak·lāstai·tob, jalta-ī.*

Dispel, v.a. *khwarawul, lire k., wrukawul.*

Dispensary, s. *dawā·khāna.*

Dispense, v.a. *weshal, kkhandal.* (-with) *mu'āf k., pulawul.*

Disperse, v.a. *khwarawul, takkhtawul tār·pa·tār k.*

Displace, v.a. *sharal, be·dzāe k.*

Display, v.a. *kkhkārah-, bartser-,* etc. *k.*

Display, s. *nandāra, tamāsha.*

Displease, v.a. *khapah-, marawar-,* etc. *k., kaṛawul, randzawul, wezārawul.*

Disposal, s. *wāk, qābū, rokh, ikhtiyār.*

Dispose, v.a. *tar,ībawul, sambālawul, gdal, īkkhodal* or *yakkhodal, īkkhawul* or *yakkhawul; kegdal* or *kkhkegdal, kekkhodal* or *kkhkekkhodal, khartsawul; warkawul, hiba k., bakkhal* or *bakhkkhal; kkhkenawul.*

Disposition, s. *tartīb, ḍaul; khwā, khoe, mizāj, lokkhai, salīqa, ṭab'a.*

Dispossess, v.a. *sharal, shūkawul, be·dzāe k.*

Disprove, v.a. *bāṭil-, darogh·jan k.*

Dispute, v.a. *jagṛa-, steza-, takrār-, qaẓiya-,* etc. *k. k.; bakṣ k.*

Disreputable, a. *be·i'tibār, nā·la·iq, ruswā.*

Disrespectful, a. *be·adab, be·makh.*

Dissatisfied, a. *nā·rāẓ, nā·khwakkh.*

Dissect, v.a. *tsīral, kūtal.*

Dissemble, v.a. *bāna-, lamghaṛa-ī,* etc. *k.*

Disseminate, v.a. *khwarawul, tār·pa·tār k.*

Dissension, s. *patna, jagṛa, steza, pasāt.*

Dissipate, v.a. *wrukawul, talaf-, ṣarf-, charcha-,* etc. *k.; mastī-, nasha·khorī-,* etc. *k.*

Dissolute, a. *chaṭ, lawanḍ, qachar.*

Dissolve, v.a. (-by fire) *wīlī k.* (-by water) *oba k.* (-an assembly) *bar·khwāst k.*

Dissuade, v.a. *man'a k., khwā girzawul.*

Distance, s. *farq.* (-of time) *mūda.* (-of place) *lār, dzāe.* (respect) *adab*

Distant, a. *lirai, prat.*

Distend, v.a. *paṛsawul, wīṛawul.* v.n. *paṛsedal, wīṛedal.*

Distention, s. *pāṛsob, waram.*

Distil, v.a. *tsātsawul.* v.n. *tsātsedal.*

Distinct, a. *biyal, judā.*

Distinction, s. *biyal·tūn, judā-ī, farq.*

Distinguish, v.a. *pejandal; zdah k., m'alūmawul; nāmer-, nām·dār-, nūm·war-,* etc. *k*

Distort, v.a. *kog k.* or *kagawul, kṛingawul, ṭīṭawul.*

Distract, v.a. *rabṛawul, hariyānawul, sargardān-, pareshān-, lewanai-,* etc. *k.*

Distress, s. *khwārī, tangsiyā, mīrtsī, randz.*

Distress, v.a. *tangawul, rabṛawal, āzārawul, zahīrawul.*

Distribute, v.a. *weshal, wesh-, brakha-, qismat-,* etc. *k.*

District, s. *tapa, pargana.*

Distrust, s. *gumān, shakk, shubha.*

Distrustful, a. *bad·gumān, shakk·man.*

Disturb, v.a. *rabṛawul, pārawul, khwadz-awul, laṛal, kkhorawul.*

Ditch, s. *kanda, kāha-ī, kaḍa-ī.*

Ditty, s. *chār·baita, ṭapa, sandara, lanḍa-ī.*

Dive, v.a. *ghūpa-, ghoṭa-,* etc. *wahal* or *k.*

Diverge, v.n. *biyaledal, girzedal, bewukkhtal.*

Diverse, a. *biyal—biyal; dzaṇe.*

Diversion, s. *nandāra, tamāsha, sail, loba.*

Divert, v.a. *girzawul, āwukkhtal; ghulawul.*

Divest, v.a. *barbanḍawul; shūkawul.*

Divide, v.a. *prekawul* or *prekṛal, tsīral, ghwutsawul; weshal, brakha-, qismat-, wanḍ-,* etc. *k.*

Dividend, s. *brakha, wesh, pucha, wanḍ.*

Divination, s. *pāl katana, koḍa, 'ilm da ghā-ib.*

Divine, a. *ilāhī, rabbānī, khudā-ī.* s. *faqīh.*

Divinity, s. *khudā-ī; fiqha.* (the-) *khudāe.*

Division, s. *wesh, brakha, ḥiṣṣa, wanḍ.* (-of land) *paṭai, ṭikai, wand, ada-ī.* (-of country) *tapa, pargana, khel.* (-of village) *kandai, mālat, cham, palaw.*

Divorce, s. *ṭalāq.* v.a. *ṭalāq k., pa kāghaz-, pa dreo kāṇro-,* etc. *ṭalāq·warkawul.*

Divulge, v.a. *tsargandawul, kkhkārah k., parda porta k., khwāla wayal, pudūlī k.*

Dizzy, a. *sargardān, akar-jan.*

Do, v.a. *kawul, kṛal, joṛawul, pa dzāe k.*

Docile, a. *el* or *īl, eman.*

Dock, s. (for vessels) *ḍanḍ, ḥauẓ, ḍab.* (the plant) *shalkhai.*

Dock, v.a. (cut short) *lanḍ-, ghūṭ-,* etc. *pre-kawul* or *k.* (-the hair) *sar·kunḍai k.*

Doctor, s. *ḥakīm, ṭabīb.* (-of law) *faqīh.* (-of divinity) *maulawī.*

Doctrine, s. *mazhab; masla; 'ilm.*

Dodge, v.a. *chal·wal-, lamghaṛa-ī-,* etc. *k.*

Doer, s. *kawūnkai, kṛūnai.*

Dog, s. *spai.* (terrier-) *pishtai.* (pointer-) *khandai.* (greyhound-) *tāzī.* (mastiff-) *khaḍal.* (mongrel) *kūtah.* (-tick) *kanṛ, kūnai, wradza.* (-fly) *manganṛ·mach.* (-in heat) *spiyama* or *spe-ama.* (-platter) *chaṭ.*

Doings, s. *kār, kṛah, kṛah·wṛah.*

Doleful, a. *gham·nāk, malāl, sūṭ·būṭ.*

Doll, s. *gūda-ī, lola-ī, nāwaka-ī, nenzaka.*

Dolt, s. *pūhaṛ, yedī·khar, kawdan, kam·'aql.*

Domain, s. *mulk, daftar; wanḍ, ada-ī.*

Dome, s. *gunbat.*

Domestic, a. *āmokhtah, eman, el* or *īl.* s. *koranai; nokar, khāna·zād.* (-economy) *kormāna.*

Dominion, s. *ḥukūmat, sardārī, khānī.*

Donation, s. *bakhkshiksh, bakkhana, khwaṛa.*

Donor, s. *warkawūnkai, bakkhawūnkai.*

Doom, s. *ḥukm, fatwā; naṣīb, qismat; ajal.*

Door, s. *war.* (-frame) *durshal.* (-leaf) *pala, tamba.* (-heel) *chūṛ.* (-keeper) *darwānchī, darwāza·wān, ghāpchī.*

Dose, s. *khwurāk.* (dry-) *paka* or *kapa.* (liquid-) *gūṭ, īnda, ghuṛap.*

Dot, s. *ṭakai, nuqta, pitsāṇrai, pūṭai.*

Double, a. *dwah·bragh, bgharg, dogānah.* (of a fox, etc.) *kālkūchaka.*

Doubt, s. *shakk, shubha, gumān.* v.a. *shakk-,* etc. *laṛal.*

Doubtful, a. *shakk·dār, shakk·man, gumānī.*

Doubtless, ad. *be·shakk, be·shubha, yaqīnan.*

Dough, s. *khamīra, ākkhalai.* (lump of-) *peṛa, ghunḍa.*

Dove, s. *qumrī, tatawa, spalama.* (ring-) *gūgushtū, kuṛkuṛa-ī.*

Dovetail, v.a. *ageyal.*

Dower, s. (portion) *dhadz, dūd, kulang.* (jointure) *mahr, kābīn.*

Down, p. *kkhkata, lānde, kkhke-a* or *kkhkiya.*

Down, s. *maidān, sama, maira.* (hair) *ghūna, tor·wekkhtah, zunba, waṛa-ī.* (-of beard) *khorma.*

Doze, v.a. *parnā-, khob-,* etc. *wṛal; ūdah-, bīdak-,* etc. *ked.*

Draft, s. *hunḍa-ī, barāt, ḥujjat.*

Drag, v.a. *rūkāgal—rūkkhkal, kashāla k.*

Dragon, s. *kkhā-mār, ajdahā, nihang.*

Dragoon, s. *turk-* or *chābuk-sawār, swor* or *spor.*

Drain, s. *mora-ī, nāla; lakkhtai.*

Drain, v.a. *wuchawul, rūkāgal—rūkkhkal.*

Dram, s. *dirham, misqāl; gūt, ghurap.*

Drama, s. *naql, swāng, pekkha.*

Draper, s. *bazzāz, parānchah.*

Drapery, s. *ṭūkai, zarūkai, pokkhāk.*

Draught, s. (gulp) *gūt, īnda, ghurap, qurt.* (beverage) *sharbat, tskkhāk* or *skāk.* (wind) *wo, bād; pū, tsapa.* (cattle) *bār-kakkh.* (copy) *naql.* (drawing) *nakhkkha.*

Draw, v.a. *rākāgal—rākkhkal.* (picture) *kāgal—kkhkal, ṭikal, kwekkhkal.*

Drawback, s. *'aib, stūnai.*

Drawers, s. *partūg, shalwār, tambān.* (hem of-) *bada.* (hole of hem) *kustīj.* (tape of-) *partūghākkh.* (leg of-) *pā-entsa.* (fork of-) *khakkhtagai.*

Drawing, s. *nakhkkha* or *naqsha; kakkhikkh, kakkha, kashāla.*

Dread, s. *yera* or *wera, bāk, khof, tars; wis-wās, andekkhnā, gram.* v.n. *weredal* or *yeredal, andekkhedal.* v.a. *tars-*, etc., *laral* or *-khwural; gram k.*

Dreadful, a. *khof-nāk, haibat-nāk; bad, bashpar, sakht.*

Dreadfully, ad. *be-shāna, be-hadda.*

Dream, s. *khob.* (fancy) *khiyāl.* (night-mare) *khapasa.* v.a. *khob ṭidal; khiyāl k.*

Dreary, a. *wairān, wijār, khushai, sunj.*

Dredge, v.a. (flour) *bornah k.*

Dregs, s. *khatbel.* (clotted-) *matra.* (-of vegetables) *gadzārai.* (-of metals) *khīra.*

Drench, v.a. *lūndawul, khushtawul, lūnd-khusht k.* (purge) *jullāb-, jār-*, etc. *war-kawul.*

Dress, s. *āghostana, pokkhāk, jāma, zarūkai, kālai, nmarai* or *nwarai.*

Dress, v.a. *āghostal, āghostawul, poslal, pokkhal.* (cook) *pakhawul.* (-a wound) *paha pore k.*

Dribble, v.n. *tsātsedal.*

Drift, s. (aim) *gharaz, matlab.* (rain and wind) *sīla-ī, jam-jakar.* (-wood, etc.) *ganda-kher, niyāz-wrai.* (-mud) *laha, lāe.*

Drill, s. *barma.* (military-) *qawā'id.* v.a. *barma-, sūrai-*, etc. *k., tsekhal; qawā'id kkhayal—kkhowul.*

Drink, v.a. *tskal* or *tskkhal* or *skal.* s. *tskkhāk*, etc.

Drive, v.a. *chalawul.* (-cattle) *biyāyal—bīwul—botlal, ramawul.* (-a horse) *zoral.* (-away) *takkhtawul, sharal, ratal, lire k.* (-a nail) *wahal, ṭakawul, mandal.* (-into) *kkhke-mandal, dūsa k.*

Drivel, v.a. *lāra ghurzawul* or *toyawul.*

Drizzle, v.n. *pūna-, rangai bārān-, narai bārān-*, etc. *oredal.*

Droll, a. *'ajab, khandā-nāk.* s. *ṭoq-mār, washt-mār, maskharāchī, pekkhe-gar, ma-landai.*

Drollery, s. *washta, ṭoqa, maskhara, pekkha.*

Droop, v.n. *mrāmedal, kumawredal; karedal, nūledal, ghamedal, malāl ked.; prewatal, ṭiṭedal.*

Drop, v.n. (distil) *tsātsedal.* (fall) *prewatal.* (-into) *kkhkewatal.* (slip) *khwa-edal* or *khwahedal.* (descend) *kūzedal.* v.a. (leap) *dangal.* (cease) *pregdal, prekkhodal* or *prekkhal.*

Drop, s. *tsātskai.* (a little) *chilka.*

Dropsy, s. *jahola, taghārak, istisqā.*

Dross, s. (-of metals) *khīra, mata.* (-of iron) *ospankharai.* (-of vegetables) *gadzārai, drūza.*

Drought, s. *sūkra, khushk-sālī.*

Drove, s. *ṭolai, park.* (-of oxen) *gūhār.* (-of buffaloes) *goram.* (-of sheep, etc.) *kandak, rama, ghela.*

Drover, s. (-of oxen) *gāhū, gorwān, gāharaī, ghobah.* (-of buffaloes) *gūjar.* (-of sheep) *shpūn.*

Drown, v.a. *ḍūbawul, gharqawul, lāhū k.*

Drowsy, a. *khob-wṛai, parnā-wṛai.*

Drub, v.a. *wahal, ṭakawul, kūṭal.*

Drug, s. *dawā, dārū, darmān; būṭai.*

Druggist, s. *pansārī.*

Drum, s. *ḍol, ḍolkai, ḍamāma.* (kettle-) *ḍambakai, tanbal, naghāra.* v.a. *ḍol-,* etc. *wahal* or *-ghagawul.*

Drummer, s. *ḍol wahūnkai, ḍa-am* or *ḍum, naghārchī.*

Drunkard, s. *sharābī, nasha-khor, 'amalī, bangī, kaipī.*

Drunken, a. *mast; be-khūd, nasha-wṛai.*

Dry, a. *wuch, khushk; tagai, tosand.* (-bread) *spora ḍoḍa-ī.* v.a. *wuchawul* v.n. *wuchedal.*

Dryness, s. *wuch-wālai, khushkī.*

Duck, s. *baṭa.* (wild-) *hila-ī.*

Duck, v.a. *ghūpa-, ghoṭa-,* etc. *wahal* or *-khwuṛal; sar ṭiṭawul.*

Ductile, a. *narm, post* or *pos, mulā-im.*

Due, a. *bāqī; wājib, munāsib.* s. *ḥaqq; qarẓ, por; maḥṣūl, chūngai, dastūr.*

Dulcimer, s. *sitār, rabāb, sārinda, ghachaka, chamtāra.*

Dull, a. *pa-ats, be-dam, be-āb; tīrah, dund; kam-'aql, gedī; sust, laṭ, shaṭal* or *shalaṭ.*

Duly, ad. *jukht, barābar.*

Dumb, a. *gung, lāl.* s. *gungai.*

Dun, v.a. *zoral, taqāẓa k.*

Dun, a. *samand.* s. *muḥaṣṣil, sazāwal.*

Dunce, s. *pūhaṛ, gedī-khar, kam-'aql.*

Dung, s. (human-) *ghul.* (orbicular of sheep, etc.) *pucha.* (-of cows and buffaloes) *ghoshoe, ghoshāk.* (horse-) *kharshan.* (birds-) *paikhāl, rīkh.* (-of kids, etc.) *poghla, pekhāṛa.* (-heap) *ḍerān, khadzala.* (mass of cow-) *sūṭa.* (fuel of cow-) *tsapiyāka.* (stack of fuel of cow-) *gohāṭa.*

Dung, v.a. *ghul k; khaṛal, loya baul-k., ḥājat ta kkhkenāstal.*

Dungeon, s. *qaid-khāna, zindān.*

Dupe, s. *ghulawulai; drohawulai, ṭiṭālai.*

Duplicate, s. *naql, joṛa.*

Duplicity, s. *palma, ṭagī, ṭiṭāl, chal-wal.*

Durable, a. *pāedār, maẓbūṭ, qā-im, ṡābit,*

Duration, s. *pāedārī, mūda.*

During, p. *tar—pore, hombra chī.*

Dusk, s. *mākkhām, shafaq.*

Dusky, a. *ṭor, mushkai, kha-aṛ, skūnr.*

Dust, s. *dūṛa, khūwra, gard* or *garz, ghubār.*

Dust, v.a. *duṛawul.* (shake) *tsanḍal.* (dredge) *bornah k.*

Dusty, a. *garz wahalai, pa dūṛo ḍak.*

Dutiful, a. *farmān-bardār, khidmatī, manūnkai.*

Duty, s. *farẓ, sharṭ.* (office) *kār.* (military) *pahra, tsoka-ī.* (tax) *maḥṣūl, bāj, chūngai, ḥaqq.*

Dwarf, s. *chūnai, poṭai, mandarai, tsongai.*

Dwell, v.n. *osedal, āstedal, pātedal.* v.a. *mīshta-, astoga-, kilai-, ṭikāo-, basiyā-,* etc. *k.*

Dweller, s. *osedūnkai. āstedūnkai, astogūnkai.*

Dwelling, s. *astoga, mīshta, dzāe, kor, makān*

Dwindle, v.n. *kamedal, la-agedal, narai-, mahīn-, bārīk-, kotāh-,* etc. *ked.*

Dye, v.a. *rangawul, rang warkawul.*

Dyer, s. *dobī, rang-rez.*

Dynasty, s. *salṭanat, khāndān, rāj.*

Dysentery, s. *ra-ama, kānga, ṛap.* (to have-) v.a. *ra-ame-, ṛap, ghurzawul, kānga niwul.*

Dyspepsia, s. *bad-hazmī; agheṛana, āṭerana.* (to have-) v.a. *agheṛal, aṭeral.*

Dyspeptic, a. *āgheṛalai, aṭeralai.*

E.

Each, p. *har·yao, yao·yo.* (-other) *yo·bel, dzabla.*

Eager, a. *tez, tod, garm*; *mayan*; *liwāl.*

Eagle, s. *bātūr, gargas.*

Ear, s. *ghwag.* (-of corn) *wagai, chala-ī.* (-ring) *chala, wālai, lakkhta-ī, barghwagai, deda, barghoṭai, mandara-ī.* (lobe of-) *narma-ī, liraga-ī, būtska-ī.*

Earless, a. *būṛai.*

Early, a. *wakhtī.* (-crop) *mahīnah.* (-morning) *saḥār* or *saḥr, ṣubḥa.*

Earn, v.a. *gaṭal, paidā k., kamā-ī k., ḥāṣil k.*

Earnest, a. *garm, tod, sā'ī, pa jid.*

Earth, s. *khāwra*; *zmaka, zamīn*; *mulk, būm*; *duniyā, jahān, naṛa-ī.*

Earthen, a. *khāwrīn.*

Earthly, a. *jahānī, duniyā-ī.*

Earthquake, s. *zalzala, larza.*

Ease, s. *āsān·tiyā, ārām.*

East, s. *nmar·* or *nwar·khātah.*

Eastward, ad. *nwar·khātah khwā.*

Easy, a. *āsān*; *sam, spuk, halak*; *āsūdah, moṛ.*

Eat, v.a. *khwuṛal.*

Eatable, a. *khwurākī.*

Eater, s. *khwuṛūnkai, khwurindah* (in comp.) *-khor.*

Eaves, s. *bala-ī, sharīfa, sarmāta-ī, tsatsoba-ī, parchata-ī.* (-dropper) *ghwag·tsārai.* (-dropping) *ghwag·tsārana.*

Eaves-drop, v.a. *ghwag tsāral.*

Ebb, s. *zawāl, prewātah, kamedana.*

Ebullition, s. *eshnā, khūṭkai, josh.*

Eccentric, a. *pa trats*; *kāwāk, lewanai.*

Echo, s. *ghag, kāngai, anga-ī, angūza, āwāz.*

Eclat, s. *raunaq, dabdaba.*

Eclipse, s. *tandar.* v.a. *tandar nīwul.*

Economy, s. *kormāna*; *tartīb.*

Ecstacy, s. *be·khūdī, be·shāna dera kkhādī.*

Eddy, s. *ghurzai, gird·āb*; *ḍab.*

Edge, s. *ghāṛa, morga, tselma, ja-ī.* (of a blade) *dam.* (to set on-) v.a. *ghākkh ṭaghawul.*

Edge, v.a. (sharpen) *tera k.* (instigate) *lamsawul.* (fringe) *jānja-ī lagawul.*

Edging, s. *jānja-ī, laman, palaw, trāṭa, maghzai.*

Edict, s. *sanad, raqam, farmān, jār.*

Edifice, s. *makān, māṇra-ī, mina, ḳanela-ī.*

Edify, v.a. *pohawul, kkhayal—kkhowul, t'alīm k.*

Edition, s. *chāp, tālīf.*

Editor, s. *murattib, mu-allif.*

Educate, v.a. *pālal, lwalawul, tarbiyat-, t'alīm-,* etc. *k.*

Education, s. *pālana, tarbiyat, t'alīm.*

Eel, s. *mār·māhai, mār·kab.*

Efface, v.a. *wrānawul, habalah k., wrukawul.*

Effect, s. *'amal, pāzah, aṣar, kār.*

Effect, v.a. *kawul, kṛal, joṛawul, 'amal-,* etc. *k.*

Effects, s. *māl, asbāb, kālī, sāmān.* (-of deceased) *tarka, pāto.*

Effectual, a. *kārī, kāmil, pūrah, kāfī·shāfī.*

Effeminate, a. *kkhadzonak, nā·mard.*

Effervesce, v.n. *eshedal* or *yashedal, khuṭ ked.*

Effervescence, s. *eshnā, khuṭkai, josh.*

Efficient, a. *pūrah, kāmil, qābil, kār·sāz.*

Effigy, s. *but, tsera, ṣūrat.*

Effluvium, s. *būe, soṛ·bū-ī*; *brās.*

Effort, s. *zor, sa'ī, miḥnat, kokshiksh.*

Effrontery, s. *be·makh·tob, be·ḥayā-ī, be·sharmī.*

Effulgence, s. *ranrā, rokkhnā-ī, brekkhnā.*

Effulgent, a. *rokkhān, dzalak·nāk, brekkh·nāk.*

Effusion, s. *rezish, toe, toedana, bahedana.*

Egg, s. *haga-ī, hā.* (-plant) *bāṭiganr.*

Egotism, s. *khpulī, khūdī, manī.*

Egregious, a. *bashpaṛ, bad, sakht, ghaṭ.*

Egress, s. *wātah, khātah, barāmad.*

Eight, a. *atah.* (eighth) a. *atam.*

Eighteen, a. *atah-las*. (18th) *at-lassem*.
Eighty, a. *atiyā*. (eightieth) *atiyā-yam*.
Either, p. *yā*. pr. *tsok, kūm, tsa*.
Eject, v.a. *sharal, bāsal—yastal, jārbāsal—jāryastal, pore-jane k*.
Ejection, s. *sharūn, yastūn, jāryastūn*.
Elaborate, a. *narai, mahīn*; *mushkil, grān*.
Elapse, v.n. *teredal*.
Elastic, a. *post, narm*; *damdār, mulā-im*.
Elated, a. *khwakkh, kkhād, kkhād-man*; *bādī kibr-jan, maghrūr*.
Elbow, s. *tsangal*.
Elder, a. *mashar*. s. *spīn-gīrai*; *pīr, shekh*.
Elect, v.a. *khwakkhawul, chunral*.
Elegance, s. *kkhāyast, kkhāyast-wālai, jorāb, krah-wrah, spetsal-tob*.
Elegant, a. *kkhāyastah, nāzak*.
Elegy, s. *wir, wainā*.
Element, s. *aslī shai*.
Elephant, s. *hātī, pīl*.
Elevate, v.a. *khejawul, porta k., pātsawul*.
Elevated, a. *ūchat, hask, lwar*.
Elevation, s. *ūchat-wālai, bulandai, taraqqai, khātah, hask-wālai*; *sarfarāzī*.
Eleven, a. *yolas*. (eleventh) a. *yolasam*.
Elicit, v.a. *kāgal—kkhkal, bāsal—yastal, m'alūmawul*.
Eligible, a. *ghwarah, lā-iq, khwakkh, pirzo*.
Elixir, s. *aksīr, 'araq*.
Elk, s. *gāwuz*.
Elocution, s. *khula-warī, khula-war-tob*.
Elope, v.n. *putedal, takkhtedal*. (-as a woman) *matiza ked*. (-with a woman) v.a. *matiz k*.
Eloquent, a. *khula-war, khog-zabān*.
Else, p. *yā*. pr. *bul, nor*. (any one-) *bul-tsok, nor-tsok*. (anything-) *bul-tsa, nor-tsa*.
Else, ad. *kawra, kana, ganra*.
Elsewhere, ad. *bul-charta, nor-charta*.
Elucidate, v.a. *kkhkārah k., prānatal, bayān k*.
Elude, v.n. *putedal, bachedal, khalāsedal*.
Elysium, s. *jannat, bihikkht*.
Emaciate, v.n. *wuchedal, karedal, zahedal*.
Emaciation, s. *dangar-tob, wuch-klak-tob*.
Emancipate, v.a. *āzādawul, khalāsawul, yalah k*.
Embalm, v.a. *murai pa masālo dakawul*.
Embankment, s. *pūla, wand, band*.
Embark, v.n. *pa bera-ī sparedal* or *khatal*.
Embarrass, v.a. *rabrawul, hariyānawul, tangawul, sargardānawul*.
Embarrassed, a. *hariyān, sargardān*.
Embassy, s. *elchī-garī*.
Embellish, v.a. *jorawul, andzorawul, ārāstah-, kkhāyastah-*, etc. *k*.
Embellishment, s. *andzor, zeba, kkhāyast, kkhāyast-wālai, daul, kkhewa*.
Embers, s. *ire*. (hot-) *khuglan, skarwata, skhwakkhtan, akhgar*. (cold-) *sare ire*.
Embezzle, v.a. *putawul. ghlā k., wrukawul*.
Emblem, s. *nakkha, nikkhān, 'alāmat*.
Embrace, s. *ghey, ghūza*.
Embrace, v.a. *ghāra-ghara-ī-, bargarandai-, bara-gara-, rogh-bar-*, etc. *k*.
Embrocate, v.a. *ghwarawul, mugal—mukkhal, tabal*.
Embrocation, s. *mālish, takor, tab*.
Embroider, v.a. *bezal* or *pezal, būtai gandal*.
Embroil, v.a. *nkkhlawul*.
Emerald, s. *zamarrud*.
Emerge, v.n. *watal, khatal*.
Emergency, s. *zarūrat*; *wāqi'a, hādisa*.
Emergent, a. *zarūr*.
Emery, s. *kurand*.
Emetic, s. *da bāka-ī-, da chāl-, da jāryasto-*, etc. *dawā, khwā-garzanai dārū*.
Emigrant, s. *musāfir, pradai*.
Emigrate, v.a. *kada wral, legdal—lekkhal*.
Eminence, s. *ūchat-wālai, hask-wālai*; *khātah, taraqqai*; *derai, ghunda-ī, kha-at, potai, rāsha, rashaka-ī*; *zbargī, loe-wālai*; *hazrat*.
Eminent, a. *ūchat*; *ghat, loe*; *zbarg*.

Emissary, s. *jāsūs, tsārī, dzarai, mukhbir.*
Emollient, a. *post, narm, mulā-im.*
Emolument, s. *gaṭa, sūd, naf'a, ḥāṣil.*
Emotion, s. *eshnā, khuṭkai; randz, dard.*
Empale, v.a. *pa sūla-ī khejawul; tsekhal.*
Emperor, s. *sulṭān, bādshāh, malik.*
Emphasis, s. *tākīd; ẓarb; drunāwai, drund-wālai.*
Emphatic, a. *tākīdī; drūnd.*
Empire, s. *salṭanat, rāj, bādshāhī.*
Employ, v.a. *mashghūlawul, lagawul; chalawul; khartṣ k., sātal, pa kār rāwṛal.*
Employer, s. *khāwind, tsakkhtan, nāyak.*
Employment, s. *kār, khidmat, mashghūlā.*
Emporium, s. *bāzār, ganj, manḍka-ī, bandar.*
Empower, v.a. *wāk-, ikhtiyār-,* etc. *warkawul.*
Empty, a. *ta-ash, khālī, ḍaḍ.*
Emulate, v.a. *sām sorai k., ghairat laral.*
Emulation, s. *ghairat, barābarī, samsorai.*
Emulous, a. *ghairat-man, himmat-nāk.*
Enable, v.a. *quwat-, ṭāqat-, zor-, tuwān-,* etc. *warkawul.*
Enact, v.a. *fármāyal, ḥukm k.*
Enamel, s. *mīnā, jaṛāo, rang, āb.*
Enamour, v.a. *mayan-, 'āshiq-, fareftah,* etc. *k.; grohedah k.*
Encamp, v.a. *dera-, muqām-,* etc. *k.*
Enchanter, s. *jādū-gar, koḍ-gar, siḥr-gar.*
Enchantment, s. *jādū, koḍa, siḥr.*
Enclose, v.a. *īsāramul* or *ḥiṣārawul, ger k.; shpol-, keṛa-, jal-, bāra-, pūla-,* etc. *taṛal* or *-k.; nghakkhtal, lifāfa k.*
Enclosure, s. *iḥāta, bāra, ḥiṣār, hadera.* (-for cattle) *bānḍa, shpol.* (-of a house) *jal, gholai.*
Encounter, v.a. *jang k.* v.n. *miliyā, ked. pekkhedal.*
Encourage, v.a. *dam-, dilāsa-,* etc. *warkawul.*
Encroach, v.a. *lānde k., dakhl k.*
Encroachment, s. *dakhl, gharaẓ.*
Encumber, v.a. *kariyābawul, dranawul, bār āchawul.*
End, s. *ākhir, khatm; anjām, tamāmī; ḥadd, sar-peza, tsūka.* v.a. *ākhir-, khatm-,* etc. *k.*
Endear, v.a. *mayan-, 'azīz-,* etc. *k., khpulawul.*
Endeavour, s. *miḥnat, was, sa'ī, kokshiksh, hatsa.*
Endless, a. *be-ḥadd, be-and; tal, mudām.*
Endorse, v.a. *ṣaḥīḥ-, dast-khaṭṭ-,* etc. *k.*
Endowment, s. *waqf, hiba; khairāt, niyāz, bakkhana; hunar.*
Endurance, s. *ṣabr, zgham, tāb, zor, ṭāqat.*
Endure, v.a. *zghamal, ṣabr k., sahal, petsal.* v.n. *pāedal, sahedal.*
Enemy, s. *dukkhman; mirtsaman.*
Energetic, a. *chālāk, takṛah, maẓbūṭ.*
Energy, s. *zor, quwat, bram, tuwān.*
Enervate, v.a. *kam-zor-, kam-quwat-,* etc. *k.*
Enforce, v.a. *maẓbūṭ-, muḥkam-,* etc. *k., zoral, chalawul, rawā-, jārī-,* etc. *k.*
Engage, v.a. *mashghūlawul, lagiyā, k., sātal, lagawul, wāda-, neṭa-, shart,* etc. *taṛal* or *k.*
Engaged, a. *lagiyā, mashghūl.*
Engagement, s. *iqrār, wāda, neṭa, shart; kār, kasb, mashghūlā; jang, muqadamma.* (-in marriage) *kojdan* or *kojda.*
Engender, v.a. *paidā k., rāwṛol.*
Engine, s. *kālai, hatiyār, ālat, ṣana'at.*
Engrave, v.a. *kandal* or *kanal, kanastal.*
Engraver, s. *muhr-kan.*
Enhance, v.a. *qīmat ziyātawul, nirkh kamawul* or *-la-agawul; khejawul, dranawul.*
Enigma, s. *ramūz, kināya.*
Enjoin, v.a. *farmāyal, kariya-, tākīd-,* etc. *k.*
Enjoy, v.a. *khwand-, maza-,* etc. *k.*
Enjoyment, s. *khwand, maza; kkhādī, khwakkhī.*
Enlist, v.a. *nokar k.; nūm līkal; mal-, mal-garai-,* etc. *k.*

Enmity, s. *dukkhmanī, 'inād, 'aks, mīrtsī.*
Enormous, a. *ghaṭ, bashpar, loe, star, nāpar.*
Enough, ad. *bas, der, kāfī, kifāyat.*
Enquiry, s. *sawāl, pukkhtana, tapos* or *tafahus, pursān, pursish, shanana.*
Ensign, s. *nakkha, nikkhān, bairaq, janḍa.*
Ensnare, v.a. *ghulawul; niwul, nkkhlawul.*
Ensue, v.n. *prewatal, khatal, kedal.*
Entangle, v.a. *arjal-barjal-, arang-barang-, tsapolai-,* etc. *k.; nkkhlawul.*
Enter, v.n. *nanawatal, dākhiledal.*
Enterprise, s. *muhimm, grān-kār.*
Enterprising, a. *himmat-nāk, zṛak-war.*
Entertain, v.a. *pālal, sātal, nmāndzal; melmastiyā-, ziyāfat-, mezmānī-,* etc. *k.*
Entertainer, s. *melmah-dost, korbah, sat kawūnkai.*
Entertainment, s. *melmastiyā, sat; tamāsha, nandāra; loba, sail.*
Enthusiasm, s. *sargarmī, mīna, 'ishq.*
Enthusiast, s. *saudā-ī; 'āshiq, liwāl.*
Entice, v.a. *ghulawul, ṭagal, lamsawul, fareb-, targhīb-,* etc. *warkawul.*
Entire, a. *tamām, pūrah, sābat, kāmil.*
Entirely, ad. *amānī, sarāsar, surup.*
Entitle, v.a. *ḥaqq-man k.; nūm igdal* or *gdal,* or *-kkhkegdal* or *-kegdal.*
Entrails, s. *laṛmānah.*
Entrance, s. *war, darwāza, khula, darah; nanawātah, dakhl.*
Entrance, v.a. *be-khūd-, farestah-,* etc. *k., damawul, hūda k., paṭ niwul.*
Entrap, v.a. *niwul, nkkhlawul, ger k.*
Entrapped, a. *niwai, nkkhalai.* v.n. *nkkhatal* or *nkkhledal.*
Entreat, v.a. *minnat k.; ghokkhtal, du'ā k.*
Entreaty, s. *minnat, du'ā, darkhwāst.*
Entrenchment, s. *bāra, sangar, gaṛa-ī.*
Enumeration, s. *shmer, shumār, ḥisāb.*
Envelop, v.a. *nghaṛal—nghakkhtal.*
Envelope, s. *lifāfa; poṭ, postekai.*

Envious, a. *ḥāsid, ḥasad-nāk.*
Environs, s. *sawād, chār-chāper.*
Envoy, s. *elchī, wakil, astādzai.*
Envy, s. *ḥasrat, ḥasad, rashk, wiyāṛ.*
Ephemeral, s. *fānī, teredūnai.*
Epicure, s. *geḍa-parwar, khūsh-khwurāk*
Epidemic, s. *wabā; 'āmm.*
Epilepsy, s. *mergai, maherga.*
Epistle, s. *nāma, chiṭa-ī, khatt, kāghaz.*
Epitaph, s. *da qabr kataba.*
Epithalamium, s. *kkhādiyāna, sandara.*
Epitome, s. *khulāṣa, mukhtaṣar, lanḍa.*
Epoch, s. *tārikh, kāl, mūda, san.*
Equal, a. *barābar, makhai, gund, yo-shān; sam, hawārah.* s. *samsorai, humdzolai, siyāl, sārai, twal, makhai.*
Equality, s. *barābar-wālai, makhai-tob; samwālai.*
Equanimity, s. *qalār-tiyā, ṣabr.*
Equestrian, a. *sparlai, sparlanai.* s. *swor* or *spor.*
Equip, v.a. *tayār k., sambālawul, mlā taṛal, wasla-, drasta-,* etc. *warkawul, dzerma k.*
Equipage, s. *sāz, sāmān, asbāb, kālī.* (retinue) *swarlī* or *sparlī, jilab.*
Equitable, a. *'ādil, rikkhtīnai, rūst-man.*
Equity, s. *inṣāf, rūstī, niyāw, 'adl.*
Equivalent, a. *barābar, twal; badal, 'iwaz.*
Equivocal, a. *shakk-man, gumānī.*
Equivocate, v.a. *palma-, hira-ī-,* etc. *k., aṛawale-khabare k., darogh-jane khabare k.*
Era, s. *tārikh, kāl, san, mūda.*
Eradicate, v.a. *mūnḍ-, wekh-, būnsaṭ-,* etc. *bāsal—yastal,* or *-khejawul,* or *-kāgal—kkhkal.*
Erase, v.a. *wrānawul, qalam pre-kāgal.*
Ere, ad. *wṛunbe, awwal, lā; pakhwā, wṛānde.* (-now) *lā tar osa.* (-while) *lā pakhwā* (-long) *pa la-age mūde kkhke.*
Erect, a. *walāṛ, negh, lak, zig, jig.*
Erect, v.a. *walāṛawul, wadrawul, khejawul.*

Err, v.a. *khaṭā k.*
Errand, s. *paighām.* (-boy) *harkārah.*
Erroneous, a. *ghalaṭ.*
Error, s. *khaṭā, wabāl, gunā, taqṣīr.*
Erudition, s. *'ilm, qābil·tob.*
Eruption, s. *eshnā, khuṭ, khuṭkai, josh.* (prickly heat-) *garmaka.* (acne-) *dzwān-aka.* (small-pox) *nanaka-ī.* (measles-) *shirai.* (tooth-) *sreh·makha.* (jet) *fawāra, dāra.*
Erysipelas, s. *surkh·bād.*
Escalade, s. *khātah pa kamandūno.* (-ladder) *kamand.*
Escape, s. *khlāṣī, tekkhta, bachāw, bach.*
Escape, v.n. *bachedal, takkhtedal, khalāṣedal, wurhedal, yalah ked.* (miss) *terwatal.*
Escheat, v.n. *lā·wāriṣ ked.*
Escort, s. *badraga*; *jalab, sparlī.*
Especially, ad. *khuṣūṣan*
Esplanade, s. *maidān, ḍāga, panḍ·ghālai.*
Espouse, v.a. *kojdan k., wādeh k., nikāḥ taṛal.* (a cause, etc.) *ākhistal, bachawul, komak warkawul.*
Essay, s. (attempt) *qaṣd.* (trial) *āzmekkht.* (endeavour) *kokshiksh, sa'ī.* (treatise) *risāla.*
Essence, s. *'araq, jawhar, aṣl.* (perfume) *'aṭr.*
Essential, a. *aṣlī*; *ẓarūr*; *sūchah.*
Establish, v.a. *muqarrar-, jārī-,* etc. *k., chalawul, rawānawul*; *qā-im-, maẓbūṭ-,* etc. *k., wudrawul, kkhkenawul, pāedār k.*
Estate, s. (land) *dawtar* or *daftar, wanḍ.* (fief) *jāgīr, jāedād.* (property) *māl, daulat, milk.* (hereditary) *mīrāṣ* or *mīrāt.* (deceased's) *pāto, taraka.* (rank) *pāya, martaba, darja.*
Esteem, s. *qadr, 'izzat*; *mīna, tapāk.*
Esteem, v.a. *qadr-,* etc. *pejandal*; *mu'tabar-, nek-,* etc. *gaṇṛal*; *mīna-,* etc. *k.*
Estimable, s. *'izzat·nāk, mu'tabar, nek.*
Estimate, v.a. *shmeral, gaṇṛal.*
Estimation, s. *rāe, khiyāl, poha, fikr, naẓar.*
Estrange, v.a. *marawar-, māṇṛai-,* etc. *k.*; *pradai-, begānah-,* etc. *k.*
Estrangement, s. *māṇṛai, marawar·tob*; *pradī·tob, begān·tūn, begānah·tob* or *begān·tob.*
Eternal, a. *abadī, dā-im, jāwīd* or *jāwīdān.*
Eternally, ad. *tal, tar·tala, tal·tar·tala, mudāman, hamesh.*
Eternity, s. *abad, azal, baqā.* (to all-) ad. *tar·abada, tar·azala.*
Ethereal, a. *āsmānī, hawā-ī.*
Ethics, s. *pand·nāma, naṣīḥat·nāma.*
Etiquette, s. *adab, makh, madāra.*
Etymology, s. *ṣarf*; *peza-ī, hezagī.*
Eulogy, s. *stāyana, ṡanā, t'arīf.*
Eunuch, s. *hijṛai, khunṣā.*
European, s. *farangai.* a. *farangī.*
Evacuate, v.a. *ta-ashawul, khālī-, khushai-,* etc. *k.*; *jārbāsal—jāryistal.*
Evade, v.a. *palma-, bāna-, hira-ī-,* etc. *k.*; *ṭagī-, chal·bāzī-,* etc. *k.* v.n. *bachedal, puṭedal, terwatal.*
Evanescent, a. *fānī, teredūnai.* (-colour) *om.*
Evaporate, v.n. *wuchedal.*
Evasion, s. *bāna, ḥīla*; *palma, hira-ī.*
Evasive, a. *bāna·war, ḥīla·bāz.*
Even, a. *barābar, yaw·shān.* (similar) *gund.* (-in weight) *twal.* (smooth) *hawārah, sam.* (odd and-) *juft·o·tāk.*
Even, ad. *hum, lā, hado, yara, kho.*
Evening, s. *mākkhām, begāh.* (to-morrow-) *ṣabā begāh.* (last-) *begāh.* (of last-) *begānai, baranai.*
Evenness, s. *barābar·wālai, sam·wālai.*
Event, s. *wāqi'a, chal, khabara, qiṣṣa,* (at all-) *hargora, kām·nā·kām, khwāh·makhwāh, kho.*
Ever, ad. *kala, chare.*
Everlasting, a. *dā-im, qā-im, lā·zawāl.*
Evermore, ad. *hamesh, mudām, tar·abada.*

Every, a. har. (-person) har·tsok. (-thing) har·tsek.

Evidence, s. gawāhī, shāhidī; dalīl; nakkha. (to give-) v.a. gawāhī- or shāhidī lal or -lawdal.

Evident, a. tsargand, kkhkārah, bartser, awtsār.

Evidently, ad. zāhiran, bartseran, pa jār.

Evil, a. bad, kharāb. s. 'aib, kharābī; balā, āfat; gunāh, wabāl. (-doer) a. bad·kirdār, gunāh·gār.

Ewer, s. kūza, kūza·ṛa-ī, khum·ra-ī, kunja-ī.

Exact, a. jukht, kaṭ·maṭ, joṛ, barābar.

Exact, v.a. zoral; taqāza k.

Exaggerate, v.a. ziyātawal, ūgdawul, mubālagha k.

Exalt, v.a. pāya pa porta k.; khejawul, pātsawul.

Examine, v.a. āzmāyal, āzmekkht k.; imtiḥān ākhistal or k.; laṭawul, shanal, katal.

Example, s. misāl, namūna; 'ibrat, siyāsat.

Exasperate, v.a. rabṛawul, zoral; pārawul; khapah k., ṭongawul, ṭongāra k., ageyal.

Excavate, v.a. kanal, kanawdal, kanastal.

Excavation, s. kanda, ḍoghal.

Exceed, v.n. ziyātedal.

Excel, v.n. pūrah-, kāmil-, ghālib-, etc. ked.

Except, p. siwā, baghair, be·la—na.

Excess, s. ziyātī, der·wālai; charcha.

Excessive, a. ḍer, ziyāt, be·shān.

Excessively, ad. be·ḥadda, be·shāna.

Exchange, s. badal, 'iwaz; adal·badal; waṭa.

Excise, s. chūngai, sāw, maḥṣūl.

Excise, v.a. tsiral, prekawul or prekṛal.

Excite, v.a. pārawul; lamsawul; pātsawul, paidā k.; ageyal, ṭongawul.

Excitement, s. cshnā; pārawūna; lamsūn.

Exclaim, v.a. nāra wahul, bāng wayal, shor k., chighawul.

Exclamation, s. nāra, sūra, chigha, ghag, zwag; wāwailā, faryād.

Exclude, v.a. sharal, lire k., ratal.

Excoriate, v.a. garawul, sūlawul, nwaṛawul, sūdah k., nūkāre wahul. v.n. sūledal, sūdah ked.

Excrement, s. ghul. (-of diarrhœa) ka-aṛ, rīkh. (-of dysentery) ra-ama, ṛap.

Excruciate, v.a. khūgawul, 'azābawul, āzārawul.

Exculpate, v.a. pulawul, be·gunāh k., bakkhal.

Excursion, s. sail; gakkht. (-foray) dāṛa.

Excuse, v.a. pulawul, bakkhal; bāna-, hira-ī-, 'uzr-, etc. k., ḥujjat k.

Execrable, a. bad, l'anatī, makrūh.

Execrate, v.a. kkhera k.

Execute, v.a. kawul, kṛal, pa·dzāe k., joṛawul, tamāmawul, pūrah k.; qatlawul, wojal or wajlal, muṛ k.; jārī k., chalawul.

Execution, s. kawūna, kṛah, joṛawuna; qatl.

Executioner, s. jallād, qātil.

Executive, a. kār guzār; mukhtār kār.

Executor, s. waṣī.

Exemplary, a. nek, sawābī; 'ibrat·nāk.

Exemplify, v.a. misal ākhistal, or -rāwṛal.

Exempt, v.a. pregdal—prekkhodal, āzādawul, pulawul, bakkhal, bachawul, khalāṣawul.

Exercise, v.a. 'amal k., chalawul, jārī k., lagawul, mashghūlawul.

Exercise, s. 'amal, ist'imāl; mashghulā, kār; sail, gakkht. (lesson) dars, sabaq. (horses) jaulān, kartab. (hawks, dogs, etc.) bāolī. (troops) qawā'id.

Exert, v.a. kokshiksh-, sa'ī-, zor-, etc. k.; staw wahal.

Exhalation, s. bṛās, bukhār, dam, lū, laṛa, piyākkla, wagma.

Exhaust, v.a. ta-ashawul, khālī-, khushai-, etc. k.; wrukawul, kharts-, ṣarf-, etc. k.; tamām-, pūrah-, etc. k.; staṛai-, be·dam-, etc. k.

Exhaustless, a. be·nihāyat, be·zawāl.

Exhibit, v.a. *kkhayal—kkhowul, prānatal, kkhkārah-, bartser-, tsargand-,* etc. *k.*

Exhibition, s. *tamāsha, nandāra.*

Exhilarate, v.a. *kkhād-, khwakkh-,* etc. *k.*

Exhort, v.a. *pand, naṣihat-,* etc. *warkawul.*

Exigency, s. *tangsiyā, lā-chārī, sakhtī, ẓarūrat.*

Exile, s. *jilā-waṭanī, be-waṭanī.* (the person) *pradai, begānah, be-waṭan.*

Exist, v.n. *shwal, kedal, osedal, maujūdedal.*

Existence, s. *shta-wālai, hastī, būd, jwand.*

Existent, a. *osan, osanai, maujūd.*

Exit, s. *wātah, watana, wartag.*

Exonerate, v.a. *pulawul, khalāṣawul.*

Exorbitant, a. *be-andāz, be-nihāyat.*

Exorcise, v.a. *damawul, hūda k., koḍ k.*

Exordium, s. *debācha, muqaddama.*

Exotic, a. *pradai, begānah, gharīb.*

Expand, v.n. *planedal, artedal.* (swell) *parsedal.* (-as a flower) *ghwaredal, khwaredal.* (spread) *wīṛedal, pheledal.*

Expanse, s. *art-wālai, plan-wālai, sor* or *psor.*

Expect, v.a. *lār katal, umed laral.*

Expectant, a. *umed-wār, muntaẓir.*

Expectation, s. *umed, āsra.*

Expedient, a. *munāsib, ghwarah, wājib.* s. *band, tadbīr, chāra, chal.*

Expedition, s. *chālākī, chustī, talwār.* (journey) *safar.* (military-) *chapāo, tākht.* (foray) *dāṛa, bota.* (against infidels) *ghazā, jihād.*

Expeditious, a. *gaṛandai, tak-lāstai, chālāk, chust, za-ar* or *zir, jalt.*

Expel, v.a. *sharal, lire k., pore-jane k., bāsal—yastal, raṭal, traṭal.*

Expend, v.a. *kharts, ṣarf-,* etc. *k., lagawul.*

Expense, s. *kharts; qīmat, bai'a.*

Expensive, a. *khartsī-, tāwānī; grān, qīmatī, qīmat-nāk.*

Experience, s. *poha, wuqūf; āzmekkht.*

Experience, v.a. *lidal, terawul, zghamal, khwuṛal, kāgal—kkhkal.*

Experienced, a. *āmokhtah, āzmūdah, pokh, wāqif, khabar-dār, zdah.*

Experiment, s. *āzmekkht, tajriba, imtiḥān.*

Expert, a. *kāri-gar, hunar-man, hokkhyār; chālāk, pokh.*

Expiate, v.a. *kafāra warkawul, tāwān warkawul.*

Expiration, s. *anjām, khatm, ākhirat.* (death) *dzān-kadan, marg.*

Expire, v.n. *mṛal, muṛ ked.; teredal; tamāmedal.* (breathe) *sā-, sāh-, dam-,* etc. *bāsal—yastal, -sharal, -pregdal—prekkhodal,* etc.

Explain, v.a. *bayānawul, pohawul, kkhayal—kkhowul, kkhkārah k.*

Explanation, s. *bayān, kkhowūna, m'anā, sharah.*

Expletive, s. *takiya-kalām.*

Explicit, a. *tsargand, ṣāf, kkhkārah, ẓāhir.*

Explode, v.n. *pṛak-chāwdal, ālwatal.* v.a. *ḍaz wahal, ālwūzawul.*

Exploit, s. *karāmat, ghaṭ-kār, zbargī.*

Explore, v.a. *laṭawul, shanal.*

Explosion, s. *ḍaz, ṭas.*

Export, v.a. *bul mulk ta āstawul* or *-legal.*

Expose, v.a. *kkhkārah-, bartser-,* etc. *k., parda porta k.*

Exposition, s. *sharah, bayān.*

Expostulate, v.a. *takrār-, ḥujjat-,* etc. *k*

Exposure, s. *kkhkārah-tob, barbanḍ-tob.*

Expound, v.a. *bayānawul, m'anā-kkhayal—kkhowul.*

Express, v.a. *wayal, lal* or *lawdal; nichoṛawul, nakkhtedzal, paz wahal, zbekkhal.*

Express, a. *tsargand, antsār; khāṣṣ.* s. *qāṣid, chapar.*

Expression, s. *khabara, wayai, sukhan, kalām; nichoṛ, paz.*

Expressly, ad. *pa qaṣd, qaṣdan.*

Expulsion, s. *sharana.*
Expunge, v.a. *qalam wahal, wrānawul.*
Exquisite, a. *pākīzah, nādir, matrah. ghwarah.*
Extant, a. *osan, osanai, maujūd.*
Extempore, ad. *sam da lāsa.*
Extend, v.n. *rasedal, ūgdedal, ziyātedal.*
Extension, s. *ūgd-wālai, ziyāt-wālai.*
Extensive, a. *loe, plan, arat, ūgd, kushād.*
Extent, s. *ūgd-wālai, plan-wālai; qadr, andāza.*
Extenuate, v.a. *kamawul, la-ugawul.*
Exterior, a. *bāhir, wardzanai.*
Extinct, a. *wruk, ter, nā-būd, nest, nishtah.*
Extinguish, v.a. *mur-, sor-, gul-,* etc. *k.*
Extirpate, v.a. *prekawul, tsīral; mund-, wekh-, būnsat-,* etc. *khejawul, -bāsal—yastal, -kāgal—kkhkal.*
Extol, v.a. *stāyal, stāyana k.* or *-wayal.*
Extort, v.a. *shūkawul, pa zor ākhistal.*
Extortion, s. *ziyātī, zulm.*
Extract, s. *'araq, jauhar.*
Extract, v.a. *bāsal—yastal, kāgal—kkhkal.*
Extraction, s. *rag, nogai, zāt, asl.*
Extraneous, a. *pradai, begūnah.*
Extraordinary, a. *'ajab, nādir.*
Extravagant, a. *khartsī, tāwānī, isrāfī, be-tartīb, chakhraba kawūnkai.*
Extreme, a. *der, be-shān, be-hadd.* s. *hadd.*
Extremely, ad. *be-hadda, be-shāna.*
Extremity, s. *sar, tsūka, peza; hadd, pūla, brid; rokh, dada, tselma, tsanda, palaw.* (distress) *tangsiyā, lā-chārī, mīrtsī.*
Extricate, v.a. *prānītel, āzādawul, khalās-awul, spardal.*
Exuberance, s. *frewānī, wadānī, der-wālai.*
Exuberant, a. *frewān, wadān, der, ziyāt.*
Exudation, s. *zyam, naw; khwale.*
Exude, v.a. *zyam-, naw-,* etc. *k.* v.n. *watal, khwale ked., zyam-,* etc. *ked.*
Exult, v.a. *salka k., wiyāral, kkhādī k.*
Eye, s. *starga.* (-sight) *nazar.* (-ball) *lema, starghalai.* (-socket) *starghālai, gogil.* (-pupil) *torai, kasai, bātūr.* (-iris) *lema.* (-brow) *wrūdza.* (-lid) *dzedzma* or *dzegma.* (-lash) *bānra.* (-witness) *gawāh, shāhid.* (-of a needle) *swam* or *spam.*
Eye diseases, s. (opthalmia) *lecha.* (albugo) *gul.* (pannus) *nakhūna.* (cataract) *parda.* (sore eyes) *lechane-starge.*

F.

Fable, s. *qissa, naql, hikāyat, matal, misāl.*
Fabricate, v.a. *jorawul, tandal.*
Fabulous, a. *darogh, wahmī.*
Face, s. *makh, tsihra, bashra, mushāda, rūe gūna.* (-to face) *makhā-makh.*
Facetious, a. *toq-mār, washtai* or *washt-mār, malandai.*
Facilitate, v.a. *āsānawul.*
Facility, s. *āsān-tiyā.*
Facing, a. *makhā-makh, wrāndai.*
Fact, s. *wāq'ia, gharaz, matlab, kār, krah.*
Faction, s. *para, janba, gundī; patna, pasāt.*
Factious, a. *pasātī* or *fasādī, takrārī.*
Factor, s. *kār kawūnkai, gumāshtah, dīwān.*
Factory, s. *kār-khāna, kotī.*
Faculty, s. *quwat, qudrat, tuwān; khāssiyat, lokkhai, khoe, tāsīr; 'aql, shu'ūr.*
Fade, v.n. *mrāwedal* or *marāwi ked., kumanre-dal, marghechan-, pezai-, malāl-,* etc. *ked.*
Fag, v.n. *rabredal, starai ked.*
Faggot, s. *gedai, panda, bālanr.*
Fail, v.a. *khatā k.* v.n. *kamedal.*
Failing, s. *'aib, qusūr, khatā, nuqsān.*
Faint, a. *māndah, tap, nā-tuwān, za'īf.* s. *pargha, be-khūdī.* v.n. *parghaz ked.*
Fair, a. *gorah, spīn; kkhāyastah, kkhkulai, pa-ī-makhai* or *pej-makhai; sāf, pāk, kkhah, jor.* (-sky) *shīn.*

Fair, s. *mela.*
Fairly, ad. *pa rāstī sara.*
Fairy, s. *parī, perai.* (the fairies) *piriyān.*
Faith, s. *īmān, dīn, khal, kesh, wisā, bāwar.*
Faithful, a. *īmān-dār, wafā-dār, rikkhtīnai.*
Faithless, a. *be-īmān, be-wafā.*
Falcon, s. (Royal-) *shahīn.* (Peregrine- or Falco sacer) *chargh, charghelai, tsarkh.* (Tercel-) *bahra-ī-bach.* See Hawk.
Falconer, s. *bāz-wān, mīr-shikār, kkhkārī.*
Fall, v.n. *prewatal, lwedal.* (-in) *drabal.* (-into) *kkhkewatal.* (slip) *khwa-edal* or *khwahedal.*
Fall, s. *prewātah, lwedana; drabai; khwai.* (foot-) *trapai.*
Fallacy, s. *darogh, ghalaṭ, kiẕb.*
Fallen, a. *prewatai, prot, lwedalai.*
Fallible, a. *gunāh-gār, quṣūr-man.*
Fallow, s. *wạḍ, shāṛ, banjaṛ.*
False, a. *darogh-jan, darghal, nā-rāst, kāẕib.* (-coin) *jūṭah, nā-sarah.*
Falsehood, s. *darogh, kiẕb; palma, fareb.*
Falter, v.n. *ṭaparedal; budrī-, tīndak-,* etc. *khwuṛal; pa jibe nkkhatal.*
Fame, s. *nūm, āwāza.*
Famed, a. *nūm-war, nāmwar, mashhūr.*
Familiar, a. *khamsor; m'alūm.* s. *āshnāe, yār, mal.*
Family, s. *kor, kaḍa, ṭabar; khānawādah, khāndān, tabār, nasl.*
Famine, s. *grānī, kahtī, ḍūkāl, qātī.*
Famish, v.n. *da lwuge mṛal.*
Famous, a. *mashhūr, nūm-war, nāmer.*
Fan, s. *babozai.* (-for flies) *chawra-ī.* (-for sifting grain) *chaj, tsap.*
Fanatic, s. *muta'ṣṣib, lewanai, nāmwar.*
Fancy, s. *qiyās, khiyāl, wahm, and.*
Fang, s. *ghākkh, dāṛa.*
Fantasm, s. *wahm, khiyāl.*
Fantastic, a. *wahmī, khiyālī; washtai, malandai, swāngī.*
Far, ad. *lire* or *liri.* (as far as) *pore* or *pori, tar—pore.* (-away) *warāya.*
Farce, s. *pekkha, ṭoqa, washta.*
Fare, s. *khwurāk, khwāṛak, sat; kreha, kirāha.* v.a. *khwuṛal sat k.* v.n. *teredal, chaledal, guẕrānedal.*
Farewell, ad. *da khudāe pa amān, salām.*
Farm, s. *paṭai, wanḍ, dawtar, zamīn, ada-ī; ijāra.*
Farmer, s. *zamīndār; ijāra-dār.*
Farrier, s. *n'al-band.*
Fart, s. *dau, ṭa-as, ṭar, tīz, pa-as, pa-aska-ī.* v.a. *aratal, tīz-,* etc. *āchawul, ṭar,* etc. *k.*
Farther, ad. *lire* or *liri, nor lire.*
Fascinate, v.a. *fareftah-, mayan-, koḍ-,* etc. *k.*
Fashion, s. *ḍaul, shān, shakl, rang, wajha, tarkīb, chāl, rasm, dod, dastūr*
Fashion, v.a. *joṛawul, tanḍal.*
Fast, a. *jalt, tez, gaṛandai, talwārī, talwārgandai, halwāk, za-ar* or *zir; maḥkam, maẕbūṭ; ṭing, klak.*
Fast, s. *roja.* v.a. *roja laral* or *-nīwul.*
Fasten, v.a. *taṛal, lagawul; ṭingawul, klakawul; kāgal—kkhkal; maẕbūṭ k.*
Fastidious, a. *bādī, kibr-jan, khāmtamā.*
Fasting, a. *nahār.* (voluntary-) *nakwa, roja.*
Fat, a. *tsorb, peṛ, peraṛ, punḍ, tanḍ, ghaṭ, kharaṭ.* (-as a child) *khamaṭ, chāgh.*
Fat, s. *spīna, wāzda.* (kidney-) *ghoz.* (melted-) *roghan, mū, ghwaṛī.*
Fatal, a. *qātil, kārī; qaẕā-ī.*
Fatality, s. *naṣīb, qaẕā, qismat, taqdīr.*
Fate, s. *ajal, marg, maut; qaẕā, qismat.*
Father, s. *plār.* (-in-law) *skhar.* (step-) *plandar.* (grand-) *nīkah.* (great grand-) *ghur-nīkah.* (great great grand-) *lā ghur-nīkah.*
Fatherless, a. *be-plār, plār-meṛai, yatīm.*
Fathom, s. *wāzak.*
Fatigue, v.a. *rabṛawul, staṛai-, stomān-, ṭap-, haukah-, māndah-,* etc. *k.*

Fault, s. *'aib, khaṭā, taqṣīr, wabāl, gunāh, quṣūr.* (to find-) v.a. *malāmatawul, ṭaqawul, raṭal, traṭal, kagal, ghandal.*

Faultless, a. *be·gunāh, be·quṣūr, be·taqṣīr.*

Faulty, a. *'aib·nāk, quṣūr·man, gunāh·gār, taqṣīrī; bad, nā·kārah.*

Favour, s. *mrasta, mihrbānī, mihrbāngī, sal, makh, sela, selwa.*

Favourable, a. *barābar, munāsib, pīrzo; makhawar, mihrbān.*

Favourite, a. *khwakkh, ghwarah, kkhkulai.*

Fawn, v.a. *chāplūsī-, ḍirpalī-, khushāmadī-, falān dast·māl-, jig·jigī-,* etc. *k.*

Fealty, s. *wafā·dārī, tābi'·dārī, kālkhwākī.*

Fear, s. *wera* or *yera, tars, khof, bāk, sahm, tara; wiswās, andekkhnā.*

Fear, v.n. *weredal, trehedel, bugnedal.* v.a. *tars-, tor-,* etc. *khwural.*

Fearful, a. *tars·nāk, khof·nāk; tarhūr, yerman.*

Fearless, a. *be·bāk, be·ḍar.*

Feasible, a. *shwunai* or *shwūnkai.*

Feast, s. *melmastiyā, ẓiyāfat, jashn.*

Feat, s. *kār, kṛah; bāzī.*

Feather, s. *baṇra, baṇraka, par.*

Feature, s. *tsihra, shakl, ṣūrat.*

February, s. *pāgaṇr.*

Fee, s. *shukrāna; ḥaqq, ajr, miḥnat; chūngai.*

Feeble, a. *nā·tuwān, ẓa'īf, kam·ṭāqat, ṭap, kam·quwat, kam·zor, 'ājiz.*

Feed, v.a. *khwurawul; tsarawul.* (eat) *khwural.* graze, v.n. *tsaredal* or *tsaral.* (-cattle) *wākkhah āchawul.* (-birds) *ṭu'amā warkawul.* (nourish) *parwaral, pālal, sātal, parwarish k.*

Feel, v.a. *laṭawul, lamsawul, masa k.* (suffer) v.n. *pohedal, m'alūmedal, zghamedal, kedal.* (bear) v.a. *khwural, līdal, kāgal—kkhkal.* (-pain) *khūgedal, dardedal.* (-the pulse) *nabẓ katal.* (-for others) *dil·sozī-, gham·khwārī-, zṛah·swai-,* etc. *k.*

Feeling, s. *poh, pahm.*

Feign, v.a. *bāna-, ḥīla-, makr-,* etc. *k.; palma-, kira-ī-, lamghaṛa-ī-,* etc. *k.*

Felicity, s. *kkhādī, khwakkhī, khush·ḥālī, khwand; barakat, bakhtawarī, nek·bakhtī.*

Fell, v.a. *prekawul, wahal, naṛawul.*

Fell, a. *sakht, kāfir, ẓālim, khūnāṛai.*

Fellow, s. *mal, malgirai, humdzolai, samsorai.* (match) *makhai, gund, dzawāb, iorah.* (contemptuous-) *lawanḍ, chaṭ, qachar, dahūs, chulur.* (in comp.) *hum-.*

Fellowship, s. *malgir·tiyā, sharākat; rogha, joṛa.*

Felon, s. *gunāh·gār, taqṣīrī, mujrim.*

Felt, s. *lamtsa-ī, krāsta, namada.*

Female, a. *zanāna, māndīna.* s. *kkhadza, artīna.* (covert-) *maṛokkha, sohāgan.*

Feminine, a. *zanānī, mādīna, kkhadza.*

Fen, s. *jaba.*

Fence, s. *bāra, panāh.* (thorn-) *shpol, jal.* (withy or twig-) *keṛa.* v.a. *bāra-,* etc. *taṛal.*

Fence, v.a. *ḍāl·bāzī-, gatka·bāzī-,* etc. *k.*

Fennel, s. *sowa, kāgah.*

Fenugreek, s. *malkhoza.*

Ferment, s. *khamīra, tomna, māya; eshnā, khuṭkai, josh; balwā, patna.*

Ferment, v.n. *khamīra-,* etc. *ked.; eshedal, khuṭ ked.*

Ferocious, a. *waḥshī, khūnaṛai, ẓālim.*

Ferocity, s. *waḥshat, khūn·khwārī, ẓulm.*

Ferret, s. *nolai.*

Ferrule, s. *ghamai, ṭekai.*

Ferry, s. *gudar, pataṇr.* (-boat) *beṛa-ī.* (-man) *māṇrgai, mahāṇrai.*

Fertile, a. *zar·khez, ghala·khez, lap·tsat, barakatī.*

Fertilize, v.a. (-land) *watar k., zor-, quwat-,* etc. *warkawul.* (-animals) *ḍakawul, blārba k.*

Ferula, s. *bet, dira, qamchī, karoṛa*

Fervent, a. *tod, garm.*

Fervour, s. *tod·wālai, todūkha, swai, garmī.*

Fester, v.n. *zawlan-, gazak-*, etc. *ked., khu-edul.*

Festival, s. *akhtar, 'id.* (-after Ramazān) *wrūkai akhtar.* (-of Abraham's sacrifice) *loe akhtar.* (-of a saint) *mela, 'urs.* (marriage-) *wādah.* (feast) *kkhādī.*

Festivity, s. *kkhādī, khush-hālī, khwakkhī.*

Festoon, s. *lar, hār, zundai, zunbak.*

Fetch, v.a. (things) *rāwral.* (animals) *rāwustal.*

Fetid, a. *skhā, gundah, bad-bū* or *bad bū-ī-dār, wrost.*

Fetter, s. *dzolana, karai, band, zandzīr.* (-for cattle) *shkel, wandar, palwākkha, ghar-wandai.*

Feud, s. *patna, badī, khāna-jangī, mīrtsī.*

Fever, s. *taba.* (-and ague) *sara taba, sara lare, sara lawe.* (intermittent-) *wārīza taba.* (remittent-) *wāra-gara taba.* (continued-) *shebara taba.* (bilious-) *zyara-ī taba.* (typhus-) *skārwa-ī taba.*

Feverish, a. *tab-jan, taba nīwulai.*

Few, a. *la-ag, kam, pūtai, pitsāwrai, tso.*

Fibre, s. *rekkha, rag, tār, pala.*

Fibrous, s. *rekkhan.*

Fickle, a. *nā-qalār, nā-pāedār, khushai.*

Fiction, s. *naql, jor karai.*

Fictitious, a. *naqlī, nāsarah, jūtah*

Fiddle, s. *satār, sāringai, chamtāra, sārinda.* (-string) *tār.* (-bow) *kamāncha.* (-key) *ghwagai.* (-bridge) *tatū, khargai.*

Fidelity, s. *īmān-dārī, rāst bāzī, wofā-dārī, namak halālī, rikkhtīn-tob.*

Fidget, v.a. *kūnātī khwadzawul.* v.n. *wis-wāsī ked., pa mawekkho laramedal.*

Fief, s. *jāedād, jāgīr, aima, dawtar.*

Field, s. *patai, wand.* (crop) *kikkht.* (plain) *maidān, dāga.*

Fiend, s. *shaitān; perai, rawai; dukkhman.*

Fierce, a. *tund, sakht, zālim, qahr-jan.*

Fiery, a. *tod, tez, garm, tāw-jan, tund, jalt.*

Fife, s. *surnāe, shpela-ī.*

Fifer, s. *surnā-chī, shpela-ī-mār.*

Fifteen, a. *pīndzah-las.* (15th) *pīndzah-lasam.*

Fifty, a. *pindzos.* (-one) *yo-pindzos*, etc.

Fig, s. *īndzar.* (wild-) *gūlar.* (Banian-) *bargat.* (Sacred-) *pīpal.*

Fight, s. *jang, muqaddama.* v.a. *jangawul.*

Fighter, s. *jangī, jangawar, jang kawūnkai; jang-yālai.*

Figurative, a. *naqlī, shaklī, majāzī, tamsīlī.*

Figure, s. *shakl, daul, sūrat, rang, shān.*

Figure, v.a. *jorawul, tandal; nakhkkha kāgal—kkhkal* or *-tikal.*

Figured, a. *būtī-dār, rangīn.*

File, s. *sohān, chausār.* (row) *qatār, para.* (catalogue) *daftar, fard.*

Filings, s. *reza, chūr.*

Fill, v.a. *dakawul.*

Fillet, s. *patai, parūkai.* (-for the head) *sar-tarūnai, sar-basta, tsapūtkai.*

Fillip, s. *chutkī.*

Filly, s. *bihāwra, biyāna.*

Film, s. *jāla-ī.* (-of the eye) *gul, nakhūna.*

Filter, s. *chāwra.* v.a. *chāwr k.*

Filth, s. *khīra, rash, chirk.*

Filthy, a. *khīran, palīt, nā-pāk, khīchan.*

Fin, s. *wazar da kab* or *-da mākī.*

Final, a. *ākhir, wrūstai, akhir; pūrah.*

Finally, ad. *ākhiran, alqissa.*

Finance, s. *mālguzārī, āmdanī.*

Find, v.a. *mūndal, biyā-mūndal, paidā k.* (-fault) *ratal, tratal, taqawul, malāma-tawul.*

Fine, s. *nāgha, tāwān, jarīmāna.*

Fine, a. *narai, mahīn, bārīk.* (-sky) *shīn, sāf.*

Finger, s. *gutta.* (thumb) *bata-* or *ghata gutta.* (fore-) *miswāka gutta.* (middle-) *miyandza gutta.* (ring-) *kamacha gutta.* (little-) *kichā gutta.* (-nail) *nūk.* (-quick) *awra-ī.*

Finis, s. *tam-tamām, ākhir, khatm.*

Finish, v.a. *tamāmawul, pūrah-, khatm-,* etc. *k.*

Fir, s. *nakkhtar.* (-cone) *gūjai.* (-seed) *chalghozai* or *janghoza* or *zaurghoza.*

Fire, s. *or.* (-fly) *orakai.* (-place) *ngharai, orghālai.* (-wood) *bālanr, khashāk.* (-brand) *shūsha-ī.* (-poker) *or larūnai.* (-stone) *shokānrai.* (-works) *ātashbāzī.* (-worshipper) *gabar.* (-lock) *bandūkh, topak.*

Fire, v.a. *or pore k., balawul.* (-a gun) *chalawul, khalāṣawul.*

Firm, a. *maẓbūṭ, klak, ṭing, pāedār.*

Firmament, s. *āsmān, kursī, tsarkh.*

First, a. *awwal* or *awwulanai, wṛūnbai* or *wṛūnbanai.* (-born) *mashar.*

Firstly, ad. *awwalan, wṛūnba-i, warkhata.*

Fish, s. *kab, māhai.* (-hook) *kunḍa.*

Fissure, s. *chāwd, darz, daṛa, chāq, rakhna.*

Fist, s. *mūṭ, mūṭai; sūk.*

Fistula, s. *nāsūr.*

Fit, s. *ghoṭa; nobat.* (fainting-) *parghaz.* (hysterical-) *da piriyāno ghoṭa.*

Fit, a. *wājib, munāsib, lāzim, lā-iq; qābil, joṛ, barābar; pirzo, yarzan, dzāe-lar.*

Five, a. *pindzah.* (fifth) a. *pindzam.*

Fix, s. *nkkhatai, balā.*

Fix, v.a. *lagawul, taṛal, joṛawul, pore k.; wudrawul, walāṛawul, muqarrar-, klak-, maẓbūṭ-,* etc. *k.; khakkhawul, njatal; khejawul, kkhkenawul.*

Flabby, a. *narm, post, sust; tsorb.*

Flag, s. *nakkha, janḍa, togh, bairagh.*

Flag, v.n. *ṭaparedal, pāte ked., staṛai ked.*

Flagrant, a. *tsargand; mashhūr; bad.*

Flake, s. *tsapak, tsaparkai.*

Flame, s. *lanba, shughla* (fire), *baṛānḍa, gharānḍa, lūkhaṛa, gharghara, bāmbaṛra, ḍānḍa-ī.*

Flank, s. *ḍaḍa, aṛkh, tsang; tselma, tsanḍa; tashai.*

Flannel, s. *shaṛa-ī, pashmīna, waṛīna.*

Flap, v.a. *tsanḍal, khwadzawul, rapawul.* v.n. *tsapedal, tsrapedal, ṭrapedal, rapedal.*

Flare, v.n. *brekkhedal, rūnredal, dzaledal.*

Flash, s. *brekkh, brekkhnā, dzalk, palwasha.*

Flask, s. *kupa-ī, kupṛa-i; kkhīkkha, khumra-ī.*

Flat, a. *sam, sat, hawār, barābar.* (pressed-) *tsaplāk, chīt.* (-taste) *be-khwand, be-maza, bilmagai, bilmangah.* (-on the back) *stūnī-stagh.* (-footed) *chapakh.*

Flatten, v.a. *samawul, hawārawul; chīt-,* etc. *k.*

Flatterer, s. *chāplūs, khūshāmad-gar, ḍirpal.*

Flattery, s. *chāplūsī, khūshāmadī, ḍirpalī.*

Flatulent, a. *bādī.*

Flavour, s. *khwand, maza, swād, tsaka.*

Flaw, s. *chāwd, darz, daṛa; 'aib, laka, dāgh.*

Flax, s. *sanr.*

Flay, v.a. *tsarman-, poṭ-,* etc., *ākhistal, -bāsal—yastal, -kāgal—kkhkal.*

Flea, s. *wruga.*

Fleam, s. *nashtar* or *neshtar.*

Fleawort, s. *ispaghol* or *isapghol.*

Flee, v.n. *takkhtedal, puṭedal.*

Fleece, s. *waṛa-ī, warg.*

Fleece, v.a. *shūkawul, lūṭawul.*

Fleet, a. *garandai, jalt, tez, zghard, halwāk.*

Fleeting, a. *teredūnai, fānī.*

Flesh, s. *ghwakkha.* (body) *dzān.* (lust) *naus, shahwat.* (-brush) *khīsa.*

Flexible, a. *narm, post, mulā-im, ṭīṭedūnai.*

Flexure, s. *ṭīṭ-wālai; kog-wālai; kaglech, kālkūch; gūṭ, grut.*

Flight, s. *tekkhta.* (-of birds) *sail, ghol.* (-of an arrow) *partaw.*

Flighty, a. *khushai, khiyālī, saudā-ī.*

Flimsy, a. *spuk, halak, narai, nā-kārah.*

Flinch, v.n. *bugnedal, weredal, haṭedal.*

Fling, v.a. *āchawul, wīshtal, ghurzawul.*

Flint, s. *bakra-ī.* (steel) *puṇḍ.* (gun-) *chaq-maq.*

Flinty, a. *sakht, klak, kānrez.*

Flirt, s. *nakhra-bāza, lashmaka-ī, shatāha.*

Flit, v.n. *ālwatal.* v.a. *kaḍa wṛal.*

Float, s. *pāyāba* or *pāyawai.* v.n. *bahedal, lāhū ked., lānbo ked.*

Flock, s. *ramma.* (leader of-) *nar-kakkh.* (-of sheep, goats, or deer) *kanḍak, ghela, psa.* (-of birds) *sail, ghol.* (-of lambs, etc.) *olah.* (a crowd of men, etc.) *ṭol, ṭolai, ṭolgai.*

Flock, v.n. *ṭoledal, yo-dzāe-, jam'a-,* etc. *ked.*

Flog, v.a. *wahal, karoṛe-,* etc. *wahal.*

Flood, s. *sailāb, niyūz* or *nīz.* (-of tears) *raṭ.*

Flood, v.a. *lāhū-, hūk-,* etc. *k., niyūz wṛal.*

Floodgate, s. *warkh, ghwagai.*

Floor, s. *zmaka, zamīn*; *takhta-bandī.*

Florid, a. *sūr.*

Florist, s. *gul-kar.*

Flounce, s. *tsanḍa, jāwja-ī.*

Flounce, v.n. *tsrapedal, ghurzedal.*

Flounder, v.n. *ṭrapedal, tsrapedal*; *rgharedal.* v.a. *ghoṭa wahal.*

Flour, s. *oṛah, maidah.* (dredging-) *bornā.*

Flourish, v.n. *ābādedal, wadānedal, tāzah-, takṛah-,* etc. *osedal.* v.a. *tsanḍal, khwadza-wul, rapawul.*

Flow, v.n. *bahedal, chaledal, rawānedal, jārī ked.*

Flower, s. *gul.* (-garden) *gul-shan.* (-bed) *gul-zār.*

Flower, v.n. *khwaredal, ghwaṛedal, ṭūkedal.*

Fluctuate, v.a. *chapa-, chalaka,* etc. *wahal.* v.n. *be-ārām-, nā-qalār-,* etc. *ked.*

Fluent, a. *jārī, rawān.* (in speech) *khula-war.*

Fluid, a. *wīlī, oba, ābī, pakhsiyāh.*

Flummery, s. *pālūda, ogrā, atob, daliya.*

Flush, v.n. *sūr-makh ked., sharmedal.*

Flute, s. *shpela-ī.*

Flutter, v.n. (-hover as a bird) *ṭrapedal, tsapedal.* (-as a leaf) *rapedal, shanedal.* (palpitate) *dṛazedal, paṛakedal, laṛzedal.*

Flux, s. *sailāb*; *rezish, nazla*; *nāstah ra-ama, dast.*

Fly, s. *mach.* (horse-) *ghobārai, bhaganr.*

Fly, v.n. *ālwatal, wurzedal.*

Foal, s. *bihānr, biyān.*

Foam, s. *zag, kaf.*

Fodder, s. *wākkhah, giyāh, 'alaf.* (-of corn) *khasīl, khwīd.* (-of maize) *ṭānṭa.* (-of rice) *palāla.* (-of pulses) *kaṭī.*

Foe, s. *dukkhman, khasam.*

Fœtus, s. *bachai, kachandai.*

Fog, s. *laṛa*; *ghubār.*

Foil, s. *gatka.* v.a. *wrānawul.*

Fold, s. *bāra, hadera.* (sheep) *bānḍa, shpol.* (of a door) *tanba, pala.* (layer) *bragh, tah.* (crease) *gundza, chunra, kṛatai.* (-of a rope) *wal, tāw, pech.* (-on fold) ad. *pabla-, wabla-* or *zabla bānde.* (in comp.) *-bragh, -chand.*

Fold, v.a. *nghakkhtal.*

Foliage, s. *pānre, zarghūn-tob.*

Folk, s. *khalq, 'ālam, makhlūq.*

Follow, v.n. *pala-pase tlal.* v.a. *pairawī-, murīdī-,* etc. *k., manal, laman nīwul*

Follower, s. *pairaw, murīd, tāb'i-dār.*

Folly, s. *nā-dānī, kam-'aqlī, nā-poha.*

Foment, v.a. *sekal, ṭakor k.* (stir up) *pātsa-wul, khejawul, porta k.*

Fond, a. *mayan.* (in comp.) *-dost, -parast.*

Fondle, v.a. *nāzawul, mīna k.*

Fondness, s. *mīna, shauq, zṛah, khwā.*

Fontanelle, s. *tandai.*

Food, s. *khwāṛah, khwurāk, shūma, qūt, ṭ'ām.* (-for a journey) *tokkha, tsawrai.* (-of cattle) *tsar, wākkhah.* (-of hawks) *tāmba.* (prepared-) *sālan, qatagh, ngholai.*

Fool, s. *nā-dān, kam-'aql, gedī-khar, lewanai.*

Foolish, a. *nā-dān, be-wuqūf, kawdan, pūhaṛ, ablah, palwanḍ.*

Foot, s. *pkkha* or *kkhpa*. (on-) *palai, pa kkhpo*. (-step) *qadam, manḍ, gām*. (-mark) *pal, manḍ*. (-fall) *trapai*. (-stool) *moṛa*.
Footman, s. *piyādah, harkarah*; *shātar*; *mlā-taṛ*.
Footpad, s. *rāh-zan, shūk-mār, lār-wahūnkai*.
Footpath, s. *tsara-lār* or *-wāṭ*.
Fop, s. *bānkā, daulī, ṭaṭai, ṭainchī*.
For, p. *dapāra*; *wāsṭa, khāṭir*. (-as much) *la de na, dzaka, ska*. (-instance) *pa misāl, laka*. (-the most part) *aksar*. (-what?) *tsa-la, wale*.
Forage, s. *wākkhah, gayāh, tsar*.
Foray, s. *dāṛa-dopa, hapa-dapa, bota, chapāo*.
Forbear, v.a. *zghamal, ṣabr-, pāl-, parhez-*, etc. *k*.
Forbearance, s. *ṣabr, zgham*.
Forbid, v.a. *man'a k*.
Forbidden, a. *man'a, ḥarām*.
Force, s. *zor, quwat, was, tuwān, bram, ṭāqat*; *ẓulm, ziyātī, jabr*.
Force, v.a. *zoral, tezal*.
Forceps, s. *ambūr, nūtsai*.
Ford, s. *gudar, pai*. v.n. *pore tlal* or *-watal*.
Fordable, a. *payāw*.
Fore, a. *wṛūnbai, wṛūnbanai, wṛāndīnai, pakhwānai, pekkhīn*.
Fore, ad. *wṛānde, wṛūnbe*.
Forefather, s. *nīkah*.
Forego, v.a. *pregdal—prekkhodal, tark k*.
Forehead, s. *wuchwalai* or *ucharlai, tandai*.
Foreign, a. *pradai, begānah, oprah*.
Foreknowledge, s. *'ilm da ghā-ib*.
Foreman, s. *peshkār*.
Forementioned, a. *mazkūr*.
Foremost, a. *wṛūnbai, wṛāndīnai, awwalanai, awwal*.
Forenoon, s. *pekkhīn, tsākkht*.
Forepart, s. *makh, sar, wṛūnbai*.
Forerunner, s. *peshraw, wṛānde tlūnai*.
Forest, s. *baur, dzangal, besha*.
Forestall, v.a. *pesh-dastī k*.
Foretell, v.a. *pāl-* or *fāl katal, ghā-ib wayal*.
Forethought, s. *dūr-andekkhī, pesh-fikrī*.
Forewarn, v.a. *wṛūnbe khabarawul, āgāh k*.
Forfeit, s. *nāgha, tāwān, jurīmāna, qurq*.
Forfeit, v.a. *nāgha-*, etc. *warkawul, bū-elal*.
Forge, s. *lohār-khāna, baṭ*.
Forge, v.a. *jāl-sāzī k*.
Forget, v.a. *herawul*.
Forgive, v.a. *bakkhal, pulawul*.
Forgiveness, s. *bakkhana*.
Forgotten, a. *her, ter-her*.
Fork, s. *dwa-kkhākha*. (pitch-) *panj-ghākkhai*.
Forked, a. *kkhākh-dār*.
Forlorn, a. *be-kas, khwār, yanādzai, lā-chār*.
Form, s. *ṣūrat, shakl, shān, rang, tartīb*.
Form, v.a. *joṛawul, tanḍal, tartībawul*.
Formal, a. *rasmī, chalanī, qānūnī*.
Formation, s. *tarkīb, sākht, joṛawūna*
Former, a. *pakhwānai, wṛūnbanai*.
Formerly, ad. *pakhwā, wṛūnbe*.
Formidable, a. *tars-nāk, khof-nāk*.
Formula, s. *nuskha*; *tarkīb*; *tartīb*.
Fornication, s. *kāsīrī, zinā-kārī, ḥarām-kārī*.
Fornicator, s. *kāsir, zinā-kār, ḥarām-kār*
Forsake, v.a. *pregdal—prekkhodal, tark k*.
Forswear, v.a. *qasam-, saugand-*, etc. *khwuṛal*; *nā-ḥaqq qasam-*, etc. *khwuṛal*.
Fort, s. *qil'a, koṭ, gaṛa-ī, bāra, ḥiṣār*.
Forth, ad. *wṛānde*; *bahar*.
Forthwith, ad. *os, pa ṭikī, sam da lāsa, pa de sā'at, wasika*.
Fortify, v.a. *mazbūṭ-, maḥkam-*, etc. *k.*; *āṛ-, ḥiṣar-, bāra-, panāh-*, etc. *k*.
Fortitude, s. *ṣabr, zgham*; *zṛah, himmat*.
Fortress, s. *koṭ, gaṛa-ī*.
Fortuitous, a. *nāgahān, ittifāqī*.
Fortunate, a. *nek-bakht, barakatī, bakhtawar, sa'ādat-man, bakhtyār*.
Fortune, s. *bakht, naṣīb, qismat*; *zamāna, rozgār*; *iqbāl, sa'ādat*; *māl, duniyā*,

daulat; *falak*, *tsarkh*. (-teller) *fāl·bīn*, *pāl·katūnkai*, *rammāl*, *d'awatī*.

Forty, a. *tsalwekkht*. (-one) *yo tsalwekkht*, etc.

Forum, s. *chauk*, *chārsū*, *bāzār*.

Forward, ad. *makhe*, *wṛānde*. a. *wṛāndai*, *makh*; *tayār*; *wīt*, *chūnkai*, *gustākh*.

Forward, v.a. *chalawul*, *rawānawul*, *āstawul*, *legal*, *rasawul*.

Foster, v.a. *pālal*, *nmāndzal*, *parwaral*. (-son) *pālalai dzoe*. (-daughter) *pālalī lūr* (-brother) *da tī* or *-to wror*. (-sister) *da tī* or *-to khor*. (-father) *plandar*, *pālūnkai plār*. (-mother) *dā-ī*, *pālūnki mor*.

Foul, a. *nā·pāk*, *palīt*, *murdār*, *kakaṛ*.

Foundation, s. *āra*, *wekh*, *bonsaṭ*, *kūnsaṭ*; *sar*, *aṣl*, *bunyād*. (pedestal) *pāya*, *asās*

Fountain, s. *chīna*, *chashma*.

Four, a. *tsalor*. (fourth) *tsaloram*. (-fold) *tsalor·bragh*. (-footed) *chār·pā*. (-score) *tsalor shili*.

Fourteen, a. *tswārlas*.

Fowl, s. *chirg*. (water-) *hīla-ī*. (-of the air) *marghah* (p. *mārghah*), *marghai*. (Cochin-) *kulang*, *kurmang*. (game-) *pandār·chirg*.

Fowler, s. *kkhkārī*.

Fox, s. *lūnbaṛ*, *troṛa-ī*, *sperlam* or *spalam*.

Fraction, s. *kasr*, *ḥiṣṣa*, *ṭoṭai*, *ṭakai*.

Fracture, s. *māt*, *daṛa*, *chāwd*.

Fragile, a. *mātedūnai*, *narai*, *nāzak*.

Fragment, s. *ṭoṭa*, *reza*, *richa*, *chur*.

Fragrance, s. *'aṭr*, *khūsh·bū-ī*.

Fragrant, a. *khūsh·bū*, *bū-ī·nāk*, *khūshbū-ī·dār*.

Frail, a. *nāzak*, *nā·tuwān*, *ẓa'īf*, *kam·zor*, *nā·pāedār*, *fānī*.

Frame, s. *kināra*, *kāna*. (door-) *dūrshil*. (mould) *qālib*.

Frame, v.a. *joṛawul*, *taṛal*.

Frank, a. *spīn*, *ṣāf*, *sādah·dil*, *rikkhtīnai*.

Frankincense, s. *lobān*, *'ad*.

Frantic, a. *lewanai*, *saudā-ī*.

Fraternity, s. *wrorī*, *wror·walī*.

Fraud, s. *ṭagī*, *fareb*, *droh*, *ghlā*, *chal*.

Fraudulent, a. *ṭag·bāz*, *farebī*, *chal·bāz*.

Fraught, s. *pūrah*, *ḍak*.

Fray, v.n. *sūledal*, *sūdah ked.*; *blosedal*.

Freak, s. *khiyāl*, *wahm*.

Freckle, s. *tarsarai*, *ta-apai*.

Free, a. *yalah*, *saṛah*, *wuzgār*, *āzād*, *khalāṣ*. (-will) *wāk*, *ikhtiyār*, *raẓā*.

Freeze, v.n. *kangal-*, *khyam-*, etc. *ked.*, *yakhedal*.

Freight, s. *bār*; *bār·bardārī*, *kreha*, *maḥṣūl*.

Frenzy, s. *sarsām*, *lewan·tob*, *paṭ*.

Frequent, a. *ḍer*, *ziyāt*, *lagiyā*.

Frequent, v.a. *rāsha·darsha-*, *tlana·rātlana-*, etc. *k.* v.n. *osedal*, *pātedal*.

Frequently, ad. *akṣar*, *ziyātī*, *ḍer dzala*, *wār·wār*.

Fresh, a. *zarghūn*, *shīn*; *tāzah*, *takṛah*, *tayār*; *nawai*; *hosā*. (complexion) *skāwr*.

Fret, v.n. *zahīredal*, *kaṛedal*, *nūledal*, *ghamedal*, *wiwāsī ked.* (-as cloth) *sūledal*. (as water) *tsaparc-*, *pache-*, etc. *ked.*

Fretful, a. *khapah*, *wiswāsī*, *nā·qalār*.

Friction, s. *sūledana*, *sūda*; *mālish*, *masha*, *mukkhana*.

Friar, s. *miyā* or *mī-ā*, *paqīr*.

Friday, s. *jum'a*, *ādīna*.

Friend, s. *āshnāe*, *yār*, *dost*, *pejandgalai*.

Friendless, a. *be·kas*, *khwār*

Friendly, a. *mihrbān*, *khair·khwāh* or *kāl·khwāh*.

Friendship, s. *āshnā-ī*, *yārī*, *yārāna*, *khpal·walī*.

Fright, s. *yera* or *wera*, *tars*, *tor*, *khof*, *trāh*, *ḍār*.

Frighten, v.a. *yerawul* or *werawul*, *trahawul*, *torawul*, *ḍārawul*.

Frightened, v.n. *weredal*, *trahedal*, *ḍāredal*. v.a. *tor khwuṛal*.

Frightened, a. *yeredalai*, *trahedalai*, *tor·khwuṛalai*, *ḍāredalai*.

Frightful, a. *tars-, khof-, tor-, haul-*, etc. *-nāk*.
Frigid, a. *soṛ, yakh*; *qarqechan, marghechan*.
Fringe, s. *tsanḍa, jāwja-ī, laman*. (frill) *sarwazana, zunḍa-ī, surkha-ī*.
Frisk, v.a. *traplal, top wahal, kharmastī-, tskhe-*, etc. *k*.
Fritter, v.n. *sharhedal*. (trifle) v.a. *jakh wahal*.
Frivolous, a. *spuk, halak, puch, khushai, nā·tsīz*.
Frock, s. *anga, khalqa, kāḍa-ī*. (quilted-) *andarka*. (long-) *qādara-ī*. (short-) *lanḍa-ī*. (woman's-) *pepna-ī, ganḍola-ī*.
Frog, s. *chindakh, changakkh, shlānda*.
Frolic, s. *loba, mastī, ṭel·ṭāl, tskhe*.
From, p. *la, da, la—na*.
Front, s. *makh, wṛāndai*. (in-) ad. *wṛānde, makhā·makh, makh·kkhke*.
Front, v.n. *wṛānde-, makh-*, etc. *ked*.
Frontier, s. *pūla, brīd, ḥadd*.
Frost, s. *kangal, yakh*. (hoar-) *parkha, asa-ī*. (-bitten) a. *qarqechan, marghechan, kaskar*.
Frosty, a. *soṛ, yakh*.
Froth, s. *zag, kaf*.
Frothy, a. *zag·jan, kaf·dār*.
Froward, a. *ḥoḍai, sar·kakkh, sar·zor, ṭakanrai*.
Frown, v.a. *brandawul, starge brandawul*.
Frozen, a. *kangal·*, or *yakh·shawai*.
Fructify, v.a. *bārdār k.*; *blārba k*.
Frugal, a. *parhez·gār*; *kam·khwurāk*.
Fruit, s. *mewa*; *bār*.
Fruitful, a. *mewa·dār*; *bār·dār*.
Fruitless, a. *be·mewa, be·bār, shanḍ*. (vain) *be·sūd, be·fā-ida, 'abas-, bar·bād, be·būd*.
Frustrate, v.a. *bāṭil-, 'abas-*, etc. *k., wrānawul*.
Fry, v.a. *talawul, teyal, wrītawul, alwoyal*.
Frying-pan, s. *taba-ī, tabakhai, teghna*.
Fuel, s. *bālanr, largai, khāshāk, khadzala, warkhaṛa*. (cowdung-) *ghoshoe*.
Fugitive, s. *takkhtedūnai*.

Fulfil, v.a. *tamāmawul, pa dzāe, pūrah-*, etc. *k*.
Full, a. *ḍak, pūrah*; *moṛ*; *sekan*.
Fuller, s. *dobī, rang·rez*.
Fully, ad. *pa kkhak shān sara, qaṭ'a-ī*.
Fulness, s. *ṭamām·tiyā, ḍak·wālai*; *moṛ·tiyā*; *art·wālai*; *sekan·tob*.
Fulsome, a. *nā·khwakkh, kraka·nāk*; *puch*.
Fumble, v.a. *wār·khaṭā k., kāwākī k*.
Fumbler, s. *pūhaṛ, kāwāk, lwāṛ*.
Fumigate, v.a. *lū-, lūgai-, lūkhaṛa-*, etc. *k*.
Fun, s. *loba, mastī*; *tamāsha, nandāra*; *ṭoqa-washta, ṭel·ṭāl*.
Function, s. *kār, 'amal*; *khidmat*; *'uhda*.
Fund, s. *sarmāya, saga, panga*.
Fundament, s. *būnsaṭ, kūnsaṭ*; *kūna, ghara, supra*.
Fundamental, a. *aṣlī, bunyādī, zātī*.
Funeral, s. *janāza*. (burial) *khakkhawūna, dafn*. (-service) *fātiḥa, pātā*. (-condolence) *lās·nīwah*. (-food) *shūma, muṛ·shūma*.
Funnel, s. *tsūkkhka, nala*; *jāba*.
Funny, a. *ṭoq·mār, washtī, wīlak*.
Fur, s. *waṛa-ī, pashm*. (-skin) *postīn*. (-coat) *nīm·tanai, nīmcha, postīncha*.
Furbish, v.a. (metals) *ṣaiqal k*. (polish) *mugal—mukkhal*. (scrape) *togal*.
Furious, a. *qahr·nāk, bṛos, lewanai*.
Furl, v.a. *nghaṛal—nghakkhtal*.
Furnace, s. *tanūr*.
Furnish, v.a. *warkawul, rasawul, paidā k.*; *sambālawul, sāzawul, ārāstah k*.
Furniture, s. *rakht, asbāb, kālai, sāmān, sāz·sāmān, partal*.
Furrow, s. *līk, karkkha*.
Further, v.a. *madad-, komak-, mrasta-*, etc. *k*.
Fury, s. *qahr, ghazab, lewan·tob*.
Fuse, v.a. *wilī k., oba k*.
Fusee, s. *bāta-ī, patīla* or *falīta*.
Fuss, s. *chal·chalā, tak·o·pū, rabaṛ*.

Futile, a. *'abas, bātil, khushai, be fā-ida, spek, nā-tsīz, be-sūd.*
Future, a. *gāndah, makh, rātlana, āyandah.*
Futurity, s. *ākhirat, 'āqibat.*
Fye, in. *toba! peṭi-mū!*

G.

Gabble, v.a. *bak-bak-, baq-baq-, baṛ-baṛ-, ṭar-ṭar-, char-char-*, etc. *k.*
Gabbler, s. *baq-baqai, baṛ-baṛai, ūnai, ṭarai.*
Gad, v.a. *hujra-gardī k.* v.n. *girzedal.*
Gadfly, s. *bhaganṛ, manganṛ-mach.*
Gag, v.a. *būja pa khule kkhke manḍal, khula bandawul.*
Gain, s. *gaṭa, sūd, fā-ida, naf'a.*
Gain, v.a. *gaṭal, mūndal.* (-over) *grohedah k.* v.n. (win) *wa-aṛ ked.* (a victory) v.a. *barai mūndal.*
Gainer, s. *gaṭa kawūnkai, wa-aṛ, barai mūndūnkai.*
Gainful, a. *sūd-man, fā-ida-man.*
Gainsay, v.a. *khilāf wayal, radd k.*
Gait, s. *yūn, chūl, tlana, chalan, raftār.*
Gale, s. *sila-ī, bād, ṭūpān.*
Gall, s. *trīkha, zahra, ṣafrā.* (-bladder) *trīkhai.*
Gall, v.a. *sūdah-, gasiyā-*, etc. *k., sūlawul.*
Gallant, a. *maṛanai, dzwān-mard, tūrzan.*
Gallant, s. *'ishq-bāz, kāsīr; yār, āshnā.*
Gallantry, s. *maṛāna, zṛahwar-tob, tūrzan-tob, zmarī-tob, dzwān-mardī; kāsīrī, 'ishq-bāzī; āshnā-ī, yārāna.*
Gallery, s. *bālā-khāna, shāhnishīn, dūnkācha, aiwān.* (mine) *surang.*
Gallop, s. *poya, tākht.*
Gallop, v.a. *pa-poyo-, pa-tākht-*, etc. *zghalawul.* v.n. *pa-poyo-*, etc., *tlal* or *-zghaledal.*
Gallows, s. *dār, sūla-ī, gahwāra.* (-rope) *tezanda-ī, zanda-ī, phā-ī.*

Galls, Gallnut, s. *māzū.*
Gamble, v.a. *jū-ārī-, jū-ā-bāzī-, qimār-bāzī-*, etc. *k.*
Gambler, s. *jū-ār-gar, jū-ā-bāz.*
Gambol, s. *ṭel-ṭāl, mastī, tskhe, loba*
Game, s. *loba, bāzī.*
Gander, s. *baṭ, qāz; pūhaṛ, yeḍī.*
Gang, s. *ṭolai, dāṛa, paṛk, tūmba, ghol, cham.*
Gangrene, s. *skhā, gazak.*
Gaol, s. *zindān, qaid-, bandī-*, etc. *khāna*
Gap, s. *kanḍāw, darghol, wut, gūṭ.*
Gape, v.n. *wītedal, chīngedal, wāzedal.* v.a. *khula chīngawul, -wāzawul* or *-wītawul.* (yawn) *aswelai-, khamiyāza-*, etc. *k.* (stare) *ghaṭ-katal.*
Gaping, a. *wīt, chīng, wāz.*
Garb, s. *toga, shān, rang; jāma, pokkhāk, libās.*
Garbage, s. *ūjrai, lirai.*
Garble, v.a. *laṭawul, chunṛal.*
Garden, s. *bāgh, bāghcha.* (flower-) *gulshan, bostān.* (-of Eden) *jannat 'adan.*
Gardener, s. *bāghwān.*
Gardening, s. *bāghwānī, bāghwān-tob.*
Gargle, v.a. *ghar-ghaṛa k.*
Garland, s. *hār, lar, amel.*
Garlic, s. *ūga.*
Garment, s. *āghostana, jāma, zaṛūkai, libās, nwarai.* (beggar's-) *gand* or *kind.*
Garner, s. *khamba, kandū, koṭa, ambār-khāna.*
Garnish, v.a. *joṛawul, andzorawul.*
Garrison, s. *qil'a, gaṛa-ī; da qil'e khalq.*
Garrulous, a. *baq-baqai, ṭarai, baṛ-baṛai.*
Gash, s. *parhār, tsīra, ghwuts, zakhm.* v.a. *tsīral, ghwutsawul, joblawul, zakhmī k.*
Gasp, v.a. *lanḍa sāh-* or *sāh pa-porta ākhistal.* v.n. *sāh khatal, sāh-lanḍah ked.*
Gate, s. *war.* (-way) *darwāza.*
Gather, v.a. *ṭolawul, jam'a-, yo-dzāe-*, etc. *k.* (select) *awrawul, chunṛal, laṭawul.* (pluck) *shūkawul.*

Gathering, s. *ṭol, ṭolai.* (-of cloth) *jung.*
Gaudy, a. *rangā-rang, rangīn.*
Gauge, v.a. *mech-, kach-,* etc. *k.*
Gay, a. *kkhād, kkhād-man, khush-ḥāl.*
Gaze, v.a. *katal, ghaṭ katal, dzīr k.*
Gazette, s. *akhbār.*
Gear, s. *kālī, sāz-sāmān, asbāb.*
Geld, v.a. *khaṣṣī, ākhtah-,* etc. *k.*; *malai k.*
Gem, s. *gauhar* or *jauhar.*
Gender, s. *jins, qism.* (masculine-) *nārīnah, nar, muẕakkar.* (feminine-) *mādīna, kkhadza, muwannaṡ.*
Genealogy, s. *shajra, nasal, nasab, aṣl, pera-ī.*
General, a. *'āmm, jārī*; *shāmil.*
General, s. *sardār, sar-guroh, mashar.*
Generally, ad. *akṡar, ziyātī.*
Generate, v.a. *paidā k.*; *zeganwul.*
Generation, s. *paidā-ikkht*; *pera-ī, pusht*; *alwād, zāwzāt*; *zamāna, daur.*
Generosity, s. *sakhāwat, sakhī-tob, sakhā, bakkhana.*
Generous, a. *sakhī, bakkhūnai.*
Genial, a. *jor, khwakkh, barābar, pīrzo.*
Genitals, s. *andām-nihānī, satar, ṣūrat, 'aurat,* (hair of-) *tor-wekkhtah.*
Genius, s. *khoe, khuṣlat, ṭab'a, khwā, mizāj, lokkhai.* (evil-) *perai, parī.* (capacity) *poha, pahm, idrāk.*
Genteel, a. *makhawar, spīndrobaī, satar-pokkh.*
Gentility, s. *makhawar-tob, sharāfat.*
Gentle, a. *ḥalīm, aṣil, ashrāf.*
Gentleman, s. *ṣāḥib-* or *ashrāf-zādah.*
Gently, ad. *ro-ro, pa-qalār.*
Gentry, s. *ra-isān, ashrāfān.*
Genuine, a. *sūchah, karah, aṣīl, khāliṣ, nughd, rikkhtīnai.*
Genus, s. *rag, qām, qism, nogai, jins.*
Germinate, v.n. *ṭūkedal, zarghūnedal.* v.a. *red k.*
Gesture, s. *ḥarakat*; *shān.*
Get, v.a. *mūndal, gaṭal, paidā k.*
Ghastly, a. *sperah.*
Ghost, s. *rawai*; *perai.*
Giant, s. *ghaṭ-khrīs, nāpaṛ-* or *gagar saṛai*; *dew, 'ifrīt.*
Gibbet, s. *dār, gahwāra.* v.a. *tezanda-ī warkawul*; *dzwarandawul.*
Giddiness, s. *sar-ghurzai, akar, sar-girzai.*
Gift, s. *bakhkshiksh, bakkhana, nazr, hiba.*
Gifted, a. *qābil, qudrat-man, zbarg.*
Gigantic, a. *khrīs, nāpaṛ, dang-, star, ghaṭ, loe.*
Giggle, v.n. *khandedal, musedal.*
Gilding, s. *ṭilā-kārī.*
Gill, s. *wakkhkai.*
Gimlet, s. *barma, tswarla-ī.*
Gin, s. *dām, lwina, lūma, lūmaka, paṛka, laṭ.*
Ginger, s. (green-) *adrak.* (dry-) *sūnḍ.*
Gipsy, s. *naṭ*; *kochī.*
Gird, v.a. *taṛal.*
Girder, s. *taṛūnai.* (-beam) *bensh, paṭsra, tīr.*
Girdle, s. *mlā-taṛūnai, mlā-band, kamar-band.* (woman's-) *tapor.* (sash) *paṭkai.*
Girl, s. *jina-ī.* (mature-) *peghla.* (betrothed-) *changhala.* (slave-) *windza.* (servant-) *mazdūra.* (kept-) *khidmat-gāra.* (dancing-) *lola-ī, kachana-ī.*
Girth, s. *paṭa-ī*; *tāng.*
Give, v.a. *warkawul, bakkhal, kkhandal.* (evidence) *lal* or *lawdal.*
Giver, s. *warkawūnkai, bakkhūnkai*; *lūnai.*
Gizzard, s. *shā-ṭinga.*
Glad, a. *khwakkh, kkhād, khush, khush-ḥāl.*
Glad-tidings, s. *zera.* (bringer of-) *zera-garai.*
Gladiator, s. *tūra-bāz, shamsher-bāz.*
Gladness, s. *khwakkhī, kkhādī, khush-ḥālī.* (-over a rival) *sakha, wiyāṛ.*
Glance, v.a. *naẓar pa za-ar terawul.* (shine) v.n. *dzal kedal.* (fly off) v.a. *tindak wahal.*
Gland, s. *stagha, ghudūd, ghūnḍārai.*

Glare, s. *ranṛā, dzalah, brekkhnā.*

Glaring, a. *kkhkārah, tsargand, awtsār.*

Glass, s. *kkhīkkha.* (-cup) *piyāla.* (mirror) *ā-īna.*

Glaze, v.a. *malma-* or *mulamm'a k., rang pore k., kāshī k.*

Glazier, s. *kāshī-gar.*

Gleam, s. *partaw, palwasha.*

Gleam, v.n. *dzalkedal, brekkhedal.*

Glean, v.a. *anṛawul, chūnṛal, drūze ṭolawul.*

Glee, s. *kkhādī, khwand.* (song) *ṭapa.*

Glimmer, s. *dzalak, palwasha.*

Glitter, v.n. *brekkhedal, dzalkedal, rūnṛedal.*

Globe, s. *duniyā, naṛa-ī, jahān.* (celestial) *tsarkh, falak, kursī.* (ball) *ghunḍai, manḍos, panḍos, mardak.*

Globular, a. *ghunḍ, ghunḍ-man.*

Globule, s. *gola-ī, mardakoṭai, ghunḍūrai.*

Gloom, s. *tyāreh, tor-wālai, tor-tam; gham, nūl.*

Glorify, v.a. *stāyal, ṡanā wayal.*

Glorious, a. *mubārak; majīd; loe, jalāl; kkhah.*

Glory, s. *nang, nūm, iqbāl.*

Gloss, s. *rang.*

Glossy, a. *brekkh-nāk, dzalak-nāk.*

Glove, s. *dastāna, da lās joṛāba.* (gauntlet) *dast-gala.* (for hawking) *bela.*

Glow, v.n. *todedal, swal.*

Glow, s. *todūkha, swai.* (-worm) *or-orakai.*

Glue, s. *slekkh; leṭa-ī.*

Glutton, s. *geḍa-war, ghārai, ghārdal, ḥirṣ-nāk, rawai.*

Gnash, v.a. *ghākkh chīchal* or *-krapawul.*

Gnat, s. *māshai, ghamāsha, jak* or *jakh.*

Gnaw, v.a. *chīchal, krapawul.*

Go, v.n. *tlal—lāṛal, drūmal* or *drūmedal, chaledal, rawānedal; kūch k., legdal.*

Goad, s. *chūka, trāṭ, konṭa-ī.*

Goal, s. *ṭikāo, mazal, borjal.*

Goat, s. *buz* or *wuz.* (he-) *psah.* (she-) *bza.* (-in heat) *wazema.* (kid) *warghūmai, chelai.* (yearling-) *serlai.* (-hair) *wajghūne.*

Gobble, v.a. *gaṛandai khwuṛal.*

Goblet, s. *kaṭorai, jām, shāh-kāsa.*

Goblin, s. *bāgū, bagalola-ī; rawai.*

God, s. *khudāe, allah, rabb.* (-forbid) *khudāe di na ka* or *-kāndi.* (-preserve us) *yā khudāya-* or *yā rabba khair ka.* (-knows), *khudāe khabar* or *-zdah.* (by-!) *khudāe go.* (good-!) *allaho akbar, subḥān allah.* (my-!) *yā dzamā khudāya.* (for God's sake) *da khudāe da pāra.* (-bless thee) *khudāe di wusāta* or *-wubakkha* or *-loe ka.* (-curse thee) *peṭī mū, pa tā n'alat, khudāe dī mīrāt ka.* (-grant) *khudāe di wuka* or *-wukī.* (-protect thee) *da khudāe pa amān.*

Godliness, s. *dīn-dārī, taqwā.*

Godly, a. *dīn-dār, namāndzī, nmūndz-guzār.*

Going, s. *tak, tlah, yūn, pand.*

Goitre, s. *ghur.*

Gold, s. *sreh-zar, zar, ṭila.* (-smith) *zargar.*

Golden, a. *zarīn.*

Gonorrhœa, s. *sozāk.*

Good, a. *kkhah, nek, pākīzah, ghwarah.* s. *kkhegaṛa, fā-ida, sūd.*

Goodness, s. *kkhah-wālai, nekī.*

Goods, s. *asbāb.* (cattle) *māl.* (clothes) *rakht.* (furniture, etc.) *kālai.*

Goodwill, s. *nek-* or *khair-khwāhī.*

Goose, s. (domestic) *baṭa.* (wild-) *qāza.*

Gore, v.a. *pa kkhkar wahal.*

Gore, s. *praṇr, jākai, malob, wīne.*

Gorge, s. *dara, tanga-ī; ghāṛa, mara-ī.*

Gormandize, v.a. *be-khrata-, be-prata-,* etc. *khwaṛal.*

Gospel, s. *injīl; ḥaqq.*

Gossip, v.a. *khushe khabare k.; khabare-atare-, khabare-mabare k.*

Gourd, s. *kadū.* (-seed) *kadū-zarai.*

Gout, s. *bād, niqris.*

Govern, v.a. *ḥukūmat-, ḥukm-*, etc. *k.* or *-chalawul.* (manage) *sambālawul.*

Government, s. *ḥukūmat, 'amal; sarkār, rāj; sardārī, khānī, malikī.*

Governor, s. *ḥākim, sardār, khān, malik.*

Gown, s. (man's) *chapan, qādara-ī.* (woman's) *peshwāz, pepna-ī.*

Grace, s. *mihrbāngī.* (favour) *mrasta.* (pardon) *bakkhana.* (beauty) *kkhāyast.* (manner) *nāz, karakkhma.* (by the grace of God) *da khudāe pa mihrbāngī sara.* (-before meals) *bismillah.* (-after meals) *d'uā, shukur.* (a form of-) *shukur alḥamdu l illah, rabbā ṣanā tā lara.* (title) *ḥazrat.*

Graceful, a. *kkhāyastah, kkhkulai, nāzak.* (in comp.) *khūsh-.*

Gracefulness, s. *kkhāyast-wālai, kkhāyast, joṛāb, kṛak-wṛak.*

Gracious, a. *mihrbān.*

Graciously, ad. *pa mihrbāngī sara.*

Gradation, s. *darja, pāya, wār.*

Gradually, ad. *ro-ro, wār pa wār.*

Graft, s. *pewand, band, qalam.*

Grain, s. *ghalla, dāna.* (a single-) *dāna.* (bruised-) *dal.* (ground-) *oṛah.* (finely ground-) *maidah.* (parched-) *nīna, pūlah.* (mixed-) *gāḍera.* (-merchant) *saudāgar, ghalla-farosh, banriyā.*

Grammar, s. *ṣarf-o-naḥw.*

Granary, s. *anbār-khāna.*

Grand, a. *loe, ghaṭ, star.*

Grandee, s. *amīr, arbāb.*

Grandeur, s. *loe-wālai, ghaṭ-wālai; zbargī.*

Grant, v.a. *warkawul, bakkhal; manal, qabūlawul.*

Granule, s. *dāna; pūṭai, pitsānrai.*

Grape, s. *angūr.* (-vine) *tāk.* (wild-) *kwar.* (dried-) *watska, mewa.*

Grapple, v.a. *parzawul, nīwul.*

Grasp, v.a. *pa qabze-, pa panje-, pa mūṭe-, pa munguli-*, etc. *nīwul.*

Grass, s. *wākkhah, gayāh, 'alaf.* (varieties of-) *drab, dūp, kabal, shama, shamekhā, ḍila, ghūnḍwagai, sargeṛṛai, sarbaga, wīga, moṭa, panai, malai, mandārū, dadam*, etc.

Grasshopper, s. *toqā, kha-argai; mlakh.*

Grate, v.a. *ṭaghawul, brekkhawul; zdoyal.* v.n. *ghaṛedal.*

Grateful, a. *shukur-guzār; khwand-nāk.*

Gratification, s. *khwakkhī; khwand.* (over another's misfortunes) *sakha, wiyāṛ.*

Gratify, v.a. *khāṭir k., nāzawul, kkhāghal.*

Gratis, ad. *weṛiyā, muft, hase.*

Gratitude, s. *shukur-guzārī.*

Gratuitous, a. *weṛiyā, muft.*

Gratuity, s. *bakhkshiksh, in'ām, shukrāna, pekkh-kakkh, khwaṛa.*

Grave, s. *gor, qabr, maqbara.* (the niche) *laḥad.* (-stone) *khadza* or *khāda.* (-digger) *qabr-kan, gor-kan.* (-badger) *gor-kakkh.* (-clothes) *kafan.*

Grave, a. *drūnd, grān; fikr-man, ghalai*

Gravel, s. *kānṛ, gṣhal, ghaṭa-shiga.*

Gravitate, v.n. *kkhkenāstal, prewatal.*

Gravity, s. *drūnd-wālai, dranāwai.*

Gravy, s. *kkhorwā.*

Gray, a. *sperah, kheṛ, khākī.* (-hair) *brag.*

Graze, v.a. *piyāyal—powul.* v.n. *tsaral, tsaredal.* (abrade) *blosedal; sūledal.*

Grazier, s. *powūnkai.* (of cows) *ghobah.* (of buffaloes) *mekkhbah, gūjar.* (of camels) *ūkkhbah, sārwān.* (of sheep, etc.) *gaḍbah, shpūn, shpankai.*

Grease, s. *ghwaṛī, mū.* v.a. *ghwaṛawul.*

Greasy, a. *ghwaṛ.*

Great, a. *ghaṭ, loe, star; zbarg.*

Greatly, ad. *nihāyat, ḍer.*

Greatness, s. *star-wālai*, etc.; *zbargī.*

Greediness, s. *ḥirṣ, ṭam'a, liwāl-tob.*

Greedy, a. *ḥariṣ, ḥirṣ-nāk, geḍa-war.*

Green, a. *shīn, zarghūn; ūm, kachah.*

Greens, s. *sāg, sābah, talkārī, tara.* (varieties

of-) *panėrak, shawtal, warkhārai, chaiwerai, tāndola, tsārmai, jawānwān*, etc. (cultivated-) *pālak, malkhoza, āorai, mūlai, gāzara, ṭepar*, etc. (dish of-) *sāginrai.*

Greet, v.a. *mubārakī wayal; salām·'alaik-, joṛ·tāzah-*, etc. *k.*

Grief, s. *gham, randz, paskhāk* or *pakhsāk, nūl; gram.*

Grievance, s. *faryād; sakhtī, dzaur, jabr, ẓulm.*

Grieve, v.n. *nūledal, randzedal, kaṛedal, ghamedal, zahīredal.* v.a. *āzārawul zahīrawul*, etc.

Grieved, a. *gham·jan, nūl·jan, randzūr, dil·gīr.*

Grievous, a. *gham·nāk; jabr·nāk, sakht, randz·nāk.*

Grill, v.a. *wrītawul, alwoyal, talawul, teyal.*

Grim, a. *sūṭ·būṭ, mushād; zīg, sakht, klak.*

Grimace, s. *pekkha, tsera, būṭ·urbūz.*

Grin, v.n. *musedal.* v.a. *dāṛe-, ghākkh-*, etc. *chīngawul.*

Grind, v.a. *oṛawul, anral, oṛeh k.*

Grindstone, s. *psān.* (-wheel) *tsarkh.* (-for corn) *mechan.* (-for spices) *tīga, silātā.*

Gripe, s. *qubẓa, da mūṭī nīwah.* (belly-) *kānga, tāo, pech.*

Gripe, v.a. *pa qabẓe-, pa mūṭī-*, etc. *nīwul.* (as birds and beasts) *pa panje-, pa manguli-*, etc. *nīwul.* (as the belly) v.n. *kānga-, tāo-*, etc. *ked.*

Gristle, s. *krachai, krachūnai, krachandūkai.*

Grit, s. *kānr, shiga; dal, drūza, gadzārai.*

Gritty, a. *shiglan, kānran, kānrez.*

Groan, v.a. *zwergai* or *zgerwai-, angahār* or *hengahar-*, etc. *k.*

Grocer, s. *pansārī, banriyā.*

Groin, s. *mghāna.*

Groom, s. *shātar, jalau·dār, nafar.*

Groove, s. *kīla, karkkha.*

Grope, v.n. *ṭaparedal.* v.a. *laṭawul.*

Gross, a. *tsorb, peraṛ; ghaṭ, lwāṛ; nāpaṛ, star.*

Gross, s. *ṭol, ṭol·ṭāl, tamām, kull.*

Ground, s. *zmaka* or *mzaka, zamīn.*

Groundless, a. *be·mūjib, nā·ḥaqq.*

Group, s. *ṭolgai, tamba, tsīṛa, paṛk, jam.*

Grouse, s. *kha-aṛārai, kha-aṛai·kauntar, kha-aṛgaṭ.*

Grove, s. *jangai, banr.*

Grovel, v.n. *rghaṛedal—rghakkhtal.*

Grow, v.n. (increase) *ghaṭedal, ziyātedal, loe ked.* (vegetate) *ṭūkedal, zarghūnedal.* (-old) *zaṛedal.* (become) *kedal.*

Growl, v.n. *ghuṛunbedal, gṛanjedal.*

Grudge, v.a. *dareghh, k.* (owe a-) *dukkhmanī-, badī-, khwā·badī-, 'inād-, kīna-*, etc. *laral.*

Gruel, s. *atob, oghra, dalya; āsh, shīra.*

Gruff, a. *sakht, tursh·rūe, suṭ·būṭ, qahr·jan.*

Grumble, v.a. *gila-, māna-*, etc. *k.* v.n. *gṛanjedal, ghuṛunbedal.* (as the bowels) *qur·qur ked.*

Guarantee, s. *ẓamānat.* (person) *ẓāmin.*

Guard, s. *pahra, tsoka-ī; pāswān, kishik: pahra·dār, tsoka-ī·dār.* (over crops and cattle) *kakkhai.* (protector) *sātūnkai, sātandoe, ĵghorai, pāslawūnai.*

Guard, v.a. *pahra-*, etc. *k.; pāswānī-*, etc. *k. gālal; kakkhī·tob k.; sātal, ĵghoral, pāslawul, khundī k.*, or *khundiyal.*

Guess, v.a. *qiyās-, khiyāl-, aṭkal-*, etc. *k., pejandal, m'alūmawul.*

Guest, s. *melmah, mezmān.*

Guidance, s. *kkhowuna, hidāyat, murshidī.*

Guide, s. *balad, lār·kkhowūnkai, būmiyā.* (spiritual) *pīr, murshid, hādī, peshwā.*

Guile, s. *ṭag·bāzī, chal·bāzī, lamghaṛa-ī-tob, ṭagī, ḥīla, fareb.*

Guilt, s. *gunāh, taqṣīr; wabāl, baza.*

Guiltless, a. *be·gunāh, be·quṣūr, be·taqṣīr.*

Guilty, a. *gunāh·gār, taqṣīrī, quṣūr·man.*

Guise, s. *ṣūrat, shakl, shān; bāna, libās; parda.*

Guitar, s. *sitāra, chamtāra.* (Fiddle.)

Gullet, s. *mara-ī, sra·ghāṛa.*

Gulp, s. *ghurap, gūṭ, īnda.* v.a. *nghardal.*

Gum, s. *chīṛ, jāwla.* (of teeth) *ūra-ī* or *awra-ī.*

Gun, s. *bandūkh, ṭopak.* (-barrel) *nala.* (-stock) *kundāgh.* (-sight) *mach, zarai, dīdwān, ghūṭa-ī.* (-match) *bāta-ī, patīla.* (-cock) *pāya.* (-trigger) *chajak.* (-priming pan) *kanḍol, māsha, ātash · khāna.* (-chamber) *khizana.* (-priming powder) *ranjak.* (-cleaning rod) *bargho, margholai.* (ramrod) *gaz, sīkh.* (-aiming rest) *sipāwa* or *sipāya.* (-powder) *dārū.* (-ball) *mardaka.*

Gunner, s. *topak·chī, bandūkh·chī*; *top·chī.*

Gush, v.n. *pa·dāro watal* or *-bahedal.* v.a. *dāra wahal.*

Gust, s. *chapa, jakar, sīla-ī.*

Gut, s. *kulma, laṛmūn*; *larai, ūjrai.*

Gutter, s. *nāwa, lakkhta-ī, wāla, tarnāo.*

Guttural, a. *ḥalqī.*

Gymnastic, a. *kushtī, pahlawānī.*

Gyves, s. *dzolana, pakhwandai, pāekara, pāela.*

H.

Haberdasher, s. *banjārī.*

Habit, s. *'ādat, yūn, 'amal*; *khoe, khaslat*; *mizāj, ṭabi'at.*

Habitation, s. *astoga, kor, dzāe, meshta, borjal.*

Habitual, a. *'ādatī, āmokhtah.*

Habituate, v.a. *'ādatī-*, etc. *k., rūgdawul.*

Hack, v.a. *kūtal, ṭoṭa·ṭoṭa-, chūr·chūr-*, etc. *k.*

Hag, s. *zaṛa-ī, jāḍa-ī.*

Haggard, a. *ṭap, ḍangar, wuch·klak, tsoṛ.*

Hail, s. *jāla, gala-ī.* v.n. *jāle-*, etc. *oredal.*

Hail, v.a. *salām·'alaik-, joṛ·tāzah-*, etc. *k.*

Hair, s. *wekkhtah.* (dressed) *sar·kunḍai.* (lock or curl of-) *tsūnra, tsunraka, zulf, wal.* (braid or plait of-) *orbal, kontsa-ī, nghakkhai.* (top knot of-) *tsaṛai.* (-of pubes) *tor · wekkhtah.* (-of the body) *zunba, ghūna.* (goat's-) *ūjghūne.* (ribbon or braid for the-) *bachawai, pekawai, peyawai.*

Hairy, a. *babar, waṛan.*

Hale, a. *takṛah·tāzah, rogh·mot, joṛ, tandurust.*

Half, a. *nīm.* (-done) *nīmgaṛai.* s. *nīmai, nīmāyah.*

Hall, s. *dālān, khūna.* (public-) *hujra.* (-of audience) *dalbār, bārgāh.*

Halloo, v.a. *chigha-, nāra-*, etc. *wahal.*

Hallowed, a. *pāk, muqaddas.*

Halo, s. *hāla, shpol.*

Halt, v.n. *wudredal*; *guḍedal*; *jah ked.* v.a. *dera-, muqām-, ṭikāo-*, etc. *k.*

Halter, s. *khapī* or *gapī, pā-ī, bāḍgol.* (headstall) *ter·sarai.* (hangman's-) *tezanda-ī, zanda-ī, pā-ī.*

Halve, v.a. *nīmawul, dwah·nīm k.*

Ham, s. (thigh) *wrūn, patūn.*

Hamlet, s. *banḍa, kaloṭai.*

Hammer, s. *pa-alk, tsaṭak.* (wooden-) *baghdar, ḍabalai.* (washerman's-) *tsobāṛai.*

Hammer, v.a. *wahal, ṭakawul, trakawul, ṭak wahal.*

Hamper, s. *khalta, kawāra, ṭokra-ī, kāra, sawada.*

Hamper, v.a. *kariyābawul, haṭālawul.*

Hamstring, v.a. *pai k.*, or *-wahal*

Hand, s. *lās*; *chaka, panja, mangul.* (-ful) *lapa* or *lapaka, paka* or *kapa.* (palm of-) *warghawai, khapaṛ.* (-breadth) *tsapak.* (closed-) *mūṭ.* (-in hand) *chak·pa·chak.* (-cuff) *karai.* (-held to receive) *mangul, changul.* (-held to take or seize) *panja.*

Handful, s. *chung, qawda.* (double-) *lapakai.*
Handkerchief, s. *rumāl, dast·māl.* (-for head) *sar·basta, sar·pechak, sar·tarūnai, tsapot-kai.*
Handle, s. *mūtai, lāstai, dasta.*
Handle, v.a. *lās lagawul, -warwral, -wahal,* etc., *latawul, niwul*; *chalawul.*
Handmaid, s. *mazdūra, khidmat·gāra, sahela-ī.* (brides-) *inga.*
Handmill, s. *mechan.* (lower stone) *kkhkatanai pal.* (upper stone) *portanai pal.* (-handle) *lāstai.* (pivot or axle) *tirak.* (axle bar) *dida, kkhārag.* (-cup) *ghāra.* (-hopper) *dol, gand.*
Handsome, a. *kkhāyastah, kkhkulai, pa-ī·makhai* or *pej·makhai.*
Handsomely, ad. *pa kkhah shān sara.*
Handsomeness, s. *kkhāyist, kkhāyist·wālai, kkhkulai·wālai, kkhkuli·tob, pej·makh·tob.*
Handy, a. *tak·lāstai*; *tayār*; *nijdai.*
Hang, v.n. *dzwarandedal, āwezānd ked.* v.a. *āwezānd k., dzwarandawul.* (a criminal) *tezanda-ī warkawul, pa dār khejawul.*
Hangman, s. *jallāt, tezanda-ī warkawūnkai, dār·kash.*
Hank, s. *tranjūkai.* (ring) *karai.*
Hanker, v.n. *liwāl-, mayan-,* etc. *ked.* v.a. *mina-, raghbat-, shauq-,* etc. *laral.*
Hapless, a. *kam·bakht, be·qismat, be·naṣīb.*
Haply, ad. *kkhā-ī, gunde*; *wī ba.*
Happen, v.n. *kedal, shwal, nāziledal, prewatal, teredal, waqi'a ked., pekkhedal.*
Happily, ad. *pa khair sara, pa kkhādī sara.*
Happy, a. *khwakkh, kkhād, kkhād·man.*
Harangue, v.a. *w'aẓ k., kalām wayal.*
Harass, v.a. *rabrawul, āzārawul, tangawul, tongawul, tongāra k.*
Harbinger, s. *peshraw, astādzai.*
Harbour, s. *bandar*; *panāh.*
Hard, a. *klak, sakht*; *grān, mushkil*; *pokh, takrah.*
Hard-hearted, a. *nā·tars, kānrai·zrah, bedard.*
Hardiness, s. *klak·wālai, maẓbūt·tiyā, takrah·wālai*; *zreh·war·tob.*
Hardly, ad. *pa mushkil sara, pa rabar sara*; *kamtar, mushkila, hila.*
Hardness, s. *klak·wālai, sakht·wālai.*
Hardship, s. *tangsa, rabar, sakhtī.*
Hardware, s. *da ospane kālī.*
Hardy, a. *klak, maẓbūt, zreh·war, maranai, takrah, ting.*
Hare, s. *soe.* (hare's form) *sozhālai.*
Harebrained, a. *khushai, lewanai.*
Hark, in. *wāwra! ghwag bāsa!* or *-nisa!* or *-kegda!*
Harlot, s. *kāsira, shatāha*; *lola-ī, kachana-ī.*
Harm, s. *tāwān, ziyān, nuqṣān.*
Harmful, a. *tāwānī, nuqṣānī, ziyānī.*
Harmonious, a. *barābar, yo·shān*; *khog.*
Harmony, s. *rogha, jora, āshtī*; *sarod, tarāna.*
Harness, s. *da ās kālī*; *sāz·sāmān.*
Harp, s. *barbat.*
Harpoon, s. *biyak.*
Harrow, s. *ghākkhawar.*
Harsh, a. *triw, trīkh*; *zig, lwār.*
Harvest, s. *faṣl.* (reaped-) *lau.* (gathered-) *khirman, dirmand.* (spring-) *orai.* (autumn-) *manai.*
Hash, v.a. *qīma k., tote k.*
Haste, s. *talwār, talwal, jaltī, shitābī.* (to make-) *talwār-,* etc. *k.*
Hasty, a. *talwārī, talwalai, jalt.*
Hat, s. *topa-ī, khola-ī.*
Hatch, v.n. *kuraka ked.*; *pa hago kkhkenāstal, bachī bāsal—yistal.*
Hatchet, s. *tabar.*
Hate, v.a. *bad manal, kagal, chinjawul, ghandal, kraka ākhistal.*
Hateful, a. *bad, kagalai, kraka·nāk, ghāndah.*
Hatred, s. *badī, khwā·badī, dukkhnī, kīna, khuṣūmat, taka, ghach.*

Haughtiness, s. *kibr, bād, maghrūrī, khpel·sarī.*

Haughty, a. *kibr·jan, bādī, khāntamā.*

Haul, v.a. *rākāgal—rākkhkal.*

Haunch, s. *kūnātai; ṭūṭa, ḍūḍa, patūn.*

Haunt, s. *borjal, meshta, astoga.*

Haunt, v.n. *osedal, āstedal.*

Hautboy, s. *sarnāe, tūrci.*

Have, v.a. *laral, darlal.*

Haven, s. *bandar, panāh.*

Havock, s. *tākht·tārāj, tālā, kharābi, wrānī.*

Hawk, s. *bāz.* (goshawk) *bāz, kaṭah·bāz, jurrah.* m. (varieties of-) *turmatai, bākkha, shaindai, lagar, jagar, regui, shikrai.* (-of the first year) *chūz.* (-of the second year) *khāna·kurīz.* (old-) *tarīnāk.* (-from the nest) *shānī.* (caught-) *dāmī.* (-perch) *chakas.* (-bells) *gingrai.* (-jessies) *tasme.* (-hood) *ṭopa-ī.* (-lure) *dalba.* (-drag) *bāolī.* (-glove) *bela.*

Hawk, v.a. *da bāz-* or *da chargh kkhkār k.*; (expectorate) *ghāṛa tāza k.* (sell) *banjārī k.*

Hay, s. *wuch wākkhah, wuch·giyāh, pashkālai.* (-of pulses) *kaṭī.* (coil of-) *beda.*

Hazard, s. *khaṭra, bāk, muhimm, andekkhnā.* (stroke) *daw, guzār.* (chance) *gumān.*

Haze, s. *dund, ghubār, ḍūp, laṛa, tyāreh.*

He, pr. *haghah, dā, dah, de, dī.*

Head, s. *sar, kala, kotai.* (-band) *sar·pechak, sar·taṛūnai.* (-piece) *paṭkai, lūnga-ī.* (-stall) *ter sarai.* (-and tail) *shīr·khaṭ.* (crown of-) *ṭopal, ṭaṭar.*

Headlong, a. *alwal; talwalai; naskor.*

Headstrong, a. *zorāwar, sar·zor, sar·kakkh, ṭakawrai, khpul·sar, hoḍai.*

Heal, v.a. *joṛawul, raghawul.* v.n. *joṛedal, raghedal.*

Health, s. *rogh·wālai, joṛ·wālai, rogh·tiyā, joṛ·tiyā, tandrustī.*

Healthy, a. *rogh, joṛ, tandrust.*

Heap, s. *ṭop, kat, rāsha, rash.* (all of a-) *sūṭ·būṭ, alwal, yak·lakhta.*

Heap, v.a. *tapal, ṭolawul, ḍera-ī-, kat-,* etc. *k.*

Hear, v.a. *āwredal; ghwag bāsal—yastal, -nīwul,* or *-kegdal—kekkhodal.* (attend) *nghwatal.* (over-) *ghwag tsāral.*

Hearer, s. *āwredūnkai, sām'i.*

Hearing, s. *āwredana, sim'a.*

Hearsay, s. *āwredali khabara, afwāh.*

Heart, s. *zṛeh, dil.* (-string) *māndara.* (-ache) *zṛeh·swai, zṛeh·nūl.* (-burning) *māṇrai, mīrtsī.*

Heartily, ad. *pa dwāṛo stargo.*

Hearty, a. *takṛah, tāzah, rogh·joṛ; zreh·war.*

Heat, s. *tod·wālai, todūkha, garmī, tāw.*

Heat, v.a. *todawul.* (warm) *teṛem k.*

Heathen, s. *but parast, kāfir.*

Heave, v.a. *khejawul; āchawul, ghurzawul, nīshtal.*

Heaven, s. *āsmān, falak; jannat, bihikkht.*

Heaviness, s. *drūnd·wālai, dranūwai.*

Heavy, a. *drūnd.*

Hedge, s. *bāra, shpol, keṛa, jal.*

Hedgehog, s. *shīshkai, zigkai.*

Heed, s. *parwā, fikr, poha, pahm, khabar.*

Heedful, a. *khabar·dār, baidār, hokkhyār.*

Heel, s. *pūnda* or *pūnḍa-ī.* (-of a door) *chūṛ.*

Heifer, s. *skhwandara, skhwandarkoṭa-ī.*

Height, s. *ūchat·wālai, hask·wālai.*

Heighten, v.a. *ūchatawul; ziyātawul.*

Heinous, a. *bad·sakht, bad·balā.*

Heir, s. *wāris, haqq·dār.* (-less) *lā·wāris.*

Hell, s. *doghakkh* or *dozakh, jahannum, saqar.*

Hellebore, s. *kūṭkī.*

Helm, s. *sīngāwaṇr, ḍapa.*

Helmet, s. *khol.*

Help, s. *madad, komak, pushtī, mrasta; tsāra, 'ilāj.* v.a. *madad-,* etc. *k.* or *-warkawul; tsāra-,* etc. *laral.*

Helper, s. *madad·gār, komakī, yār, mal.*

Helpless, a. *lā·tsūr, nā·tuwān, 'ājiz.* (-from wounds) *zmol, zam·zmolai, kanḍ·kapaṛ.*

Helter-skelter, a. *gaḍ·waḍ, lānde·bānde.*

Hem, s. *laman, jānja-ī*; *trāṭa, maghzai.* (corner of a dress) *pitskai.*

Hem, v.a. *ganḍal, bezal.*

Hemp, s. *saur.*

Hen, s. *chirga.*

Hence, ad. *la de na, dzaka*; *la de dzāya.* in. *lire! lire sha!*

Henceforth, ad. *wṛānde.*

Her, pr. *hagha, dā, da, de, di.*

Herald, s. *jār·chī, munadī kawūnkai.*

Herb, s. *būṭai.* (pot-) *sāg.*

Herbage, s. *wākkhah, giyāh.*

Herd, s. *ramma, ṭol, ṭolai, tolgai, paṛk.* (-of cows) *gāhar, gohār.* (-of buffaloes) *goram.*

Herdsman, s. (-of oxen) *gāhū, ghobah.* (-of buffaloes) *gūjar, mekkhbah.* (-of sheep, etc.) *gaḍbah, shpūn.*

Here, ad. *dalta, dale, hīsta.*

Hereafter, ad. *la de na wrusto, biyā.*

Hereby, ad. *pa de, la de na.*

Hereditary, a. *mīrāṣī.* (-tenant) *mīrāṣ khor.*

Herein, ad. *pa de kkhke.*

Heresy, s. *rāfiẓī·tob, darogh.*

Heretic, s. *rāfiẓī, khārijī, darogh·jan.*

Herewith, ad. *de sara.*

Heritage, s. *mīrāṣ* or *mīrāt.*

Hermaphrodite, s. *kkhadzūnak, khunṣā, hijrai.*

Hermit, s. *gokkha nishīn.*

Hernia, s. *tsūhra, khoṭa bād.*

Hero, s. *bahādur, maṛanai, turzan.*

Heroism, s. *maṛanī·tob, tūrzan·tob.*

Heron, s. *baglai.*

Hesitate, v.n. *wṛānde·wrusto ked., stāra prewatal, shakk·man-, wiswāsī-, andekkh·man-,* etc. *ked.*

Heterodox, a. *khārijī*; *mukhālif.*

Heterogeneous, a. *gaḍ·waḍ, argajah*; *mukhālif, 'aks, nā·muwāfiq.*

Hew, v.a. *prekawul* or *prekṛal, kūtal*; *tsaurang k.*

Hiccough, s. *haṭkai.*

Hidden, a. *puṭ, pinham.*

Hide, v.n. *puṭedal.* v.a. *puṭawul.*

Hide, s. *tsarman, poṭ, tsarm.*

Hideous, a. *bad, nā·kūrah, haul·nāk.*

Hie, v.n. *drūmal, za-ar* or *zir-, gaṛandzi-,* etc. *tlal—lāṛal.*

High, a. *ūchat, hask*; *lwaṛ*; *dang.*

Highlander, s. *rohīlai, kohistānai, da ghreh saṛai, ghartsanai.*

Highly, ad. *ḍer, nihāyat, be·shāna.*

Highminded, a. *kibr·jan, bādī.*

Highness, s. *ūchat·wālai, hask·wālai*; *lwaṛtiyā*; *dang·wālai.* (title) *hazrat.*

Highway, s. *bādshāhī lār, saṛak.*

Highwayman, s. *lār wahūnkai, shūk·mār, rāh·zan, ghal.*

Hilarity, s. *kkhādī, khush·hālī, khandā, mastī.*

Hill, s. *ghar, koh.* (low spur of-) *pukkhta, kha-aṭ.*

Hillock, s. *ghunḍa-ī, ḍera-ī, taraka-ī, pota-ī.*

Hilt, s. *mūṭai, lāstai, qabẓa.*

Hinder, v.a. *aṭālawul, kariyābawul, man'a k.*

Hindermost, a. *wrustai, wrustanai, akhīr, pastanai, ākhirīn.*

Hindrance, s. *aṭāl, kariyāb, āṛ, harakat.*

Hinge, s. *qabẓa, chūṛ.*

Hint, s. *ishārat, kināyat.*

Hip, s. *ṭuṭa, ḍūḍa.* (-bone) *kkhna.*

Hire, s. *ajr, ujrat, mihnat, mazdūrī, kreha.*

Hireling, s. *mazdūr.*

Hiss, v.a. (as snake, etc.) *pakh wahal.* (as meat on the fire) *sakkha-, dzadz-,* etc. *wahal.*

History, s. *tawārīkh, riwāyat, taẕkira.*

Hit, v.a. *wahul, lagawul.* v.n. *jangedal, lagedal.*

Hither, ad. *dalta, rāhīsta, de khwā, de palaw.*

Hitherto, ad. *tar osa, tar osa pore.*

Hive, s. *kor, khūna.* (bees-) *gabīna, garbīnai.* (wasps-) *kkhor.* (ants-) *megalūn.*

Hoar, a. *sperah, brag, spīn.*

Hoard, v.a. *ṭolawul, gaṭal, ambār-, jam'a-,* etc. *k.*

Hoard, s. *jam'a, panga, saga, anbār, māya.*

Hoarse, a. *bog, ḍaḍ.*

Hobble, v.n. *guḍedal, pa kharpotso tlal—lāṛal; ṭaparedal.*

Hocus-pocus, s. *chal-wal, jādū, koḍ.*

Hodge-podge, a. *gaḍ-waḍ, aṛang-baṛang argajah.*

Hodiernal, a. *nananai.*

Hoe, s. *kodāla-ī, saspor, sakkhsora, kasha-ī.* (small) *rambai.*

Hog, s. *kharbīshoe, sarkūzai.* (wild-) *soḍar, maṭah.*

Hoist, v.a. *khejawul, ūchatawul, porta k.*

Hold, v.a. *niwul.* (take) *ākhistal.* (-fast) *klak niwul, ṭīngawul.* (contain) *dzāyawul.* (consider) *gaṇṛal.* (keep-) *sātal, sambālāwul, khundī k.* v.n. (remain) *osedal, pātedal.* (cling) *nkkhatal.* (contain) *dzā-edal.* (connect) *lagedal.*

Holder, s. *ākhistūnai; sātandoe, sātūnkai; dzāyūnkai, larūnkai.* (in comp.) *-dār, -gīr, -khor.*

Hole, s. *sūṛa, sūṛai.* (pit) *ḍoghal, ṭūbkai* or *ṭublai, kanda.* (opening) *khula, swam* or *spam.*

Holiday, s. *akhtar, 'īd.*

Hollo, in. *o! ai! yā! yāe!* v.a. *nāra wahul.*

Hollow, a. *ta-ash* or *t-ish, khālī; ḍaḍ, kāwāk; khushai.*

Hollow, s. *tahana, jawara; kanda, kas.*

Holy, a. *pāk; nek, pārsā.*

Holy Ghost, s. *rūḥu l-quds, ruḥ-ullah.*

Homage, s. *tāb'i-dārī, salāmī.*

Home, s. *borjal, kor, dzāe, astoga, mīshta, ṭikāo.* (country) *waṭan, mulk, wilāyat, dzāe-dzāegai.* (-made) *koranai, khānagī.*

Homeless, a. *be-kor, dar-ba-dar, khāwre-pasar.*

Homely, a. *khamsor, sādah; lwāṛ.*

Homogeneous, a. *barābar, yaw shān, yaw jins.*

Hone, s. *belāw, belho, barjo, psān.*

Honest, a. *rikkhtīnai, nek, karah, sam.*

Honesty, s. *rikkhtīn-tob, nekī, rāstī.*

Honey, s. *shāt* or *shahad.* (-comb) *gabīna.*

Honeycombed, a. *zang wahalai, chinji khwuṛalai.*

Honour, s. *nang, nūm, 'izzat, makh, abrū.*

Honourable, a. *nang-yālai, 'izzat-nāk; nūmwar; makhawar.*

Hood, s. *ṭopa-ī, khola-ī, kulāh.* (woman's-) *paṛūnai, oṛanai.* (snake's-) *chaja.*

Hoof, s. *sum.* (cloven-) *swa, kkhongarai.*

Hook, s. *kunḍa.* (flesh-) *nukhakkh.*

Hoop, s. *chambar, chak.*

Hoot, v.a. *chighawul.*

Hop, v.a. *tskhawul, tskhe k., ṭīndak-, ṭop-,* etc. *wahul.*

Hope, s. *umed, āsra; khal.* v.a. *umed-,* etc. *laral.*

Hopeful, a. *umed-wār.*

Hopeless, a. *nā-umed.*

Horde, s. *ulas, tapa.*

Horizon, s. *ufuq.*

Horizontal, a. *prot, mlāst, sam.*

Horn, s. *kkhkar, kkhākh.*

Horned, a. *kkhkarawar, kkhākh-dār.*

Hornet, s. *ḍanbara, ḍanḍāra, ghālbūza.*

Horrible, a. *bad sakht; kagalai, ghāndah; khof-, haul-, tars-,* etc. *-nāk.*

Horripilate, v.n. *ghūna zigedal.*

Horror, s. *wera* or *yera, tor, tars.*

Horse, s. *ās.* (pack-) *yābū, ṭaṭū.* (ambling-) *yarghah.* (-dealer) *dallāl.* (-breaker) *chābuk sawār.* (-man) *spor* or *swor.* (-shoe) *nāl.*

Horticulture, s. *bāghwānī, gul karana.*

Hose, s. *joṛāba, meza.* (leather) *māsa-ī.*

Hospitable, a. *melmah·dost, ḍoḍī·mār.*

Hospital, s. *bīmār·khāna; langar·khāna.*

Hospitality, s. *melmastiyā.*

Host, s. *korbah, melmah·dost; meṛah, tsakkh-tan; lakkhkar, ganr·khalq*

Hostage, s. *yarghamāl.*

Hostess, s. *korbana, merman.*

Hostile, a. *dukkhman, mukhālif.*

Hostility, s. *dukkhmanī, badī, 'adāwat.*

Hot, a. *tod, garm.*

Hound, s. *tāzī-* or *kkhkārī spai.* v.a. *spī pase k.*

Hour, s. *sā'at, gaṛai.*

Hourly, ad. *har sā'at, sā'at pa sā'at.*

House, s. *kor, khāna.* (storied-) *mānra-ī, angaṛ.* (premises) *ḥawela-ī, myana.* (-holder) *korbah, dawtarī.* (-wife) *korbana, merman.* (-keeping) *kormāna.* (-hold) *ṭabaṛ, kor, khāndān, khān-o-mān, kaḍa.* (-tax) *lūgī·tāwān.* (-ruins) *kanḍar.* (-rent) *kreha, tāwān.* (-breaker) *ghal, gūṭ mātawūnkai, kanḍar kawūnkai.* (court of a-) *gholai.* (side of a-) *chana.*

Hovel, s. *jūngaṛa, kaḍala, manah.*

Hover, v.n. *tsrapedal, rapedal; girzedal.*

How, ad. *tsanga? tsa ranga? pa tsa shān?*

However, ad. *walekin, wale, mangar.*

Howl, v.a. *ghapal, angolā k., nāra wahal.*

Hubbub, s. *zwag·zwūg, chagh·chugh, nāre·sūre, hāṛa·hūṛa, dagh·dagha.*

Hue, s. *rang, laun.* (-and cry) *kūhā.*

Hug, v.a. *ghāṛa·ghaṛa-ī k.*

Huge, a. *loe, ghaṭ, star; nāpaṛ, khrīs.*

Hum, v.n. *bonredal.* v.a. *zwag k.*

Hum, s. *bonra.* (conversation) *gangosai, shālwak* or *kkhkālwak.*

Human, a. *basharī, insānī, nāsūt.* (-being) s. *wagaṛai, gawai; bashar, insān.*

Humane, a. *nek·khoe, mulā-im, raḥm·dil.*

Humanity, s. *saṛī·tob, ādmiyat, insāniyat; nek·khaṣlatī, mom·dilī.*

Humble, a. *'ājiz, nā·tsīz, gharīb, kamīn.*

Humbly, ad. *'ājizī sara.*

Humbug, s. *allam·ghallam, shkharā.*

Humid, a. *lūnd; nam·nāk, zyam·nāk, naw-jan.*

Humidity, s. *lūnd·wālai; zyam, nam, naw.*

Humiliation, s. *'ājizī, gharībī, nā·tsīzī; spuk·tiyā, makh·torī.*

Humility, s. *'ājizī, gharībī, nā·tsīzī, kamīn·tob.*

Humorous, a. *ṭoqī, washtī, khandā·bāz.*

Humour, s. *khwā, khoe, mizāj.* (matter) *zwa, zahūb, khīrai, rīm.* (fun) *washta, ṭoqa.* (moisture) *zyam, nam, naw.*

Humour, v.a. *nāzawul, nāz wṛal, khāṭir k.*

Hump, s. *kūb* or *kwab.* (-backed) *kūbai, chūghai.*

Hundred, s. *sal* or *sil.* (more than one-) *saw.* (one hundred) *sil.* (two, three, four, etc. hundred) *dwah-, dre-, tsalor-,* etc., *-sawa.*

Hunger, s. *lwaga, liwāl·tob.*

Hungry, a. *wagai, liwāl, naghlānd.*

Hunt, v.a. *kkhkār k.* (search) *laṭawul, shanal.*

Hurl, v.a. *ghurzawul, wīshtal, āchawul.*

Hurrah, in. *shābāsh! āparīn!*

Hurricane, s. *silu-ī, ṭūfān.*

Hurry, v.a. *talwār-, talwal-, jaltī-, gaṛandai-,* etc. *k.*

Hurt, s. *khūg, zakhm, parhār; tāwūn, nuqṣān. ziyān.* a. *zakhmī, parhār·jalai, jobal.* v.a. *khūgawul, jobalawul, zahīrawul, tā-wān-, nuqṣān-,* etc. *k.*

Hurtful, a. *tāwūnī, ziyān·kār, nuqṣānī; muzirr, wrān·kār, stukh.*

Husband, s. *meṛah, tsakkhtan, khāwand.*

Husbandman, s. *zamīndār, kikkht·gar.* (hired-) *charekār, dihqān.*

Husbandry, s. *kar, kikkht·garī, zamīndārī.* (thrift) *kormāna, khāna·dārī; sātana, bachawūna.*

Hush, in. *chip! chup!*
Husk, s. *būr, pot, bat; sūṛī, būṭ-sūṛī.*
Hut, s. *jūngaṛa, kuḍala, tsapar, manah.*
Hyacinth, s. *nargis, kangas.* (colour) *sausan.*
Hyena, s. *kog, sar-ṭiṭai, kaftār.*
Hypochondriasis, s. *khapqān, saudā-ī.*
Hypocrisy, s. *makr, riyā.*
Hypocrite, s. *makrai, makr-jan, riyā-kār.*
Hypothesis, s. *qiyās, rāe, andāza, gumān.*
Hysterics, s. *pariyān, da pariyāno ghoṭa.*

I.

I, pr. *zah, khpul; mā.*
Ice, s. *kangal, yakh.*
Idea, s. *khiyāl, rāe, fikr, poha, and.*
Identical, a. *be-dū, hūbahū, kaṭ-maṭ, pa ṭikī.*
Identity, s. *ṣūrat, shān; pejandgalī; yo-wālai.*
Idiom, s. *iṣṭilāḥ, iṣṭilāḥī khabara, chalana.*
Idiomatic, a. *iṣṭilāḥī, chalanī, riwājī.*
Idiot, s. *gedī, kam-'aql, nā-dān, nā-poh.*
Idle, a. *wuzgār, khālī, be-kār.* (lazy) *nā-rāst, sust, laṭ.* (useless) *'abaṣ, be-fā-ida.* (trifling) *be-hūdah, wuch-puch, nā-kārah.*
Idleness, s. *nā-rāstī, sustī, laṭ-wālai.*
Idol, s. *būt, tsera.*
Idolater, s. *but parast, mushrik.*
Idolatry, s. *but parastī, shirk.*
Idolize, v.a. *parastī k.* (admire) v.n. *gro-hedal.*
If, c. *ki, agar.* (as-) *laka chi, ghūnde, ganra, goyā.*
Ignite, v.n. *baledal, swal.* v.a. *balawul, sedzal, or pore k., swadzawul.*
Ignoble, a. *lānde-zāt, kam-aṣl, bad-aṣl, spuk, pāsū, bad-zāt.*
Ignominious, a. *ruswā, bad-nūm, nā-kārah, bad.*
Ignominy, s. *bad-namūsī, sharmindagī, ruswā-ī, makh-torī.*
Ignorance, s. *nā-dānī, be-khabarī, nā-pohī, jel.*
Ignorant, a. *nā-dān, nā-poh, jāhil; be-khabar.*
Ignorantly, ad. *nā-dānista, be-khabara.*
Ill, a. *bad, nā-kārah, nā-sāz, nā-kkhanai, kharāb.* (sick) *nā-rogh, nā-joṛ, randzūr, bīmār.*
Illegal, a. *nā-rawā, ḥarām.*
Illegitimate, a. *ḥarāmī, ḥarāmūnai, ḥarām zādah.*
Illiberal, a. *shūm, shūm-shaghāl, bakhīl.*
Illiterate, a. *nā-lwustai, jāhil, āmī.*
Ill-natured, a. *bad-khoe, bakhīl, sūṭ-būṭ.*
Illness, s. *nā-joṛ-tiyā, nā-rogh-tiyā, āzār, bīmārī.*
Ill-timed, a. *be-wakht, be-ṭāng.*
Illumination, s. *rokkhnā-ī, ranṛā-ī; chirāgh-dān.*
Illuminate, v.a. *rokkhān-, ranṛā-,* etc. *k., chirāgh-dān k.*
Illusion, s. *khām khiyāl, ghalatī, fareb.*
Illustrate, v.a. *kkhoyal—kkhowul, tsarganda-wul, kkhkārah k., bayānawul, tamṣil k.*
Illustration, s. *bayān, kkhowūna, miṣāl.*
Illustrious, a. *nūm-war, nāmdār, nāmī.*
Im-, negative prefix. (in comp.) *be-, nā-, kam-.*
Image, s. *but, tsera; ṣūrat, shakl.*
Imaginary, a. *khiyālī, wahmī, gumānī.*
Imagination, s. *khiyāl, qiyās, fikr, gumān, rāe.*
Imagine, v.a. *qiyās-, fikr-,* etc. *k.*
Imbecile, a. *kam-'aql, nā-tuwān, palwand.*
Imbibe, v.a. *tskkhal* or *skal, dzbekkhal, randal; wuchawul.*
Imbue, v.a. *rangawul; kharob k.; ḍakawul.*
Imitate, v.a. *pairawī k., naql k., swāng k.*
Imitator, s. *pairaw; nāqil; swāngai.*
Immaculate, a. *be-gunāh, be-'aib, pāk ṣāf, spin-spetsalai, nog.*
Immaterial, a. *be-wujūd, nābūd; khushai, nā-kār.*
Immature, a. *ūm, khām, kachah, umghalan, nīma-khwā, nīmgaṛai.*

Immediately, ad. *os, pa de sā'at, sam da lāsa, pa ṭikī, dam dar ḥāl.*
Immemorial, a. *la yād na bāhar, da yāda ter.*
Immense, a. *be-ḥadd, be-nihāyat, be-shān; loe, ghaṭ, star, bashpaṛ, nāpaṛ.*
Immensely, ad. *be-qiyāsa, be-shāna, be-kacha*, etc.
Immerse, v.a. *ḍūbawul, gharqawul, ghūpa-, ghoṭa-*, etc. *warkawul.*
Imminent, a. *nijdai, rātlūnai, prewatūnai.*
Immoderate, a. *be-ḥisāb, be-kach, be-andāzah; nā-parhez-gār.*
Immodest, a. *be-sharm, be-ḥayā, be-makh.*
Immodesty, s. *be-sharmi, be-ḥayā-tob, be-makh-tob.*
Immolate, v.a. *qurbān-, ṣadqa-, zār-*, etc. *k.* (-oneself) v.n. *qurbān-*, etc. *ked.*
Immoral, a. *bad-kār, bad-kirdār, ḥarām-kār.*
Immortal, a. *be-marg, jāwīdān.*
Immortality, s. *baqā, jāwīdānī.*
Immortalize, v.a. *jāwīdān k., pātai k.* v.n. *pāedal, jāwīdān ked., pātai ked.*
Immovable, a. *mazbūṭ, qā-im, pāedūnai.*
Immunity, s. *khalāṣī, āzādi, najāt.*
Immutable, a. *be-tabdīl.*
Impair, v.a. *kamawul, spukawul, wrānawul.*
Impart, v.a. *pohawul, khabarawul; warkawul.*
Impartial, a. *rāst-kār, 'ādil, rikkhtīnai, ṣādiq, niyāw kawūnkai, be-mrasta.*
Impassable, a. *be-lār, be-gūdar, band.*
Impatient, a. *be-ṣabr, be-zgham; jalt, tund, tez.*
Impeach, v.a. *d'awa k., tuhmat pore k.*
Impede, v.a. *haṭālawul, kariyābawul, nkkhlawul, man'a k.*
Impediment, s. *haṭāl, kariyāb, āṛ, nkkhatai.*
Impel, v.a. *zoral, tezal, zghalawul, chalawul.*
Impend, v.n. *dzwaṛandedal, nijdai rasedal.*
Impending, a. *nijdai; dzwaṛand.*
Impenitent, a. *nā-toba-gār, nā-pakkhemān.*
Imperative, a. *ḥukmī, farẓī; amr.*

Imperceptible, a. *puṭ, nā-m'alūm.*
Imperfect, a. *nīmgaṛai, ūm, nīma-khwā.*
Imperial, a. *bādshāhī.* (hair on chin) *charekār.*
Imperious, a. *kibr-jan, khāntamā, khpul-sar.*
Imperishable, a. *pāedār, qā-im, lā-zawāl, pātedūnai, be-marg.*
Impertinent, a. *be-dzāe, be-adab, wilakai.*
Impervious, a. *klak, ṭing; be-lār, band.*
Impetuous, a. *tund, tez, gaṛandai, jalt.*
Impetus, s. *zor, quwat.*
Impious, a. *be-dīn, kāfir.*
Implacable, a. *be-raḥm, sakht-dil, kāṇrai-zṛah, nā-pīrzo da pakhulā, bad-dukkhman.*
Implant, v.a. *khakkhawul, njatal.*
Implement, s. *kālai, hatiyār, sāz.*
Implicate, v.a. *nkkhlawul, gaḍawul; malgarai-, sharīk-*, etc. *k.*
Implicit, a. *kāmil, pūrah, tamām.*
Implore, v.a. *minnat-, d'uā-*, etc. *k.*
Imply, v.a. *m'anā-, dallīl-*, etc. *laral, nakkha-, ishārat-*, etc. *k.*
Import, s. *m'anā; da pradī mulk māl.*
Import, v.a. *da pradī mulk māl khpul waṭan ta rāwṛal.*
Important, a. *drūnd, grān, ẓarūr.*
Importune, v.a. *taqāẓā k., lagiyā ghokkhtal.*
Impose, v.a. *āchawul, lagawul, kegdal.* (upon) *ghulawul, ṭagal, fareb-*, etc. *warkawul.*
Impost, s. *tāwān, sāw, bāj; maḥṣūl, nāgha.*
Impostor, s. *ṭag, chal-bāz, bāna-khor, farebī, darghal, sādū, ḥīla-bāz.*
Imposture, s. *ṭagī, ghulat, fareb, droh.*
Impotent, a. *nā-tuwān, 'ājiz; nā-mard.*
Impoverish, v.a. *khwār-, gharīb-*, etc. *k.*
Impracticable, a. *na-kedana, na-shwūnkai.*
Imprecate, v.a. *kkhera-, n'alat-, bad-d'uā-*, etc. *k.*
Impregnate, v.a. *ḍakawul; blārba k.*
Impress, v.a. *ṭāpa-, chāpa-*, etc. *k.*, or *-wahul; kkhkc-manḍal.* (-on the mind) *tākīd k.*

Impression, s. *ṭāpa, chāpa*; *nakkha, dāgh*; *gumān, khiyāl, fikr.*
Imprint, v.a. *ṭāpa-, chāpa-*, etc. *k.*; *dāghawul.*
Imprison, v.a. *qaid-, band-*, etc. *k.*
Improbable, a. *la 'aqla lire* or *-bāhir.*
Improper, a. *nā·munāsib, nā·kkhanai, nā·sāz, nā·rawā, nā·kār, kānah.*
Improve, v.a. *joṛawul, raghawul.* v.n. *joṛedal, raghedal.*
Improvement, s. *kkhegaṛa, joṛ·tiyā.*
Improvident, a. *be·tadbīr, kotāh·andesh.*
Imprudent, a. *be·khabar, be·fikr.*
Impudent, a. *be·adab, gustākh*; *be·ḥayā.*
Impulse, s. *zor, quwat, ḥarakat.*
Impulsive, a. *tund, tez, gaṛandai, talwalai.*
Impure, a. *nā·pāk, palīt, murdār.*
Impute, v.a. *lagawul, pore k.*
In, p. *danana, kkhke, pa kkhke.*
In-, negative prefix. (in comp.) *be-, lā-, nā-.*
Inability, s. *nā·tuwānī, lā·tsārī, 'ājizī.*
Inaccessible, a. *nā·mūndanai.*
Inaccurate, a. *ghalaṭ, nā·durust.*
Inactive, a. *sust, laṭ, shaḍul*; *be·kār*; *prot.*
Inadequate, a. *kam, la-ag*; *nā·qābil.*
Inadmissible, a. *nā·qabūl, band, man'ah.*
Inadvertent, a. *be·khabar, be·fikr.*
Inanimate, a. *be·dzān, be·sāh, muṛ.*
Inapplicable, a. *nā·munāsib, nā·sāz.*
Inattentive, a. *be·parwā, be·khabar.*
Inaugurate, v.a. *kkhkenawul, wudrawul.*
Inauspicious, a. *bad·bakht, shūm·bakht, asī.*
Incalculable, a. *be·shumār, be·ḥisāb, be·kach.*
Incantation, s. *jādū, koḍa, siḥr, dam, kūda, pāṛ, mantar, du'ā, t'awīz.*
Incapable, a. *nā·qābil, nā·tuwān, be·was.*
Incautious, a. *be·tadbīr, nā·khabar·dār.*
Incendiary, s. *shūsha-ī mār,* or *lagawūnkai,* or *pore kawūnkai.*
Incense, s. *'ūd.* (-dish) *majmir.*
Incense, v.a. *khapah k., kaṛawul.*
Incentive, s. *sabab, bā'is*; *lamsūn.*
Incessant, a. *lagiyā, mudām, hamesh.*
Incessantly, ad. *har sā'at, sā'at pa sā'at.*
Incest, s. *mor-, khor-, lūr-*, etc. *ghoḍī.*
Incident, s. *wāqi'a, ḥādisa, chal, wārida.*
Incidentally, ad. *nā·gumāna, nā·gahāna.*
Incision, s. *tsīra, zakhm, parhār.*
Incite, v.a. *lamsawul*; *pārawul*; *agayal.*
Inclination, s. *khwā, mīna, zṛeh, shauq.*
Incline, v.a. *khwā ta k., mayan k., zṛeh lagawul*; *ṭīṭawul.* v.n. *khwā ta ked.*, etc.
Include, v.a. *shāmil-, yo·dzāe-, dākhil-*, etc. *k.*; *dzāyawul.*
Incog, ad. *pa puṭa.*
Incoherent, a. *be·joṛ, be·hūdah, be·khud.*
Income, s. *āmad, ḥāsil.*
Incommode, v.a. *taklīf warkawul.*
Incomparable, a. *be·siyāl, lā·sānī, be·misāl.*
Incompatible, a. *mukhālif.*
Incompetent, a. *nā·qābil, nā·tuwān.*
Incomplete, a. *nīmgaṛai, nā·tamām.*
Incomprehensible, Inconceivable, a. } *be·qiyās, shandah, la 'aqla lire* or *-bāhir.*
Inconclusive, a. *be·isbāt, be·dalīl*; *nā·zbād, nā·sābit.*
Incongruous, a. *be·joṛ, nā·sāz, be·ṭikānah, be·hūdah, bar·khilāf, nā·muwāfiq.*
Inconsiderate, a. *be·liḥāz, be·parwā, be·ghaur, be·fikr, be·tadbīr, ghāfil.*
Inconsistent, a. *be·jor*, etc. (*v.* Incongruous.)
Inconsolable, a. *gham·jan, nūl·jan, be·tasallī.*
Inconstant, a. *nā·pāedār, nā·qalār, be·wafā.*
Incontestible, a. *sābit, zbād, lā·dzawāb, qat'a-ī.*
Incontinent, a. *be·parhez, bad·laman, bad·parhez.*
Incontrovertible, a. *zbād*, etc. (*v.* Incontestible.)
Inconvenience, s. *be·ārāmī, rabaṛ, taklīf, harj.*
Inconvenient, a. *be·dzāe, nā·kārah, nā·munāsib.*

Incorporate, v.a. *yadawul, yo·dzāe k., laral.*
Incorrect, a. *nā·durust, ghalat, darogh·jan.*
Incorrigible, a. *bad·sakht, hets da kkhah, lā·'ilāj.*
Incorruptible, a. *be·fanā, pāedār.*
Increase, v.a. *ziyātawul, wadānawul, derawul.* v.n. *ziyātedal, wadānedal, deredal.*
Increase, s. *ziyāt·wālai, wadānī, der·wālai.*
Incredible, a. *be·i'tibār, shandah.*
Incrust, v.a. *lewawul.*
Incubate, v.n. *kuraka kkhkenāstal; pakhedal.*
Inculcate, v.a. *pohawul, pahmawul, tākīd k., kkhayal—kkhowul.*
Incumbent, a. *farz, lāzim, wājib, zarūr.*
Incur, v.n. *pīrzo-, lā·iq-,* etc. *ked.* v.a. *rāwral, lagawul, āchawul, ākhistal.*
Incurable, a. *lā·'ilāj, lā·dawā, lā·tsār.*
Incursion, a. *chapāo, dāra·dopa, hapa·dapa, tākht·tārāj, halla.*
Indebted, a. *qarz·dār, porawurai*
Indecent, a. *pūch, chūnkai; be·hoyā, be·nang; nā·lā·iq, nā·munāsib· be·adab, be·pardah.*
Indeed, in. *rikkhtiyā! khudāe·go! āyā! he!* ad. *hado, yara, kho.*
Indefatigable, a. *mihnatī, sā'ī, kokshikshī.*
Indefinite, a. *be·ṭikānah, be·kach.*
Indemnity, s. *badal, tāwān, nāgha.* (-for blood) *diyat.* (-for abduction) *swara.*
Indenture, s. *iqrār·nāma, 'ahd·nāma.*
Independent, a. *khpul·sar, da khpul wāk khāwand; yāghī, sar·kakkh.*
Indescribable, a. *lā·bayān.*
Index, s. *nakkha, nikkhān; dalīl.* (-of a book) *fihrist.* (-finger) *kkhowūnai; mis·wāka gutta.*
India, s. *hind, hindūstān.* (language of-) *hindko.* (Mussalmān native of-) *hindkai.* (Pagan native of-) *hindū.*
Indian-corn, s. *jūwār, ghaṭ jūwār, maka-ī.*
Indicate, v.a. *kkhayal—kkhowul.*
Indication, s. *kkhowūna; nakkha; dalīl.*
Indifferent, a. *be·parwā, be·khabar; khushaı.*
Indifferently, ad. *hase, be·parwā·ī sara.*
Indigent, a. *khwār, hājat·man, muhtāj, muflis.*
Indigestion, s. *bad·hazmī, agheṛ, aṭer.*
Indignant, a. *khapah, qahr·jan, qahr·nāk.*
Indignity, s. *spuk·tiyā, makh·torī, sharmin·dagī.*
Indigo, s. (-plant) *wasma.* (-dye) *nīl.* (-maker) *nīl·gar.*
Indirect, a. *kog, tratskan, girzedalai.*
Indirectly, ad. *pa trats; pa chal sara; pa wasile sara.*
Indiscreet, a. *be·tadbīr, be·sha'ūr, kam·'aql.*
Indiscriminate, a. *gaḍ·waḍ, alwal.*
Indispensable, a. *zarūr, lāzim, wājib; farz.*
Indisposed, a. *nā·khwakkh, nā·rāz; nā·rogh, nā·joṛ.*
Indisputable, a. *lā·radd, qat'a-ī, yaqīnī.*
Indistinct, a. *dund; puṭ; nā·sāf.*
Individual, a. *biyal, judā, mufrid, yawādzai.* s. *tan, kas, saṛai, wagaṛai, gawai.*
Individuality, s. *wātka-ī, yawādzai·wālai, yo·wālai, biyal·wālai, judā.*
Individually, a. *biyal·biyal, yaw·yaw, judā*
Indolent, a. *sust, laṭ, nā·rāst, shalaṭ.*
Indubitable, a. *be·shakk, be·shubka, be·gumān.*
Induce, v.a. *lamsawul, targhīb warkawul.* (bring on) *rāwral, paidā k., khejawul, porta k.; 'amal-, pāzah-,* etc. *k.*
Indulge, v.a. *nāzawul, khātir k.; pālal, nmāndzal; bakkhal, mihrbāngī k.*
Indulgent, a. *mihrbān, khātir·dār, nāz wrūnkai, narm, bakkhūnkai.*
Indurate, v.n. *klakedal, ṭingedal.*
Industrious, a. *mihnatī, kokshikshī.*
Industry, s. *mihnat, koshish, mushaqqat.*
Inebriate, v.a. *nasha warkawul, be·khūd-, be·hokkh-,* etc. *k.; mast k.*
Ineffable, a. *lā·bayān, be·bayān.*

Inefficacious, a. *be·pāzah, nā·kārah, 'abas, be·tāsir, be·asr, khushai, spuk.*
Inequality, s. *lwar·jawar·tiyā, zig·wālai, nā·hawār·tiyā.*
Inert, a. *be·harakat; be·pāzah; sust, lat.*
Inestimable, a. *be·bahā, be·qīmat; grān.*
Inevitable, a. *muqarrar, qat'a-ī.*
Inexcusable, a. *be·'uzr, be·hujjat, lā·dzawāb.*
Inexhaustible, a. *be·pāyān, be·hadd, be·nihāyat, be·and, be·hisāb.*
Inexorable, a. *sakht, nā·tars, kānrai·zrah.*
Inexpedient, a. *be·dzāe, nā·munāsib, nā·kkhanai, nā·sāz.*
Inexperienced, a. *nā·wāqif, nā·āmokhtah, nā·'ādat, nā·āshnā, nā·balad.*
Inexpert, a. *kam·ustāz, be·hunar, kachak.*
Inexplicable, a. *lā·bayān, nā·m'alūm.*
Infallible, a. *nā·khatā, qādir, nā·ghalat.*
Infamous, a. *bad, bad·namūs, makh·tor.*
Infamy, s. *bad·namūsī, makh·torī, ruswā-ī.*
Infancy, s. *māshūm-,* or *m'asūm·wālai, bachai-, tandai-,* etc. *-tob.*
Infant, s. *māshūm, tandai, bachai, kachotai, warkotai, kamkotai, wrūkai, pa-ī-rawai.*
Infantry, s. *piyādah, mlā·tar; paltan.*
Infatuated, a. *lewanai, fareftah, khushai.*
Infatuation, s. *lewantob, fareftagī, khushī·tob.*
Infect, v.a. *banganul, bonrawul, gazak k., nahal, lagawul.*
Infer, v.n. *pohedal.* v.a. *ganral.*
Inference, s. *khulāsa, hāsil, natīja.*
Inferior, a. *kam·pāyah, kam·asl, kamtar, spuk, adnā; lāndai, kūz, lur, kkhkatanai.*
Infernal, a. *doghakkhī, jahannamī.*
Infidel, s. *kāfir, be·dīn, be·īmān, be·islām.*
Infidelity, s. *kufr, be·dīnī, be·īmānī.*
Infinite, a. *be·nihāyat, be·hadd, be·and, be·shān, be·pāyān, be·kach, be·shumār.*
Infirm, a. *tap, nā·tawān, kamzor, za'īf.*
Inflame, v.a. *balawul, swadzawul.* v.n. *baledal, sedzal, swal.*
Inflammation, s. *swai.*
Inflate, v.a. *pūkal, parsawul.* v.n. *parsedal.*
Inflect, v.a. *titawul, kagawul, arawul, girzawul.*
Inflexible, a. *klak, sakht, zig, krosand; khpulsar, sar·kakkh, takanrai, kodai.*
Inflict, v.a. *pore k., āchawul, rasawul, lagawul, warkawul, kawul, kral.*
Influence, s. *pāzah, 'amal, asr, tāsir.*
Influenza, s. *dūmai, nazla, zukām, sāreh, yakhnī.* (to have-) *sareh-, yakhnī-,* etc. *nahal.*
Inform, v.a. *khabarawul, āgāh k.; pohawul, kkhayal—kkhowul.*
Information, s. *khabar; āgāhī.*
Informer, s. *mukhbir, tsārai.*
Infringe, v.a. *mātawul.*
Infuse, v.a. *āchawul, gadawul; lamdawul; damawul, dam warkawul.*
Ingenious, a. *hikmatī, hunar·man, pohānd.*
Ingenuous, a. *rikkhtūnai, nek, karah, sādah, spīn, rāst, sum, pāk·sāf.*
Inglorious, a. *spuk, halak, be·nām, be·nang.*
Ingraft, v.a. *pewand-, qalam-,* etc. *lagawul; kkhke·mandal, khakkhawul, lagawul.*
Ingrate, a. *namak·harām, nā·shukr·guzār.*
Ingratiate, v.a. *lār ākhistal* or *-mūndal.*
Ingredient, s. *juz, shai; gada.*
Ingress, s. *nanawātah, dakhl.* (-and egress) *wātah·nanawātah, rāshah·darshah.*
Inhabit, v.a. *astoga-, mīshta-,* etc. *k.* v.n. *osedal, āstedal.* (colonize) v.a. *ābādawul.*
Inhabitant, s. *osedūnkai, astogūnkai.*
Inhale, v.a. *sāh-, dam-,* etc. *pa·porta ākhistal* or *-rākāgal—rākkhkal.*
Inherent, a. *zātī, aslī, jibillī.*
Inherit, v.a. *mīrās-* or *mīrāt ākhistal* or *-mūndal.* v.n. *mīrāt·khor ked.*
Inheritance, s. *mīrās* or *mīrāt.*
Inheritor, s. *mīrāt khor, wāris.*
Inhospitable, a. *bakhīl, shūm, be·makh.*

Inhuman, a. *nā-insān, nā-tars, be-dard.*

Inimical, a. *mukhālif, bad-niyat, dukkhman, khwā bad.*

Inimitable, a. *be-nazīr, be-misāl.*

Iniquitous, a. *bad, nā-haqq, be-insāf.*

Iniquity, s. *badī, be-insāfī, nā-haqqī, zulm, gunāh, pasāt, wabāl, baza.*

Initial, a. *wrūnbanai, awwalanai.*

Initiate, v.a. *jārī k., chalawul, rawānawul; āmokhtah k., lagawul, lwalawul; bāolī warkawul.*

Injection, s. *naniyasteh; huqna.*

Injudicious, a. *be-tadbīr, be-shu'ūr, nā-lā-iq, nā-kkhanai, nā-kkhāyistah.*

Injunction, s. *hukm, amr, kariya, tākīd.* (prohibition) *qadaghan.*

Injure, v.a. *tāwān-, ziyān-,* etc. *rasawul; āzārawul, khūgawul; wrānawul, habatah k.*

Injurious, a. *mozī, muzirr; ziyān-kār, nuqsānī, tāwānī; randz rasawūnkai, stukh.*

Injury, s. *nuqsān, ziyān, tāwān, īzā, zarar.*

Injustice, s. *be-insāfī, nā-haqqī, zulm.*

Ink, s. *siyāhī.* (red-) *shangrip.* (-stand) *mashwānra-ī.*

Inlaid, a. *jarāo.*

Inmate, s. *osedūnkai, astogūnkai; hamsāyah, kilai-wāl.*

Inn, s. *srāe, rabāt.*

Innate, a. *zātī, aslī, jibillī.*

Innocent, s. *māshūm* or *m'asūm, be-gunāh, pāk sāf, spīn, nek, be-qusūr, be-taqsīr.*

Innovation, s. *nawai dastūr, -chalan,* etc.

Innumerable, a. *be-shumār, be-hisāb.*

Inoculate, v.a. *rag wahal.*

Inoffensive, a. *be-gunāh, be-qusūr; gharīb.*

Inordinate, a. *be-andāzah, be-kach, be-hadd.*

Inquietude, s. *nā-qalār-tiyā, be-ārām-tiyā.*

Inquire, v.a. *pukkhtedal, pukkhtana-, tapos-* or *tapakus-, sawāl-,* etc. *k.* (-into) *latawul, shanal.*

Inquirer, s. *tālib, pukkhtana-, pursān-, talab-,* etc. *kawūnkai.*

Inquiry, s. *tapos, pursān, tālāsh, tahqīqāt.*

Inroad, s. *dūsa, dāra-dopa, chapāo, halla.*

Insane, a. *lewanai, saudā-ī, khushai.*

Insanity, s. *lewantob, saudā.*

Insatiable, a. *hirs-nāk, gharai, bad-linūl.*

Inscribe, v.a. *likal, kāgal—kkhkal.*

Inscription, s. *lik; sar-nāma.*

Insect, s. *chinjai, khazanda.*

Insensible, a. *be-hokkh, be-khud, be-khabar, be-hiss; be-parwā, be-dard.*

Insert, v.a. *nanabāsal—nanayistal, kkhke-bāsal—kkhke-yistal, mandal, kkhke-mandal; gayayal; khakkhawul, njatal.* (write) *kāgal—kkhkal, likal.*

Inside, s. *danana; bātin; larmūn.*

Insidious, a. *darghal, drohai, tag-bāz, farebī, hīla-bāz.*

Insight, s. *wuqūf, shnākht, pejāndah, poh, lidah, kātah, m'arifat.*

Insignia, s. *nakkhe, 'alāme, nikkhānūna.*

Insignificant, a. *nā-tsiz, spuk, khushai.*

Insincere, a. *nā-rāst, makar, be-īmān, be-wafā, nā-khālis, dwah-rangai.*

Insinuate, v.a. *nana-* or *kkhke-bāsal—yastal; ishārat k., gumān rāwṛal.*

Insipid, a. *be-khwand, balmangah* or *balmagai.*

Insist, v.a. *zoral, tākīd k.; jah k.*

Insolent, a. *be-adab, gustākh, sar-kakkh.*

Insolvent, a. *nā-dār, dīwālī.*

Inspect, v.a. *katal, lidal, goral, tamāsha-, nandāra-, mulāhaza-,* etc. *k.*

Inspection, s. *katana, lidah, tamāsha,* etc.

Inspector, s. *nāzir, dāroghah, katūnkai.*

Inspiration, s. *ilhām, ladūn, wahī; sāh, dam, rākkhkalai sāh* or *-dam.*

Inspire, v.a. *ilhām k.; sāh ākhistal* or *-rākāgal—rākkhkal.*

Instal, v.a. *kkhkenawul, wudrawul, muqarrar k., walārawul.*

Instalment, s. *qisṯ, ūgṛā-ī.*
Instance, s. *wāqi'a*; *nakkha*; *misāl.* (for-) *pa misāl.*
Instant, s. *lahza, dam, drang.* a. *hāzir*; *hāl.*
Instantly, ad. *pa ṯakī, os, pa de sā'at, sam da lāsa, dam dar hāl.*
Instead, ad. *pa dzāe, pa badal, pa 'iwaz.*
Instigate, v.a. *lamsawul, lamsūn k.*
Instigation, s. *lamsūn, targhib.*
Instigator, s. *lamsūnai.*
Instinct, s. *shu'ūr, 'aql, hokkh, sud.*
Institute, v.a. *wudrawul, muqarrar k., taṛal, jārī k., walāṛawul.*
Instruct, v.a. *bwalawul, kkhayal—kkhowul, tarbiyat-, kkhowuna-,* etc. *k.*; *pohawul.*
Instruction, s. *kkhowuna, sabaq, t'alīm,* etc.
Instructor, s. *ākhūn, ustāz, mu'allim.*
Instrument, s. *kālai, hatiyār, ālat.* (agent) *wasīla, wāsiṯa.* (cause) *bā'is, 'illat, sabab.* (deed) *sanad, qibāla.*
Instrumental, a. *komakī, madad·gār.*
Insufficient, a. *kam, la-ag*; *nāqis, nā·qābil.*
Insult, v.a. *spuk wayal, kanzal* or *kkhkandzal, be·'izzat-, be·makh-,* etc. *k.*
Insuperable, a. *mushkil, grān, na·shwūnai.*
Insurgent, s. *balwā·gar, yāghī·gar, pasātī.*
Insurrection, s. *balwā, pasāt, patna.*
Integral, a. *pūrah, amānī, sābat.*
Integrity, s. *rikkhtīn·tob, nekokārī, rāstī.*
Integument, s. *tsarman, postakai, poṯ*; *paṯ, khwar.*
Intellect, s. *'aql, hokkh, poha, pahm.*
Intelligence, s. *khabar*; *poh, hokkhyār·tiyā.*
Intelligent, a. *pohānd, pahm·nāk, 'aql·man, hokkhyār, khabar·dār.*
Intemperance, s. *bad·parhezī, bad·pālī*; *bad·mastī, bad·'amalī.*
Intemperate, a. *bad·parhez·gār, sharābī, nasha·khor, bad·'amal, bad·kār.*
Intend, v.a. *niyat-, qasd-, irāda-,* etc. *k.*
Intense, a *ḍer, nihāyat, sakht, bad.*
Intensity, s. *ḍer·wālai, zor, ziyātī,* etc.
Intent, a. *lagiyā, mashghūl.* s. *maṯlab, niyat, qasd, muda'ā, murād.*
Intention, s. *niyat,* etc. (*v.* Intent.)
Intentionally, ad. *pa qasd.*
Inter, v.a. *khakkhawul.*
Intercede, v.a. *bakkhana-, khalāsī-,* etc. *ghokkhtal, shafā'at k.*; *gwākkh-* or *gwākkh·grandai k.*
Intercept, v.a. *nīwul, lānde k., stūnawul*; *nkkhlawul, hiṯālawul.*
Intercessor, s. *sipārish-, shafā'at-,* etc. *kawūnkai*; *gwākkh·grandai, mandz·garai.*
Interchange, s. *badal, adal·badal, len·den.*
Intercourse, s. *'ilāqa, lār, suhbat, rūshak·darshak.*
Interdict, v.a. *qadaghan-, man'a-,* etc. *k.*
Interest, s. *kār, gharaz, maṯlab*; *kkhegaṛa, sūd, gaṯa, naf'a, fā-ida*; *brakha, wesh, hissa.*
Interested, a. *gharaz·man, khpul·maṯlab, gharazī.* (self-) *khpul·gharaz.*
Interesting, a. *khwand·nāk, maza·dār, dil·chasp.*
Interfere, v.a. *gharaz k., lās lagawul, -āchawul, -wawṛal,* or *-pa kkhke khwadzawul.*
Interim, s. *mandz, miyān, miyandz.*
Interior, a. *danananai, darūnī, bāṯinī.*
Interlace, v.a. *agayal, lānde·bānde k., gayayal.*
Interlude, s. *tamāsha, nandāra, swāng.*
Intermeddle, v.a. *lās lagawul,* etc., *dast·andāzī k., dakhl-, gharaz-,* etc. *k.* (*v.* Interfere.)
Intermediate, a. *mandzwai.*
Interminable, *be·sar, be·and, be·hadd.*
Intermission, s. *nobat, wār*; *nāgha*; *fursat.*
Intermit, v.n. *pa·nobat-, pa·wār-,* etc. *rātlal.*
Intermittent, a. *wārī.* (-fever) *wareza.*
Internal, a. *bāṯinī, darūnī, danananai.*
Internals, s. *laṛmānah.*
Interpose, v.n. *pa·mandz rātlal—rāghlal.*

v.a. *pa·mandz kegdal,* or *kkhkegdal—kekkh-odal,* or *kkhkekkhodal,* etc.; *gwākkh-* or *gwākkh·grandī k.*

Interpret, v.a. *tarjuma k., pohawul, kkhayal—kkhowul, m'anā kkhkārah k.*

Interrogate, v.a. *pukkhtedal, sawāl·dzawāb-, tapos-,* etc. *k.*

Interrupt, v.a. *kariyābawul, hiṭālawul, band·awul, nkkhlawul, ḥarakat k.*

Interruption, s. *kariyāb, hiṭāl, harj, khalal, nkkhatai, ḥarakat.*

Interstice, s. *darz, rakhna*; *khūna*; *gruṭ.*

Interval, s. *mandz, miyān*; *wār.*

Intervene, v.n. *pa·mandz rātlal—rāghlal*; *gwākkh-* or *gwākkh·grandī k.* ——

Intervention, s. *pa·mandz rātlana*; *gwākkh.*

Interview, s. *dīdan, līdah, kātah, mulāqāt.*

Intestate, a. *be·waṣīyat.*

Intestine, s. (large-) *kulma, laṛmūn.* (small-) *larai, ūjrai.*

Intimate, a. *khamsor, gaḍ*; *wāqif*; *balad.* s. *yār, āshnāe, mal, rafīq.*

Intimate, v.a. *khabarawul*; *wayal.*

Intimately, ad. *pa kkhah shān sara.*

Intimation, s. *khabar*; *nakkhh, ishārat.*

Intimidate, v.a. *yerawul* or *werawul.*

Into, p. *pa kkhke, kkhke, pa mandz kkhke.*

Intolerant, a. *be·ṣabr, be·zgham.*

Intoxicate, v.a. *be·khūd k., nasha warkawul*; *mast k., kaipī k.*

Intoxication, s. *nasha, kaip*; *be·khūdī, mastī.*

Intractable, a. *sar·kakkh, sar·zor, khpul·sar, ṭakaṛai, hoḍai.*

Intrenchment, s. *sangar, bāra, morcha.*

Intrepid, a. *maṛanai, tūrzan, zṛah·war, be·bāk, dilāwar, bahādur.*

Intricate, a. *grān, mushkil*; *kog·wog, pech·dār*; *arjal·barjal, tsapolai.*

Intrigue, s. *joṛikkht, sāzish, kār·sāzī*; *lār, 'alāqa, rāz·o·niyāz, yārāna.*

Intrinsic, a. *ẕātī, aṣlī.*

Introduce, v.a. *nana-* or *kkhke bāsal—yastal.* (-a person) *pekkhawul.* (a custom) *chala·wul, jārī k.* (to a place) *rāwastal.*

Introduction, s. *nanayistah*; *mulāqāt*; *de·bācha.*

Intrude, v.a. *ḍūsa k., nanawatal, lās laga·wul, -āchawul,* etc.

Intrust, v.a. *spāral, pāslawul, hawāla k.*

Intuition, s. *ilhām, ladūn*; *m'arifat, poh, pahm.*

Intwine, v.a. *agayal, gayayal, nghaṛal—nghakkhtal.*

Inundate, v.a. *hūk-, lāhū-,* etc. *k., niyūz, nīz-,* etc. *wṛal.* (-a field) *khaṛob k.*

Inundation, s. *sailāb, nīz* or *niyūz, tughiyānī,* etc.

Inure, v.a. *āmokhtah-, 'ādat-,* etc. *k., rugd·awul.*

Invade, v.a. *halla-, dāṛa-, chapāo-, ḍūsa-,* etc. *k.* v.n. *khatal, prewatal, pre·mātedal.*

In vain, ad. *'abaṣ, be·fā-ida.*

Invalid, a. *bāṭil, 'abaṣ, nā·kārah, nāqiṣ.* s. *nā·joṛ, nā·rogh, randzūr, ẓa'īf.*

Invaluable, a. *be·bahā, grān·bahā, be·qīmat.*

Invariable, a. *be·tabdīl, be·biyal·tūn, pāedār.*

Invariably, ad. *har·kala, mudāman, hamesha.*

Invasion, s. *halla, chapāo, tākht, ḍūsa, dāṛa.*

Invective, s. *peghor, kanzal* or *kkhkandzal kkhera, malāmat, tuhmat, tor.*

Inveigle, v.a. *ghulawul, ṭagal, damawul, dam-, fareb-,* etc. *warkawul.*

Invent, v.a. *joṛawul, nawai·ḥikmat bāsal—yastal, nawai paidā k.*

Invention, s. *ḥikmat, chal.*

Inventory, s. *siyāha, daftar, fard.*

Inverse, a. *aṛawul, naskor, wājgūn, 'aks, apūṭah, chapah.*

Invert, v.a. *aṛawul, naskorawul, 'aks-,* etc. *k.*

Invest, v.a. *warkawul, bakkhal*; *poslawul, āghūstawul*; *īsārawul* or *ḥiṣārawul, yer k.*

Investigate, v.a. *tapahus* or *tapos-*, *pukkh-tana-*, *pursān-*, *taḥqīq-*, etc. *k.*, *pukkhtedal*, *laṭawul*, *shanal.*

Inveterate, a. *kuhand*, *pakhwānai*, *zoṛanai*; *pokh*, *klak*, *sakht.*

Invidious, a. *ḥasad-nāk*, *kīna-war*, *wiyāṛ-jan.*

Invigorate, v.a. *quwat warkawul*, *quwat-nāk-*, *mazbūt*, *takṛah-*, *tāzah-*, etc. *k.*

Invisible, a. *puṭ*, *ghā-ib*; *wruk.*

Invite, v.a. *sat k.*, *balal.*

Inviting, a. *dil-kakkh*, *dil-chasp*, *dil-rubā*; *maza-dār*, *khwand-nāk.* s. *sat kawuna.*

Invocation, s. *d'uā*; *d'uwat*; *ghokkht.*

Invoice, s. *siyāha*, *bījak*, *chalān.*

Invoke, v.a. *d'uā k.*, *balal*, *nūm ākhistal*, *ghokkhtal.*

Involuntary, a. *be-ikhtiyār*, *be-was*, *be-nāk.*

Involve, v.a. *āchawul*, *nkkhlawul*, *nīwul.*

Inward, a. *dananunai*, *darūnī*, *bāṭinī.*

Inwrought, a. *jaṛāo*; *kūṭalai.*

Irascible, a. *qahr-nāk*, *ghuṣṣa-nāk*, *tund.*

Ire, s. *ghuṣṣa*, *ghazab*, *qahr*, *bṛos-wālai.*

Irksome, a. *sakht*, *grān*, *drūnd*, *rabaṛ-jan.*

Iron, s. *ospana.* (-slag) *ospankhaṛai.* (bar-) *kashai.* (-monger) *lohār*, *āhan-gar.*

Iron-gray, a. *nīlai.*

Irony, a. *ṭoqa*, *khandā*, *pekkha.*

Irradiate, v.n. *dzalakedal*, *rūṇredal.*

Irrational, a. *be-hūdah*, *nā-poh*, *be-'aql.*

Irregular, a. *be-tartīb*, *be-ā-īn*, *be-qā'ida*; *nā-lā-iq.*

Irrelevant, a. *be-dzāe*, *be-nisbat*, *nā-kārah.*

Irreligious, a. *be-dīn*, *bilmāz*, *be-mazhab.*

Irremediable, a. *lā'ilāj*, *lā-chār*, *lā-dawā.*

Irreproachable, a. *be-gunāh*, *be-malāmat.*

Irresistible, a. *zorāwar*, *mazbūt*, *be-band.*

Irresolute, a. *be-himmat*, *nā-qalār*, *nā-mard.*

Irretrievable, a. *ter*, *wruk*, *lāṛ*; *lā-'ilāj.*

Irreverent, a. *be-adab*, *be-makh.*

Irrigate, v.a. *oba-*, *watar-*, *kharob-*, *lūnd-*, etc. *k.*

Irritable, a. *khapah-nāk*, *bṛos*, *khaṛ.*

Irritate, v.a. *pārawul*, *ṭongawul*, *agayal*, *rabṛawul*, *ṭongāra k.*

Irritation, s. *khapgī*; *ṭongāra*; *pārawūna*; *dard*, *pasāt*, *swai.*

Irruption, s. *halla*, *tākht*, *ḍūsa*, *dāṛa*; *khuṭ*, *eshnā*; *dāra*, *jawāra.*

Island. s. *bela*, *jazīra.* (sandbank) *chara.*

Isolated, a. *biyal*, *yawādzai*, *judā.*

Issue, s. *anjām*, *natīja*, *ḥāṣil*; *pāzah*; *gaṭa*; *awlād*, *zawzāt*; *lār*, *wātah*; *war*, *khula.*

Issue. v.n. *watal*, *bahedal*, *chaledal*, *prewatal.* (-an order) v.a. *chalawul*, *jārī k.*

It, pr. *haghah*, *dā*, *dah*, *de*, *di*, *e.*

Itch, s. *khārikkht*, *koe*, *kaha*; *pishak*, *spūnrai.* v.n. *khārikkhtedal*, *kaha-*, etc. *ked.*

Item, s. *shai*, *tsiz*, *kālai.*

Itinerate, v.n. *girzedal.* v.a. *gakkht-*, *sail-*, etc. *k.*

Itself, pr. *khpul*, *khpul dzān.*

J.

Jackal, s. *gīdaṛ*, *sūrlanḍ*, *shaghāl.*

Jackdaw, s. *qāghah.*

Jacket, s. *kurta*, *nīm-tana-ī.*

Jade, s. (horse) *ṭap-ḍangar ās.* (woman) *pūhaṛa-*, *shalaṭa-*, etc. *-kkhadza*, *gashta-ī*, *baghara-ī.*

Jagged, a. *zīg*, *lwāṛ.*

Jail, s. *qaid-khāna*, *bandī-khāna*, *zindān.*

Jailer, s. *da qaid-khāne dārogha.*

Jam, s. *zokkha*, *khog-pakhalai*, *murabba.* v.a. *bandawul*, *ṭingawul*, *klakawul.*

January, s. *māh.*

Jar, s. *loṭkai*, *mangai*, *khum*, *maṭkai*, *batakai.* (-of leather) *daba*, *kupa-ī*, *jāba.*

Jargon, s. *wucha-pucha-*, *gaḍa-waḍa-*, *aṛa-baṛa-*, etc. *-khabara*, or *-wrāsha.*

Jasmine, s. *rāmbel-chāmbel.*

Jaundice, s. *ziyaṛai.*

Jaunt, s. *sail, gakkht.*

Javelin, s. *bala, barcha, neza, shalgai.*

Jaw, s. *jāma.* (upper-) *portana-ī jāma.* (lower-) *kkhkatana-ī jāma.* (-angle) *kaj.*

Jay, s. *shīn-ṭagh.*

Jealous, a. *bad-gumān, wiyāṛ-jan, sūndah.*

Jealousy, s. *bad-gumānī, wiyāṛ, rashk.*

Jeer, v.a. *khandā pore k.*

Jehovah, s. *allah, yāhū, khudāe ta'ālā.*

Jelly, s. *zokkha; māya.*

Jeopardy, s. *khaṭra, wera, muhimm.*

Jerk, v.a. *pṛakawul; ṭel wahal.*

Jest, s. *ṭoqa, washta, malanḍa, maskhara.*

Jester, s. *ṭoq-mār, washtai, malanḍai, maskharā-chī, pekkhe-gar.*

Jesus, s. *īsā.* (-Christ) *ḥaẓrat īsā.*

Jet, s. *dāra, fuwāra, shutraka.* (-bead) *shaba.* (-black) a. *tak-tor.*

Jew, s. *jahūd.*

Jewel, s. *gāṇra, kālai, zewar.*

Jeweller, s. *zar-gar.*

Jingle, s. *shṛang, gṛanj, krach.* v.n. *shṛangedal, gṛanjedal.*

Job, s. *kār.* (a little-) *kārgoṭai.*

Jockey, s. *chābuk-sawār.*

Jocose, a. *ṭoqī, washtī, khandā-bāz* or *-rūe.*

Jocularity, s. *washta-ṭoqa, khandā-bāzī.*

Jocund, a. *khūsh-rūe, kkhād, khūsh-ḥāl.*

Jog, v.a. *ṭakaṛ-, tel-, gasa-,* etc. *wahal.* v.n. *ṭaparedal.*

Join, v.a. *joṛawul, lagawul, pewand k., gaḍ awul.* v.n. *gaḍedal, yo dzāe ked.*

Joint, s. *joṛ; band, pewand; ghūṭa.*

Jointure, s. *mahr, dahadz, dod.*

Joke, s. *ṭoqa, washta, malanḍa.*

Jollity, s. *kkhādī, khūsh-ḥālī.*

Jolly, a. *kkhād, kkhād-man, khwakkh; rogh-moṭ.*

Jolt, s. *ṭakaṛa, ḍaka, ṭel; tīndak, budrī.*

Jot, s. *ṭakai, pūṭai, batsarai, ṭoṭa, ẓarra.*

Jovial, a. *khwakkh,* etc. (*v.* Jolly.)

Journal, s. *roz-nāmcha.*

Journey, s. *safar, pand.* (a day's-) *mazal* or *manzil.*

Joy, s. *kkhādī, khūsh-ḥālī.* (over rival) *sakha.*

Joyful, a. *kkhād-man, khūsh-ḥāl.*

Joyfully, ad. *pa kkhādī sara, khūsh-ḥālī-, khwakkhī-,* etc. *-sara.*

Jubilee, s. *akhtar, 'īd; kkhādī, mela.*

Judge, s. *ḥākim, qāẓī, munṣif.*

Judge, v.a. *'adālat-, inṣāf-, niyāw-,* etc. *k.; qiyās-, fikr-,* etc. *k.; gaṇral.*

Judgment, s. *ḥukm, fatwā; 'aql, poha.* (opinion) *fikr, rāe, qiyās.* (-seat) *maḥkama.* (-day) *ḥashr, ākhirat, qiyāmat.*

Judicature, s. *ḥukm, qaẓā.*

Judicial, a. *shara'ī.*

Judicious, a. *hokkhyār, pohānd, 'aql-man.*

Jug, s. *kūza, kūza-ṛa-ī, khumra-ī, kanja-ī.*

Juggler, s. *bāzī-gar, jādū-gar, hod-gar.*

Juice, s. *oba, pa-ī, ras, gūṛa-ī, rub; naw, zyam, nam.*

July, s. *pashakāl, sāwaṇr.*

Jumble, v.a. *gaḍ-waḍ k.*

Jump, v.a. *ṭop-, trap-,* etc. *wahul, dangal.*

Juncture, s. *joṛ, band, pewand; wakht, tāng.*

June, s. *hāṛ.*

Junior, a. *kishar.*

Jurisdiction, s. *ḥukūmat, 'amaldārī, wāk.*

Jurisprudence, s. *fiqha.*

Jury, s. *jirga m'arika.* (-man) *jirgata.*

Just, a. *'ādil, munṣif, rikkhtīnai, rāst; jukht, barabar, sam.* ad. *surup, faqaṭ.*

Justice, s. *inṣāf, 'adālat, niyāw, dād.*

Justifiable, a. *rawā, wājib.*

Justification, s. *ḥujjat.*

Justify, v.a. *'uẓr-, ḥujjat-,* etc. *rāwṛal.*

Justly, ad. *pa ḥaqqa, pa rikkhtiyā.*

Justness, s. *rikkhtīn-tob, rāstī, nekī.*

Juvenile, a. *kishar*, *dzwān*. s. *jaṛrai*, *zalmai*, *halak*, *woṛkai*.

Juvenility, s. *jaṛrī-tob*, *halak-wālai*, *dzwānī*, *zalmī-tob*.

K.

Keen, a. *terah*, *dam-dār*; *jalt*, *tez*, *tund*. (acid) *brekkhan*. (eager) *garm*, *tod*, *linăl*.

Keenness, s. *terah-wālai*; *tund-wālai*, etc.

Keep, v.a. *sātal*, *jghoral*, *khundiyal*, *khundī k.*; *pālal*, *parwaral*, *nmāndzal*. (-watch) *gālal*. (observe) *manal*. (-back) *pātai k.*, *pātawul*, *stūnawul*. (possess) *laral*. (-an engagement) *pūrah-*, *adā-*, etc. *k.*

Keep, v.n. *pātedal*, *pātai ked.*, *pāedal*, *osedal*.

Keeper, s. *sātandoe*, *sātūnkai*, *jghorai*, *pālūnkai*, *khundī kawūnkai*.

Keeping, s. *sātana*, *pālana*, *jghorana*. *khundī kawūna*; *pāedana*, *osedana*, *pātedana*.

Keepsake, s. *yād-gār*, *yād-dāsht*.

Kernel, s. *chaka-ī*, *maghzai*, *zaṛai*.

Kettle, s. *dechka*, *deg*, *khum*. (earthen-) *katwa-ī*.

Kettledrum, s. *naghāra*, *ḍamāma*, *ḍūkāṛa*, *ḍambakai*, *tambal*.

Key, s. *kunja-ī*. (-hole) *da jandre khula*.

Kick, v.a. *lata-*, *laghata-*, etc. *wahal*.

Kid, s. *warghūmai*, *chelai*, *serlai*, *psharlai*, *wuzgarai*.

Kidnap, v.a. *botlal—bīwul*, *bota k.*, *takkhtawul*.

Kidney, s. *pukkhtawarga*. (-bean) *lobiyā*.

Kill, v.a. *wajal* or *wajlal*, *muṛ k.*, *qatlawul*. (for food) *ḥallālawul*.

Killed, a. *maqtūl*, *wajalai*, *muṛ kaṛai*; *ḥallāl kaṛai*.

Killer, s. *qātil*, *wajlūnai*, *khūnī*, *muṛ-* or *marg kawūnkai*. (in comp.) *-kush*.

Killing, s. *khūn-*, *muṛ-*, *marg-*, *qatl-*, etc. *-kawūna*, *wajlana*.

Kiln, s. *paja*; *baṭ*.

Kin, s. *ragai*, *khpul*, *khekkh*, *'azīz*.

Kind, a. *mihrbān*; *makhawar*.

Kind, s. *ẕāt*, *aṣl*, *rang*, *nog*, *qism*, *shān*.

Kindle, v.a. *balawul*, *pūkal*, *swadzawul*. v.n. *baledal*, *swal*, *sedzal*.

Kindly, ad. *pa mihrbāngī sara*.

Kindness, s. *mihrbānī* or *mihrbāngī*.

Kindred, s. *khpal-walī*, *khekkhī*. a. *yo-shān*, *ragai*, *hum-rang*, *hum-jins*.

King, s. *bādshāh*, *shāh*, *sulṭān*.

Kingdom, s. *bādshāhat*, *salṭanat*, *rāj*.

Kingfisher, s. *māhī-khwurak*, *babozai*.

Kinsman, s. *khpul*, *khekkh*. (paternal-) *plār ganai*. (maternal-) *mor-ganai*.

Kiss, s. *kkhkul*, *macha*, *chapa-ī*. v.a. *kkhkulawul*, *machawul*, *chapa-ī-*, *kkhkul-*, etc. *k.*, *koka-ī-*, *khula-*, etc. *-akkhistal*.

Kitchen, s. *langar*, *jal-nāna-ī*, *ngharai*.

Kite, s. *ṭapūṭs*. (paper-) *godā*, *patang*.

Kitten, s. *pishongaṛai*.

Klick, v.a. *ṭak wahal*.

Knack, s. *ḥikmat*, *chal*, *pech*, *kārī-garī*.

Knapsack, s. *dzola-ī*, *gūḍai*, *bana-ī*, *butskha*.

Knave, s. *ṭag*, *darghal*, *chaṛland*, *farebī*, *be-īmān*, *chal-bāz*, *chal-walai*.

Knavery, s. *ṭagī*, *ṭag-bāzī*, *chal-bāzī*, etc.

Knavish, a. *ṭag-bāz*, *be-īmān*, *farebī*.

Knead, v.a. *aghagal—akkhal*. (-the limbs) *manḍal*, *kkhke-manḍal*, *chāpī k.*

Knee, s. *zangūn*, *ḍoga*. (-cap) *zangānak-starga*.

Kneel, v.a. *ḍoga-*, *zangūn-*, etc. *-lagawul*. v.n. *pa ḍogo-*, *zangūno-*, etc. *-kkhkenāstal*.

Knife, s. *chāṛeh*. (pen-) *chaṛūka-ī*, *chāqū*.

Knit, v.a. *gayayal*, *agayal*; *ḍūr k.* (-the brows) *starge brandawul*.

Knitting, s. *ḍūṛ*. (-needle) *dūk*.

Knob, s. *ghūṭai*, *pūṭai*, *ghūndai*; *pāṛsob*, *māṭus*, *pūpaka*; *rasaula-ī*, *ghunḍāṛai*.

Knock, v.a. *ṭraq-*, *ṭap-*, *ṭak-*, etc. *-wahal*.

(-up against) *ṭakaṛ-, ḍika-*, etc. *-khwuṛal.* v.n. *blosedal, lagedal, jangedal.*

Knot, s. *ghūṭa, taṛa, bandanr.*

Know, v.a. *m'alūmawul, pejandal, gaural, zdah k.* v.n. *khabaredal, pohedal, zdah ked.*

Knowing, a. *zdah, khabar-dār, kokkhyār, pokh, wāqif.*

Knowingly, ad. *pa 'aql sara, pa khabar sara.*

Knowledge, s. *poha, 'aql, khabar, 'ilm.*

Known, a. *zdah, pejāndah, m'alūm.*

Knuckle, s. *band, da gūte band.* (-bone) *bujal, ṭaka, arghund.*

L.

Label, s. *sar-nāma, ṭika.*

Laboratory, s. *kār-khāna.*

Laborious, a. *miḥnatī, kokshikshī ; mushkil, grān, sakht.*

Labour, s. *miḥnat, kokshiksh, sa'ī, mushaqqat, mazdūrī ; rabaṛ ; kār, kasb, pesha.* (childbirth) *langa, langedana.* (-pain) *stam.*

Labour, v.a. *miḥnat-, mazdūrī-*, etc. *k.* (be in-) v.n. *langedal.* (worry oneself) v.n. *rabṛedal.* (to strain) v.a. *stam-wahal.*

Labourer, s. *mazdūr ; kasb-gar.*

Labyrinth, s. *kaga-waga, warta, mār-pech.*

Lac, s. (gum) *da pala-ī chiṛ.* (dye) *lāk.* (100,000) *lak.*

Lace, s. *jālaka-ī, jāla-ī, muqaish.*

Lacerate, v.a. *shlawul, wrarawul, chāk k.; mātawal, ghwutsawul.*

Laceration, s. *shledah, wraredah, chāwd ; tsīra, parhār, zakhm.*

Lack, v.n. *muḥtāj-, ḥājat-man-*, etc. *ked.* v.a. *ghokkhtal.*

Lad, s. *halak, zanrai, ghunḍāyah, zalmai.*

Ladder, s. *andarpāya, pawṛa-ī, pārchang.*

Lade, v.a. *bār āchawul, legdal—lekkhal, ḍakawul.*

Ladle, s. *kaṛecha-ī, harkāra.* (small-) *qāshogha, tsontsa-ī, chamcha-ī* or *tsamtsa-ī.*

Lady, s. *bībī, merman, ṣāḥiba.* (-fly) *bībī-pāto bakhmala-ī.*

Lag, v.n. *pātedal, ṭaparedal.*

Laity, s. *'āmmiyān.* (one of the-) *'āmmī.*

Lake, s. *loe ḍanḍ, tālāw* or *tālāb.*

Lamb, s. *wrai, ga-aḍūrai.* (wether-) *wuch-kūl.*

Lame, a. *guḍ, khūg, kaṛam.*

Lameness, s. *guḍ-wālai.*

Lament, v.a. *afsos-, ghum-, wāwailā-*, etc. *k.*, *juṛal, wīr-, hāe-hāe-, hāe-hūe-, jaṛā-*, etc. *k.*, *wainā wayal.*

Lamentation, s. *afsos, jaṛā, wīr, sānda, faryād*, etc.

Lamenter, s. *wīṛa-jalai, wainā wayūnkai*, etc.

Lamp, s. *chirāgh, ḍiwa.* (-stand) *ḍiwat.* (-black) *kajal, lūgai.* (-black cup) *masa.* (-wick) *bāta-ī.*

Lance, s. *neza, bala, barcha.*

Lance, v.a. *tsiral ; tsīkhal, tetsal.*

Lancet, s. *nishtar* or *nekkhtar.*

Land, s. *mzaka* or *zmaka, zamīn.* (country-) *mulk, hewād.* (own-) *waṭan, būm.* (table-) *bāwra-ī, būṭa, steza.* (ploughed-) *sādīn* (sown-) *shudyāra.* (bare-) *ḍaga, ṭikūrkai.* (fallow-) *waḍ.* (waste-) *shāṛ.* (patch of-) *paṭai ; pūṭa.* (irrigated-) *watar, ābī.* (unirrigated-) *lalamī.* (inundated-) *khaṛob.* (marsh-) *jaba.* (village-) *ada-ī, wanḍ.* (church-) *sīra-ī, bogarai.*

Land, v.n. *kūzedal.* v.a. *kūzawul.*

Landholder, s. *dawtarī* or *dofturī, jāgīr-dār, zamīn-dār, brakha-khor.*

Landlord, s. *dawtarī, zamīn-dār, nāyik ; korbah, merah, khāwand, tsakkhtan, māl-dār.*

Landmark, s. *tsalai, pūla.*

Lane, s. *kūtsa.*

Language, s. *jiba, wrūsha.*

Languid, a. *ṭap, staṛai, stomān, māndah, haukah ; sust, laṭ, shalat, kāṛai-wāṛai.*

Languish, v.n. *mṛāxedal* or *mṛāmedal, wuchedal, kamanṛedal; kaṛedal, nūledal, zahedal; staṛai-, stomān-, zahīr-,* etc. *ked.*

Languor, s. *sustī, stomānī, māndagī.*

Lantern, s. *fānūs.*

Lap, s. *gheg, ghūzai; laman, pitskai, dzola-ī.*

Lap, v.a. *tsaṭal.* (wrap) *ngharal—nghakkhtal.*

Lapidary, s. *mukr-kan.*

Lapse, v.n. *teredal, ghuzāredal, ter watal.*

Large, a. *loe, star, ghaṭ, 'azīm.*

Largeness, *loe-, star-,* etc., *-wālai.*

Largesse, s. *bakhkhshikhsh, bakkhana, in'ām, khairāt.*

Lark, s. *kha-rāṛa, kopla, agan.*

Larynx, s. *ḥalq, wucha-ghāṛa; stūnai.*

Lascivious, a. *mast, shokhī, shahwatī, hawasnāk.*

Lasciviousness, s. *mastī, shahwat, naus, hawos.*

Lash, s. *bachawai, bachokai, bachakarai; karoṛa.*

Lash, v.a. *karoṛa wahal; taṛal.*

Lass, s. *jina-ī, peghla, lūr, khoraka-ī.*

Lassitude, s. *sustī, stomānī.*

Last, a. *wrustai, wrustanai, ākhir, pasīn.*

Last, v.n. *pāedal, chaledal, pātedal, osedal.*

Lasting, a. *pāedār, qā-im, mazbūṭ.*

Lastly, ad. *wrusto, ākhir.*

Latch, s. *kūl, aṛam, aṛamai*

Latchet, s. *rog, tasma.*

Late, a. *nā-wakht, pasīn; osanai; mutawaffī.*

Lately, ad. *osan, nan wradz, da la-ago wradzo.*

Lateness, s. *nā-wakhtī; lārghah, drang.*

Latent, a. *puṭ, ghalui.*

Later, a. *nawai.*

Lather, s. *zag, kaf.*

Latitude, s. *plan-wālai, art-wālai, sor* or *psor.*

Latitudinarian, s. *be-shar'a, āzād-ṭab'a saṛai.*

Latter, a. *wrusṭanai, pasanai* or *pasina*

Lattice, s. *jālakai, shabaka, j'afarī.*

Laud, v.a. *stāyal, stāyana k.,* or *-waya!.*

Laugh, v.a. *khandal, khandā k.*

Laughter, s. *khandā, qak-qaka, hanṛ-hanṛ.*

Launch, v.a. *obo ta kūzawul; ghwurzawul, chalawul, āchawul, wishtal.*

Lave, v.a. *wīndzal* or *mīndzal, wlal, lambawul.*

Lavish, a. *khartsī, isrāfī, musrif.*

Lavish, v.a. *kharts-, tāwān-, isrāf-,* etc. *k.*

Law, s. *fiqha.* (divine-) *shar'a, sharī'at.* (rule) *qā'ida, qānūn, ā-īn, rasm.* (justice) *'adālat, inṣāf, niyāw.* (right) *ḥaqq, rawā.* (Afghan-) *pukkhtūn-walī.*

Lawful, a. *rawā, ḥallāl.*

Lawsuit, s. *muqaddama, d'awa, qaẓiya.*

Lawyer, s. *qāẓī, faqīḥ.*

Lax, a. *sust, prānatai, spaṛdalai, arat.*

Laxative, a. *pos-, narm-,* etc. *-kawūnkai.* s. *pos-jāṛ, narm-jullāb, mūnzij.*

Lay, v.a. *gdal* or *igdal, yakkhodal* or *ikkhodal, yakkhal* or *ikkhal, kegdal* or *kkhkegdal, kekkhodal* or *kkhkekkhodal, kekkhal* or *kkhkekkhal.* (-hold of) *ākhistal, nīwul.* (-down) *tsamlawul.* (-on) *āchawul, lagawul.* (-in) *ṭolawul, gaṭal.* (-out) *gazawul* or *ghazawul.*

Lay, s. *ghazal.*

Layer, s. *bragh, tah.* (-of bricks) *rada.*

Layman, s. *'āmmī.*

Laziness, s. *sustī, nā-rāstī, laṭ-wālai.*

Lazy, a. *sust, nā-rāst, laṭ, shatal* or *skalaṭ.*

Lead, s. *sīka, sīsa; mas.* (red-) *sendūr.* (white-) *sapeda.*

Lead, v.a. *rāwustal, biyāyal—bīwul, botlal—bīwul.*

Leader, s. *sardār, nāyak, sar-guroh, peshwā.*

Leaf, s. *pānṛa.* (-of a book) *waraq.* (-of a door) *pala, tanba.*

League, s. *para, janba, gundī; bandanṛ.*

wāda, lafz̤, taṛa, jorikkkht, qaul. (measure) *farsakh.*

Leak, v.n. *tsātsedal.*

Leaky, a. *tsātsedūnai, māt.*

Lean, a. *narai, ḍangar, khwār, lāghar.*

Lean, v.a. *takiya k., ḍaḍa lagawul.*

Leanness, s. *ḍangar·tob, narai·wālai.*

Leap, v.a. *dangal, traplal, ṭop wahal.*

Leap, s. *ṭop, dang, trap.*

Learn, v.a. *zdah k., yādawul.*

Learned, a. *zdah, yād, āmokhtah; 'ālim, pohānd.*

Learner, s. *shāgird, ṭālib, sabaq lwustūnai.*

Learning, s. *'ilm.*

Lease, s. *gānṛa, ijāra.*

Least, a. *kisharīn, kamtarīn, la ṭolo na la-ag* or *-wūṛ.* (at-) ad. *bāre, kho, ākhir.*

Leather, s. *tsarman.* (-dresser) *dabbāgh.* (-worker) *tsamyār, mochī.* (-strop) *rog, tasma.* (-bottle) *chāgul, ja-ī, batak.* (-scraper) *zarbiyāng.*

Leave, v.a. *pregdal, prekkhodal, prekkhal; rukhṣat ākhistal.* v.n. *rawānedal, tlal—lāṛal.*

Leave, s. *rukhṣat, ijāzat, ḥukm, izan.*

Leaven, s. *khamīra, māya, tomna.*

Leavings, s. *jūṭa, pāte, pas·khurdah.*

Lecher, s. *kāsīr, lawanḍ, qachar, chaṭ.*

Lecture, s. *sabaq, dars.* v.a. *sabaq wayal.*

Ledge, s. *ghāṛa, morga, ja-ī, ḍaḍa; kamar.*

Leech, s. *jawara.*

Leek, s. *gandana.*

Leer, v.a. *pa·trats katal; pa·zarana-ī katal.*

Lees, s. *khaṭbel, matra.*

Left, a. *pātai, bāqī.* (not right) *kīṇr, gats.* (-handed) *gatsai.* v.n. *pātai ked.*

Leg, s. (whole) *kkhānga.* (below knee) *paṛkai, lengai.* (-of a table, etc.) *pāya, kkhpa* or *pkkha.* (-of drawers) *pāentsa.* (-of mutton, fowl, etc.) *patūn.*

Legacy, s. *mīrāt, waṣiyat, hiba.*

Legal, a. *shara'ī, rawā.*

Legate, s. *astādzai, wakīl, elchī.*

Legation, s. *elchī·garī; jirga, m'arika.*

Legend, s. *rawāyat, qiṣṣa, taẕkira.*

Legerdemain, s. *bāzī·garī, jādū·garī, naz̤ar·bandī.*

Legion, s. *ḍala, ganṛ 'ālam; tuman, dasta, ulus.*

Legislate, v.a. *ḥukm-, ā-īn-, qānūn-,* etc. *chalawul.*

Legislator, s. *ḥākim, sharī'yat·jārī kawūnkai.*

Legislature, s. *sarkār, 'adālat.*

Legitimate, a. *rawā, ḥallāl.*

Legume, s. *palai.*

Leisure, s. *wazgār·tiyā, furṣat.*

Lemon, s. *nībū, tursh nārinj.*

Lend, v.a. *por warkawul, qarz̤ warkawul.* (a thing itself to be returned) *'āriyatī warkawul.*

Lender, s. *qarz̤-, por-,* etc. *-warkawūnai.*

Length, s. *ūgd·wālai.*

Lengthen, v.a. *ūgdawul.*

Lenient, a. *mulā-im, narm, ḥalīm.*

Lenity, s. *mulā-im·tob, narm·wālai, raḥm.*

Lent, s. *roja.* (Muhammadan) *ramz̤ān.*

Lentils, s. *moṭ, mahe; chanṛa; ma-ī; lobiyā.* (cooked-) *paitī, rāṛa.*

Leopard, s. *prāng, baur, baurgai, yūz.*

Leper, s. *koṛī, bragai, pesai.*

Leprosy, s. *koṛ, brag, pes.*

Less, a. *la-ag, kam, lāndai.*

Lessen, v.a. *la-agawul, kamawul.* v.n. *la-agedal, kamedal.*

Lesson, s. *dars, sabaq; pand, naṣīḥat.*

Lest, c. *mabādā, hase di na wī, kkhā-ī.*

Let, v.a. *pregdal, prekkhodal, prekkhal, prekkhawul.* (-go) *yalah-, khalāṣ-, āzād-,* etc. *k.* (hire) *karīh* or *kreha-,* etc. *warkawul.* (allow) *izan-, ḥukm-, rukhṣat-,* etc. *warkawul.*

Let, s. *ḍr, kariyāb, kiṭāl.*

Lethargy, s. *sustī, laṭ-wālai.*

Letter, s. *ḥarf; khaṭṭ, chīṭa-ī, ranwāna.*

Levee, s. *dalbār.*

Level, a. *sam, hawār, barābar, sat.* v.a. *samawul, naṛawul, hawārawul.*

Lever, s. *aṛam, dah-marda.* (-for water) *ḍīngara-ī* or *dingla-i.*

Levity, s. *spuk-wālai, halak-wālai.*

Levy, v.a. *ṭolawul, yaw dzāe-, jam'a-,* etc. *k.*

Lewd, a. *bad-mast, shahwat-nāk.* (-woman) *lashmaka-ī, shatāha.*

Lewdness, s. *mastī, shahwat.*

Lexicon, s. *lughat.*

Liable, a. *shwūnkai, pīrzo.*

Liar, s. *darogh-jan, darghal.*

Libel, s. *peghor, tor, tuhmat, bad-namūsī, ruswā-ī, malāmat.*

Liberal, s. *sakhī, bakkhūnkai, warkawūnai.*

Liberate, v.a. *āzādawul, khalāṣawul, pregdal, wurhawul, yalah k.*

Liberated, a. *yalah, āzād, khalāṣ.*

Libertine, s. *lawanḍ, chaṭ, lūtsak, qachar.*

Liberty, s. *yalah-tob, khalāṣī, āzādī; wāk, ikhtiyār; rukhṣat, ijāzat.*

Libidinous, a. *bad-mast, shahwat-nāk.*

Library, s. *kitāb-khāna.*

License, s. *izan, ḥukm, parwāna, sanad.*

Licentious, a. *bad-laman, bad-parhez-gār, bad-kār, ḥarām-kār; sar-kakkh.*

Lick, v.a. *tsaṭal.* (beat) *wahal, ṭakawul.*

Lid, s. *bargholai, sar-pokkh.*

Lie, s. *darogh.* v.a. *darogh wayal.*

Lie-down, v.n. *mlāstal, tsamlāstal, gazedal* or *ghazedal.* (-concealed) *ghalai kedal.*

Lieutenant, s. *nā-ib, qā-im muqām, jam'a-dār.*

Life, s. *dzān, jwāk, jwand; jwandūn, rozgār, zindagānī, ḥayāt.*

Lifeless, a. *be-dzān, be-sāh, muṛ.*

Lifetime, s. *'umr, jwandūn, ḥayāt.*

Lift, v.a. *porta k., khejawul, ūchatawul.*

Ligament, s. *pala, rag.* (-of the heel) *kūchai, spīna.* (-of horse's leg) *pai.*

Ligature, s. *taṛūn, ṭaṛa, band, paṭa-ī, skoe.*

Light, s. *ranṛā, rokkhnā-ī.* a. *rokkhān, rūṇr; spuk, halak.* v.a. *rūṇrawul, rokkhān k.* (-a fire) *balawul.* v.n. *rūṇredal, rokkhān ked.* (-as fire) *baledal.* (descend) *kūzedal, prewatal, nāziledal.*

Lighten, v.a. *spukawul, kamawul.* v.n. *rūṇredal, brekkhedal, dzalqedal.*

Lightness, s. *spuk-wālai.*

Lightning, s. *brekkhnā, barq.*

Like, a. *gund, miṣāl, ghūndai, rang, shān.* ad. *laka, pa shān, ghūndī, hase.* s. *pasand, khwakkh.*

Like, v.a. *khwakkh-, pasand-, qabūl-,* etc. *k.* v.n. *khwā-ta ked.*

Likelihood, s. *shān, shakl, ṣūrat, gumān.*

Likely, a. *shwūnai.* ad. *kkkā-ī, ghūnde.* (most-) *aghlab, ghāliba.*

Liken, v.a. *miṣāl-, tamṣīl-,* etc. *k., barābarawul, joṛawul.*

Likeness, s. *tsera, ṣūrat, taṣwīr, miṣāl, tamṣīl.*

Likewise, ad. *hum, 'alāwa, ziyāt la de na.*

Liking, s. *mīna, shauq, khwā.*

Lily, s. *sausan.* (water-) *nīlofar.*

Limb, s. *band, andām.* (-of a tree) *kkhākh, khṛand.*

Lime, s. *chūna; kūnai.* (-kiln) *paja.*

Limestone, s. *da chūne kāṇrai.* (nodulated-) *qurut-kāṇrai.*

Limit, s. *ḥadd, brīd, pūla, ṭikāna.* v.a. *ḥadd-,* etc. *taṛal.*

Limp, v.n. *guḍedal, ṭaparedal, ṭapal.*

Limpid, a. *spīn, pāk, ṣāf, narai.*

Line, s. *līk, līka, karkkha, khaṭṭ.* (rope-) *pa-aṛai, biyāsta, rasa-ī.* (row) *qaṭār, para, tsīṛa.* (clothes-) *tsakai, paikal, saha, tanāw.* (-of a book) *jadwal.*

Lineage, s. *aṣl, nasl, mūnḍ, nasab.*

Lineament, s. *ṣūrat, khāl-o-khaṭṭ, rang, ḍaul.*

Linen, s. *khāmtā, karbās.* (-draper) *bazzāz.*
Linger, v.n. *karedal, zahīredal, nūledal.* (delay) v.a. *drang-, lārghah-, dzand-,* etc. *k.* v.n. *pātedal, taparedal, pātai ked.*
Linguist, s. *pa jibo āmokhtah* or *-maranai.*
Lining, s. *astar, zerāstar.*
Link, s. *kara-ī.* (torch) *mash'al, shonta-ī.*
Linseed, s. *alsī, da saur zarai* or *-tukhm.*
Lintel, s. *darshal, sarāna.*
Lion, s. *zmarai* or *mzorai, babar-zmarai, sher.*
Lip, s. *shūnda.* (-of a cup) *morga.* (hare-) *shūnd-pārah kandā.*
Liquid, a. *narai, oblan.* (melted) *wīlī.*
Liquidate, v.a. *pūrah-, adā-,* etc. *k.*
Liquor, s. *oba; 'araq; sharāb.*
Liquorice, s. *khwaga-wala.*
Lisp, v.a. *tatarai-, gūngūra-, nkkhati jiba-,* etc. *wayal.*
List, v.a. *ghokkhtal; āwredal* or *ārwedal.*
List, s. *siyāhī, fard, fihrist; jārja-ī.*
Listen, v.a. *āwredal, nghwatal, ghwag bāsal—yastal, -keydal—kekkhodal, -nīwul,* etc. (spy) *ghwag tsāral.*
Listless, a. *be-dzān, be-sāh, be-dam, sust, lat.*
Literal, a. *lughawī; aslī; rikkhtīnai, jukht.*
Literary, a. *'ilmī; kitābī.*
Literati, s. *mullāyān.*
Literature, s. *'ilm, 'ilm-o-fazal.*
Litigate, v.a. *d'awa-, qaziya-,* etc. *k.*
Litigious, a. *jagrāū, qaziya-kār, takrārī.*
Litter, s. *dola-ī, ambāla-i.* (camel-) *kajāwa.* (grass) *wākkhah.* (refuse) *khazala, khāshāk.*
Little, a. *la-ag, kam.* (small) *wor, wurūkai, patai.* ad. *la-og-kūti* or *lakūtī, pitsāurai, khāsha, zarra.*
Littleness, s. *la-og-wālai, wurūk-wālai.*
Live, v.a. *jwand-, jwāk-, rozgār-,* etc. *k., jwandūn-, 'umr-,* etc. *terawul.* v.n. *jwandai ked., osedal.*
Livelihood, s. *rozī, rozgār, rizq, guzrān.*
Lively, a. *chālāk, chust; khush-tab'a, shokhīn.*
Liver, s. *īna, dzigar.*
Livery, s. *jāma, libās, bāna.*
Livid, a. *sperah, ziyar, shīn.*
Living, a. *jwandai; jān-dār.* s. *rozgār, rozī, guzrān, rizq.*
Lizard, s. *samsara, tsarmakkhkai, khadama-ī, karborai.* (iguana) *ghwāranduna-ī, ghwārixi.*
Lo, in. *gora! wāh!*
Load, s. *bār, potai.* (half-) *anda-ī.* (for head) *pand, pandūkai.*
Load, v.a. *bārawul, leydal—lekkhal; dakawul.*
Loadstone, s. *āhan-rubā.*
Loam, s. *mata-khāwra, matīna-zmaka.*
Loan, s. *qarz, por.* (of a thing itself to be returned) *'āriyat.*
Loath, a. *nā-rāz, nā-khwakkh, daregh-man.*
Loathe, v.a. *bad manal, kagal, ghandal, kraka ākhistal, chinjawul.*
Loathsome, a. *kraka-nāk, kagalai, chinjan, makrūh, ghandah.*
Loathing, s. *kraka, kagah, ghandana, chinjana.*
Local, a. *makānī, khāss.*
Lock, s. *jandra, qulf.* (-of hair) *zulf, tsūnra, tsunraka, kojak, wal.* (-plaited) *kontsa-ī, orbal.* (-of wool) *wara-ī.* (-of goat's hair) *ojghūna.* (-of a gun) *chaq-maq.*
Lock, v.a. *jandra lagawul* or *-band k.* (stick) v.n. *nkkhatal, jangedal.*
Locker, s. *sandūq, taunra-ī, kandū-rai.*
Locket, s. *t'awīz.*
Locomotion, s. *harakat; sail, girzedūn.*
Locust, s. *mlakh.*
Lodge, s. *jūngara, takiya, dzāe, āstāna, kor.*
Lodge, v.n. *osedal, āstedal.* v.a. *tikāo-, astoga-, kilai-,* etc. *k., dzāe nīwul.* (place) *gdal,* etc.
Lodger, s. *osedūnkai, āstedūnkai, astogūnkai.*
Lodging, s. *tikāo, dera, dzāe.*
Loft, s. *kota, bām, chat.*
Lofty, a. *ūchat, lask, darg, buland, lwar.*

Log, s. *garga, mūnḍ, tsaṭ.*

Logic, s. *manṭiq, da dalīlūno 'ilm.*

Loins, s. *mlā, shā-lanḍa, ḍūḍa.* (side of-) *ta-ashai.*

Loiter, v.a. *drang-, lārghah-, dzanḍ-,* etc. *k.* v.n. *ṭapal, ṭaparedal, pātedal, pātai ked.*

Loll, v.a. *takiya-, aram-,* etc. *k., loṭ-poṭ k.* v.n. *tsamlāstal, rghaṛedal—rghakkhtal.* (hang out) *walalai dzwaṛandedal.*

Lonely, a. *yawādzai, tsaṛah, biyal, tanhā.*

Long, a. *ūgd.* (duration) *ḍer-pā.* (distance) *ḍer, lire* or *liri.* (-ago) ad. *lire-lārghah, larghūne.* (as long as) ad. *hombra chi, tso chi, tar haghah pore chi.*

Long, v.n. *linwāl-, ūgai-, mayan-,* etc. *ked.* v.a. *ghokkhtal.*

Longevity, s. *zoṛ-tiyā, zoṛ-wālai.*

Longing, s. *linwāl-tob*; *mīna, armān, shauq, raghbat, khwā.*

Look, s. *katal, līdal, goral, kasal, nazar k.*

Look, s. *kātah, līdah, nazar, nigāh.*

Looking, s. *katana, līdana* (-glass) *āhīna.* (-for the thumb) *ārsa-ī, shast.*

Looks, s. *ṣūrat, shakl.*

Loom, s *rach, shāna*

Loop, s. *palwākkha, ghaṛwandai, ghuryāsha.*

Loose, a. *prānatai, art, āzād, yalah, khushai, ghaṛand*; *spaṛdalai.*

Loose, v.a. *pregdal, prekkhodal*; *khalāṣawul. āzādawul, yalah k., spaṛdal, prānītal*; *arat k.*

Looseness, s. *art-wālai.* (-of bowels) *nāstah.*

Lop, v.a. *prekawul* or *prekṛal, ghūṭ-, lanḍ-,* etc. *k.*

Lord, s. (God) *khudāe, rabb.* (master) *mālik, tsakkhtan, meṛah.* (owner) *khāwand, ṣāḥib.* (spiritual-) *sayad, pīr, ḥaẓrat.* (temporal) *sardār, khān, malik.*

Lordly, a. *khāntamām, kibr-jan.*

Lordship, s. *sardārī, khānī, malikī.* (your-) *ḥaẓrat.*

Lose, v.a. *wrukawul.* (at play, etc.) *bāelal,* v.n. *pa-aṛ ked.* (-in trade) *ziyān-, tāwān-,* etc. *k.*

Loser, s. *pa-aṛ, bāelūnai.*

Loss, s. *ziyān, tāwān, nuqṣān, troṭa, talaf.*

Lost, a. *wruk, puṭ*; *bāelalai.*

Lot, s. *qismat, naṣīb, bakht.* (share) *brakha-wesh, wanḍ.* (die) *hisk, pucha, qur'a.*

Lottery, s. *qur'a-bāzī, sharṭ.*

Loud, a. *ūchat-āwāz, shor-nāk, tāo-jan.*

Loudly, ad. *pa tāo sara.*

Lounger, s. *nā-rāst*; *hujrai.*

Louse, s. *spaga.* (-nit) *richa.* (crab-) *broṛa.* (cattle-) *konr, kūnai, kana, wrādza.*

Lousy, a. *spagan.* (mean) *gandah.*

Love, v.n. *mayan-, 'āshiq-,* etc. *ked.* v.a. *mīna-, muḥabbat-, 'ishq-,* etc. *laral* or *k.*

Love, s. *mīna, muḥabbat, 'ishq*; *mayan-tob, 'ishq-bāzī, āshnā-ī, yārī.*

Lovely, a. *kkhkulai, kkhāyastah, pej-makhai* or *pa-ī-makhai.*

Lover, s. *yār, āshnāe, mayan, 'āshiq, m'ashūq.*

Low, a. *kūz, lāndai, kkhkatah, lar, past.* (mean) *spuk, dūn, gandah.* (-stature) *mandarai.* (-price) *wel, arzān.* (-spirited) *malūl, zahīr* (-breed) *kam-aṣl, lāndai-ẓāt, pāsū.*

Low, v.n. *ghurchedal, ghuṛunbedal.* v.a. *naṛal, nāra-, ḍarān-,* etc. *wahal.*

Lower, a. *kkhkatanai, kūz, lar, lāndai.*

Lower, v.a. *kūzawul, kkhkatah-, lāndai-,* etc. *k.*; *ṭīṭawul.* (lessen) v.a. *spukawul, kamawul.* (as the sky) v.n. *toredal, ṭīṭedal.* (frown) v.a. *brandawul, brand katal.*

Lowland, s. *sama, maidān*; *tahana.*

Lowly, a. *gharīb, kamīn, ḥalīm.*

Lowness, s. *kūz-, kkhkatah-,* etc. *-wālai.*

Loyal, a. *khair-khwāh, wafā-dāṛ, namak-ḥalāl.*

Lucid, a. *ṣāf, spīn*; *tsargand, kkhkārah.*

Luck, s. *bakht, qismat, naṣīb.*
Lucky, a. *bakhtāwar, barakatī, nek·bakht.*
Lucrative, a. *sūd·man, fā ida·man, naf'a·nāk.*
Lucre, s. *duniyā, daulat, māl, sūd.*
Ludicrous, a. *khandā·nāk, washtī, ṭoqī.*
Lug, v.a. *rākāgal—rākkhkal, kashāla k.*
Luggage, s. *asbāb, partal*; *balā·batar.*
Lukewarm, a. *taṛam.*
Lull, v.a. *lala-ī-, lalo-, ṭāṭa-ī, ḍing·ḍinga-ī-,* etc. *k.*; *khob-, ārām-,* etc. *rāwṛal*; *damawul, ūdah k.*; *saṛawul, kamawul.*
Lumbago, s. *tsak.*
Lumber, s. *balā·batar, be·kkhai, nā·pakār.*
Luminous, a. *rokkhān, rūṇr.*
Lump, s. *ghaṭai, ghūnḍūrai, peṛa, chaka-ī, chakṛa-ī.* (all of a-) *sūṭ·būṭ, aluwal.*
Lunacy, s. *lewan·tob, saudā.*
Lunatic, s. *lewanai, saudā-ī.*
Luncheon, s. *nihārai, nwaṛa-ī, da paste doḍa-ī.*
Lungs, s. *sagai, paṛpūs.*
Lurch, v.n. *tsangzan ked.*
Lure, v.a. *ghulawul, ṭagal*; *pa dalbe nīwul, pa ṭam'e-* or *pa tāmbe-,* etc. *nīwul.*
Lurk, v.n. *ghalai kkhkenāstal, puṭedal.* v.a. *pasūnai-, tsawai-,* etc. *nīwul.*
Lurking-place, a. *pasūnai, tsawai, puṭgana-ī.*
Luscious, a. *khog, khwand·nāk, maza·dār.*
Lust, s. *shahwat, mastī, nas, naus.*
Lustful, a. *shahwat·nāk, mast.*
Lustre, s. *raṇrā, dzalak, brekkhnā.*
Lustrous, a. *rūṇr, brekkh·nāk, dzalak·nāk.*
Lusty, a. *zorāwar, tuwānā, qwwat·nāk, tandrust*; *maghzan, gogar, kaṭah, peṛ, chāgh.*
Lute, s. *shpela-ī, birdla-ī.*
Luxuriance, s. *prewānī, ziyātī, wadānī, ḍerwālai, ābādī.*
Luxuriant, a. *prewān, ziyāt, wadān, ḍer.*
Luxurious, a. *nafs·parast, ārām·ṭalab.*
Luxury, s. *moṛ·tiyā, ārām·tiyā.*
Lynx, s. *pṛāng·pīsh, yūz*

M.

Mace, s. *amsā, lawaṛ, ḍāng, ḍāngora-ī, gruz, koṭak.*
Macerate, v.a. *khuṛīnawul, pastawul, khushtawul, lānd sātal.*
Machination, s. *band, taṛa, joṛikkht.*
Machine, s. *kālai, hatiyār.*
Mad, a. *lewanai, saudā-ī, khushai.*
Madam, s. *bībī, merman.*
Madder, s. *rodang majīt.*
Madness, s. *lewan·tob, saudā.*
Magazine, s. *zakhīra, khazāna, ganj.*
Maggot, s. *chinjai, kikkhai.*
Magic, s. *jādū, koḍa, siḥr.*
Magician, s. *jādū·gar, koḍ·gar, siḥr·gar.*
Magistrate, s. *ḥākim, 'amal·dār.*
Magnanimity, s. *himmat, zṛeh.*
Magnanimous, a. *himmat·nāk, zṛah·war.*
Magnet, s. *āhan·rubā, chumbak·kāṇrai.*
Magnificence, s. *raunaq, dabdaba, tamtarāq.*
Magnificent, a. *raunaq·dār.*
Magnify, v.a. *ziyātawul, ghaṭ-, loe-,* etc. *k.* (praise) *stāyal, ganā wayal.*
Magnitude, s. *loe-, ghaṭ-, star-,* etc. *-wālai.*
Maid, s. *jina-ī, peghla.* (bond-) *wīndza, kanīza.* (servant-) *mazdūra, chūra-ī, sahela-ī.* (bride's-) *wreyaza* or *wre-uza, wrā·bāṇra-ī, mānja-ī, inga.*
Mail, s. *zghara*; *chalqat, zira.* (a man in-) *zghar·yālai.*
Maim, v.a. *guḍawul, khūgawul, kaṛam k.*; *jobalawul, ghwutsawul, zam·zmolai k.*
Maimed, a. *guḍ, khug, jobal, ghwuts, kaṛam, zam·zmolai, zakhmī, parhār·jalai, parhār·jan, māt·guḍ, sukṛuk.*
Main, a. *wṛūnbanai, awwalanai, wṛūnbai.*
Mainly, ad. *akṣar, ziyāt, ḍer, ghāliban, aghlab.*
Maintain, v.a. *iqrār-, d'awa-,* etc. *k.*; *wayal.*

(defend) *jghoral, khundī k.* (support) *parwaral, pālal, sātal.*

Maintenance, s. *rozī, khwurāk, parwarish.*

Maize, s. *jwār, ghaṭ·jwār.* (ear of-) *wagai.* (ear cone of-) *shata-ī.*

Majestic, a. *shāhī, bādshāhī*; *loe, ghaṭ, 'azīm.*

Majesty, s. *dabdaba, raunaq, jalāl*; *ḥazrat*; *salṭanat.*

Major, a. *loe, mashar*; *ziyāt, akṣar.*

Make, v.a. *joṛawul, kawul, paidā k.* (-amends) *tāwān warkawul.* (-away with) *wrukawul, puṭawul*; *wajlal, muṛ kawul.* (-good) *pūrah-, adā-,* etc. *k.* (-known) *khabarawul.* (-of, or understand) *pohedal.* (-out) *tsargandawul, kkhkārah-, daryāft-,* etc. *k.* (-over) *spāral, pāslawul, gumāral.* (-sure of) *yaqīn ganṛal.* (mix) *gaḍawul.* (-up, as a quarrel, etc.) *pakhulā k., gwākkhal, gwākkh·grandī k.* (collect) *ṭolawul.* (-towards) *khwā·ta-, lorī·ta-,* etc. *tlal—lāṛal.* (-much of) *nāzawul, nmāndzal.*

Make, s. *shakl, ḍaul, ṣūrat.*

Maker, s. *joṛawūnkai.* (in comp.) *-gar -sāz, -kār.*

Making, s. *joṛawūna, sākht.*

Malady, s. *maraẓ, āzār, bīmārī, randz, nā·joṛ·tiyā, nā·rogh·tiyā.*

Male, a. *nar, nārīnah.* (-of cattle for breeding) s. *mīndah* or *kindah.* (stallion) *turum.*

Malediction, s. *kkhera, bad·d'uā, l'anat.*

Malefactor, s. *gunāh·gār, bad·kār.*

Malevolence, s. *khwā·badī, kīna, badī.*

Malevolent, a. *khwā·bad, kīna·war.*

Malice, s. *kīna, badī, bughẓ.*

Malignant, a. *kīna·war, bad.*

Malinger, v.a. *bāna-, lamghaṛa-ī-,* etc. *k.*

Mallet, s. *molai, ḍabalai, baghdar.* (washerman's-) *tsobāṛai.*

Maltreat, v.a. *bad·sulūk k., be·makh k., wahal.*

Mamma, s. *aba-ī, ada-ī, mor.*

Mammon, s. *daulat, duniyā, nafs.*

Man, s. *saṛai, wagaṛai, gawai*; *bashar, insān, bandah.* (wild-) *banṛ·mānū.*

Manacles, s. *da lās karī.*

Manage, v.a. *chalawul, kawul, sambālawul, tadbīr k., band taṛal.*

Manageable, a. *da kawulu, da sambālawulu,* etc. *pa qābū, gharīb*; *spuk, āsān.*

Management, s. *kār·sāzī, tadbīr, intiẓām.*

Manager, s. *kār·sāz, pesh·kār, dāroghah.*

Mandate, s. *ḥukm, farmān, farmā-ikkht.*

Mane, s. *wrag, yāl, okkhī, owī.*

Mange, s. *khārikkht, pam, pūn, garg, pa-akh.*

Manger, s. *ākhor.*

Mangle, v.a. *mātawul, kanḍ·kapar-, ṭoṭe-ṭoṭe-, chūr·laṭ-, char·chūr-, daṛ·daṛ-,* etc. *k.*

Mango, s. *am.* (-tree) *da am wana.*

Mangy, a. *paman, pa-akhai, gargai.*

Manhood, s. *dzwānī, zalmī·tob*; *mardī.*

Maniac, s. *lewanai, saudā-ī.*

Manifest, a. *tsargand, kkhkārah, bartser, ẓāhir.* v.a. *tsargandawul, kkhkārah-,* etc. *k., kkhayal—kkhowul.*

Manifestly, ad. *bartseran, pa jār* or *-ẓāhir.*

Manifestation, s. *tsargand·tob, kkhkārah·wālai*; *iẓhār, jār.*

Manifesto, s. *ishtihār, jār, iẓhār·nāma.*

Manifold, a. *ḍer, bragh·bragh, braghan.*

Mankind, s. *sarai, wagaṛai, gawai, insān, bashar.*

Manliness, s. *saṛī·tob, maṛan·tob, nārīn·tob.*

Manly, a. *maṛanai, nārīnah.*

Manner, s. *shān, ṭaur, toga, rang, yang, wajha*; *ḍaul, chāl·chal, ṭaraḥ.*

Mannerly, a. *sulūkī, makhawar, adabī.*

Manners, s. *chāl, ādāb, khoe·khaṣlat, makh.*

Manœuvre, s. *chal, ḥikmat*; *tadbīr, band*; *fareb, lamghaṛa-ī.*

Manor, s. *daftar, jāgīr, mulk*; *wanḍ, ada-ī.*

Mansion, s. *koṭa, mena.* (storied) *mānra-ī, ḥawela-ī.*

Manslaughter, s. *marg, khūn, qatl.*

Manslayer, s. *qātil, khūnī, marg kawūnkai.*

Mantle, s. (man's-) *chogha, kosai, junga-kaṛi sharạ-ī; lūnga-ī, shamla, shāl.* (woman's-) *tsādar, paṛūnai, pachorai, chāyal, oḍana-ī, yaklā-ī.*

Manual, a. *dastī, da lās.* s. *kitāb.* (in comp.) *-nāma.*

Manufacture, s. *ḍast-kārī, joṛikkht, sākht.*

Manufacturer, s. *joṛawūnkai, kārī-gar.*

Manufactory, s. *kār-khāna.*

Manure, s. *sara, sarā.*

Manuscript, s. *dast-khaṭṭ; qalamī kitāb.*

Many, a. *ḍer, gaṇr.* (too-) *ziyāt.* (how-) *tso, tsomra.* (so-) *hombra, daghombra.* (as many as) *hombra chi.* (-coloured) *rangā-rang.* (-times) *ḍer dzala, wār-wār.*

Map, s. *nakhkkha, naqsha.*

Mar, v.a. *wrānawul, kharāb-, habatah-,* etc. *k.*

Marble, s. *mardaka.* (-stone) *marmar.*

March, s. *kūch, safar, pand.* (month) *chetar.*

Mare, s. *āspa, mādyān.*

Margin, s. *ghāṛa, morga, tselma, tsanḍa, ja-ī, laman.* (-of a book) *ḥāshiya.*

Marine, a. *daryābī.*

Mark, s. *nakkha; dāgh.* v.a. *nakkha lagawul; dāghawul; naẓar-, fikr-,* etc. *k.*

Marked, a. *nakkha-dār; dāghī; mashhūr.*

Market, s. *bāzār, ganj, haṭa-ī, manḍha-ī.*

Marketable, a. *bāzārī; chalanī.*

Marl, s. *maṭa-khāwra, maṭīna-zmaka.*

Marquee, s. *khaima, ḍera.*

Marriage, s. *wādah, nikāḥ.* (-feast) *kkhādī.* (-procession) *janj, wrā.* (-male guest) *jānjī, wrā-bāṇrai, mānjī.* (-female guest) *wrā-bāṇra-ī, wre-aza, mānja-ī.* (-gift) *belak.*

Married, a. (-man) *wādah-kaṛai.* (-woman) *wādah-shawī.* (under coverture) *maṛokkha.* v.n. *wadedal.*

Marrow, s. *māghzah, maghz.*

Marry, v.a. *wadawul, nikāḥ taṛal.* (-a husband) *tsakkhtan-, meṛah-,* etc. *k.* (-a wife) *kkhadza k.*

Marsh, s. *jaba.*

Marshy, a. *jaba-nāk, lūnd, zyam-nāk.*

Mart, s. *bāzār, ganj, haṭa-ī.*

Martial, a. *jangī, lakkhkarī.*

Martyr, s. *shahīd.*

Martyrdom, s. *shahādat.*

Marvel, v.n. *ḥariyānedal, ḥaryān* or *ḥairān ked., rabṛedal.*

Marvellous, a. *'ajab, 'ajīb, 'ajūbah, badī'a.*

Masculine, a. *nar, nārīnah, saṛai.*

Mash, s. *oghra, atūb, daliya.* v.a. *paz wahal.*

Mask, s. *parda, tsera; libās, swāng; fareb, bāna, chal.* v.a. *parda-,* etc. *k.; puṭawul, pokkhal.*

Mason, s. *rāj, m'imār.*

Mass, s. *ghunḍa, peṛa, chakṛa-ī; dala-ī, ḍera-ī.*

Massacre, s. *qatl, qatl-i-'āmm.* v.a. *qatlawul.*

Massive, a. *loe, ghaṭ, star; drūnd.* (-person) *kharīs, nūpaṛ, punḍ, gagar.*

Mast, s. *tīr, loe stan da jahāz.*

Master, s. *khāwand, tsakkhtan, meṛah, nāyak, mālik.* (-of a house) *korbah.* (tutor) *ākhūn, ustād.* (school-) *mullā, mu'allim.*

Master, v.a. *lānde k., sambālawul, barai mūndal.*

Mastery, s. *barai; ḥukūmat.*

Masticate, v.a. *jowul* or *joyal, chīchal, krapawul.*

Mastiff, s. *khadal, ghaṭ ghartsanai-spai.*

Mat, s. *pūzai, pūhaṛ, anḍerai.*

Match, s. (contest) *bāzī, sharṭ.* (equal) *makhai, joṛah, gund, siyāl; sārai, samsorai, hum-dzolai.* (gun-) *patīla, bāta-ī.* (fire-) *shonṭa-ī; shūsha-ī.* (marriage) *kojdan.* (-maker) *rebār, dallāl, mandz-garai.*

Match, v.a. *barābarawul, joṛawul, lagawul; jangawul.* v.n. *barābaredal, joṛedal, lagedal.*

Matchless, a. *be-misāl, be-siyāl, be-nazīr, lā-sānī.*

Mate, s. *mal, mal-garai, joṛah, yār.*

Material, a. *jismī, tan-dār; zarūr, grān.*

Materials, s. *kālī, hatyār, asbāb, sāmān.*

Materially, ad. *ḍer, ziyāt, nihāyat.*

Maternal, a. *moranai.* (-relation) s. *mor-ganai.*

Mathematics, s. *'ilm da riyāzī.*

Matrix, s. *qālib, sāncha.*

Matrimony, s. *wādah.* (state of-) *wādah-tūn.*

Matron, s. *mor, merman, bībī, spīn-sara.* (-of a house) *korbana.* (-under coverture) *maṛokkha.*

Matted, a. *arjal-barjal, tsapolai, nkkhatai.*

Matter, s. *jism, māda, jauhar.* (affair) *kār, khabara.* (thing) *tsīz, shai.* (pus) *ziwa* or *zawa, zahūb, rash.* (dirt) *khīra, chirk, chikhai.* (concern) *gharaz.*

Mattock, s. *kodāla-ī, sakkhsora, saspor, kasha-ī.*

Mattress, s. *tolā-ī, nihālī, toshak, taltak.*

Mature, a. *pokh, pūrah, kāmil.*

Maturely, ad. *pa fikr-, ghaur-,* etc. *-sara.*

Maturity, s. *pokh-wālai, kamāl.*

Maul, v.a. *wahal, ṭakāwul, kūṭal, mātawul.*

Maund, s. *man, las daṛa-ī.*

Maw, s. *jajūra.*

Mawkish, a. *balmangah* or *balmagai, be-khwand.*

Maxim, s. *matal, wayai, qānūn, masla.*

May, s. *jeṭ.*

Maze, s. *kaga-waga, pech-o-kham.*

Meadow, s. *warsho, chaman, kurūgh.*

Meagre, a. *ḍangar, narai, rangai, mahīn.*

Meal, s. *oṛah.* (fine-) *maidah.* (coarse-) *dal.* (rice-) *khamacha.* (pulse-) *rāṛa.*

Mean, a. *bakhīl, shūm; spuk, dūn; landai-zāt, kam-asl; mandzwai, āwsaṭ.* s. *mandz.*

Mean, v.a. *m'anī-, maṭlab-,* etc. *laral; qasd k.*

Meander, v.n. *girzedal, pechedal.*

Meaning, s. *m'anī, maṭlab; qasd, mudd'ā.*

Meanness, s. *bakhīlī, shūm-wālai, spuk-tiyā.*

Means, s. *m'arifat, wasīla, wāsiṭa; kabala.* (property) *panga, saga, māya; māl, kharts.* (manner) *wajha, shān, rang, ṭaur.* (by no-) *hets-chare, kruṭ.* (by what-) *pa tsa shān.*

Meantime, } ad. *pa de mandz kkhke.*
Meanwhile, }

Measles, s. *sharai, sara-malha.*

Measure, v.a. *mech-, kach-,* etc. *k.* (weigh) *jokal, talal.* (divide) *weshal.*

Measure, s. *mech, kach; tol, andāza, joka, wesh.* (action) *kār, chal, band, tarkīb.* (grain-) *kuṛai, ogai, daṛa-ī.* (verse) *wazn.* (-in music) *tāl, tāng.* (-for land) *pa-aṛai.* (beyond-) ad. *la hadda ter.*

Measureless, a. *be-kach, be-andāzah, be-hadd, be-shān, be-qiyās.*

Meat, s. *ghwakkha.* (food) *khwurāk, ḍoḍa-ī, ghiza.*

Mechanic, s. *kasb-gar, pesha-war.*

Mechanism, s. *tarkīb, joṛikkht, sākhtagī.*

Medal, s. *ṭughma; nakkha.*

Meddle, v.a. *gharaz k., lās lagawul, -āchawul, -war-wṛal,* etc.

Medial, a. *mandzwai, miyānah.*

Mediate, v.a. *gwākkhal, gwākkh-grandī k.*

Mediation, s. *gwākh; sipārish.*

Mediator, s. *gwākkh-grandai; mandz-garai.*

Medical, a. *ṭibbī.* (-man) s. *ṭabīb.*

Medicine, s. *dawā, dārū, durmal.* (science of-) *ṭibb.* (practice of-) *ṭibābat, ṭabībī.*

Mediocrity, s. *nīmgarī-tob, ausaṭ.*

Meditate, v.a. *fikr-, ghaur-, andekkhnā-,* etc. *k.*

Medium, a. *mandzwai, miyānah.* s. *wasīla, wāsiṭa, m'arifat.*

Medley, s. *gāḍera, argajah, gaḍ-waḍ.*

Meek, a. *halīm, gharīb, post, narm.*

Meekness, s. *halīm-tob, gharībi, post-wālai.*

Meet, a. *pīrzo, wājib, munāsib, lā-iq.*

Meet, v.n. *pekkhedal, nrānde-, miliyā-*, etc. *ked.*; *jangedal, lagedal, yo·dzāe ked.* (find) v.a. *mūndal.*

Meeting, s. *majlis, ṭolai*; *mulāqāt, didan*; *jirga, jumā'at.* (-place) *borjal, ṭikāo.*

Meetness, s. *pīrzonvuna, pīrzo·nālai, lā-iq·nālai, munāsibat.*

Melancholy, a. *gham·jan, malāl*; *saudā-ī.* s. *nūl, gham*; *saudā.*

Mellow, a. *pokh, khurīn, pos*; *paṭakh.*

Melodious, a. *khush·āwāz, khush·bāng.*

Melody, s. *sarod, badalla, tarāna.*

Melon, s. (water) *hindwāna, tarbūza.* (musk) *kharbūza*; *dastambol.* (sweet-) *khaṭakai, sarda, kand·yālai.* (wild-) *kākoṛa, kāl·kūnḍa-ī.* (bitter-) *tarkha kākoṛa.*

Melt, v.a. *wilī k.*; *oba k.* v.n. *wilī ked.*; *oba ked.*

Member, s. (-of the body) *andām, band.* (partner) *sharīk, brakha·khor.* (-of an assembly) *majlisī, jirgatū.* (clause) *juz, faṣl.*

Membrane, s. *parda, jāla-ī.* (-of belly) *spekkhta.* (-of the heart) *dzān·khwal.*

Memoir, s. *taẕkira, tawārīkh.*

Memorable, a. *qābil-* or *lā-iq da yād.*

Memorandum, s. *yād·dāsht, yād·gārī.*

Memorial, s. *yād·gār*; *'arẓī, darkhwāst.*

Memory, s. *yād, ḥifẓ.*

Menace, v.a. *raṭal, traṭal, ḍabawul, ḍāral.*

Mend, v.a. *joṛawul, raghawul.* (-clothes) *bezal, pezal.* v.n. *joṛedal, raghedal.*

Mendicant, s. *faqīr, gadāe*; *ṭālib*

Menial, s. *nokar, chūrai, mazdūr.*

Menses, s. *ḥaiẓ, zaṛūkī.*

Menstrual, a. *ḥaiẓī.* (-woman) *ḥaiẓ·dāra, ḥāiẓa, bilmāza.* (-cloth) *ḍerān.*

Mensuration, s. *mech, kach.*

Mental, a. *bāṭinī, qalbī.*

Mention, v.a. *yādawul*; *wayal, khabarawul.*

Mercantile, a. *da saudāgarī, tijāratī.*

Mercenary, a. *khpul·gharaẓ, duniyā·parast, zar·āshnāe.* (-soldier) *mlā·taṛ.*

Merchandise, s. *māl, jins, saudā*; *saudāgarī, banj, bipār* or *wapār, tijārat.*

Merchant, s. *saudā·gar, wapārī, banjārī*; *seṭ*; *parāchah.*

Merciful, a. *mom·dil, raḥm·dil.* (-God) *raḥīm, raḥmān, karīm.*

Merciless, a. *be·raḥm, be·dard.*

Mercury, s. *pārā, sīmāb.*

Mercy, s. *raḥm, raḥmat, khwā·khūgī.*

Merely, ad. *sirp, surup, ta-ash, khālī, faqaṭ.*

Meridian, s. *gharma, ṭakanra·gharma.*

Merit, s. *ḥaqq, qadr, yarz*; *s̤awāb.*

Meritorious, a. *wājib, lā-iq*; *s̤awābī.*

Merriment, s. *kkhādī, khush-ḥālī, khandā, washta·toqa.*

Merry, a. *kkhād, kkhād·man, khush·ḥāl, khandā·rūe.*

Mesh, s. *tor, jāla-ī, shabaka.*

Mess, s. *qatagh, ngolai.* (-of herbs) *sāginrai.* v.a. *ḥānḍa-ī·wālī k.*; *chūka k.*

Message, s. *khabar, paighām, karya.*

Messenger, s. *astādzai, qāṣid, harkārah.*

Messmate, s. *hānḍa-ī·wāl*

Metallic, a. *kānī.*

Metaphor, s. *mis̤āl, majāz, kināyat.*

Metaphysics, s. *'ilm da maujūdāt.*

Mete, v.a. *weshal*; *mech-, kach-*, etc. *k.*

Metempsychosis, s. *tanāsukh.*

Meteor, s. *lūk, laka-ī, shughla.*

Method, s. *tartīb, shān, rang, ḍaul, ḥikmat, toga, yang*; *ṭaur, ṭarīqa.*

Methodise, v.a. *tartībawul.*

Metre, s. *wazn, mech, mīzān.*

Metropolis, s. *pāe·takht, dāru·l·mulk.*

Mettle, s. *garand·wālai, tund·wālai*; *maṛāna.*

Mettlesome, a. *gaṛandai, tund, tez*; *maṛanai.*

Mew, v.a. *miyāw k.*

Midday, s. *gharma, ṭakanra·gharma, nīma·wradz.*

Middle, a. mandzwai, miyānah. s. mandz or miyandz. (-finger) mandza-gūta.

Middling, a. nīmgaṛai, hass.

Midge, s. māshai, ghamāsha. (water) jak, jakh.

Midnight, s. nīma-shpa, shūma.

Midst, a. mandzwai, miyānah.

Midway, s. nīma-lār, pa lārī.

Midwife, s. qābila, dā-ī.

Mien, s. tsihra, ṣūrat; rang, ḍaul; chāl, yūn.

Might, s. quwat, zor, was, twān, bram, qudrat.

Mighty, a. zorāwar, mazbūt, twānā, qawī.

Mitigate, v.a. kaḍa wṛal, lcgdal—lekkhal, kūch-, naql-, etc. k.

Milch, a. lunga, pa-ī-wara.

Mild, a. ḥalīm, narm, pos, khog; cman.

Mildew, s. chanrāsa, chata-ī.

Mildness, s. ḥalīm-tob, narmī, pos-wālai, etc.

Military, a. jangī, lakkhkarī.

Milk, s. pa-ī, shaudah. (sour-) khaidak, pranr. (curdled-) māstch. (butter-) shomle or shlonbe, kha-areṛai. (whey) tarwe. (candle-) matar or matra, kaṛa. (-pail) dowra-ī, lawaghūna. (-maid) ghobana. (-man) ghobah. (-and water) lassī. (first-) wargah.

Milk, v.a. lwashal.

Milkless, a. wucha, zāṛa-ī.

Mill, s. (hand-) mechan. (water-) jaranda, āsiyā. (oil-) gānra-ī. (-stone) da mechani gaṭa.

Miller, s. jarand-garai, muzd-garai, āsiyā-wān.

Millet, s. ghokkht, gdan, kārah.

Million, s. las laka.

Mimic, s. pekkhe-gar, malanḍai, swāngai.

Mimicry, s. pekkha, malanḍa, swāng.

Mince, v.a. qīma-, ṭoṭe-ṭoṭe-, reze-reze-, etc. k., warjal

Mind, s. zṛah, dil, dzān; 'aql, poha, palm, hokkh; khwā; gharaẓ; fikr, rae; yād. (presence of-) ausān, bidārī. (out of one's-) ausān-tlalai.

Mind, v.a. yād laral, manal, fikr-, etc. k.

Mindful, a. yādawar, khabar-dār, hokkhyār.

Mine, s. kān; surang, naqab. pr. dzamā, khpul.

Mine, v.a. kān-kanal, -kanaudal or -kanastal, surang wahal. (-a house) kanḍar mātawul or k.

Miner, s. kān-kanūnkai; surang wahūnkai, naqab-zan; kanḍar kawūnkai.

Mingle, v.a. yaḍawul, laṛal, ṛaqawul.

Minister, s. (-of state) wazīr. (agent) wakīl, nāẓir, nā-ib, gumāshtah, dīwān.

Minister, v.a. khidmat k.; warkawu

Ministry, s. khidmat.

Minor, a. kashar or kishar; la-ag, kam.

Minority, s. kishar-tob, wuṛūk-wālai; la-ag, kam.

Minstrel, s. muṭrib, sandar-bol, sarodī, mīrāṣī, ḍum.

Mint, s. ṭaksāl, ẓarb-khāna. (the plant) n'anā, pūdina.

Minute, s. laḥẓa, sā'at, dam. (note) yād-gār.

Minute, a. warai, mahīn, bārīk; pūṭai, pitsānrai.

Minutely, ad. pa kkhah shān sara.

Miracle, s. karāmat, m'ujaza.

Miraculous, a. 'ajab, 'ajīb, karāmatī.

Mirage, s. sarāb.

Mire, s. khaṭa, chikaṛ, chakṛaba.

Mirror, s. ā-īna, shīsha, hindāra. (-for the thumb) shasht, ārsā-ī.

Mirth, s. kkhādī, khush-ḥālī, khwakkhī, khandā.

Miry, a. chikṛan, khaṭolan.

Misapply, v.a. be-dzāe lagawul, 'abaṣ k.

Misapprehension, s. nā-pohī, khaṭā.

Misbegotten, a. ḥarāmī, pa khaṭā paidā, or ghalaṭ-paidā.

Misbehaviour, s. *bad·chāl, bad·sulūkī, nā·rāstī.*

Miscarry, v.n. *wrukedal.* (abort) v.a. *geḍa ghurzawul, ziyān-, tāwān-,* etc. *k.*

Miscellaneous, a. *biyal, judā; be·tartīb, gaḍ·waḍ.*

Miscellany, s. *jung, gaḍera, arg̣aja.*

Mischief, s. *tāwān, nuqṣān, ziyān; dukkh·manī, badī; pasāt, shar, sharārat; wīta, shokhī.*

Mischievous, a. *mozī, muzirr, ziyān·kār, ta·wānī; bad, kharāb, sharīr.* (-boy) *wītakai.*

Misconduct, s. *bad 'amalī, -kārī, -chalan,* etc.

Miscreant, s. *kāfir, bad·zāt, mardūd.*

Misdeed, s. *gunāh, quṣūr, taqṣīr, wabāl*

Miser, s. *shūm, bakhīl, tang·dast.*

Miserable, a. *khwār, tabāh, kharāb·khastah.* (worthless) *nā·kārah, nā·tsīz, nā·kas.*

Misery, s. *khwārī, tabāhī, khasgī* or *khastagī, nā·kasī, tangsiyā, nā·chārī, muflisī.*

Misfortune, s. *āfat, balā, bad-, kam-, tor-,* etc. *-bakhtī, nāzila, muṣībat.*

Mislay, v.a. *wrukawul, be·dzāe kegdal* or *kkhkegdal.*

Mislead, v.a. *ghulawul, gumrāh k.*

Mismanage, v.a. *be·tadbīrī k., wrānawul, kharābawul.*

Miss, v.a. *khaṭā k.* v.n. *ter watal.*

Missing, a. *puṭ, wruk.*

Mission, s. *āstawuna, risālat.*

Missionary, s. *āstādzai.*

Misspell, v.a. *peza-ī-, hezgī-, hijgī-,* etc. *pa khaṭā wayal* or *-k.*

Mist, s. *laṛa, dund, gard, ghubār.*

Mistake, s. *khaṭā, būlāwa, ghalaṭ.*

Mistress, s. *merman, korbana; m'ashūqa, yāra, āshnāya, 'aurata.*

Mistrust, s. *shakk, bad·gumān, wiswās.* v.a. *shakk-,* etc. *laral.*

Mistrustful, a. *shakk·man, bad·gumānī, wis·wāsī, be·i'tibār, stūra·prewatai.*

Misty, a. *dund, gard·jan, ghubārī.*

Misunderstanding, s. *nā·pohī, nā·pahmī; mānṛai, marawar·tiyā; mīrtsī, badī.*

Mite, s. *pūṭai, batsarai, pitsāṇrai; richa.*

Mitigate, v.a. *la-oyawul; kamawul, saṛawul.*

Mix, v.a. *gaḍawul; laṛal, ṛaqawul.*

Mixed, a. *gaḍ; laṛalai.*

Mixture, s. *gaḍ, gāḍera; murakkab.*

Moan, s. *zwergai* or *zgerwai, bilāṇra, heng, angahār.* v.a. *zwergai-,* etc. *k.*

Moat, s. *kanda, kāha-ī, khandaq.*

Mob, s. *paṛk, ṭolai, ḍala, ghol, gaṇr.*

Mob, v.a. *ger k., īsārawul* or *hiṣārawul.*

Mock, v.a. *pekkhe k., khandā pore k*

Mockery, s. *pekkha, khandā, ṭoqa.*

Mode, s. *shān, rang, toga, ṣūrat, wajha; chāl, chalan, ṭaur, dastūr, rasm, ṭarīqa.*

Model, s. *naqsha, namūna; nakkha, ḍaul; qālib, kālbūt.* v.a. *pa nakkhe-,* etc. *joṛa·wul.*

Moderate, v.a. *sambālawul, kamawv*

Moderate, a. *mandzwai, miyānah, muwāfiq.*

Moderation, s. *ṣabr, zgham, parhez.*

Modern, a. *nawai, osanai, osan.*

Modest, a. *sharm-, ḥayā-, ghairat-,* etc. *-nāk, sharm·sār; nek, pāk·laman.*

Modesty, s. *sharm, ḥayā,* etc.

Modify, v.a. *ṣūrat-,* etc. *warkawul; bad·lawul.*

Modulate, v.a. *āwāz joṛawul, sarod k., tarāna-, sandara-, zamzama-,* etc. *wayal.*

Moiety, s. *nīm, nīmai, nimāyah.*

Moist, a. *lūnd, zyam·nāk, nam·nāk, naw·jan.*

Moisten, v.a. *lūndawul* or *lamdawul.*

Moisture, s. *lūnd·wālai, zyam, naw, nam.*

Mole, s. *potai, ghunḍa-ī, ḍera-ī, kha-aṭ; dam·dama.* (-of the skin) *ta·apai, khāl.*

Molest, v.a. *pārawul, rabṛawul, zoral.*

Molestation, s. *āzār, rabaṛ, ṭongāṛa, blos,* etc.

Mollify, v.a. *narmawul, pastawul, saṛawul.*

Molten, a. *wilī, wilī shawai.*

Moment, s. *lahza, dam, sā'at, drang*; *parwā, fikr, gharaz.*

Momentary, a. *teredūnai, nā-pāedār.*

Momentous, a. *drūnd, grān, mushkil*; *zarūr, muhimm.*

Monarch, s. *bādshāh, amīr, sultān.*

Monarchy, s. *bādshāhī, saltanat.*

Monday, s. *pīr, gul.*

Money, s. *rok, tanga, naghd* or *naqd, paisa, rūpa-ī.* (-changer) *sarrāf.*

Moneyed, a. *daulat-man, dunyā-dār, māl dār, da rūpo paiso khāwand.*

Moneyless, a. *ta-ash lās, be-daulat, muflis.*

Mongoose, s. *nolai.*

Mongrel, a. *nīmchah, dwah-ragah.*

Monition, s. *nasīhat, pand.*

Monitor, s. *nāsih, pand warkawūnkai.*

Monkey, s. *bīzo, shādo.*

Monopoly, s. *khāss, saudā, ijāra.*

Monotonous, a. *yaw-shān, yaw-wazn.*

Monsoon, s. *parshakāl.*

Monster, s. *dew, dad, rawai*; *banr-mānū.*

Monstrous, a. *haul-nāk, 'azīm, 'ajīb.*

Month, s. *myāsht.* (solar-, used with reference to agriculture and the seasons, commencing at April) *wīsāk, jet, hār, pashakāl, bādro, asū, kātak, mangar, poh, māh, paganr, chaitar.* (lunar-, used with reference to dates, festivals, etc.) *hasan husen, safara, wrūnba-ī khor, dwayma khor, driyma khor, tsalorama khor, da khudāe, myāsht, da sho qadr* or *da barāt myāsht, da roje myāsht, da wurūkī akhtar myāsht, khālī* or *miyāna, da loe akhtar myāsht.*

Monthly, ad. *myāsht pa myāsht, māh-wārī.*

Monument, s. *tsalai, nikkhān, nakkha.* (tomb) *maqbara, qabr, khāda.*

Mood, s. *hāl, shān*; *rang, khoe.*

Moody, a. *khapah, malāl, sūt-būt.*

Moon, s. *spogma-ī.* (new-) *myāsht.* (-less) *tarogma-ī.* (-light) *spogma-ī, rabanra.* (-stroke) *bar.* (-struck) *bar-wahalai.*

Moor, s. *habshī, zangī.* (marsh) *jaba.*

Moor, v.a. *langar āchawul, lagawul, taral.*

Mope, v.n. *ghamedal, nūledal*; *malāl kedal.*

Mopish, a. *gham-jan, nūl-jan, malāl.*

Moral, a. *pāk, pākīzah, nekokār.* s. *nasīhat, pand*; *hāsil, gharaz.*

Morality, s. *nekī, nekokārī, rikkhtīn-tob.*

Moralize, v.a. *pand wayal, nasīhat wayal.*

Morals, s. *nek-chalan, nekokārī, sīrat.*

Morally, ad. *pa haqq, pa rikkhtiyā.*

Morass, s. *jaba, bokkhtana, taramna, yala.*

Morbid, a. *kharāb, wrān*; *nā-jor, nā-rogh.*

More, a. *ziyāt, nor.* (-and more) *nor ziyāt.* (-or less) *la-ag ziyāt.*

Moreover, ad. *bal, balki, wale, nor, siwā la de na.*

Morning, s. *sahr* or *suhār.* (-star) *starga.* (to-morrow-) *sabā* or *subha.*

Morose, a. *sūt-būt, bad-khoe, trīw-makh, tursh-rūe, bakhīl.*

Morrow, s. *sabā, subha.* (day after-) *bul-sabā.*

Morsel, s. *nwara-ī, gola*; *pitsānrai, pūtai.*

Mortal, a. *fānī, tlūnai, teredūnai.* (human) *insānī, basharī, wagarai.* (deadly) *qātil, kārī, halāhil.*

Mortal, s. *sarai, wagarai, garai, insān, bashar.*

Mortality, s. *ajal, marg, maut*; *sarī-tob, bashriyat, insāniyat.*

Mortar, s. *baghara-ī.* (cement) *kūnai, gach.*

Mortgage, v.a. *gānra-, graw-,* etc. *k.*

Mortification, s. *gazak, skhā-wālai*; *randz, da zrah nūl, paskhāk.*

Mortify, v.n. *gazak-, skhā-,* etc. *ked., wrostedal.* v.a. *karawul, sedzal, āzārawul.*

Mosque, s. *jumā'at, masjid.*

Moss, s. *da wano waran khwar*; *babar wākkhah chi da wano pa pot bānde tūkegī.*

Most, a. *aksar, ziyāt, nihāyat.*

Mostly, ad. *aksar, ziyātī, aghlab, ghāliban.*
Mote, s. *khas, khasanrai, khāsha.*
Moth, s. *or-pukkht, patang*; *da zarūko chinjai.*
Mother, s. *mor, aba-ī, ada-ī.* (-in-law) *khwākkhe.* (grand-) *nyā, anā.* (great grand-) *warla-anā, da nyā mor.* (great great grand-) *lā-warla-anā, da nyā nyā.* (step-) *ba-an-mor, maira-mor.* (-less) *yasīr, be-mor, mor-murai.* (-of pearl) *sipa-ī.*
Motion, s. *harakat, khwadzedana.*
Motive, s. *sabab, bā'is, matlab, mūjib, kabl.*
Motley, a. *brag, gag, chrag-brag, brag-yālai*; *gad-wad*; *rangīn.*
Motto, s. *'alāma, nakkha.*
Mould, s. *qālib, kālbūt, sāncha.* (mildew) *zang, chanrāsha.* (earth) *khāwra.* (manure) *sara.*
Mould, v.a. *jorawul, tandal, sūrat-, daul-,* etc. *warkawul.*
Moulder, v.n. *sharhedal, wrostedal, khāwre ked.*
Mouldy, a. *zang-jan, chanreshan.*
Moult, v.a. *kurīz k., rajawul.* v.n. *rajedal.*
Mound, s. *dera-ī, ghunda-ī, potai, kha-at, rāsha, rashaka, tall.*
Mount, v.n. *khatal.* (-upon) *sparedal.* v.a. *khejawul.* (-a jewel) *jarāo k.*
Mountain, s. *ghar, koh.* (-ridge) *ghākkhai, kamar.* a. *ghartsanai, kohistānī.* (-goat) s. *ghartsah.*
Mountaineer, s. *kohistānai, rohilai, ghartsanai.*
Mountainous, a. *ghartsan, kohistān.*
Mourn, v.a. *jaral, wīr k., wainā woyal.* v.n. *karedal, nūledal, ghamedal.*
Mourner, s. *wīr-jalai, gham-khor.*
Mournful, a. *wīr-nāk, gham-nāk.*
Mourning, s. *wīr, jarā*; *gham, nūl*; *wainā wayana.*
Mouse, s. *magakūrai.* (-hole) *sūra.*
Mouth, s. *khula.* (small-) *khulga-ī.*
Mouthful, s. *nwara-ī, mara-ī, gola.*
Move, v.a. *khwadzawul.* v.n. *khwadzedal.*
Movement, s. *harakat, khwadzedana.*
Mow, v.a. *lau k., randal, rebal.*
Mower, s. *lau-garai.*
Much, a. *der, prewān.* s. *prewānī, der wālai.* (how-) *tsomra.* (so-) *hombra.* (so much so) *tar daghah pore.*
Mucilage, s. *chīr, salekkh, leta-ī, l'uāb.*
Mucilaginous, a. *salekkh-nāk, laha-jan. l'uāb-dār, chīran.*
Mucus, s. *laha, l'uāb.* (-of nose) *karmeza, kanr, kharmat, grang.* (-of bowels) *rama, rap.* (-of urethra, etc.) *maza-ī.*
Muck, s. *sara, derān, khīrai, rash.*
Mud, s. *lāha, khata, chīkar.* (-for building) *paskha.*
Muddy, a. *khatolan, kha-ar, chikran.*
Muffle, v.a. *ngharal—nghakkhtal, putawul, pokkhal.*
Mug, s. *piyāla, kandolotai.*
Mulberry, s. *tūt.* (royal-) *shāh-tūt.* (seed less-) *be-dāna tūt.* (black-) *tor-tūt.* (white-) *spīn-tūt.* (grey-) *bor-tūt.*
Mulct, v.a. *tāwān-, nāgha-,* etc. *ākhistal.*
Mule, s. *khachar* or *kachar, qātir.*
Multiform, a. *rangā-rang.*
Multiplication, s. *bragh, zarb, jor.*
Multiplicity, s. *prewānī, der-wālai. ziyāt-wālai.*
Multiply, v.a. *zarb-, bragh-,* etc. *k., hisāb-jorawul.* (increase) v.a. *ziyātawul, wadā-nawul, derawul.* v.n. *ziyātedal, wadānedal, deredal.*
Multitude, s. *lakkhkar, pauz* or *fauj, dala, ganr khalq* or *-'ālam.*
Mumble, v.a. *bar-bar-, pus-pus-, gunr-gunr-,* etc. *k.*
Mummy, s. *momiyāe.*
Munch, v.a. *krapawul, jowul* or *joyal, chīchal.*
Mundane, a. *duniyā-ī.*

Munificence, s. *sakhī-tob, sakhāwat, bakkhan-tob.*

Munificent, a. *sakhī, sakhāwatī, bakkhana kawūnkai.*

Murder, s. *marg, khūn, qatl.* (price of-) *diyat.* v.a. *khūn-*, etc. *k.*, *muṛ k.*, *wajal* or *wajlal.*

Murderer, s. *khūnī, qātil, marg kawūnkai.*

Murderous, a. *khūn-khwār, khūnāṛai.*

Murky, a. *tor, dund, tīrah, gard-jan.*

Murmur, v.a. *baṛ-baṛ-*, *ṭar-ṭar-*, etc. *k.* (complain) *māna-*, *gila-*, etc. *k.* (-as a brook) *juṛ-juṛ k.* (as the belly) *quṛ-quṛ k.* s. (-of conversation) *gangūsai, pus-pus, zwag-zwūg, kkhkālwa.*

Murrain, s. *ṭak, ṭak-sarai.*

Muscle, s. *ghwakkha, līnda-ī.*

Muscular, a. *ghwakkha-war, gagar, mazai, khrīs.*

Muse, v.a. *fikr k.* v.n. *fikr-man ked.*

Museum, s. *'ajā-ib-khāna.*

Mushroom, s. *kha-arcṛai, gūmāndū, samā-rūgh.*

Music, s. *sarod, zamzama, tarāna.*

Musical, a. *sarodī, khush-āwāz.*

Musician, s. *sarod-gar, muṭrib, ḍum, mīrāṣī.*

Musk, s. *mukkhk.* (-pod) *mush-kunda-ī.* (-rat) *mukkhkai magak, mukkhkīn magak.*

Musket, s. *ṭopak, bandūkh.*

Muslin, s. *malmal.*

Must, v. imp. *boya chi, zarūr* or *lāzim dai chi.* (he must do it) *boya chi wu e kawī* or *kī.* Must is also expressed by using the past participle of the verb with *boya.* Ex. (it must be done) *kṛellai boya.* Or it is expressed by using the infinitive alone with the third person singular present tense of the auxiliary *yam.* Ex. (we must go) *mūnga ta tlal dī.*

Mustard, s. *sharsham.* (wild-) *awrai.* (-tops) *ghandal.* (-seed) *mandaw.* (-threshed stalks) *kāmbūra.*

Muster, v.a. *shmeral, shmāral, ṣān niwul.*

Musty, a. *wrost, skhā*; *chanreshan.*

Mutable, a. *nā pāe-dār, be-qalār.*

Mute, a. *gung, lal*; *chup, ghalai.*

Mutilate, v.a. *mātawul, prekawul, kharāb k.*, *jobalawul, ghwutsawul, kaṛam k.*

Mutineer, s. *yāghī-gar, pasātī.*

Mutinous, a. *yāghī, sar-kakkh.*

Mutiny, s. *yāghī-garī, balwā, pasāt.*

Mutter, v.a. *baṛ-baṛ-*, *ṭar-ṭar-*, *pus-pus-*, etc. *k.*

Mutton, s. *da ga-aḍe ghwakkha.* (shoulder of-) *walai.* (leg of-) *patūn.*

Mutual, a. *da dwāṛo palo* or *-lorīo* or *-khwāo*; *ṭarafain, jānibain.*

Mutually, ad. *yaw bul sara, dzabla.*

Muzzle, s. *poza, ūrbūz, tambez.* (-for the mouth) *tambūzak, tambezai, korai.* v.a. *khula bandawul, tambūzak*, etc. *taṛal* or *-logawul.*

Myriad, s. *las zara*; *tūmān.*

Myself, pr. *zah khpul, khpul-dzān.*

Mysterious, a. *puṭ, nā-m'alūm, ghā-ib.*

Mystery, s. *ghā-ib, puṭa-khabara.*

N.

Nail, s. *mekh, mogai.* (-of finger, etc.) *nūk.*

Nail, v.a. *ṭakawul.* (pay cash) *rok warkawul.*

Naked, a. *barbanḍ* or *barmanḍ, lūts.* (stark-) *lūts-pūts, lūts-lapaṛ, lūts-laghaṛ.*

Nakedness, s. *barbanḍ-tob, laghaṛ-tob, lūts-wālai.*

Name, s. *nūm, nām.* v.a. *nūm kegdal* or *kkhkegdal.* (mention) *nūm akhistal, yāda-wul.*

Named, a. *nūmedah, nūmāndai.*

Namely, ad. *y'ane, maglan, ganre.*

Namesake, s. *ham·nām, pa nāmah sharīk.*
Nap, s. *ṭūk.* (sleep) *khob, parnā, churt.*
Nap, v.a. *khob-, parnā-,* etc. *wṛul.* v.n. *khob zangedal.*
Nape, s. *tsaṭ; wuja.*
Napkin, s. *rūe·māl, dast·māl.*
Narration, s. *bayān; qiṣṣa, rawāyat, naql.*
Narrator, s. *nāqil, qiṣṣa kawūnkai.*
Narrow, a. *tang.* v.a. *tangawul.* v.n. *tangedal.*
Narrowly, ad. *pa sakhtī sara; pa fikr sara.*
Narrowness, s. *tang·wālai; tangsiyā; bakhīl·tob.*
Nasty, a. *nā·kārah, makrūh, koyalai; nā·pāk, palīt, khiran, murdār.*
Nation, s. *qām, ulus, tabar, firqa.*
National, a. *qāmī; waṭan·dost.*
Native, a. *aṣlī, ẕātī; waṭanī, mulkī, wilāyatī.* s. *woṭanī, wilāyatī, balad.* (-country) *waṭan, wilāyat.*
Nativity, s. *paidā-ikkht, zeyedah.*
Natural, a. *ẕātī, ṭab'-i.* (-son) *ḥarāmī.*
Naturalize, v.a. *khpulawul, sharik k.*
Naturally, ad. *pa·khpula.*
Nature, s. *khoe, khaṣlat, lokkhai, mizāj, ṭab'a, ṭabī'at.* (world) *naṛa-ī, duniyā, 'ālam.*
Naught, s. *hets.*
Naughty, a. *bad, kharāb, nā·kārah.*
Nausea, s. *mīkkh·mīkkhai, kaha, koe, bāka-ī, kraka, kūz·kātah.*
Nauseate, v.a. *chinjawul, kūz katal* or *-goral.* v.n. *chinjedal, mīkkh·mīkkh ked.*
Nauseous, a. *chinjan, kraka·nāk, bad·khwand.*
Naval, ad. *jahāzī, dariyābī.*
Navel, s. *nū* or *nūm.*
Navigate, v.a. *jahāz chalawul.*
Nay, ad. *nah, yah, āyā.*
Near, a. *nijdai.*
Nearness, s. *nijdekī.*
Neat, a. *pākīzah* or *pāzīkah, sādah, spetsalai.*
Neatness, s. *pākīzagī, spetsal·tob, joṛāb.*
Necessarily, ad. *kkhā-ī, boya, khwāh·ma-khwāh.*
Necessary, a. *lāzim, ẓarūr, bāedah, wājib.* (it is-) *boya chi, lāzim dai.* s. *chār·choba.* (to go to the-) *awdas k.*
Necessitous, a. *ḥājat·man, muḥtāj, darmāndah.*
Necessity, s. *ḥājat, ẓarūrat.*
Neck, s. *mara-ī, ghāṛa, markanḍa-ī.* (nape) *ormeg.*
Necklace, s. *amel, hār, psol.* (-ring) *oga-ī.*
Necromancer, s. *siḥr·gar, koḍ·gar, jādū·gar.*
Necromancy, s. *siḥr, koḍa, jādū.*
Nectar, s. *āb da ḥayāt, da kawṡar oba.*
Need, s. *ḥājat, ghokkht, ẓarūrat.* v.a. *ḥājat-,* etc. *laral, ghokkhtal.*
Needful, a. *ḥājat·man; lāzim, ẓarūr, pa·kār.*
Needle, s. *stan.* (eye of-) *swam* or *spam,* (packing-) *sparkhai.* (knitting-) *dūk, sīmak.* (-work) *ganḍal, skoe.*
Needless, a. *'abaṡ, be·fā-ida, nā pakār, be·kkhai.*
Needy, a. *muḥtāj, ḥājat·man.*
Nefarious, a. *bad, nā·kārah, nakkhanai.*
Negative, a. *nahī, nafī.* v.a. *man'a-, nahiya-,* etc. *k.*
Neglect, s. *ghaflat, be·fikrī, be·khabarī, be·parwā-ī.*
Negligent, a. *ghāfil, be·khabar, be·parwā.*
Negotiate, v.a. *sawāl·dzawāb-, m'amala-, jirga-, kār·rozgār-, khabara-,* etc. *k.*
Negotiator, s. *dallāl, rebār, mandz·garai.*
Negro, s. *ḥabashī, zangī.*
Neigh, s. *shashurai, hanr.* v.n. *shashuredal, hanredal.*
Neighbour, s. *gawānḍai, hamsāyah.*
Neighbourhood, s. *gawānḍ, cham.*
Neither, c. *na yo na bul.*
Nephew, s. (sister's son) *khora-e.* (brother's son) *wrārah.* (clansman's son) *'azīz.*
Nerve, s. *pla, rag, wuja; himmat, zṛeh, quwat.*

Nerveless, a. *be-himmat, be-zṛeh, nā-mard.*
Nervous, a. *yer-man, harānd, yaredūnkai.*
Nest, s. *jāla, āshiyāna.*
Net, s. (fish-) *jāla.* (bird-) *jāl.* (-for hay, etc.) *trangaṛ, korai, lad, shalita.*
Nether, a. *lar, lāndai, kūz.*
Nettle, v.a. *pāraṙul, ṭongaṙul, khapah k.* s. *jalbang.* (-rash) *laṛama.*
Never, ad. *hechare, haḍo, kets-kala, la-sara.*
Nevertheless, ad. *walekin, magar, sara la de.*
Neuter, a. *hijrai.* (-verb) *lāzimī.*
Neutral, a. *biyal, judā.*
New, a. *nawai, tāzah, osanai.* (-cloth) *kora, shaḍala, batī ḍaka.*
News, s. *khabar.* (good-) *zerai, sār.* (-paper) *akhbār.*
Next, a. *nijdai.* (the-) *bul.* (-time) *biyā.*
Nib, s. *tsūka, peza.* (beak) *makkhūka.*
Nibble, v.a. *chichal.*
Nice, a. *khwand-nāk, maza-dār.* (accurate) *jukht, barābar, joṛ.* (fine) *narai, bārik.* (delicate) *nāzuk.*
Nicely, ad. *pa maze sara. pa kkhah shān sara.*
Niche, s. *ṭāq, ṭāqcha, darai, rap.*
Nick, s. *barghanḍ, jghanḍ, kanḍaw.* (-of time) *ṭāng, neṭa, puk, mūda.*
Nickname, s. *laqab.*
Niece, s. (brother's daughter) *wrera.* (sister's daughter) *khordza.* (clanswoman's daughter) *khor-lanṛa.*
Niggard, a. *bakhīl, shūm, tang-dast.*
Nigh, a. *nijde, tsakha* or *khatsa.*
Night, s. *shpa.* (all-) *kara-ī-shpa.* (last-) *begāh, barūyah, begana-ī-, parūna-ī-, barana-ī-*, etc. *shpa.* (to-) *nan-shpa, mākkhām, begāh.* (dark-) *tora-shpa, taro-gma-ī.* (moonlight-) *spogma-ī, raṇrā-shpa.* (-blind) a. *shaw-kor* or *sham-kor.* (-blindness) *sham-kor-tiyā.* (-attack) *sho-khūn.* (-watching) *shaw-gīra.*
Nightingale, s. *bulbul, kastūra.*

Nightmare, s. *khapasa* or *khapaskai, rawai.*
Nimble, a. *gaṛandai, chust, chālāk, tak-lāstai, jalt, tez, zghard.*
Nine, a. *nahān.* (ninth) *nuham.* (-fold) *nuk-bragh, nu-chand.*
Nineteen, a *nu-las.* (nineteenth) *nuk-lasam.*
Ninety, a. *nawe.* (ninetieth) *nawiyam.*
Nip, v.a. *shūkawul.* (pinch) *skūnḍal.* (-with cold) *sedzal, wahal.*
Nippers, s. *ambūr, nūtsai.*
Nipple, s. *tai.*
Nitre, s. *kkhora.* (nitrous) a. *kkhoran.*
No, ad. *na, yah, āyā.* (-one) *hets-tsok.*
Nobility, s. *amīr-tob, sāwū-tob, sharāfat.*
Noble, a. *aṣīl, sāwū, ashrāf; loe, ghaṭ, zbarg.* s. *amīr, arbāb, khān.*
Nobly, a. *amīr-shān.*
Nobody, s. *hets tsok, hets kas; nā-tsīz, nā-kas, lā shai.*
Nocturnal, a. *da shpe.* (-pollution) *shaiṭān khaṭā.*
Nod, v.a. *sar ṭiṭawul.* v.n. *khob zangedal.*
Node, s. *pūrsob, stagh, ghunḍārai, margharai.*
Noise, s. *ghag, zwag, ghāw, shor, chagh, bāng*, etc. (to make a-) *ghagawul, chagh-awul, zwag-*, etc. *k.* v.n. *ghagedal, chagh-edal.*
Noisome, a. *kagalai, gandah, kraka-nāk, bod.*
Noisy, a. *shor-mār, ghag-mār, shor-pusht, ghāw-nāk, zwag-nāk.*
Nominal, a. *khiyālī, nāmī.*
Nominate, v.a. *muqarrar k., wudrawul, kkhkenawul; nūm ākhistal* or *-kkhayal—kkhowul.*
Nomination, s. *muqarrar kawuna, wudra-wuna.*
None, a. *hets.*
Non-existence, s *nisht-wālai, nestī.*
Non-existent, a. *nishtah, nest.*
Nonplus, v.a. *kariyānawul, rabṛawul lā-dzawāb-, lā-chār-, band-*, etc. *k.*

Nonsense, s. *wucha-pucha-, be-kūda-, dūza-*, etc. *-khabara, qatāra, shkhara, kiti-piti*, etc.

Nonsuit, v.a. *bāelawul, pa-aṛ k.*

Nook, s. *gūṭ, gokkha.*

Noon, s. *gharma, ṭakanra-* or *ṭakanḍa-gharma.*

Noose, s. *pulwākkha, gharwandai, gharāsha, pakhwandai, kamand, zanda-ī.* (-of hair) *lūma, lūmaka.*

Nor, c. *na.* (nor one nor the other) *na yo na bul.*

North, s. *shamāl, quṭb, kkhai ṭaraf.* (-star) *quṭb storai.*

Northward, a. *quṭb khwā* or *-lorai* or *-dada*, etc.

Nose, s. *poza.* (-bag) *tobra.*

Nosegay, s. *gul-dasta.*

Nostril, s. *spegma, spenga.*

Not, ad. *na.* imp. *ma.* (-at all) *la sara, hado.*

Notable, a. *mashhūr, nūm-war; lā-iq da yād.*

Notch, s. *barghanḍ, ighand, wut.*

Note, s. *nakkha, 'alāmat.* (letter) *khaṭṭ, chiṭa-ī.* (bond) *ḥujjat, tamassuk.* (voice) *tarāna, bāng, āwāz.* (musical-) *zīr, trang, wazn.* (memo.) *yād-dāsht.* (marginal-) *ḥāshiya.*

Note, v.a. *qiyās-, fikr-, ghaur-*, etc. *k.* (write) *likal, kāgal—kkhkal, darj k.* (look) *kutal, goral, lidal, nazar k.*

Noted, a. *mashhūr, nūm-war, nūm-dār.*

Nothing, s. *hets, hets shai; nā-tsīz.*

Notice, s. *nazar, liḥāz, mulāḥiza; khabar, ittilā'a, jār.* v.a. *nazar-*, etc. *k.*

Notify, v.a. *khabarawul, jār wahal.*

Notion, s. *khiyāl, gumān, fikr, wahm.*

Notoriety, s. *zwag, shuhrat, āwāza.*

Notorious, a. *mashhūr, m'alūm, tsarganā.*

Notwithstanding, c. *walekin, magar, sara la de, har tsomra, bā-wujūd.*

Noun, s. *ism. nūm.*

Nourish, v.a. *sātal, pālal, nmāndzal, parwaral.*

Nourisher, s. *pālūnkai, sātūnkai*, etc.

Nourishing, s. *pālana, sātana.* a. *quwat-nāk.*

Nourishment, s. *parwarish, pālana; khwurāk.*

Novel, a. *nawai.* s. *qiṣṣa, naql.*

November, s. *magar.*

Novice, s. *shāgird, nawai āmokhtah, kāchah.*

Now, ad. *os, dā sā'at.* (-adays) *nan-wradzi.*

Nowhere, ad. *hets-charta, hets-dzāe.*

Nowise, ad. *hets-shān, hets-rang.*

Noxious, a. *ziyānī, nuqṣānī, tāwānī, mozī, muẓirr.*

Nudity, s. *barbanḍ-tob, luts-wālai.*

Nugatory, s. *'abaṡ, nā kārah, lā ḥāṣil, be-fā-ida.*

Nuisance, s. *wabāl, mozī, muẓirr.*

Null, a. *'abaṡ, bāṭil, spuk, khushai.*

Numb, a. *ūdah, be-ḥiss.* (with cold) *qarqe-chan, marghechan.*

Number, s. *shumār* or *shmer, ḥisāb, 'adad.* v.a. *shmeral* or *shmāral, ḥisāb k.*

Numberless, a. *be-shumār, be-ḥisāb.*

Numeration, s. *shumār* or *shmer, ḥisāb.*

Numerous, a. *ḍer, ganr, frewān, wadān.*

Nuptial, a. *nikāḥī.* (-ceremony) *wādah.* (-knot) *nikāḥ.* (-song) *kkhādiyāna.* (-feast) *kkhādī.*

Nurse, s. *dā-ī.* v.a. *pālal, tai warkawul.*

Nurture, s. *parwarish, pālana.* v.a. *pālal, parwaral.*

Nut, s. *jauz.* (Nutmeg) *jauza.*

Nutriment, } s. *khwurāk, khwāṛah, ghizā,*
Nutrition, } *parwarish.*

Nutritious, a. *quwat-nāk, quwat bakkhūnkai.*

Nymph, s. *hūra, parī.*

O.

O (sign of vocative), *o, wo, ai, yā.* in. *āh, e, eh, he, hāe.* (in pain) *wāe, wā-ī.*

Oak, s. *balūṭ.* (-apple) *māzū.*

Oakum, s. *sanr, paṭ.*

Oar, s. *chapa*.

Oath, s. *qasam, saugand, ḥalaf*.

Obdurate, a. *sakht, be·dard, be·raḥm*; *ṭak-anrai, hoḍai, khpul·sar, sar·kakkh*.

Obedient, a. *farmān·wṛūnkai, ḥukm·manūn-kai, tābiʻa·dār*.

Obeisance, s. *salām, ādāb*; *sijda*.

Obelisk, s. *munāra, tsalai, stan*; *khaza* or *khāda*.

Obese, a. *peraṛ, tsorb, ghaṭ, punḍ, lwāṛ, peṛ*.

Obey, v.a. *manal, ḥukm pa·dzāe rāwṛal, tābiʻa·dārī k*.

Object, s. *shai, tsīz*; *gharaẓ, niyat, maṭlab*.

Object, v.a. *ʻuẕr-, takrār-, ḥujjat-*, etc. *k.*; *daregh k*.

Objection, s. *ʻuẕr, ḥujjat, takrār*; *daregh*.

Oblation, s. *qurbān, ṣadqa, dzār*; *naẕr, niyāz*.

Obligation, s. *farẓ, sharṭ, wājib*; *neṭa, wāda, taṛa, bandanr, lafẕ, qaul*; *minnat, khāṭir-dārī*.

Oblige, v.a. *minnat·dār-, khāṭir·dār-*, etc. *k*. (force) *zoral, be·was k*.

Obliged, a. *minnat·dār, iḥsān·man*.

Obliging, a. *khāṭir·dār, makhawar, mihrbān*.

Oblique, a. *tratskan, kog, kṛing*.

Obliterate, v.a. *wrānawul, wrukawul, wahal*.

Oblivion, s. *her·wālai, nisiyān*.

Oblivious, a. *her·man, be·fikr, nisyān·ka-wūnkai*.

Oblong, a. *ūgd*.

Obloquy, s. *peghor, tuhmat, tor, malāmat*.

Obnoxious, a. *moẕī, muẓirr, be·kkhai*. (liable) *shwūnkai, lāndai, maghlūb*.

Obscene, a. *pūch, palīt, murdār, pūhaṛ, nā·pāk*.

Obscure, a. *tor, tīrah*; *dund, kha-aṛ, gard·man, gard·jan*; *puṭ, nā mʻalūm*; *kam ẕāt* or *-aṣl*, or *-nogai*, etc.

Obscurity, s. *tyāra, tor·tam, ẓulmat*.

Obsequies, s. *fātiḥa* or *pātā, lās·nīwah, dʻuā*.

Obsequious, a. *khūshāmad·gar, ḍirpalai, jig·jigiyā*.

Observance, s. *makh, adab, khidmat*; *ʻamal, istʻimāl*; *dastūr, rasm, ṭariqa*.

Observation, s. *naẓar, mulāḥiẓa*; *līdah, kātah*; *khabara, wayai*.

Observe, v.a. *katal, goral, līdal, naẓar k. manal*; *wayal, khabara k*

Obsolete, a. *ghair istʻimāl, -chalan, -riwāj*, etc. *mansūkh, band, bāṭil*.

Obstacle, s. *aṛ, band, nkkhatai, kariyāb*.

Obstinate, a. *sar·kakkh, khpul·sar, hoḍai, kaṭai*.

Obstreperous, a. *jang·yālai, shorī, takanrai pasātī*.

Obstruct, v.a. *kaṭālawul, kariyābawul, nkkhla-wul, bandawul, manʻa k*.

Obstruction, s. *aṛ, band, nkkhatai*.

Obtain, v.a. *mūndal, gaṭal, biyā·mūndal*. v.n. *jārī ked.*; *chaledal, lagedal*.

Obtrude, v.a. *ḍūsa k*. v.n. *be·dzāe nana-watal, -rāghlal, -prewatal*, etc.

Obtuse, s. *pa-ats* or *p-uts*. (stupid) *pūkaṛ, kawdan*. (not pointed) *lwāṛ, ghaṭ*.

Obviate, v.a. *girzawul, manʻa k., lār nīwul*.

Obvious, a. *tsargand, kkhkārah, ẓāhir, bartser*.

Occasion, s. *her, plū, dzal, guẕār*; *nobat, neṭa, mūda, wakht*. (cause) *bāʻiṡ, sabab* (need) *pa·kār, ẓarūr, gharaẓ*.

Occasion, v.a. *paidā k., rāwṛal, khejawul, kawul, kṛal*.

Occasionally, ad. *kala·kala, kala·nā·kala*.

Occupation, s. *kār, kasb, mashghulā, chār*.

Occupy, v.a. *mashghūlawul, lagawul, dzāya-wul*; *dzāe nīwul, ākhistal, lānde k.*; *ʻamal k*.

Occur, v.n. *kedal, prewatal, nāziledal, wāqiʻa ked*. (-to the mind) *yādedal*.

Occurrence, s. *wāqiʻa, chal, ḥādiṡa, ittifāq*.

Ocean, s. *baḥr, qālī-* or *qārī dariyāb*.

Ochre, s. *ziyaṛa·khāwra*. (red-) *bagwa, sra·khāwra*.

October, s. *kātak*.

Odd, a. *'ajab, 'ajīb.* (not even) *tāk* or *ṯāq.* (-and even) *tāk·o·juft.*

Odds, s. *farq, biyal·tūn, biyal·wālai, tafāwat.* (strife) *patna, steza.* (gain) *zor, aghlab.* (-and ends) *balāe·batar.*

Ode, s. *ghazal. landa-ī, sandara, chār·bait.*

Odious, a. *makrūh, kagalai, ghāndah, kharāb, nā·khwakkh, nā·pasand, khwā·bad.*

Odium, s. *malāmat, peghor, tor, tuhmat; kīna, badī, khwā·badī.*

Odoriferous, a. *khush·bū-ī·dār, bū-ī·nāk.*

Odour, s. *bū-ī, bo* or *boe.* (sweet-) *khush·bū-ī* or *khush·boe.*

Œsophagus, s. *sra·ghāṛa, ḥaiq.*

Of, p. *da.* (on account-) *dapāra dz.*

Off, ad. *lire* or *liri.* (-hand) *sam da lāsa.* (to go-, come-, etc.) v.n. *lire ked.* (to go off, as a gun, etc.) v.n. *khalāṣedal, chaledal.* (well-) a. *mor.* (-and on) ad. *kkhkata·porta.*

Offal, s. *ūjarai, larai; murdār; jūṭa, pas·khurda.*

Offence, s. *gunāh, taqṣīr, wabāl.* (pique) *mānrai, marawar·tiyā; randz, khapagī.*

Offend, v.a. *gunāh-,* etc. *k., marawar-,* etc. *k., khapah-,* etc. *k.*

Offended, a. *marawar, khapah, bezār.*

Offender, s. *gunāh·gār, taqṣīrī.*

Offensive, a. *bad, nā·pasand, kharāb; moẕī, muẓirr.*

Offer, v.a. *warkawul.* (sacrifice) *qurbān-, ṣadqa-,* etc. *k.* (devote) *nazr-, niyāz-,* etc. *gdal* or *īgdal.* (present) *nazrāna-, pekkh·kakkh-,* etc. *warkawul.* (attempt) *qaṣd-, niyat-,* etc. *k.* (propose) *wayal, pukkkhtedal.*

Offering, s. *qurbān, ṣadqa, dzār; nazr, niyāz.*

Office, s. *kār, khidmat; dzāe, 'uhda, manṣab.* (-room) *daftar·khāna.* (good-) *sulūk, mrasta.* (bad-) *bad·sulūk, badī.*

Officer, s. *sardār, 'uhda·dār, manṣab·dār.*

Official, a. *sarkārī, khidmatī.*

Officiate, v.a. *khidmat k., nā-ib·garī-, qā-im·muqāmī-,* etc. *k.*

Officious, a. *harbaṛai, talwalai; khidmatī.*

Offspring, s. *alwād, zāwzād, farzand, tung.*

Often, ad. *wār·wār, bār·bār, ḍer·dzala.*

Ogle, v.a. *zarana-ī-, dzīr-,* etc. *k., pa·zarana-ī katal, starge wahal, pa·trats katal.*

Oh, in. *āh! eh! he! hāe! wāe! wāh!*

Oil, s. *tel.* (-man) *telai.* (-press) *gānra-ī.* (-cake) *kal.* (-jar) *daba.* (hair-) *pulel* or *fulel.*

Oily, a. *ghwaṛ, tel·jan.*

Ointment, s. *malham, paha, tab.*

Old, a. *zoṛ, kuhand.* (-man) *spīn·gīrai, būḍā.* (-woman) *spīn·sara, būḍa-ī.* (-age) *zoṛ·tiyā, zoṛ·wālai.*

Olive, s. *kkhona* or *kkhawana, zaitūn.*

Omelet, s. *khāgina.*

Omen, s. *pāl.* (good-) *akhtar.*

Ominous, a. *bad·pāl, bad·shugūn.*

Omission, s. *khaṭā, quṣūr, ter·wātah.*

Omit, v.a. *terawul, herawul, pregdal.*

Omnipotent, a *qādir, kirdigār.*

Omnipresent, a. *ḥāẓir·o·nāẓir, har dzāe.*

On, p. *pa, bānde, pre, par, da bānde, da pāsa, pre·bānde.* (in front) *wrānde, makh·kkhke.*

Once, ad. *yaw dzal, -heṛ, -wār, -guzār,* etc., *yawa·plā.* (-before) *pakhwā, wrānde.* (at-) *os, pa ṭikī, pa de sā'at.* (all at-) *yak·lakhta, nātsāpa, tsaṭ·waṭ.*

One, a. *yaw.* (in comp.) *yak.* (every-) *har·yaw.*

Oneness, s. *yaw·wālai, yaktā-ī.*

One's-self, pr. *dzān, khpul·dzān; nafs.*

Onerous, a. *drūnd, grān, mushkil, sakht.*

Onion, s. *piyāz.*

Only, ad. *sirp* or *surup, faqaṭ, khālī, ta-ash.* a. *yawādzai, tsaṛak, biyal.*

Onset, s. *halla, tsot, guẕār, brīd.*

Onward, ad. *wrānde, makh·kkhke.*

Ooze, v.n. *tsātsedal, watal.* s. *lāha, khaṭa.* (green-) *ūbṛa-ī.* (moisture) *zyam, naw.*

Opaque, a. *dūnd, kha-aṛ, ganr, gūr.*

Open, a. *prānītai, wāz, arat.* (clear) *ṣāf, spīn.* (apparent) *tsargand, kkhkārah.* (-as a door) *lire* or *liri.*

Open, v.a. *prānītal, artawul.* (undo) *spaṛdal.* (spread-) *khwarawul, ghwarawul.* (-as a flower) v.n. *khwaredal, ghwaṛedal.* (as a door) v.a. *lire k.*

Opening, s. *prānītana*; *spaṛakkhtana*; *khwaredana*, etc. (orifice) *khula, sūṛa.*

Openly, ad. *pa tsargand, pa jār* or *-ẓāhir.*

Openness, s. *art·wālai*; *tsargand·tob.*

Operate, v.a. *kār-, 'amal-, pāzah-, aṣar-,* etc. *k.*

Operator, s. *kār·kawūnkai, fā'il*; *kār·guẓār.*

Opinion, s. *fikr, rāe, tadbīr, khiyāl, gumān, qiyās*

Opiniative, a. *khpul·rāe, khpul·sar, kibr·jan.*

Opium, s. *apīm, afiyūn, tiriyāk.*

Opponent, s. *mudda'ī, mukhālif, ẓidd*; *dukkhman.*

Opportune, a. *munāsib, jukkt, pa·dzāe, pa·wakkt.*

Opportunity, s. *wakkt, ṭāng, neṭa, nobat, sā'at, puk.*

Oppose, v.a. *man'a k., haṭālawul, bandawul, lār nīwul, jangawul, muqābala k.* v.n. *makhā·makh-*, etc. *ked., jangedal.*

Opposite, a. *makhā·makh, wṛāndy*; *mukhālif, 'aks.*

Opposition, s. *ẓidd, hoḍ*; *jang, dukkhmanī, badī.*

Oppress, v.a. *zoral, ẓulm-, jafā-,* etc. *k., āzārawul.*

Oppression, s. *ẓulm, jafā, dzaur, zorāwarī, zabardastī, zor, ziyātī.*

Oppressor, s. *ẓālim, jafā·kār, zorāwar.*

Opprobrious, a. *bad, nā·kārah, bad·namūs, ruswā-ī.*

Option, s. *wāk, ikhtiyār, khwakkh, pasand, raẓā.*

Opulent, a. *daulat·man, māl·dār, duniyā·dār.*

Or, c. *yā.* (-else) *ki·na, kanra*; *ganre.*

Orach, s. *sārma.*

Oracle, s. *kalām.* (person) *zbarg.*

Oral, a. *zabānī, wayai.*

Orange, s. *nāranj.* (colour) *sūr·bor.*

Oration, s. *w'aẓ, khabara, taqrīr.*

Orator, s. *w'aẓ kawūnkai, taqrīrī, sukhan·sāz.*

Orb, s. *tsarkh.* (-of sun, etc.) *kakoṛai, ṭakai, chakla-ī, qurṣ.*

Orbicular, a. *ghunḍ, ghunḍ·man.*

Orbit, s. *daur, daurān.*

Orchard, s. *bāgh.*

Ordain, v.a. *muqarrar k., wudrawul, farmāyal, wayal.*

Ordeal, s. *āzmekkht, imtiḥān.*

Order, s. *tartīb, tadbīr*; *ḥukm, farmā-ikkht, farmān, amr*; *qām, ẓāt, nog, rang*; *dastūr, ṭarīqa, rasm.* (in order that) *tso chi.*

Order, v.a. *farmāyal, ḥukm k.*

Orderly, a. *ārāstah, pa tartīb, pa qā'ida.*

Ordinance, s. *ḥukm, amr*; *shar'a, qānūn*; *sunnat*; *qā'ida, ā-īn.*

Ordinary, a. *'āmm, jārī, chalanī*; *spuk, halak.*

Ordnance, s. *top, top·khāna.*

Ordure, s. *ghul, murdār, khīrai.*

Ore, s. *khāwra, kānrai.* (copper-) *da tāmbe kānrai.* (iron-) *da ospane khāwra.*

Organ, s. *ālat, 'aẓū.* (musical-) *bāja.*

Organize, v.a. *joṛawul, tarkīb k., tanḍal.*

Orifice, s. *khula, sūṛa.* (small-) *swam* or *spam.*

Origin, s. *aṣl, nogai, munḍ, wekh, bunsaṭ.*

Original, a. *aṣlī, awwal, nog.*

Originally, ad. *wṛūnbe, pa aṣl, pa awwal.*

Originate, v.a. *paidā-, jārī-,* etc. *k., chalawul, bāsal—yastal, kāgal—kkhkal.*

Ornament, s. *zewar, kālai, gānra* or *gahana, zeb, zīnat*; *andzor, kkhewa, singār.* (-for the head) *t'awīẓ, gul, dāṛa-ī, ṭīk.* (-for the ear) *lakkhta-ī, wāla-ī.* (-for the nose) *pezwān, natka-ī, chār·gul, pīsha-ī.* (-for the neck) *amel, ūga-ī, baḍa-ī,* (-for the arm) *kaṛa, wakkhai, kanganr, bangṛai, gūjra-ī, bāhū, ma-aṭkai.* (-for the feet) *pāckara, pakhwandai, pāenzeb.* (-for the finger) *tsalai, gūṭa, anrwat, shasht, ārsā-ī.*

Ornament, v.a. *joṛawul, andzorawul, dzān-, ḍaul-,* etc. *joṛawul, kkhewa-, singār-,* etc. *k.*

Orphan, s. *yatīm, yasīr, plār·meṛai, mor·meṛai.*

Orpiment, s. *hartāl, zarnīkh.*

Orthodox, a. *momin, sunnī, īmān·dār, chār·yārī; sūchah, rikkhtīnai, rāst·man.*

Oscillate, v.n. *dzwaṛandedal, zangedal, rapedal.* v.a. *ṭāl khwuṛal* or *-wahal.*

Oscillation, s. *zangedana, ṭāl, zāngo.*

Ostensible, a. *tsargand, kkhkārah, jār* or *ẓāhir.*

Ostentation, s. *lāpa, dzān kkhkārah·kawūna, dzān stāyana.*

Ostentatious, a. *lāpai, ṭatai, dzān kkhkārah kawūnkai, dzān stāyūnkai* or *-stāyana kawūnkai.*

Ostler, s. *ṭeliyā, nokar, nafar.*

Other, pr. *nor, bul.* (-wise) ad. *nor·shān, būl·shān; ka·na, ganra, kanra.*

Otter, s. *saglāwū* or *sanglāo, sīndlāo.*

Ought, v. imp. *boya chi, kkhā-ī chi.*

Ounce, s. *nīma·chīṭāka-ī.*

Our, ours, pr. *dzamūnga* or *dzamūga.*

Ourselves, pr. *mūng* or *mūg·khpul.*

Out, ad. *bāhir, warchane* or *wardzane.* (expelled) a. *sharalai.* (expended) a. *pūrah, tamām.* (extinguished) a. *muṛ, soṛ.* (get out!) in. *lire sha, biyarta sha.*

Outcast, s. *sharalai, sharūnai, pradai*

Outer, a. *bāhir; pradai, begānah, oprah.*

Outlaw, s. *farārī ghal, yāghī·gar, sharūnai.*

Outlet, s. *khula, lār; warkh; ghwagai.*

Outline, s. *nakhkkha* or *naqsha, kīl, karkkha.*

Outlive, v.n. *pāedal, pātedal, bachedal.*

Outrage, s. *zor, zulm, ziyātī, jafā, be·satrī.*

Outright, ad. *sam da lūsa, tsaṭ·waṭ; amānī, pūrah, pāk·ṣāf.*

Outside, s. *bāhir, makh.* (without) p. *war chane* or *wardzane.* (on the-) p. *pās, dapāsa, bānde.*

Outstrip, v.a. *pa zghākkht-* or *pa daw-,* etc. *lānde k.,* or *-wrusto pregdal.*

Outward, a. *bāhir, bartser, oprah.*

Outwardly, ad. *bartseran, pa jār, ẓāhiran.*

Outwit, v.a. *ṭagal, ghulawul.*

Oval, a. *ūgd, ghunḍ·munḍ.*

Oven, s. *tanūr.*

Over, p. *pās, bānde, da bānde.* (across) *pore* (above) *da pāsa.* (more-) *ziyāt, ḍer.*

Overbalance, v.n. *dranedal, sangzan ked.*

Overbearing, a. *zabardast, zorāwar, ẓālim; kibr·jan, maghrūr, khpul·sar, khpul·rāe.*

Overcast, a. *ganr, gūr, puṭ, tor, siwrai·kaṛai.*

Overcome, v.a. *lānde k., pa-aṛ k., baraı mūndal, wahal, mātawul.*

Overflow, v.n. *toyedal* or *toe ked., lāhū ked.*

Overhaul, v.a. *laṭawul, atsanral, shanal.*

Overhear, v.a. *āwredal, ghwag tsāral.*

Overleap, v.a. *pore dangal.*

Overlook, v.a. *katal, līdal, goral.* (forgive) *bakkhal, pulawul.* (pass over) v.n. *ter watal.*

Overplus, s. *ziyātī, bāqī, junga.*

Overpower, v.a. *lānde k., pa-ar k.*

Overrate, v.a. *ziyāt ganral* or *-shmeral.*

Overrule, v.a. *ḥukm mātawul* or *-wahal.*

Overrun, v.a. *tākht·tārāj-, lūṭ-, tālā-, wairān-,* etc. *k.* (spread) v.n. *khwaredal, ghwaredal, wīṛedal.*

Overseer, s. *peshkār, dārogha.* (of crops) *kakkhai.*

Overset, v.a. *naskorawul, aṛawul.*

Oversight, s. *khaṭā, ter·wat.*

Overt, a. *tsargand, kkhkārah, prānitai, ẓāhir.*

Overtake, v.a. *lānde k., nīwul.*

Overthrow, v.a. *mātawul, wahal, pa-aṛ·*

lānde-, etc. *k.*; *naṛawul*, *ghūrzawul*. (ruin) *pāe-māl-*, etc. *k.*, *litāṛawul*. (in wrestling) *parzawul*.

Overthrow, s. *māt*, *shikast*, *pa-aṛ*.

Overture, s. *sawāl*, *pukkhtana*, *khabara*.

Overturn, v.a. *naskorawul*, *aṛawul*, *peṛmakh k.*

Overwhelm, v.a. *ḍūbawul*, *gharqawul*.

Owe, v.n. *porawṛai-*, *qarẓ-dār-*, etc. *ked*.

Owl, s. *gūngai*, *chagharū*.

Own, pr. *khpul*.

Own, v.a. *khpulawul*, *taṛal*; *manal*, *ganṛal*; *qabūlawul*, *iqrār k.* v.n. *qā-il ked*.

Owner, s. *khāwand*, *meṛah*, *tsakkhtan*, *mālik*.

Ox, s. *ḍangar*; *ghwāe* or *ghwayai*, *ghutskai*.

Oxymel, s. *sikanjabīn*, *turanjabīn*.

Oyster, s. *kastūra*.

P.

Pace, s. *qadam*, *yūn*, *gām*; *chāl*, *tag*, *raftār*.

Pacify, v.a. *pakhulā k.*, *saṛawul*, *rogha-joṛa-*, etc. *k.*; *tasallī-*, *dilāsa-*, etc. *warkawul*.

Pack, s. *bār*, *peṭai*, *panḍ*, *laḍ*. (half-) *anḍai*. (-ropes) *wākkhkai*, *siyala-ī*. (-sack) *malaw*, *ghundai*, *tsaṭa*. (-net) *trangaṛ*, *korai*, *lad*, *shalīta*. (-saddle) *kata*, *pālān*. (party) *paṛk*, *ṭolai*.

Pack, v.a. *dzāyawul*, *taṛal*, *ṭolawul*, *nghaṛal* —*nghakkhtal*.

Packet, s. *gūṭla-ī*, *panḍūkai*, *panḍa*, *geḍai*.

Packthread, s. *natsai*, *muzai*.

Pad, s. *manjala* or *manjīla*; *bālikkhtah*, *bālikkhtgoṭai*, *moṛa*.

Paddle, v.a. *chape wahal*. (in water) *lānbo k.*

Padlock, s. *jandra*, *qulf*.

Pagan, s. *but-parast*, *kāfir*, *gabr*.

Paganism, s. *but-parastī*, *kāfir-tob*.

Page, s. *ṭeliyā*, *nokar*, *jilaw-dār*; *mra-e*, *ghulām*. (-of a book) *safha*.

Pageant, s. *tamāsha*, *nandāra*.

Pail, s. *taghār*, *gaḍhal*, *ḍol*, *salal*, *maṭkai*. (milk-) *donra-ī*, *lawaghūna*.

Pain, s. *khūg*, *daṛd*, *zakhm*, *'azāb*, *swai*. v.a. *khūgawul*, *daṛdawul*, *zakīrawul*. v.n. *khūgedal*, *daṛdedal*, *zakīredal*, *swal*.

Painful, a. *dard-man*, *zakhmī*, *khūg-man*.

Pains, s. *kokshiksh*, *mihnat*, *sa'ī*. (-of childbirth) *da langedo dard*.

Paint, v.a. *rangawul*, *rang lagawul*.

Painting, s. *rangawūna*; *tsera*, *taṣwīr*, *naqsha*.

Pair, s. *bragh*, *qulba*, *joṛa*.

Palace, s. *dargāh*, *bārgāh*, *daulat-khāna*.

Palatable, a. *khwand-nāk*, *maza-dār*.

Palate, s. *tālū*. (soft-) *kūmai*.

Pale, s. *sperah*, *sperchan*, *be-rang*; *ziyaṛ*, *shīn*, *spīn*; *kha-aṛ*, *īro-rang*. (stake) s. *mogai*.

Palisade, s. *keṛ*, *bāra*.

Pall, s. *tsādar*, *kapan* or *kafan*.

Palliate, v.a. *spukawul*, *kamawul*, *la-agawul*.

Pallid, a. *sperah*, *sperchan*, *ziyaṛ*, *shīn*, *kheṛ*.

Palm, s. *warghawai*, *khapar*, *lapa* (measure) *tsapak*. (-tree) *khajūr*.

Palpable, a. *tsargand*, *kkhkārah*, *bartser*.

Palpitate, v.n. *rapedal*, *laṛzedal*, *ḍrakedal*.

Palpitation, s. *laṛza*, *dradzedana*, *ḍrakedana*, *rapedana*. (-of heart) *khafqān*.

Palsied, a. *shall*, *guzan wahalai*.

Palsy, s. *guzan*.

Paltry, a. *spuk*, *khushai*, *nā-kārah*.

Pamper, v.a. *nāzawul*; *maṛawul*.

Pamphlet, s. *risāla*, *wor* or *wūr kitāb*, *juz*.

Pan, s. (metal) *tabakhai*, *dechka*, *kaṛahai*, *baṭ*. (pottery) *lokkhai*, *katwa-ī*, *taba-ī*, *maṭkai*. (of wood) *kkhānak*, *kachkol*.

Panacea, s. *aksīr*.

Pancake, s. *paṛāta*, *weshala*, *kāk*, *kakoṛai*.

Pander, s. *barwā*, *dallāl*. v.a. *dallālī k.*

Pane, s. (-of glass) *ā-īna*.

Panegyric, s. *stāyana, sanā, t'arīf.*

Panegyrist, s. *stāyana-, sanā-,* etc. *goe* or *-wayūnkai.*

Pang, s. *tsirīka, brekkh, dard.* (death-) *dzān-kandan.*

Pangolin, s. *kishor.*

Panic, s. *tor, tara, haibat, wera, khof.* (-struck) *tor khwūralai, weredalai.*

Pannier, s. *kawāra, kāra, kajāwa.*

Pant, v.a. *sā pa landa ākhistal.*

Pantaloons, s. *partūg, tambān, shalwār.* (the string) *partūghākkh.* (the hem) *bada.* (the leg) *pāentsa.* (the fork) *khakkhtag.*

Panther, s. *prāng, baur, baurgai.*

Pantry, s. *ambār-khāna.*

Pap, s. (teat) *tai.* (paste) *leta-ī, oghra, atob.*

Papa, s. *bābā, bābū*; *plār.*

Paper, s. *kāghaz.*

Par, s. *barābar-wālai, twal, gundī.*

Parable, s. *matal, misāl.*

Parade, s. *dabdaba, tamtarāq.* (military) *qawā'id, sān.* (-ground) *qawā'id-gāh, maidān.*

Paradise, s. *jannat, bihikkht.*

Paradox, s. *da 'aqla lire, arawulī khabara.*

Paragraph, s. *juz, qit'a.*

Parallel, a. *sam, barābar, sara sam.*

Paralysis, s. *guzan, shall.* (-of face) *laqwa.*

Paralytic, a. *shall, guzan-wahalai.*

Paramount, a. *mashar, ghat, loe.*

Paramour, s. *yār, āshnāe, m'ashūq.*

Parapet, s. *mard-rau, kangūra*; *sangar, bāra, panāh.*

Paraphrase, s. *tarjūma, sharah.*

Parasite, s. *khūshāmad-gar, dirpal*; *tufailī, lwegand, taghārai.*

Parboil, v.a. *nīm-josh k., nīma-khwā eshawul.*

Parcel, s. *gātla-ī, butskha, butskhaka.* (-of land) *bakhra, wesh, patai.*

Parch, v.a. *wrītawul, talawul, alwoyal, teyal, karawul.* v.n. *wuchedal, wrītedal, karedal.*

Parched, a. *wrīt, teyalai, alwoyalai,* etc. (-grain) s. *nīna, pūlah.*

Parchment, s. *raqq.*

Pardon, s. *bakkhal, m'uāf k.*

Pare, v.a. *khriyal, togal, tarāshal.* (-the nails) *nūkūna ākhistal.* (a tree) *lakkhte prekawul* or *-shūkawul.*

Parent, s. *mor, plār.*

Parentage, s. *asl, kor, nogai, khāndān, khūna nasal, nasab.*

Paring, s. *tarāza, chūr.*

Parish, s. *tapa, kandai, cham, mālat, wand.*

Parity, s. *barābarī, samsor-tiyā, siyālī, gundī.*

Park, s. *kkhkār-gāh.* (artillery-) *top-khāna.*

Parley, v.a. *sawāl-dzawāb-, khabare-,* etc. *k.*

Parliament, s. *da ulus jirga, da qām majlis.*

Parlour, s. *dar-dālān.*

Paroxysm, s. *ghota, nobat, bārī.*

Parrot, s. *totā, totī.*

Parry, v.a. *girzawul, bachawul, daf'a-, lire-,* etc. *k., bandawul, man'a k.*

Parsimonious, a. *kam-kharts, tang-dast, bakhīl.*

Parson, s. (moslem-) *imām.* (pagan-) *bām-bawr.* (christian) *pādrī.*

Part, s. *brakha, hissa, wesh.* (-of debt) *ūgrā-ī, qist.* (place) *dzāe, zmaka.* (piece) *tota.* (side) *janba, para, taraf.* (-of speech) *kalima.* (for the most-) *aksar.* (own-) *khpul-dzān.* (a small-) *la-ag-shān.* (to take in ill-) *bad manal.* (to take in good-) *kkhah manal.*

Part, v.a. *biyalawul, dwah-dzāe k., judā k.* (share) *weshal.* (-with) *pregdal, prekkhodal, prekkhawul, prekkhal, tark k.* v.n. *biyaledal, dwah-dzāe-, judā-,* etc. *ked., lwukkhtal.* (take leave) *rukhsatedal.*

Partake, v.a. *brakha ākhistal.* v.n. *malgarai-, sharīk-, brakha-khor-,* etc. *ked.*

Partaker, s. *brakha-khor, sharīk*; *malgarai, mal.*

Partial, a. *ṭaraf·dār, janba·dār*; *mayan*; *nīmgaṛai.*

Partiality, s. *ṭaraf-, janba-*, etc. *-dārī, wrasta, pās·wālai*; *mīna, sela*; *khwā.*

Participate, v.n. *malgarai-, sharīk-, gaḍ-*, etc. *ked.*

Participle, s. (active-) *ismi·fā'il.* (passive-) *ismi·mafa'ūl.*

Particle, s. *ṭikai, pitsānṛai, pūṭai, zarra, reza.*

Particular, a. *khāṣṣ.* s. *khabara*; *tafṣīl*; *juz·o·kul.* (in-) ad. *khuṣūṣan, pa ṭikī.*

Partisan, s. *para-, janba-, gundī-*, etc. *-dār*; *malgarai, mal, sharīk*; *yār, komakī.*

Partition, s. *wesh, taqsīm*; *parda, dīwāl.*

Partly, ad. *la-ag·shān, nīme·nīme, yaw la-ag tseh.* [*ambāz.*

Partner, s. *mal, malgarai, sharīk, brakha·khor,*

Partnership, s. *malgīrī, malgir·tiyā, shirākat, ambāzī.*

Partridge,. s. (black-) *tārū.* (grey-) *tangzarai* or *tangzarai.* (Greek-) *zarkah.*

Parts, s. (talents) *'aql, poha, sha'ūr, dānish.* (regions) *hewād, zmaka, mulk.* (districts) *tapa, pargana.* (private-) *ṣūrat, tor·wekkhtah, andām·nihānī, da parde dzāe.*

Parturition, s. *lang·wālai, langedana.* (delivery) *khalāṣī.*

Party, s. *ṭolai, paṛk.* (person) *kas, tan.* (meeting) *majlis.* (convivial-) *ṣuḥbat.* (side) *para, janba, gundī, ṭaraf.* (family-) *cham, firqa, khel, qām.*

Pass, v.n. *teredal, chaledal, tlal—lāṛal.* (-over) *pore watal.* (-by) *ter watal.*

Pass, s. (ford) *gūdar.* (ferry) *patanṛ, gūdar,* (hill-) *ghākkhai, kotal.* (defile) *tanga-ī, darra.* (road) *lār.* (permit) *parwāna.* (state) *ḥāl, nobat.* (stroke) *guzār, dāw, wār.*

Passage, s. *lār, darak, gūdar*; *safar.*

Passenger, s. *musāfir, rāh·rau.*

Passion, s. *qahr, ghuṣṣa.* (lust) *nafs, hawas, shahwat.* (love) *mīna, 'ishq.* (suffering) *quwat, zgham, ṣabr.* (ardour) *tāo.*

Passionate, a. *qahr·jan, ghaẓab·nāk*, etc. *bṛos, khīr, tund-, tod-, tez-*, etc. *mizāj* or *-khoe.*

Passive, a. *be·ḥarakat, prot, walāṛ.* (in grammar) *mafa'ūl, majhūl.*

Passport, s. *rawāna, parwāna.*

Past, a. *ter, tilai, tlalai.* (-and forgotten) *ter·o·her.*

Paste, s. *bati, leta-ī*; *atob.* (-board) *kānṭī.*

Pastern, s. *lās, kkhpa.* (-leathers) *pakh wandai.* (-joint) *gīṭa-ī.*

Pastime, s. *tamāsha, loba, bāzī, mashghulā.*

Pastor, s. *shpūn, gūjar.* (spiritual-) *imām, hādī, shekh, pīr.*

Pastry, s. *weshala, parāṭa, ghunzākkha.*

Pasture, s. *wākkhah, giyāh, 'alaf, tsar.* (-ground) *tsarā·gāh, maira, warsho.* v.n. *tsaredal.* v.a. *tsarawul, piyāyal, powul.*

Pasturing, s. *tsar, piyāyana, powuna.*

Pat, a. *jukht, joṛ, sam, barābar, drust.* s. *ṭas, ṭaq, trak.* v.a. *lās wahal pa chā bānde, dilāsa warkawul k.* (slap) *ṭas*, etc. *wahal, ṭaqawul.*

Patch, v.a. *joṛawul.* (-cloth) *bezal* or *pezal, ganḍal, ṭūkai-, khakkhtagai-*, etc. *pore ganḍal.* s. *ṭūkai, marīnṛa, pīna, joṛ, pewand*, etc.

Patent, s. *sanad, parwāna, farmān.*

Paternal, a. *plāranai.* (-relation) *plār·ganai.*

Path, s. *lār, wāṭ.* (bye or foot-) *tsaṛa lār* or *-wāṭ.*

Pathetic, a. *zṛeh·swai, khwā·khugai, dziyar·swai.*

Patience, s. *ṣabr, zgham, sah.* (to have) v.a. *ṣabr-*, etc. *laral*, or *k.*

Patient, a. *ṣābir, zgham-, ṣabr-*, etc. *-nāk.* s. *bīmār, marīẓ, nā·joṛ, randzūr, nā·rogh.*

Patriarch, s. *mashar, spīn·gīrai*; *nīkah, zbarg.*

Patrimony, s. *mīrāt, dawtar, milk.*

Patriot, s. *watan-dost.*
Patrol, s. *shab-gakkht*; *qarāwal.*
Patron, s. *murabbī, pushtī, nāyik.* (-saint) *pīr.*
Patten, s. *kanrāwa.*
Patter, v.a. (as rain) *darahār-, shirahār-*, etc. *k.*, or *-wahal.*
Pattern, s. *nakkha, namūna*; *qālib.*
Paucity, s. *kam-tiyā, tangsiyā, qīmatī, kākhtī, qātī.*
Pauper, s. *gadā, faqīr, nā-aār, nā-kas.*
Pause, v.a. *dama k., fikr k.* v.n. *wudredal.*
Pave, v.a. *farsh-bandī k.*
Pavilion, s. *khaima.*
Paw, s. *mangul, panja, changul.*
Pawn, v.a. *graw-, gānra-*, etc. *k.*
Pay, s. *talab, tankhwāh, mawājib*; *kharts, mazdūrī, shukrāna* (-master) *bakhshī, khizānchī.*
Pay, v.a. *talab-*, etc. *warkawul.* (discharge) *adā-, pūrah-*, etc. *k.*
Pea, s. *matar, krāk.* (chick-) *chanra.*
Peace, s. *rogha, jora, āshtī, khair, khairiyat, aman, ārām-tiyā, āsūdagī.*
Peaceable, a. *eman, gharīb, kam-sharr.*
Peaceful, a. *āsūdah. ārām. be-patna be-pasāt.*
Peach, s. *shaftālū.*
Peacock, s. *tāūs, mor.*
Peak, s. *tsūka, peza, sar.*
Peal, s. *daz, ghurunb.*
Pear, s. *tāngū, nāk, nāshpātai.*
Pearl, s. *marghalara, marwarīd, durr.* (mother of-) *māhī-ghwag, sadaf.* (-diver) *marjīwanrah.*
Peasant, s. *zamīndār, dihqān, charekār.*
Pease, s. *chanra, mot, mahe, ma-ī* or *mayī, māsh.* (split-) *dāl.* (ground-) *rāra, gir-gira.* (-pod) *palai.* (-husks) *sūrī, būt-sūrī.* (cooked-) *paitī.*
Pebble, s. *gīta-ī, dabara, kānrota.*

Peck, v.a. *tongawul, tongāra k., makkhūka wahul.*
Peculiar, a. *khāss*; *matrah*; *'ajīb.*
Peculiarity, s. *khāssiyat, lokkhai, khoe, khaslat.*
Pecuniary, a. *naghdī* or *naqdī.*
Pedagogue, s. *ustād, mullā, ākhūn.*
Pedestal, s. *pāya, āra, asūs, wekh, dunkācha, kkhpa.*
Pedigree, s. *pera-ī, pusht, asl, nasab.*
Pedlar, s. *banjārī.*
Peel, v.a. *pot-, khwar-*, etc. *bāsal—yastal* or *-kāgal—kkhkal.* v.n. *nwaredal.*
Peep, v.a. *pa-puta-, pa-zarana-ī-*, etc. *katal.*
Peep, s. *put-nazar, zarana-ī, dzīr.*
Peer, s. *sārai, makhai, samsorai, siyāl, gund*; *arbāb, sardār, khān, malik.*
Peerage, s. *kursī-nāma*; *shajara.*
Peerless, a. *be-misāl, lā-sānī, be-siyāl, nādir*, etc.
Peevish, a. *sūt-būt, būt-ūrbūz, trīkh-rūe, khapak.*
Peg, s. *mogai, mekh, sparkhai.*
Pelf, s. *tanga, taka, paisa*; *duniyā. daulat, māl.*
Pelican, s. *kotān.*
Pellet, s. *ghundaskai, pandoskai, mardakai, gola-ī.* (-of goat's, etc. dung) *pucha.*
Pellicle, s. *tsaparkai.*
Pelt, v.a. *wīshtal, lawastal, āchawul, ghur-zawul.*
Pelvis, s. *tabakhai, spokhadza.*
Pen, s. (writing-) *qalam.* (cattle-) *bānda. shpol.*
Penalty, s. *tāwān, nāgha, jarīmāna, sazā.*
Penance, s. *kafārat.*
Pencil, s. *salā-ī, sīkh, dūk.*
Pendant, a. *dzwarand, āwezānd.* s. *zundai, zunbak.*
Penetrate, v.n. *nanawatal, ore-pore watal.*
Penetration, s. *nanawātah, dakhl*; *poh, 'aql.*

Penis, s. *tsūkkhai, ḍaga, zakar.* (virilis) *ghenr.* (child's-) *tsakkhkūṛai, cholak.*
Penitence, s. *toba, pakkhemānī, istighfār.*
Penitent, a. *toba·gār, pakkhemān.*
Penknife, s. *chāqū, chaṛūka-ī.*
Penman, s. *kātib, kkhkūnkai.*
Pennant, s. *janḍa, bairagh, nakkha.*
Penny, s. *paisa, ṭanga, ḍāng, damṛa-ī.* (-weight) *shirshā-ī, dwa rata-ī.*
Pension, s. *wazīfa; jāgīr.*
Pensioner, s. *wazīfa·khor, jāgīr·dār.*
Pensive, s. *fikr·man, andekkh·man.*
Pentateuch, s. *tauret, kitāb da ḥazrat mūsā.*
Penurious, a. *shūm, bakhīl, tang·dast.*
Penury, s. *tabāhī, khwārī, tangsiyā.*
People, s. *'ālam, khalq, wagaṛī, mardum.* (tribe) *ulus, qām, khel.* v.a. *ābādawul, wadūnawul.*
Pepper, s. *mrich.* (red-) *sra·mrich.* (cubeb-) *ḍanbara.*
Perambulate, v.n. *girzedal.* v.a. *gakkht k.*
Perceive, v.a. *lidal, m'alūmawul.* v.n. *pohedal. rasedal, pejandal.*
Perception, s. *fikr, poha, hokkh, wuqūf.*
Perch, s. (-for birds) *chakas.* v.n. *kkhkenāstal.*
Perchance, ad. *gora, gunde, ganre, kkhā-ī.*
Percolate, v.a. *chanral, ghalbelawul.*
Percussion, s. *ṭaq, ṭakar.*
Perdition, s. *kharābī, halākī, tabāhī.*
Peremptory, a. *qaṭa'ī, pūrah, kāfī shāfī.*
Perennial, a. *pāedār, dā-im; yo·kālanai, kālanai.*
Perfect, a. *pūrah, tamām, kāmil; pāk, be·aib.*
Perfection, s. *kamāl, kāmil·tob, tamāmī, pūrah·wālai.*
Perfectly, ad. *amānī, sarāsar.*
Perfidious, a. *be·wafā, be·īmān, namak·ḥarām.*
Perfidy, s. *be·īmānī, be·wafā-ī, namak·ḥarāmī.*
Perforate, v.a. *sūṛai k., tetsal, sīkhal.*
Perform, v.a. *kawul, kṛal, pūrah-, adā-,* etc. *k., guzāral, tamāmawul, pa dzāe rāwṛal.*
Performance, s. *kār, kṛah, kawūna, adā.*
Perfume, s. *khūshbūī, 'aṭr.* (oil-) *fulel.*
Perfumer, s. *'aṭṭār.*
Perhaps, ad. *gunde, wī ba,* etc. (v. Perchance.)
Peril, s. *khaṭra, wera, khof, muhimm.*
Perilous, a. *khaṭar·nāk, wera·nāk, khof·nāk.*
Period, s. *wakht, ṭāng, nobat, mūda, neṭa, maḥal, wār, plā, keṛ.*
Periodical, a. *wārī, nobatī.*
Perish, v.n. *mṛal, muṛ-, halāk-, fū·fanā-,* etc. *ked.*
Perishable, a. *fānī, nā·pāedār, teredūnai.*
Perjure, v.a. *nā·ḥaqq-,* or *darogh qasam-,* or *nā·ḥaqq saugand-,* etc. *khwuṛal.*
Permanent, a. *pāedār, mazbūṭ, qā-im, lā·zawāl.*
Permanently, ad. *pāedārī sara, tar·tala.*
Permission, s. *izn, ḥukm, ijāzat.*
Permit, s. *parwāna.* v.a. *rawā laral; ḥukm-, izn-,* etc. *warkawul.*
Pernicious, a. *tāwānī, nuqṣānī, niyānī; moẓī, muẓirr.*
Perpendicular, a. *negh, walāṛ, lak, jig.*
Perpetrate, v.a. *kawul, kṛal.*
Perpetual, a. *dā-imī, mudāmī, jāwīdān.*
Perpetually, ad. *har·kala, tal, tar·tala, ham·esha.*
Perplex, v.a. *rabṛawul, hariyānawul, sargar·dānawul, hak·pak-, hekkh-, huts-,* etc. *k.*
Perplexity, s. *rabaṛ, hariyānī, sargardānī,* etc.
Perquisite, s. *gaṭa, shukrāna, dastūrī.*
Persecute, v.a. *āzārawul, zoral, tangawul, khūgawul, zulm-,* etc. *k.*
Persecution, s. *zor, zulm, ziyātī; taqāza.*
Persecutor, s. *zālim, jafā·kār, zorūnkai.*
Perseverance, s. *himmat, sa'ī, kokkhikkh.*
Persevere, v.a. *himmat-,* etc. *k.* v.n. *lagiyā osedal.*
Persist, v.a. *ḥujjat-, takrār-,* etc. *k.* v.n. *lagiyā osedal, qā-im-,* etc. *osedal.*
Person, s. *sarai, wagaṛai, gawai, kas, tan.*

(self) *khpul, dzān.* (body) *ṣūrat, andām, tan.*
Personal, a. *khpul, khāṣṣ.*
Personality, s. *ṣūrat, nātka-ī, pejandgalī.*
Personally, ad. *pa khpula, pa dzān.*
Personate, v.a. *ṣūrat-, libās-, swāng-,* etc. *k.,* or *-ākhistal* or *-joṛawul.*
Perspiration, s. *khwala.*
Perspire, v.n. *khwale ked.*
Persuade, v.a. *rāwustal, raẓā k., tasallī,* etc. *warkawul; lamsawul; ma-ilān-,* etc. *k.*
Persuasion, s. *tasallī, dilāsa; targhīb, lamsūn.*
Pert, a. *shokh, wītak, be-makh, be-adab.*
Pertinacious, a. *ḥujjatī, takrārī, hoḍai, ṭakanrai.*
Pertinent, a. *joṛ, munāsib, wājib, jukht, lā-iq.*
Perturbation, s. *nā-qalār-tiyā, wiswās; gram.*
Perusal, s. *lwustana; katana, mulāḥiẓa.*
Peruse, v.a. *lwustal; katal, naẓar-,* etc. *k.*
Pervade, v.n. *phelcdal, khwaredal, wīṛedal.*
Perverse, a. *hoḍai, khpul-sar, ṭakanrai, haṭ.*
Pervert, v.a. *girzawul, aṛawul, be-lār k.*
Pest, s. *balā, wabāl, janjāl; wabā.*
Pester, v.a. *tangawul, zoral, janjāl k.*
Pestiferous, a. *moẓī, muẓirr, ziyān-kār*
Pestilence, s. *wabā, tāwūn* or *ṭa'ūn.*
Pestle, s. *molai, pāeko, hokla-ī.*
Pet, s. *marawar-tiyā, mānrai; mayana.*
Petition, v.a. *'arẓ-, sawāl-, darkhwāst-,* etc. *k.,* or *-laral,* or *-ghokkhtal; 'arẓī āchawul.*
Pettish, a. *khapah, mānrī-gar, marawar.*
Petty, a. *woṛ, kachoṭai; spuk, nā-tsīz.*
Petulant, a. *shokh, be-adab; wītak, chūnkai.*
Pewter, s. *qal'a-ī, jas.*
Phalanx, s. *palṭan, ghol, ṭol, paṛk, tamba.*
Phantom, s. *wahm, khiyāl, siwrai; rawai.*
Phenomenon, s. *awtsār; 'ajab-kār* or *-chal.*
Phial, s. *kkhīkkha.*
Philanthropist, s. *khair-khwāh, insān-dost.*
Philology, s. *'ilm da ṣarf-o-naḥw.*
Philosopher, s. *ḥakīm, ṣūfī, 'ālim, failsūf.*
Philosopher's stone, s. *kīmiyā, aksīr, pāras.*
Philosophy, s. *'ilm da maujūdāt.*
Philter, s. *ṭoṭka, t'awīz, mantar.*
Phlegm, s. *balgham, khrāshkai, grolbai.*
Phlegmatic, a. *balghamī, soṛ-mizāj.*
Phlogistic, a. *khushk, wuch, tod, garm.*
Phœnix, s. *'unqāe, humāe, quqnūs.*
Phrase, s. *khabara, wayai; lughat, 'ibārat.*
Phraseology, s. *'ibārat, maḥāwara.*
Phthisis, s. *narai-randz, diqq, sill.*
Physic, s. *dawā, dārū, darmān.* (science) *ṭibb.* (practice) *ṭibābat, ṭabībī.*
Physical, a. *ẓātī, jibillī, ṭaba'ī.*
Physician, s. *ṭabīb, ḥakīm.*
Physics, s. *'ilm da maujūdāt, ḥikmat.*
Pick, v.a. (pluck) *shūkawul, laṭawul, ṭolawul.* (select) *chunral, anrawul, chīndah k., khwakkhawul.* (-up) *ākhistal, porta k.* (teeth, etc.) *ṭunbal.* (-knot, etc.) *spaṛdal, prānatal.* (-a quarrel) *gwākkhal, gwākkhedal.*
Pickaxe, s. *kodāla-i, kaha-ī.*
Pickle, s. *āchār.*
Pickpocket, s. *gan-kap, uchakkah-ghal.*
Picture, s. *tswra, taṣwīr, nakhkkha, ṣūrat.*
Piebald, a. *ablaq, chrag-brag, brag-yālai.*
Piece, s. *ṭoṭa, reza, ṭūk.* (patch) *ṭūkai, pīna, marlūra.* (land) *paṭai, wanḍ.* (joint) *joṛ, pewand.*
Piecemeal, a. *biyal, judā, yo-yo.* ad. *ṭoteṭoṭe, chūr-chūr, daṛ-daṛ.*
Pier, s. *pushta, band; pāya, stan.*
Pierce, v.a. *sūrai k., sīkhal, tetsal, zanal, tsarkh k.; orc-porc-, pore-rāpore-,* etc. *bāsal—yastal.*
Piety, s. *taqwā, zuhd, dīn-dārī, īmān-dārī.*
Pig, s. *kharbishoe, kharbishkatai, sarkūzai.* (-of iron) *sala.*
Pigeon, s. *kauntar,* or *kotar,* or *kawtar.*
Pigmy, s. *lweshtīnak, chūnai, potai.*
Pike, s. *neza, balla, barcha, shalgai.*

Pile, s. ḍera-ī, kat, ṭop, rashaka; mogai.
Pile, v.a. ḍera-ī-, tūda-, dalai-, rāsha-, etc. k.
Piles, s. baṙāsīr, maṙekkhī.
Pilfer, v.a. puṭaṙul, ghlā k.
Pilgrim, s. ḥājī, ḥajj kaṙūnkai, ziyārat kaṙūnkai.
Pilgrimage, s. ḥajj, ziyārat.
Pill, s. gola-ī, mardakai.
Pillage, s. lūṭ, tālān, tākht-o-tārāj, chaṙr.
Pillage, v.n. lūṭaṙul, lūṭal, natal, nūtāraṙul.
Pillar, s. stan; tsalai.
Pillory, s. shikanja, kāṭ, tsarkh.
Pillow, s. bālakkht, takiya. (small-)bālakkht-goṭai.
Pimp, s. baṛwā, dallal, dahūs.
Pimple, s. nanaka-ī, dāna. (on face) dzṙānaka.
Pin, s. stan; salā-ī.
Pincers, s. ambūr. (small) nūtsai.
Pinch, s. skūnḍāra; pūṭai, pitsāṉrai, chūndai.
Pinch, v.a. skūnḍal or tskūnḍal.
Pine, s. nakkhtar, sanobar. (-torch) shonṭa-ī.
Pine, v.n. kaṛedal, nūledal, dzaṙredal, ghamedal, pakhsedal, zahīredal, zahedal.
Pinion, s. ṙazar, tsāng; baṉra, kkhāh-par. (fetter) dzolana, kara-ī.
Pinion, v.a. sūṭ-būṭ taṛal.
Pinnacle, s. tsūka, peza, sar; kangūra.
Pioneer, s. bel-dār.
Pious, a. taqṙā-, īmān-, dīn-, etc. -dār, or -larūnkai, nmāndzī, nmūndz kaṙūnkai, or -guzār.
Pipe, s. shpela-ī, nala. v.a. shpela-ī ghagaṙul.
Pique, s. māṉrai, maraṙar-tiyā, khṙā-badī, zṛeh-badāṙai.
Piss, v.a. baul-, ṙāṛa baul-, mutiyāze-, etc. k.
Pistol, s. tamāncha.
Pit, s. ḍoghal, ṭublai, jwar-ghālai. v.a. jangaṙul.
Pitch, s. rūndzaṛah. (degree) ḥadd, nobat.
Pitch, v.a. ṙudraṙul, ṙalāṛaṙul, khcjaṙul.
(cast) āchaṙul, ṙīshtal, laṙastal, ghurz-aṙul.
Pitcher, s. loṭkai, mangai, maṭ, maṭkai.
Pitchfork, s. kkhākha-ī, dre-kkhākha-ī, sānga-ī.
Pith, s. māghzah, zaṛai.
Pitiful, a. khṙā-khūgai. (paltry) spuk.
Pitiless, a. be-dard, be-raḥm.
Pittance, s. ṭukṛa, nṙaṛa-ī, rozī.
Pity, s. zṛah-sṙai, khṙā-khūgī, dard, raḥm, gham; afsos, daregh.
Pivot, s. tīrak, salā-ī; ḍīḍa, khulborai.
Place, s. dzāe, zmaka, makān. (stead) 'iṙaz, badal. (rank) pāya, martaba. (office) 'ukda. (residence) astoga, meshta.
Place, v.a. gdal or īgdal, yakkhodal, yakkhal, yakkhaṙul, kegdal or kkhkegdal, kekkhodal, etc.
Placenta, s. preṙān.
Placid, a. khog, narm, pos or post.
Plague, s. ṙabā, tāṙūn; āfat, balā; ṙabāl; janjāl. v.a. rabṛaṙul, āzāraṙul, pa balā ākhtak k.
Plain, a. sam, hawār, barābar, sat. (simple) sādah, ṣāf, spīn. (unmixed) torai, spor; karah, sūchah. s. maidān, sama.
Plainly, ad. spīn, ṣāf, rikkhtiyā.
Plaint, s. gila, māna, māṉrai; faryād, ṙāṙailā.
Plaintiff, s. mudda'ī, faryādī.
Plaintive, a. gila-man, māṉrī-gar, māna kaṙūnkai.
Plait, s. tā, taha, ṙal, bragh; jūhaṛa, kraṭai, gundza, chīchaṛ. v.a. odal; āgayal, chunṛal.
Plan, s. tadbīr, ḥikmat, band, chal; nakhkkha or naqsha, namūna. v.a. joṛaṙul, band taṛal, chal k.
Plane, s. randa. (-tree) chinār.
Plane, v.a. togal, khrayal or khriyal, randa k.
Planet, s. storai.
Plank, s. takhta.

Plant, s. *būṭai, ḍakai.*

Plant, v.a. *lagawul, khakkhawul; wudrawul, lakawul, walāṛawul.*

Plantain. s. *kela.* (herb-) *isapghol* or *spaghol.*

Plantation, s. *jangai, banr.*

Plaster, s. *lew, akhāṛah, gach, khaṭa; malham, paha, tab, ẓamād.* v.a. *lewawul, akheral, tapal, khaṭa k.*

Plat, s. (-of ground) *paṭai, pāṛa, ḍaga.*

Plate, s. *rikeba-ī, raghai, bishqāb.* (-of iron for baking on) *tabakhai, teghna.* (earthen ditto) *taba-ī.*

Plated, a. *mulamma.*

Platform, s. *dūnkācha, garwanj; manah.*

Platter, s. *kkhānak, taghārai, tabakhai, tālai.*

Plaudit, s. *shābbāshī, āparīn.*

Plausible, a. *khog-khulai, chalwalai, khula-war.*

Play, s. *loba, bāzī; nandāra, tamāsha; jūārī.*

Play, v.a. *lobe k.* (gamble) *jūārī k.* (-the fool) *malande k.* (act) *pekkhe k.* (music) *sarod-, tarāne-,* etc. *ghagawul.* (in comp.) *-kawul, -kṛal.*

Playfellow, s. *hum-dzolai.*

Playful, a. *mast, shokhīn.*

Plaything, s. *da lobe kālai.*

Plea, s. *ḥujjat, dalīl, 'uẓr, d'awa, hira-ī.*

Plead, v.a. *wayal, lal, lawdal, 'uẓr-,* etc. *k.*

Pleasant, a. *khwand-nāk, kkhah.*

Pleasantness, s. *khwand, maza, kkhādī.*

Pleasantry, s. *khandā, washta, ṭoqa.*

Please, v.a. *rāẓī-, khwakkh-, kkhād-,* etc. *k.*; *khwand warkawul.*

Pleased, a. *khwakkh, khūsh-ḥāl, kkhād, kkhād-man.*

Pleasure, s. *khwakkhī, kkhādī, khūsh-ḥālī, khwand.* (will) *raẓā, marẓī.* (spiteful-) *sakha, wiyāṛ.*

Plebeian, a. *'āmm, adnā, kam-ẓāt.* s. *'āmmī.*

Pledge, s. *graw, gānra.* (word) *wāda, lafẓ, bandaur, taṛa.* (token) *nakkha, yād-gār.*

Pleiades, s. *perūne, jambaq storī.*

Plenary, a. *pūrah, tamām, amānī*

Plenipotentiary, s. *kul mukhtār, wāk-dār.*

Plenitude, s. *pūrah-wālai; ḍer-wālai.*

Plentiful, a. *ḍer, ziyāt, prewān, wadān.*

Plenty, s. *ḍer-wālai, prewānī, ziyāt-wālai, abādī, wadānī.*

Pliable, / **Pliant**, } a. *narm, post, mulā-im.*

Plight, s. *ḥāl, ḥālat, chal.* v.a. *graw-, gānra-,* etc. *k.*; *wāda-, neṭa-, lafẓ-,* etc. *taṛal.*

Plod, v.a. *miḥnat-, kokshiksh-,* etc. *k.* v.n. *ṭaparedal.*

Plot, s. *band, sāzish, joṛikkht.* (-of land) *paṭai, wanḍ.* (stratagem) *chal, lamghaṛa-ī.*

Plot, v.a. *joṛawul, band taṛal, sāzish-,* etc. *k.*

Plough, s. *yiwa* or *īwa, yoya, qulba* or *yiwe.* v.a. *īwe* or *yiwe k.*

Ploughshare, s. *pāla, saspār, spāra.*

Plover, s. *ṭīṭārai.*

Pluck, v.a. *shūkawul.* (-out) *kāgal—kkhkal, bāsal—yastal.*

Plug, s. *būja, shoṛa, mūnrai, ḍīḍa, khulborai.*

Plum, s. *bera, bada bera, sāwū bera, makhranai.*

Plumage, s. *banre, wazar.*

Plume, s. *zundai.* (-head) *qarqara.*

Plume, v.a. *banre joṛawul, dzān joṛawul.*

Plummet, s. *sahūl, chāwul.*

Plump, a. *tsorb, chāẖ, ghaṭ, punḍ.*

Plunder, v.n. *lūṭ-, tālā-, nātār-,* etc. *k., natal.*

Plunge, v.a. *ḍūbkai-, ghoṭa-, ghūpa-,* etc. *warkawul* or *-wahal* or *-khwural.*

Plural, a. *jam'a.*

Ply, s. *tā, bragh, chūnra, chīchar, gundza.*

Ply, v.a. *chalawul, lagawul, kawul, kṛal.*

Pocket, s. *jeb; kīsa, dzola-ī.*

Pock-mark, s. *ta-ap, ta-apai.*

Pod, s. *palai, ghoza.*

Poem, s. *ghazal, chār bait, sandara.*

Poet, s. *shā'ir, qaṣīda, goe, sandar goe.*
Poetry, s. *sh'ir, bait, naẓm.*
Poignant, a. *tez, tund, sakht.*
Point, s. *peza, tsūka, sar.* (dot) *ṭakai, dāna, nuqta.* (spot) *dāgh, tsirīka, laka.*
Point, v.a. *terah k., peza-,* etc. *joṛawul; naẓar lagawul.* (-out) *kkhayal—kkhowul.*
Pointed, a. *peza-dār* or *-larūnkai.*
Poise, v.a. *talal, jokal, barābarawul.*
Poison, s. *zahr.* v.a. *zahr warkawul.*
Poisonous, a. *zahr-nāk.*
Poke, v.a. *negh wahal; laṭawul.*
Poker, s. (fire-) *or laṛūnai.* (goad) *chūka.*
Pole, s. *lakaṛa.* (barge-) *bala-ī.* (balance-) *ḍānḍa-ī.* (North-) *quṭb.* (-star) *da quṭb storai.*
Police, s. *band-o-bast, intiẓām.* (superintendent of-) *koṭwal.* (-office) *tānra.* (-man) *tsoka-ī dār.*
Policy, s. *intiẓām, tadbīr, ḥikmat 'amalī.*
Polish, v.a. *mugal—mukkhal, togal, ṣaiqal k.*
Polite, a. *makhawar, sulūkī, mihrbān; dilbārī.*
Politeness, s. *makh, makhawarī, sulūk.*
Politic, a. *ḥikmatī, tadbīrī.*
Political, a. *mulkī; 'amalī, tadbīrī.*
Politician, s. *tadbīrī, jirgatū.*
Politics, s. *tadbīr da mulk* or *-salṭanat,* etc.
Poll, s. *sar, koṭai.* (-tax) *jiziya.* v.a. *land-, ghūṭ-,* etc. *prekawul.*
Pollute, v.a. *nā-pāk-, palīt-, murdār-, kakaṛ-,* etc. *k.* (-oneself) *mūṭak wahal.* (-oneself in sleep) *āwdas awukkhtal, shaiṭān khaṭā k.*
Pollution, s. *nā-pākī, palītī,* etc.; *shaiṭānī khaṭā.*
Polytheism, s. *but parastī, shirk.*
Polytheist, s. *but parast, mushrik.*
Pomegranate, s. *anangai, anangūṛai, anār.* (wild-) *narsiwai.*
Pommel, v.a. *wahal, ṭakawul, kūṭal.*
Pomp, s. *dabdaba, tamtarāq, sāmāna.*
Pompous, a. *khāntamā, sar hawā.*
Pond, s. *ḍanḍ, nāwar, wasta, wangara.*
Ponder, v.a. *fikr-, ghaur-,* etc. *k.*
Ponderous, a. *drūnd, grān.*
Pony, s. *ṭaṭū, yābū.*
Pool, s. *ḍanḍūkai; ḍab, kol.*
Poor, a. *khwār, gharīb, muflis, nā-kas*
Poorly, a. *nājoṛ, nārogh, bīmār.* ad. *nīmgaṛai.*
Pop, s. *ṭas, ṭak, ḍaz, ṭar,* etc. v.a. *ṭas-,* etc. *wahal.*
Poppy, s. *koknār, khāsh khāsh.* (wild-) *redai.*
Populace, s. *ulus, 'āmmiyān, 'awām.*
Popular, a. *'āmm, jārī, chalanī, riwāj.*
Population, s. *ābādī, wadānī; 'ālam, khalq, ulus.*
Populous, a. *ābād, wadān.*
Porch, s. *manḍaw, dahlīz.*
Porcupine, s. *shkūnr.*
Pore, s. (-of the skin) *ghūna.* (to roughen or erect the-) v.n. *ghūna zīgedal.* (aperture) *sūṛa.*
Pore, v.a. *lagiyā katal* or *-goral—līdal, dzīr k.*
Porous, a. *sūṛa-war.*
Porpoise, s. *tsūtsa, sūs.*
Port, s. *bandar.* (door) *war, darwāza.* (mien) *yūn, chāl.* (aperture) *darbacha, karka-ī.*
Portable, a. *spuk, kalak, da wṛalo.*
Portal, s. *darwāza, āstāna.*
Portend, v.a. *dalīl k., āgāhī k., pāl kkhayal—kkhowul.*
Portent, s. *dalīl, āgāhī, pāl* or *fāl; bad fāl, bad shugun.*
Porter, s. *ḥammāl, mazdūr.* (gate-) *darwāzawān, ghāw-chī.*
Portico, s. *manḍaw, dahlīz, jilau khāna.*
Portion, s. *brakha, ḥiṣṣa, wesh, wanḍ, qismat.*
Portly, a. *ghaṭ, juṣṣa-war, jasīm, khrīs, gagar, star.*

Portmanteau, s. khurjīn, yakhdān, rakht·dān, dzola-ī, gūdai.

Portrait, s. tsera, taṣwīr, ṣūrat.

Pose, v.a. pa-aṛ k., lā dzawāb k., hariyānawul.

Position, s. shān, wajha, ḥāl, ṣūrat.

Positive, a. yaqīn, qaṭaʻī, be·shakk, be·shubha. (stubborn) khpul rāe, khpul·sar. (real) aṣlī, sūchah.

Possess, v.a. laral, darlal.

Possession, s. qābū, qabẓa. (to take-) v.a. qābū-, etc. k., khpulawul, ākhistal, lānde k. (to give-) bakkhal or bakhkkhal, warkawul, kkhandal.

Possessor, s. meṛah, tsakkhtan, mālik, khāwand. (in comp.) -larūnkai, -dār, -man, -war, etc.

Possibility, s. imkān, kedana, shwah.

Possible, a. mumkin, shwūnkai, kedūnkai. (to be-) v.a. imkān laral, shwal.

Possibly, ad. gunde, kkhā-ī, bā-īda, wī ba.

Post, s. (office) kār, khidmat, ʻuhda. (station) dzāe, makān. (military-) tsoka-ī, tānra. (pillar) stan, tsalai. (mail-) ḍāk. (-man) qāṣid, ḍāk·wālā. (express-) chapar.

Post, v.a. (station) wudrawul, kkhkenawul, -walāṛawul.

Posterior, a. wrustai, wrustanai, pastanai.

Posteriors, s. kūnāṭī.

Posterity, s. alwād, zurriyāt, nasl. (to the latest-) naslan bʻad nasl.

Postpone, v.a. drang-, lārghah-, multawī-, etc. k., muʻaṭṭal-, barkhwāst-, nāgha-. etc. k.

Postscript, s. tatimma.

Posture, s. shān, wajha, ṣūrat, ṭaur.

Pot, s. lokkhai. (metal-) kaṛahai, deg, dechka. khumra-ī. (earthen-) hānḍa-ī, kaṭwa-ī, kawdīk. (water-) mangai, maṭkai, loṭkai. (-lid) barghəlai, sar·pokkh. (-herb) sāg, sabzī, wākkhah.

Potato, s. ālū.

Potent, a. zorāwar, mazbūṭ, quwat·nāk, tuwānā.

Potentate, s. bādshāh, amīr, sardār, malik.

Potion, s. sharbat, nosh, tskkhāk or skāk.

Potsherd, s. kaudai, kaudarai.

Pottage, s. sāgīnrai, sāg, āsh. (-of meat, etc.) qatagh, ngolai, sālan.

Potter, s. kulāl, kumhār.

Pottery, s. kaṭwa-ī lokkhai. (glazed-) kāshīn.

Pouch, s. jeb, kīsa; dzola-ī, bana-ī, gūdai· toshdān.

Poultice, s. leṭa-ī, paha, tab.

Poultry, s. chirg, chirgūṛī.

Pounce, v.a. pa panjo wahal.

Pound, s. nīm ser.

Pound, v.a. ṭakawul, kūṭal, dzabal, dar daṛ-, chūr chūr-, etc. k.

Pour, v.a. toyawul, āchawul. (-out) sandzal. (-as rain) v.n. oredal, tsātsedal. (-over) v.n. toyedal or to-edal.

Pout, v.a. būṭ ūrbūz nīwul.

Poverty, s. khwārī, tabākī, muplisī, iplās, tangsiyā or tangsa.

Powder, s. oṛah, maidah, chūr. (gun-) dārū. (-horn) kkhkar. (medicine) paka, kapa, kharpaṭ.

Powder, v.a. oṛawul, maidah-, oṛeh-, etc. k. (dust) bornah k.

Power, s. zor, quwat; was, ṭāqat; tuwān, bram. (authority) wāk, majāl, ikhtiyār, ḥukm. (possession) qābū, qabẓa.

Powerful, a. zorāwar, tuwānā, mazbūṭ, zabardast.

Pox, s. bād-i farang, garmī, juẓām. (small-) nanaka-ī.

Practicable, a. shwūnkai, mumkin, da kawulo.

Practical, a. ʻamalī, istʻimālī, kṛūnai.

Practice, s. ʻādat, ʻamal, yūn, dastūr, chāl chal.

Practise, v.a. kawul, ʻādat-, etc. k., mashq k.

Praise, s. stāyana, ṣanā, ṣifat, tʻarīf. v.a. stāyal, stāyana, etc. wayal or k.

Prance, v.a. *trapal, ṭop wahal, khharmastī k., tsk͟he k.*

Prank, s. *khharmastī, ṭel ṭāl, laṭah per.*

Pray, v.a. *nmūndz k.*, or *-guzāral; du'a-, minnat-*, etc. *k., darkhwāst k., ghokkhtal.*

Prayer, s. *nmūndz; du'ā.* (-for Lent) *tarāwe.*

Preach, v.a. *w'az k.; khutba lwustal.*

Preamble, s. *debācha, muqadamma.*

Precarious, a. *nā-pāedār, teredūnai, zawālī.*

Precaution, s. *dūr-andeshī, wṛānde katana.*

Precede, v.n. *wṛānde tlal.*

Precedent, a. *wṛāndīnai.* s. *misāl, nakkha.*

Preceding, a. *pakhwānai, wṛūnbanai.*

Precept, s. *matal, misāl; ḥukm, kariya; pand, naṣīḥat.*

Preceptor, s. *ākhūn, ustāz; nāṣiḥ, pand warkawūnkai.*

Precinct, s. *ḥadd, pūla, brīd.*

Precious, a. *qīmat-nāk, grān-bahā, matrah: 'azīz.*

Precipice, s. *kamar, kanda, gaṛang, tāk.*

Precipitate, a. *jalt, tez, jalt-bāz, talwār-gandai, talwalai, haṛbaṛai.*

Precipitate, v.a. *āchawul, wīshtal, ghurzawul, lawastal; dangawul; jaltī-, ṭalwār-, z-ir-* or *za-ar-*, etc. *k.* v.n. *ghurzedal, prewatal, kkhkenāstal.*

Precipitation, s. *jaltī, talwār, be-ṣabrī.*

Precise, a. *jukht, drust, joṛ, pūrah.*

Precisely, ad. *jukht, joṛ, rikkhtiyā, bedū.*

Precision, s. *barābar-wālai, jukht-wālai, taḥqīq.*

Preclude, v.a. *man'a-, band-, pore jane-*, etc. *k., stanawul, sharal.*

Precursor, s. } *peshrau, wṛānde tlūnai.*
Predecessor, s. }

Predestination, s. *taqdīr, qazā.*

Predicament, s. *ḥāl; nobat, chal.*

Predicate, s. *khabar, ṣifat, m'aqūl.*

Predict, v.a. *pesh khabarī-, khabar da ghā-ib-*, etc. *wayal, fāl wīcul, fāl katana k.*

Predominate, v.n. *ghālib-, ghalaba-, ziyāt-, ganṛ-, ḍer-*, etc. *ked.*

Preface, s. *debācha, muqadama.*

Prefer, v.a. *khwakkhawul, ghwarah k., kkhak ganṛal, kkhāghal: sar buland-, sar farāz-, sar bālā*, etc. *k.*

Preferable, a. *ghwarah, kkhak.*

Preference, s. *khwakkh; mrasta.*

Preferment, s. *sar farāzī, pāya pa porta.*

Prefix, v.a. *wṛānde-, pa makh-*, etc. *lagawul.*

Pregnant, a. *brūlba* or *blārba, ḍaka, warla, shigāra, bār-dāra.* (full) *ḍak, pūrah.* (to make-) v.a. *blārba-*, etc. *k.*

Prejudice, s. *ṭarafdārī, mrasta; mīna, khwā, mā-ilān; bad gumānī, khwā badāwai; tāwān, ziyān.*

Prejudicial, a. *tāwānī, ziyānī, nuqṣānī, bad, muẓirr.*

Prelate, s. *imām, mujtahid.*

Preliminary, a. *wṛūnbanai, awwalanai.*

Premature, a. *be-wakht, be-ṭūng; nīma khwā, kachandai, nīmgaṛai.*

Premeditate, v.a. *pesh fikrī-, pesh bandī-*, etc. *k.; qaṣd-, niyat-*, etc. *taṛal* or *k.*

Premier, a. *mashar.* s. *wazīr; sarghanah.*

Premium, s. *sūd, naf'a; in'ām, bakhkshiksh; shukrāna, muzd.*

Preparation, s. *tayārī, dzerma, tadbīr.*

Prepare, v.a. *tayārī-*, etc. *k., joṛawul, tayārawul.*

Preponderate, v.n. *dranedal, drūnd ked., ziyātedal, ḍeredal.*

Preponderation, s. *dranāwai, ḍer-wālai*, etc.

Preposition, s. *ḥarf.*

Prepossess, v.a. *mayan-, mā-ilān-*, etc. *k.*

Prepossession, s. *mayan-tob, mīna.*

Preposterous, a. *be-hūdah, abtar, wuch pūch; naskor, aṛawulai.*

Prepuce, s. *chichaṛa, da tsūkkha-ī tsarman*

Prerogative, s. *ḥaqq, wāk, ikhtiyār*

Presage, s. *pāl, dalālat, āgūhī, nakkha.*

Prescience, s. *khabar da ghā-ib, ghā-ib·dānī.*

Prescribe, v.a. *nayal, farmāyal, ḥukm k., kkhayal—kkhowul.* (medically) *nuskha likal, -kāgal—kkhkal.* (fix) *taṛal, muqarrar k.*

Presence, s. *ḥuẓūr, khidmat.* (-of mind) *baidārī, ausān, hokkhyār·tiyā.*

Present, a. *ḥāẓir, maujūd; osan, osanai.* (at-) ad. *dā sā'at, os.* s. *bakhkshiksh, naẕr, pekkhkakkh, nazrāna, shukrāna.*

Present, v.a. *bakhkkhal* or *bakkhal, kkhandal, warkawul.* (show) *bartser-, kkhkārah-, ẕāhir-,* etc. *k.* (-a gun) *naẕar lagawul.* (introduce) *pekkhawul, wṛānde-, makhā makh-,* etc. *k.*

Presently, ad. *os, dasṭı, pa de sā'at.*

Preservation, s. *sātana, ĵghorana, khundī·tob, bachawūna.*

Preservative, a. *sātūnai, sātandoe, ĵghorai, bachawūnkai.*

Preserve, v.a. *sātal, ĵghoral, khundiyal, khundī k., bachawul.*

Preserver, s. *sātandoe, ĵghorai, khundī·kawūnkai, bachawūnkai.*

Preside, v.a. *sardārī-, mīr majlisī-, masharī·tob-,* etc. *k.*

President, s. *sardār, mashar; mīr majlis.*

Press, v.a. (squeeze) *nachoṛawul, paz wahal, nakkhtedzal.* (-down) *drabal.* (-into) *kkhke·manḍal.* (knead the limbs) *manḍal.* (urge) *zoral, tezal.* (vex) *tangawul, dabawul.* (-to the bosom) *bargaṛandī k.*

Press, s. (oil-) *gāṇṛa-ī.* (book-) *shikanja.* (a crowd) *ḍala, gaṇṛ 'ālam.*

Pressure, s. *zor; bār; tangsiyā, grān·tiyā.*

Presume, v.a. *gauṛal, qiyās-, khiyāl-, gumān-,* etc. *k.; dam wahal, gustākhī k.*

Presumptuous, a. *kibr·ĵan, shokh, gustākh.*

Pretend, v.a. *bāna-, chal-, ḥīla-, lamghaṛa-ī-, tagī-, hira-ī-,* etc. *k.*

Pretender, s. *bāna·khor, chal·bāz.* (claimant) *d'awa·dār, mudda'ī.* (boaster) *lāpai.*

Pretension, s. *d'awa; ḥujjat.*

Preternatural, a. *karāmatī, zbarg.*

Pretext, s. *bāna, chal, hira-ī, palma, 'uẕr.*

Pretty, a. *kkhāyastah, kkhkulai, pej·makhai* or *pa-ī·makhai.* ad. *tsa la-ag* or *la-ag tsa, nijde.*

Prevail, v.a. *barai mūndal, lānde-, pa-aṛ-,* etc. *k.* v.n. *ziyātedal; jārī ked., chaledal.*

Prevalence, s. *zor, ziyātī, ghalba.*

Prevalent, a. *ziyāt; jārī; zorāwar, wa-aṛ; ghālib.*

Prevaricate, v.a. *palma-, hira-ī-, guzmuzai-,* etc. *k.*

Prevent, v.a. *man'a k., kariyābawul, haṭālawul, bandawul, āṛawul.*

Preventer, s. *mān'i, man'a kawūnkai.*

Prevention, s. *man'a, haṭāl, kariyāb, āṛ, band.*

Previous, a. *pukhwānai, wṛūnbanai, wṛāndīnai, awwalanai.*

Previously, ad. *pukhwā, wṛūnbe, wṛānde, qabl, awwal.*

Prey, s. *kkhkār, māta.* (booty) *lūṭ.* (beast of-) *dad, waḥsh.*

Price, s. *bai'a, baya, bahā, qīmat.* (-current) *nirkh.*

Prick, v.a. *tsekhal, sikhal, stan-, chūka-,* etc. *wahal, sūṛai k.*

Prickle, s. *āzghai* or *āghzai, khār.*

Prickly, a. *āzghan* or *āghzan.*

Pride, s. *kibr, mastī, wiyāṛ.* (proper-) *nang, ghairat.*

Priest, s. *imām, shekh, pīr, mullā*

Priestcraft, s. *mullā·tob.*

Priesthood, s. *imāmat, pīr khāna.*

Primarily, ad. *wṛūnbe, awwal.*

Primary, a. *wṛūnbanai, awwalanai.*

Prime, a. *awwal, aṣlī, khāṣṣ, sāwū, karah, sūchah.*

Prime, v.a. *ranjak āchawul.*

Primitive, a. *zor, pakhwānai, awwalanai*; *aṣlī, zātī*.
Primogeniture, s. *mashar-tob, loe-wālai, loyat*.
Prince, s. *shāh-zādah, malik*.
Princess, s. *shāh-zāda-ī, malika*.
Principal, a. *mashar, awwal, sardār*; *sar, loe, ghaṭ*. s. *panga, saga, māya, aṣl*; *sardār, sar, sarghanah, mashar*.
Principality, s. *ṣūba, rāj, qalam-rau*.
Principally, ad. *akṣar, awwalan, khuṣūṣan*.
Principle, s. *aṣl, awwal sabab, jauhar*; *bā'iṣ, jihat*; *mazhab, dīn*; *qānūn, ā-īn*.
Print, v.a. *chāp k., chāpa wahal*.
Prior, a. *wṛūnbanai, wṛāndenai, pakhwānai, awwalanai*.
Priority, s. *awwaliyat, wṛāndīn-tob*.
Prison, s. *qaid-* or *bandī khāna, zindān*.
Prisoner, s. *qaidī, bandī, asīr*; *nazar-band*.
Privacy, s. *khilwat, parda, parda-pokkhī, puṭ-wālai, yawādzī-tob, biyal-wālai*.
Private, a. *puṭ, yawādzai, tanhā, tsaṛah, biyal*.
Privately, ad. *pa puṭa, pa parde*.
Privation, s. *nisht-wālai, nābūdī*.
Privilege, s. *ḥaqq*; *khalāṣī, āzādī*.
Privities, s. *ṣūrat, satr, tor-wekkhtah, andām nihānī, da sharm dzāe*.
Privy, a. *khabar-dār, baidār, wāqif, āgāh*. s. *chār-choba-ī, jāe-zarūr*.
Prize, s. *in'ām*; *bāzī, shart, daw*; *lūṭ, gaṭa, tālā*. (-fighter) *pahlawān*.
Prize, v.a. *kkhah-, 'azīz-, grān-*, etc. *ganṛal*.
Probability, s. *ṣūrat, shakl*; *kedana*.
Probable, a. *shwūnkai, kedūnkai*.
Probably, ad. *gunde, kkhā-ī, wī ba* or *ba wī*.
Probation, s. *āzmekkht*; *umed-wārī*.
Probationer, s. *umed-wār*.
Probe, v.a. *sīkh-, salā-ī-*, etc. *wahal, tsekhal, sīkhal, sūghawul*.
Probity, s. *nekī, rikkhtīn-tob, rāstī*.
Problem, s. *masla, sawāl*.
Problematical, a. *shakk-man, shakkī*.
Proboscis, s. *khartam* or *khartūm, sūndak*.
Proceed, v.n. *tlal—lāṛal, chaledal, rawānedal, drūmedal, teredal*; *watal, paidā ked*. v.a. *kawul, kṛal*.
Proceeding, s. *kār, kṛah, 'amal, mu'amala, chal*.
Proceeds, s. *gaṭa, sūd, paidā-ikkht*.
Process, s. *tarkīb, chalan, shān, ṭaur, rang*; *jagṛa, mu'amala, muqadamma*.
Procession, s. *swarlī*; *tamāsha*.
Proclaim, v.a. *munādī k., ḍamāme-, jār-*, etc. *wahal, mashhūr-, jārī-*, etc. *k*.
Procrastinate, v.a. *drangī-, dzanḍ-, lārghah-, multawī-*, etc. *k*.
Procreate, v.a. *zegawul, rāwṛal, paidā k*.
Procurable, a. *muyassar, da mūndalo, da paidā kawulo, mūndūnai*.
Procure, v.a. *mūndal, paidā k., rāwṛal, rasawul*.
Procurer, s. *dallāl, rebār*.
Prodigal, a. *khartsī, iṣrāfī, tāwān kawūnkai*.
Prodigality, s. *kharts, tāwān, iṣrāf, chakhṛaba*.
Prodigious, a. *'ajīb, 'azīm, loe, ghaṭ, nāpaṛ*.
Prodigy, s. *'ajab, shanda*; *subḥān allah*.
Produce, v.a. *rāwṛal, paidā k*.
Produce, s. *ḥāṣil, paidā-ikkht*; *sūd, gaṭa, naf'a*.
Productive, a. *rāwṛūnkai, paidā kawūnkai*. (-land) *ghala-kheza, ghala-būda, zorāwara, lap-tsaṭa*. (-cattle) *paia-wara*. (-tree) *mewa-dāra*. (-animal) *zeganda-ī*.
Profane, v.a. *nāpāk-, palīt-, murdār-, bilmāz-*, etc. *k*.
Profane, a. *bilmāz, ḥarām, nā-rawā*, etc.
Profess, v.a. *manal, wayal, iqrār k., lal, lawdal*.
Professedly, ad. *pa tsargana, pa jār* or *ẓāhir*.
Profession, s. *iqrār, qaul*; *kār, kasb*.
Professor, s. *ustād, mullā, mu'allim*.

Proffer, v.a. *nazr-, nazrāna-, pekkhkakkh-*, etc. *warkawul*; *wrānde-, pekkh-*, etc. *k.*; *'uzr k.*

Proficient, a. *pokh, hokkhyār, kārī-gar, khabar-dār.*

Profile, s. *tratskan ṣūrat, tratskana tsihra.*

Profit, s. *sūd, gaṭa, kkhegaṛa, fā-ida, naf'a, būd.* v.a. *gaṭal, sūd-*, etc. *mundal*

Profitable, a. *sūd-man, fā-ida-man.*

Profligate, a. *lawanḍ, bad-kār, chaṭ, qachar.*

Profound, a. *jawar, star*; *ghaṭ, loe*; *narai, bārīk.*

Profundity, s. *jawar-tiyā, star-wālai*; *loeyat*, etc.

Profuse, a. *tāwānī, khartsī*; *ḍer, frewān, wadān.*

Profusion, s. *tāwān, kharts*; *frewānī, wadānī*, etc.

Progenitor, s. *nīkah, plār-nīkah.*

Progeny, s. *awlād, zānzād, farzand, nasl, tūng.*

Prognostic, s. *nakkha, 'alāmat, dalīl.*

Prognosticate, v.a. *pesh khabarī k., fāl katal.*

Progress, v.n. *tlal—lāṛal, chaledal, rawānedal.* s. *tlana, chalan, rawānagī.*

Progression, s. *chāl, tah, yūn, raftār.*

Progressive, a. *chaland, rawān.*

Prohibit, v.a. *man'a-, qadaghan-, kariya-*, etc. *k.*

Project, s. *tadbīr, band, ḥikmat, tajwīz.*

Projection, s. *tsūka, peza*; *ghunḍa*; *pāṛsob.*

Prolapsus ani, s. *būṛa-ī, watana da kulme.*

Prolific, a. *zeganda-ī*; *mewa-dāra*: *tukhmreza.*

Prolix, a. *ūgd, ṭūland* or *tūlānd.*

Prolong, v.a. *ūgdawul, ṭūl k.*; *ziyātawul.*

Prominent, a. *ūchat, khatalai*; *tsargand, kkhkārah.*

Promiscuous, a. *gaḍ waḍ, laṛalai, argajah.*

Promise, s. *wāda, lafz, qaul, bandanr, oe, wela.* v.a. *wāda-*, etc. *taṛal* or *k.*

Promising, a. *shwūnai, kkhah, nek-bakht, kkhāyastah, joṛ.*

Promissory, a. *sharṭī, qarārī.* (-note) *tamassuk.*

Promontory, s. *khatalī zmaka, peza, sar.*

Promote, v.a. *ziyātawul, khejawul*; *sar farāz-, sar buland-, pāya pa porta-*, etc. *k.*

Promotion, s. *sar farāzī, sar bulandī.*

Prompt, a. *chust, chālāk, tayār, gaṛandai.*

Prompt, v.a. *kkhayal—kkhowul*; *yād warkawul*; *lamsawul.*

Promptitude, s. *chālākī, chustī, tayārī.*

Promulgate, v.a. *munādī k., ḍamāme-, jār-*, etc. *wahal, mashhūr k.*

Prone, a. *pa-aṛ-makh*; *prot*; *ṭīṭ*; *mā-ilān, tayār.*

Prong, s. *kkhākha-ī, dwa kkhākha-ī.*

Pronoun, s. *zamīr.*

Pronounce, v.a. *wayal*; *ḥukm-, fatwā-*, etc. *k.*

Proof, s. *dalīl, ḥujjat, zbād* or *isbāt.* a *āzmayalai, pokh, āzmūdah.*

Prop, s. *pusht, pushtībān, aṛam, aṛamkai.*

Propagate, v.a. *zegawul, paidā-, jārī-*, etc. *k.*

Propel, v.a. *zghalawul, chalawul, rawānawul*; *āchawul, wīshtal, ghurzawul.*

Propensity, s. *shauq, raghbat, khwā, mīna, mā-il.*

Proper, a. *khāṣṣ*; *rawā*; *kkhah, kkhāyastah, joṛ, wājib, munāsib, pīrzo, drust.*

Properly, ad. *aṣlan* or *pa aṣl*; *pa kkhah shān sara, pa rikkhtiyā.*

Property, s. *māl, milk*; *khoe, khaṣlat, lokkhai, khāṣṣiyat, ṣifat.*

Prophecy, s. *ghā-ib go-ī, da ghā-ib khabara.* v.a. *ghā-ib wayal, da ghā-ib khabarawul.*

Prophet, s. *paighāmbar, nabī, rasūl.*

Propitiate, v.a. *khwā saṛawul* or *-kkhah k., mihrbān k., pakhulā k.*; *kafārat-, ṣadqa-, qurbān-*, etc. *k.*

Propitious, a. *mubārak, nek, mihrbān.*

Proportion, s. *brakha, andāza, qadr, wesh.* v.a. *barābar-*, etc. *k.*, *samawul*; *weshal.*

Propose, v.a. *'arz-, sawāl-, darkhwāst-*, etc. *k.*; *tapos* or *tapahus-, pukkhtina-*, etc. *k.*

Proprietor, s. *merah, tsakkhtan, khāwand, mālik, nāyik.*

Propriety, s. *kkhāyast·wālai, drust·wālai, nek chalan, munāsibat, lā-iqat, pīrzo·wālai.*

Prorogue, v.a. *barkhwāst-, mauqūf-, nāgha-*, etc. *k.*

Prose, s. *nasr.* (-writer) *nasr nawīs.*

Prosecute, v.a. *chalawul, kawul, lagiyā k.* v.n. *lagedal, mashghūledal, lagiyā osedal.* (sue) v.a. *d'awa-, faryād-*, etc. *k.*, *ghāra-, grewa-*, etc. *nīwul.* v.n. *pase prewatal, pase lagedal.*

Prosecutor, s. *mudda'-ī, laman-, ghara-*, etc. *nīwūnkai, d'awa-*, etc. *kawūnkai.*

Proselyte, s. *murīd, m'utaqid.*

Prospect, s. *nandāra, līdah, nazar.* (likelihood) *ṣūrat.* (hope) *umed.*

Prosper, v.n. *barakatī-, bakhtawar-*, etc. *osedal* or *-ked.*; *wadānedal, ābādedal, maredal.*

Prosperity, s. *barakat, bakht, nek bakhtī*; *ābādī, wadānī, mor·tiyā.*

Prosperous, a. *barakatī, iqbāl·man, sa'ādat·man, bakhtawar*; *mor, ābād, wadān.*

Prostitute, s. *kachna-ī, lola-ī.*

Prostitution, s. *kachna-ī·tob, lola-ī·tob.*

Prostrate, a. *pa-armakh, prot.* v.n. *pa-armakh prewatal.* v.a. *sijda k.*; *narawul, ghuzārawul*; *parzawul.*

Prostration, s. *pa-armakh·tob*; *sijda*; *kam-zor·tiyā.*

Protect, v.a. *bachawul, panāh k., nanawātah manal, sātal, jghoral, khundī-, khasamāna-*, etc. *k.*; *pālal, nmāndzal.*

Protection, s. *panāh*; *sātina*, etc. (asylum) *nanawātah.*

Protector, s. *sātandoe, jghorai*; *pālūnkai*; *nāyāk.*

Protest, v.a. *iqrār k., lal, lawdal*; *ratal, tratal*; *nāre-, faryād-*, etc. *k.*

Protract, v.a. *ūgdawul*; *drang-, lārghah-*, etc. *k.*

Protrude, v.n. *bāhar watal, khatal.*

Protuberance, s. *ghundakai, pārsob, pūpaka.*

Proud, a. *kibr·jan. bādī, mast, khāmtamā, maghrūr.*

Prove, v.a. *ṣābit-, ṣubūt-, zbād-, rikkhtiyā-*, etc. *k.* (try) *āzmāyal, āzmekkht k.* (happen) v.n. *kedal, shwul, prewatal, khatal.*

Provender, s. *wuch wākkhah dapāra da tsārwo.*

Proverb, s. *matal, miṣāl, masal.*

Proverbial, a. *matalī*; *mashhūr.*

Provide, v.a. *rāwral, paidā k., tadbīr-, tayār-, dzerma-*, etc. *k.*, *khabar ākhistal, khabar-gīrī k.*; *warkawul*; *shart taral.* (-against) *pesh·fikrī k.*

Provided, c. *pa shart, pa ṣūrat, pa ḥāl.*

Providence, s. *khudāe, rabb, razzāq.* (foresight) *dūr·andeshī, pesh·fikrī.*

Provident, a. *dūr·andesh, khabar·dār.*

Providentially, ad. *da khudāe pa ḥukm sara, da rabb pa mihrbāngī sara.*

Province, s. *ṣūba, pargana, tapa*; *kār, khid-mat*; *gharaz.*

Provision, s. *tadbīr, fikr*; *dzerma, tayārī.*

Provisions, s. *khwurāk, khwārah, ṭa'ām, ghizā.* (-for a journey, etc.) *azūqa, tokkha, tantosh, tsawrai.* (-for an army, etc.) *rasad, zakhīra, sūrsāt.*

Provisional, a. *shartī.*

Proviso, s. *shart.*

Provocation, s. *pārawuna, ṭongāra*; *gwākkh.*

Provoke, v.a. *pārawul, zoral, āgayal, gwākkhal, khapak k.*

Prowess, s. *marāna, maranī·tob, tūrzan·tob, bahādūrī, dzwānmardī.*

Prowl, v.n. *ghalai girzedal, gakkht k.*

Proximate, a. *nijde, nizd, rātlūnai.*

Proximity, s. *nijdekī* or *nizdekī.*

Proxy, s. *badalī, 'iwazī*; *nā-ib.*

Prudent, a. *khabardār, pokh, hokkhyār.*

Prune, v.a. *prekawul, tarāshal, shūkawul.* (-as birds) *banre joṛawul, waza-ar tsandal.* s. *ashāṛai, kishta.*

Pry, v.a. *zarana-ī-, tsār-, jāsūsī-, dzīr-*, etc. *k.*

Psalm, s. *zabūr*; *stāyai.*

Puberty, s. *dzwānī, bulūghat, zalmī·tob.*

Public, a. *'āmm, mashhūr*; *tsargand, kkhkārah.* s. *khalq, 'āmmiyān, ulas* or *ulūs.*

Publicity, s. *shuhrat, gaḍa.*

Publicly, a. *pa tsargand, pa jār* or *pa ẓāhir.*

Publish, v.a. *mashhūr-, ẓāhir-, gaḍ-*, etc. *k.*

Pucker, s. *jung, gundza, chunr, kṛatai, chīchaṛ.*

Puddle, s. *tsaparai, ḍanḍūkai.*

Puff, s. *pū, pūk.* (-of wind) *tsapa.* v.a. *pūkal, pūk wahal*; *paṛsawul, tyak k.*

Pugilist, s. *mūka-ī-* or *sūk wahūnkai, musht-zan.*

Puisne, a. *kashar, kachoṭai.*

Puissant, a. *zorāwar, quwat·nāk*

Pull, v.a. *rākāgal—rākkhkal.* (-out) *kāgal—kkhkal, bāsal—yastal.* (-along) *kashāla k.* (-down) *naṛawul.* s. *kakkh, rākkhkah*

Pullet, s. *chirgūṛai, chūchai.*

Pulley, s. *tsarkha-ī.*

Pulp, s. *māghzah.*

Pulpit, s. *mimbar.*

Pulsate, v.n. *drazedal.* v.a. *tsiṛīke wahal.*

Pulsation, s. *draz, tsiṛīka.*

Pulse, s. *nabẓ, rag.* (to feel the-) *nabẓ katal.* (pea) s. *chanṛa, moṭ, māhe, māsh, ma-ī* or *mayī.*

Pulverize, v.a. *oṛawul, oṛah-, maidah-*, etc. *k.*

Pump, v.a. *oba pa nalo rākāgal—rākkhkal* or *-bāsal—yastal*; *maṭlab-, rāz-*, etc. *bāsal—yastal.*

Pumpkin, s. *kadū.* (-seed) *kadū zaṛai.*

Pun, s. *laṭīfa, dwa ma'nī khabara.*

Punch, v.a. *sūṛai k.*; *sūk wahal.*

Punctual, a. *pūrah, sūchah, rikkhtīnai.*

Punctuality, s. *rikkhtīn·tob, rāstī.*

Punctually, ad. *jukht pa neṭe* or *-wakht.*

Puncture, s. *sūṛa, tsīra.*

Pungent, a. *tez, tund.*

Punish, v.a. *sazā warkawul, wahal, tāwan ākhistal.*

Punishment, s. *sazā, 'uqūbat, siyāsat.*

Puny, a. *kachoṭai, kuchinai, kharmandai, poṭai, woṛ, khamachah, woṛūkai.*

Pupil, s. *shāgird, murīd, chelah.* (-of eye) *torai, bātor, kasai, lema, ṭagh.*

Puppet, s. *godā, goda-ī, nāwaka-ī, nenzaka, nāzaka.*

Puppy, s. *kūtrai, kungarai.*

Purchase, v.a. *pa bai'e ākhistal, pīral, pīrodal.*

Purchaser, s. *pa bai'e ākhistūnkai, pīrūnkai.*

Pure, a. *pāk, ṣāf, karah, sūchah, khāliṣ, torai, kkhah*; *pāk laman, nek, pākīzah* or *pāzīkah*; *pūrah.*

Purely, ad. *surup, ta-ash, khālī.*

Purgative, a. *mushil, jullābī.*

Purgatory, s. *i'raf.*

Purge, s. *jullāb, jāṛ.* v.a. *jullāb-*, etc. *warkawul.* v.n. *nāstah lagedal, pa dastūno kkhkenāstal.*

Purification, s. *pākawuna.* (ceremonial) *awdas, tebūn,* or *temūn,* or *tayammum, ṭahārat.*

Purify, v.a. *pākawul, pāk-, pākīzah-, ṣāf-,* etc. *k., spetsal* or *spedzal.*

Purity, s. *pākī, pakīzagī, pāk-, ṣāf-,* etc. *-wālai, spetsal·tob*; *rikkhtīn·tob.*

Purple, a. *arghawānī, tor sūr.*

Purport, s. *ma'nī, ma'nā, maṭlab.*

Purpose, s. *niyat, qaṣd, irāda, murād, gharaẓ.* (on-) ad. *pa qasd.* (to what-?) *tsa la, tsa dapāra, wale.* (to the-) *ṣawāb, joṛ, jukht.* v.a. *niyat-*, etc. *taṛal,* or *laral,* or *k.*

Purr, v.a. *khur wahal, khur khur k.*

Purse, s. *hamiyānī, kīsa, būtskhaka.*
Purslain, s. *warkhāṛai, khulfa* or *khurfa.*
Pursuant, a. *muwāfiq.* (-to) ad. *pa mūjib.*
Pursue, v.n. *pase zghaledal—zghākkhtal; pase tlal, -lagedal, -ked.*, etc.
Pursuit, s. *zghākkht, tekkhta; mashghūlā, kār; kokshiksh, tapos, talāsh.*
Purulent, a. *zawlan.*
Purvey, v.a. *khwurāk-, rasad-, sūrsāt-, zakhīra-*, etc. *ṭolawul.*
Pus, s. *zawa* or *ziwa, ra-ash, zahūb, khīrai.*
Push, v.a. *ṭel-, ḍakka-*, etc. *wahal.*
Pusillanimous, a. *nāmard, yer-man.*
Pustule, s. *nanaka-ī, dāna; kharai.*
Put, v.a. *gdal* or *īgdal, īkkhodal, īkkhawul, īkkhal, kkhkegdal*, etc., *lagawul.* (-away) *lire k., sharal.* (-off) *mu'aṭṭal-, drang-*, etc. *k.* (-on) *āghostal, pa dzān-*, etc. *k.* (-out) *muṛ k.* (-together) *joṛawul, yo dzāe k., ṭolawul.* (-up with) *wṛal, zghamal.*
Putrefy, v.n. *wrostedal, pūdah-, skhā-*, etc. *ked.; shaṛhedal.*
Putrid, a. *wrost, skhā, pūdah.*
Puzzle, v.a. *hariyānawul, rabṛawul, hak pak k., ḥairān* or *hariyān-, sarāsīmah-*, etc. *k.* s. *pech, ghūṭai, kaga waga.*

Q.

Quack, s. *lāpai, nīmgaṛai ṭabīb, -mullā*, etc.
Quack, v.a. *qā qā k.*
Quadrilateral, a. *chār-gūṭlai.*
Quadruped, s. *tsārwai, dāba, sutūr.*
Quadruple, s. *tsalor bragh, tsalor chand.*
Quaff, v.a. *skal, tskal* or *tskkhal.*
Quagmire, s. *bokkhtana, khaṭa, palanda, taramna.*
Quail, s. *mṛaz, uwaṛaz.*
Quaint, a. *'ajīb; laṭīf, nāzuk, bārīk.*
Quake, v.n. *larzedal. rapedal, pṛakedal.*

Qualification, s. *lā-iqat, qābilyat.*
Qualified, a. *lā-iq, qābil, yarzan.*
Quality, s. *khoe, khaṣlat, ṣifat, ṭab'a, lokkhai.* (rank) *martaba, pāya, darja, kor.*
Qualm, s. *bāka-ī, chāl.* (-of conscience) *gram.* (to have a-) *bāka-ī-*, etc. *k.* *gram ked.*
Quantity, s. *qadr, andāza, wazn.*
Quarrel, v.a. *jang-, jagaṛa-, qaẓiya-*, etc. *k.*
Quarrelsome, a. *jang-yālai, jagṛāū, bādī.*
Quarry, s. (game) *kkhkār.* (stone-) *da kāṇo kān.*
Quart, s. *ser.*
Quarter, s. *pao, tsalorama brakha.* (side) *khwā, lorai, tsalma, rokh; aṛakh, tsang, ḍaḍa.* (district) *palaw, cham, khel, kandai, mahalla.* (asylum) *panāh, nanawātah, āmān, amn.* (lodging) *dzāe, ustoga, borjal, ṭikāo.*
Quash, v.a. *mātawul.* (annul) *bāṭil k.*
Quaver, v.n. *trangedal; larzedal, rapedal, pṛakedal.*
Quay, s. *pushta, dunkācha.*
Queen, s. *malika.* (-at chess, etc.) *wazīr.*
Queer, a. *'ajab, 'ajīb.*
Quell, v.a. *kkhkenawul, saṛawul, mātawul, lānde-, man'a-*, etc. *k.*
Quench, v.a. *saṛawul, muṛ k.*
Query, s. *sawāl, tapos* or *tafaḥus*
Quest, s. *talāsh, ṭalab, togā pū.*
Question, s. *sawāl, tapos, pukkhtana; gumān, shakk, shubha.* v.a. *pukkhtedal, sawāl-*, etc. *k., gumān-*, etc. *laral.*
Questionable, a. *shakk-man, gumānī.*
Quibble, s. *hira-ī, palma, lamghaṛa-ī, ḥīla, chal.*
Quick, a. *za-ar* or *zir, jalt, gaṛandai, chālāk, zghard, tez, talwār-gandai.* (alive) *jwandai.* s. *ūra-ī, jwanda-ī ghwakkha.*
Quicken, v.a. *jwandai k.; za-ar* or *zir-*, etc. *k.*
Quickly, ad. *zir zir, pa talwār, pa gaṛandī.*

Quickness, s. *talwār, garand-wālai.*
Quicksand, s. *bokkhtana, ghal shiga.*
Quicksilver, s. *pārā, sīmāb.*
Quiet, a. *chup, ghalai; qalār, ārām.* s. *qalār-tiyā, ārām-tiyā, āsūdagī.*
Quietly, ad. *ro ro, pa qalār sara.*
Quietness, s. *ghalī-tob; ārām-tiyā; gharībī.*
Quill, s. *banra, shāh par* or *kkhāh par.*
Quilt, s. *brastan; nāla-ī, tolā-ī, toshak.*
Quince, s. *biha-ī* or *bī.* (-seed) *bī dāna.*
Quinsy, s. *haspa, khunāq.*
Quintessence, s. *jauhar, asl; khulāsa.*
Quit, v.a. *pregdal, prekkhodal, prekkhal, tark k.*
Quite, a. *pūrah, amānī, sarāsar, tamām, wārah, tol tāl.* (in comp.) *tak-, tap-,* etc.
Quiver, s. *larza, parak.* (-for arrows) *shkhwalai, tar kakkh.*
Quiver, v.n. *larzedal, rapedal, parakedal.*
Quota, s. *brakha, wesh, hissa.*
Quote, v.a. *sanad rāwral, da bul chā khabara* (or *wayai*) *yādawul.*

R.

Rabbit, s. *khargosh, koranai soe.*
Rabble, s. *dala, park, ganr khalq.*
Race, s. *manda, zghākkht.* (generation) *asl, nasl, zāt, khāndān, kor, noga.*
Rack, s. *shikanja, tsarkh, pāna, kāt.* v.a. *pa shikanjo-,* etc. *khejawul, 'azābawul.*
Radiance, s. *brekkhnā, ranrā, palwasha.*
Radiant, a. *brekkh-nāk, rūnr, dzalkan.*
Radiate, v.n. *brekkhedal, dzalkedal, rūnredal.*
Radical, a. *aslī, zātī.*
Radish, s. *mūla-ī, turp.*
Raffle, v.a. *pa hisk-, pa pucho-, pa qur'o-,* etc. *khartsawul.*
Raft, s. *jāla, bera.*
Rafter, s. *bensh, lakara, patera.*
Rag, s. *chirra, parūkai, pārcha, purza, khartsorai.*
Rage, s. *qahr, ghussa, ghazab, tāo; saudā.*
Ragged, a. *tūkī tūkī.* (in rags) *gand* or *kind poksh.* (uneven) *zīg, lwār jawar, kandai kandarai.*
Raging, a. *ghazab-nāk, qahr-jan, khapah, eshānd.*
Rail, v.a. *ker-, bāra-, shpol-,* etc. *taral* or *-lagawul.* (abuse) *peghor warkawul, kanzal* or *kkhkandzal.* (blame) *malāmatawul, ratal, tratal.*
Raiment, s. *āghostan, zarūkai, wrarai, jāma, pokkhāk, libās.*
Rain, s. *bārān.* (slight-) *rangai bārān, pūna.* (heavy-) *ganr bārān, shebah.* (spring shower) *hakkhma, wasa.* (hot weather-) *parshakāl.* (-bow) *shna kāsa, sra kāsa, da būda-ī tāl.*
Rain, v.n. *oredal, tsātsedal, bārānedal.*
Raise, v.a. *pātsawul, khejawul, porta k.* (erect) *walārawul, wudrawul, lakawul.* (educate) *pālal, nmāndzal, parwaral.*
Raisin, s. *watska, mewa.*
Rake, s. *pāra, ghākkhawar, panj-gakkhai; lawand, chat, kāsīr, lūtsak.*
Rake, v.a. *ghākkhawar girzawul, panj-gakkhai wahal; kāsīrī-,* etc. *k.* (search) *latawul.* (collect) *tolawul.*
Rally, v.a. *tīngawul, sambālawul, jorawul, mazbūt k., komak rasawul.* (jeer) *khandā-, toqa-,* etc. *k*
Ram, s. *mag, ga-ad.* (fighting) *ghuch.*
Ram, v.a. *mandal, kkhke mandal.*
Ramble, v.n. *girzedal, sail k.*
Rambler, s. *gashtai, āwārah, lawand.*
Ramify, v.n. *khwaredal, wīredal, pheledal.*
Rammer, s. *pācko, dabalai, bargho.*
Rampant, a. *mast, shokhin.*
Rampart, s. *kkhahr panāh, bāra, sangar.*

Rancid, a. *skhā, wrost, trīw, trīkh.*

Rancour, s. *kīna, bughz, khwā badī, 'inād.*

Random, a. *tawakkulī, qismatī.* (at-) ad. *hase.*

Range, v.a. *sail-, gakkht-*, etc. *k.* v.n. *girzedal.* (set) *tartībawul, sambālawul.*

Rank, s. *martaba, pāya, dzāe, darja*; *para, ṣaff, qaṭār.* a. *wrost, skhā, bad·būī·dār.* v.a. *para-*, etc. *taṛal*; *gaṇṛal, shmeral.*

Rankle, v.n. *baledal, yashedal, khūyedal* or *khū-edal, swal.*

Ransack, v.a. *laṭawul, shanal*; *tālā-, lūt-*, etc. *k.*

Ransom, s. *būnga.*

Rant, v.a. *lāpe shāpe wahal· baq baq-, baṛ baṛ-*, etc. *k.*

Rap, v.a. *wahal, trakawul, tak wahal, ṭakawul.*

Rapacious, a. *lūṭ·bāz, ghārat·gar*; *khūnāṛai.*

Rape, v.a. *bikr mātawul, pa zabardastī ghowul.* (-seed) *awrai.*

Rapid, a. *gaṛandai, za-ar* or *zir, jalt, tez, tund.*

Rapidity, s. *jaltī, talwār, tundī, tezī.*

Rapine, s. *lūṭ, ghārat, tālān, tākht tārāj.*

Rapture, s. *ḍera khush·ḥālī, josh, eshnā.*

Rare, a. *nādir, matrah, kam paidā.* (thin) *narai.*

Rarify, v.a. *narai-, mahīn-, bārīk-*, etc. *k.*

Rarely, ad. *kamtar, la-ag.*

Rascal, s. *ḥarāmī, laṛalai, bad·m'āsh, charland.*

Rash, a. *talwalai, talwār·gandai, jalt, be·tadbīr, zir.* (-on the skin) *garmaka, laṛama, sra makha, jarmoṛa, nanaka-ī, dzwānaka.*

Rasp, v.a. *sohān-, chausār-*, etc. *wahal*, or *k.*; *sūlawul, zīgawul, zdoyal.*

Rat, s. *magak, magah, samandai.* (musk-) *mukkhkai magak.*

Rate, s. *bai'a, qīmat, nirkh*; *andāza, ḥisāb*; *shān, ṭaur.* v.a. *bai'a-*, etc. *taṛal*; *andāza-*, etc. *k.*, *gaṇṛal.* (scold) *raṭal, traṭal, dāṛal.*

Rather, ad. *wṛūnbe, awwal, lā.*

Ratify, v.a. *qabūlawul, muqarrar k*

Ratio, s. *andāza, wazn.*

Rational, a. *'aql·man, pohand*; *munāsib.*

Rationality, s. *'aql, pok, pahm, sha'ūr.*

Rattle, v.a. *shṛangawul, gṛanjawul, ga-arahā· k.* s. *chanṛ chanṛai, gṛanjāū.*

Ravage, v.a. *tālā-, wairān-, ūjāṛ-, kkhpo lānde-*, etc. *k.*, *latāṛawul, natal.*

Rave, v.a. *be·khūde khabare k.*, *baṛ baṛ k.*

Raven, s. *kāgh.*

Ravenous, a. *liwāl, wagai, naghländ.*

Ravine, s. *khwaṛ, kanda, kas.*

Ravish, v.a. *bikr shlawul* or *-mātawul*; *pa zor ākhistal*; *satr ākhistal.*

Raw, a. *ūm* or *om, nīma·khwā, nīm·pokh, kachah.* (abraded) *sūdah, sūlawulai.* (-cold) *soṛ.*

Rawness, s. *om·wālai*; *sāṛa.*

Ray, s. *palwasha, partaw, dzalak, shughla.*

Raze, v.a. *naṛawul, kkhpo lānde-, litāṛak-*, etc. *k.*

Razor, s. *ustura, pāka-ī.* (-strap) *paṭaka*

Reach, v.n. *rasedal, rātlal, rāghlal.* (touch) *lagedal, jangedal.* (-out) *ghazedal* or *gazedal.* (fetch) v.a. *rāwṛal.*

Reaction, s. *zor, quwat.*

Read, v.a. *lwustal, kitāb katal.*

Readiness, s. *tayārī, chālākī.*

Reading, s. *lwustūn.* (-the Qurān) *qirāt.*

Ready, a. *tayār, chālāk, ḥāẓir.*

Real, a. *rikkhtīnai, aṣlī, sūchah, karah.*

Reality, s. *rikkhtiyā, rikkhtīn·tob, ḥaqīqat.*

Realize, v.a. *mūndal, gaṭal*; *paidā-, ḥāẓir-*, etc. *k.*

Really, ad. *rikkhtiyā, khudāe go.*

Realm, s. *mulk, rāj, bādshāhī*; *hiwād.*

Reap, v.a. *lau k.*, *rebal, rawdal*; *mūndal, gaṭal.*

Reaper, s. *lau·garai*; *gaṭūnkai.*

Rear, s. *wrūstai, shā, dumbāl.* (in the-) ad. *wrūsto, pa shā, pastana.*

Rear, v.a. *khejawul, pātsawul, walāṛawul.* v.n. *walāṛedal, pātsedal, khatal.* (-up) *negh-, lak-, jig-,* etc. *walāṛedal* or *-ked.* (nourish) *parwaral, pālal, nmāndzal.*

Reason, s. *'aql, poh, pahm.* (cause) *sabab, kabl, bā'is; mūjib, wāsiṭa, jihat.* (proof) *dalīl; ḥujjat.* (right) *ḥaqq, inṣāf.* v.a. *baḥs-,* etc. *k.*

Reasonable, a. *wājib, munāsib, kkhāyastah, kkhah.*

Rebel, s. *yāghī-gar, sar-kakkh.* v.a. *yāghī-garī-, sar-kakkhī-,* etc. *k.* v.n. *yāghī-,* etc. *ked.*

Rebellious, a. *yāghī, tughiyān.*

Rebound, v.a. *tīndak wahal, top wahal.*

Rebuke, v.a. *malāmatawul, ratal, dāṛal;* (-oneself) *gram k.*

Recall, v.a. *biyā balal, stūnawul* or *stanawul; yādawul.*

Recant, v.a. *rāe badlawul.* v.n. *girzedal, jārwatal, stūnedal* or *stanedal; munkiredal.*

Recapitulate, v.a. *biyā bayānawul.*

Recede, v.n. *wrusto ked., stunedal, haṭedal, pastana ked., jārwatal.*

Receipt, s. *rasīd, ḥujjat, tamassuk.*

Receive, v.a *ākhistal; manal.*

Recent, a. *nawai, osanai, nan wradzanai.*

Recently, ad. *os, pa zir mūde.*

Receptacle, s. *khūna, dzāe, kor, makān.*

Reception, s. *ākhistah; manana; istiqbāl; melmastiyā.*

Recess, s. *ṭāq, ṭāqcha, rap, dara-ī; gūṭ, gokkha.* (suspension) *barkhwāst, wazgār-tiyā, t'aṭīl.*

Recipe, s. *nuskha.*

Reciprocal, a. *da dwāro paṛo, -loro, -ḍaḍo,* etc., *ṭarfain, jānibain.*

Recite, v.a. *bayānawul, yādawul, naql k.*

Reckon, v.a. *shmeral, shumāral, ḥisābawul; ganṛal.* v.n. *pohedal, pahmedal.*

Reclaim, v.a. *joṛawul, sambālawul, ābādawul, wadānawul.*

Recline, v.n. *tsamlāstal, tsamlal, mlāstal. ghazedal* or *gazedal.*

Recluse, s. *gokkha-nishīn.*

Recognisance, s. *iqrār-nāma.*

Recognition, s. *pejāndah, pejandgalī.*

Recognize, v.a. *pejandal.*

Recoil, v.a. *tīndak wahal.* v.n. *stanedal, pa biyarta jārwatal.*

Recollect, v.a. *yādawul; zdah k.*

Recollected, s. *yād, zdah.*

Recommend, v.a. *sipārish k., spāral.*

Recompense, v.a. *tāwān-, badal-,* etc. *war-kawul.*

Reconcile, v.a. *pukhlā k., rogha jora k., khwā saṛawul; manal, barābarawul.*

Record, s. *daftar, tawārīkh.* v.a. *līkal, darj k.*

Recorder, s. *qānūn-goe, sarishta-dār.*

Recount, v.a. *bayānawul.*

Recover, v.n. *raghedal, joṛedal.* v.a. *biyā-mūndal.*

Recovery, s. *raghedana, joṛedana; biyā-mūndah.*

Recreation, s. *sail, tamāsha, loba, wazgār-tiyā.*

Recriminate, v.a. *chighawul, sāra kanzal k., lagiyā sara peghorūna warkawul.*

Recruit, v.a. *hosā-,* etc. *k., dama warkawul; pūrah-,* etc. *k., nawai nokar k.*

Rectify, v.a. *joṛawul, sam-, drust-,* etc. *k.*

Rectitude, s. *rikkhtīn-tob, nekī, rāstī, ṣawāb.*

Rectum, s. *chustai, kulma.*

Recumbent, a. *mlāst, prot, ghazedalai.*

Recur, v.n. *rātlal, rāghlal; yādedal.*

Red, a. *sūr, lāl, surkh, rat.*

Redeem, v.a. *khalāṣawul, āzādawul, bach-awul.*

Redress, v.a. *tāwān warkawul, dādrasī-, niyāw-,* etc. *k.*

Reduce, v.a. *kamawul, landawul, saṛawul*; *rāwṛal.*

Reduction, s. *kam·tiyā, la-ag·wālai*; *troṭ, zwam.*

Redundant, a. *ziyāt, ḍer.*

Reed, s. *ḍūrma, darwai, nal, shpelai, lūkha.*

Reel, s. *aṭerān, tsarkhai.* (-of thread) *aṭa* or *aṭeka.* (dance) *atanṛ.*

Refer, v.a. *pukkhtedal, spāral, līdal—goral, katal, lagawul, nisbat laral.* v.n. *lagedal.*

Reference, s. *nisbat, 'alāqa, ta'alluq, lār.*

Referee, s. *munṣif.*

Refine, v.a. *pāk-, ṣāf-, spīn-,* etc. *k., narai-,* etc. *k.*

Refit, v.a. *joṛawul.*

Reflect, v.a. *fikr-, ghaur-,* etc. *k.*; *sewrai-, 'aks-,* etc. *āchawul.*

Reflux, s. *jārwātah, stūnedah.*

Reform, v.a. *nawai joṛawul, ārāstah k.*

Refractory, a. *yāghī, sar·kakkh, ṭakanṛai.*

Refrain, v.a. *parhez k., dzān sātal.* v.n. *ḍaḍa ked.*

Refresh, v.a. *hosā-, tāzah-,* etc. *k., dama warkawul, khwā saṛawul.*

Refreshment, s. *khwūrāk, naharai, ṭa'ām*; *ārām, dama.*

Refuge, s. *āsra, panāh*; *nanawātah, amn.*

Refugee, s. *nanawātai, panāh·gīr.*

Refulgent, a. *rūnṛ, rokkhān, brekkh·nāk.*

Refund, v.a. *stūnawul* or *stanawul, biyarta-, pastana-,* etc. *warkawul*; *tāwān warkawul.*

Refuse, v.a. *namanal, naqabūlawul, daregh-, ibā-,* etc. *k.* or *-rāwṛal.*

Refute, v.a. *bāṭil-, radd-,* etc. *k.*; *gram k.*

Regain, v.a. *biyā mūndal.*

Regal, a. *bādshāhī.*

Regard, v.a. *naẓar-, nigāh-,* etc. *k., katal*; *manal*; *fikr-,* etc. *k., khabar ākhistal*; *ganṛal.*

Regardless, a. *be·khabar, be·parwā.*

Regent, s. *qā-im muqām, nā-ib.*

Regimen, s. *pāl, parhez, tīmār.*

Regiment, s. *palṭan.* (-of horse) *risāla.*

Region, s. *zmaka, mulk, kiwād.*

Register, s. *daftar, sijill, shajara.*

Regret, s. *afsos, daregh, armān, tartāb, sto mānī, pakkhemānī.* v.a. *afsos-,* etc. *k.* v.n. *stomānedal, pakkhemān ked.*

Regular, a. *barābar, sam, hawār, drust*; *qānūnī, ā-īnī, intiẓāmī.*

Regulation, s. *ā-īn, qānūn*; *tartīb.*

Reject, v.a. *lire k., shaṛal*; *jārbāsal—jāryastal*; *nā·qabūl*; *nā·khwakkh-,* etc. *k.*

Reign, v.a. *bādshāhī-, rāj-, ḥukm-,* etc. *k.*

Reimburse, v.a. *warkawul, tāwān-, badal-, 'iwaẓ-,* etc. *warkawul, stūnawul, pūrah-,* etc. *k.*

Rein, s. *wāga, mlūna*; *jilab, bāḍgoī.*

Reinstate, v.a. *pa dzāe kkhkenawul* or *-muqarrar k.*

Rejoice, v.a. *kkhādī-, khūsh·hālī-,* etc. *k.* v.n. *kkhādedal, khūsh·hāledal, kkhād·man ked.* (spitefully) v.a. *sakha-, wiyāṛ-,* etc. *k.*

Rejoin, v.a. *joṛawul, lagawul.* v.n. *gaḍedal*

Reiterate, v.a. *dubāra-, biyā biyā-, wār wār-,* etc. *wayal.*

Relate, v.a. *bayānawul, wayal, qiṣṣa k.*; *nisbat-, 'alāqa-,* etc. *laral.* v.n. *lagedal.*

Relation, s. *bayān, qiṣṣa*; *nisbat-, 'alāqa-, khpul, khekkh, 'azīz.* (paternal-) *plār·ganai.* (maternal-) *mor·ganai,* etc.

Relationship, s. *khpul·walī, khpulwī, 'azīz·walī* or *'azīz·galī, khekkhī*; *ragai, haḍ.*

Relative, s. *khpul, khekkh,* etc. (*v.* Relation). a. *nisbatī.*

Relax, v.a. *arat-, sust-,* etc. *k.*

Relaxation, s. *arat·wālai, sust·wālai*; *sustī*; *wazgār·tiyā.*

Release, v.a. *āzādawul, khalāṣawul, wurhawul, yalah k., pregdal, prekkhodal, prekkhal.*

Relent, v.n. *narmedal, mulā-im ked.*

Relentless, a. be·rahm, sang·dil, kāṇrai zrah.
Reliance, s. bāwar, umed, takiya, tawakkul.
Relief, s. madad, komak; ārām; badlī.
Relieve, v.a. madad-, komak-, etc. rasawul; ārām warkawul; badlī k.
Religion, s. dīn, īmān, mazhab, kesh.
Religious, a. dīn·dār, īmān·dār, nmāndzī, nmūndz·guzār; dīnī, mazhabī.
Relinquish, v.a. pregdal, prekkhodal, prekkhal. tark k.
Relish, v.a. khwand-, maza-, etc. warkawul, maza·dār-, khwand·nāk-, etc. k.
Reluctance, s. daregh, stomānī.
Reluctant, a. nārāz, stomān.
Rely, v.a. bāwar-, takiya-, tawakkul-, etc. k.
Remain, v.n. pātedal, vāedal, osedal, pātai ked.
Remainder, s. bāqī, pātai.
Remains, s. pas·khurda, jūṭa. (mortal-) muṛai.
Remark, v.a. nazar-, nigāh-, etc. k., yādawul, wayal.
Remarkable, a. 'ajīb, 'ajab; mashhūr.
Remedy, s. 'ilāj, dawā, tsāra, darmān, tadbīr. v.a. 'ilāj-, etc. k., joṛawul, raghawul.
Remember, v.a. yādawul, yād laral pejandal; zdah k.
Remembrance, s. yād; pejāndah.
Remind, v.a. yād warkawul.
Remiss, a. sust, ghāfil, soṛ, narm.
Remit, v.a. bakkhal, pulawul, mu'āf k. (send) āstawul, legal. (lessen) kamawul, la-agawul.
Remittance, s. bakkhana · āstawūna; kamawūna.
Remnant, a. bāqī, pātai.
Remonstrance, s. 'arzī; takrār; gila.
Remorse, s. paskhāk or pakhsāk, pakkhemānī.
Remote, a. liri or lire, prat.
Remove, v.a. liri k., khejawul; kaḍa wṛal, legdal—lekkhal, kūch k.

Remunerate, v.a. ajr-, ujrat-, mihnat-, etc. warkawul; tāwān-, shukrāna-, etc. warkawul.
Rend, v.a. shlawul, tsīral, tsāk k., mātawul, wrarawul.
Render, v.a. kawul, kṛal, rāwṛal.
Rendezvous, s. borjal. v.n. toledal, yo dzāe ked.
Renew, v.a. biyā kawul, -rāwṛal, -ākhistal, etc. nawai-, tāzah-, etc. k.
Rennet, s. tomna, māya; siyalai.
Renounce, v.n. munkiredal, jārwatal. v.a. inkār-, etc. k., pregdal, prekkhodal, prekkhal.
Renowned, a. nāmwar, mashhūr.
Rent, a. shledalai, tsīralai. s. tsāk, tsīra, darz. (hire) kreha, kirāka; ijāra.
Rent, v.n. shledal or tsīredal; wraredal.
Renunciation, s. inkār, tark.
Repair, v.a. joṛawul, pewand-, marammat-, etc. k.
Repartee, s. ḥāzir dzawābī.
Repast, s. naharai, nāshta, ḍoḍa-ī.
Repay, v.a. badal-, tāwān-, etc. warkawul; qarz-, por-, etc. khejawul; pūrah-, adā-, etc. k.
Repeal, v.a. bāṭil-, radd-, etc. k.
Repeat, v.a. biyā-, dubāra-, etc. wayal, bagānawul, mukarrar wayal.
Repeatedly, ad. biyā qa biyā, daf'atan.
Repel, v.a. liri k., shaṛal, raṭal, haṭālawul.
Repent, v.a. toba būsal—yastal. v.n. stomānedal, pakkhemān ked.
Repentance, s. toba, stomānī, pakkhemānī.
Repentant, a. toba·gār, stomān, pakkhemān.
Repine, v.n. kaṛedal, nūledal, ghamedal.
Replete, a. pūrah, ḍak, moṛ.
Reply, v.a. dzawāb-, pāsukh-, etc. warkawul.
Report, s. khabar, āwāza; bāng; ḍaz, ghag. v.a. khabarawul, khabar warkawul; bāng wayal; ḍaz wahal, ghagawul.

Repose, v.n. *tsamlāstal, mlāstal, ghazedal*; *ūdah ked*. v.a. *khob-, ārām-*, etc. *k.*

Reprehensible, a. *malāmatī, nākārah.*

Represent, v.a. *'arẓ k.*; *kkhayal—kkhowul.*

Representation, s. *'arẓī*; *tsera, ṣūrat*; *tamāsha.*

Representative, s. *wakīl, nā-ib, qā-im muqām.*

Reprimand, v.a. *malāmat k., ṭaqawul, raṭal.*

Reprisal, s. *bota, bramta.*

Reproach, v.a. *peghor warkawul*; *gila k.*

Reprobate, s. *gumrāh, mardūd, wruk lāṛ.*

Reprove, v.a. *malāmatawul, traṭal, raṭal, dāṛal.*

Reptile, s. *chinjai, khazanda.*

Republic, s. *da ulas* or *ulūs jirga*; *da jirgo ḥukūmat.*

Repudiate, v.a. *inkār k., sharal, kkhayal.*

Repugnance, s. *kraka*; *daregh.*

Repugnant, a. *mukhālif, kagalai.*

Repulse, v.a. *mātawul, takkhtawul, haṭālawul.*

Reputable, a. *mu'atabar, i'tibārī.*

Reputation, s. *nūm, nang, abrū, i'tibār.*

Request, v.a. *darkhwāst-, 'arẓ-, sawāl-*, etc. *k., ghokkhtal, pukkhtedal.*

Require, v.a. *ghokkhtal, ḥājat taral.*

Requisite, a. *pakār, lāzim, ẓarūr.*

Rescue, v.a. *khalāṣawul, wurhawul, bachawul.*

Resemblance, s. *barābarī, mushābahat.*

Resembling, a. *ghondi, pa shān, pa rang.*

Resent, v.a. *bad manal.*

Resentment, s. *kīna, badī, dukkhmanī.*

Reserve, v.a. *sātal, khundiyal, khundī k.*

Reservoir, s. *ḥauẓ, baha-ī, ḍanḍ, tālāw.*

Reside, v.n. *āstedal, osedal, pātedal.* v.a. *astoga-, meshta-*, etc. *k.*

Resident, s. *osedūnkai, astogūnkai, āstedūnkai.*

Residue, s. *bāqī, pātai*; *tarka.*

Resign, v.a. *pregdal, prekkhodal, prekkhal*; *tark k.*; *spāral, pāslawul*; *bakkhal.*

Resignation, s. *tark, prekkhodana*; *spārana, spārakkhtana*; *tawakkul*; *ist'ifā.*

Resin, s. *rāndzaṛah, chūṛel*; *jāwla.*

Resist, v.a. *maẓbūṭī-, barābarī-, jang-*, etc. *k.* v.n. *ṭing-, klak-, maẓbūṭ-*, etc. *wudredal*, or *ked., haṭedal.*

Resolute, a. *maẓbūṭ, klak, ṭing, zṛah-war.*

Resolution, s. *qaṣd, niyat.*

Resolve, v.a. *qaṣd k., niyat taral.*

Resort, v.a. *rāsha darsha k.*

Resound, v.n. *ghagedal, ghṛunbedal.*

Resource, s. *chāra, 'ilāj*; *chal, ḥikmat.*

Respect, s. *'izzat, adab*; *nisbat, 'alāqa.* (with respect to) *pa ḥaqq kkhke.* (in many respects) *pa ḍero khabaro kkhke.* (in every respect) *pa hare khabare.* v.n. *grohedal*; *manal.*

Respectable, a. *mu'tabar, 'izzat-nāk.*

Respectful, a. *adab kawūnkai.*

Respective, a. *khāṣṣ*; *khpul khpul.*

Respire, v.a. *sāh ākhistal.*

Respite, s. *furṣat*; *wazgār-tiyā*; *nāgha.*

Response, s. *dzawāb, pāsukh.*

Responsibility, s. *ẓimma*; *tāwān.*

Responsible, a. *ẓimma-dār, tāwān warkawūnkai.*

Rest, s. *ārām-tiyā, qalār-tiyā*; *ārām, qalār* or *qarār, furṣat.* (pause) *wār. dama.* (sleep) *khob.* (prop) *aṛam.*

Rest, a. *bāqī, pātai*; *nor, nor ṭol.*

Restive, a. *sar-kakkh, sar-zor, ṭakanṛai.*

Restless, a. *be-ārām, nā-qalār.*

Restore, v.a. *biyā pa dzāe waläṛawul, pa biyarta warkawul.*

Restrain, v.a. *sambūlawul, bandawul, man'a k., īsārawul, haṭālawul.*

Result, s. *ḥāṣil*; *'amal*; *khatah*; *pāzah.*

Resume, v.a. *biyā ākhistal.*

Resurrection, s. *ākhirat, ḥashr, qiyāmat.* (day of-) *wradz da ḥashr*, etc.

Retail, v.a. *bel bel-, la-ag la-ag-*, etc. *khartsawul, lāgī k.*

Retain, v.a. *sātal, laral, khundī k.*

Retaliate, v.a. *badal-, jazā-, qiṣāṣ-*, etc. *ākhistal; bota-, bramta-*, etc. *k.*

Retard, v.a. *haṭālawul, kariyābawul; drang-, lārghah-, multawī-*, etc. *k.*

Retch, v.a. *bāka-ī-, qai-, chāl-*, etc. *k., jārbāsal—jāryistal, kūz katal, zmake ta goral.*

Reticular, a. *jāl·dār, jālī.*

Retinue, s. *swarlī; jalab.*

Retire, v.n. *wrusto-, biyarta-*, etc. *ked., haṭāledal, pastana jārwatal* or *-tlal—lāṛal, pātsedal; puṭedal.*

Retired, a. *puṭ, yawādzai, bel* or *biyal.*

Retirement, s. *yawādzī·tūn, bel·tūn.*

Retract, v.n. *girzedal, landedal.* v.a. *inkār-, bāṭil-*, etc. *k., jārbāsal—jāryastal.*

Retreat, v.n. *takkhtedal, haṭāledal, biyarta-*, etc. *ked.* s. *tekkhta, māt.* (cover) *puṭgana-ī, psūnai, tsawai.* (asylum) *panāh, nanawātch.*

Retrench, v.a. *kamawul, la-agawul, landawul.*

Retribution, s. *sazā, siyāsat, badal, jazā.*

Retrieve, v.a. *sambālawul, biyā mūndal.*

Return, v.n. *girzedal, jārwatal, stūnedal, āwukkhtal, pastana rātlal—rāghlal.* v.a. *pa biyarta āstawul, stūnawul.*

Return, s. *jarwātah; badal.* (profit) *sūd, gaṭa.* (answer) *dzawāb.* (form) *ṣūrat ḥāl.*

Reveal, v.a. *tsargandawul, kkhkārah k., parda porta k., wayal.*

Revel, v.a. *mastī-, bad mastī k*

Revenge, v.a. *badal-, qiṣāṣ-*, etc. *ākhistal.*

Revengeful, a. *kīna·war.*

Revenue, s. *bāj, khirāj, maḥṣūl, sāw.*

Revere, v.a. *zbarg gaṇral* or *-manal.* v.n. *grohedal.*

Reverence, s. *grohedana, manana; sat, adab; salām, sijda.*

Reverse, v.a. *naskorawul, aṛawul, apūṭah k.*

Reverse, a. *naskor, aṛawulai; apūṭah.* s. *āfat, balā, bad-* or *tor bakhtī.*

Review, v.a. *nandāra-, tamāsha-, dzer-*, etc. *k.*

Revile, v.a. *kanzal, kanzal k., kkhkandzal, peghor warkawul.*

Revolution, s. *tsarkh, daur; balwā, pasāt.*

Revolve, v.n. *churledal, tsarkhedal, girzedal.* v.a. *fikr-, ghaur-*, etc. *k.*

Reward, s. *ujrat, miḥnat; bakkhana, in'ām; ṣawāb, barakat.*

Rheumatism, s. *bād, wo.*

Rhinoceros, s. *genḍai.*

Rhubarb, s. *rewand.* (fresh) *rawāsh.*

Rhyme, s. *radīf, naẓm*

Rib, s. *pukkhta-ī.*

Riband, s. *paṭa-ī, rekkha; pekawai.*

Rice, s. *wrīja.* (-in the husk) *shola.* (broken-) *khamacha.* (boiled-) *kamoda, chalāū.* (-straw) *palāla.* (-field) *shol·gara, shālī·zār, kadhal.* (-planting) *nihālī.*

Rich, a. *māl·dār, duniyā·dār, daulat·man.*

Riches, s. *māl, duniyā, daulat.*

Rick, s. *dala-ī, ḍera-ī.*

Rid, v.a. *liri k., jārū k., ta-ashawul, khalāṣawul, āzādawul, wurkawul, rihā k.*

Riddle, s. *mu'amma.* (sieve) *ghalbel.*

Ride, v.n. *swaredal* or *sparedal.* v.a. *swarlī k.*

Rider, s. *swor* or *spor; sparlanai.*

Ridge, s. *kamar, pushta* or *pukkhta, ghākkhai.*

Ridicule, s. *khandā, ṭoqa, pekkha, malanḍa.*

Ridiculous, a. *khandā·nāk, ṭoqī, malanḍai.*

Rifle, v.a. *shūkawul, natal, lūṭawul.*

Rig, v.a. *joṛawul, tartībawul.*

Right, a. *rikkhtiyā, drust, jukht, rāst, joṛ, wājib, rawā, barābar, kkhāyastah, kkhah.* (-hand) *kkhai.* in. *jukht! joṛ! drust!* etc. s. *ḥaqq; wāk, ikhtiyār; māl, milk; 'adl, inṣāf; kkhai.* v.a. *joṛawul, samawul*, etc.

Righteous, a. *nek, nekokār, rikkhtīnai, rāst·bāz, pāk, ṣawābī.*

Righteousness, s. *nekī, rāstī, rikkhtīn·tob, ṣawāb.*

Rightful, a. *ḥaqq-dār, haqq-man.*

Rigid, a. *klak, lak, zīg, negh, sakht, tsak, ṭīng.*

Rigidity, s. *klak-wālai, zīg-wālai*, etc.

Rigour, s. *sakhti* ; *sāṛah, yakhnī* ; *larza.*

Rigorous, a. *sakht, zīg* ; *soṛ, yakh.*

Rim, s. *ghāṛa, morga, tsanda, ja-ī.* (wheel-) *kīra-ī garda-ī* ; *drakaṛ.*

Rind, s. *baṭ, paṭ, poṭ, khwar, postakai.*

Ring, s. *kara-ī.* (finger-) *tsalai.* (nose-) *peznān, natka-ī* (ear-) *chala, wālai* (neck-) *oga-ī*

Ring, v.n. *trangedal, shrangedal, granjedal*

Ringdove, s. *gūgushtū, qumrī, spalama, tatawa, kur-kura-ī.*

Ringleader, s. *sarguroh, sarghanah, nāyak*

Ringlet, s. *tsūnra, tsunraka, zulfa, gesū.*

Ringworm, s. *pishak, spūnrai.*

Rinse, v.a. *wīndzal* or *mīndzal, wlal.*

Riot, s. *balwā, pasāt, kharkhakkha.* (revel) *khar mastī, bad mastī, ṭel ṭāl.*

Riotous, a. *balwā-gar, vasātī, sar-kakkh* ; *mast*

Rip, v.a. *tsīral, tsāk k., shlawul.*

Ripe, a. *pokh, khūrīn.*

Ripple, s. *tsaparkai, pacha.*

Rise, v.n. *pātsedal, vorta ked., walāṛedal, khatal.*

Rise, s. *khātah, taraqqa-ī.*

Risk, s. *khatra, muhimm, bāk, yera.*

Rite, s. *ṭarīqa, rasm* ; *maẕhab, sunnat.*

Rival, s. *dukkhman, raqīb.* (-wife) *ba-an*

Rivalry, s. *dukkhmanī, raqībī.*

River, s. *sīnd, dariyāb, nahar.*

Rivulet, s. *lakkhtai, aṛākh, wela.*

Road, s. *lār, rāh, wāṭ.*

Roam, v.n. *girzedal, rammedal, khushai girzedal.*

Roan, a. *samand.*

Roar, v.a. *nāra-, tanr-, ḍarān-*, etc. *wahal.* v.n. *gharedal, ghuṛunbedal.*

Roast, v.a. *wrītawul, kabābawul, talawul, teyal.*

Rob, v.a. *shūkawul, lūṭawul, natal, ghlā k., lār wahal.*

Robber, s. *ghal, shūk-mār, lār wahūnkai.*

Robbery, s. *ghlā.* (highway-) *shūka.*

Robe, s. *jāma, āghostan, libās* (-of honour) *khalāt* or *khil'at.*

Robust, a. *maẓbūṭ, takṛah, mazai, gagar*

Rock, s. *tīga, gaṭ.*

Rock, v.a. *khwadzawul, ṭāl wahal, jūṭa-ī warkawul, zangawul, shanawul.* v.n. *zangal, zangedal, khwadzedal, shanedal.*

Rocky, a. *kānredz, sanglākh, gaṭīn*

Rod, s. *lakkhta, hamsā* or *amsā.*

Rogue, s. *ṭag, ṭag-bāz, chal-bāz, farebī.*

Roguery, s. *ṭagī, ṭag-bāzī, chal-bāzī, fareb.*

Roll, v.a. *nghaṛal—nghakkhtal.* (-on the ground) v.n. *rghaṛedal—rghakkhtal, lots pots ked.*

Roll, s. *nghakkht* ; *wal, pech, tāo.* (-of paper) *dasta, fard.* (list) *daftar, sijill.* (plait) *bragh.*

Roller, s. *māla, mandānro.* (bandage) *paṭa-ī.*

Romance, s. *qiṣṣa* ; *darogh-jana khabara.*

Romantic, s. *'ajab, 'ajīb* ; *khiyālī.*

Romp, v.a. *ṭel ṭāl-, khar mastī-, laṭah per-*, etc. *k., khajūnko-, tskhe* or *tske-*, etc. *k.*

Roof, s. *chat, tsapar, bām, koṭa.* (of mouth-) *tāla.*

Rook, s. *qāghah.*

Room, s. *khūna, dzāe, koṭa.* (public-) *ḥujra.*

Roomy, a. *arat, prānatai.*

Roost, s. *chakas, basera.* v.a. *basera k.*

Root, s. *welkh, wula, mūnḍ* ; *bonsaṭ, kūnsaṭ, bunyād.*

Root up, v.a. *wekh-, mūnḍ-*, etc. *bāsal—yastal, -kāgal—kkhkal* ; *mūnḍ-, bonsaṭ-*, etc. *khejawul.*

Rooted, a. *khakkh, maẓbūṭ, njatai.*

Rope, s. *pa-aṛai, rasa-ī.* (hair-) *wākkhkai, siyala-ī.* (palm-leaf-) *būnr, biyāsta.*

Rosary, s. *tasbiḥ, tasbe.* (one bead of-) *tasba.*

Rose, s. *gul.* (wild white-) *phulwāṛai.*

Rosin, s. *ṛāndzaṛah.*

Rot, v.n. *wrostedal, sharhedal, skhā ked., bonredal.*

Rotate, v.n. *tsarkhedal, churledal, girzedal.*

Rotation, s. *tsarkh; daur.* (in-) ad. *wār pa wār sara.*

Rotten, a. *wrost, skhā, sharhedalai, bonredalai*

Rough, a. *lwāṛ, zīg, klak· zmokht, trīkh, brekkhan.*

Round, a. *ghund, ghund·mund.* s. *gakkht; guzār.* p. *chāpera.* (to turn-) v.n. *girzedal; churledal.*

Roundness, s. *ghund·walai.*

Rouse, v.a. *pātsawul, wikkhawul, baidār k.*

Rout, v.a. *takkhtawul, mātawul, tār pa tārawul.* s. *tekkhta, māt, tār pa tār, shikast.*

Route, s. *lār, rāh.*

Rove, v.n. *girzedal.* v.a. *sail-, gakkht-,* etc. *k.*

Row, s. *para, kat, qatār, tsīṛa, ṣaff.*

Row, v.a. *chape wahal.*

Royal, a. *bādshāhī.*

Rub, v.a. *magal—mukkhal, mālish k.*

Rubber, s. *māla, mukra.* (flesh) *khīsa.*

Rubbish, s. *khadzala, khāshāk, waṛkhara.*

Ruby, s. *l'al, yāqūt.*

Rudder, s. *singāwanr, sukkān.*

Ruddy, a. *sūr, l'al* or *lāl.*

Rude, a. *be·adab; nā·dān; lwāṛ.*

Rudiment, s. *aṣl, wekh, mūnḍ.*

Rue, v.n. *toba·gār-, pakkhemān-, stomān-,* etc. *ked.*

Rue, s. (wild) *spelanai, spānda, sipand.*

Rueful, a. *toba·gār, stomān; gham·jan, malūl.*

Ruffian, s. *ṭag, ḥarāmī, khūnāṛai, ghal.*

Ruffle, v.a. (-the feathers) *banre tārawul.* -(the skin) *ghūne zīgawul.* (crumple) *jungawul.* (disturb) *pārawul.*

Rug, s. *ghālīcha* or *qālīcha; namad, lamtsai; krāsta, kosai, shaṛa-ī.*

Rugged, a. *zīg, lwāṛ, klak; kāuredz, sanglākh.*

Ruin, v.a. *wrānawul, kharābawul, ujāṛawul. līțāṛawul, habatah-, abtar-, chauṛ-, ṛang-,* etc. *k.*

Ruination, s. *wrānī, kharābī.*

Ruinous, a. *wrān, wujāṛ, māt gud,* etc.; *tāwānī, ziyānī, nuqṣānī.*

Ruins, s. *kanḍar, kharāba.*

Rule, s. *qānūn, qā'ida, ṭarīqa, ā-īn, lār; 'amal, ḥukm, ḥukūmat.*

Ruler, s. *ḥākim, sardār, khān, amīr; misṭar, saṭar-* or *jadwal kakkh, lauḥa.*

Rumble, v.a. *juṛ juṛ-, qur qur-,* etc. *k.* v.n. *ghaṛedal, ga-aredal, ghuṛunbedal.*

Ruminate, v.a. *shkhwand wahal* or *k.*; *fikr k.*

Rummage, v.a. *laṭawul, shanal.*

Rumour, s. *āwāza, khabara, afwāh.*

Rump, s. *kūnāṭai, surīn; ḍuḍa* or or *ṭūṭa.*

Rumple, v.a. *jungawul, mātawul, kraṭī-,* etc. *k.*

Run, v.n. *zghaledal—zghākkhtal, drūmedal.* v.a. *manḍe wahal.* (-away) v.n. *takkhtedal.* (-on) *chaledal.* (flow) *bahedal, rawānedal.* (-after) *pase zghaledal* or *-prewatal.* (-over) *toyedal* or *to-edal.* (-out) *watal; tamāmedal.* (-down) *lāndī k.*; *kagal, ghandal.* (-up) *khatal.* v.a. *khejawul.* (-away with) *takkhtawul.*

Runaway, s. *takkhtedūnai.*

Rupee, s. *rupa-ī.*

Rupture, s. *māt.* (disagreement) *wrānī.* (hernia) *tsūhṛa.*

Rural, a. *dihātī, dzangalī.*

Rush, v.a. *halla-, ḍūsa-,* etc. *k.* v.n. *khatal; watal.*

Rust, s. *zang.*

Rustic, a. *dihqānī, gawār, lwāṛ.* s. *kilī-wāl, dihqān, ghunḍāyah.*
Rustle, v.a. *sharahār-, ga-arahār-,* etc. *k.*
Rut, s. *kīla, līk, karkkha.* (heat) *mastī.*
Ruthless, a. *be-raḥm, be-dard, kāṇrai zṛak.*
Ruttish, s. *shahwat-nāk, mast.* (-female) *tera, sema.* (in comp.) *-cma* or *-yama.*

S.

Sable, a. *tor*; *mushkai.* (-fur) *samūr, postīn.*
Sabre, s. *shamsher, tūra, tegh.*
Sack, s. *tsaṭa, ghundai, jwāl.*
Sack, v.a. *tālā-, lūṭ-, nātār-,* etc. *k., natal.*
Sacred, a. *pāk, majīd, muqaddas.*
Sacrifice, s. *qurbān, ṣadqa, dzār.*
Sad, a. *gham-jan, dil-gīr, āzurdah, malūl.*
Saddle, s. *zīn, kāṭī.* (-pad) *ṭogham* or *toghal, kejam, qajarī.* (-cloth) *zīn-pokkh.* (-girth) *tātang, tāng.* (-pad) *kho-gīr.* (-bag) *khūrjīn.* (-pommel) *ngūbai, kāsh, āna.* (-straps) *kānjogha.* v.a. *zīn taṛal.*
Saddler, s. *sarrāj, zīn sāz.*
Sadness, s. *gham, nūl, dil-girī*; *saudā.*
Safe, a. *salāmat, amn amān, khair ṣalāḥ.* (-guard) *panāh, pushta.* (meat-) *tsakai.*
Saffron, s. *gūngū, kangū, z'afarān.*
Sagacious, a. *hokkhyār, pohānd, 'aql-man.*
Sagacity, s. *poh, pahm, sha'ūr.*
Sage, s. *'āqil, dānā, 'aql-man.* s. *ḥakīm, zbarg.*
Sail, s. *bādwān.*
Sailor, s. *mallāḥ, jahāzī.*
Saint, s. *walī, abdāl, zbarg, pīr.* (the saints) *auliyā, āstāna-dārān.*
Sake, p. *dapāra, wāsta*; *la kabla.*
Salacious, a. *mast, shahwat-nāk.*
Salmander, s. *samandar.*
Salary, s. *ṭalab, mwājib, tankhwāh.*
Sale, s. *plor, prolana, prowuna, kharts, bai'a.*
Saline, a. *mālgīn, kkhora-nāk, kkhoran.*

Saliva, s. *lāṛa* or *lāṇra, tūk, tūkai.*
Salivate, v.a. *khula rāwṛal.*
Sallow, a. *ziyaṛ*; *skāṇr.*
Sally, v.a. *tākht-, tsoṭ-, kalla-,* etc. *k.*
Salt, s. *mālga.* (-collector) *mālgbah.* (-meat) *lāndai.* a. *mālgīn, namkīn.* (-less) *balmagai, balmangak.*
Saltpetre, s. *kkhora.*
Salubrious, a. *kkhah muwāfiq.*
Salutary, a. *sūd-man, fā-ida-man.*
Salutation, a. *d'uā, salām.*
Salute, v.a. *salām-, salāmī-,* etc. *k.*
Salvation, s. *khalāṣī, najāt, rihā-ī.*
Salve, s. *malham, paha, tab.*
Same, a. *haghah, daghah.* (in comp.) *yo-, hum-.* (the-) ad. *bedū.*
Sameness, s. *yo shānī, yoyat, barābarī.*
Sample, s. *namūna, nakkha.*
Sanctify, v.a. *pāk-,* etc. *k.*; *muqaddas ganṛal.*
Sanction, s. *ḥukm, izn, ijāzat.* v.a. *ḥukm-,* etc. *k.*
Sanctuary, s. *dargāh*; *panāh.*
Sand, s. *shiga, reg.* (-bank) *char.*
Sandal, s. *tsapla-ī, gāwlai.* (-wood) *chandaṇr.*
Sandy, a. *shiglan.*
Sane, a. *hokkhyār, hokkh-man, khabar-dār.*
Sanguinary, a. *khūnāṛai, khūn khwār*
Sanguine, a. *sūr*; *qawī*; *umed-wār.*
Sap, s. *pa-ī, oba, gūṛa-ī, rub.*
Sap, v.a. *surang wahal*; *mūnḍ bāsal—yastal.*
Sapient, a. *'aql-man, dānā.*
Sapling, s. *khalai, buzghalai*; *nihāl*; *keṛa.*
Sarcasm, s. *tarkha khabara, ṭ'an ṭ'an.*
Sash, s. *paṭka, lūnga-ī, mlā wastanai*; *jāl.*
Satan, s. *shaiṭān, iblīs.*
Satiate, v.a. *maṛawul, ḍakawul.*
Satiety, s. *moṛ-wālai, moṛ-tiyā, maṛa khwā.*
Satin, s. *aṭlas, dariyā-ī.*
Satire, s. *ṭoqa, pekkha.*
Satisfaction, s. *raẓā-mandī, khāṭir khwāhī.*
Satisfactory, a. *khāṭir khwāh, joṛ, ghwarah.*

Satisfy, v.a. *rāẓī-, khāṭir jam'a-*, etc. *k.*; *maṛawul, saṛawul*; *pohawul.*

Saturate, v.a. *khaṛob-, serāb-*, etc. *k.*; *khusht k.*

Saturday, s. *khālī, shamba.*

Sauce, s. *chāshnī*; *kkhornā.*

Saucepan, s. (metal) *dechka, kaṛahai.* (pottery) *kaṭwa-ī, kodai.*

Saucy, a. *be-adab, shokhīn, wīlak, chāṛdīnak.*

Sausage, s. *kulma.*

Savage, a. *dzangalī, wahshī*; *ẓālim, khūnāṛai.*

Save, v.a. *bachawul, sātal, khundī-, sarfa-*, etc *k*

Saving, s. *sūd, gata, sarfa.* ad. *siwā, baghair*

Saviour, s. *bachawūnkai, shafī.*

Savour, s. *khwand, maza, tsaka.*

Saw, s. *ara.* (-dust) *chūr.*

Say, v.a. *wayal, khabare k.*; *lal* or *lawdal.*

Sayer, s. *wayūnkai*; *lūnai* or *lūnkai.*

Saying, s. *wayana*; *khabara, wayai.*

Scab, s. *khīg, waṛ, khwaṛ.*

Scabbard, s. *teka, kāṭī, miyān.* (-mounting) *pāenak, mūnāl, taknāl.*

Scaffold, s. *manā*; *garwanj*; *dunkācha.*

Scald, v.a. *swadzawul.* v.n. *swal, sedzal.* (-head) s. *ganja.*

Scaldheaded, a. *ganjai, sudar, lendak.*

Scale, s. *tala.* (-cup) *pala.* (fish-) *khwar, tsaparkai.* (gradation) *kach, mech.* (skin) *khwar, poṭ.*

Scale, v.n. *khatal.* (peel) *lwaredal, nwaredal.*

Scales, s. *tala, tarāzū, mīzān.* (beam) *ḍānḍa-ī.*

Scan, v.a. (verse) *wazn k., jokal, talal.* (examine) *katal, āzmāyal, shanal, laṭawul.*

Scandal, s. *tukmat* or *tūmat, tor, peghor, ruswā-ī.*

Scanty, a. *la-ag, kam, rangai, pitsānrai.*

Scar, s. *dāgh*; *ta-apai*; *ṭakai*; *nughai.*

Scarce, a. *la-ag, kam, matrah, pitsānrai.*

Scarcely, ad. *kamtar, pa mushkil sara, kila.*

Scarcity, s. *kam-tiyā, tangsiyā, kākhti* or *qahṭī.*

Scare, v.a. *yerawul, trahawul, bugnawul.*

Scarecrow, s. *tsera.* (bogie) *bau, bagalola-ī.*

Scarf, s. *paṭka, lūnga-ī*; *oḍana-ī, dū-paṭa.*

Scarify, v.a. *kkhkar laqawul, wīne būsal—yastal.*

Scarlet, a. *sūr, lāl.*

Scatter, v.a. *khwarawul, tār pa tārawul.*

Scavenger, s. *jārū kakkh.* (at shrines, etc.) *mīnjawar.*

Scene, s. *nandāra, tamāsha.* (place) *dzāe.*

Scent, s. *bo, bū-e* or *bū-ī* v.a. *bū-ī k., bū-ī ākhistal.*

Scheme, s. *tadbīr, ḥikmat, band, chal, lamghaṛa-ī*; *maṭlab, niyat.*

Schism, s. *khalal, pasāt, mīrtsī*; *rifẓ.*

Schismatic, a. *rāfiẓī, khārijī*; *pasātī.*

Scholar, s. *shāgird, ṭālib*; *'ālim, mullā*

School, s. *maktab, madrasa.* (-boy) *dzanrai.* (-master) *ākhūn, mullā, ustād, mu'allim.* (-fellow) *ham dars, ham sabaq, ham dzolai.*

Science, s. *'ilm, ḥikmat, hunar*

Scirrhus, s. *yaga.*

Scissors, s. *biyātī, qainchī, ghachī.*

Scoff, v.a. *kanzal-, ṭoqe-, pekkhe*, etc.

Scold, v.a. *raṭal, traṭal, dāṛal, ṭaqawul, malāmatawul, peghorawul.*

Scope, s. *niyat*; *gharaẓ*; *araṭ-wālai*; *dzāe.*

Scorch, v.a. *kaṛawul, alwoyal, lūgharan-, lūlapah-, kaskar-, sūngaṭ-, saṭkūrai-*, etc. *k.*

Score, v.a. *shmeral, shumāral, ḥisābawul*; *kīkal, karkkha kāgal—kkhkal, -būsal—yastal.* (scratch) *gargal, garawul.*

Score, s. *karkkha, khaṭṭ*; *ḥisāb*; *shil*; *sabab.*

Scorn, v.a. *spuk ganral.*

Scorpion, s. *laṛam.*

Scoundrel, s. *bad ẓāt, ḥarāmī.*

Scour, v.a. *mugal—mukkhal, togal, skoyal, zdoyal.*

Scourge, v.a. *karoṛa-, qamchī-, dira-*, etc. *wahul.*

Scout, s. *dzarai, tsārī, jāsūs, yalak·dār.* v.a. *tsāral, tsār-, zarana-ī-*, etc. *k.*

Scowl, v.a. *starge brandawul.*

Scramble, v.a. *lūṭ māt k.*

Scrap, s. *ṭoṭa, reza; pūṭai, pitsānrai.*

Scrape, v.a. *garawul, togal, khriyal, gargal.*

Scrapings, s. *tarāshe.* (pot-) *koyanai, koela.*

Scratch, v.a. *garawul, gargal, skoyal.*

Scream, v.a. *chigha-, nāra-, sūra-*, etc. *wahal.*

Screen, v.a. *parda-, panāh-*, etc. *k., puṭawul, pokkhal; bachawul.*

Screw, s. *pech, marwat.*

Scribe, s. *kātib, līkūnkai, kkhkawūnkai.*

Scrip, s. *bana-ī, gūdai, dzola-ī.*

Scripture, s. *kitāb-i majīd.* (C.) *tauret, zabūr, injīl.* (H.) *shāstar.* (M.) *qurān, furqān.*

Scrofula, s. *anjīr.*

Scroll, s. *daftar, fard, ṭomār; nghakkhtai kāghaz.*

Scrotum, s. *khoṭa, da khoṭo pūkanra-ī.*

Scrub, v.a. *mugal—mukkhal, togal.*

Scruple, v.a. *shakk-, shubha-, gumān-*, etc. *laral.*

Scrupulous, a. *wahmī, wiswāsī, shakkī.*

Scrutinize, v.a. *āzmāyal, laṭawul, shanal, talal.*

Scrutiny, s. *āzmekkht, shanana, imtiḥān.*

Scuffle, v.a. *parzawul, ṭel wahal, sara nkkhlawul.*

Sculk, v.n. *ghalai ked., puṭedal.*

Sculptor, s. *naqqāsh, but sāz, sang tarāsh.*

Scum, s. *jakh, rag, kaf.*

Scurf, s. *pa-akh, poṭakai, khig.*

Scurrilous, a. *jiba·war, kanzal kawūnkai.*

Sea, s. *dariyāb, qālī dariyāb, baḥr.*

Seal, s. *muhr.* (-stone) *ghamai.* (-cutter) *muhr kan.* v.a. *muhr lagawul.*

Seam, s. *joṛ, skoe, ganḍal, darz.*

Sear, v.a. *dāghawul.*

Search, v.a. *laṭawul, shanal, talāsh k.*

Season, s. *wakht* or *waqt, mūda, neṭa; mausam* or *mosim, faṣl.*

Season, v.a. *namkīn-, maza·dār-*, etc. *k., maṣālak-*, etc. *warkawul* or *-āchawul; pokh-, maẓbūṭ-*, etc. *k.*

Seasonable, a. *joṛ, jukht, barābar.*

Seasonably, ad. *pa wakht, pa neṭe, pa mūde.*

Seasoning, s. *maṣālah* or *masāla; mālga.*

Seat, s. *kursī, da nāst dzāe; dzāe, muqām.* v.a. *kkhkenawul* or *kenawul.*

Secede, v.n. *jārwatal, stūnedal.*

Seclude, v.a. *belawul, yawādzai-, judā-*, etc. *k.*

Seclusion, s. *tanhā-ī, bel·tūn; ghalī·tob.*

Second, a. *dwayam, ṣānī, bul.* s. *pal, laḥẓa; mal, yār, komakī, pushtī, madad·gār.* v.a. *madad k., pushtī-, komak-*, etc. *warkawul.*

Secondly, ad. *ṣānī-an, biyā, bul.*

Secrecy, s. *parda, parda pokkhī, ghalī·tob, tara-ī, puṭ-wālai.*

Secret, a. *puṭ, pinham.* (in-) ad. *pa puṭa, pa tara-ī, pa parde.* s. *rāz, sirr, puṭa khabara.*

Secretary, s. *munshī.*

Secrete, v.a. *puṭawul, pokkhal; paidā k.*

Secretion, s. *rezish.*

Secretly, ad. *pa puṭa, pa parde, pa tara-ī.*

Sect, s. *firqa, maẕhab, ummat; ẕāt, noga.*

Sectary, s. *rāfiẓī, khārijī.*

Section, s. *juz, faṣal, sipāra; para, janba, gundī.*

Secular, a. *duniyā-ī, 'āmmī.*

Secure, a. *salāmat, amn, amān; maẓbūṭ, qā-im, ṭīng.* v.a. *sambālawul, maẓbūṭ-*, etc. *k., sātal, khundī k.*

Security, s. *salāmatī, panāh, amānat.* (bail) *ẓāmin.* (bond) *ẓamānat.* (false-) *be-khabarī.*

Sedan, s. *ḍola-ī, anbāla-ī.* (camel-) *kajāwa.*

Sedate, a. *qalār, ghalai.*

Sedentary, a. *be·ḥarakat, nāst.*

Sediment, s. *khatbel, matar.*

Sedition, s. *yāghī-garī, balwā-tob, patna, pasāt.*

Seditious, a. *pasātī, balwā-sāz, balwā-gar, yāghī-gar, yāghī, mufsid, sar-kakkh.*

Seduce, v.a. *ghulawul, darghalawul, be-lāri k.*

Seduction, s. *darghal-tob, ghulawuna, fareb.*

See, v.a. *katal* or *kasal, goral—līdal, nazar k.* (perceive) v.n. *pohedal, rasedal.* in. *gora!*

Seed, s. *tukhm, dāna.* (-of stone fruit, melons, etc.) *zarai.* (progeny) *alwād, zāwzad* or *zawzāt, tūng.* (sperm) *manī, mardī.*

Seeing, s. *līdah, kātah. nazar.* a. *bīnā.* (-that) ad. *dzaka.*

Seek, v.a. *latawul, talāsh k.*; *ghokkhtal, d'uā-,* etc. *k.*

Seem, v.n. *kkhkāredal, m'alūmedal.*

Seemingly, ad. *pa kkhkārah, pa līdah, pa kātah.*

Seemly, a. *munāsib, kkhāyastah, jor, lā-iq.*

Seize, v.a. *nīwul, ākhistal, qabz-, giriftār-,* etc. *k.*

Seldom, ad. *kamtar, kala nā kala.*

Select, v.a. *khwakkhawul, chunral, anrawul, pasand-, qabūl-, chīndah-, ghwarah-,* etc. *k.*

Self, pr. *dzān, khpul.*

Selfish, a. *khpul gharaz, khpul matlab, gharazī, gharaz-man, khpul nafs.*

Sell, v.a. *khartsawul, prowul, ploral* or *prolal, pa bai'e warkawul.*

Seller, s. *khartsawūnkai, prowūnkai,* etc.

Semen, s. *mardī, manī.*

Senate, s. *jirga*; *majlis*; *dīwān.*

Senator, s. *jirgatū, majlisī.*

Send, v.a. *āstawul, legdal* or *legal.* (-for) *rābalal, balal, ghokkhtal, talab k.*

Senior, a. *mashar, loe.*

Senna, s. *sana makī.*

Sensation, s. *hiss, dzān, sāh, sud.* (to have-) v.n. *pa dzān pohedal.* v.a. *hiss-,* etc. *laral.*

Sense, s. *'aql, poha, pahm*; *m'anī*; *hokkh, sud, khabar.* (to have-) v.a. *'aql-,* etc. *laral.*

Senseless, a. *be-hiss,* etc.; *be-hūdah, be-m'anī.*

Sensible, a. *baidār, hokkhyār, khabar-dār.*

Sensitive, a. *dzān-dār, jwandai.*

Sensual, a. *nafsānī, shahwatī, mast.*

Sensuality, s. *nafs parastī, mastī*; *shahwat, nafs.*

Sentence, s. *hukm, fatwā.* (of Quran) *āyat.* v.a. *hukm-,* etc. *k.*

Sentiment, s. *fikr, rāe, pona.*

Sentinel, s. *pāsbān, pahra-dār, tsoka-ī-dār.*

Separate, v.a. *biyalawul* or *belawul, judā k.* v.n. *biyaledal, bwukkhtal, bwaredal.* a. *bel* or *biyal, judā.*

Separately, ad. *biyal biyal, judā-judā.*

Separation, s. *biyal-tūn, judā-ī, biyal-wālai.*

September, s. *asū.*

Sepulchre, s. *gor, qabr*; *lahd.*

Sequel, s. *'āqibat, ākhir*; *khatm.*

Sequester, v.a. *biyalawul*; *qurq k.*

Seraglio, s. *zanāna, haram srāe.*

Serene, a. *qalār, ārām*; *spīn, shīn, sāf.*

Series, s. *qatār*; *hār, lar*; *silsila.*

Serious, a. *drūnd, grān, muhimm.*

Sermon, s. *w'az*; *khutba, pand, nasīhat.*

Serpent, s. *mār.* (python) *kkhāh mār.* (viper) *mangor, mangarai.* (amphisbœna) *latka, landa-ī*

Serpentine, a. *mār pech, walandai, kog wog, kālkūchan.*

Servant, s. *nokar, khidmat-gār, mazdūr.*

Serve, v.a. *nokarī-, khidmat-, mazdūrī-,* etc. *k.* v.n. *kedal, lagedal, chaledal.*

Serviceable, a. *pa-kār, fā-ida-man, sūd-man.*

Servile, a. *khūshāmad-gar, chāplūs, dirpal.*

Servility, s. *khūshāmad-garī, chāplūsī,* etc.

Sesamum, s. *kunzala.*

Session, s. *majlis, jalsa, mahkama.*

Set, s. *jora*; *firqa*; *para, gundī.* a. *jarāo.* v.a. *gdal* or *īgdal, īkkhodal, īkkhal, kegdal* or *kkhkegdal,* etc. *layawul, jorawul, khejawul, kkhkenawul* or *kenawul.* v.n.

kūzedal, prenatal. (-out) *ranānedal, drūmal, drūmedal, tlal—lāṛal.*
Settle, v.a. *astoga k., dzāe nīnul, ābādawul.* (fix) *muqarrar k., wudrawul, kkhkenawul.* (arrange) *tartībawul, atsanṛal, samawul, barābarawul.* (compose) *saṛawul.* (-an account) *pūrah-, adā-,* etc. *k.* (-a difference) *pakhulā k., gwākkh-grandī k.* (-down) v.n. *kenāstal* or *kkhkenāstal.*
Settled, a. *qalār, ārām; nāst, prot; pūrah, adā.*
Settlement, s. *bandobast.* (colony) *ābādī.* (marriage-) *kābīn.* (-of dispute) *rogha, joṛa, faiṣal.*
Seven, a. *owah.* (seventh) *owam.*
Seventeen, a. *owah-las.*
Seventy, a. *awwyā.* (seventieth) *awwyāyam.*
Sever, v.a. *prekawul, biyalawul; lwaṛawul.*
Several, a. *dzani, b'azi, tso, ḍer.*
Severally, ad. *yaw yaw, biyal biyal, judā judā.*
Severe, a. *sakht, tez, tund, klak.*
Sew, v.a. *gandal, skoe k.* (darn) *bezal, pezal.* (-up) *agayal.*
Sex, s. *jins, ẕāt.*
Sexton, s. *muazzin; mīnjawar* or *mujāwir.*
Shabby, a. *spuk, khwār; pūhaṛ; khushai.*
Shade, s. *sorai, siwrai.*
Shadow, s. *sorai; 'aks; panāh.*
Shaft, s. *tīr, ḍānḍa-ī, stan.* (-of a well) *koṭa.* (-of a carriage) *bāzū, gānḍa-ī.*
Shaggy, a. *babar, waṛan.*
Shagreen, s. *kīmukht.*
Shake, v.a. *khwadzawul, tsandal, kkhorawul, rapawul.* (-down) *drabal.* v.n. *khwadzedal, rapedal, laṛzedal, kkhoredal.*
Shallow, a. *pāyāo* or *pāyāb; nādān, nīmgaṛai.*
Sham, s. *bāna* or *bahāna, lamghaṛa-ī, chal, ṭagī.* a. *jūṭah, nāsarah, darogh-jan.* v.a. *bāna-,* etc. *k.*
Shame, s. *sharm, hayā; sharmindagī; makh, ghairat.*
Shameful, a. *ruswā, bad; sharmsār, sharmnāk; ghairat-man* or *ghairat-nāk.*
Shameless, a. *be-sharm, be-hayā, be-nang, be-makh,* etc.
Shampoo, v.a. *chāpī k., manḍal.*
Shank, s. *kkhanga; tsānga; kkhākh; lasta.*
Shape, s. *shakl, ṣūrat, ḍaul, rang.*
Share, s. *brakha, wesh, ḥiṣṣa, wanḍa.* (plough-) *pāla, saspār.*
Share, v.a. *weshal.* v.n. *sharīk ked.*
Sharer, s. *brakha-khor, sharīk.*
Sharp, a. *terah, tez.* (sour or acid) *triw, trīkh, brekkhan.* (active) *chālāk.* (clever) *pohānd.*
Sharpen, v.a. *terah-,* etc. *k.*
Sharper, s. *ṭag, ṭag-bāz, darghal.*
Shatter, v.a. *chūr chūr-, daṛ daṛ-, ṭoṭe ṭoṭe-, reze reze-, kanḍ kapar-,* etc. *k.*
Shave, v.a. *khriyal* or *khrayal; togal.*
Shaving, s. *ṭoṭkai, tarāza, tūtankai.*
Shawl, s. *shāl.* (-for waist) *abra.*
She, pr. *hagha, dā, de, da, e.*
Sheaf, s. *geḍa-ī.*
Shear, v.a. *skūstal, skūl-* or *skwal k., kaṭeyal.*
Shears, s. *biyātī, khorkhal, kāz, skūlai.*
Sheath, s. *teka, miyān; kāṭī.*
Shed, s. *chopāṛ, jūngaṛa, kadala, manḍaw, kūḍa-ī.*
Shed, v.n. *rejedal; to-edal* or *toyedal.* v.a. *āchawul, ghurzawul, toyawul.*
Sheep, s. *ga-aḍ, ga-aḍūrai.* (long-tailed-) *herṛai, berṛai, barra.* (-owner) *ga-aḍbah.* (-cot) *shpol, bānḍa.* (ewe-) *kada, meg.* (ram) *mag, ga-aḍ.* (wether) *wuch-kūl.*
Sheer, a. *ṣāf, pāk.*
Sheet, s. *tsādar, dū-paṭa.*
Shelf, s. *ṭāq, ṭāqcha, daraz, rap.*
Shell, s. *gūjai, sīpa-ī.* (cowrie) *kunjaka, kawḍa-ī.* (fruit) *poṭ, postakai.*
Shelter, s. *panāh, amn* or *aman; nanawātah.*

v.a. *panāh-*, etc. *warkawul*; *pokkhal*, *puṭawul*.

Shepherd, s. *shpūn*. (-boy) *shpankai*.

Sherbet, s. *guṛobai*, *sharbat*.

Shield, s. *spar*, *ḍāl*, *salaṭ*. (-handle) *dast-māya*, *da guda-ī laṛ*. (boss) *patrai*.

Shield, v.a. *bachawul*, *jghoral*, *sātal*, *panāh-*, etc. *k*.

Shift, s. *ḥikmat*, *chal*, *band*, *chāra*. (evasion) *hira-ī*, *lamghaṛa-ī*, *ḥila*, *bāna*. (shirt) *ganḍolai*, *pepna-ī*, *khata*, *qamīṣ*.

Shift, v.a. *khwadzawul*, *badalawul*, *girzawul*. v.n. *khwadzedal*, *girzedal*, *āwukkhtal*.

Shine, v.n. *brekkhedal*, *dzalkedal* or *dzaledal*, *rūnredal*, *rokkhānedal*.

Shining, a. *brekkh-nāk*, *rokkhān*, *rūnr*, *dzalkān*.

Ship, s. *jahāz*, *beṛa-ī*.

Shirt, s. *qamīṣ*, *khata*, *ganḍolai*, *pepna-ī*.

Shiver, v.n. *rapedal*, *regdedal*, *larẓedal*. s. *larẓa*. (break) *mātawul*. (*v.* Shatter.)

Shoal, s. *ṭolai*, *sail*, *ghol*, *pāyāo*; *char*.

Shock, s. *ḍaka*, *ṭakar*.

Shocking, a. *makrūh*, *kraka-war* or *-nāk*.

Shoe, s. *panra*, *pāezār*, *jūṭa-ī*; *mochanra*, *kokkha*, *jista*. (-maker) *mochī*, *tsamyār*. (horse-) *na'l*. (to put on-) v.a. *pa kkhpo k.*, *na'l k.* or *-lagawul*.

Shoot, v.a. *wīshtal*, *ṭopak-*, etc. *khalāṣawul* or *chalawul*. v.n. *ṭūkedal*, *zarghūnedal*.

Shop, s. *dūkān*, *haṭa-ī*; *kār-khāna*. (-keeper) *dūkān-dār*, *banriyā*, *kaṭrī*.

Shore, s. *ghāṛa*. (near-) *rā-pori ghāṛa*. (far-) *pori ghāṛa*.

Short, a. *lanḍ*, *kotāh*. (less) *kam*, *la-ag*. (size) *mandarai*, *khamachah*.

Shorten, v.a. *lanḍawul*; *kamawul*. v.n. *lanḍedal*; *kamedal*.

Shortly, ad. *pa lanḍa*, *za-ar* or *zir*, *pa drang sā'at*.

Shot, s. (small) *chara*. (bullet) *mardakai*. (cannon-) *gola-ī*. (stroke) *guẓār*. a. *wīshtai*.

Shoulder, s. *oga*. (-blade) *walai*.

Shout, v.a. *nāra-*, *chigha-*, etc. *wahal*, *bāng wayal*.

Shove, v.a. *ṭel-*, *ḍaka-*, *ṭakar-*, *ṭāl-*, etc. *wahal*.

Shovel, s. (iron) *yūm* or *yīm*, *kara*. (wooden) *rashbel*.

Show, s. *nandāra*, *tamāsha*. v.a. *kkhayal*—*kkhowul*, *kkhkārah-*, *bartser-*, etc. *k.*, *tsargandawul*; *pohawul*, *pahmawul*.

Shower, s. *jaṛa-ī*, *bārān*. (spring-) *wasa*. (heavy-) *shebah*. (slight-) *pūna*. v.n. *woredal*, *bārānedal*, *tsātsedal*.

Showy, a. *raunaq-dār*, *kkhāyastah*, *ḍaulī*.

Shred, s. *rekkha*, *paṛūkai*, *reza*, *purza*.

Shrewd, a. *pokh*, *hokkhyār*, *chirg*, *kāgh*.

Shriek, v.a. *nāra-*, *sūra-*, *chigha-*, etc. *wahal*.

Shrine, s. *ziyārat*, *āstāna*, *dargāh*.

Shrink, v.n. *haṭedal*; *stanedal*; *bugnedal*; *jārwatal*. (as the belly) *wuchedal*, *kawt ked*.

Shrivel, v.n. *wuchedal*, *kawt ked.*, *chichar ked*.

Shroud, s. *kafan*, *tsādar*.

Shrub, s. *būṭai*, *jāṛa*, *ḍakai*. (thorny-) *karkanra*.

Shrubbery, s. *janga-ī*, *jāṛ*.

Shudder, v.n. *laṛzedal*, *ghūne zīgedal*, *regdedal*. v.a. *gagaṛodze nīwul*; *kraka ākhistal*.

Shuffle, v.a. *ṛaqawul*, *laṛal*, *gaḍ-waḍawul*. (equivocate) *janra-*, *hira-ī-*, *lamghaṛa-ī-*, etc. *k.*, *palma wayal*. (in gait) v.n. *ṭaparedal*.

Shun, v.a. *parhez k.*, *ḍaḍa ākhistal*. v.n. *bugnedal*, *takkhtedal*, *ḍaḍa ked*.

Shut, v.a. *bandawul*, *lagawul*. (as a door) *pori k*. (as the eyes) *puṭawul*. (as a book) *ṭap wahal*.

Shutter, s. *parda*, *takhta*. (-of a door) *tamba*, *pala*.

Shy, a. *yer-man*, *harānd*; *sharmsār*. v.n. *bugnedal*.

Sick, a. *nā-rogh*, *nā-joṛ*, *bīmār*, *randzūr*

(-of) *bezār, starai stomān.* (-of food, etc.) *sekan.* (-at stomach) *mīkkh mīkkh, chinjedalai.*

Sickle, s. *lor, lawa* or *lawāor.*

Sickly, a. *maraẕī, za'īf, nā-rogh.*

Sickness, s. *nā-joṛ-tiyā, bīmārī, āzār, randz.*

Side, s. *palaw, tselma, rokh, khwā, lorai; aṛkh, ḍaḍa, tsang; ghāṛa; ṯaraf, para, janba.* (-piece) *bāzū.*

Sideways, ad. *pa trats.*

Sieve, s. *ghalbel, parwezai; chaj, tsap.*

Sift, v.a. *ghalbelawul, chaj-,* etc. *wahal; chunṛal, chānṛawul; laṭawul, shanal.*

Sigh, v.a. *aswelai k.*

Sight, s. *naẕar; līdah, kātah; tamāsha, nandāra.*

Sign, s. *nakkha, 'alāma.* v.a. *dast khaṯṯ k.*

Signal, s. *nakkha, ishārat, nikkhānī.*

Signet, s. *muhr, ghamai.*

Significant, a. *m'anī-dār, m'anawī.*

Signification, s. *m'anī, maṯlab.*

Signify, v.a. *m'anī laral.*

Silence, s. *ghalī-tob.* in. *chup!*

Silent, a. *ghalai, chip.*

Silently, ad. *ro ro, ghalai ghalai.*

Silk, s. *rekkham.* (-worm) *da rekkham chinjai.* (-cocoon) *pela, ghoza.*

Silken, a. *rekkhmīn.*

Silly, a. *sādah, kawdan, nādān.*

Silver, s. *spīn zar.* (-smith) *zar-gar.*

Similar, a. *barābar, ghondai, gund, yaw shān.*

Simile, s. *matal, miṡāl, tashbīh.*

Simper, v.n. *musedal.*

Simple, a. *sādah, sarah, karah; spor, torai.*

Simpleton, s. *pūhaṛ, kawdan, gedī khar.*

Simply, ad. *sirp* or *surup, khālī, ta-ash.*

Sin, s. *gunāh, wabāl, taqṣīr, khaṯā, baza.*

Since, ad. *laka chi; pas, dzaka chi.* (-when?) *kala, la kūma.*

Sincere, a. *rikkhtīnai, rāst-bāz karah, sādah.*

Sinew, s. *pai, pla, rag, wuja.*

Sinful, a. *gunāh-gār, taqṣīrī.*

Sing, v.a. *sarod-, sandare-,* etc. *wahal.*

Singe, v.a. *swadzawul.* v.n. *swal, sedzal.*

Singer, s. *sarodī, muṯrib, sandar-goe.*

Single, a. *yo, yawādzai, witar, tsaṛak, tāk.* (-fold) *yawastawai, yak-tā.* (unmarried) *lawanḍ.*

Singly, ad. *yo yo.*

Singular, a. *wāḥid; 'ajab.*

Sinister, a. *nā-rāst, bad, kog, tratskan.*

Sink, v.a. *ḍūbawul, gharqawul.* v.n. *ḍūbedal, gharqedal.*

Sinner, s. *gunāh-gār, bad-kār, taqṣīrī.*

Sip, v.a. *skal* or *tskal* or *tskkhal, chūpal, zbekkhal.* (taste) *tsaṭal, tsakal.*

Sir, s. *ṣāḥib, jī, bābū, lālā.*

Sire, s. *plār; ḥaẕrat.*

Sister, s. *khor.* (husband's) *ndror.* (by brother) *bābī, wrandār, wandyār.* (by husband's brother) *yor.* (wife's) *kkhīna, khwakkhīna.* (foster-) *da to khor.* (tribal-) *khoringa.* (-hood) *khoringa-ī.*

Sit, v.n. *kenāstal* or *kkhkenāstal.*

Site, s. *dzāe, zmaka.*

Sitting, s. *nāstah* or *kkhkenāstah.*

Situation, s. *dzāe 'uhda, darja; khidmat, kār.*

Six, a. *shpag.* (sixth) *shpagam.*

Sixteen, a. *shpāṛas.* (sixteenth) *shpāṛasam.*

Sixty, a. *shpetah.* (sixtieth) *shpetam.* (-one) *yaw shpetah.* (-two) *dwah shpetah,* etc.

Size, s. *qadr, andāza; slekkht; batī.*

Skein, s. *tranjai, tranjūkai, aṭa* or *aṭeha.*

Sketch, s. *naqsha* or *nakhkkha, taṣwīr.* v.a. *naqsha-,* etc. *kāgal—kkhkal,* or *-likal,* or *-bāsal—yastal.*

Skewer, s. *sīkh, sīkhcha, salā-ī, sparkhai.*

Skilful, a. *qābil, pokh, kārī-gar, hunar-man.*

Skill, s. *hunar, kārī-garī, qābiliyat.*

Skim, v.a. *zag liri k.* or *ākhistal.* (-over) *naẕar pa zir terawul.*

Skin, s. *tsarman, poṭ.* v.a. *tsarman-*, etc. *liri k.*, or *-bāsal—yastal* or *-kāgal—kkhkal.*

Skip, v.a. *trapa-, ṭop-*, etc. *wahal, khajūnko-, tskhe*, etc. *k.*

Skirmish, s. *ṭas ṭūs, ḍandūkār.*

Skirt, s. *laman, ja-ī, pītskai* ; *ghāṛa, tselma.*

Skittish, a. *be-qalār, yer-man* ; *mast, shokhīn.*

Skull, s. *kapara-ī, kakara-ī.*

Sky, s. *āsmān.* (clear-) *shīn āsmān.* (dark-) *ganr* or *gūr āsmān.*

Slab, s. *takhta.* (stone-) *tīga, siyādza.*

Slack, a. *sust, arat, prānatai* ; *laṭ, nā-rāst.*

Slake, v.a. *saṛawul.*

Slander, s. *tuhmat* or *tūmat, tor, peghor palma.* v.a. *tūmat-, tor-*, etc. *pori k., peghor warkawul, palma wayal.*

Slanting, a. *tratskan, sar jawar, rewand.*

Slap, v.a. *ṭas-, tsāpeṛa-, kṛap-*, etc. *wahal.*

Slash, v.a. *ghwutsawul, tsīral* ; *wahal* ; *tsanḍal.*

Slattern, a. *pūhaṛ, shaṭal* or *shalaṭ, shānlai wāwlai.*

Slaughter, s. *qatl, khūn, qatli'āmm.*

Slave, s. *mra-e, ghulām, agar.* (f.) *windza, barda, agara.*

Slavery, s. *mra-e-tob, ghulāmī.*

Slay, v.a. *qatlawul, muṛ k., wajal* or *wajlal.* (-for food) *halālawul.*

Slayer, s. *qātil, khūnī.*

Sleek, a. *tsorb, chāgh* ; *ghwaṛ* ; *ṣāf, spetsalai, spīn.*

Sleep, s. *khob.* v.a. *khob k.* v.n. *ūdah-, bīdah-*, etc. *ked.* (to put to-) v.a. *ūdah k., tsamlawul.*

Sleepy, a. *khob-nāk, parnā-, khob-*, etc. *-wṛai* ; *drane starge.*

Sleeve, s. *lastūnrai, āstīn.*

Slender, a. *narai, trandz, nāzuk, mahīn, bārīk.*

Slice, s. *tarāzaṭ, oṭkai.*

Slide, v.n. *kkhwahedal* or *kkhwa-edal, kkhakedal, laghzedal.*

Slight, a. *la-ag, kam* ; *spuk, halak.* (v. Slender). v.a. *spuk ganṛal, spuk nazar k.*

Slim, a. *narai, trandz.* (v. Slender).

Slime, s. *chiqaṛ, khaṭa, lāha.* (vegetable-) *ubṛa-ī.*

Slimy, a. *chiqran, kkhwai.*

Sling, s. *machoghna* or *machaloghza, trankūtsa.* (the cup of a-) *gāṭa-ī.* (cradle) *zāngo, gahwāra, amel* or *ḥamā-il.* v.a. *wīshtal.*

Slip, v.n. *kkhwahedal.* (v. Slide). (-away) *teredal.* (-from the memory) *heredal.* (-from sight) *puṭedal.* (-from the hand) *khalāṣedal, yalah ked.*

Slip, s. *kkhwahedana, laghz* ; *khaṭā, ter wat* ; *ṭoṭa, rekkha, paṭa-ī* ; *qalam.*

Slipper, s. *panṛa, kokkha, paizār* or *pāezār, jista.*

Slippery, a. *kkhwai, laghzan, chiqran.*

Slit, v.a. *tsīral, shlawul, chawul, chāk k.* s. *tsīra, chāwd, daṛa, chāk* or *chāq.*

Sloping, a. *tratskan, rewand, sar jawar, sar lwaṛ.*

Slothful, v.a. *sust, laṭ, nā-rāst, kāhil, shaḍal.*

Slough, s. *chiqaṛ* or *qīchaṛ, bokkhtana* ; *khwar, postakai, tsarman.*

Sloven, s. *pūhar, palīt, shalaṭ* or *shaṭal.*

Slow, a. *sust, laṭ, ro, qalār.*

Slowly, ad. *ro ro, qalār qalār.*

Sluggard, a. *shaḍal, laṭ, ārām ṭalab.*

Sluice, s. *warkh, ghwagai* ; *mūra-ī.*

Slur, s. *dāgh, laka* ; *tor, peghor.* v.a. *dāghawul, wrānawul.*

Slut, s. *pūhaṛa, shalaṭa-* ; *hujra-ī, gashta-ī* ; *spa-ī.*

Sly, a. *chalwalai, chal-bāz.*

Smack, v.a. *ṭas-, ṭaq-, tsāpeṛa-*, etc. *wahal.* (taste) *tsaka, khwand, maza.*

Small, a. *woṛ, la-ag, warūkai, waṛkoṭai, pūṭai, mandarai, kachoṭai, kuchinai, kharmandai.*

Smallness, s. *la-ag·walai, wṛūk·wālai.*

Smallpox, s. *nanaka-ī.* (scar) *ta-apai.* (chicken) *katswak.*

Smart, a. *chālāk, chust, tez, tund.* v.a. *swai k.* v.n. *swal, sedzal.*

Smear, v.a. *lewawul, tabal, ghwaṛ k.*; *akheṛal.*

Smell, s. *bū, bū-ī.* v.n. *bū-ī tlal.* v.a. *bū-ī k.*

Smile, v.n. *musedal.* v.a. *muskai k.*

Smite, v.a. *wahal.*

Smith, s. *lohār, āhan·gar.* (gold-) *zar·gar.*

Smoke, v.a. *lū-, lūgai-*, etc. *k.* (as tobacco) v.a. *skal* or *tskkhal.*

Smoky, a. *lūghaṛan.*

Smooth, a. *sam, hawār, barābar*; *narm.* v.a. *samawul, atsanṛal, hawārawul*, etc.

Smother, v.a. *sāh bandawul, ghāṛa-, mara-ī-*, etc. *-khapa k., sāh ḍūbawul.*

Smut, s. *pūch go-ī.* (mildew) *tor, chanṛāsha.*

Snail, s. *shāpeṭai, gūjai, da kārghah paaska-ī.*

Snake, s. *mār.* (-charmer) *pāṛū.*

Snap, v.a. *chīchal*; *māṭawul*; *chuṭkī k.* (-as a dog) *ghapal, dāṛal.*

Snare, s. *dām.* (different kinds) *lūma, lūmaka, lwīna, jāl, ghūndārai, paṛka, talaka, laṭ, kuṛka-ī, honṛā.*

Snarl, v.a. *ghapal, dāṛal.*

Snatch, v.a. *pa ḥamle ākhistal, shūkawul, ghoṭa k., tsapa wahal.*

Sneak, v.n. *ghalai ked., puṭ girzedal.*

Sneer, v.a. *spuk naẓar k., poza-*, or *ūrbūz būṭawul.*

Sneeze, v.n. *pranjedal, prachedal.* v.a. *ngai k., ngal.*

Snipe, s. *karak, ṭamṭīl.*

Sniff, v.n. *sūnṛedal, sūghedal.*

Snore, v.a. *kha-ar wahal, kha-arkai k.*

Snort, v.n. *prashedal, sūnṛedal.*

Snot, s. *kaṛbeza* or *kaṛmeza.*

Snout, s. *poza, ūrbūz, tambūza.*

Snow, s. *wāwra.* v.n. *wāwre oredal* or *-prewatal.*

Snub, v.a. *dāṛal, raṭal, ṭaqawul.*

Snuff, s. *sūnṛ.* (tobacco) *nās, naswār.* v.n. *sūnṛedal.* v.a. *naswār k.*

Snug, a. *puṭ, ghalai*; *khwakkh, moṛ.*

So, ad. *hase, dā·hase, dā rang, hase shān, laka.* (-much) *hombra, tsombra.* (-much so) *tar de ḥadda pori.* (-long as) *tso chi, hombra chi.* (-be it) *wī di, hase di wī.* (it may be-) *wī ba, hase ba wī.* (-that) *tso chi.* (-often as) *har kala chi.* (-and so) *palānkai.*

Soak, v.a. *lūndawul, khushtawal.* (-up) v.a. *wuchawul, tskhal.*

Soap, s. *ṣābūn.* v.a. *ṣābūn lagawul.*

Sob, v.a. *zgerwai* or *zwergai-, salga-ī* or *sugala-ī-, ārkhakkh-, alhang-*, etc. *k., kūk wahal, jaṛal, pa raṭo raṭo jaṛal.*

Sober, a. *parhez·gār, parhezī*; *hokkhyār, baidār.*

Sociable, a. *majlisī, ṣuḥbatī, melmah·dost.*

Society, s. *ṣuḥbat, majlis*; *shirākat, malgartiyā, malgīrī, malgar·tob.*

Sod, s. *chūm, lūṭa.*

Sodden, a. *khuṛīn, post, oblan.*

Sodomite, s. *kūnī, kūnīgai.*

Sodomy, s. *kūnī·tob, bacha·bāzī, halak·bāzī, liwāṭat, ighlām.*

Soft, a. *pos* or *post, narm, mulā-im.*

Softly, ad. *ro ro, pa qalār.*

Soil, s. *mzaka* or *zmaka, khāwra.* (country) *waṭan, wilāyat*; *mulk, hiwād.* (manure) *sara.* v.a. *palīt-, khīran-, kakaṛ-*, etc. *k.*

Sojourn, v.n. *āstedal, osedal.* v.a. *astoga, mesht-, ṭikāo-*, etc. *k., dzāe nīwul*; *musāfiri k.*

Sojourner, s. *osedūnkai, astogūnkai*; *musāfir.*

Solace, s. *tasallī, ārām*; *k͟hwakk͟hi*. v.a. *tasallī-*, etc. *warkawul, pokk͟hal*.

Solder, v.a. *qalā'ī k., joṛawul*.

Soldier, s. *spāhī, lakk͟hkarī*. (heavy armed-) *puṭ spāhī*. (light armed-) *tsaṛah spāhī*. (irregular) *mlā taṛ, jazāelc͟hī*.

Soldiership, s. *spāhī-garī*; *spāhī-tob*.

Soldiery, s. *lakk͟hkar, fauj* or *pauj, ḍal*.

Sole, a. *yawādzai, tsaṛah*; *yak-tā*. s. *k͟hapaṛ, tala, warg͟hawai*. (-of a shoe) *talai*.

Solely, ad. *sirp* or *surup, ta-as͟h, faqaṭ*.

Solemn, a. *grān, drūnd*; *'ibrat-nāk*.

Solemnize, v.a. *manal*; *'urs-, 'īd-, 'ibādat-*, etc. *k., qā-im-, rawā-*, etc. *laral*.

Solicit, v.a. *g͟hokk͟htan, minnat-*, etc. *k*.

Solicitation, s. *g͟hokk͟ht, minnat, dark͟hwāst, sawāl*.

Solicitous, a. *andekk͟h-man, wiswāsī, fikr-man*.

Solicitude, s. *andekk͟hnā, wiswās, fikr, g͟ham*.

Solid, a. *klak, ṭing, sak͟ht, drūnd, gauṛ, pok͟h, k͟hyam*.

Solidity, s. *klak-*, etc. *-wālai, dranāwai*.

Solitary, a. *yawādzai, tanhā, biyal, tsaṛah*.

Solitude, s. *tanhā-ī, biyal-tūn*; *dzangal, ba-yābān*; *gokk͟ha, k͟hilwat*.

Solve, v.a. *prānatal, tsargandawul*; *wīlī k*.

Solvent, a. *zar-dār, māl-dār*; *wīlī kawūnkai*.

Some, a. *la-ag, la-ag ḍer*; *dzane, tsok, kūm, tsa*.

Somebody, s. *palānkai, tsok, kūm, kas, tan*.

Somehow, ad. *yaw s͟hān sara, tsa c͟hal sara*.

Something, s. *s͟hai, tsīz*. a. *la-ag ḍer, pitsāṇrai*.

Sometimes, ad. *kala kala*.

Somewhat, a. *la-ag, kam, pitsāṇrai*. ad. *la-ag-kāṭī* or *lukāṭī, tsak͟ho, la-ag s͟hān*.

Somewhere, ad. *c͟hare*.

Son, s. *dzoe*. (-in law) *zūm, zūmgai*. (grand-) *nwasai*. (great grand-) *karwasai*. (step-, by father) *parkaṭai*. (step-, by mother) *ba-anzai*. (brother's-) *wrārah*. (sister's-) *k͟hora-e* or *k͟horaye*. (only-) *kas͟hai*.

Song, s. *sandara, sarod, badala, ṭapa, tarāna*.

Sonnet, s. *c͟hār baite g͟hazal, lanḍa-ī, sandara*.

Soon, ad. *zir, pa zir mūde, pa la-ag sā'at kk͟hke*.

Sooner, ad. *wrūnbe, awwal*.

Soot, s. *lūgai, mas, dūna*; *koyina*.

Soothe, v.a. *tasallī warkawul, k͟hwā saṛawul, pok͟hal*.

Soothsayer, s. *pāl-* or *fāl-goe*, or *-katūnkai*.

Sooty, a. *lūg͟haṛan*.

Sop, s. *nwaṛa-ī*. v.a. *c͟hūka k., k͟hus͟htawul*.

Sorcerer, s. *jādū-gar, koḍ-gar, siḥr-gar*.

Sorcery, s. *jādū, koḍa, siḥr*.

Sordid, a. *s͟hūm, bak͟hīl, tang-dast, stag͟h*

Sore, s. *parhār, zak͟hm*. a. *zak͟hmī, k͟hūg*.

Sorrel, s. *tarūkai*.

Sorrow, s. *g͟ham, nūl*; *randz, afsos*; *pakk͟he-mānī, stomānī*; *armān, tartāb*. v.n. *g͟ham-edal, nūledal, randzedal, pakk͟hemānedal, stomānedal*. v.a. *afsos-, armān-*, etc. *k*.

Sorrowful, a. *g͟ham-jan, g͟ham-nāk, nūl-jan, dil-gīr*.

Sorry, a. *toba-gār, pakk͟hemān, stomān*. (vile) *nā-kārah, k͟hus͟hai, hets s͟hai*.

Sort, s. *qism, rang, s͟hān, noṛa*. v.a. *c͟hunṛal, atsanṛal, tartībawul, c͟hīndah k*.

Sot, s. *bangī, s͟harābī, nas͟ha-k͟hor*.

Soul, s. *rūḥ, nafs, dzān*. (souls) *arwāḥ*.

Sound, a. (honest) *sūc͟hah, karah, rikk͟htīnai*. (healthy) *joṛ, rog͟h moṭ, tandrust*. (safe) *salāmat, pūrah, ṣābit, amānī*. (right) *juk͟ht, barābar, sam*.

Sound, s. *g͟hag, zwag, bāng, ḍaz*. v.a. *g͟hagawul, zwag k., bāng wayal, ḍaz wahal*.

Soundly, ad. *pa kk͟hah s͟hān sara*.

Soundness, s. *tandrustī, salāmatī, ṣiḥḥat*.

Soup, s. *kk͟horwā*.

Sour, a. *trīw*.

Source, s. *munḍ, wek͟h, aṣl, sar, bonsaṭ*.

Souse, v.a. *lūndawul, k͟hus͟htawul*; *ḍūbawul*.

South, s. *suhel, k͟hūṛ-taraf*.

Sovereign, s. *bādshāh, sultān, amīr.*
Sow, v.a. *karal, kar k.* (-for another) *bogarai k.*
Space, s. *dzāe.* (-of time) *mūda, wakht, 'arṣa.*
Spacious, a. *arat, prānītai, dzāe·war.*
Spade, s. *yūm* or *yīm, kara.*
Span, s. *lwesht, langor, anang, gaḍozai.*
Spar, s. *bensh, tīr, largai.* (small-) *chaṇra; aṛam, aṛamkai.*
Spar, v.a. *jang k., sūkūno sara wahal, lāsuna sara tsanḍal.*
Spare, v.a. (save) *bachawul, bakkhal, pulawul.* (forego) *pregdal, prekkhodal, prekkhal.* (give) *warkawul.*
Spare, a. (scanty) *kam, la-ag, rangai.* (slender) *narai, trandz.* (short) *lanḍ, tang.* (unoccupied) *khālī, wuzgār.* (superfluous) *ziyāt, pāltū.*
Sparing, a. *kam·kharts, tang·dast.*
Spark, s. *batsarai, batsarkai, ghuṛutskai.*
Sparkle, v.n. *brekkhedal, dzalkedal, rūṇredal.*
Sparkling, a. *brekkh·nāk, dzalkūn, rūṇr.*
Sparrow, s. *chaṇr chaṇr, chughuk.*
Spasm, s. *ghoṭa, tāo, pech.*
Spatter, v.a. *tsiṛīke wahal; dāghawul, palītawul.*
Spavin, s. *haḍai, oba.*
Speak, v.a. *wayal, khabare k., lal.*
Spear, s. *neza, balla, barcha, shalgai.*
Special, a. *khāṣṣ.*
Specie, s. *zar, naghd* or *naqd.*
Species, s. *zāt, rang, qism, noga.*
Specific, a. *zātī, nogai.* s. *mujarrab.*
Specimen, s. *namūna, nakkha, miṣāl.*
Speck, s. *ṭikai, laka, tsiṛika, dāgh.*
Speckled, a. *ṭik·yālai, brag·yālai.*
Spectacle, s. *tamāsha, nandāra.*
Spectacles, s. *chashme, chashmake.*
Spectator, s. *nandārchī, tamāsha·bīn.*
Spectre, s. *rawai, khapaskai; sīwrai.*

Speculate, v.a. *fikr-, qiyās-, khiyāl-,* etc. *k.*
Speculative, a. *fikr·man, khiyālī, aṭkalī.*
Speculator, s. *aṭkal·bāz, saudāgar.*
Speech, s. *jiba, wayai, wayana, khabara, wrāsha, sukhun.*
Speechless, a. *gūng, lāl, lā dzawāb.*
Speed, s. *talwār, talwal, jaltī, gaṛandī·tob.*
Speedily, ad. *pa talwār, pa gaṛandī, pa jaltī.*
Speedy, a. *gaṛandai, za-ar* or *zir, jalt, tez.*
Spell, s. *jādū, koḍ, mantar.*
Spell, v.a. *paiza-ī-, pakkhoya-, hijgī-,* etc. *k.*
Spend, v.a. *kharts-, ṣarf-,* etc. *k., lagawul.* (pass) *terawul.* (emit) *khalāṣawul, chalawul.* v.n. *chaledal, kamedal, teredal, khalāṣedal.*
Spendthrift, s. *khartsī, tāwānī, iṣrāfī.*
Sphere, s. *tsarkh; ghūndai.*
Spherical, a. *ghūnd, ghūnd·man.*
Spice, s. *maṣālah* or *masāla.*
Spider, s. *jolā.* (tarantula-) *ghaṇra.*
Spigot, s. *būja, khulborai, ḍiḍa.*
Spike, s. *wagai, khosha.* (nail) *mogai.*
Spill, v.a. *toyawul, ghurzawul, āchawul.* v.n. *toyedal* or *to-edal, prewatal, bahedal.*
Spin, v.a. *tsarkha k.; tsarkhawul, churlawul, girzawul.* v.n. *tsarkhedal, churledal, girzedal.*
Spinach, s. *pālak.*
Spindle, s. *dūk, barandai, jalak, tsarkhai, tsarkhalgai, girzandai, tsākkhai.* (stalk) *tīla-ī, nāṛa.*
Spinning, s. *tsarkhawuna.* (-wheel) *tsarkha.*
Spire, s. *munāra.*
Spirit, s. *rūḥ, nafs, dzān; dam, sāh; zṛah, dil; himmat, maṛāna; nang, ghairat; khoe, mizāj; 'araq, jauhar.*
Spirited, a. *zṛah·war, maṛanai, himmat·nāk, nang·yālai, ghairat·nāk* or *ghairat·man.*
Spiritual, a. *rūḥānī, bāṭinī.*
Spit, v.a. *tūkal, tū-, tūkāṛrai-,* etc. *ghurzawul.*

Spit, s. *sīkh, sīkhcha.*

Spite, s. *kīna, ẓidd, khwā badī, 'adāwat, 'inād, 'aks, rakha, droh, ghach.* (in spite of) *par 'aks, par khilāf.*

Spiteful, a. *kīna-war, khwā bad, 'inādī.*

Spittle, s. *tū, tūk, tūkānrai, lāṛa, lānra.*

Splash, v.a. *tsiṛīke-, charaq-,* etc. *wahal, lawastal.*

Spleen, s. *torai.* (spite) *kīna, khwā badī.*

Splendid, a. *rokkhān, dzalkān*; *loe, ghaṭ.*

Splendour, s. *raunaq, dabdaba, tamtarāq.*

Splice, s. *joṛ, pewand.* v.a. *joṛawul, pewand k.*

Splint, s. *tūtankai.* (-in horses) *haḍai.* (surgical) *takhta, kalokkhta, kalola, skanḍa.*

Splinter, s. *ṭoṭkai, daṛa, kak, tarāza.*

Split, v.n. *chāwdal, shledal.* v.a. *chawul, shlawul.* (peas, grain, etc.) *dal k., dalawul.*

Spoil, v.a. *wrānawul, kharābawul, habatah-, 'abas-, ṛang-, abtar-,* etc. *k.* (plunder) *lūṭawul, shūkawul, natal, tālā-,* etc. *k.* s. *lūṭ, tālā, shūka, ghārat, gaṭa.*

Spontaneously, ad. *pakhpula.*

Spoon, s. *chamcha-ī* or *tsamtsa-ī* or *tsontsa-ī, qashoghā.* (large) *kaṛecha-ī, harkāra.*

Sport, s. *loba*; *khandā, ṭoqa washta*; *kkhkār.* v.a. *lobe k.*; *khandā-,* etc. *k.*; *kkhkār k.*

Sportsman, s. *kkhkārī.*

Spot, s. *ṭakai, laka*; *dāgh, 'aib, tsiṛīka*; *dzāe.*

Spotted, a. *chrag brag, gag, ṭak-yālai, brag-yālai.*

Spout, s. *tsūkkhka, tsakkhkūṛai.* (of water, etc.) *dāra, fawāra*; *charaq.* v.n. *pa dāro-,* etc. *watal* or *-bahedal.* v.a. *dāra-,* etc. *wahal.*

Sprain, s. *wal, tāo, pech.* v.a. *wal-,* etc. *khwuṛal.*

Sprawl, v.n. *rghaṛedal—rghakkhtal, lots pots ked.*

Spread, v.a. *khwarawul, wīṛawul, phelawul.* v.n. *khwaredal, wīṛedal, pheledal.*

Sprig, s. *lakkhta, kkhākhcha.*

Sprightly, a. *chust, chālāk*; *kkhād, kkhād-man*; *mast, shawkhīn.*

Spring, s. (season) *sparlai, bahār.* (source) *chīna, chashma.* (leap) *ṭop, trapa, dang, ghurzang.* (elasticity) *dam.* (instrument) *kamāncha.* (bound) *tīndak, khachūnai.*

Spring, v.a. (leap) *ṭop-,* etc. *wahal, dangal, traplal.* (bound) *tīndak-,* etc. *wahal.* (germinate) v.n. *ṭūkedal, zarghūnedal.* (issue) v.n. *khatal, watal, jārī ked.*

Sprinkle, v.a. *charqāo k., tsātsawul, tsiṛīk-awul.* (-from mouth) *pūg wahal.*

Sprout, s. *khalai, buzghalai, ghandal, tegh.* v.n. *ṭūkedal, zarghūnedal, ghundzedal.*

Spruce, a. *ḍaulī, joṛābī, spīn spetsalai, kṛah wṛah, kkhāyastah, pāk ṣāf.*

Spruceness, s. *joṛāb, kkhāyast, kkhāyast-wālai.*

Spur, s. *mamrez* or *mahmeza.* (cock's-) *khāro.* v.a. *tezal, pūnḍa-* or *pūnḍa-ī-. mamrez-,* etc. *wahal.*

Spurious, a. *jūṭah, nā-sarah, nā-karah.*

Sputter, s. *tsir, sakkhā, dzaz.* v.a. *tsir-,* etc. *wahal.*

Spy, s. *tsārī, jāsūs, zarai, mukhbir.* v.a. *tsāral, tsār-, zarana-ī-, jāsūsī-,* etc. *k.*

Squabble, v.a. *jagṛa-, qaẓiya-, steza,* etc. *k.*

Squalid, a. *palīt, gandah, khīran, murdār.*

Squall, s. (wind) *sīla-ī, jakaṛ, jam jakaṛ.* (cry) *chigha, jaṛā.* v.a. *chighawul, jaṛal.*

Squander, v.a. *iṣrāf-, talaf-,* etc. *k., wru-kawul.*

Square, a. *chār gūṭlai, chār kunjai, murabb'ah.*

Squash, v.a. *chīt pīt k., paz wahul.*

Squeamish, a. *mekkh mekkh.*

Squeeze, v.a. *nachoṛawul.* (-out) *nakkhtedzal.* (press) *manḍal.* (flatten) *chīt k.*

Squint, v.a. *pa kago-, pa kṛingo-, pa cha-pako-,* etc. *stargo katal.*

Squirrel, s. *bilūngaṛai, gidaṛai, bilawṛai.*

Squirt, s. *pichkāra-ī.* v.a. *pichkāra-ī wahal.* (-from the mouth) *pūg wahal*; *mazmaza k.*

Stab, v.a. *pa chāṛe-*, etc. *negh wahal*; *sūk wahal.*

Stable, a. *pāedār, qā-im, mazbūṭ.* s. *ṭabela.*

Stack, s. *dala-ī, ṭop, ḍera-ī.*

Staff, s. *lakaṛa*; *amsā*; *ḍānda-ī.* (shepherd's) *aṛamkai, konṭai.* (stem) *chaṛ.*

Stage, s. *mazal* or *manzil.* (degree) *darja.* (platform) *manā*; *dunkācha*; *gaṛwanj.*

Stagger, v.n. *rapedal, laṛzedal*; *gaḍ waḍ tlal, ṭaparedal*; *hak pak ked., kariyānedal.*

Stagnant, a. *band, walāṛ.* (-water) *ḍab.*

Stain, s. *dāgh, laka, tsiṛīka.*

Stair, s. *pārchang, pawṛa-ī, andarpāya.*

Stake, s. (peg) *mogai.* (post) *dār, sūla-ī.* (at play) *daw, sharṭ.*

Stale, a. *zoṛ, begānai, baranai.*

Stalk, s. *nāṛa, tila-ī*; *mūnḍ, ḍakai.*

Stall, s. *dzāe, khūna*; *ākhor.*

Stallion, s. *sānr, turum.*

Stammer, v.n. *tartaredal.* v.a. *guzmuzai k.*

Stammerer, s. *tartarai, chāṛā, tatai.*

Stamp, s. *chāp*; *muhr*; *manḍā*; *rang.* v.a. *chāp wahal*; *muhr lagawul*; *manḍal, manḍa wahal.*

Stampede, s. *ghwa-e-manḍ.*

Stand, v.n. *wudredal, walāṛedal, pātsedal.* (-fast) *tam ked.* (-at bay) *hatedal, jah* or *jig ked.* (erect) *neghedal, lak ked.*

Standard, s. *nakkha, nikkhān, togh, janḍa, bairaq* or *bairagh.*

Standing, a. *walāṛ, negh*; *lak*; *jig*; *pāedār.*

Staple, s. *saudā.* (lock-) *kūl, aṛam.* (hook) *kunḍa.*

Star, s. *storai.* (planet) *starga.*

Starch, s. *batī.* v.a. *batī ḍakawul.*

Stare, v.a. *ghaṭ katal.*

Starling, s. *sarkhaka.*

Start, v.n. *rawānedal, tlal—lāṛal, drūmedal, drūmal.* (fear) *bugnedal, tarhedal.*

Startle, v.a. *bugnawul, trahawul, yerawul.*

Starve, v.n. *da lwuge mṛal* or (v.a.) *-muṛ k.*

State, v.a. *bayānawul, wayal, lal, lawdal.*

State, s. *hāl, hālat*; *shān, shauqat*; *rāj, mulk.*

Statement, s. *ṣūrat hāl, bayān, wayai*; *hisāb.*

Station, s. *dzāe*; *mazal*; *darja, martaba.* v.a. *wudrawul, kkhkenawul, walāṛawul*

Statue, s. *but, tsera.*

Stature, s. *qadd, qāmat.* (tall) *dang.* (short) *mandarai.*

Statute, s. *qānūn, qā'ida, ā-īn.*

Stay, v.n. *osedal, pātedal, pātai-, tam-*, etc. *ked., āstedal.* (prevent) *man'a k., haṭālawul, kariyābawul.*

Stead, s. *dzāe, badal, 'iwaz.*

Steadfast, Steady, a. } *mazbūṭ, qā-im, pāedār, qalār.*

Steal, v.a. *ghlā k., puṭawul.* (-upon) *chapāo k.* (-away) v.n. *puṭedal.*

Stealth, s. *ghalī-tob, puṭ-wālai*; *ghlā.* (by-) *ghalai ghalai, puṭ puṭ.*

Steam, s. *bukhār, barās.*

Steep, a. *ūchat, hask*; *jawar*; *iwaṛ, kamar.*

Steep, v.a. *khushtawul, lūndawul.*

Steer, s. *skhwandar, skhwandarkai.*

Steer, v.a. *chalawul, kkhayal—kkhowul.*

Stem, s. *kkhākh, kharand, ṭanga, ḍanḍara, mūnḍ.* (of grasses, etc.) *nal, nāṛa.*

Stem, v.a. *bandawul, man'a k., haṭālawul.*

Stench, s. *bad-bū-ī, skhā-bū-ī, soṛ-bū-ī.*

Step, s. *qadam, gām*; *chāl, yūn*; *pāya, darja*

Sterile, a. *shanḍ.* (as land) *kkhora-nāk.*

Stern, a. *trīkh, sakht, klak.* s. *shā, wrusta.*

Stew, s. *pulāo, qorma, dam pukht.*

Steward, s. *dīwān, kārdār.*

Stick, s. *largai, hamsā*; *lawaṛ, ḍāng, koṭak.*

Stick, v.n. *nkkhatal, nkkhledal, chaspedal, lagedal.* (pierce) v.a. *sīkhal, tetsal.* (-into) *njatal, kkhkc-manḍal, khakkhawul, kkhke-bāsal—kkhke-yastal.*

Stickle, v.a. *takrār-, ḥujjat-*, etc. *k.*

Stiff, a. *ṭīng, klak*; *lak, negh*; *zīg, lwāṛ*; *tsak.*

Stifle, v.a. *sāh bandawul.*

Stigma, s. *tor, tuhmat, peghor*; *dāgh, laka.*

Stigmatize, v.a. *tor-, tuhmat-*, etc., *pori kawul, peghor warkawul.*

Still, a. *ghalai, chup*; *walāṛ, qalār*; *band, be·ḥarakat.* (water) *ḍab.* ad. *tar osa, os hum, lā.* s. *khum.*

Stimulate, v.a. *zoral, tezal*; *wīkkhawul, pātsawul, baidār k.*; *lamsawul.*

Sting, s. *nekkh*; *lasha.* v.a. *nekkh wahal.*

Stingy, a. *shūm, bakhīl, tang·dast, sakht.*

Stink, v.n. *bad-, skhā-, soṛ-*, etc. *bū-ī tlal.*

Stipulate, v.a. *wāda-, bandawr-, neṭa-*, etc. *k.*, or *-ṭaṛal.*

Stir, v.a. *khwadzedal, kkhoredal.* v.a. *laṛal, ṛaqawul, khwadzawul, kkhorawul.*

Stirrup, s. *rikāb.* (-leather) *dawāl, tasma.*

Stitch, s. *skoe.* v.a. *ganḍal, skoe k., skoyal, agayal.*

Stock, s. *tsaṭ.* (tree) *mūnḍ, gharand.* (-for legs) *kāṭ.* (source) *aṣl, noga.* (gun-) *kundāgh.* (store) *panga, saga, māya.*

Stocking, s. *jorāba, moza.* (leather-) *māsa-ī.*

Stocks, s. *kāṭ.* (torture-) *pāna, kunda.* (to put in the-) *pa kāṭ khejawul, pāna ṭakawul.*

Stomach, s. *geḍa, kheṭa*; *ūjrai.* (crop) *jajūra.*

Stone, s. *kāṇrai, gaṭ, ṭīga, giṭai.* (-of the bladder) *gīṭa-ī.* (grave-) *khāda* or *khaza.* (ring-) *ghamai.* (-of fruit) *haḍ.* v.a. *pa kāṇro-, pa gaṭo-*, etc. *wīshtal* or *-muṛ k., sangsār k.*

Stony, a. *kāṇredz, sanglākh, trāṛah.*

Stool, s. *peṛa-ī, moṛa.* (purge) *dast, nāstah.*

Stoop, v.n. *ṭīṭedal.* v.a. *sar ṭīṭawul.*

Stop, v.a. *pātawul, pātai k., man'a k., bandawul, īsārawul*; *wudrawul, walāṛawul*; *kiṭālawul, hariyābawul*; *nkkhlawul.* v.n. *pātedal, pātai ked., osedal*; *bandedal*; *īsāredal*; *wudredal, walāṛedal*; *nkkhledal, nkkhatal.*

Stopper, s. *būja, shoṛa, mūṇrai*; *khulborai, ḍiḍa.*

Store, s. *ambār, ganj, ḍerai*; *saga, panga, māya.* (-house) *koṭa, ambār·khāna, khazāna.* v.a. *ṭolawul, jam'a k., yandzāe k.*

Stores, s. *zakhīra, sūrsāt, rasad*; *tokkha, tsawrai*; *asbāb, sāmān*; *hatiyār, kālī.*

Stork, s. *ḍing.*

Storm, s. *sīla-ī, tūpān* or *ṭūfān.* v.a. *halla-, ḥamla-*, etc. *k.* (-by night) *shaw·khūn k.*

Story, s. *qiṣṣa, naql.* (stage) *mazal, maḥal.*

Stout, a. *mazbūṭ, ghaṭ, kaṭah*; *gagar, khrīs, nāpaṛ*; *lwāṛ, punḍ, tanḍ.*

Stow, v.a. *dzāyawul, kkhke·mandal, kkhkegdal, kkhekkhodal, kkhekkhal.*

Straddle, v.n. *chīnge kkhpe tlal—lāṛal.*

Straggle, v.n. *khor khor-*, or *khwarai khwarai-, tār pa tār-*, etc. *girzedal.*

Straight, a. *sam, negh, sat.*

Straightway, ad. *sam da lāsa.*

Strain, v.a. *ghalbelawul, chāṇrawul.* (labour) *stam wahal.* (endeavour) *ḥadd k.*

Strainer, s. *chāṇra, ghalbel, parwezai.*

Strait, s. *tanga-ī*; *tangsiyā, tangī, sakhtī.*

Strange, a. *pradai, begānah*; *'ajab.*

Stranger, s. *nā-āshnāe, nā·balad, pradai.*

Strangle, v.a. *mara-ī-, ghāṛa-*, etc. *khapa k.*

Strap, s. *tasma, rog.* (-of churning staff) *barangai.* (shoulder-) *paṭa*

Stratagem, s. *chal, ḥīla, fareb, lamghaṛa-ī.*

Stratum, s. *bragh, tā.*

Straw, s. *khas, khasaṇrai, kāna-ī.* (Maize-) *ṭānṭa.* (Rice-) *palāla.* (Mustard-) *kāmbūra.* (Pulse-) *kaṭī.* (broken-) *būs* or *būsī.*

Stray, v.n. *wrukedal, gumrāh-, be·lār-, khaṭā-*, etc. *ked., khushai, girzedal.*

Streak, s. *kil, līka, karkkha.* (-of light) *partaw, palwasha.*

Stream, s. *dāra, sailāb, chala, chalānda.* v.n. *bahedal, chaledal, jārī ked.*

Street, s. *lār, kūtsa.*

Strength, s. *zor, quwat, bram, tuwān, ṭāqat.*

Strengthen, v.a. *zor-*, etc. *warkawul, mazbūṭ-, klak-*, etc. *k.*

Strenuous, a. *sar·garm, mazbūṭ, klak.*

Stress, s. *zor, quwat; dranāwai, bār.*

Stretch, v.a. *rākāgal—rākkhkal, ūgdawul.* (-out) *ghazawul.* v.n. *ūgdedal; ghazedal.*

Strew, v.a. *khwarawul, rejawul* or *rejdawul, satrai watrai-, tār pa tār-, khwarai-*, etc. *k.*

Strict, a. *sakht, klak, ṭing, tang; jukht, joṛ.*

Strictly, ad. *pa rikkhtiyā.*

Stride, s. *tūlānd.* v.n. *pa tūlānd tlal—lāṛal.*

Strife, s. *patna, steza, mīrtsī, jogṛa, 'adāwat.*

Strike, v.a. *wahal, jangawul.*

String, s. *mazai.* (tie) *tanra-ī.* (-of beads) *laṛ, hār.* (-of cattle) *qaṭār.* v.a. *pewdal.*

Stringy, a. *rekkha·dār.*

Strip, s. *paṭa-ī, pāra, tarāza, rikkhkai, paṛūkai.*

Strip, v.a. *barbandawul; shūkawul.*

Stripe, s. *karkkha.* (blow) *guzār.* (whip) *karoṛa.*

Stripling, s. *halak, janrai; zalmai, ghundāyah.*

Strive, v.a. *miḥnat-, kokshikkh-*, etc. *k.; ẓidd-, qaṣd-*, etc. *k.*

Stroke, s. *guzār.* (at play) *daw.* v.a. *lās wahal* or *-girzawul*, etc.

Stroll, v.n. *girzedal.* v.a. *sail-, gakkht-*, etc. *k.*

Strong, a. *mazbūṭ, klak, mazai, zorāwar.*

Structure, s. *tarkīb, joṛawūna; shakl, ṣūrat.*

Struggle, v.a. *parzawul; jang k.; miḥnat k.*

Strumpet, s. *gashta-ī, baghara-ī, hujra-ī, kāsīra, kūtsa gashta, kachana-ī, lola-ī.*

Strut, v.n. *pa ḍaul tlal—lāṛal*, or *-girzedal.*

Stubble, s. *drūza, kharīz, nāṛ, ṭānṭa.*

Stubborn, a. *ṭakanrai, khpul·sar, hoḍ, jah, sar·kakkh, khpul·rāe.*

Stud, s. *ghūṭa-ī, gul·mekh.* (of horses) *galla.*

Student, s. *shāgird, ṭālib da 'ilm.*

Study, v.a. *fikr k.; zdah k.*

Stuff, s. *tsīz, shai; asbāb, sāmān, kālai; rakht, zaṛūkai, ṭukai; be·hūda-, khusha-ī-, pūcha-, ḍūza-*, etc. *khabara.*

Stuff, v.a. *manḍal, kkhke·manḍal.*

Stumble, v.a. *tindak-, ṭakar-, budrī-, kangas-, skandarī-*, etc. *khwuṛal.*

Stump, s. *mūnḍ, khanḍ, tsaṭ.* (-of a tooth) *daṛa, wekh.*

Stun, v.a. *parghazī-, gans-, dap-, sar·kawdan-, be·hokkh-*, etc. *k.*

Stupefy, v.a. *be·hokkh-, be·khūd-*, etc. *k.*

Stupid, a. *kawdan, palwand, gedī khar, nā·poh, kam 'aql.*

Sturdy, a. *mazai, mazbūṭ, gagar, nāpaṛ, ghaṭ, khṛīs.*

Stutter, v.n. *tartaredal.*

Sty, s. (in the eyelid) *gholawunkai.*

Style, s. *inshā, 'ibārat; nūm, laqab.* v.a. *wayal, balal* or *bolal, nūm ākhistal* or *-warkawul, -lagawul.*

Subdue, v.a. *lāndi k., qābū k., wahal.*

Subject, s. *r'ayat, tābi'a·dār; khabara, maṭlab, mazmūn.* (in grammar) *fā'il.* v.a. *lāndi k., r'ayat-*, etc. *k.*

Sublime, a. *ūchat, buland; ghaṭ, loe*

Submissive, a. *tābi'a·dār, farmān wrūnkai.*

Submit, v.a. *farmān wṛal, ḥukm manal, tābi'a·dārī k.; pekkhawul, wrāndi gdal* or *-kkhkegdal*, etc.

Subordinate, a. *kishar; kkhkatanai, lāndīnai.*

Suborn, v.a. *pa mok-* or *pa baḍe gaṭal* or *-mūndal, -paidā k.*, etc. *baḍa-*, etc. *warkawul.*

Subscribe, v.a. *manal, qabūlawul, nūm līkal, dast khaṭṭ k.*

Subscription, s. *manana, dast khaṭṭ; bakkhana, bakkhshikkh.*

Subsequent, a. *wrustai, wrustanai, pasanai, akhir.*

Subsequently, ad. *wrusto, pas, ākhir.*

Subservient, a. *madad·gār, komakī, madad-*, etc. *warkawūnkai.*

Subside, v.n. *kamedal, la-agedal; kkhkenāstal, prewatal.*

Subsidy, s. *pekkh·kakkh, khirāj, n'al·bandī.*

Subsist, v.n. *pāedal, osedal, pātedal, pātai ked.* v.a. *rozgār-, guzrān-*, etc. *k.*; *pālal, nmāndzal.*

Subsistence, s. *rozī, rozgār, guzrān, jwand, jwandūn.*

Substance, s. *shai, tsīz*; *māl, duniyā, daulat*; *sar, aṣl*; *khulāṣa, jauhar*; *māya, saga.*

Substantial, a. *pāedār, mazbūt*; *maujūd, aṣlī*; *māl·dār, daulat·man.*

Substantiate, v.a. *rikkhtiyā-, rikkhtīnai-, ṣābit-, zbād-*, etc. *k.*

Substantive, s. *shai, nūm*; *aṣl.*

Substitute, s. *badal, 'iwazī.*

Subterfuge, s. *hira-ī, bāna, lamghara-ī, palma.*

Subtile, a. *narai, bārīk, mahīn.*

Subtle, a. *hokkhyār, pokh*; *chal·bāz, ḥīla·bāz.*

Subtract, v.a. *ākhistal, prekawul, bāsal—yastal.*

Subvert, v.a. *wrānawul, naskorawul, naṛawul.*

Succeed, v.a. (follow) *pairawī k.* v.n. *pase lagedal, pase rātlal—rāghlal.* (prosper) v.a. *was chalawul, bakht mūndal, kār gaṭal.* (conquer) v.a. *pa-aṛ k., barai mūndal.* v.n. *wa-aṛ ked., was chaledal.*

Success, s. *wa-aṛāna, barai, bakht, barakat, gaṭa.*

Successful, a. *wa-aṛ, barakatī, bakhtāwar.*

Succession, s. *wār, dzāe nīwah.*

Successive, a. *wārī, pa wār rātlūnai.*

Successively, ad. *wār pa wār, pala pase.*

Successor, s. *pairaw, qā-im muqām.*

Succour, s. *mrasta, madad, komak.*

Succulent, a. *objan, pa obo ḍak, scrāb.*

Succumb, v.n. *la brama prewatal, lāndī ked.*

Such, p. *hase, dā·hase, done.* (-a one) *palānkai, tsok.*

Suck, v.a. *chūpal, zbekkhal.* (-the breast) *randal.*

Suckle, v.a. *tai warkawul.*

Suckling, s. *tai rawdūnkai, tandai* or *tankai.*

Suction, s. *chūpana*; *rākkhkana.*

Sudden, a. *nāgahān, nā·gumān, tsaṭ waṭ.*

Suddenly, ad. *nāgāh, nātsāpa, nā·gumāna.*

Sudorific, a. *khwale rāwṛūnkai, da khwalo dawā.*

Sue, v.a. *d'awa-, muqaddama-*, etc. *k.*; *ghokkhtal, minnat k.*

Suffer, v.a. *zghamal, wṛal, khwuṛal, rākāgal—rākkhkal.* v.n. *zghamedal, petsal, sahal, sahedal.* (allow) *pregdal, prekkhodal, prekkhal*; *ijāzat-, izn-, ḥukm-, rukhṣat-*, etc. *warkawul.*

Sufferer, a. *khūg·man, dard·man, randzūr.* (in comp.) *-khor, -kakkh, -man*, etc.

Suffering, a. *khūg*; *zgham·nāk, ṣabr·nāk.*

Sufficient, a. *bas, kāfī, ḍer*; *lā-iq, qābil.*

Suffocate, v.a. *sāh-, dam-*, etc. *bandawul.*

Sugar, s. *shakara, tarī, nabāt.* (raw-) *gūṛa.* (-candy) *qand.* (-cane) *ganna, ponḍa, khū.*

Suggest, v.a. *ishārat-, 'arẓ-, kkhowuna-*, etc. *k., wayal.*

Suit, v.a. *joṛawul, barābarawul, samawul, lagawul, dzāe laral, pīrzowul.* v.n. *barābaredal, lagedal, pīrzo ked., pa·kār rātlal—rāghlal.*

Suit, s. (-of clothes) *joṛa.* (-of cards) *rang.* (law-) *d'awa, muqaddama, jagṛa.* (petition) *'arẓ, sawāl.* (retinue) *swarlī, jalab.* (wish) *ghokkht, darkhwāst.*

Suitable, a. *joṛ, barābar, munāsib, wājib, pīrzo, kkhāyastah, kkhah, yarzan.*

Suitor, s. *mudd'aī*; *ṭalab·gār.*

Sulky, a. *marawar, mānṛī·gar, khapah.*

Sulphur, s. *gogaṛ, gogird.*

Sultry, a. *dūp, garm.*

Sum, s. *ṭol ṭāl, jam'a, mablagh, kull.* v.a. *ḥisāb k.*

Summary, s. *mujmal, khulāṣa.* a. *land.*

Summer, s. *oṛai, dubai, tābistān.* (-house) *chopāṛ.*

Summit, s. *sar, peza, tsūka.*

Summon, v.a. *balal, rābalal, ṭalab k.*

Summons, s. *ṭalab nāma; bālah, balana.*

Sumptuous, a. *grān qīmat, be-bahā; shāh kharts.*

Sun, s. *nwar* or *nmar.* (-beam) *partaw.* (-shine) *pitāo, gharma.* (-rise) *nwar khātah.* (-set) *nwar prewātah.* (-dial) *da sirrī tsalai.* (-flower) *da nwar gul.*

Sunday, s. *itwār, yak shamba.*

Sundry, a. *aṛgajah, balāe batar, dzane, b'aze, biyal.*

Superabundant, a. *ḍer, ziyāt, frewān.*

Superb, a. *'aẓīm, be bahā, be siyāl, lā ṣānī.*

Supercilious, a. *kibr-jan, maghrūr, khāntamā.*

Superficial, a. *nīmgaṛai, kachah; bāhir, wardzane.*

Superficies, s. *makh, zmaka, maidān, zamīn.*

Superintendent, s. *nāẓir, kār kawūnkai, dāroghah, sardār, mīr majlis.*

Superior, a. *mashar; ghwarah; loe, ghaṭ, star; bar, pāsanai, portanai.*

Supernatural, a. *la 'aqla bāhir, khilāf la 'ādata.*

Superscription, s. *sar-nāma.*

Supersede, v.a. *bāṭil k., lāndi k.*

Superstition, s. *wahm, bāṭil īmān.*

Supine, a. *sat, stūnī-stagh.* (careless) *be parwā, sust; laṭ, nā-rāst.*

Supper, s. *da māskhutan ḍoḍa-ī; shūma.*

Supplant, v.a. *sharal, pa-chal sara be dzāyawul.*

Supple, a. *narm, mulā-im, pos* or *post.*

Suppliant, a. *niyāz-man, minnat-dār.*

Supplication, s. *minnat, du'ā.*

Supply, v.a. *warkawul, rasawul, rāwṛal, paidā k.*

Support, v.a. *wṛal, zghamal, petsal.* (nourish) *pālal, nmāndzal.* (keep) *sātal, jghoral, khundī k.* (assist) *pushtī-, komak-, āṛ-, mrasta-,* etc. *k.*

Support, s. *āṛ, pushta; komak, mrasta; parwarish.*

Supporter, s. *pushtībān, takiya; pālūnkai, sātūnkai, sātandoe, jghorai.*

Suppose, v.a. *gaṇṛal, angeral, qiyās-, fikr-, khiyāl-,* etc. *k.* v.n. *pohedal.*

Suppress, v.a. *kkhkenawul, lāndi k., man'a k., māṭawul, bandawul.* (conceal) *puṭawul.*

Suppurate, v.n. *zawlan ked., khūyedal, pakhedal.*

Supreme, a. *ṣadar; kull mukhtār, loe, ghaṭ.*

Sure, a. *yaqīn, rikkhtīnai, wāq'ī; maẓbūṭ, pokh.*

Surely, ad. *rikkhtiyā, yara, be-shakka.*

Surety, s. *ẓāmin.* (the thing) *ẓamānat.*

Surface, s. *makh, zmaka, maidān, zamīn.*

Surfeit, s. *agheṛ, ateṛ, sekan.* v.a. *agheṛal, ateṛal, be prate-, be-khrate-,* etc. *khwuṛal.* v.n. *sekan ked.*

Surge, v.n. *ghurzedal.* v.a. *chape wahal.*

Surgeon, s. *jarrāḥ, ṭabīb.*

Surly, a. *bakhīl, trīkh-* or *tursh rūe, sūṭ būṭ.*

Surname, s. *da qām-, da khel-, da khāndān-,* etc. *nūm* or *nāma; laqab, nūm.*

Surplus, s. *pātai, ziyātī, bāqī.*

Surprise, v.a. *hariyānawul, rabṛawul; chapāo k.* v.n. *be-khabar rasedal, nātsāpo prewatal.*

Surrender, v.a. *pāslawul, spāral.*

Surround, v.a. *ẓsārawul, gerawul.*

Survey, v.a. *mech-, kach-,* etc. *k.; katal, kasal, goral—līdal, naẓar-,* etc. *k.*

Survive, v.n. *pāedal, jwandai pātai ked.*

Suspect, v.a. *shakk-, shubha-, gumān-,* etc. *laral.*

Suspend, v.a. *dzwarandawul, āwezānd k.* (-from office) *mu'attal-, man'a-, band-,* etc. *k.*

Suspense, s. *shakk, shubha, wiswās, andekkhnā.*

Suspicion, s. *gumān, shubha, shakk; tuhmat, tor, peghor, sigāl.*

Sustain, v.a. *wral, zghamal, petsal, khwural, kāgal—kkhkal.* (aid) *madad-, pushtī-, komak-,* etc. *warkawul.* (keep) *sātal, jghoral, khundī k.* (cherish) *pālal, nmāndzal.*

Sustenance, s. *rozī, khwurāk, parwarish.*

Swagger, v.a. *dūze-, lāpe-, lāpe shāpe-,* etc. *wahal.*

Swallow, s. *totakarai.* (swift) *totakai.* (sand martin) *totakarkai.*

Swallow, v.a. *nghardal, terawul.*

Swallow-wort, s. *spalma-ī.*

Swamp, s. *jaba.*

Swan, s. *qāz.*

Swarm, s. *tol, park, lakkhkar, ganra gūnra.* (-of bees) *ghubār.* (-of locusts) *lakkhkar.*

Swarthy, a. *skānr; ghanum rang.*

Swathe, v.a. *ngharal—nghakkhtal, pata-ī taral.* (a babe) *seznī taral, blegdal.*

Sway, v.a. *hukm chalawul, hukūmat k.* (bias) *mā-il-, mailān,* etc. *k., rāwastal.*

Swear, v.a. *qasam-, saugand-,* etc. *khwural.* (-falsely) *darogh-, nāhaqq-,* etc. *qasam khwural.*

Sweat, v.n. *khwale ked.*

Sweep, v.a. *jārū k.*

Sweeper, s. *jārū·kakkh, shāhī khel, musallī, chūrai.* (-of a mosque, etc.) *mīnjawar.*

Sweepings, s. *khāshāk, khadzala, kharshan, warkhara.*

Sweet, a. *khog, shīrīn, khwand·nāk.*

Sweetheart, s. *yār, yāra; mayan, mayana; 'āshiq, 'āshiqa; m'ashūq, m'ashūqa; āshnāe, āshnāya.*

Sweetish, a. *khog·nāk, khog·lorai.*

Sweetmeat, s. *qanāt, mityā-ī, shīrīnī.* (varieties) *amrasa, ghunzākkhai, dzalobai, rewra-ī, lapū, datāsa, halwā, pāpar,* etc. etc. (-seller) *halwā-ī.*

Sweetness, s. *khog·wālai, khog·lor.*

Swell, v.n. *parsedal, pundedal, tyak ked.*

Swelling, s. *pārsob.*

Swift, a. *garandai, jalt, tez, zir.*

Swim, v.a. *lānbo wahal* or *k.* v.n. *pa lānbo tlal—lāral, rawānedal, chaledal*

Swimmer, s. *lānbo·zan.*

Swindler, s. *darghal, tag, sādū.*

Swing, s. *tāl, gahwāral.* (cradle) *zāngo.* (whirligig) *banre·chagh.* v.a. *tāl wahal, zangawul.* v.n. *zangal, zangedal.*

Switch, s. *lakkhta, kera.*

Swivel, s. *zambūrak, shāhīn.*

Swoon, s. *parghaz.* v.n. *parghazī prewatal.*

Swoop, v.a. *pa chape-, pa ghote-, pa guzār-,* etc. *wahal* or *-niwul.*

Sword, s. *tūra, tegh.* (-spear) *sela.* (-knot) *zundai, kīlak.*

Swordsman, s. *tūrzan, tūra·bāz.*

Sycophant, s. *khūshāmad·gar, dirpal.*

Sylvan, a. *dzangalī, dashtī.* s. (satyr) *banr mānū.*

Symbol, s. *nakkha, nikkhān, 'alāmat.*

Sympathy, s. *khwā·khūgī, zrah swai*

Symptom, s. *nakkha,* etc. (*v.* Symbol).

Synod, s. *jirga-* or *majlis da shekhāno* or *-da imāmāno* or *-da mullāyāno.*

Syntax, s. *nahw.*

Syringe, s. *pichkāra-ī, huqna.*

Syrup, s. *gūra-ī, qiwām, zokkha, rub.*

System, s. *qānūn, ā-īn, qā'ida, tarīqa.*

T.

Table, s. *mez, takhta; naqsha.* (-cloth) *dastar·khwān.* (-cover) *chāndanī.*

Tablet, s. lauḥ, takhta.

Tacit, a. ghalai, chup.

Tactics, s. da jang ḥikmat.

Tail, s. lama, laka-ī. (-bone) laka lamai. (-less) lanḍai. (fat tailed) a. lamawur.

Tailor, s. darzī, khaiyāṭ.

Taint, v.a. bourawul, wrost-, skhā-, etc. k.

Take, v.a. ākhistal, nīwul, lāndī k. (-in) dzāyawul. (suppose) gaṇral. (effect) pāzah k. (carry) yawsal, wṛal. (lead) botlal—bīwul. (-off) bāsal—yastal. (-out) kāgal—kkhkal. (-care of) sātal, ĵghoral, khundī k. (-down) kūzawul. (-care) pahm k.

Talc, s. abraq, da shige gul, zarbarakh.

Tale, s. qiṣṣa, naql, rawāyat. (-bearer) chughl·khor, mawās.

Talent, s. 'aql, sha'ūr, poh, hunar.

Talk, v.a. wayal, khabare k. s. wayana, khabara; wrāsha, wayai; gangosai.

Tall, a. ūchat, hask, dang, lwaṛ.

Tallow, s. ghwaṛ, spīna, mū.

Talon, s. nūk, mangul, changul, panja.

Tambourine, s. tambal, ḍūmbakai, ḍūmkai.

Tame, a. āmokhtah, el, koranai. v.a. āmokhtah k., elawul.

Tamper, v.a. lās lagawul, lamsawul, lamsūn k.

Tan, v.a. dabbāghī k., tsarman joṛawul or -pakha k. (-by the sun) v.n. swal, sedzal.

Tank, s. ḍanḍ, ḥauẓ, tālāo, nāwar.

Tanner, s. dabbāgh, tsamyār.

Tantalize, v.a. pa umed nā umed k.

Tap, v.a. ṭak-, trak-, etc. wahal. (pierce) tsikhal, sūrai k.

Tape, s. paṭa-ī; niwāṛ.

Taper, s. bāta-ī, patīla. a. gāo dum, trandz.

Tar, s. rāndzaṛah, chūṛel.

Tardy, a. sust, laṭ, drangai.

Tardiness, s. sust·wālai, drang, dzanḍ.

Target, s. mūkha, nakkha, kuhāṛa; ḍāl, spar.

Tarnish, v.a. khīran-, kakaṛ-, murdār-, etc. k.

Tarry, v.n. osedal, pātedal; walāṛedal, wudredal; lārghak-, dzanḍ-, drang-, etc. k.

Task, s. kār, mashghūlā; dars, sabaq; miḥnat.

Tassel, s. zunḍai, zunbak.

Taste, s. khwand, maza, tsaka; tsakindan. v.a. khwand-, etc. -wahal, ākhistal, or -k., tsakal.

Tattle, v.a. bak bak-, baṛ baṛ-, ṭar ṭar-, etc. k.

Taunt, v.a. pekkhe-, ṭoqe-, khandā-, etc. pore k.

Tawny, a. skāṇr, ghanum rang.

Tax, v.a. bāj-, khirāj-, sāw-, maḥṣūl-, etc. lagawul or -ṭaṛal. (cattle-) s. sargalla, goshī. (land-) kulang, sarghala, sar·sabzī. (house-) lūgī·tāwān, khāna·shumārī. (poll-) jaziya.

Tea, s. chāe. (-cup) piyāla

Teach, v.a. kkhayal—kkhowul, pohawul; lwalawul, tarbiyat-, t'alīm-, etc. k., āmokhtah-, 'ādat-, zdah-, etc. k.

Teacher, s. ākhūn, ustād, mu'allim.

Tear, v.a. shlawul, tsīral, wrarawul, chāk k. v.n. shledal, tsīredal, wraredal. (-out) kāgal—kkhkal, bāsal—yastal.

Tear, s. okkha. (-ful) a. okkhan.

Tease, v.a. pārawul, tangawul, ṭongawul.

Tedious, a. drūnd, grān, sakht.

Teem, v.n. gaṇr kcd., ḍeredal, wadānedal.

Tell, v.a. wayal, khabarawul; bayānawul; kkhayal—kkhowul. (-tales) chughlī k.

Temerity, s. be·adabī; be·tadbīrī; be·bākī.

Temper, s. khoe, khaṣlat, lokkhai, mizāj, ṭab'iyat. (-of metals) āb, dam.

Temperate, a. barābar, joṛ, muwāfiq; parhez·gār; m'utadil, na tod na soṛ.

Tempest, s. sila-ī, tūpān or ṭūfān.

Temple, s. 'ibādat·gāh, masjid, jumā'at. (-of Mecca) qibla, k'aba. (-of Jerusalem) bait ul muqaddas. (-of the head) lweganda, ṭck.

Temporal, a. duniyā-ī, fānī, jahānī.

Temporary, a. teredūnai, la-ag wradzanai.

Temporize, v.a. *drang-, lār<u>gh</u>ah-, multawī-,* etc. *k.*

Tempt, v.a. *<u>gh</u>ulawul, dar<u>gh</u>alawul, lamsawul, tar<u>gh</u>īb-,* etc. *warkawul.*

Ten, a. *las.* (tenth) a. *lasam.* (-fold) *las bra<u>gh</u>*; *las pa yo.* (-times) *las heṛa, las <u>dz</u>ala.*

Tenable, a. *klak, ṭīng, maḥkam, maẓbūṭ.*

Tenacious, a. *klak, ṭīng, sa<u>kh</u>t*; *bo<u>kkh</u>t, sle<u>kkh</u>t-nāk*; *<u>sh</u>ūm, ba<u>kh</u>īl*; *<u>kh</u>pul rāe.*

Tenant, s. *hamsāyah, faqīr, ijāra-dār, āsāmī.*

Tend, v.a. *sātal, <u>jgh</u>oral*; *<u>kh</u>abar ā<u>kh</u>istal, <u>kh</u>idmat k* (-flocks) *<u>sh</u>panī k.* v.n. *girzedal, mā-il-, mailān-,* etc. *ked.*

Tendency, s. *mā-il-, <u>kh</u>wā*; *<u>gh</u>araẓ*; *maṭlab, mudd'ā.*

Tender, a. *nāzuk, narm, mulā-im, post.*

Tendon, s. *pala, rag, wuja.* (-of horse's leg) *pai.* (-of the heel) *spīna, kū<u>ch</u>ai.*

Tendril, s. *zela, bela.*

Tenesmus, s. *kānga, tāo, pe<u>ch</u>.*

Tenet, s. *masla*; *bāwar, īmān*; *ṭarīqa.*

Tenor, s. *m'anī*; *yūn, <u>ch</u>alan.* (in music) *<u>dz</u>īr.*

Tense, a. *rā<u>kkh</u>kalai, klak, ṭīng.*

Tent, s. *ḍera, tambū, <u>kh</u>aima.* (nomad's) *kigḍa-ī.* (-in surgery) *bāta-ī.* (-rope) *māndara, mazai.*

Tenth, a. *lasam.* (-part) s. *lasama bra<u>kh</u>a.*

Tepid, a. *taṛam, nīm garm.*

Term, s. *<u>kh</u>abara, wayai, lafẓ.* (time) *neṭa, mūda.* (stipulation) *<u>sh</u>arṭ, taṛa, wāda, banda<u>nr</u>.* (limit) *ḥadd.* (phrase) *'ibārat.* (good terms) *ro<u>gh</u>a joṛa, pa<u>kh</u>ulā.*

Termagant, s. *jība-wara, jang-yāla-ī.*

Terminate, v.n. *tamāmedal, pūrah ked., anjāmedal.* v.a. *tamāmawul,* etc.

Terrace, s. *dunkā<u>ch</u>a.* (-of a house) *<u>ch</u>at, bām.*

Terrible, a. *haul-nāk, <u>kh</u>of-nāk.*

Terrify, v.a. *yerawul, tarhawul.*

Territory, s. *mulk, zmaka, hiwād.*

Terror, s. *yera* or *wera, tor, <u>kh</u>awf.* (-struck) *tor <u>kh</u>wuṛalai.*

Test, v.a. *āzmāyal* or *āzmoyal, āzme<u>kkh</u>t k.*

Testament, s. (Old) *tauret.* (New) *injīl,* (will) *waṣiyat nāma.*

Testicle, s. *and, haga-ī, <u>kh</u>oṭa.*

Testify, v.a. *<u>sh</u>āhidī-, gawāhī-,* etc. *lal* or *lawdal,* or *-warkawul.*

Testimonial, s. *rāẓī-nāma*; *gawāhī-nāma.*

Testimony, s. *gawāhī, <u>sh</u>āhidī.*

Tether, v.a. *taṛal.* s. *<u>sh</u>kal* or *<u>sh</u>kel, wandar.*

Text, s. *matan, aṣl.* (of Qurān) *āyat.*

Texture, s. *tarkīb, joṛawuna, sā<u>kh</u>t.*

Than, ad. *la—na.*

Thank, v.a. *<u>sh</u>ukr k., -bāsal—yastal, -guẓāral, -pa <u>dz</u>āe rāwṛal,* etc.

Thankful, a. *<u>sh</u>ukr guẓār.*

That, pr. *ha<u>gh</u>ah, e, kūm, dā.* c. *<u>ts</u>o <u>ch</u>i, dapāra da.*

Thatch, s. *<u>ts</u>apar, <u>ch</u>at.*

Thaw, v.n. *oba ked.*; *wīlī ked.*

The, art. *ha<u>gh</u>ah, da<u>gh</u>ah, dā.*

Theft, s. *<u>gh</u>lā.*

Theme, s. *masawda* or *musawadda*; *man<u>sh</u>ā.*

Then, ad. *hāla, pas*; *tro, bāre*; *nor, biyā.*

Thence, ad. *<u>dz</u>aka, la ha<u>gh</u>e na.* (-forth) *pas, pas la ha<u>gh</u>e na.*

Theology, s. *fiqha.*

Theory, s. *'ilm, qiyās, <u>kh</u>iyāl.*

There, ad. *halta, hore, horta, ha<u>gh</u>a <u>kh</u>wā.*

Thereabout, ad. *la-og ḍer* or *la-ag ziyāt, nijde, ta<u>kh</u>mīnan.*

Therefore, ad. *pas, <u>dz</u>aka, tro.*

Thick, a. *<u>gh</u>aṭ, ṭīng, lwāṛ*; *ga<u>nr</u>, tat, ṭal.* (-as the voice) *bog, ḍaḍ.*

Thicket, s. *jangai, jāṛ, jāmbṛa, karka<u>nr</u>.*

Thief, s. *<u>gh</u>al, u<u>ch</u>akah, <u>ch</u>akah <u>gh</u>al.*

Thigh, s. *wrūn, patūn, <u>kkh</u>ānga.*

Thimble, s. *gūtma.*

Thin, a. *narai, mahīn, bārīk, tran<u>dz</u>, nāzak.* (lean) *ḍangar, <u>kh</u>wār.* (scanty) *rangai.*

Thing, s. *shai, tsiz, kālai.*

Think, v.a. *fikr-, qiyās-, khiyāl-,* etc. *k.*; *gumān-, andekkhnā-,* etc. *k.*; *ghaur-, parwā-,* etc. *k.*; *ganral, angeral.* v.n. *pohedal.*

Third, a. *driyam* or *dre-am.* (-part) s. *driyama brakha.*

Thirst, v.n. *tagai ked.* s. *tanda, tagai·wālai.*

Thirsty, a. *tigai.*

Thirteen, a. *diyārlas.*

Thirty, a. *dersh.* (thirtieth) *dersham.* (thirty-one) *yo dersh.* (-two) *dwah dersh,* etc.

This, pr. *dā, daghah, dah, de, hāyah.* (-very one) *bedū, pa ṭikī.*

Thistle, s. *āzghakai, kārīza.*

Thither, ad. *halta, hore, horta, warhīsta, hagha khwā.*

Thong, s. *tasma, rog.*

Thorax, s. *taṭar, gargas, gogal, sīna.*

Thorn, s. *āzghai* or *āghzai, khār.* (-bush) *ghana, karkanra.* (-apple) *dātūra.* (-apple seed) *tora dāna.* (thorns) *ghane.*

Thorny, a. *āzghan* or *āghzan, khār·dār.*

Thorough, a. *pūrah, pokh, bashpaṛ, amānī.*

Thou, pr. *tah, tā, de, di.*

Though, c. *agarchi, sirā la de na.* (as-) *laka chi.*

Thought, s. *fikr, qiyās, khiyāl*; *ghaur, khabar, parwā*; *gumān, sigāl*; *andekkhnā.*

Thoughtful, a. *fikr·man, andekkh·man.*

Thoughtless, a. *be·fikr, be·parwā, be·khabar.*

Thousand, a. *zar.* (two-) *dwah zara,* etc.

Thraldom, s. *qaid, band, nkkhatai.*

Thrash, v.a. *wahal, ṭakawul, kūṭal.* (-corn) *ghobal k.*

Thrashing-floor, s. *khirman, dirmand.*

Thread, s. *spanrsai, tār, mazai.* v.a. *pewdal, peyal.*

Threaten, v.a. *ḍabawul, ḍabka k.*

Three, a. *dre* or *dri.* (-fold) *dre bragh*; *dre pa yo.*

Threshold, s. *āstān, dargāh*; *dahlīz.*

Thrice, ad. *dre heṛa, -dzala, -plā, -guzāra,* etc.

Thrifty, a. *kam kharts, kam tāwān kawūnkai, bachāū, kifāyat kawūnkai.*

Thrive, v.n. *wadānedal, ābādedal, maṛedal.*

Throat, s. *mara-ī, markanḍai, ghara-ī.* (fauces) *ghāra, halq.*

Throb, v.a. *tsiṛīka wahal.* v.n. *ḍrazedal.*

Throne, s. *takht, masnad, gadda-ī.*

Throng, s. *ṭol, paṛk, ḍala, ganra gūnra.*

Through, p. *pore, pa mandz kkhke.* (-and through) *pore ore, ore rāpore.* (by means of) *pa m'arifat, la kabla.*

Throughout, ad. *amānī, sarāsar.*

Throw, v.a. *wīshtal, āchawul, ghurzawul, lawastal.* (-up) *jārbāsal—jāryastal*; *pregdal, prekkhodal, prekkhal, tark k.*

Thrust, v.a. *negh wahal*; *ṭel-, ḍaka-, sūk-,* etc. *wahal.* (-into) *manḍal, kkhke·manḍal*; *nana-,* or *kkhke·bāsal—nana-,* or *kkhke·yastal.*

Thumb, s. *ghaṭa-gūta.*

Thump, v.a. *ḍab-, ṭak-, sūk-, gasa-,* etc. *wahal.*

Thunder. s. *tālanda, tanrā.* (-bolt) *tandar, ṭaka.* v.n. *ghuṛunbedal, ghaṛedal.*

Thursday, s. *pānshamba, da ziyārat wradz.*

Thus, ad. *hase, dā·hase, hase shān, dā shān, dā rang.* (-much) *done, hombra, daghombra.*

Thwart, v.a. *wār khaṭā k., wrānawul, aṛawul, 'aks-, ẓidd-,* etc. *k.*

Thyself, pr. *tah khpul.*

Tick, s. (sound) *ṭak, ṭas.* (louse) *kūnai, kana, konr, wrādza.*

Ticket, s. *chīṭa-ī*; *sar·nāma.*

Tickle, s. *takha.* v.a. *takhawul, takhnawul.* v.n. *takhedal, takhnedal.*

Tidings, s. *khabar.* (good-) *zera, zerai.* (the bearer of good-) *zera·garai.*

Tidy, a. *ḍaulī, spīn spetsalai.*

Tie, s. *taṛūn, taṇra-ī, wandanai.* v.a. *taral, lagawul.*

Tiffin, s. *nāshta, nahārai.*

Tiger, s. *zmarai* or *mzarai.*

Tight, a. *tang, chust, rākkhkalai, klak.*

Tighten, v.a. *tangawul, klakawul, rākāgal—rākkhkal.*

Till, p. *tar haghah pore.* (when ?) *tar kala pore.* (-now) *tar osa pore.*

Till, v.a. *kar-, īwe-,* or *yawe-,* etc. *k., zmaka āṛawul.*

Tillage, s. *kar, īwe,* or *yiwe,* or *yawe.*

Timber, s. *largai*; *bensh.*

Time, s. *wakht* or *waqt.* (season) *neṭa, mūda, nobat, ṭāng.* (age) *'umr, kāl*; *zamāna, daur.* (turn) *wār, heṛ, plā, dzal, guẓār.* (leisure) *wuzgār·tiyā, furṣat.* (-in music) *tāl, wazn.* (at all times) *har wakht, har kala.*

Timid, a. *yer·man, harānd, wiswāsī, yere-dūnkai.*

Tin, s. *qal'aī.* (-man) *qal'aī·gar.*

Tinder, s. *khū, khpah, badagāl.*

Tinge, s. *rang.* v.a. *rangawul.*

Tingle, v.n. *shṛangedal.* (tickle) *takhnedal.* (with pain) *swal, brekkhedal.*

Tiny, a. *woṛ, woṛkoṭai, pūṭai, kharmandai.*

Tip, s. *sar, peza, tsūka, nūka.*

Tire, v.n. *staṛai-, stomān-, haukah-, māndah-,* etc. *ked.* v.a. *staṛai-,* etc. *k.*

Tiresome, a. *drūnd, grān, rabaṛ·nāk.*

Tithe, s. *'ushr.* (-to servants) *chūngai.*

Titillate, v.n. *takhnedal, koc-, kaha-,* etc. *ked.*

Titillation, s. *takhai, koc, kaha, megī megī.*

Title, s. *nūm, nāma, laqab, khitāb.* (right) *ḥaqq.*

Titter, s. *muskai.* v.n. *musedal.*

Tittle, s. *ẓarra, khas, pitsāṇrai, pūṭai, ṭakai.*

Tittle-tattle, s. *gap shap, bak bak, lāv shāp, zwag pak.*

To, p. *ta.* (-day) *nan.* (-morrow) *sabā* or *ṣabāḥ.* (-night) *nan begā, mākkhām.* (-morrow night) *sabā begā.* (-me) *rā ta.* (-thee) *dar ta.* (-him, etc.) *war ta.*

Toad, s. *chīndakh.* (-stool) *kha-areṛai, gū-māndū.*

Toast, v.a. *wrītawul, alwoyal, teyal, talawul.*

Tobacco, s. *tambākū.* (-pipe) *chilam.*

Toe, s. *da kkhpe* or *pkkhe gūta.*

Together, ad. *yaw dzāe, dzabla, sara.*

Toil, v.a. *miḥnat-, kokshiksh-, tagāpū-,* etc. *k.*

Toilette, s. *kkhewa, singār.*

Token, s. *nakkha, nikkhān, 'alāmat.*

Tolerate, v.a. *wṛal, zghamal*; *rawā gaṇral, prcydal, prekkhodal, prekkhal.*

Toll, s. *maḥṣūl, chūngai, tāwān.*

Tomb, s. *qabr, gor, maqbara.* (the niche) *laḥad.* (the tablet) *khaza* or *khāda.*

Tone, s. *zwag, ghag, āwāz, bāng.* (elasticity) *dam.*

Tongs, s. *ambūr.*

Tongue, s. *jiba.*

Tonsil, s. *da jibe laṛ, haḍ.*

Too, ad. *hum, lā.* (-much) *ḍer, ziyāt.*

Tool, s. *kālai, hatiyār, ālat.*

Tooth, s. *ghākkh.* (molar-) *dāṛa, da jāme ghākkh.* (decayed) *chinjo khwaṛalai ghākkh.* (-pick) *ghākkh ṭanbūnai* or *sūra-yūnkai* or *shūkayūnkai, khilāl.* (-brush) *miswāk.* (-ache) *ghākkh khūgai, da ghākkh dard.* (-less) *kaṛshap, kanḍās.*

Top, s. *sar, tsūka, peza.* (on-) *dapāsa, da-bāndi, pa porta.* (toy) *tsarkhandūkai, challkha-ī, churlanda-ī, lāḍū, bahna.*

Topic, s. *maẓmūn, manshā, mudd'ā.*

Topknot, s. *tsaṇra-ī.*

Topsyturvy, a. *naskor, aṛawulai, pa-aṛ·makh.*

Torch, s. *shūsha-ī*; *mashāl.* (-of pine wood) *shonṭa-ī.*

Torment, s. *'aẓāb, āzār.* v.a. *'aẓābawul, āzārawul, khūgawul, kaṛawul.*

Torpid, a. *sust, laṭ*. (-with cold) *marghechan, qarqechan*.

Torrent, s. *dāra, sailāb, nīz* or *niyāz, chalānda*.

Tortoise, s. *shamshata-ī, kashap*.

Torture, s. *'azāb*. (instruments of-) *shikanja, pāna, kāṭ, tsarkh*. v.a. *'azābawul; pāna warkawul, pa shikanjo-, pa kāṭ-, pa tsarkh-*, etc. *khejawul*.

Toss, v.a. *ghurzawul, āchawul, lawastal*. v.n. *ghurzedal*. (-money) v.a. *shīr khaṭ k*.

Total, a. *ṭol, amānī, pūrah, tamām, wāṛah*. s. *ṭol ṭāl, jam'a*.

Totally, ad. *amānī, sarāsar*. (in comp.) *tak-, ṭap-*, etc.

Totter, v.n. *ṭaparedal*.

Touch, v.a. *lās lagawul* or *-warwṛal; masa-, lams-*, etc. *k*. v.n. *lagedal, jangedal, blodal, blosedal*.

Touchy, a. *tod-*, or *tund mizāj*.

Tough, a. *klak, sakht, ṭīng*.

Tour, s. *daur, safar, gakkht; sail*.

Tow, s. *sanr, da sanro paṭ*.

Towards, p. *khwā ta, lorī ta, makh ta, ḍaḍe ta, palaw ta*, etc. (-me) *rākīsta*. (-thee) *dar kīsta*. (-him, her, it, them) *war kīsta*.

Towel, s. *dast·māl, rūmāl*.

Tower, s. *bruj* or *burj*.

Town, s. *kkhahr, kilai, dih*.

Townsman, s. *kkhahr-wāl, kilī-wāl, da kkhahr-, da kilī-*, etc. *saṛai*.

Toy, s. *da lobe kālai*. v.a. *lobe k.; nāz k*.

Trace, s. *nakkha, darak, belga*. v.a. *belga bāsal—yastal; nakhkkha* or *naqsha kāgal—kkhkal* or *līkal*.

Track, s. *pal, manḍ, darak; lār, rakkh*. v.a. *pal-*, etc. *goral—līdal-, -mūndal, -laṭawul*, etc.

Tract, s. *maidān, zmaka; mulk, kiwād*. (treatise) *risāla, nāma*.

Tractable, a. *narm, gharīb, mulā-im*.

Trade, s. *saudāgarī, warkṛah rākṛah, lāgī, saudā; kasb, kār*. v.a. *saudāgarī-*, etc. *k*

Trader, s. *saudāgar, wapārī, banjārī, parānchah*. (travelling-) *rawānī, lohānī*.

Tradesman, s. *kasb·gar, pesha·war*.

Tradition, s. *ḥadīṣ, khabara, naql, wayai*.

Traditional, a. } *wayali* or *rāghlali khabara*,
Traditionary, } *da pero pa pero khabara*.

Traduce, v.a. *tor-, tuhmat-*, etc. *pore k. peghor warkawul, bad·nāmawul, kagal, ghandal*.

Traffic, v.a. (*v*. Trade.)

Tragical, a. *gham·nāk, haibat·nāk, haul·nāk*.

Trail, v.a. *rākāgal—rākkhkal, kashāla k*.

Train, v.a. *āmokhtah k.; bāolī warkawul; kkhayal—kkhowul, lwalawul; pālal*.

Train, s. (escort) *swarlī, jalab*. (-of a dress) *laman*. (series) *qaṭār*.

Trait, s. *'ādat; nakkha; karkkha*.

Traitor, s. *namak ḥarām, ṭag, darghal*.

Trammel, s. *jāl, lūma, dām; paikaṛa*.

Trample, v.a. *litāṛawul, kkhpo lāndi-, pāemāl-, ghwa-emanḍ-*, etc. *k., ghobalawul*.

Trance, s. *parghaz, da periyāno ghoṭa, bekhūdī*.

Tranquil, a. *qalār, walāṛ, ārām*.

Tranquillize, v.a. *ārāmawul, qalārawul, saṛawul, walāṛawul*.

Transact, v.a. *mu'āmala-, kār-, rozgār-*, etc. *k., chalawul, lagawul, jārī k., rawānawul*.

Transaction, s. *kār, rozgār, m'uāmala, khabara*.

Transfer, v.a. *wṛal, rasawul; spāral, pāslawul*.

Transfix, v.a. *ore pore tetsal* or *-sikhal, pewdal*.

Transgress, v.a. *mātawul; khaṭā k*.

Transient, a. *teredūnai, nā-pāedār, fānī*

Translate, v.a. *tarjuma k., naql k*.

Transmit, v.a. *āstawul, legal, rasawul*.

Transparent, a. *ṣāf, shaffāf; bārīk*.

Transpire, v.n. *tsargandedal, kkhkārah ked., watal, khatal, m'alūmedal.*

Transport, v.a. *wral, yosal; botlal—bīwul; legdal—lekkhal; jalā-watan k.*

Transpose, v.a. *arawul, badlawul, gadwadawul.*

Transverse, a. *tratskan, kog.*

Trap, s. *dām.* (net-) *jāl, dwah gaza.* (noose-) *lūma, lūmaka, ghundārai.* (springe) *laṭ, talaka, qurqa-ī.* (catch-) *park, konrā.* (ambush) *psūnai, tsawai, putgana-ī.* v.a. *nīwul, nkkhlawul.*

Trappings, s. *kālī, asbāb.* (armour) *drasta, wasla.* (horse-) *bargastwān.*

Trash, s. *balāe batar, khadzala, khāshāk.*

Travel, v.a. *safar-, sail-, musāfirī-,* etc. *k.*

Traveller, s. *musāfir.*

Tray, s. *khwān, khwāncha, sīnī.*

Treacherous, a. *be-īmān, be-wafā, darghal-bāz.*

Treachery, s. *be-īmānī, darghal-tob.*

Treacle, s. *gūra, awlū, kak; tiriyāq.*

Tread, v.a. *kkhpa-* or *pkkha-, qadam-,* etc. *gdal,* or *-īgdal,* or *-kkhkegdal.* (-upon) *latārah-, laṭ paṭ-, kkhpo lāndi-,* etc. *k.* (as birds) v.n. *khatal.* (-corn) v.a. *ghobal k.* (after one) *pala pase tlal.*

Treason, s. *namak harāmī, pasāt, darghal-bāzī, ghadr.*

Treasure, s. *khazāna, ganj, daulat.*

Treasurer, s. *khazānchī.*

Treasury, s. *khazāna, tūng; makhzan.*

Treat, v.a. (parley) *sawāl dzawāb-, khabara-,* etc. *k.* (use) *sulūk-, mu'āmala-,* etc. *k.* (guest) *ziyāfat-, melmastiyā-, sat-,* etc. *k.* (-well) *kkhah sulūk k.* (-badly) *bad sulūk k.* (-a disease) *chāra-, 'ilāj-,* etc. *k.* (manage) *jorawul, chalawul.* (mention) *yādawul, bayānawul.*

Treaty, s. *'ahad, qaul-qarār, tara, bandaur.*

Treble, a. *dre bragh, dre chand.* (in music) *dzīr* or *zīl.*

Tree, s. *wana, drakhta.* (small-) *dakai.* (Mulberry-) *tūt.* (Sissoo-) *shewa.* (Acacia modesta) *palosa.* (Acacia Arabica) *kikar.* (Pine-) *nakkhtar.* (Cedar-) *diyār.* (Plane-) *chinār.* (Melia sempervirens) *shanda-ī, bukāyanra.* (Seris-) *srīkh.* (Willow-) *wala.* (Olive-) *kkhona.* (Tamarisk-) *ghaz.* (Bauhinia variegata) *koliyār,* etc. etc.

Tremble, v.n. *rapedal, regdedal, larzedal.*

Tremendous, a. *haibat-nāk; bashpar, loe.*

Tremor, s. *larza, gagarodza.*

Trembling, s. *rapedūn, larzedana.*

Trench, s. *kanda, kaha-ī.*

Trencher, s. *kkhānak, pīna, taghār.*

Trepidation, s. *larza, rapedana, gagarodza.*

Trespass, s. *gunāh, wabāl, taqṣīr, khaṭā.*

Trial, s. *āzmekkht, imtiḥān.*

Triangle, s. *dre gokkha, muṣallaṣ.*

Tribe, s. *qām* or *qaum, firqa, tabār, khel.*

Tribulation, s. *gham, randz, mīrtsī, paskhāk, āfat, balā.*

Tribunal, s. *maḥkam, 'adālat.*

Tribute, s. *pekkh-kakkh, khirāj, bāj, 'ushr.*

Trice, s. *pal, laḥza.*

Trick, s. *fareb, lamghara-ī, ghulat, ṭagī, chal.* (habit) *'ādat, khoe.* v.a. *ṭagal, ghulawul.*

Trickle, v.n. *tsātsedal.*

Triennial, a. *dre kālanai.*

Trifle, s. *khasanrai, nā-tsīz, lā shai, kets.*

Trifle, v.a. *lobe k., 'abaṣ k., jakh wahal.*

Trifling, a. *spuk, khushai, be-hūdah, pūch.*

Trim, v.a. *jorawul, atsanral, drust k.*

Trinity, s. *taṣlīṣ, ṣalāṣa.*

Trinket, s. *kālai, zewar, gānra.*

Trip, v.a. *tīndak-, ṭakar-, budrī-, kangas-, skandarī-,* etc. *khwaral.*

Tripe, s. *ūjarai, kulma.*

Triple, a. *dre bragh, dre chand, dre ṭarafah.*

Tripod, s. *dre pāya, darbala-ī.*

Trite, a. *zor, pakhwānai, mashhūr.*

Triturate, v.a. *oṛawul, oṛah-, maidah-*, etc. *k. dalawul, dzabal.*

Trivial, a. *spuk, khushai, adnā.*

Triumph, v.a. *barai mūndal*, or *-gaṭal.* (joy over enemy) *wiyāṛ-, sakha-*, etc. *k.*

Troop, s. *paṛk, ghol, galla, tanba, ṭol, ṭolgai.* (-of horse) *risāla.*

Trooper, s. *bār-gīr, turk sawār.*

Trophy, s. *ghanīmat, lūṭ, shūka, gaṭa.*

Trot, v.a. *pa ḍugland-, pa dachko-*, etc. *tlal.*

Trouble, s. *rabaṛ, miḥnat, diqq-dārī, randz, āzār, dzaur.* v.a. *rabṛawul, āzārawul, diqq k.*

Troublesome, a. *rabṛūnai, rabaṛ-nāk, diqq-dār, janjālī.*

Trough, s. *pūl, nāwa, tarnāo.*

Trowel, s. *karanḍa-ī.*

Trowsers, s. *partūg, shalwār, tambān.* (-band) *partūghākkh.* (-hem) *baḍa.* (-fork) *khakkhtag.* (-leg) *pāentsa.*

Truant, a. *gashtai, khushai, hujrai.*

Truce, s. *m'arika, rogha joṛa, ṣulḥa.*

Trudge, v.n. *ṭaparedal, ro ro tlal.*

True, a. *rikkhtiyā, rikkhtīnai, sūchak, karah, rāst, pokh, pūrah.*

Truly, ad. *pa rikkhtiyā*; *yara.*

Trumpet, s. *tūrai, būq.*

Trunk, s. (box) *ṣandūq, tawura-ī.* (tree) *mūnḍ, tanga, garga.* (body) *ṣūrat, tan.* (snout) *khaṛtam, sūnḍak.*

Trust, s. *bāwar, i'tibār, sā-wīsā, khal*; *umed, takiya, āsra, tawakkul*; *amānat, ḥawāla*; *por, qarẓ, nasiyah.*

Trust, v.a. *bāwar-*, etc. *k.* or *lural*; *amānat-*, etc. *gdal* or *īgdal, spāral, pāslawul*; *por-*, etc. *warkawul.*

Trustee, s. *ẓimma-dār, amānat-dār.*

Trusty, a. *i'tibārī, īmān-dār, wafā-dār.*

Truth, s. *rikkhtiyā, rāstī.*

Try, v.a. *āzmāyal* or *āzmoyal, āzmekkht k., s'aī-, kokhikkh-*, etc. *k.*, *was chalawul*; *'adālat k.*

Tub, s. *taghār, ḍol, saṭal, gaḍkal.*

Tube, s. *shpela-ī, nala, tsūkkhka.*

Tuesday, s. *naha, sih shamba.*

Tuft, s. *zunḍa-ī, ghūncha.* (-of hair) *tsaṛa-ī* or *tsawra-ī*; *parcham* or *parkham.* (bird's) *chār khwalak.* (-of grass, etc.) *kalokkhta.*

Tug, v.a. *rākāgal—rākkhkal.*

Tuition, s. *tarbiyat, t'alīm*; *parwarish.*

Tumble, v.n. *prewatal, lwedal.* (roll on the ground) *rghaṛedal—rghakkhtal, lots pots k.* v.a. *bāzī-garī-, naṭ-bāzī-*, etc. *k.*

Tumour, s. *pāṛsob, ghumba, ghunḍārai, stagh.*

Tumult, s. *balwā, ghulghula, zwag-zūg, shor, shor-shaghab.*

Tune, s. *sarod, tarāna, badala, wazn.*

Turban, s. *pagṛa-ī, paṭkai, dastār, manḍos.* (end of-) *shaklai, shamla.*

Turbid, a. *kha-aṛ, lāha-jan, khaṭolai.*

Turbulence, s. *pasāt, shor.*

Turbulent, a. *pasātī, shor-nāk.*

Turf, s. *chim, lūṭa, kulūkh.*

Turmeric, s. *korkamān.*

Turn, s. *tsarkh, daur.* (twist) *tāo, wal, pech, wawwat.* (time) *wār, guzār*; *heṛ, plā, dzal.* (walk) *sail, gakkht.* (bend) *kaglech, kālkūch.*

Turn, v.n. *girzedal, tsarkhedal, churledal, āwukkhtal, badledal.* (-back) *jārwatal, stūnedal*, or *stanedal, pastanah ked.* (become) *kedal, shwal.* v.a. *girzawul, tsarkhawul, churlawul.* (-back) *stūnawul.* (-over) *aṛawul.* (-out) *shaṛal.* (-from) *shā k., pregdal.*

Turnip, s. *tepar, shalgham*

Turpentine, s. *rāndzaṛah.*

Turret, s. *bruj*; *kangūra.*

Tutor, s. *ākhūn, ustād, mu'allim.*

Twang, s. *ṭang, trang.* v.n. *ṭangedal, trangedal.*

Tweezers, s. *nūtsai.*

Twelve, a. *dwah·las*. (twelfth) *dwah·lasam*. (-month) *kāl, dwah·las myāshti*.
Twenty, a. *shil*. (twentieth) *shilam*. (-one) *yaw·wisht*. (-two) *dwah·wisht*, etc.
Twice, ad. *dwah kera, -guzāra, -dzala, -wāra*, etc.
Twig, s. *lakkhta*.
Twilight, s. *shafaq*; *sapede*.
Twins, s. *jora, bragh*. (one of-) *braghūnai*.
Twine, s. *mazai, tār*.
Twine, v.a. *pech-, tāo-, wal-*, etc. *khwural*.
Twinkle, s. (of time) *pal, lahza*. (-of a star) *palwasha*. v.n. *dzalkedal* or *dzaledal*.
Twirl, v.a. *churlawul, tsarkhawul, tsandai* or *tsandawul*.
Twist, s. *pech, wal, tāo, marwat*. v.. *pech-*, etc. *warkawul*. (fold) *nghakkhtal*. (bend) *ṭīṭawul, krīngawul*.
Twitter, v.a. *chaur chaur-*, etc. *k*.
Two, a. *dwah, dwe*.
Type, s. *nakkha, 'alāmat, noga, misāl*.
Tyrannize, v.a. *jabr-, zulm-*, etc. *k*.
Tyranny, s. *zulm, zor, ziyātī, zabardastī, jafā*.
Tyrant, s. *zālim, jābir, jafā·kār*.
Tyro, s. *shāgird, mubtadī, nawai āmokhtah*.

U.

Udder, s. *ghulāndza*.
Ugly, a. *bad·sūrat, bad·shakl, mushād*.
Ulcer, s. *nāsūr*; *yaga*.
Ultimate, a. *ākhir, wrustanai pasīn*.
Ultimately, ad. *ākhir, wrusto, pas*.
Umbrage, s. *sorai* or *siwrai, gūr, gaur, chatr*. (offence) *marawar·tiyā, māurai*; *mīrtsī*.
Umbrella, s. *chatra-ī*.
Umpire, s. *mandz·garai, munsif*.
Un-, neg. prefix. (in comp.) *be-, nā-, lā-*, etc.
Unable, a. *nā·turān, nā·qābil*.
Unanimous, a. *yo zrah, yo jihat, yo ittipāq, pa yawe khule* or *-jibe*.
Unavailing, a. *'abas, be·fā,ida, nā·pakār*.
Unawares, ad. *nātsāpa, nāgāh, yak lakhta*.
Unbecoming, a. *nā·lā·iq, nā·munāsib, na·kkhanai, nā·kkhandah*.
Unbelief, s. *kufr, be·īmānī, kāfir·tob*.
Unbeliever, s. *kāfir, be·dīn, be·īmān*.
Unbosom, v.a. *prānatal, wayal, parda liri-*, or *porta k., tsargandawul*.
Unbroken, a. *amānī, pūrah, salāmat*.
Unbutton, v.a. *tanra-ī-, palwākkha-, ghūṭa-ī-gharāsha-*, etc. *prānatal* or *spardal*.
Unceremonious, a. *khamsor, be·takalluf*.
Uncertain, a. *nā·m'alūm, be·ṭikānā*.
Unchaste, a. *bad laman, shatāh, nā·pāk*.
Uncircumcised, a. *nā·solaṭ* or *nā·sunnat, shopā*.
Uncivil, a. *be·adab, be·makh, lwār, dzaban*.
Uncivilized, a. *lwār, pūhār, shār*.
Uncle, s. (paternal) *trah, kākā, ākā*. (maternal) *māmā, nwe*.
Unclean, a. *palit, nā·pāk, khīran, murdār*.
Unclouded, a. *shīn, sāf*.
Uncomfortable, a. *be·ārām, nā·khwakkh*.
Uncommon, a. *nādir, matrah, kamtar*.
Unconcerned, a. *be·parwā, be·khabar, be·gham, be·fikr*.
Uncouth, a. *lwār, pūhār, shār, dzaban*.
Uncover, v.a. *barbandawul, bargholai-, sar·pokkh-*, etc. *liri k*. (the head) *sar tor k*. (the face) *be·satr-, be·parde-*, etc. *k*. (a roof) *spardal*.
Unction, s. *mālish, mukkhana*.
Unctuous, a. *ghwar*.
Uncultivated, a. *ghair ābād, shār, wujār, wairān*.
Undecided, a. *wiswāsī, andekkh·man*; *nā·ta·mām, nīmgarai, nīma·khwā*.
Undefiled, a. *pāk, pākīzah, sāf*.
Undeniable, a. *lā·radd, qat'a-ī*.

Under, ad. and p. *lāndi, dalāndi, kkhkata, kkhkiya.* (-part) s. *talai, lāndi khwā.* (-most) a. *lāndinai, kkhatanai.*
Undergo, v.a. *wṛal, zghamal, khwuṛal.*
Underhand, ad. *pa puṭa, pa tara-ī, pa parde.*
Undermine, v.a. *surang wahal; naṛawul; wekh-, mūnḍ-,* etc. *wahal* or *khejawul.*
Underneath, ad. *dalāndi, kkhkata, kkhkiya.*
Underrate, v.a. *lāndi-, spuk-, nā·tsiz-,* etc. *ganṛal, ghandal, kagal.*
Understand, v.a. *pohedal, pahmedal, rasedal.*
Understanding, s. *poha, pahm, 'aql; joṛikkht, maṣlahat.*
Undertake, v.a. *ākhistal, porta k., khejawul, kawul, chalawul, lās lagawul.*
Undertaking, s. *kār, mu'āmala.*
Undervalue, v.a. *spuk-, kam-, nā·tsiz-,* etc. *ganṛal.*
Underwood, s. *jangai, dzangal, jāṛ, karkanṛ.*
Undivided, a. *pūrah, tamām, amānī.*
Undo, v.a. *spaṛdal, prānital, khwarawul.*
Undone, a. *spaṛdalai* or *spaṛai; wrān, kharāb.*
Undoubted, a. *yaqīn, be·shakk aw shubha.*
Undress, v.a. *jāme-,* etc. *bāsal—yastal.*
Undulate, v.n. *laharedal, ghurzedal.*
Uneasy, a. *be·ārām, nā·qalār; andekkh·man, wiswāsī.*
Unemployed, a. *kariyāb, khushai, be·kār, aṭāl, wazgār.*
Uneven, a. *lwaṛ jawar, kandai kawdarai, kkhkata porta, nā·hawār.*
Unexampled, a. *be·siyāl, lā·ṣānī, be·miṣāl.*
Unexpected, a. *nā·gahān, nā·gumān.*
Unexpectedly, ad. *nā·tsāpa, nāgāh.*
Unfair, a. *nā·rāst, nā·ṣāf.*
Unfaithful, a. *be·īmān, be·wafā.*
Unfeeling, a. *be·dard, kānṛai zṛah, be·rahm.*
Unfit, a. *nā·lā-iq, nā·qābil.*
Unfold, v.a. *prānatal, spaṛdal, tsargandawul, kkhkārah k.* v.n. *khwaredal, ghwaṛedal, ṭūkedal.*
Unforeseen, a. *nā·m'alūm, nā·līdah.*
Unfortified, a. *be·panāh, khushai.*
Unfortunate, a. *kam·bakht, bad·naṣīb, lā·chār, stāra prewatai.*
Unfounded, a. *bāṭil, be·kūdah.*
Unfruitful, a. *shanḍ, be·mewa, nā·mewa·dār.*
Unfurnished, a. *khushai, be·sāz, be da kālo.*
Ungird, v.a. *mlā prānital.*
Ungodly, a. *be·dīn, nā·khudā·tars.*
Ungovernable, a. *sar·zor, sar·kakkh, yāghī.*
Ungrateful, a. *namak ḥarām, nā·shukr·guẓār, nā·ḥaqq·shinās.*
Unguarded, a. *be·khabar, ghāfil.*
Unhappy, a. *khapah, malūl, dil·tang, nā·khwakkh, nā·kkhād.*
Unhealthy, a. *nā·joṛ; nā·muwāfiq.*
Unheard, a. *nā·āwredah.*
Unholy, a. *ḥarām, nā·pāk, bilmāz, nā·rawā.*
Uniform, a. *barābar, sam, hawār, yaw·shān.* s. *jāma, joṛa, libās.*
Unimaginable, a. *be·qiyās.*
Uninhabited, a. *ghair·ābād, wairān, wujāṛ.*
Union, s. *joṛ, pewastūn, taṛūn; rogha, joṛa, ittipāq; joṛakkht, malgar·tiyā.*
Unit, s. *yaw.* (Unity) s. *yaw·wālai, yak·tā-ī.*
Unite, v.a. *joṛawul, lagawul, pewand k.*
United, a. *pewastah; yaw zṛah, yaw jihat.*
Unitedly, ad. *pa ittipāq sara.*
Universal, a. *kullī, amānī, muṭlaq.*
Universally, ad. *bil·kull, sarāsar, tamāmī.*
Universe, s. *duniyā, jahān, naṛa-ī.*
Unjust, a. *be·inṣāf; nā·ḥaqq.*
Unknowingly, ad. *pa nā·dānī sara, nā·pohī sara, be·khabarī sara.*
Unlawful, a. *ḥarām, nā rawā, nā·ḥaqq.*
Unlearned, a. *jāhil, nā·lwustai, 'āmmī.*
Unless, ad. *magar* or *mangar, ganṛa* or *kanṛa* or *ka na.*
Unload, v.a. *bār·kūzawul, ta-ashawul.*
Unlucky, a. *kam·bakht, be·naṣīb, shūm·bakht, bad·bakht, stāra prewatai.*

Unmarried, a. *lawanḍ, nā·wādah kaṛai.* (f.) *peghla, nā·wādah·shiwi.*
Unmeaning, a. *be·m'anī, be·hūdah.*
Unmoved, a. *paedār, qā-im, mazbūṭ, ṭīng.*
Unoccupied, a. *khālī, khushai ; wazgār.*
Unpack, v.a. *prānītal, spaṛdal, ghwarawul.*
Unprotected, a. *khushai, be·panāh, be·wasīla.*
Unravel, v.a. *prānītal, spaṛdal, ghwaṛawul, khwarawul, wīṛawul.*
Unreasonable, a. *be·dzāyah, nā·munāsib.*
Unripe, a. *om, nīma·khwā, nīm·pukhtah, nīmgaṛai, kachah, khām.*
Unrivalled, a. *be·siyāl, lā·ṡānī, be·misāl.*
Unroll, v.a. *prānītal, spaṛdal, ghwaṛawul, khwarawul, wīṛawul.* v.n. *ghwaṛedal, wīṛedal, khwaredal.*
Unruly, a. *sar·zor, sar·kakkh.*
Unsafe, a. *khaṭr·nāk, be·amn.*
Unsatisfactory, a. *nā·sāz, nā·pīrzo.*
Unsatisfied, a. *nā·rāẓ, nā·khwakkh.*
Unseasonable, a. *be·dzāe, be·ṭāng, be·khratai. be·wakht.*
Unseen, a. *puṭ, ghā-ib, nā·līdah.*
Unserviceable, a. *nā·pakār, nākārah.*
Unsheltered, a. *khushai, be·panāh.*
Unshod, a. *abl, kkhpa·* or *pkkha·abla.*
Unsuccessful, a. *pa-aṛ, bāelūnkai.*
Untamed, a. *dzangalī, waḥshī ; lwāṛ, dzaban.*
Untidy, a. *shaḍal, pūhāṛ, shāwlai·wāwlai.*
Untie, v.a. *prānītal, spaṛdal.*
Until, p. *tar—pore, tso chi.* (-when ?) *tar kala pore.* (-now) *tar osa pore.*
Untimely, a. *be·ṭāng, be·wakht, be·khratai.*
Unto, p. *ta, la, lara, wa—ta,* etc. (-me) *rā ta, rā lara, lā la, lā lara, mā ta,* etc. (-thee) *dar ta, da la, dar lara, tā ta, wa tā ta, tā wa tā,* etc. (-him, her, it, them) *war ta, wa la, war lara, haghah ta, hagho ta,* or *-la,* or *-lara.*
Untold, a. *be·ḥisāb, be·shumār ; nā·wayalai, nā·guftah.*
Untoward, a. *nā·kārah ; aṛawulai ; bad.*
Untrue, a. *darogh·jan, jūṭah, nā·rāst.*
Untruth, s. *darogh, kiẕb, nā·rāstī.*
Untwist, v.a. *spaṛdal, prānītal, khwarawul.*
Unusual, a. *kam·ist'imāl, kam·chalan, shāẕẕ.*
Unveil, v.a. *be·satr-, be·parde-,* etc. *k., bar·banḍawul.*
Unwary, a. *be·khabar, ghāfil.*
Unwearied, a. *tāzah, nā·staṛai, hosā.*
Unwell, a. *nā·joṛ, nā·rogh.*
Unwieldy, a. *loe, ghaṭ, star, drūnd.*
Unwilling, a. *nā·rāẓ, daregh·man.*
Unworthy, a. *nā·lā-iq, nā·pīrzo.*
Up, p. *bāndi, porta, pās.* (-on) *pa-, par-, pri-,* etc. *bāndi.* (-to) *-ta, -la, -lara, -pore.* (-and down) *lar bar, kūz pās, kkhkata porta, lāndi bāndi, lwaṛ jawar.*
Upbraid, v.a. *malāmatawul, peghorawul, ṭaqawul, raṭal, traṭal, dāṛal.*
Uphold, v.a. *sambālawul, khejawul, porta nīwul, pushtī-, komak-,* etc. *warkawul.*
Uplift, v.a. *khejawul, porta ākhistal* or *k.*
Upon, p. *bāndi, dapāsa, dabāndi, pa·bāndi, pri·bāndi.*
Upper, a. *bar, pāsanai, portanai.*
Upright, a. *walāṛ, negh, jig, lak ; rikkhtīnai, rāst·man, nek.*
Uprightness, s. *walāṛ·tiyā, negh·wālai,* etc. ; *nekī, rikkhtīn·tob, rāstī.*
Uproar, s. *balwā, ghāl·o·ghūl, shor·shaghab.*
Upset, v.a. *naskorawul, aṛawul, naṛawul, āchawul, ghurzawul ; toyawul, sandzal.* v.n. *naskoredal, naṛedal, lwedal, prewatal ; toedal.*
Upshot, s. *anjām, gaṭa, ḥāṣil.*
Upside-down, a. *naskor, aṛawulai.*
Upwards, ad. *pās, porta, bar ; ziyāt.*
Urbanity, s. *makhawarī, nek sulūkī.*
Urge, v.a. *zoral, tezal, chalawul, rawānawul ; tākīd-, taqāza-,* etc. *k.* ; *lamsawul.*
Urgent, a. *ẓarūr, tang, sakht.*

Urine, s. *baul, mitiyāzi, peshāb.*

Usage, s. *sulūk.* (custom) *rasm, dastūr.* (habit) *'ādat, chalan.* (rule) *ā-īn, qā'ida.*

Use, s. *kār, fā-ida*; *'amal, ist'imāl.*

Use, v.a. *pa·kār rāwṛal, lagawul, chalawul*; *'amal-*, etc. *k.*; *sulūk-*, etc. *k.*

Useful, a. *fā-ida·man, sūd·man, pa·kār.*

Useless, a. *nā·kārah, 'abas, khushai, be·fā-ida.*

Usual, a. *ist'imālī, jārī, chalanī.* (as-) *pa·dastūr.*

Usually, ad. *aksar, aghlab.*

Usurer, s. *sūd·khor, ribā·khor.*

Usurp, v.a. *shūkawul, nā·haqq ākhistal, pa·zor-, pa·zabardastī-*, etc. *-lāndi k.*, *-dzān ta ākhistal.*

Usurpation, s. *shūka, pa·zor-*, etc. *ākhistana.*

Usury, s. *sūd, ribā.*

Utmost, a. *nihāyat, hadd.*

Utter, a. *nihāyat, bashpaṛ, amānī.*

Utter, v.a. *wayal, lal, lawdal*; *chalawul, jārī k.*

Utterly, ad. *sarāsar, amānī, tamāmī.*

Uvula, s. *kūmai, laṛ.*

Uxorious, a. *kkhadza·dost* or *·parast.*

V.

Vacant, a. *ta-ash, khālī, khushai.*

Vacate, v.a. *ta-ashawul, khālī-*, etc. *k.*

Vacation, s. *t'atīl, farāghat, wazgār·tiyā, furṣat.*

Vagabond, s. *lawanḍ, lūtsak, chaṭ, kūtsa·gard, kujrai, awārah, qachar.*

Vagary, s. *khiyāl, wahm.*

Vague, a. *nā·m'alūm, khushai.*

Vain, a. *'abas, bātil, be·fā-ida*; *wiyāṛ·jan, bādī, khpul·rāe, khāntamā, bād·hawā.*

Vainly, ad. *'abas, be·fā-ida.*

Valiant, a. *maṛanai, tūrzan, zṛah·war, bātor, dilāwar, bahādur, zmarai.*

Valid, a. *mazbūṭ, mahkam, qā-im*; *joṛ, drust, rikkhtīnai, zbād.*

Valley, s. *dara, sama, maidān.*

Valour, s. *maṛāna, tūrzan·tob, zṛah·war·tob, maṛanī·tob, zmarī·tob, bahādurī.*

Valuable, a. *qīmat·nāk, grān bahā.*

Value, v.a. *bai'a-, qīmat-*, etc. *twṛal* or *-lagawul* or *k.*; *qadr-, 'izzat-*, etc. *pejandal, ganṛal.*

Valve, s. *ghwagai, warkha*; *war, tamba, pala.*

Van, s. *pesh·khaima*; *harāwul, qarāwul.*

Vanish, v.n. *puṭedal, lwukkhtal—lwuṛedal, wrukedal*; *ālwatal*; *wuchedal.*

Vanity, s. *wiyāṛ, dam, lāpa shāpa*; *be·hūdagī, spuk·tiyā*; *khpul·sarī, bād hawā-ī.*

Vanquish, v.a. *pa-aṛ-, māt-, lar-, lāndi-*, etc. *k.*, *barai mūndal.*

Vapid, a. *be·khwand, balmagai, balmangak.*

Vapour, s. *bukhār, bṛās*; *laṛw*; *lūgai*; *ghubār.*

Variable, a. *nā·qalār, nā·pāedār, nīma khwā.*

Variance, s. *dukkhmanī, mīrtsī, kharkhakkha*; *patna, pasāt, 'aks*; *gwākkh*; *zidd.*

Variation, s. *biyal·wālai, farq.*

Variegated, a. *rangā·rang, brag·yālai.*

Variety, s. *rang pa rang, raqam pa raqam*, etc.

Various, a. *biyal·biyal, rangā·rang, shānā·shān, judā·judā, dzane.*

Varnish, v.a. *rangawul, rang lagawul, batī ḍakawul, lāk-, slekkh-*, etc. *lagawul.*

Vary, v.n. *badledal, āwukkhtal, girzedal, biyaledal.* v.a. *badlawul, āwukkhtal*, etc.

Vassal, s. *hamsāyah, faqīr, r'aīyat.*

Vast, a. *loe, ghaṭ, star, 'azīm.*

Vastly, ad. *nihāyat, be·shāna.*

Vat, s. *hauz.*

Vault, s. *gunbata, qubbu.* (cellar) *tah khāna.* (cave) *smats, ghār.* (tomb) *qabar, lahad.*

Vault, v.a. *ghurzang-, tīndak-, ṭop-, khachūnai-*, etc. *wahal, dangal*; *gunbata-*, etc. *joṛawul.*

Vegetable, s. *wākkhah, ḍakai, būṭai.* (greens) *sāg, sabzī.*

Vegetate, v.n. *ṭūkedal, zarghūnedal.*

Vehement, a. *sakht, tod, tund, tez.*

Vehicle, s. *gāḍa-ī*; *swarlī* or *sparlī.* (means) *m'arifat, wasīla, wāsiṭa.* (in medicine) *badragha* or *badraga.*

Veil, v.a. *parda-, maizar-, oḍana-ī-, bolqa* or *burq'a-*, etc. *pa-sarawul, satr pokkhal* or *k.*, *puṭawul, pokkhal.*

Vein, s. *rag, nas.* (jugular) *kkhāh rag.*

Velocity, s. *garand-wālai, za-ar-* or *zir-tiyā, jaltiyā.*

Velvet, s. *bakhmal, makhmal.*

Venal, a. *zar dost, zar parast.*

Vend, v.a. *khartsawul, ploral* or *prolal, prowul.*

Venerable, a. *zbarg, loe.*

Venerate, v.a. *manal, zbarg ganral.* v.n. *grohedal.*

Venery, s. *gho, ghowuna, kor-wālai, jimā'a, suḥbat.* (chase) *kkhkār.*

Venesection, s. *rag wahana.*

Venetian, s. *karka-ī.*

Vengeance, s. *badal, qiṣāṣ*; *qahr, qiyāmat, balāe.* (to take-) v.a. *badal-*, etc. *ākhistal.* (with-) *pa qahr.*

Venial, a. *da bakkhalo, da pulawulo*; *rawā.*

Venom, s. *zahr.*

Venomous, a. *zahr-nāk, zahr-dār.*

Vent, s. *sūra, khula, lār, war.* (of a chimney) *dūd-* or *lū-kakkh.* (-of a canal) *warkh, ghwagai.* (to give-) v.a. *khalāṣawul, pregdal, prekkhodal, prekkhal.*

Ventilator, s. *bād-kakkh, bād-rau.*

Venture, s. *khaṭra.* (chance) *daw.* (fate) *naṣīb.* (at a-) *pa tawakkul.* v.a. *himmat-, qaṣd-*, etc. *k.*; *daw k.*

Venturesome, a. *himmatī, himmat-nāk, bakht-bāz.*

Venus, s. (star) *gūp, da melmana starga, zuhra.*

Veracity, s. *rikkhtīn-tob, rāstī, ḥaqq.*

Verb, s. *f'il.* (active-) *f'il i mut'addī.* (passive-) *f'il i majhūl.* (neuter-) *f'il i lāzimī.*

Verbal, a. *zabānī, wayalai.* (-noun, active participle) *ism i fā'il.* (-gerund) *ism i maṣdar.* (present participle) *ḥāṣil bil maṣdar.*

Verbatim, ad. *khabara pa khabare, ḥarf pa ḥarf, ṭakai pa ṭakī, ḥarfan ḥarfan.*

Verdant, a. *shīn, zarghūn, tar o tāzah.*

Verdict, s. *ḥukm, fatwā, faiṣala.*

Verdigris, s. *zangār.*

Verdure, s. *shīn-wālai, shīn wākkhah, sabzī.*

Verge, s. *ghāṛa, morga, tsanḍa, laman, ja-ī.*

Verge, v.n. *girzedal, mailān ked.*, *rasedal, lagedal, jārwatal, āwukkhtal.*

Verify, v.a. *rikkhtīnai-, zbād-, tahqīq-*, etc. *k.*

Verily, ad. *rikkhtiyā, yara.*

Verity, s. *rikkhtiyā, rikkhtīn-tob, rāstī.*

Vermicelli, s. *māeche.*

Vermin, s. *mozī dzanāwar, chinjī-n.injī, khazande-mazande, mlakh-magak*, etc.

Vernacular, s. *mulkī, waṭanī, wilāyatī*; *da waṭan wrāsha* or *-jiba.*

Verse, s. *naẓm, sh'ir, bait.* (-of Quran) *āyat.*

Version, s. *naql, tarjuma.*

Vertigo, s. *gīrzedana da sar, akar, pa stargo tyāra, sar churlai* or *-girzai.*

Very, ad. *ḍer, ziyāt.* (this-) *bedū, pa takī.*

Vesicle, s. *tanrāka.*

Vespers, s. *nmākkhām.*

Vessel, s. *lokkhai, kaṭwa-ī.* (blood-) *rag.* (boat) *beṛa-ī, jahāz.*

Vestibule, s. *manḍaw, dahlīz.*

Vestige, s. *nakkha, pal, ṭakai.*

Vesture, s. *aghostan, nwaraī, pokkhāk. jāma.*

Vetch, s. *chaura, moṭ, kṛāk.*

Veteran, a. *zoṛ, pokh, pūrah.*

Vex, v.a. *pārawul, ṭongawul, rabṛawul, kaṛawul.*

Vexation, s. *ṭongāṛa, rabaṛ, khapagī, diqqat.*

Vexatious, a. *rabaṛ·nāk, khūg·nāk, janjālī, āzār rasawūnkai.*

Vial, s. *kkhīkkha.*

Vibrate, v.n. *rapedal, regdedal, pṛakedal; zangal, zangedal, kkhoredal.*

Vice, s. *badī, 'aib, sharārat.* (instrument) *zambūr.*

Viceroy, s. *qā-im muqām, nā-ib; nāẓim, nawwāb.*

Vicinity, s. *nijdekī, gāwanḍ.*

Vicious, a. *bad, nākārah, bakhil, 'aib·nāk.*

Vicissitude, s. *wār, nobat, wakht, ṭāng.*

Victim, s. *qurbān, jār* or *dzār, ṣadqa.*

Victor, s. *bar, wa-aṛ, ghālib, pa-aṛ kawūnkai.*

Victorious, a. *wa-aṛ, bar, barai mūndūnkai,* or *-mūndalai,* or *-gaṭalai.*

Victory, s. *barai, wa-aṛūna.*

Victuals, s. *khwurāk, khwāṛak, qūt, ṭa'ām, ghiẓā.*

Vie, v.a. *barābarī k., was chalawul, ḥadd k.*

View, s. *naẓar, nandāra, tamāsha, līdah, kātah, dzīr, mulāḥiẓa; niyat, maṭlab, gharaẓ.* v.a. *goral, līdal, katal, kasal, naẓar-,* etc. *k.* (to have in-) v.a. *niyat-,* etc. *laral.* (to consider) v.a. *ganṛal.*

Vigil, s. *sho·gīrī, tsoka-ī.*

Vigilance, s. *baidārī, khabar·dārī, hokkhyār·tiyā.*

Vigilant, a. *baidār, khabar·dār, hokkhyār, wīkkh.*

Vigorous, a. *zorāwar, quwat·nāk, tawānā, qawī.*

Vigour, s. *zor, quwat, barm* or *bram, tuwān, ṭāqat, tāo.*

Vile, a. *bad, kharāb, nā·kārah, dūn, khwār, spuk, palīt, murdār.*

Vilify, v.a. *tor-, tuhmat-,* etc. *pore k., peghor warkawul, kanzal* or *kkhkandzal, ghandal, kagal, bad nāmawul, ruswā k.*

Village, s. *kilai, dih.*

Villager, s. *kilī·wāl, da kilī saṛai.*

Villain, s. *bad·m'ash, bad·ẓāt, ḥarāmī, chular-charlanḍ.* (farm servant) *dihqān, charekār.*

Villainous, a. *bad, nā·kārah, ḥarām·kār.*

Villainy, s. *sharārat, pasāt, bad·ẓātī, ṭagī, namak·ḥarāmī.*

Vindicate, v.a. *ṣābitawul, pūrah-, zbād-, rikkhtiyā-, qā-im-,* etc. *k.*; *'uẕr rāwṛal.*

Vindication, s. *iṣbāt, zbād; 'uẕr.*

Vindictive, a. *kīna·war.*

Vine, s. *tāk, kwar.* (-yard) *raz.*

Vinegar, s. *sirka.*

Violate, v.a. *mātawul; wrānawul.*

Violence, s. *zor, ẓulm, jabar, zabardastī, jafā; sakhtī, tūndī; qahr, ghaẓab.*

Violent, a. *sakht, tund, tez; qahr·nāk, ghaẓab·nāk.*

Violin, s. *rabāb, sārinda, ghichaka.*

Viper, s. *mangor, mangarai.*

Virgin, s. *peghla, ja-an, jūna-ī, jina-ī, bākira.*

Virility, s. *mardī, quwat da bāh.*

Virtually, ad. *pa wāq'ī, pa aṣl, pa rikkhtiyā.*

Virtue, s. *nekī, nekokārī, ṣawāb.* (quality) *lokkhai, ṣifat, khoe, khaṣlat, khāṣṣiyat.*

Virtuous, a. *nek, nekokār, ṣawābī, pāk, pāk·laman, nek·khoe, ·khaṣlat, ·bakht,* etc.

Virulent, a. *sakht, tund, tez, jābir, qātil.*

Visage, s. *makh, tsihra, rūe, gūna, bashra, ṣūrat.*

Viscid, a. *barwai, bokkht, slekkh·nāk, chaspān.*

Visible, a. *kkhkārah, tsargand, bartser, awtsār, ẓāhir.*

Vision, s. *naẓar, līdah, kātah.* (dream) *khob, khiyāl.*

Visionary, s. *khiyālī, wahmī.*

Visit, v.a. *līdah-, kātah-, dīdan-, mulāqāt-,* etc. *k.* (a shrine), *ziyārat k.*

Vital, a. *jwandai; da marg aw jwāk.*

Vitality, s. *dzān, jwandūn, jwāk.*

Vitals, s. *laṛmānah, dzigar, īna.*

Vitiate, v.a. *spukawul, habatah k., wrānawul, kharābawul, tabāh k.*

Vitriol, s. *totā*. (blue-) *nīla·totā*. (green-) *shna·*, or *sabza·totā*.

Vituperation, s. *malāmat, peghor, tor, tuhmat. kanzal*, or *kkhkandzal*.

Vivacious, a. *kkhād, khūsh·hāl, khanda·rūe*.

Vivid, a. *rūnr, rokkhān, brekkh·nāk*; *jwandai*.

Vocabulary, s. *lughat, da kalimo kitāb*.

Vocation, s. *kār, kasb, pesha*.

Vocative, s. *nidá, bāng, ghag*.

Vociferate, v.a. *bāng wayal, nāra-, chigha-, sūra-*, etc. *wahal, chighawul*.

Vogue, s. *chāl, chalan, dastūr*. (in-) *rawā*.

Voice, s. *āwāz, bāng, zwag, ghag*. (active-) *sīgha i m'arūf*. (passive-) *sīgha i majhūl*.

Void, a. *ta-ash, khālī, khushai*; *'abas, bātil*.

Void, v.a. *jārbāsal—jāryastal, ghurzawul*. (-at stool) *ghul k., kharal*.

Volition, s. *wāk, ikhtiyār, ghokkht*.

Volley, s. *shilak, bār, dandūkār*.

Voluble, a. *jiba·war*; *chālāk*.

Volume, s. *kitāb, jild*; *qadr, andāza*.

Voluntarily, ad. *pa khpula*.

Voluntary, a. *khpul·wāk, khpul·ikhtiyār*.

Voluptuary, s. *geda·parast, shahwat·parast*.

Voluptuous, a. *geda-* or *kheta-, shahwat-, nafs-*, etc. *parast*.

Vomit, v.a. *jārbāsal—jāryastal, qai-, bāka-ī, chāl-*, etc. *k., kūz katal, zmake ta katal, -goral*, etc.

Voracious, a. *līwāl, wagai*.

Vortex, s. *ghurzai, gharq·āb, gird·āb*.

Votary, s. *ghulām, mra-e*; *hājat·man, niyāz·man*; *parastār, manūnkai*.

Vote, s. *lafz, qaul, khabara, wayai*. v.a. *khwakkhawul, qabūlawul, pasandawul*.

Vouch, v.a. *gawāhī-, shāhidī-*, etc. *warkawul*, or *-lal*, or *-wandal*; *dalīl-, hujjat-*, etc. *warkawul*; *wayal*.

Voucher, s. *hujjat, dalīl, sanad*; *gawāh, shāhid*.

Vouchsafe, v.a. *bakkhal, warkawul, mihrbāngī k*.

Vow, s. *neta, wāda, shart, qaul, lafz*; *nazr, niyāz*. v.a. *neta-*, etc. *k.* or *-taral*; *nazr-*, etc. *warkawul, -warwral*.

Vulgar, a. *'āmm*. (mean) *spuk, nā·kārak*. (the-) *'āmmiyān, 'awāmm*.

Vulture, s. *ganjai, gargas*.

Vulva, s. *kus*.

W.

Wabble, v.n. *khwadzedal, zangedal*.

Wad, s. *būja, dīda, shora*; *manjīla*.

Waddle, v.n. *arte-* or *chīnge kkhpe tlal—lāral*.

Wade, v.n. *pa obo kkhke girzedal*.

Wafer, s. *tika-ī, chaka-ī, tsaparkai*.

Waft, v.a. *rasawul, ālwūzawul, āstawul*.

Wag, s. *pekkhe·gar, toq·mār, malandai, maskharāchī, washtai*.

Wag, v.a. *khwadzawul, tsandal, rapawul*.

Wage, v.a. *kawul, kral, chalawul, ākhistal*.

Wager, v.a. *shart taral, daw k*.

Wages, s. *talab, tankhwāh, mihnat, kharts, muzd, mazdūrī*; *muwājib*.

Wagon, s. *gāda-ī, 'arāba*.

Wagtail, s. *māmūlaka, shīn·topa-ī, ziyarānaka*.

Wail, s. *wīr, wainā, wāwailā, jarā, sānda*.

Wailing, a. *wīra·jalai, jarānd*.

Waist, s. *mlā, landa*.

Wait, v.n. *osedal, pātedal, pātai ked., wudredal*; *hāzir osedal*. (-upon) v.a. *khidmat k*.

Waiter, s. *khidmat·gār*.

Waive, v.a. *pregdal*, etc. *tark k*.

Wake, v.n. *wīkkhedal, pātsedal, baidār ked*. v.a. *wīkkhawul, pātsawul, baidār k*.

Wakeful, a. *wīkkh, baidār, khabar·dār*.

Walk, v.n. *tlal—lāṛal, drūmal* or *drūmedal, chaledal, girzedal, pa kkhpo tlal.*

Walk, s. *sail, gakkht*; *chāl, yūn*; *lār.*

Wall, s. *dīwāl.* (side wall of a house) *chana.* (-eyed) a. *chaghar.* (to build a-) v.a. *dīwāl wahal* or *-khejawul.*

Wallet, s. *bana-ī, gūḍai, dzola-ī, chamta.*

Wallow, v.n. *rghaṛedal—rghakkhtal, lots-pots ked.*

Walnut, s. *akoṛ, ghoz.* (-soft) *chaghzī.* (-hard) *maṭāk.*

Wan, a. *ṭap, ziyaṛ, sperah.*

Wand, s. *amsā, lakkhta.*

Wander, v.n. *khushai-, dar ba dar-,* etc. *girzedal, rammedal*; *be-lār-, gumrāh-,* etc. *ked.*

Wane, v.n. *kamedal, zahedal, la-ag-, zawāl-,* etc. *ked., prewatal.*

Want, s. *ghokkht, ḥājat, darkhwāst.* (penury) *tangsiyā, khwārī.* (deficiency) *troṭa, waṭa.*

Want, v.a. *ghokkhtal, ḥājat laral*; *pukkhtedal. sawāl-, darkhwāst-,* etc. *k.*

Wanting, a. *kam, nāqiṣ, nīmgaṛai, ḥājat-man.*

Wanton, a. *mast, shokh, shahwat-nāk, bad-laman, shatāh, lashmakai, be-ḥayā.*

War, s. *jang, jadal*; *patna, kharkhakkha.* (civil-) *khāna-jangī.* (religious-) *ghazā, jihād.*

Warble, v.a. *chaur-chaur-, chighāra-, bul-ghāk-,* etc. *k.*

Ward, v.a. *sātal, jghoral, khundī k.* (-off) *raf'a-daf'a k., bachawul.*

Ward, s. *kandai, mūlat, maḥalla, cham.*

Ware, s. *māl, jins, saudā, asbāb, shai, tsīz.* (-house) *kār-khāna, māl-khāna, ambār.* (hard-) *da ospane kālī.* (crockery-) *kaṭwī lokkhī.*

Warily, ad. *pa hokkhyār-tiyā-, pa baidārī-, pa pahm-, pa khabar-dārī-,* etc. *-sara.*

Warlike, a. *jangī.*

Warm, a. *tod, garm.* (luke-) *taṛam.*

Warmth, s. *tod-wālai, todūkha, garmī.*

Warning, s. *khabar, āgāhī.* (example) *'ibrat.* (to give-) v.a. *khabar-,* etc. *k.*; *'ibrat war-kawul.* (to take-) v.a. *'ibrat ākhistal.*

Warp, v.a. *pech-, tāo-,* etc. *warkawul.* v.n. *kagedal.*

Warp, s. *pūda, tār*; *tanasta, kanrai.*

Warrant, s. *parwāna, sanad, barāt, ḥukm-nāma.*

Warrant, v.a. *wayal*; *wāk-, ikhtiyār-,* etc. *warkawul*; *rawā-, rikkhtiyā-, sūchah-,* etc. *ganral* or *k.*; *pushtī-, madad-,* etc. *war-kawul.*

Warrantable, a. *rawā, lāzim, shara'ī.*

Warranted, a. *shartī, qarārī.*

Warrior, s. *ghāzī, jangī, mujāhid.*

Wart, s. *zakha.*

Wary, a. *hokkhyār, pokh, chirg, kāgh, gharand.*

Wash, v.a. *wīndzal* or *mīndzal, wlal.* (-one-self) *lambal, ghusl k.* (-for prayers) *awdas-, wazū-,* etc. *k.*

Washerman, s. *dobī.* (woman) *dobanra.* (-of the dead) *ghāsil.* (-his boiler) *khūm.* (-mallet) *tsobārai.*

Wasp, s. *ḍanḍāra, ḍanbara, sra macha-ī, ghālboza.*

Waste, v.a. *'abaṣ kharts k., iṣrāf-, tāwān-, talaf-,* etc. *k., wrukawul.* v.n. *wuchedal, kaṛedal, zahedal.*

Waste, a. *wairān, wujāṛ, kharāb, shāṛ.* s. *maira, shāṛa*; *tāwān, iṣrāf, talaf.*

Wasteful, a. *muṣrif, iṣrāfī, talaf kawūnkai.*

Watch, v.a. *tsoka-ī-, pahra-, pāswānī-,* etc. *k.*; *sho-gīrī-, baidārī-,* etc. *k., kashak gālal, jghoral.*

Watch, s. *gaṛa-ī, sā'at.* (-maker) *gaṛa-ī-,* etc. *-sāz* or *-joṛawūnkai.* (-house) *tānra.* (-tower) *bruj.* (-man) *pāswān, tsoka-ī-dār, pahra-dār.* (-man over fields, cattle, etc.) *kakkhai.* (-word) *nakkha, lafz.*

Watchful, a. *khabar·dār, baidār, hokkhyār.*

Water, s. *oba, āb.* (-carrier) *mashkī, saqāo.* (-bag) *mashk, ja-ī; palānra.* (-course) *khwar, kanda, kas, shela.* (-closet) *chār·choba.* (-cresses) *tartezak, halam.* (-fall) *dāra, tsādar.* (-fowl) *hīla-ī.* (-lily) *nīlofar.* (-man) *mahanrah, mānrgai.* (-melon) *hind·wāna, tarbūza.* (-mill) *jaranda, āsiyā.* (-pot) *loṭkai, mangai.*

Watery, a. *ob·lan, ob·jan, abī; lūnd khūsht, zyam·nāk.*

Wattle, s. (hedge) *keṛ.* (bird's-) *jajūra, ghuṭ·yālai.*

Wattle, v.a. *ogayal, gayayal* or *gayawul.*

Wave, s. *chapa, mauj, lahar.*

Wave, v.n. *zangal* or *zangedal; laharedal.* v.a. *tsanḍal, kkhorawul, shanawul.*

Waver, v.n. *rapedal, tsrapedal; wṛāndi wrusto-, be·qalār-, be·ārām-,* etc. *ked.*

Wavering, a. *nā·qalār.*

Wax, s. *mūm.* (-cloth) *mūm·jāma.* (sealing-) *lāk.*

Way, s. *lār; ṭaur, shān, toga, rang; ṭarīqa, dastūr, chalan.*

Waylay, v.a. *lār nīwul, psūnai k.*

Wayward, a. *sar·kakkh, khpul·sar; wītak, shokh.*

We, pr. *mūng, mūg, mū.*

Weak, a. *nā·tuwān, kam·zor, 'ājiz, ẓa'īf, zahīr, kam·quwat, kam·ṭāqat, māndah.* (low) *spuk, khwār, nā·tsīz.* (as tea, etc.) *narai, malīn.*

Weakness, s. *kamzor·tiyā, na·tuwānī, 'ājizī.*

Wealth, s. *duniyā, daulat, māl, zar.*

Wealthy, a. *duniyā·dār, daulat·man, zar·dār, tuwān·gar.*

Wean, v.a. *la to na ghūṭ k.*

Weanling, s. *zāṛai, ghūṭkai, būhārai.*

Weapon, s. *wasla, drasta, hatiyār, kālai.*

Wear, v.a. *āghostal, pa dzān k.,* or *-āchawul.* (rub) v.n. *sūledal.* (waste) *zaṛedal.* (last) *chaledal, teredal, pāedal.*

Wearisome, a. *drūnd, grān, staṛai kawūnkai.*

Weary, a. *staṛai, stomān, haukah.*

Weather, s. *āsmān, bād, hawā, mosam, wradz.* (-cock) *bād numāe* or *-kkhowūnkai.*

Weave, v.a. *ūdal* or *odal.*

Weaver, s. *jolāh, dahor.* (-loom) *shāna, rach.* (-beam) *palcṭanr* or *paṭelanr.* (shuttle) *mākū.* (-brush) *māla.* (-paste) *batī.* (-yarn) *tanasta.* (-yarn beam) *hata.* (-web) *būda* or *pūda.* (-reeds) *nala, dūrma.* (-spindle) *garzanai.* (-reel) *nicha.*

Web, s. *tanasta, kanrai, būda.* (spider's-) *jāla-ī.*

Wed, v.a. *wadawul, wādah k., nikāḥ taṛal.* v.n. (applied to the woman) *wadedal, wādah ked.*

Wedding, s. *wādah, nikāḥ.* (-party) m. *janj.* f. *wrā.* (-guest) m. *jānjī, mānjī, wrā·bānrai.* f. *wre-aza* or *wreyaza, wrā·bānra-ī, mānja-ī.*

Wedge, s. *pāna, shpetai.*

Wednesday, s. *chār shamba.*

Weed, s. *wākkhah.* v.a. *lalūn-, goḍ-,* etc. *k.*

Weeding, s. *lalūn, goḍ, pūjī.* (-hoe) *rambai.*

Week, s. *hafta.*

Weekly, ad. *hafta pa hafte.*

Weep, v.a. *jaṛal, okkhe toyawul.* (mourn) *wīr-, wāwailā-,* etc. *k., wainā wayal.*

Weeper, s. *wīra·jalai, wainā wayūnkai; jaṛand.*

Weeping, s. *jaṛā; wīr, wāwailā.*

Weevil, s. *gūnr, buza.*

Weigh, v.a. *talal, tol k., jokal.*

Weight, s. *tol, jok; wazn, andāza; drandwai, drūnd·wālai; bār.* Bazar weights (two lbs.) *ser.* (oke = 7 sers) *ogai.* (quarter oke) *kuṛhai.* (4 sers) *daṛa-ī.* (10 daṛī or maund) *man.* (8 maunds) *kharwār.* (¼ ser) *pāo.* (½ ser) *dwah pāwa.* (¾ ser) *dre pāwa.* (1¼ ser) *pīndzah pāwa.* (1½ ser) *yo·nīm ser.* (1¾ ser) *pāo kam dwah sera.*

(2 sers) *dwak sera.* (2¼ sers) *pāo bāndī-* or *pāo dapāsa—dwak sera.* (2½ sers) *dwak-nīm sera*, etc. (2 oz.) *chīṭāka-ī.* (1 oz.) *nīma chīṭāka-ī.* (⅛ oz.) *shirshā-ī.* (¼ oz.) *nīma shirshā-ī.* (2 drs.) *paisa.* Jeweller's weights. *rata-ī* = 1·8 gr.; *māsa* = 8 *rata-ī*; *misqāl* = 4 *māsa* + 3½ *rata-ī*; *tola* = 12½ *māsa* or 180 grs.

Weighty, a. *drūnd, grān.*

Welcome, a. *mubārak, kkhah, khwakkh, khair.* s. *mubārakī, du'ā da khair, rogh-baṛ, bara-gaṛa, bar-gaṛandī.* in. *har-kala har-kala! pa khaira-* or *pa khair sara rāghlai ye! khairāt dī rāwuṛ!* v.a. *joṛ tāzah sara k., mubārakī warkawul.* (to be-) v.n. *pa khaira-*, or *pa khair sara rāghlal.*

Welfare, s. *khairiyat, tandrust-wālai, kkhe-gaṛa, bihbūdī, bihtarī; wadān-wālai, ābād-wālai.*

Well, s. *kūhai, chāh.* (-with lever) *ḍingara-ī, yak-langa.* (-with steps) *baha-ī.* (-with wheels) *arhaṭ.*

Well, a. *kkhah, joṛ, rogh; nek, khwakkh, mubārak.* ad. *kkhah, pa kkhah shān sara.* (very-) *ḍer kkhah.* (-done!) *ākh* or *ākhkkh, ākhkkhai.* (-then) *biyā, nor.* (as-) *hum.* (as well as) *laka chi.* (-nigh) *nijde.* (-born) a. *sānū, aṣil.* (-wisher) *khair-khwāh, du'ā-goe.*

Wen, s. *baura-ī, kala-ī, rasaula-ī, ghumba.*

Wench, s. *wīndza, mazdūra, khidmat-gāra, sahela-ī; ja-an, jina-ī, peghla, kkhadza; kachana-ī, lola-ī.*

West, s. *nwar prewātah, qibla, maghrab.* (-ward) *nwar prewātah khwā.*

Wet, a. *lūnd, khusht, naw-jan, nam-nāk.*

Wether, s. *wuch-kūl.*

Wetness, s. *lūnd-wālai, khusht-wālai; nau, zyam.*

Wetnurse, s. *dā-ī.*

What, pr. *kūm, tsok, tsa.* (-else?) *nor tsa.* (-then?) *biyā.*

Whatever, pr. *har kūm, har tsok*, etc.; *kūm chi, har chi.*

Wheat, s. *ghanum.*

Wheedle, v.a. *ghulawul, darghalawul, dam warkawul.* (coax) *jigī-, hāṛe-, jāna-*, etc. *k.*

Wheel, s. *tsarkh.* (-spoke) *tīrai, palai, shpeshtai.*

Wheel, v.n. *girzedal, churledal, tsarkhedal.*

Wheeze, v.a. *sāh pa ūchata ākhistal, sāh shṛangawul.*

Whelp, s. *bachai, kutrai.*

When, ad. *kala, kūm wakht.*

Whenever, ad. *har kala chi, har-*, or *kūm wakht chi.*

Where, ad. *charta, kūm dzāe, kūma khwā.* (no-) *hets charta, hets dzāe.*

Whereas, ad. *dzaka chi, la de na, balki, wale.*

Whereat, ad. *pas, biyā, nor, pa de.*

Wherefore, ad. *pas, dzaka, la kabla.*

Wherever, ad. *har charta chi, har-*, or *kūm dzāe chi.*

Whet, v.a. *terah-, tez-*, etc. *k.*

Whether, c. *ki, yā, khwāh.*

Whetstone, s. *psān, belko* or *belāo, barjo, tsarkh.*

Whey, s. *tarwe, lassī; mājūban* or *mā ul joban.*

Which, pr. *kūm, kūm yaw.*

While, s. *wakht* or *waqt, mūda.*

Whilst, ad. *tso chi, hombra chi, tar haghah pore chi.*

Whim, s. *wahm, khiyāl.*

Whine, v.a. *pṛang-, rangaṭ-, kūk-*, etc. *wahal.*

Whip, s. *karoṛa, dura, tāziyāna, qamchīna.* v.a. *karoṛa-*, etc. *wahal* or *-lagawul.*

Whirl, v.a. *girzawul, churlawul, tsarkhawul.* v.n. *girzedal, churledal, tsarkhedal.*

Whirligig, s. *baṛen-chagh, jalandarai, churla-ī, bāmbūra.*

Whirlpool, s. *ghurzai, gird·āb, gharq·āb.*
Whirlwind, s. *borbūka-ī.*
Whiskers, s. *kāna-ī.*
Whisper, v.a. *pus pus k., ro ro pa ghwag kkhke wayal.*
Whistle, v.a. *shpela-ī wahal* or *-ghagawul.*
Whit, s. *ṭakai, khasanrai, pūṭai, pitsānrai, zarra.*
White, a. *spīn, saped* or *safed.*
White-ant, s. *oenak.*
Whiteness, s. *spīn·wālai.*
Whither, ad. *charta, kūma khwā.*
Whitlow, s. *kharai, shīnai.*
Whizz, s. *sagh.* v.a. *sagh k.*
Who, pr. *tsok, kum.* (-ever) *har tsok chi.*
Whole, a. *pūrah, amānī, tamām ; drust, salāmat.* s. *ṭol, wāṛah.* (-sale) *ṭālah.*
Wholesome, a. *kkhah, ghwarah, joṛ, muwāfiq.*
Wholly, ad. *amānī, sarāsar, bil·kull, muṭlaq.*
Whore, s. *kachana-ī, lola-ī, kāsira, shatāha.*
Whoremonger, s. *kāsīr, zinā·kār.*
Why, ad. *wale? tsa la?*
Wick, s. *bātai, patīla.*
Wicked, a. *bad, bad·kār, gunāh·gār, sharīr.*
Wickedness, s. *badī, bad·kārī, sharārat, gunāh.*
Wicket, s. *kaṛka-ī, tambaṛa-ī.*
Wide, a. *plan, arat, psorawar* or *sarah·war.* (-open) *chīng, wīt.* (-as a door) *liri.*
Widen, v.a. *plananwul, artawul ; chīngawul, wītawul.*
Widow, s. *kūnḍa.* (-hood) *kūnḍ·tūn.*
Widower, s. *kūnḍ.*
Width, s. *plan·wālai, art·wālai, psor, sor.*
Wield, v.a. *chalawul, girzawul.*
Wife, s. *kkhadza, artīna, merman, kor, ṭabar.* (cotemporary-) *ba-an.* (under coverture) *maṛokkha.* (brother's-) *wrandār* or *wandyār, bābī.* (son's-) *ngor.* (husband's brother's-) *yor.*
Wild, a. *dzangalī, wahshī, dashtī, sahrānai ; khiyālī, wahmī ; be·tartīb, nā·parhez·gār ; be·qaid, sar·kakkh.* s. *dzangal, maira, ṣahrā.* (-beast) *dad, wahsh.*
Wilderness, s. *dzangal, dakkht, ṣahrā, maira.*
Wile, s. *bāna, chal, lamghaṛa-ī, ḥīla, fareb.*
Wilful, a. *khpul·sar, khpul·rāe, sar·kakkh.*
Wilfully, ad. *pa qaṣd.*
Will, s. *marẓī, raẓā ; wāk, ikhtiyār ; khwakkhī, kāl·khwāhī ; was, ḥukm.* (testament) *waṣiyat·nāma.* (good-) *nek·khwāhī, khair·khwāhī, nek·sigālī.* (bad-) *bad·khwāhī, bad·sigālī.*
Will, v.a. *ghokkhtal, khwakkhawul ; farmāyal.*
Willing, a. *rāẓī, raẓā·man, khwakkh.* (God-) *da khudāe pa ḥukm sara, inshā allahu ta'ālā.*
Willingly, ad. *pa khwakkhī sara, pa dwāṛo stargo.*
Wily, a. *chal·bāz, farebī, bāna·khor, ḥīla·bāz.*
Win, v.a. *gaṭal, mūndal, wral, pa-aṛ k.* v.n. *ghālib-, wa-aṛ-,* etc. *ked.* (-a battle) *barai mūndal.* (-over) *rāwustal, grohedah k.*
Wind, s. *bād, wo, hawā.* (breath) *sāh, dam.* (to take) v.a. *dama k.,* or *-niwul, sāh ākhistal.* (hot-) s. *lū, paro, tod bād.* (cold-) *sūla-ī, soṛ bād.*
Wind, v.a. *tsarkhawul.* (envelope) *nghaṛal—nghakkhtal.* (twist) *tāwawul ; tāo-, pech-, wal-,* etc. *warkawul ; tāo-, kālkūch-,* etc. *khwaṛal.* v.n. *girzedal, kagedal.*
Winding, a. *pech·dār, wahlandai, kog·wog.* s. *tāo, pech, kalkūchaka, kag·lech.* (-sheet) *kafan, tsādar.*
Window, s. *darbacha* or *darīcha, kaṛka-ī.*
Windpipe, s. *wucha ghāra, halq.*
Windy, s. *bādī, hawā·dār.*
Wine, s. *sharāb.* (-bibber) *sharāb·khor.*
Wing, s. *wazar, tsānga, banra ; bāzū.*
Wink, s. *chashmak, ghamza.* v.a. *zegma-* or *zezma-, starga-,* etc. *wahal.* (blink) *dzambal, brandawul.* (-at faults) *starge puṭawul.* (hint) *ishāra k.*

Winner, s. *gaṭūnkai, wa-aṛ, pa-aṛ kawūnkai.*
Winning, s. *gaṭana, wa-aṛāna.*
Winnow, v.a. *chaj-, tsap-*, etc. *k.* or *-wahal, ālūzawul.*
Winter, s. *jamai* or *jimai, sāra.*
Wipe, v.a. *masḥa k., pāk-, ṣāf-*, etc. *k., mugal—mukkhal, jārū k.*
Wire, s. *tār.* (-drawer) *jandra, tār-kakkh, rākkhko.* (to draw-) v.a. *tār kāgal—kkhkal.*
Wisdom, s. *'aql, poha, pahm, sha'ūr, wuqūf.*
Wise, a. *'aql-man, pohand, dānā, kokkhyār, 'āqil.* s. *shān, rang, ṭaur, toga.*
Wisely, ad. *pa 'aql-*, etc. *-sara.*
Wish, s. *ghokkht, ārzū, mudd'ā, hanḍa, shauq.* v.a. *ghokkhtal, ārzū-*, etc. *laral.*
Wishful, a. *ārzū-man, rāghib, liwāl.*
Wisp, s. *kalokkhta.*
Wit, s. *zīrakī.*
Witch, s. *jādū-gara, koḍ-, siḥr-*, etc. *-gara.* (-craft) *jādū-*, etc. *-garī.*
With, p. *sara, khatsa* or *tsakha.*
Withal, ad. *sara la de, ziyāt la de na.*
Withdraw, v.a. *stanawul, pa biyarta ākhistal.* v.n. *jārwatal, stanedal, biyarta ked.*
Wither, v.n. *mṛāmedal* or *mṛāwedal, wuchedal, kamawredal, pezai-, marghechan-*, etc. *ked.*
Withers, s. *mandaw, wulai.*
Withhold, v.a. *stanawul*; *khundī k.*
Within, p. *danana, pa kkhke.*
Without, p. *bāhir, warchani* or *wardzani.* (not possessed of) *be-, lā-, nā-, ghair-*, etc.
Withstand, v.a. *āṛ-, man'a-*, etc. *k.* v.n. *wudredal, teredal, pāedal, ṭing ked., walāṛedal.*
Witness, s. *gawāh, shāhid*; *gawāhī, shāhidī*; *gawāhī-*, etc. *-lānai* or *-lūnkai*, or *-war-kawūnkai.* v.a. *katal, goral—lidal.* (to give-) v.a. *gawāhī-*, etc. *lal* or *-lawdal*, or *-warkawul.* (to be-) v.n. *gawāh-*, etc. *ked.*
Wittol, s. *dakūs, bagharai.*
Witty, a. *zīrak, tez-pahm.*
Wits, s. *'aql, hokkh, ausān.* (out of his-) *ausān-tlalai.*
Wizard, s. *jādū-gar, bāzī-, koḍ-, siḥr-*, etc. *-gar.*
Woe, s. *gham, randz*; *afsos, daregh.*
Woeful, a. *gham-jan, gham-nāk, andekkh-man.*
Wolf, s. *sharmakkh, lewah.*
Woman, s. *kkhadza, artīna, arwata, 'aurata, zanāna.* (lying in-) *langa, zarghāla, tsal, wekkhta-ī.*
Womb, s. *riham, gawranai.*
Wonder, v.a. *'ajab k.* v.n. *hariyānedal.*
Wonder, s. *hariyānī* or *ḥairānī.* (-struck) *hak-pak, hak-hariyān.*
Wonderful, a. *'ajab, 'ajīb, badī'ah.*
Wont (to be), v. imp. Is expressed by the continuative past tense of verbs. Ex. *rātah ba* or *ba rātah*, he used to come or was wont to come.
Wont, s. *'ādat, dastūr.*
Wood, s. *largai.* (forest) *bawr.* (grove) *jangai.* (fire-) *bālawr, khāshāk.*
Wool, s. *waṛa-ī, pashm.*
Woollen, a. *waṛīnah, pashmīnah.*
Woolly, a. *waṛan, babar.*
Word, s. *khabara, wayai, lafẓ, wayana.* (news) *khabar.* (-of honour) *qaul.* (in a-) *gharaẓ.*
Work, s. *kār, kasb*; *khidmat, miḥnat*; *shughl, mashghūlā.* (effect) *pāzah, 'amal.*
Work, v.a. *kār-*, etc. *k., kawul, kṛal.*
Workman, s. *kār kawūnkai, kasb-gar, kārīgar.*
Workmanship, s. *kārī-garī.*
World, s. *duniyā, jahān, naṛa-ī, 'ālam.*
Worldly, a. *duniyā-ī*; *duniyā parast.*
Worm, s. *chinjai, khazanda.* (Guinea-) *nārū.* (Tape-) *kadū zaṛai.* (intestinal) *wagha.* (Ascarides) *kikkha.* (-of a still) *marwat.*

Wormwood, s. *tarkha, mastiyāra.*
Worn, a. *zor; be-dzān, be-ḥāl.* (frayed) *sūdah, sūledalai.* (exhausted) *ṭap, staṛai.*
Worry, v.a. *pārawul, ṭongawul, kaṛawul, zoral.*
Worse, a. *nor bad.* (-than he) *la haghah na bad.*
Worship, s. *'ibādat, sijda.* (title) *ḥazrat.* v.a. *parastī-, 'ibādat-,* etc. *k.*
Worsted, a. *pa-aṛ, māt, bāelalai.* s. *ojghūnai, waṛa-ī; natsa-ī* or *antsa-ī, wākkhkai.* (ball of-) *spandakh.*
Worth, s. *bai'a, bahā, qīmat; qadr; kkhegaṛa.* v.n. *arzedal.*
Worthless, a. *be-fā-ida, nā-kārah, 'abas, khushai, nā-tsīz, habatah, hets da kkhah.*
Worthy, a. *kkhāyastah, kkhah, lā-iq, wājib, yarzan, pīrzo.*
Wound, s. *parhār, zakhm.* v.a. *jobalawul, ghwutsawul, zakhmī k.*
Wounded, a. *parhār-jalai, jobal, ghwuts, zakhmī, zam-zwolai.* v.n. *jobaledal, ghwuts-,* etc. *ked.*
Wrangle, v.a. *jagṛa-, qaẓiya-, steza-,* etc. *k.*
Wrangler, s. *jagṛān, jang-yālai, qaẓiya-kār, ḥujjatī, takrārī.*
Wrap, v.a. *nghaṛal—nghakkhtal.*
Wrapper, s. *lifāfa.*
Wrath, s. *qahr, ghaẓab, bros-wālai.*
Wrathful, a. *qahr-jan, ghaẓab-nāk, bros, khīr.*
Wreak, v.a. *āchawul, ghurzawul, khalāṣawul, chalawul, mātawul, lagawul.*
Wreath, s. *tāo, wal, pech; hār, laṛ.*
Wreck, s. *tālān, tabāhī, kharābī, halākat.*
Wrench, v.a. *tāo-, pech-,* etc. *warkawul; kāgal—kkhkul, bāsal—yastal; shūkawul.*
Wrest, v.a. See preceding word.
Wrestle, v.a. *parzawul k.*
Wrestler, s. *pahalwān, parzawul kawūnkai.*
Wretch, s. *kam-bakht, bad-naṣīb, khāna kharāb.*
Wretched, a. *khwār, tabāh, be-kas, lā-chār.*
Wretchedness, s. *khwārī, tabāhī, tor-bakhtī.*
Wright, s. *darūzgar, tarkāwr.* (in comp.) *-gar.*
Wring, v.a. *tāwawul; nichoṛawul.*
Wrinkle, s. *chīchaṛ, jūhaṛa, gundza.*
Wrist, s. *maṛwand, band.*
Write, v.a. *līkal, kāgal—kkhkal.*
Writer, s. *kātib, līkūnkai, kkhkūnkai.*
Writing, s. *līkal, kkhkal, khaṭṭ.*
Writhe, v.n. *pechedal, lamghaṛa-ī ked.*
Wrong, a. *nā-rawā, nā-ḥaqq, nā-kkhanai, be-inṣāf; ghalaṭ, khaṭā, bad.* s. *ẓulm, zabardastī, jafā, nā-ḥaqqī, nuqṣān, nā-rawā-ī, ẓarar.* (right or-) *ḥaqq nā-ḥaqq.*
Wry, a. *kring, kog, tsoṛ.*

Y.

Yard, s. *gholai, angawr, hadera; gaz.*
Yarn, s. *spawrsai, mazai.*
Yawn, v.a. *aswelai k., argamai k.*
Yea, ad. *ho, āre.*
Year, s. *kāl.* (this-) *sag-* or *saganai kāl,* or *sakh-* or *sakhanai kāl.* (next-) *rātlūnai-* or *malkai kāl.* (last-) *paṛos-,* or *paṛosag-,* or *paṛosyanai kāl.* (-before last) *waṛam kāl.* (three years ago) *lā waṛam kāl.* (-by year) *kāl pa kāl.* (every-) *har kāl.* (whole-) *kāl-o-tlin, wāṛah kāl, kāl-o-sar.* (old, in comp.) *-kālah, -kālanai.*
Yearn, v.n. *kaṛedal, nūledal, liwāl ked., pechedal, pakhsedal.*
Yeast, s. *khamīra, tomna, māya.*
Yell, v.a. *chigha-, sūra-, nāra-,* etc. *wahal.*
Yellow, a. *ziyaṛ.*
Yelp, v.a. *ghapal.*
Yes, ad. *ho, āre; ayā!*
Yester, ad. *parūnai, begānai.* (-day) *parūn, parūna-ī wradz.* (day before-) *waṛama wradz.* (two days before-) *lā waṛama.*

wradz. (-night) *begāh*, *begāna-ī-* or *parūna-ī-shpa*. (night before-) *warma shpa*.

Yet, c. *wale*, *walekin*, *lekin*, *magar*. (beside) *'alāwa*, *siwā*, *lā*. (still) *os hum*, *tar osa*. (again) *biyā*.

Yield, v.a. *rāwṛal*, *warkawul*, *paidā k*. (consign) *spāral*, *pāslawul*. (consent) *manal*, *qabūlawul*. (give way) v.n. *kamedal*.

Yoke, s. *jugh*, *ṭauq*. (fastening rope) *sarbānḍa*. (-peg) *jaghūnḍai*. (couple) *qulba*, *joṛa*, *juft*.

Yonder, ad. *halta*, *hori* or *hūri*, *hūrita*, *horta*.

You, pr. *tāsū*, *mo*.

Young, a. *dzwān*. s. *bachai*.

Youngster, s. *halak*, *jauṛai*, *zalmai*.

Youth, s. *dzwān*, *zalmai*, *ghunḍāyah*; *dzwānī*, *zalmī-tob*.

Z.

Zeal, s. *garmī*, *shauq*, *ghairat*, *tapāk*.

Zealot, s. *zāhid*, *shekh*, *ghairat-man*.

Zealous, a. *garm*, *tund*, *tez*.

Zephyr, s. *bād da ṣabā*, *nasīm*; *narai wo* or *-bād*.

Zest, s. *khwand*, *maza*.

Zigzag, s. *kaga waga*, *kṛīng pṛīng*.

Zinc, s. *jas*, *jasta*.

THE END.